International Relations

International Relations

Concepts and Trends

Shibashis Chatterjee
Anindya Jyoti Majumdar
Sulagna Maitra

Orient BlackSwan

Boxes, Figures, and Tables

Boxes

Figures

Table

Abbreviations

ANZUS	Australia, New Zealand and United States Security Treaty
ARF	ASEAN Regional Forum
ASEAN	Association for Southeast Asian Nations
AU	African Union
CAN	Andean Community
CBM	confidence-building measures
CEDAW	Convention on the Elimination of All Forms of Discrimination against Women
CENTO	Central Treaty Organization
CFCs	Chlorofluro Carbons
CIA	Central Intelligence Agency (US)
COP	Conference of Parties
CPI (M)	Communist Party of India (Marxist)
CRC	Convention on the Rights of the Child (UN)
CSRV	conflict-related sexual violence
CTBT	Comprehensive Test Ban Treaty
DAP	Deutsche Arbeiterpartei (German Workers' Party)
DRC	Democratic Republic of Congo
ECO	Economic Cooperation Organization
ECOSOC	Economic and Social Council (UN)
ECOWAS	Economic Community of West African States
EU	European Union
EVD	Ebola Virus Disease
GATT	General Agreement on Tariffs and Trade
GCC	Gulf Cooperation Council
GHGs	greenhouse gases
IADS	Inter-American Defense System

IBRD	International Bank for Reconstruction and Development
ICBMs	Inter-Continental Ballistic Missiles
ICJ	International Court of Justice
ICTR	International Criminal Tribunal for Rwanda
ICTY	International Criminal Tribunal for the Former Yugoslavia
IDP	internally displaced person
IFC	International Finance Corporation
IGO	Inter-Governmental Organisation
ILO	International Labour Organization
IMO	International Monetary Fund
INF	Intermediate-range Nuclear Forces
IPCC	Intergovernmental Panel for Climate Change
IPE	international political economy
IR	International Relations
IRBMs	Intermediate Range Ballistic Missiles
IRW	intervention-reconstruction-withdrawal
ISIS	Islamic State of Iraq and Syria
J&K	Jammu and Kashmir
JEM	Justice and Equality Movement (Sudan)
LAC	Line of Actual Control
LAFTA	Latin American Free Trade Association
LGBTQIA	Lesbian, Gay, Bisexual, Transgender, Queer, Intersex, and Asexual
LoC	Line of Control
LSE	London School of Economics and Political Science
LTTE	Liberation Tigers of Tamil Eelam (Sri Lanka)
MFN	Most Favoured Nation
MNCs	multinational corporations
MQM	Muttahida Qaumi Movement (Pakistan)
MVSN	Milizia Volontaria per la Sicurezza Nazionale (National State Voluntary Militia; Italy)
NAFTA	North American Free Trade Agreement
NAM	Non-aligned Movement
NAS	National Academy of Sciences (US)
NATO	North Atlantic Treaty Organization

NDA	National Democratic Alliance
NEP	New Economic Policy (of Lenin)
NFP	National Fascist Party (Italy)
NGO	non-governmental organisation
NIEO	New International Economic Order
NPT	Nuclear Non-Proliferation Treaty
NSDAP	Nationalsozialistische Deutsche Arbeiterpartei (National Socialist German Workers' Party)
NSG	Nuclear Suppliers' Group
NWFZ	Nuclear Weapons Free Zones
NNWS	Non-Nuclear Weapon States
NWS	Nuclear Weapon States
OAU	Organization of American States
OLF	Oromo Liberation Front (Ethiopia)
OPEC	Organization of the Petroleum Exporting Countries
PAFTA	Pan-Arab Free Trade Area
PCA	Permanent Court of Arbitration
PCIJ	Permanent Court of International Justice
PNAC	Project for the New American Century
POJK	Pakistan-occupied Jammu and Kashmir
R2P	responsibility to protect
RMA	revolution in military affairs
RPF	Rwandan Patriotic Front
RSDLP	Russian Social Democratic Labour Party
SAPs	Structural adjustment programs
SCO	Shanghai Cooperation Organization
SDGs	Sustainable Development Goals
SEATO	South East Asian Treaty Organization
SGBV	sexual and gender-based violence
SLA	Sudan Liberation Movement
START	Strategic Arms Limitation Talks
TNEs	transnational enterprises
TPLF	Tigrayan Peoples Liberation Force (Ethiopia)
UCDP	Uppsala Conflict Data Program
ULFA	United Liberation Front of Asom
UN	United Nations

Philip Noel-Baker, the Nobel Peace Prize winner, was instrumental in setting up the International Relations programme at the London School of Economics and Political Science (LSE) in 1920. Subsequently, the Montague Burton Chairs in International Relations came up at LSE and Oxford University, and departments were also opened in Geneva and the United States, which gradually placed the academic study of the discipline on a more solid foundation.

This brief prefatory note serves to make three things clear at the outset. *First*, while the idea of world politics is old, the subject of international relations is a new one. *Second*, the subject is quintessentially Western in impulse and origin, and the theoretical, ontological, and epistemic bases of the discipline bear this out till date. *Third*, IR had self-consciously started as a study of war, in order to gain knowledge to usher in peace.

These three facts have a number of significant consequences for the way the discipline has evolved. *First*, the relatively slow birth of IR as a systematic field of enquiry led to problems of institutional location and division of labour. As Brian Schmidt argues, 'The task of demarcating the disciplinary boundaries of the field is an important prerequisite to establishing authority over its object of inquiry' (Schmidt 2013, 5–6). The primary debate here is between two major positions, one that locates IR as a sub-discipline or branch of Political Science, and another that visualises it as a multidisciplinary field of study, borrowing freely from many domains of knowledge. This issue cuts very deep. To move IR closer to Political Science would mean accepting the primary cognitive categories of the latter, and, more crucially, responding to the central debates of the parent discipline in a self-conscious manner. All the central debates in Political Science, therefore, find their way into IR. The reverse, it may be noted, is seldom the case. This has also meant that those who clamour for autonomy need to make their case, both at the ontological and the methodological levels. Settled disciplines have their codes, and code sharing is not easy for a discipline that claims autonomy on the basis of its multidisciplinary character.[2]

[2]Brian Schmidt has drawn attention to how the early proponents of the discipline struggled with the eclectic moorings of the field (Schmidt 2013, 6). The study by Olson and Groom (1991) describes how IR developed in close association with a number of disparate fields like international law, diplomatic history, the peace movement, moral philosophy, geography, and anthropology. The problem of coherence owing to multiple borrowings and varied sources was

Second, the European origins of the discipline have meant that Western concerns, attitudes, and problems have always dominated the field, and it was only in the 1970s that the postcolonial world started to gain the recognition that was due to it. However, the non-Western world lagged behind in the discipline, emerging in the footnotes and on the margins of a narrative dominated overwhelmingly by the West. This meant that even when the subject took up postcolonial concerns, these were mostly understood in Western terms, which, incidentally, dominated both the mainstream and radical tendencies within the discipline. It is only in the last decade or so that a body of postcolonial IR has started asking questions regarding the alien moorings and Western domination of the subject, although it is far from clear how the discipline might respond to these critiques.

Third, the fact that IR began as a field to understand European wars meant that military and political security remained its overriding concerns. Although the scope of security was broadened subsequently, and its depth deepened as many new units were added to the state, IR retained its familiar cast as a subject primed on territorial separateness, the pursuit of military power and security, and an analytical demarcation of the inside and the outside of the state.

Fourth, it was only in the late 1990s that some scholars began to claim the advent of a new epoch of global politics that sought to challenge some of the operating codes of International Relations, primarily due to the technological and economic transformations brought about by globalisation. The history of the discipline, however, shows a quite remarkable resilience as the proponents of global politics have failed to dislodge the dominant orthodoxy of the field. We do not make the claim that IR has not changed over the millennia. Indeed, new issues have crowded the agenda, and fresh approaches were crafted to make sense of them. However, the centrality of the state, power, territoriality,

---

also highlighted by Quincy Wright (1955), who identified eight 'root disciplines' and six disciplines with a 'world point of view', contributing to the making of the discipline. Likewise, Kenneth Thompson regretted that 'there was nothing peculiar to the subject matter of international relations which did not fall under other separate fields' (Thompson 1952, 433). The interdisciplinary character of the field, and the fact that other disciplines studied various dimensions of its subject matter, have sometimes led to the question of whether 'international relations is a distinctive discipline' (Kaplan 1961).

The next great debate within the discipline was one that pitted science against tradition. In a way, this was the most important discussion in methodological terms, as it significantly impacted the way the discipline took shape in the United States and elsewhere. The debate was not peculiar to IR, though; by the 1950s, all social science disciplines had been pervaded by the impact of behaviouralism, which sought to model social sciences on the natural sciences, displaying a commitment to a unified methodology. The philosophical legitimacy to this increasingly quantitative enterprise was provided by logical positivism, which sought to separate values from facts and tried to discover laws that explained particular events as instances of a general rule. While the early onslaught of the empiricists was spiritedly resisted by more traditional-minded scholars who drew attention to the crucial role played by history, ethics, and culture, the methodological baits were successfully laid in favour of the scientists. Causal theories, hypothesis testing through standard statistical tests, accuracy, and predictability became the defining aspects of a modern and scientific IR that drew much of its methodological inspiration from Economics and Statistics. The seductive charm of systems theory and groundbreaking early research on deterrence further reinforced the trend. While the debate polarised the quantifiers and generalists in the field, the deeper epistemological issues were hardly referred to, and, perhaps most crucially, the underlying ontological concerns remained entirely unaddressed (Knorr and Verba 1961).

While the underlying issues were rather profound, the debate was carried within extremely narrow limits, and there were hardly any significant contributions from either side that took care to delve into larger philosophical issues. Thus, the criticisms levelled against positivism within the philosophy of sciences did not enter the terrain at all. It did not occur to the participants that while there was a lot happening in the realm of 'tools and techniques', there was neither any attempt to clarify how beliefs conditioned the way one might discover knowledge about the world, nor any concern with our assumptions regarding the constitution of the world that we wish to find and create. Despite the serious underlying problems, the debate remained limited in scope, with minimal contributions from both sides addressing broader philosophical concerns. In a significant way, our epistemic positions on theory decide not only what we consider the subject matter and its constituent parts (ontology), but also how we wish to make sense of it (methods). Needless to say, even the more developed version of the debate has not buried these questions for good.

Major philosophers of science, such as Karl Popper, Thomas Kuhn, and Imre Lakatos, have all been invoked in judging knowledge formation within IR, particularly after the neorealism of Kenneth Waltz became the dominant theoretical approach by the middle of 1985. John Vasquez, a positivist scholar who had a major disagreement with realism, came up with a significant work that described realism as a degenerative research programme. In *The Power of Power Politics* (1983), Vasquez targeted a body of realist scholarship on the balance of power and alliances, and argued that realists were trying desperately to save their core assumptions by endlessly proliferating auxiliary propositions that only explained anomalies and failed to provide new theoretical insights or empirical content. The chaotic expansion of theoretical propositions immunised realism against falsification. Following Lakatos, Vasquez pronounced a harsh verdict on realist research, the post-Waltzian scientific micro-foundations notwithstanding.

All the realists targeted by Vasquez struck back (Elman and Elman 1997; Walt 1997; Waltz 1997). While some found fault with the very idea of a Lakatosian test (Waltz, in particular) to determine knowledge through accumulation, others claimed that their work passed such a benchmark, contrary to Vasquez's accusations. On balance, IR seemed to be more comfortable with the Kuhnian idea of paradigm over Lakatos's notion of research programmes. Realism was thus declared to be not one research programme but many, which shared basic tenets but developed very different theories. In some ways, the inter-paradigm debate and the Lakatosian debate were parallel activities taking place within the mainstream. The inter-paradigm debate was ontological and pitted realism, liberalism, and critical perspectives against each other. Its emphasis was less on epistemological issues. The debates on research programmes galvanised the paradigms from within and contributed to sharpening many theoretical formulations. This was more an epistemic affair. However, the gains notwithstanding, these debates proved inconclusive in the long run. The assessment of whether the research was progressive or degenerative rested entirely on the position of the theorist. Those who criticised research programmes from the outside used terms and interpreted evidence in a manner fundamentally at odds with those who defended these from within.

THE POST-POSITIVIST DEBATE

The post-positivist turn in IR complicated matters further. At one level, it has generated an unprecedented theoretical eclecticism, with continental philosophers being claimed and appropriated at random. At another level, for the initial period, there was a complete scission between the rationalist and post-positivist schools, particularly those writing within the postmodern/post-structuralist genres. Over time, there has developed a stalemate of sorts, but the fundamental rift remains (Der Derian 2009; Devetak 1996b; George 1994, 1995). Post-structuralists viewed social events as texts with multiple interpretations, shaped by cultural and historical contexts and highlighting how dominant meanings suppress alternative ones, in the process establishing unquestioned truths. Knowledge-making is thus always intensely political, and the meaning of terms depended on how actors drew on discourses. Language positioned players in relation to particular discourses; as the discourse shifted, so did the meaning. The widespread acceptance of dominant narratives was fuelled by expert support, influencing agreement and ensuring successful replication. Discourse formation and legitimacy are therefore achieved through technologies of power. Post-positivist scholars of IR were deeply indebted to Michel Foucault's analysis of power. For Foucault, modern power is not vertical or pyramidal; it is neither modelled on force nor on commodity. Rather, power is capillary and inextricably intertwined with subject-producing discourses. Power crafts institutions in ways that act upon human minds and bodies and structures individuals systematically. In this way a state, through its architecture, its organisation, and its practices, can be imagined as a disciplinary site that brings particular discourses (truth regimes), such as the institution of sovereignty, to legitimate its existence and to determine its activities.

According to Sorensen, 'I believe that this is a core metatheoretical debate in IR after the Cold War' (Sørensen 1998, 86). For the post-positivists, the scientific enterprise is cognitively misguided, blatantly hegemonic, hostile to variety, and inherently anti-political. In place of a search for scientific certitude and the timeless laws of world politics, it encourages researchers to interrogate and interrupt the taken-for-granted character of dominant academic discourses and media representations of all domains of world politics. In line with its overall commitment, post-structural scholars work on fault-lines and interstices, revealing the contingent and dubious nature of all truth claims, and the accompanying crisis of meaning. The debate rages on, dividing the discipline further.

Scholars are divided on how the schism is to be read. On the one hand, positivists like Robert Keohane have taken the split as insuperable. In his oft-quoted terms,

> These authors, of whom the best-known include Hayward Alker, Richard Ashley, Friedrich Kratochwil, and John Ruggie, emphasize the importance of the 'intersubjective meanings' of international institutional activity (Kratochwil and Ruggie, 1986: 765). In their view, understanding how people think about institutional norms and rules, and the discourse they engage in, is as important in evaluating the significance of these norms as measuring the behavior that changes in response to their invocation. (Keohane 1988, 381)

Postmodernists like Jim George and Roxanne Lynn Doty have also come to a similar conclusion from the other end. Scholars like Alexander Wendt and Sorensen, on the other hand, have refused to accept this binary, as they consider the extreme variants of both positions to be antithetical. Sorensen argues, 'It is clear, then, that both the static objectivism of extreme positivism and the voluntaristic subjectivism of extreme post-positivism contain serious problems. It is fortunate, therefore, that a middle ground which avoids these extremes can be found' (Sorensen 1998, 89). This commonsensical truce, however, is problematic. In fact, Ole Weaver, in one of the most penetrating analyses of the inter-paradigm debate, quite rightly saw the fourth debate (post-positivism) as a resurrection of the fundamental methodological divide that has remained constant in IR, which was initially described rather aptly as the science *versus* tradition debate. From Robert Kaplan's efforts to fashion a systems theory to Kenneth Waltz's neorealism, and from inter-War liberalism to neoliberal institutionalism, the attempt has been to provide IR with a robust scientific cast. Post-positivists strongly resist this 'scientific enterprise', and even those like Wendt, who attempted to reconcile viewpoints, did not effectively challenge the dominance of rationalist methodologies.

For post-positivists, mainstream IR will therefore never problematise certain realities as these are inevitably taken for granted and naturalised in the discipline. Furthermore, IR, as a field of study, is often viewed as the most hierarchical of the social sciences due to its focus on the perspectives of elites and those in power. Its theories invariably work top-down. It also safeguards the state from the wider society. Post-positivists, however, make the crucial point that no matter how elite-driven international politics is, its decisions and dynamics reach everyone and have an impact on the range of possibilities available to the masses. Global economic flows impact urban cartography and the economic well-being of the classes. Human movements and significant displacements of populations are often the result of global processes. Post-structural IR creates possibilities to interrogate such developments within the discipline. For post-structural IR theorists, the debate is therefore not just over the specification of terms; it is centred on the very meaning of social categories as claimed by the rational approaches. Rationalists and reflectivists offer fundamentally opposed answers to questions of meaning, theory, knowledge, and evidence. The possibility of striking a middle ground, though superficially attractive, seems hardly convincing.

FROM INTERNATIONAL RELATIONS TO GLOBAL POLITICS?

How much has the agenda of international relations changed over the years? The world has witnessed the rise and fall of great powers, the discovery of weapons of mass destruction like nuclear weapons, which fundamentally reshaped many of the traditional precepts of war and crisis stability, and unprecedented technological breakthroughs that not only created a new world of virtual reality but also collapsed distances, leading to fundamental alterations in our understanding of time and space. We have also seen remarkable ups and downs in ideological discourses and political systems, tectonic shifts in the international political economy and trading regimes, and a plethora of new actors emerging in world politics, contending and cooperating with, and supplanting, the state. Since the 1990s, a host of new metaphors has populated the discipline, all of which, in some ways, complicate the nation-state-oriented international order. It is commonly argued that the state now cohabits a very complex world of multinational corporations, the media, financial institutions, social movements, regional and sub-regional groupings, and international organisations. Some scholars see in this trend an inevitable transformation of the underlying nature of world politics, and they boldly reject the term IR as an appropriate description of this altered agenda. Their preferred coinage is 'global politics', a term that loosens the state-centric order and flattens its settled chrono-politics of linear time. The transactions of transnational firms, global media houses, corporate governance, and social movements do not depend on a determined cartography of nation-states with their fixed borders and independent claims of sovereignty. There has been a fundamental shift in the economic, technological, and social foundations of world politics towards a de-territorialised dynamic, which the traditional state-centric discipline of IR is unable to comprehend. What is needed is a massive change in both ontological references and cognitive categories, which can explain the steady substitution of the claustrophobic idea of the international with the liberating notion of the global.

A closer look reveals that although the world has changed dramatically in the past twenty-five years, many hallmarks of the post-1945 world persist. The world is still organised into nation-states, and most of these states care a good deal about controlling their borders scrupulously, admit or deny migrants by their sovereign will, display a healthy sensitivity to their entitlements, feel uncomfortable at the thought of any global scrutiny of their human rights records, and find it difficult to mount any collective action on deterritorialised problems that affect them severely. The United Nations has remained hostage to the political chicanery conducted by the great powers behind closed doors, and the idea of a world government is as bleak today as it was before. The alarming rise of terrorism across the world has hardened states considerably, and international borders have become more restrictive in several quarters. The world is certainly more global than ever in terms of technology and the intrusiveness of corporate capitalism, although, critically enough, it remains state-centric by virtue of authority and jurisdiction. Although non-state actors have greatly increased in global politics, the fundamental norms of the international order remain largely unchanged. However, many of our traditional theories and concepts stand considerably challenged as major transformations continue to mark the international economy and humanity struggles in the face of a host of vulnerabilities that can neither be grasped nor fought by state-oriented frames of reference. The impact of satellite and digital technologies, the proliferation of social media, the expansion of corporate governance across the world, extreme climate and environmental problems, and pandemics impact powerfully on global politics and require new conceptual toolkits. As some of the chapters of this book will show, the global and the international intermesh in world politics, where new institutions, norms, and practices defy the mandate of nation-states without replacing the international order.

POSTCOLONIAL IR?

A group of scholars, widely divergent in their theoretical interests and ideological moorings, have questioned the inadequacies of IR in studying the non-Western world. One of the arguments here is that the most pertinent basis of conflict in the Global South remains internal or domestic, arising out of either distributional inequalities or problems of recognition. Postcolonial states have forged national identities by linking territory, citizenship, and nationalism, while holding exclusive legal sovereignty. Several factors, such as the ones mentioned above, have significantly contributed to numerous lengthy civil conflicts with international implications. This stems from the sharp difference between historical realities and artificial political systems, especially Western ideas of sovereignty, frequently challenged by ethnic disputes. The unresolved questions of identity configured within artificial and rigid state borders compound such conflicts. No conventional paradigm of academic IR, including a constructivist engagement of identity discourses, has been able to comfortably explain such disputes, given the discipline's self-consciously Western genealogy. Hence, what needs to be problematised in the non-Western world is the domestic, for its international relations in general and discourses of conflict in particular remain firmly rooted in the constitution of the inside.

Therefore, IR must interrogate the 'postcolonial', for a proper understanding of the non-Western world is a precondition for explaining its conflicts. The meaning of the concept of 'post' is problematic. It can either signify a period of time, one that begins after the end of colonialism or the formal transfer of political power to the colony, or refer to an orientation, a structure of feeling, or even a form of subjectivity, which transcends the colonial in the ideational and existential senses of the term. The other reading insists that it is superficial to consider formal political independence as constituting the moment of the postcolonial, since it does not lead to any fundamental change in the social and economic dynamics of life. Hence, a conventional reading of the non-Western is often marred by the use of cognitive categories like the trajectories of modernity, capital, and the norms of international society, which are derivatives of Western experiences. This intersubjective understanding has been brilliantly captured by Stuart Hall:

> So, postcolonial is not the end of colonisation. It is after a certain kind of colonialism, after a certain moment of high imperialism and colonial occupation—in the wake of it, in the shadow of it, inflected by it—it is what it is because something else has happened before, but it is also something new. (Hall 1997, 189)

What is lost in these narratives is the central and constitutive role played by colonialism, subjugation, and empire-building in the making and unmaking of the subjectivities of people who underwent such tumultuous experiences throughout the non-Western world. Neither the colonial nor the postcolonial can be neatly separated. Western influence on the institutions and practices of the non-Western world is complemented by the non-West's own contribution to these influences. Postcolonial scholars state that a proper understanding of the modern international order requires a study of the dialectical flows between the colony and the colonial power, one that historicises the political categories taking shape in the postcolonial world by paying attention to the distinctiveness of the non-Western societies. This calls for a conscious distancing from received categories and their application across time and space. Interrogating the idea of the postcolonial is the first precondition to understanding what postcolonial IR might connote (Seth 2011).

The non-Western world, in other words, demands 'non-Western' forms of knowledge. This epistemological claim, however, is exceedingly difficult, if not outright impossible, to sustain. The fact that dominant interests define what constitutes knowledge, who the knowing subject is, what can be known about the subject (IR), and how knowledge is acquired remains fundamentally true. Within IR, this process has led a dominant community of scholars to privilege a positivist and empirical conception of theory, which is frankly naturalistic in inspiration. For a long time, they maintained their stranglehold over the discipline, successfully marginalising alternative approaches. Proponents of indigenisation find these theories and their products hegemonic and impoverished. Like the debate between rationalist and post-positivist IR, the clash between Western and non-Western IR will not admit to an easy resolution. Principled positions are better than a half-hearted truce, although they may result in pulverising the discipline further. One position is to throw open the disciplinary gates, disown the gatekeepers, and prioritise the everyday experiences of the amateur in favour of the hierarchical and rule-bound readings of the expert, to indigenise by refraining from mimicking the West, moving carefully between decontextualised cosmopolitan passivity and the atavistic nativism of the local, acknowledging the legitimacy of non-Western modes of thinking and knowledge creation, being dialogic, and delving into traditions, histories, and local practices (Behera 2010, 106–11).

Others would draw a distinction between ontology and epistemology, arguing that IR needs to listen carefully to the global histories of modernity and colonialism, which requires, among other things, a healthy infusion of historical specificity into a discipline that has long claimed an immutability of structures. Steve Smith has recently argued for a refurbished IR, predicated on accepting normativity, power and social relations, the material and the ideational, and rejecting IR as an American social science, its asocial scientism, and the lure of embracing the powerful (Smith 2015 [2011]). But like every other social science discipline and the humanities at large, IR has also witnessed an unprecedented efflorescence in its methodological and theoretical underpinnings in the past two decades. The inspiration for this variegated impulse has mostly come from the West. Is this a significant deficiency when it comes to interrogating the non-Western world? Crucially, one needs to question the ethnic and geographic meaning of 'the West', invoked as an epistemic term. In all aspects of life and across various levels of collective existence, the idea of the West has been problematised and challenged. Some of these have indeed surfaced in the non-Western world, but the overwhelming majority of the voices of dissent and denial have germinated in the 'West' itself.

THE LEVELS OF ANALYSIS PROBLEM IN IR

The disjuncture between unit- and system-level analysis is manifestly sharp in the larger body of IR theory. This has been a major debate in

IR theory that actually conflates two separate debates, namely levels of analysis and agent *versus* structure. Classical realism was unit-based, but structural realism prioritised the role of the structure. Liberal IR theory is essentially agent-specific. Constructivism, on the other hand, is based on the idea of the co-constitution of agency and structure. The Marxist or critical theory perspectives are again structural, with little independent treatment given to agential freedom. In contrast, postmodernist or post-structuralist discourses are typically agential, given their suspicion of meta-structures or all forms of grand narratives. A similar situation obtains in the sphere of foreign policy analysis, most of which belongs to one of two categories. *First*, the bulk of the literature uses agency-specific explanations of foreign policy behaviour that are remotely related to systemic or structural factors. The *second* genre of literature is based on decision-making studies, either case-specific or conceived as historical or diplomatic narratives. Against such clean, dichotomous frames, the models of structure-agency interaction have assumed greater prominence in recent years even within the folds of the structural realism that continues to dominate IR theory.

Turning to levels of analysis, the critical benchmark is still Kenneth Waltz's classic, *Man, State and War* (1959), where he distinguished among three levels with distinctive properties, namely the individual, the state, and the international system, which can be used as explanatory variables in international relations. In the early 1960s, David J. Singer wrote a couple of critical essays that set the terms of the debate (see Singer 1960, 1961). Later, Martin Hollis and Steve Smith wrote a philosophically enriching account on the subject (see Hollis and Smith 1990) and the constructivist Alexander Wendt protracted the debate further.

At the basic level, explanations in international relations can occur on several levels. Dominant national leaders and influential statesmen or bureaucrats have often influenced and impacted foreign policy decisions and organisational choices. The personalities of dictators like Adolf Hitler and Joseph Stalin have been invoked by many analysts explaining World War II. The personal chemistry of leaders has likewise been shown to either facilitate or problematise relations between states. The mutual dislike that US President Nixon and Indian Prime Minister Indira Gandhi had for each other was claimed as a key factor in exacerbating negative relations between the two states in the early 1970s, particularly over the Bangladesh War of 1971. The excellent personal rapport between French President Francois Mitterrand and German Chancellor Helmut Kohl, in sharp contrast, contributed significantly to cementing the bonds of Franco-German partnership at the heart of the European integration process. Leaders ruling for a long time develop variable relations of trust or discomfort with their counterparts that apparently cast a shadow on how relations evolve between states. Yet, the impact of personalities can only offer a limited understanding. Personalities operate within political and economic systems and even the strongest of leaders needs a favourable ecosystem to be effective. The pulls and pressures of the international system also constrain decision-makers and limit their available range of choices.

The domestic pathology of states may likewise contribute critically to the actions of states in world affairs. The theory of democratic peace says that liberal democratic states do not make war with each other, while they fight fiercely, and mostly win, against authoritarian states. Realists like Barry Posen, Van Evera, and Jack Snyder have recognised the limitations of pure structural effects in explaining specific national policies, and have accordingly sought to plug the gap by offering various additional explanations. Thus, Posen (1984) used organisational theory, Snyder (1991) developed a typology of domestic regimes, and Van Evera (1999) invoked militarism as adjunct-explanations to structural realism. The new school of neoclassical realism developed by William Wohlforth, Randall Schweller, Fareed Zakaria, and Gideon Rose, for example, has used domestic factors in addition to standard external variables to explain the foreign policies of states. The constructivist scholarship of norms and identities has also used the societal level as the causal lever, arguing that norms, collective identities, and practices grow out of the processes of socialisation and selective social filtering that calls for close attention to the properties of states and societies on the one hand, and their complex interactions on the other. Liberals like Andrew Moravcsik have developed a sophisticated theory of societal preferences that tie together the properties of individuals, groups, and states in explaining why certain policies prevail over others.

Kenneth Waltz and John Mearsheimer have steadfastly argued that international politics must be understood at the systemic level. Waltzian structural realism is based on modern, neoclassical economic theory, which makes a conscious distinction between the theories of markets and firms. While the theory of competitive markets is said to be structural or interactional, the theory of firms is a unit-level explanation of behaviour. Structural realism is similarly a theory of international politics, of the environment/context, or of the operational dynamics of the system structure, which comes into existence through the mutual interaction of units (states). Therefore, as per Waltz's theoretical dictum, a structural theory (or systemic theory) of world politics is conceptually distinct from the theory (or theories) of foreign policy analysis. According to Waltz, the two theories run on separate or parallel courses, unless their unification is brought about by a major theoretical innovation. Mearsheimer has largely accepted this script, with only one difference: he thinks that Waltz underestimated the structural effects of anarchy on state behaviour by prioritising security over power as the goal of states. Mearsheimer considers the logic of anarchy far more prohibitive, as it pushes states towards power maximisation at all times. However, the account put across here is purely structural or systemic; the organising principle (anarchy or the absence of authority) sends signals to all units that respond according to their capabilities.

Marxists use another level of analysis in international relations, namely class. While Karl Marx did not develop an account of classes operating in an international system of states and his Olympian universalism made a concrete analysis difficult, his idea was that capitalism had to be replaced and a radically different order put in place globally. V. I. Lenin subsequently introduced an international dimension to this class analysis by showing that finance capital morphed into monopoly capital as capitalism exhausted domestic markets quickly, and then sought new markets or territories to maintain profits. Leading capitalists, however, were now facilitated by their parent states, and this led ultimately to colonialism and imperialism. But dominant capitalist countries were bound to stagnate, and new ones would come up. The latecomers would also need new markets and territories for profits, and this would ultimately culminate in a war of imperialism. Lenin considered this a structural contradiction, inevitable in its effects, while Karl Kautsky, a famous Czech-Austrian Marxist, disagreed. He thought that imperial powers would divide and share the booty peacefully. Additionally, Lenin also mentioned the tendency for a labour aristocracy to develop, bought off and co-opted by the capitalists. He therefore prescribed the precedence of a revolutionary seizure of power before settling the issues of an international political economy. On the other hand, Antonio Gramsci, in his masterful analysis, contrasted developed and backward capitalist societies and explained how the hegemony of consensual domination by capital, defined as the collective commonsense of the masses, was successfully established in the developed capitalist states. This caused people to voluntarily embrace opposing beliefs, a change only reversible through the counter-hegemony of progressive working-class ideas.

Critical IR theorists like Robert Cox and Stephen Gill argued that such hegemony was indeed global, and unless the historic blocs of capitalist forces were countered by those of the working classes and other oppressed categories of people, the international system would remain a capitalist one. Another branch of leftist scholars who came up mostly in Latin America in the 1960s and 1970s, called the dependency school or the world systems theory (Wallerstein 1974, 1980, 1989), used a structural perspective to make sense of international relations. They found the global political economy to be capitalist in organisation, the existence of the Soviet bloc notwithstanding, wherein a developed core specialising in manufacturing commodities used their favourable terms of trade to exploit and dominate a vast periphery of underdeveloped economies that comprised overwhelmingly of the postcolonial states, through a layered extraction of surplus capital using a network of middlemen. The dependency school mapped dominant military powers on this octopus-like canvas of the international system.

Agents and Structures

The question of structure and agency remains one of the most vexing and complicated problems in the philosophy of the social sciences. This study does not wish to revisit the philosophical debate, since it is rather superfluous in terms of its scope and objective. However, a brief analysis of the issues involved here is essential for introducing the perspective developed and used in the study. Put simply, the issue of structure and agency concerns the locale and nature of explanation of social phenomena. It is about the constitution of valid effects or outcomes in social reality. There are two broad tendencies in all social sciences regarding the explanation of social effects or outcomes. While some approaches emphasise the structural factors, others predominantly privilege the agential ones. Structure basically means the context, the setting or environment, within which a social phenomenon takes place. However, most structural perspectives cut deeper. They claim that there is a definite structural ordering of the system under investigation, which appears as a pattern of regularities and whose identity cannot be grasped by studying the ephemeral or surface phenomena alone. Such deep structures are not the mathematical aggregate or sum of the units, but have an identity of their own. Different social sciences employ their own variants of structure. In IR, the structural realists take anarchy to be the system's structure, and the pattern of distribution of capabilities to be the critical variable. The dependency scholars, on the other hand, took exchange relations to constitute such a structure. The difference between these two conceptions of structure will be explained in the following section.

Structural perspectives are essentially built on natural science models. In physics, for example, the axiomatic assumption is that the natural order is patterned in a way that makes a predictable outcome possible by studying a new initial condition and the knowledge of the structuring principles of the universe (Hay 2002, 94). The truth of the natural sciences is based on the transcendental or trans-historical nature of such governing axioms. The problem is different in the social sciences, where no such governing axioms can be identified, because the very idea of the 'social' is both ontologically and epistemologically contested. This is not to suggest that the social world is completely unpatterned; however, the discernible regularities of this world are indeterminate. The structures of the social world are therefore, unlike the natural world, not set in the stronger, determinant sense.

Agency, on the other hand, refers broadly to action, or social outcome. Colin Hay defines it as 'the ability or capacity of an actor to act consciously and, in so doing, to attempt to realise his or her intentions' (Hay 2002, 94). But it is more than action. It implies, most significantly, an actor's choice or autonomy. Decisions thus become a function of an actor's conscious choice. In Political Science or Sociology, agential autonomy is usually taken to mean the autonomous capacity for conscious deliberation enjoyed by a rational individual (rationality, however, is an auxiliary assumption, and does not necessarily refer to utility maximisation). The idea of agency in IR, however, is more complex, since the individual is not the common or popular unit of analysis. Therefore, the more acceptable practice is to equate the standard unit of analysis, or the state, with agency. Theories of foreign policy, though, look at the notion of agency differently. Here, the perspective is closer to Sociology and Political Science, because agency often refers to the psychological attributes or predispositions of a particular decision-maker (or a person/human being), while structure refers to the macro variables, both domestic and external. The final section of this chapter will elucidate this further.

In most contexts, a series of structural and agential factors are at work, and the usual tendency is to think of their relationship in oppositional terms. Thus, to the extent that an event is given to structural explanation, agential factors are to the same degree thought to be incidental or superfluous. There are scholars who believe that to formulate one form of explanation is to necessarily deny the legitimacy of the other. However, such dichotomous or mutually exclusive accounts have little purchase on explaining the reality. It is more convenient to acknowledge the mutually supportive role of both. Here, structure is viewed as a context within which social outcomes take place. By itself, it is inaccessible to the actors concerned. Agency is more direct since agential factors emphasise the action of the actors directly involved in producing a particular social effect. The blending of the structural and the agential factors vary according to the questions posed, and the nature of the problems that give rise to these questions. Therefore, the explanations are never theory-neutral, and it is here that much of the controversy and confusion remain unresolved.

Without getting embroiled in the major issues concerning the philosophy of knowledge, the problem can be couched in simple, pragmatic terms. The critical issue in this debate is to frame it properly, or to understand what the debate is itself about. To argue that the structure-agency controversy is a problem that can be empirically solved is to misplace the debate, because to insist that the relative claims and counterclaims of structure- and/or agency-based accounts can be resolved by evidence is to collapse the empirical and the ontological. The intensity of the mutual divide is weakened considerably if the empirical claim is given up completely.

In simplest terms, then, the conflict between structure and agency is not one to be adjudicated or resolved by concrete or hard evidence. The unfortunate reality is that most scholars remain extremely inconsistent on this issue. They at times advance contending ontological accounts of reality rather than viewing it as a puzzle to be empirically resolved. However, on other occasions they seem to abandon ontology in favour of empiricism, arguing that the choice of ontology hinges on differences in the empirical observation of reality. Alexander Wendt is particularly guilty of such inconsistency and confusion. Thus, in a chapter co-written with Ian Shapiro, Wendt writes,

> The differences among ... 'realist' models of agency and structure—and among them and their individualist and holist rivals—are differences about where the important causal mechanisms lie in social life. As such, we can settle them only by wrestling with the empirical merits of their claims about human agency and social structure.... These are in substantial part empirical questions. (Wendt and Shapiro 1997, 181)

Again, the authors complain, 'The advocates of individualism, structuralism and structuration theory have all done a poor job of specifying the conditions under which their claims about the relationship of agency and social structure would be falsified' (ibid.). Wendt further degrades the significance of ontology when he states that 'ontology talk is necessary, but we should also be looking for ways to translate it into propositions that might be adjudicated empirically' (Wendt 1999, 37).

The fact is that empirical evidence cannot settle disputes over ontological accounts. The realists, liberals, constructivists, and dependency scholars all differ in their respective delineations of reality; the problems they identify follow from their articulation of what they see. Divergent accounts of ontology inevitably clash. But their conflict/s cannot be resolved by an appeal to data, as empirical facts cannot license such disputes. Following the works of Anthony Giddens, Archer, and Roy Bhaskar, IR scholars like Steve Smith, Alexander Wendt, David Dessler, and Heike Pottomaki, among others, have developed a philosophically rich account of agents, structures, and levels at play. This is not the place to discuss this literature. We need to conclude by emphasising that explanations can be attempted at all levels; while multiple levels are welcome, care must be taken to discriminate between levels properly. The empirical cases are crucial in deciding which level is the appropriate one to use, and researchers need to follow standard protocols when they offer aggregate or multimodal explanations in the field.

The conclusion, therefore, is unremarkable. The evolution of IR as a field of enquiry shows notable trends. It evolved during the inter-War period in the West as a systematic study aimed at finding answers to the problem of war. Its birth was therefore overlaid by security considerations. This remains the chief orientation of the discipline even now. IR is essentially about security explorations at various levels of human existence. Although concerns about the political economy and the complex interplay of commerce and defence have assumed greater importance over the years, security issues remain firmly in focus. But military or hard security matters are no longer the obsession of the field; IR as a discipline has done much to expand the subject of security, both in depth and coverage. To these, the post-Cold War period has added concerns of globalisation and identity/community. The so-called marginal voices—those of women, refugees, and the environment—have subsequently become more important, and can be heard even in the bastion of the most conservative settings of the discipline.

To conclude, IR remains lodged in Political Science, a partnership that is uneasy and often volatile in nature. In a way, the tensions have their source in the rather different understandings of 'politics' that political scientists and IR scholars carry. Justifiably enough, we restrict our judgement to IR. On the surface, IR continues to view politics either cynically or as lacking moral content, reinforcing statist categories. It affirms the long-held tradition of reasoned self-reflection as the basis of politics and the image of the rational individual as its chosen model. Power and competition, instrumental and egoistic cooperation, uncomplicated binaries of the self and the other are its attributes. But this is only a surface reading. The subtext of IR is rich and complex, where all the apparently settled categories are questioned, not necessarily for rejection, but often—and this is perhaps the most crucial point—for fresh vindication and more powerful re-affirmation. Cultural metaphors shape IR in problematic, repetitive ways, yet they also foster more stable, secure environments for reimagining them. The story of IR is the tragedy of the other—the settled discourses retrench at the very moment of their displacement; their rejuvenation comes in times of peril. Politics as power, instrumentality/transaction, or culture clash are not attractive metaphors, and more importantly, bear no promise of the emancipation of the human subject, which is the only ethically viable notion of politics at all times. The promise of a politics of emancipation in international politics hangs in the balance, with no prospect of a drastic transformation in sight.

2

Mainstream International Relations Theories
Political Realism and Liberalism

Shibashis Chatterjee

Like all social sciences, International Relations (IR) is a plural discipline. The multiplicity of IR manifests in many forms, and at various levels. IR theory is often regarded as distinctively underdeveloped compared with other, more developed or mature social science disciplines (Alker 1996; Waever 1996). Scholars have been unable to come to a consensus on the nature, range, and purpose of theory in IR, and there is wide support for non-theoretical scholarship in the field. The disagreement takes familiar forms. *First*, the issue is methodological: the science *versus* tradition debate lingers on in IR theory, although rigid partisans have declined in number on both sides and the present mood prefers a division of labour, dialogue, and reconciliation. The *second*, and more profound, disagreement concerns the ontological as well as epistemological differences across competing theoretical paradigms. The contestation became more complicated in the post-Cold War period when all the conventional theories were found wanting in terms of their ability to predict or explain the massive transformation that followed the Cold War, and a large number of new theoretical positions arose to challenge the predominance of the mainstream. But we need to know the mainstream before chronicling its decline.

This chapter studies two dominant theories of IR, political realism and liberalism, and will critically engage with their conceptual range and highlight some of their obvious deficiencies. Apart from political realism, which is a very self-consciously IR theory, all other approaches are unique adaptations of, or later importations into, the discipline. Even liberalism, the first major theoretical moment in the institutional history of the discipline emerging from the West, is not so much a pure IR construction as it is an adaptation of an older and profound philosophical tradition. These can broadly be described as the mainstream theories of IR, both equally diverse (Donnelly 2000; Dunne 2001; Dunne and Schmidt 2001; Richardson 2001; Viotti and Kauppi 1990). Some would also include the dependency approach within the mainstream, or, more correctly, as the dominant alternative to the mainstream, since the more contemporary radical approaches not only challenge the dominance of realism and liberalism, but also question the radicalism of the dependency school. However, we shall discuss dependency theory as part of Marxist and neo-Marxist approaches to IR in Chapter 4.

POLITICAL REALISM

Political realism, the dominant orthodoxy of the field, took root in the dark hours of the liberal tragedy. The philosophy of realism has its roots in antiquity, dating back to the works of Thucydides and Kautilya. But within the academic discipline of IR, political realism became a dominant force only after World War II, alongside the rising politico-military fortunes of the United States. The philosophy of political realism was best expressed and popularised by Hans J. Morgenthau, a Jewish German migrant to the United States, who authoritatively spelled out six basic principles of realism in his *Politics Among Nations* (1948). Political realism, however, has an exceedingly rich heritage, comprising masterpieces by E. H. Carr (1947), Richard Niebuhr (1932), John Herz (1951), Henry Kissinger (1994), and Robert Gilpin (1981), among many others.

The philosophy of realism draws its appeal from its pragmatism and sparseness. Its central theoretical categories, despite all their varieties and internal differences, are statism, survival, and self-help, each inextricably linked to the other (Dunne and Schmidt 2001, 150–55). The realist storyline, simply put, is the following: the international order (or system) is anarchic, devoid of a central regulatory authority, and populated by basic units that are the sovereign territorialised nation-states. The states are Weberian constructs—they monopolise the legitimate means of violence within a given territory. States contain the political community—citizens—who are defined along the axes of sovereignty and exclusive territoriality. Within the state is a realm of order, progress, and development, under the heavy hand of authority. Outside the state is the sphere of uncertainty, war, and anarchy, where no authority stands. The states, as rational actors, are solely motivated by their perceived national interest. The interplay of sovereign wills in an anarchic set-up leads to coalitions and countervailing coalitions, which can only be equilibrated by a balance of power.

Realists marry power with security, although the relationship is complex and divides realists themselves into defensive and offensive variants. But all realists tend to agree that a balance of power among dominant states secures the stability and equilibrium of the system as a whole. Morgenthau's classical realism, which borrowed heavily from Reinhold Niebuhr's Augustinian pessimism, emphasised the universal *animus dominandi* in men (and, by extension, of states), which gave rise to competition and war unless disciplined through the efficient balance-of-power arrangements worked out through ingenious diplomacy. The other aspects of classical realism concerned the insistence on defining national interest by power; separating moral or ethical pronouncements from power-based interest; the autonomy of politics; and a passionate case for prudence as the only moral standard in international affairs (Morgenthau 1948, 4–15).

There are four basic attributes of political realism: the primacy of the state; the international system as anarchy; the centrality of power; and pragmatism as morality. *First*, realism is about the primacy of the state, conceived as a collective and rational actor. Realists recognise the primacy of groups and group interactions in human life. The fact that human beings are organised into nation-states makes the state the primary unit of analysis in human life. While realists do not necessarily deny the presence of multiple power centres within the state, or the fact that foreign policy is not always an optimal rational choice, they firmly caution against any disaggregated analysis of the state. The policy pronouncements of the sovereign executive are taken as the voice and position of the state. Realists do not deny the existence of non-state actors, flows, and networks in the international system; however, they consider these actors subordinate to the state, since the latter retains the legal power to regulate and even terminate the activities of the former within its territorial bounds. As stated earlier, the state is understood as being a territorial entity that has a legitimate monopoly over society's means of violence. It is also viewed as having a distinctive legal or international personality that separates it from all other organisations. It is defined primarily as a security institution, having the responsibility to guarantee the life of its borders. Guarding external sovereignty from dangers emanating from the international system, be it from other states or powerful non-state entities, is the existential basis of the state (Morgenthau 1948, 4–15).

Realists are divided over the role of the state in the political economy. Some realists like Robert Gilpin believe that the state is vital to securing the health of the domestic economy and managing international relations in a manner conducive to the prosperity of the domestic population (Gilpin 1981). But many other realists do not grant any specific economic function to the state other than agreeing that a state-based order provides the foundation of a normal free-trading international economy (Guzzini 1998). The domestic market cannot function without the legal guarantees of authority. Although international authority is anarchic and devoid of any central authority, states make rules and norms for the regulation of the international market forces. Realists have also strongly rebutted claims that globalisation and modern information technology have made the state redundant. On the contrary, they have argued that while the state has lost power to its organisational rivals in some areas, it has discovered strength in many new ones. And, most crucially, in the fundamental task of maintaining security and order, the state remains uncontested, despite the numerous structural changes rocking the global order (Hirst and Thompson 1996; Krasner 1996–97).

The *second* feature of realism is the claim that the international system is anarchic, that is, there is no central regulatory authority to maintain law and order. States are understood as being self-help units, having the responsibility to protect their territory and population against possible predation by other states. While anarchy does not theoretically foreclose the option of collective security, realists believe that it would not be prudent of states to plan their security through external and altruistic guarantees. Anarchy induces a sameness in state behaviour and institutional arrangements of security, independent of space and time. Those states that fail to align their policies with the signals emitted by the anarchic international system risk military defeat or domination by strong and resourceful states. It should be remembered that classical realists had no systematic account of anarchy. They derived the state's obsession with power and security from human nature. Morgenthau argued that, much like individuals, states are driven by dark and pessimistic impulses. They share a universal desire to dominate others and, in the absence of reliable security assurances, are unable to trust their neighbours. Realists argued that peace/security was the precondition for prosperity, commerce, and development. And given the fact that there was no supra-authority standing above and controlling the states, states could not leave the business of security to others.

Third, realists believe that national interest, defined as power, is the most important principle driving meaningful foreign policies. Power is the master variable in all forms of realism, although realists do not agree on its measurement and nature. They argue that any attempt by a powerful state to dominate others would invariably provoke countervailing tendencies, and the resultant forces would lead to a balance of power among them. This balance of power, for most classical realists, had to be carefully constructed through conscious state action, be it via the internal mobilisation of resources or through alliance-building exercises. Strong states endowed with a massive amount of resources could afford to mobilise them against powerful adversaries. Weak states, on the other hand, had to come together and join with comparatively strong states to guarantee their security against powerful predators. Most realists argue that states must consider material resources and morale in calculating the 'balance'. In other words, states must find a balance against actual capabilities and not against anticipated intentions. This is because while capabilities are concrete and thus 'real', intentions are ambivalent, liable to be misleading and to change in a short time. Relying on a subjective assessment of intentions against the concrete calculation of capabilities would imperil state security, as there are no permanent friends or enemies in international relations. But realists are also divided over the goals of state behaviour. Defensive realists argue that states seek security and do not need infinite power to reach this goal. Offensive realists, however, disagree and contend that states must aim at the maximisation of power rather than optimal security. Their point is that while hegemonic states would willingly hold on to the present distribution of power to guarantee security, revisionist states want to alter the distribution of power itself, and seek as much power as may be required to achieve this. There is no way to settle this debate theoretically within the paradigm.

One school of realism—the power transition theory—does not consider balance of power an attribute of the paradigm. Scholars like A. F. K. Organski and Robert Gilpin argue that in every historical period, systems are stabilised by the hegemonic state and not by any balance between great powers (Gilpin 1981; Lemke 2002; Organski 1958). Hegemons rise and fall over time due to their growth differentials. At critical conjunctures, when the rate of decline of a hegemonic power is superseded by the rise of a challenger, systemic wars tend to break out, moving the system towards a new equilibrium in keeping with the interests of that new hegemonic power. It is the rise of the new hegemon that pacifies and stabilises the system. This power provides the primary public goods and takes up the responsibility of maintaining the basic rules of the game. While the two variants are clearly at loggerheads, both emphasise the role of the material capacity held by great powers to stabilise the given order (Morgenthau 1948, 4–15).

Fourth, realists do not consider realism a moral approach to politics. A closer scrutiny reveals, though, that realism is not totally devoid of values. While realists reify the value of national security, a closer examination shows that there are differences between personal and national security, well appreciated by the realist school. For realists, national security pre-empts other fundamental norms, and thus security is understood as providing the very foundation of a healthy and productive human society. The need for security arises because some people often violently threaten the physical existence of their fellow beings. Security is therefore essentially thought of as protection against all forms of physical danger or threats to bodily injury of any kind. However, security also means the preservation of the means of existence, and hence protection against any threat to such means of survival. Personal security is an absolutely essential precondition to the production and successful reproduction of human life. National security, on the other hand, applies to the populations of countries, and it is therefore both a political and a personal good.

The idea of national security is premised upon the search for personal security. In its philosophical defence, Thomas Hobbes stated that the state was essentially a security arrangement with a monopoly of legitimate force or authority to perform its security role. According to Hobbes, the solution to the problem of domestic insecurity was to change the organising principle of the domestic sphere from anarchy to hierarchy. However, this had an effect in producing an international state of nature comprised of armed states. For Hobbes, the price of living under international anarchy was less threatening than domestic insecurity. This resulted in the dilemma that the security of the citizen within came with the insecurity of the people outside. However, the realists argue that responding to the demands of international anarchy and the security of the people does not necessarily mean jeopardising the security of the citizen by going back to the state of nature in the domestic sphere. In this resolve, the commitment to 'security' by realists remains uncompromised (Chatterjee 2011, 335–36).

Classical realism, however, did not go uncontested within the discipline. The first major crisis to strike realism took the form of the behavioural revolution in IR, which challenged the methodological inadequacies of the realist school. But this was a minor skirmish. The behaviouralists could neither challenge the realist ontology nor convincingly argue their case (Hollis and Smith 1990; Knorr and Rosenau 1969).

The second serious challenge to realism came from interdependence scholars like Robert Keohane and Joseph Nye and pluralists like Graham T. Allison, who challenged some of its basic assumptions. Keohane and Nye argued that the global system was not anarchic but marked by a complex interdependence based on a web of interactions amongst state and various non-state actors, and that states were not obsessed with power considerations, the agenda of international politics was not set automatically, and that while states were important, they were not exclusive actors in world politics (Keohane and Nye 1971, 1977). Allison's work on decision-making challenged the rational and unitary nature of the realist state and concluded that no particular national interest was obvious from a decision-maker's perspective. Organisational frames of reference, competition, and bargaining amongst crucial players, as well as irrational factors often decided the nature of decisions, rather than the cold, abstract notion of interest defined by power (Allison 1971; Allison and Zelikow 1999). Both theoretically and empirically, the 1970s looked bleak for political realism.

The third related crisis took the form of the dependency challenge. Whereas realists draw attention to the competition for power between states, dependency scholars examine the political economy underlying the system of states. They alleged that mainstream IR theories had no staple political economy; instead, they took the surface phenomena as real. Somewhat true to their Marxist inspiration, dependency scholars highlighted the critical role of the global economy as the main motor driving international relations. While not disregarding the nation-state altogether, they subordinated state activities to the constraints imposed by the political economy. Dependency scholars took a structuralist view of the international system, viewing international structures as essentially capitalist and divided into two parts: the core and its periphery. These are defined by the degree of development or underdevelopment of their modes of production. The core comprised the great (Western) powers while the periphery included the vast majority of Third World states. Dependency scholars were not consciously IR theoreticians, but wrote primarily from developmental and historical-sociological perspectives. Yet, their criticism was significant for the realists. Realism was exposed as devoid of structural underpinnings and as essentially a theory of superstructures (Frank 1972; Hobden 1998; Wallerstein 1974, 1980, 1989).

By the end of the 1970s, the realists had responded. The counter-offensive came from three distinctive sources: *first*, Kenneth Waltz published *The Theory of International Politics* (TIP) in 1979, which marked the most authoritative statement of a structural realist position, popularly dubbed as neorealism. *Second*, Robert Gilpin, following the little-noticed work of Organski and Kugler, developed the hegemonic stability theory in 1981, which provided a distinctive political-economic perspective to realism. *Third*, Stephen Krasner developed a complex theory of regimes in 1983 that sought to accommodate the role of institutions, norms, and practices. By the 1980s, realism had reclaimed its dominance within the discipline, and its detractors were on the defensive.

Neorealism was committed to constructing 'a theory of international politics that remedies the defects of present theories' (Waltz 1979, 1). Waltz began his text by constructing reductionist theories through a deductive structuralism that promised to produce a grand theory of IR. He sought to model his realism upon neoclassical economic theory to reveal the systemic order underlying contemporary international politics. The kernel of Waltz's neorealist or structuralist perspective is contained in the following propositions:

1. A system is composed of a structure and of interacting units. The structure is the system-wide component that makes it possible to think of the system as a whole (ibid., 79).
2. How units stand in relation to each other, and the way they are arranged or positioned is not a property of the unit. Rather, the arrangement of the unit is the property of the system (ibid., 80).
3. The structure of the system acts as a constraining and disposing force, and because it does so, systemic theories explain and predict continuity within the system (ibid., 72).

Waltz's concept of political structure consists of three analytical components: the principle according to which the system is ordered or organised; the differentiation of units and the specification of their functions; and the degree of concentration or diffusion capabilities within the system (Ruggie 1983, 264–65). Waltz's central propositions are as follows:

1. The fundamental feature of the international realm is anarchy or the absence of central rule. The units are functionally alike, and so there is no functional differentiation of units (states). All states are self-help units and organisations that provide security. These units are placed within the international system through the distribution of capabilities among them (ibid.).
2. International structures will change if the organisational principle changes, or, failing that, through variations in the capabilities of units. There are intra-systemic changes brought about by shifts in the configuration of capabilities, that is, the number of powers inhabiting the system, but these changes are not systemic in nature. While intra-systemic changes result from changes in the distribution of capabilities, systemic change is prevented by the structure of anarchy itself. Structural realism therefore offers a systemic reading of world politics, which is about a continuity of patterns, recurrences, and repetitions, and not change (ibid., 273–74; Waltz 1979, 69, 93, 271).

Neorealism continues to exert a considerable influence on IR theory. But it has attracted at least as much critique as praise. Its primary limitations are four-fold. *First*, the parsimony of the theory makes it too abstract to be useful for the daily affairs of world politics. Big changes and large trends do not come often or easily. Within a certain distribution of capabilities, it might explain continuity and similarity, but it has no perspective for change and a limited explanatory reach. *Second*, neorealism of the Waltzian variety is sociologically naïve and lacks proper consideration of domestic variables. It black-boxes too much too easily, without offering sufficient reasoning. *Third*, Waltz's contrast between system and units is problematic, for he misses the centrality of interactions or dynamic density that are crucial, and have enormous significance for both states and the system. He pushes interactions to the unit level, a move that makes the unit a dumping ground for all that is unexplained or outside the structure. And *fourth*, Waltz's neorealism, like its classical counterpart, is devoid of any theory or perspective of change. The debates following the publication of TIP amongst realists and between realists and liberals are concerned, in one way or another, with these four limitations of Waltz's work (Ashley 1984, 225–86; Buzan, et al. 1993).

Balance of power remains the central concept for neorealists.[1] Waltz insists that the theory of the balance of power is the central political theory in international politics, and termed it a law. He explains balance of power through two factors: structure and anarchy. Thus, balance of

---

[1]Both classical and neorealist accounts are balance of power theories, the classical version being agential and the latter taking a systemic perspective. Both theories take balance, rather than bandwagon, as the natural tendency for states and the international system, although Randall Schweller's balance of interest theory finds *joining with*, rather than *opposing*, the dominant state to be the common strategic behaviour for unthreatened revisionist states, while neoclassical realist theorists like William Wohlforth and Fareed Zakaria allow a healthy role to domestic factors as additional triggers of balancing policies.

Against conventional realist theories are staked a number of approaches, such as the long cycle theory of Modelski and Thompson, the capitalist world-economy paradigm of Wallerstein and Chase-Dunn, the power transition theory of Organski and Kugler, Gilpin's theory of hegemonic war and change, Doran's power cycle theory, Vayrynen's theory of economic cycles and the power transition, and Midlarsky's theory of hierarchical equilibrium. In their own ways, these refute the centrality of balance of power and emphasise the role of war and change, particularly the rise and fall of dominant or hegemonic states, in stabilising a given international system.

power arises from the structure of the international system and not from diplomacy. Despite several critiques, no recent neorealist scholar has dismissed the research agenda of neorealism on the ground of the limitations they have detected. Rather, they have strengthened the realist position so as to make it virtually unassailable (Chatterjee 2014, 5).

What can a state do when faced with a powerful adversary or a coalition of adversaries? Unlike hierarchical systems, anarchy features a balance of power where states counter each other's influence to avoid being dominated by the strongest. This prevents them from passively following a dominant power; instead, they prioritise their own security and autonomy. Simply put, states, when faced with opposition, oppose their adversary instead of joining the strongest power. Waltz argues that 'bandwagoning' refers to allying with the stronger power, that is, the one capable of establishing hegemony. The balance of power theory believes, however, that such an alliance will be dangerous for the survival of weaker states, who should instead (of bandwagoning) oppose or try to find a balance against the hegemon. Stephen Walt has attempted to validate this crucial assumption by examining the pattern of alliance-formation in West Asia between 1955 and 1979, and that of India and Pakistan (Walt 1988). Walt's findings support Waltz's central proposition that states normally seek a balance and do not bandwagon: 'These studies revealed that states form alliances primarily to *balance* against other states, and that "bandwagoning" behaviour—that is, alignment with the dominant state or coalition—was relatively rare' (ibid., 277).

Unlike the Waltzian balance of power theory defined on capabilities, Walt premised his theory on threats. He maintains: 'By focusing solely on the distribution of capabilities, structural balance-of-power theory ignores the *other factors* that statesmen will consider when making alliance ... as a result, the theory cannot explain why balances often fail to form' (Walt 1988, 279). Walt modifies a crucial assumption of structural theory, affirming that states 'seek allies to balance *threats*, and that power is merely one element in their calculations—albeit an important one' (ibid.). Accordingly, 'an imbalance of threat occurs when the most threatening state or coalition is significantly more dangerous than the second most threatening state or coalition' (ibid., 280). The degree of threat depends on the aggregate power, geographic distance/proximity, offensive capability, and the aggressive intent of a threatening state or coalition. States are found to balance against threats, not capabilities.

Unless factors like distance, intention, and offensive capabilities are factored in, there can be no accurate or substantive explanation of state behaviour (Chatterjee 2014, 5–6).

Most significantly, Walt's treatment of the subject is so intricate and subtle, it successfully turns choice into inevitability. The essence of Waltzian structuralism lies in the fact that he links the balance of power theory to the prevailing condition of structural anarchy. Thus, balance of power can be avoided in both the most unlikely circumstances—either the survival instinct of states in a condition of unregulated anarchy must disappear, or the structure of anarchy itself has to change.

To summarise, Waltz views the international system as a self-help system and treats states as defensive actors, inasmuch as their primary, though not exclusive, intention is self-preservation. Thus, while states are not necessarily self-aggrandising, they are compulsively seeking their own security in an anarchic milieu where the probability of threat(s) to their survival (as independent states) is always real. Thus, states are forced to view other states as potential threats, which makes balance of power the only theory of international politics that can explain the systemic or structural logic of the anarchic order fully. Having ruled out the possibility of any third kind of system—other than the hierarchical and the anarchic—Waltz could confidently discuss the self-perpetuation of the internal system, as states can logically only be self-help units within an anarchic system lacking an authoritative or commanding sovereign regulator. Essentially, balance of power is a balance of capabilities, and states have to judge the capabilities of other states continuously to maintain this balance. Balance, again, is defined by the number of poles in the balance, which refer to the number of states that can seriously threaten the existence of others. Contrary to many neorealists (and realists), Waltz believed that a bipolar balance was the ideal mechanism for the international system, since it was easier to manage with fewer interested and capable players.

Waltz did not seek to provide a theory of foreign policy, and therefore his perspective will not account for major variations in interactions at the state level caused by local or specific factors (Telhami 2002; Waltz 1996). What, then, is the value of neorealism as a theory of security if it cannot explain major foreign policy outcomes in different parts of the world? Waltz did not consider this a limitation. In his defence, he provided a two-fold text, claiming that neorealism successfully possesses both. *First,* he emphatically stated that no theory can ever claim to explain 'everything', and neorealism was no exception. *Second*, the validity of neorealism did not depend on empirical cases, but rested on the internal consistency of propositions constituting the theory, while its utility depended on its capacity to generate a sophisticated research programme on security at the systems level.

Contrary to the claims of interdependency, functionalist, and pluralist scholars, Waltz believed there was no fundamental change in the logic of the system. Such an alteration was not possible without the contemporary international system changing from an anarchic into a hierarchical one. Although neorealism theoretically considered a global government based on collective security, it was no more likely than classical realism to replace the balance of power with a new world order or a stateless society (Chatterjee 2008, 182). However, the primary purpose of the neorealist intervention was to deny the possibility of any alteration, owing to the structural attributes of the system and the logic of survival of the units.

How do we see this structural effect independent of the foreign policy of states? What are its templates? How do they vary over time? These are complex questions that at once problematise the distinction between structural and foreign policy theories. Unless interaction capacity as a process variable is interposed between the structure and the units, neither the so-called structural effect—that moves the units—nor variations in the distribution of power can be properly explained. Structural theories employ the concept of polarity to define a system; poles are defined by concentrations of power at the unit level. They change when the number of states (or units) inhabiting a system, which have the power to inflict unacceptable damage on their adversaries, vary. But how does power accumulate in a state? A pure structural theory of world politics is unable to account for this.

It is necessary to take a close look at the debates between structural and neo-classical realists. According to Waltz (1979, 1996), his theory of international politics differs in purpose from foreign policy theories. A structural theory of world policies explains why different states behave similarly, while foreign policy theory explains why similarly placed states behave differently. This is simple enough from Waltz's perspective. Waltz argues that powerful states, like oligopolistic firms, cannot avoid the effects of global systems, but can manipulate them for their benefit.

How convincing is his distinction in practice? It is here that the debate gets stronger. It is true that all kinds of states, regardless of their domestic composition, are primarily interested in physical survival. Even in domestic politics, all individuals normally agree to guarantee physical safety above all else. But then what? Like individuals, states, which are national collectives of individuals, differ on the choice of strategy and the means of survival. Hence, realists must introduce secondary assumptions that have a crucial bearing on the motives and costs of behaviour. A few analytical illustrations are instructive at this stage. Faced with a threatening environment, states can balance, bandwagon, hide, or even seek to transcend the situation. Again, for a state, security might mean either holding on to their position or seeking to dominate their adversary (hegemony). Further, in a multipolar system, states might either chain-gang[2] or pass the buck. These forms of state behaviour are apparently sanctioned by structural realism (neorealism), but they are definitely not all the same. This seems to suggest that beyond establishing the universal desire of states to obtain security and survival through the means of self-help, which include internal as well as external balancing (in the form of alliances), structural realism has little to say about what a state will actually do in its foreign policy behaviour.

Structural realists can still argue that such indeterminacy is not peculiar to their theory. Great powers are expected to balance and maintain the stability of the system. If some great powers refrain from doing so, the explanation will have to be sought at lower (domestic) levels. Similarly, weaker powers are supposed to be susceptible to the constraints imposed by the system structure. If they leave their security to chance, they will be abandoning their primary responsibility, whose outcome may be catastrophic. Such an inability, however, is an exceptional condition, and requires explanation at the domestic level. It is not for a systemic theory to explain such deviations.

---

[2]When alliances are rigidly structured, chain-ganging in international relations forces allies to join wars, thereby leading to considerable escalation of conflict. This tendency leads to the security dilemma, best typified in the run-up to World War I; it demonstrates how entangling alliances can turn local conflicts into global wars. Chain-ganging stands in contrast to buck-passing, where states refuse to take the risk of confrontation and instead offload the responsibility of constraining a threat onto other actors (Christensen and Snyder 1990).

Yet, deviations and irregularities occur in foreign affairs. These cannot be explained without considering non-systemic factors. We need to appreciate two fundamental points. *First*, systemic or structural effects are not free-standing; as Wendt has shown so clearly, the structure and units constitute each other. Therefore, there is rarely a pure structural effect. *Second*, the constraints and opportunities of the system structure are invariably filtered and mediated through variables at the domestic level. That states often do not behave as per the prediction of structural realists is because of the role played by domestic variables.

The relatively recent debate within structural realism between Waltz and Mearsheimer, or what has come to be called the offensive *versus* defensive realism(s), has been much contested. The major disagreement is over the ontology of realism. Defensive realists claim that states are primary; against this, the offensive brigade argues that the structural effects of anarchy are more thorough and forbidding than the former would admit, thereby leading to an inexorable and incessant drive for power and domination within the system. Interestingly, both schools derive their conflicting propositions from shared assumptions—that the international system lacks self-regulation; rational and egoistic states are the primary actors populating the international system; and material capabilities are the primary currency of power. While defensive realists offer a better explanation of how complacent great powers behave, their offensive counterparts model the behaviour of revisionist powers more accurately (Snyder 2002). We need to look at this more closely.

Anarchy has different implications as realists differ on the actors who inhabit such an anarchist realm. Realists like Mearsheimer take a pessimistic view of such actors, akin to the classical realism of Morgenthau (Mearsheimer 2001). Offensive realists provide a fearful view of an interminable conflict between states, which is invariably exploitative, hateful, cynical, and hegemonic in orientation (Chatterjee 2005b, 5498). Mearsheimer's states have an insatiable appetite for power, which ironically becomes a basic precondition for security. Mearsheimer suggests two reasons for this: *first*, it seems impossible to measure power accurately and feel confident about the relative positions of states. States are never sure of the amount of power that could secure them against their rivals. *Second*, the calculation of power is never static. It is even more difficult to project relative power positions over twenty- or thirty-year periods. A defensive realist like Waltz, on the other hand, has a more relaxed view of anarchy. While his states are egoists, they are not cynical or inherently exploitative, eternally restive, or inevitably hegemonic in character. Neither Waltz nor Mearsheimer consider subjective, psychological, or ideological factors, and without this, their conclusions are incomplete and partly illogical.

Such a structural theory offers no explanation for what makes or unmakes great powers. A better explanation comes from power transition theorists like Organski and Kugler, Gilpin, Mandelbaum, Modelski, William Thompson, the historian Paul Kennedy, Immanuel Wallerstein, and Charles Doran. Power transition and hegemonic stability theories argue that the rise and fall of great powers can be explained by the differential rates of economic growth of these states, coupled with their satisfaction—or dissatisfaction—with the existing status quo. The transition occurs when the economic decline of an existing great power corrodes its military capability, while its challenger's economic rise translates into steady military ascendancy. The point at which the former's decline intersects with the latter's ascent is the moment of systemic transformation. The change may involve massive wars, or may be peaceful if the declining power accommodates the challenger. In a vital sense, these theories direct attention to the domestic configuration of great powers. Their key variable is economic growth, which includes technological innovation that allows states to acquire the hard power capabilities to challenge their adversaries, and ultimately push for a decisive power transition. While transition theorists have emphasised dynamics ignored by the neorealists, they did not pay sufficient attention to domestic politics as a key variable in assessing the relative power distribution within an international system.

Neoclassical realists, in contrast, argue that the notion of a smoothly functioning mechanical transmission belt is inaccurate and misleading. The international distribution of power can drive the behaviour of countries only by influencing the decisions of real officials, and we need to explore how each country's policymakers actually understand their situation. Capabilities do not translate into behaviour automatically. This gap has been largely filled by neoclassical realists like Randall Schweller, William C. Wohlforth, and Fareed Zakaria, who gave weight to both the international distribution of power and domestic politics from within a broad realist perspective. Picking up from the earlier generation, Zakaria, in his compelling study of US foreign policy in the late nineteenth century, *From Wealth to Power* (1998), argues that wealthy states tend to build large armies in order to use the tools at their disposal to gain control over their environment. Wohlforth and Thomas J. Christensen also refer to the shifting distribution of power behind major foreign policy choices.

Neoclassical realists also highlight the need for a nuanced understanding of a state's range of foreign policy goals and ideas, and draw attention to state-society relations, using the rich historical and sociological works of Charles Tilly and Michael Mann. Thus, Zakaria and Wohlforth's work have shown that both power distribution and the perception of that distribution matters in the foreign policy of great powers. They argue that while decision-makers may be idiosyncratic, no foreign policy can be successful if it goes against the grain of the actual distribution of power within the international system. In fact, contrary to popular interpretations, all realists consider power distribution the ultimate variable in the game of great power politics. Neorealists, however, do not explore the impact of the deep structure, and seek to explain the nature of the system's effects and not the adaptive choices. Power transition theories see domestic structures as transmission belts, while neoclassical theorists explain the 'adaptive preferences' of great powers under a given distribution of power (Christensen 1996; Rose 1998; Schweller 1998; Wohlforth 1993; Zakaria 1998).

Critique of Realism

The chief limitation of such realism is its reliance on unverifiable assumptions of human nature, which it depicts as lustful and power hungry, given to domination and control. Moreover, there is no possibility of breaking out of this cycle of domination and fear, and a fatal desire to pre-empt the consequences of mutual mistrust by overpowering each other leads to an unending spiral of violence. Realism based on human nature, therefore, is too pessimistic, and does not adequately explain those aspects of world affairs that build on voluntary cooperation, mutual trust, and interdependence.

There will be little development if we live in a constant state of fear and conflict. The fact is that there is actually more cooperation than conflict, and contrary to the prescriptions of realism, most states have a far more relaxed attitude vis-à-vis others. This critique, however, is only partially true; for the great powers in the world, politics is often based on realist precepts. Moreover, realists do not argue that conflicts will necessarily erupt; they speak more in terms of the potential of conflict and the dynamics that influence the policies of states (Bandyopadhyaya 1993).

The assumptions of the classical realism of Morgenthau, in particular, seem problematic as there can be no objective and scientific validation of human nature and the psychopathology of states. There is also the related problem of extrapolating individual traits onto macro entities like states. Realist positions on morality and ethics have also been questioned. On the one hand, realism contrasts power and morality, which is untenable theoretically since all notions of power build on certain moral standards. On the other hand, realist precepts tend to dwarf the normative dimensions of international relations and rationalise behaviour unconcerned with the moral and ethical development of the people. This breeds a culture of pessimism and conservatism that prevents deeper relations from developing across states and societies. But states are not only competitors in an anarchic system, they are also partners in a global civil society bound by international law. Theorists of the English school (the International Society approach) show how states are influenced both by material/systemic factors and normative constraints. States are both rational and social and, like individuals, have legitimate interests that others can recognise and respect. Observing a principle of reciprocity in their mutual relations can prove beneficial to states. The notion of benefits is also not as narrow as the realists would have it; mutual recognition, respect, and legitimacy of ideas are potent benefits for all states.

The realist case for the 'anarchy problematic' has been challenged by constructivists like Wendt. While many scholars agree that the international realm lacks a legitimate body of authority, the meaning and consequences of such a fact are not necessarily based on realist injunctions. Countering neorealist ideas, Wendt argues that self-help does not follow logically or causally from the principle of anarchy (Chatterjee 2019, 113), but is socially constructed. 'Self-help and power politics are institutions and not essential features of anarchy. Anarchy is what states make of it' (Wendt 1987). Thus, Wendt argues that anarchy is a form of social culture that is constituted by agents, and whose meaning varies across time and space. Consequently, the anarchy of enemies is different from that of rivals or friends.

Realists are divided over the role of domestic politics. Both classical realists and neorealists underplay its significance. Waltz, in his seminal text *Man, the State, and War* (1959), argued that neither personalities nor state structures can explain the continuity in state behaviour across millennia. The standard realist ploy is to contrast anarchy and hierarchy as two opposing modes of organising space. But neoclassical realists have accepted the pivotal role of domestic factors in shaping the foreign policies of states (Rose 1998). They have shown how concepts like security dilemmas and alliance-making are critically related to domestic considerations and political compulsions. Moreover, liberals and pluralists have exposed the superficiality of the statist perspective held by realists. They have documented how domestic preferences have shaped states' attitudes towards neighbours in several major areas, and the critical role played by key institutions as well as leaders and bureaucrats in the decision-making processes pertaining to foreign affairs. Constructivists have corroded the realist claim to unitary national interest, while liberals, Marxists, and critical theorists have analysed how national interest is defined, claimed, and legitimated by the dominant interests and groups in society. Most realists are unable to account for the role played by domestic variables in any systematic manner. But many new-generation realists are far more attentive to this deficiency in their approach, and recent realist scholarship has attempted to bridge the divide in areas like security dilemma, grand strategy, and coalition-building.

The realist idea of balance of power is also fraught with conceptual ambiguities and contradictions. For instance, theorists like Organski and Vasquez have shown that this concept means different things to different people, has been deployed differently by Morgenthau in several contexts, and is mathematically imprecise and historically controversial. The constant refinement of and emendations in the concepts of balance (and alliances) have made the concept immune to falsification, and considerably compromised its analytical worth.

Neoliberals contend that state behaviour is caused less by anarchy and more by institutions, learning, and other factors that encourage cooperation. Scholars like Robert Keohane and Robert Axelrod accepted Waltz's central assumptions—that the international order is anarchic, and states are rational and egoistic actors who work for their own benefit—but demonstrated that states could widen their perception of self-interest through economic cooperation and involvement in international institutions (Axelrod 1984; Keohane, 1983, 1986). Realists are unable to understand how the webs of interaction and complex interdependence affect world politics.

Critical theorists, such as Robert W. Cox, critique the failure of neorealism to explain change. They argue that realists are mistaken in considering the structure of international relations as a timeless, universal category, when it is actually time-bound and historical in nature. In contrast, critical theorists focus on the creative interplay of ideas, material factors, and social forces as a way to understand the genealogy of structures and their possible transformation. Realism unfortunately legitimates the existing status quo of strategic relations among states, and thus rationalises the politics of the dominant. Critical theorists also negate the underlying positivistic and scientific methods used by realists. Cox, for example, denies that theories are objective and neutral. In all systems, the dominant defines moral standards and the regime of truth. Hence, all orders are exclusionary in effect, reflecting a built-in interest in domination and control (Cox 1981, 1983).

Realism, and particularly neorealism, has been severely criticised by postmodern and post-structural scholars of IR. Richard Ashley and R. B. J. Walker, for example, have criticised the assumptions, methodology, and central attributes of neorealism (Devetak 1996b). Seeing in neorealism a departure from the classical heritage, they targeted its scientific, rational, objective, and empiricist cast. They also found the realist understanding of power narrow and superficial, unable to explain the processes of subjectification and how power creates its own field of play. These scholars have denied the sanctity of the domestic/international divide, calling it a false dichotomy. Perhaps most significantly, they have accused realism of creating a discourse within which the conventional categories of the discipline acquire meaning. They argue that alternative ideas are not allowed to flourish within the discipline, given the epistemic hegemony of realism as 'the theory' that provides the fundamental truths of international politics (Ashley 1984; Walker 1993).

Feminist scholars have also critiqued realism. An important component of the theories of both Morgenthau and Waltz is their intellectual connection to early realist thinkers such as Thucydides, Machiavelli, Hobbes, and Jean-Jacques Rousseau. Feminist analyses of this genre have revealed that their work was always built on a hyper-masculinity underlying a militarised conceptualisation of the state, which views the feminine as a symbolic threat. Feminists argue that early state formation marked the effective centralisation of political authority and processes of accumulation, which were achieved through the institutionalisation of gender exploitation and the ideological legitimisation of such gendered practices. National politics as well as the theory and practice of international war and peace have been gendered throughout modern history, and gendered elements at all levels of world politics are critical causal and constitutive factors in war (Sjoberg 2012). Feminists have also argued that the structure of the international system is gender-hierarchical and not anarchic. For many feminists, at the heart of the 'structure of international politics' is a gender divide; gender inequalities within a state are constitutive of aggression in international relations, and gender subordination, rather than a competition for power, among states is a constant aspect of human nature and the defining motor of international interaction (Sjoberg 2012; Tickner 1992, 58).

Realism and South Asia: Applying Theory to Practice

Most strategic analysts would describe the South Asian security predicament in the new millennium in broad realist terms. According to them, South Asia remains a conflict-prone subcontinent. These conflicts, however, are related to the history of the region. In this sense, the post-Cold War era has neither caused any new conflict, nor ended any old ones. South Asian conflicts can be broadly divided into three categories: conflicts over territory, ethnicity, and resource-sharing. The key conflict in the region remains the rivalry between India and Pakistan, primarily over the territory of Jammu and Kashmir, but also concerning issues of community and identity. The root of the conflict lies in the imperial past. Pakistan was the result of the politics of faith, whereby the Muslim League, under the leadership of Mohammad Ali Jinnah, sought to create a homeland for the Muslims of the subcontinent, to safeguard them against the numerical, political, and cultural domination of the Hindus led by the Indian National Congress. The resulting communal discord saw a temporary solution in the partition of the country, with the birth of the sovereign states of India and Pakistan. Soon after, the two states were embroiled in conflict over the fate of the province of Kashmir, which Pakistan claimed legitimately belonged to her, despite India's legal possession of the territory.

Wars fought in 1948 and 1965 failed to settle the matter. The 1948 war resulted in the division of the territory into Pakistan-occupied Azad Kashmir and the Indian province of Jammu and Kashmir (J&K), divided by the Line of Control (LoC). In 1971, India won a decisive war against Pakistan that resulted in the splitting of East Pakistan into the separate country of Bangladesh. India's conflict with Pakistan is also on strategic issues like control of the Siachen Glacier, and an intense arms race is underway to ensure military balance between them. This arms race assumed a new character when both states acquired nuclear weapons, and missiles with which to deliver such weapons, in the 1990s. After the Pokhran and Chagai Hill explosions of 1998, India and Pakistan settled into a deterrent relationship that largely ruled out the possibility of a full-scale war. Pakistan, however, continues a war of attrition by allegedly equipping militants in the Kashmir Valley with arms, training, money, and protection to carry out terrorist strikes against India. Pakistan has sought to balance India by allying with China, while India has in turn reached out to the US as a counter strategy.

India's foreign policy in the post-Cold War era is also distinctly realist as its national elite, like those in Pakistan and China, looks to realism as the theory guiding their foreign relations. If recent empirical trends are any indication, there is no prospect of a major deviation from pragmatist or maximalist versions of realism in Indian foreign policy. In the last two decades, both the National Democratic Alliance (NDA) and the United Progressive Alliance (UPA) governments have sought to transform India into a major power in world politics. Their strategic investments have thus bolstered the state's critical power resources, securing their influence and safety. This approach attempts to increase the projection of India's power by augmenting her economic strength. In fact, the possibility of India transforming into a big power hinges on the relation between economic performance and strategic assets. This, however, is not a direct relationship. Economic capability provides the foundation for strategic depth; the conversion of economic gains to strategic assets, on the other hand, requires conscious policy decisions. Those decisions depend in turn on how external and domestic constraints are negotiated. For a rising power, the structural constraints inherent in the international system are of critical importance. Established powers tend to prevent new aspirants from becoming powerful states. In an extended unipolar system (such as we see in the present epoch), India's diverse ties with the US are an effort to grapple with the structural dynamics of this system. It seems that India views a mixed strategy of bandwagoning, hiding, and soft balancing with the US as a means to gain greater prominence.

The power that India seeks depends on two other crucial factors. *First*, how India manages her relationship with China, as relations between the two Asian giants have soured and there have been frequent border clashes since 2017. Once again, there is no simple solution in sight. India had long preferred a strategy of balancing and engaging China, both strategically and economically, depending on the nature of the issue at hand. While the cost of this complex strategy is mitigated by the hegemonic role played by the US, India's recent switch to direct balancing and restraining economic relations has complicated matters further. The efficacy of this mixed strategy hinges critically on how the US, as the leading military power in the world, plays its role in the future.

The *second* issue concerns India's challenges in South Asia, most important of which is the menace of terrorism emanating from both Afghanistan and Pakistan. India's record of managing her immediate neighbourhood is poor. Until she devises a strategy of optimal returns vis-à-vis her immediate neighbours, her potential for becoming a major power will remain constrained. The increasingly intrusive role that the Chinese are playing in the subcontinent is also troubling. Realists argue that as a rising power, India's foreign policy is more concerned with structural issues and great powers at present. This is also the perspective of the national elites, and lack of attention to the domestic bases has hobbled India's aspirations considerably.

Liberal Theories of IR

The liberal approach signalled the beginnings of the discipline of IR. However, it was quickly discredited by the realist onslaught. It is crucial to highlight, though, that realism has never eclipsed liberalism. The enduring debate between the two has been a central feature of mainstream political thought. Of the diverse strands of liberal theory, three deserve detailed elaboration: commercial liberalism, democratic peace theories, and liberal institutionalism. Commercial liberalism is the oldest, and can be traced back to the writings of classical liberal political economists like Adam Smith, Richard Cobden, and Lord Bryce. The functionalist, interdependence, and integration theories are variations on the theme of commercial liberalism. The origins of democratic peace theory can be found in the political writings of Immanuel Kant, most prominently in his pamphlet *The Perpetual Peace* (Chatterjee 2014, 7). Several contemporary liberal thinkers have invested in this idea. As an approach, liberal institutionalism comes closest to the neorealist genre of scholarship. Although in broad agreement with some of the basic assumptions of neorealist theory, liberal institutionalists draw their own, very different conclusions (Baldwin 1993; Keohane 1986).

The initial moment of the discipline was captured by the liberal internationalists (see Brown 1997). The liberals were critical of a number of ideas and practices that have conditioned international politics, from the eighteenth century in particular. They were opposed to autocratic and despotic rule, trade protectionism, and the perils of ultra-nationalism. Undoubtedly, these liberal ideas were far from being genuinely universal in scope, and were seldom sufficiently reflective. Their trepidations regarding dictatorial rule often did not go far enough; they were hesitant to welcome mass democracies and feared threats to property rights if the lower classes were genuinely empowered. Likewise, their censoring of nationalism was limited to European forms, and they did not endorse the project of decolonisation. Although liberals like Hobson were critical of finance capitalism, liberal IR scholars did not extend it to any systematic explanation of global political economy. Mostly concerned with the perils of war in Western Europe, they sought democracy, commerce, and collective security arrangements that could bring about lasting peace in the continent. Heirs to the broad philosophical arguments of Hume and Kant, they were inspired equally by the classical British political economists and utilitarian arguments. They conceived the international order as a modernist project, progressive and amenable to reform; preferred the associational logic of society to the authoritarian argument of the state; and were undecided on how far to endorse the claims of sovereignty.

They had six arguments to offer. *First*, democratic norms would lead to peace; *second*, absolute power had to be made accountable through institutional checks and balances, separation of powers, and a free press; *third*, there was no essential distinction in the way societies function nationally and globally, and it was wrong to underestimate the role of domestic pathologies in theories of war and peace; *fourth*, aggressive nationalism had to be contained as it could move societies towards militarisation and war; *fifth*, free market exchanges naturally demanded an open trading system based on comparative advantage; and *sixth*, international institutions mattered in world politics as blind submission to the demands of national interest did not lead to an optimal outcome for all.

Norman Angell articulated the liberal perspective during the early twentieth century when he argued that chauvinistic nationalism prevented states from reading and understanding the genuine benefits derived from peaceful interdependence and commerce. If a community of free traders controlled policy, both nationalism and war would be rejected as relics of the past (Angell 1912). While liberals like Angell emphasised the wealth-generating consequences of a free trade order as the surest deterrent to war, the peace induced through the benefits of trade would also lead to better resource distribution. When people are by and large doing well and happy, there is little scope for crooked politicians to exploit the rhetoric of war as a survival strategy, or point to harmful external links as a justification for poor growth. Free market policies strengthen peace by ensuring that communities have a direct stake in maintaining stability. The neoliberal case for globalisation is based on this logic—globalisation is supposed to make war irrelevant by enabling states to realise the enormous potential for gain through following free market policies both at home and abroad.

Sadly for the liberals, their prescriptions were not followed during the inter-war years and their immediate aftermath. Their reading of democracy was sociologically naïve as they paid little attention to the tensions between the liberal and democratic aspects of their theory; nor could they anticipate the arrival of a system of mass mobilisation like fascism through apparently democratic means. Likewise, their understanding of nationalism was hollow and failed to account for mass sentiments and anger following national humiliation after the wars. While their understanding of the dangers of aggressive nationalism was fundamentally correct, they offered no alternative to the idea of the nation as the centre of collective political imagination. They also failed to appreciate the global effects of free market capitalism, which not only created problems of asymmetric interdependence that were politically exploited by illiberal forces, but also abandoned specific social classes during massive economic downturns. Keynesianism and welfare liberalism took time to develop, and could not save liberal internationalists from falling into disrepute.

Finally, these early liberals were, paradoxically, paying attention to institutional design on the one hand, and yet not theorising domain specificities carefully. They grossly underestimated the dynamics of national power and the primacy of military capabilities in world affairs, believing that global institutions would generate enough beneficial effects to mitigate the attractions of competitive national responses. The rise of fascism and the lessons of World War II dealt a severe blow to such institutionalism, and it took years for the liberals to create a more robust account of working through institutions within a decentralised international system of states.

Democratic peace theory builds on the legacy of Immanuel Kant. Kant's basic argument was that if states became republics, they would have a natural propensity to maintain peace. He believed that nations had to give up espionage, tactics of secret diplomacy, and standing armies before republicanism could usher in peace. Kant's famous three articles of peace mandated that states must adopt republican constitutions; the world must gradually become a confederation of republics; and, conforming to the idea of universal hospitality, the basic rights of civility must be available to every person, regardless of citizenship. However, Kant was no impractical dreamer; he was of the opinion that republics ought to battle autocratic states, and in some cases, democratic states could well be the aggressor, fearing mischief and the loss of their hard-earned freedom to dictatorial regimes. His Perpetual Peace is not a foreign policy argument; rather, Kant's view is systemic as he considered lasting peace the result of socialised global norms that were learnt as much by statesmen as by local societies.

Michael Doyle's pioneering study on the philosophical lineages of democratic peace theory identifies two other strands of argument in addition to Kant's pacifism. Doyle notes that Joseph Schumpeter had identified a case for international peace in the modernising, individualising, and rationalising tendencies of industrial capitalism, which automatically discarded the atavistic feudal interests of aristocratic classes and the landed gentry. Schumpeter considered modern capitalism as organically anti-war, since no one could rationally benefit from devastation and the snapping of commercial ties. Machiavelli, according to Doyle, advanced yet another variant of liberal imperialism, which argued that republican states benefitted from the inherent balance of its constitutional structure that did not allow any one class to dominate others. His central contention was that a liberal state would be expansionist, for it feared illiberal empires and could not risk the rise of non-republican states (for details, see Doyle 1986).

In the 1980s and 1990s, scholars like Doyle, Bruce Russett, James Oneal, Zeev Maoz, David Lake, Morgan, and Campbell developed the democratic peace theory and soon, scholars began to claim that their conviction that democracies do not fight wars with each other was akin to a law. If the central argument holds true, then the most effective panacea to the historical problem of war is surely democratisation. Democracies are internally peaceful, resolving their differences through mutual discussion, debate, and negotiation. This culture of democratic deliberation is expected to be followed between democratic states as well. Moreover, democracies are not only driven by norms, but are also highly institutionalised. Most crucially, democracies are transparent, mainly due to their free media. This aids peace as it provides transparency in the political process, opening it up to public scrutiny, which would be seen and appreciated by other states. Even authoritarian states would come to appreciate liberal democracy if their interests collided. People are either divided or united in such moments of crisis. If divided, vigorous diplomacy can prevent war; if, however, people stand firm, the detractor can be warned of dire consequences, should it use force.

The normative and institutional arguments are not mutually exclusive, but complementary. The normative aspect states that while shared norms between democracies rule out war as a legitimate means of resolving differences, institutional mechanisms can actually make this happen (Owen 1994, 119, 124). By itself, the normative model is inconsistent with militarised disputes between democratic dyads. If democratic states view each other as having shared norms, a key element of which precludes the use of force against one another, what explains the covert use of force between them? The normative model therefore cannot stand on its own, but requires the support of the institutional model. It is often institutional dynamics that either enable decision-makers in a democratic state to use calibrated force against another democratic government, or prevents them from acting strongly—even when the power elite considers the use of force morally desirable (Ray 1995, 37).

Needless to say, democratic peace, like all theories, is deeply contested. Liberal peace theory is particularly open to criticisms of hegemonic design, and its efficacy is limited to only a few mature Western liberal democratic states. Theoretically, the proponents have failed to adjudicate between the monadic and dyadic versions of the theory, that is, whether democracies are inherently peaceful, or if they sustain peace only with like-minded states. Empirically, it is often seen that weak democracies are prone to violent foreign policy options for consolidation. Again, it is not clear whether peace is the result of democratic orientations, structures, norms, and institutions, or the effects of a power difference (Chatterjee 2014, 8).

Let us study a few of the central shortcomings of this theory. Sebastian Rosato has, for example, advanced a critique against the normative argument of the theory as a causal explanation, stating that 'democracies do not reliably externalize their democratic norms of conflict resolution, nor do they generally treat each other with trust and respect when their interests clash' (Rosato 2003, 588). Christopher Layne, in contrast, finds the structural explanation flawed, arguing that 'institutional constraints do not explain the democratic peace. If democratic public opinion really had the effect ascribed to it, democracies would be peaceful in their relations with all states, whether democratic or not' (Layne 1994, 12). In fact, Kant's central argument was that enlightened public opinion affects how costs are recognised and calculated by the public. In other words, the moderating consequences of a democratic state structure require pre-existing belief systems that enable that very effect in the first place. It is a fact that public opinion in a democracy may not always support the cause of peace; but there is also enough evidence to suggest that in democratic societies, people are less disposed to put their trust in illiberal regimes.

A more powerful set of criticisms comes from scholars who doubt if the theory is as universal as its proponents claim. The record of liberal democracies is not as peaceful as the theory predicts. Even if liberal democracies have not fought each other, they have participated in many wars with different kinds of states. Liberal democratic states have been, and continue to be, imperial outfits, engaging in warfare even when there is no overwhelming threat to their interests, and subjugating weaker nations with little respect for their rights (Levy 2002, 359–61).

Again, it is not clear whether democratisation can promote regional peace in states ruled by conservative aristocratic elites for years and which experienced a democratic transition for only a limited period. These might be postcolonial states lacking indigenous democratic institutions and practices, or post-socialist countries with remnants of party nomenklatura controlling the newly democratic institutions. As Snyder and Mansfield's work suggests, many states retain powerful residues of old regime elites who tend to hijack the political process from time to time. Such leaders are prone to subversive tactics while maintaining a façade of democracy, and often engage in virulent mobilisation along ethnic or national lines for regime survival. These leaders are often prone to perverse democratising tendencies, particularly given the weak institutions in most such societies. An ultra-nationalist public and belligerent pressure groups often prefer a military option to cooperation, and the limited time frame available to such leadership further encourages the adoption of risky, hardline strategies (Snyder and Mansfield 1995).

Mohammad Ayoob and Kaveji Holsti have shown in their research on Third World conflicts that democratisation often aggravates social cleavages in the fragmented societies of Africa and in parts of the Balkans (Ayoob 1991; Holsti 1996), where ethnic groups feel encouraged to displace members of rival communities or withhold their participatory rights. Democratisation might therefore encourage a dangerous brand of identity politics, exacerbate ethnic discord, and fuel secessionist tendencies, resulting in greater conflict rather than peace. It might even work against moderate regimes and encourage the use of plebiscitary tactics. As the empirical record of a large number of Third World states show, democratisation has often brought to power radical forces, which openly oppose the politics of reconciliation and adjustment. Fundamentalists may also occupy power through the democratic route. In all such cases, democratisation can hardly be claimed as a positive incentive to peace.

Neoliberal institutionalists come closest to the neorealists, as both agree on the prevalence of anarchy, the centrality of the state, and the competition for power based on rational and egoistic calculations. Baldwin mentioned six important differences between the two theories:

they disagree on the costs of anarchy, relative *versus* absolute gains, view military security and other domains like political economy or the environment as fundamentally different sites of institutional cooperation, the role of institutions, the significance of ideas and perceptions, and the priority of state goals. Most crucially, neoliberals believe that anarchy is not as prohibitive in its effects as the realists would have it; that states are capable of cooperating with each other over political and economic issues (if not that easily over security matters); institutionalised cooperation often resolves a lack of trust and free-riding tendencies; and that institutions clarify choices, induce transparency, reduce opportunity costs, and make targeted retaliation against regime detractors possible. Life under anarchy, then, is not as hopeless as the realists argue, as anarchy can be moderated and redefined through conscious means.

Liberal institutionalism, however, suffers from one great deficiency: it works well only with good realism, that is, it succeeds only when it has the blessing of the great powers. Satisfied realists are willing to cooperate, and neoliberal institutionalists add little by specifying the conditions under which such cooperation can occur (Chatterjee 2014, 8). First-generation scholars of liberal internationalism like Robert Keohane (1984) and Robert Axelrod (1984) pioneered the development of complex prisoner dilemma game models that differed from those employed by structural realists. They argued that while a trust deficit under anarchy indeed encouraged sub-optimal outcomes among competitive players, unlike the classic illustration that used a one-time game model, actors had to engage with each other unceasingly; therefore, as many rounds were played, the rational egoists understood better why sub-optimal solutions did not work, how insurance strategies could be developed, how, by lengthening the 'shadow of the future', the motivation to cheat and abandon cooperation could be effectively neutralised; and why cooperation benefitted all, despite the absence of altruism and good faith.

Second-generation scholars like Jennifer Sterling-Folker and Martha Finnemore developed sophisticated institutional designs addressing the problem of defection and the autonomy of institutional explanations to show how, in many domains of international politics (including the use of weapons of mass destruction), institutions have significantly lowered transaction costs, improved transparency, identified rule-breakers and defectors, enabled targeted retaliation, and ensured that a myriad actors kept to their transactions despite their many differences. Liberal institutionalists agree that cooperation under anarchy is a daunting task, and refute critiques like Mearsheimer who view institutions as dependent variables and as a reflection of what the great powers want from them. They also reject the popular belief that institutions are effective only when backed by great powers. Liberals have painstakingly shown that institutions contribute significantly to the strength of great powers, investing them with prestige while helping them to save on costly resources. These scholars also draw attention to the daily work of international bureaucrats, stressing that it is vital to keep the essential services running and make benefits available to member-states (for details, see Sterling-Folker 2007).

Neoliberal institutionalism is a robust approach in IR, particularly in the burgeoning field of international political economy (IPE). With globalisation and the rise of the liberal international trading order based on the World Trade Organization (WTO), the liberal school has gained in strength and found patronage from powerful capitalist states and their think tanks. Liberal trade theory has become an orthodoxy in IPE, and even detractors who critique such theories as hegemonic and exploitative find it difficult to decry their theoretical puzzles and methodological accomplishments. Liberal institutionalism, however, has had less purchase in security studies, where realists have dominated. The realists' arguments are predictable: Mearsheimer alleges that institutions are not independent variables but are almost always captured by powerful states, thereafter contributing to advancing their interests against the less powerful nations. Grieko states that liberal theory, which utilises Vilfredo Pareto's theory of optimality, works in softer areas like political economy, where the gains made through cooperation are more critical than how those gains are divided amongst us. When it comes to security, relative gains are prioritised over absolute gains. Where there is little trust and no way to punish bad actors, competitors fear betrayal and repeated disadvantage, thereby making rational cooperation unlikely.

Finally, we come to a brief discussion of two liberal tracks. *First*, Andrew Moravcsik has developed a theory of societal preferences as the basic argument of liberal international relations theory. He shows that liberalism in IR is no different from the general theory of liberalism, as it argues that the state is a representative institution of society; society is always prior to, supreme, and more fundamental than the state; and states 'represent some subset of domestic society, whose views constitute state preferences'. The state is only relatively autonomous; its nature is decided by the social preferences dominating it. Domestic social coalitions that capture the state use political institutions as a 'transmission belt', translating their preferences into policies (Moravcsik 1997, 518–20). The moot point is variations in the power and influence that groups and individuals have in collective settings. The national interest of a state is not an abstraction, but reflects the preferences of the dominant groups that have captured political institutions.

For Moravcsik, the second core liberal assumption is that 'the interdependence among state preferences influences state behavior'. This always varies, and liberalism offers an explanation for this variation. Against realists, liberals argue that strategic interests in world politics may be largely subjective and look to international institutions and third parties as a force for managing conflict and disciplining behaviour, thereby allowing state behaviour to be prompted by absolute gains considerations. At the same time, they do not claim that every state pursues its most significant interests without regard for the actions of other states. Liberalism is fundamentally a theory of societal preferences that are interactional in nature. Liberals argue that international affairs require states to agree to a set of purposes, without which there can be no motivation for any action, either cooperative or conflicting in nature.

John Ikenberry has shown that the order set up in the modern era is liberal, since it is based on the Enlightenment values of modernity, science, industrial technology, progress, rule of law, and democracy. The major challenges to this order came in the first half of the twentieth century, which saw two World Wars and massive dislocations. However, this did not alter the central commitments of the leading architects of the post-World War order, who drew on ideas of market economics and open trading systems, and created the Bretton Woods institutions[3] to govern the international political economy along liberal lines. The best

[3]The Bretton Woods institutions are international financial organisations created post-World War II to foster global economic growth and stability. Established at the 1944 Bretton Woods Conference in New Hampshire, the IMF and World Bank are two key institutions here. Overseeing the global monetary system and ensuring financial stability is the IMF's mandate; the World Bank aids developing nations with financial and technical assistance for

years of this liberal international order ironically coincided with the politics of the Cold War, because it was cohesive and manageable since it was limited largely to the US, West European states, and Japan, who found the order advantageous and the American leadership legitimate. They also forged a security community that agreed to a peaceful resolution of their mutual differences, and—in principle—to the ideas of private property, rule of law, representative democracy, limited multilateralism, and an open trading system. The Soviet Union and Eastern Bloc remained opposed to this, and the participation of China and the postcolonial world was also marginal.

The end of the Cold War in 1991 changed this. For the first time, the liberal order became genuinely global, and we witnessed states with their different problems and challenges entering the system. The earlier consensus was lost, and many new states refused to accept American leadership; however, as the US became the leading power, it increasingly put pressure on those states. Most crucially, American liberals campaigned for integrating states like China and Russia within the new liberal world order, hoping to make them responsible role partners and stakeholders in the long run. While China and Russia did accept the liberal international economy and joined institutions such as the WTO, they ended up weakening liberal norms significantly. As America declined economically and its overstretched military might suffered, the Chinese and Russians began to challenge the American-led international order.

While Ikenberry and Charles Kupchan do not believe that the liberal order is on its last legs, they foresee major transformations. The rise of right-wing populist regimes have dealt a severe blow to its resilience. The Trump Presidency ushered in a period of dispersal from within as the American President took steps to withdraw the United States from several multilateral forums and institutions that were crucial to the liberal international order. The rise of China and the enormous economic strains imposed by the COVID-19 pandemic might make it impossible to rejig the liberal order in the short, or even the medium term.

Liberal IR theories were the first to be developed within the discipline in the modern era. Liberals have made a lasting contribution to world politics, particularly in their analyses of international institutions, the

---

development initiatives. The global economic order is significantly shaped by these institutions working together.

structures and agencies of global political economy, and the role of democracy in international affairs. The immediate post-World War II period saw the gradual development of a series of approaches like functionalism, neo-functionalism, complex interdependence, and regime theory, which shared significant common ground with liberalism. In the post-Cold War era, the democratic peace thesis became the closest thing to a law in IR theory, and liberal institutionalism emerged as a sophisticated approach. Theorists like Keohane and Axelrod developed liberal institutionalism into a powerful research programme, complementing realism, and deployed game theory and rational choice explanations of behaviour that included both state and non-state actors. The post-globalisation period saw the addition of new actors as attention shifted to issues and problems that were transnational in character, which could not be tackled by the sovereign nation-state. Liberals have shown that while the scales have often shifted, the mode of reasoning, namely methodological individualism, has remained as relevant as ever. In other words, problems of collective choice are rampant at all levels of collective existence, and institutions need to be devised to find solutions to them.

APPLYING LIBERAL IR THEORY TO SOUTH ASIA

Case 1: The Indo–US Nuclear Deal and the Indian Left

Mainstream state preferences concerning the Indo-US nuclear deal can be summarised along the following lines. *First*, the nuclear deal recognises the substantial convergence of interests between the United States and India. This agreement is based on the practical reality of differences in national military power, economic strength, societal values, and cultural perspectives. Therefore, it is incorrect to assume that relationships between nations remain static. The unique attributes of each country affect its alliances and interactions, hindering the formation of permanent bonds. *Second*, the deal is justified on the basis of India's changing economic needs, which have been fundamentally altered after decades of liberalisation policies and globalisation. Although India has so far demonstrated its resilience vis-à-vis the new global economic structure, it has to accept American (and European) transnational corporations as the prime movers of this economic growth, and as the source of much-needed investment capital, technology, and research capabilities. Material compulsions and crude pragmatism leave India with little option but to recognise the imperatives of the global economy, and take every opportunity that comes her way to access the full range of technology indispensable for her growth in the long run. The nuclear deal offers India a chance to escape the constraints imposed by the nuclear Non-Proliferation Treaty (NPT), which has, along with other international agreements, debarred India from importing a range of sophisticated technology vital to her long-term development.

The Indo–US nuclear deal was seen as a possible solution to India's growing energy requirements, in keeping with the high growth rates registered in the post economic liberalisation era (for a detailed analysis, see Chatterjee 2009, 186–203). The adverse environmental consequences of burning fossil fuels and India's limited coal and natural gas reserves point to the need for identifying alternative, cost-efficient sources of fuel. The mainstream elites believe that civilian nuclear energy, which it considers 'clean energy', would contribute substantially to this end. Although the possibility of catastrophic nuclear accidents has not been entirely ruled out, the predominant perspective is one of optimism regarding the safety of nuclear plants. Besides, proponents of this view also identified enormously beneficial technological and scientific effects of the civilian nuclear deal, which is expected to benefit the entire economy.

When it came to national security considerations, the deal was considered perfectly acceptable for three broad reasons. *First*, the deal would have forced India to separate civilian and defence facilities and place the former under International Atomic Energy Agency safeguards. But India would retain the right to identify the specific facilities and programmes in this regard. *Second*, the deal would grant India the right to reprocess imported fuel. And *third*, India could use the existing stockpile of weapons-grade plutonium and fissile material from the Cirus and Dhruva reactors to make more nuclear weapons.

This mainstream view belongs to elite social groups in metropolitan India who identify globalisation and liberalisation as the primary avenues leading to economic fortune, and consider close links with the United States as representing that prosperity. The upwardly mobile elite belonging to these social groups are therefore the principal beneficiaries of this deal. As a result, the Congress, one of the main spokespersons for these groups among the mainstream political parties, views the nuclear deal as the litmus test of India's foreign policy commitment to the US-designed world order, of which it is an organic part. These social preferences are symptomatic of aspirations towards the status of a great power, and the conceptualisation of its concomitant role, to which we will turn next.

The Indo–US civilian nuclear deal, or the need for a strategic relationship between the two countries, must be understood not merely as a geo-strategic decision inspired by the systemic compulsions of the contemporary global distribution of power. The deal is better understood as a culmination of the shared social and economic interests of the dominant elite in both states, and is thereby projected as a natural policy choice in the evolving relationship of the two democracies. Therefore, the liberal model of foreign policy decision-making, which disaggregates the apparently unitary articulations of national interest, is a more useful analytical approach to explain the nuclear deal within the framework of the growing Indo–US partnership.

The left parties' position on the deal, which many consider dysfunctional and detrimental to India's national interest, has to be understood in the context of the mainstream politics discussed above. While the opinion of individual leaders belonging to the Communist Party of India (Marxist)—or CPI(M)—may have varied, a large body of literature generated by the left delineates a consistent position on the issue. A detailed analysis of these documents highlights an alternative foreign policy paradigm for the Indian states, one that is based on a particular reading of the national interest concomitant with the societal preferences held by leaders of the left parties.

The left paradigm of India's foreign policy continues to be structured along dependency lines, albeit with certain modifications. Military strategy is therefore denied independent status here. Foreign policy is conceptualised as almost entirely driven by domestic elite interests, in close connection with favourable global forces. It is no accident, therefore, that the left related the nuclear deal to wider concerns like the globalisation-liberalisation policies and even farm reforms. Thus, in an article titled 'Nuclear Deal: Larger Game Plan Exposed', the editorial team of *People's Democracy* placed the civilian nuclear deal within a far larger context. It quoted the address of the American Ambassador to India at the Indo–US Economic Summit on 18 September, where he spoke of a 'broader, longer term vision for US–India relations that touches all fields of human endeavour for which the civil nuclear (deal) is important, but only one part of the larger whole'. This was, for the left, the 'blue print for an emerging strategic alliance' between USA and India, the implications of which not only meant subservience to US strategic and foreign policy interests, but was also destined to propel the country towards rampant liberalisation, which would adversely affect the overall economic interests of the average Indian.

The key point to note here is that the left constantly and categorically maintained that the policy of close interaction between the US and India is the brainchild of a narrow, restrictive elite whose business and commercial interests are inextricably intertwined with that of the United States. This perspective, with its allegations of class bias, problematises the very idea of national interest. The mainstream perspective on the nuclear deal, together with its endorsement of a close strategic alliance between India and the US, is alleged to be predicated on the business and commercial interests of India's dominant elites, who have wilfully cloaked it in the language of invariant strategic needs to hoodwink the masses.

Case II: India–Pakistan Relations and Democratic Peace Theory

Political trends in Pakistan between 1969 and the onset of the India–Pakistan War of 1971 revealed the limitations of the democratic peace theory and highlighted the complexities and problems of incipient democratisation under a military regime, as anticipated by scholars like Mansfield and Snyder (2002). The political system appeared to open up in 1970; martial law was relaxed and the directive of March 1970 lifted curbs on political activity, culminating in the 1970 elections. But these events did not fundamentally alter Pakistan's political orientation. Pakistan lacked both democratic institutions and norms, and it was the military that ultimately prevented Pakistan's move towards democracy. Yahya Khan's regime did not allow the verdict of the national election to materialise, once again thwarting the values of political participation and representation. However, the impetus towards democratisation unleashed a dynamic that could be neither anticipated nor controlled, and therefore had a destabilising effect within the polity. This also induced greater instability and intensified domestic cleavages, leading to more violence. Democratisation did not lead to domestic peace within Pakistan or bilateral peace in India–Pakistan relations. It threatened the interests of the social groups in power in Pakistan and encouraged their inflexible view of their own interests.

Democratisation under a military regime also caused enormous structural strain on the polity. In sharp contrast to the norms of peaceful conflict resolution and negotiation of differences within the domestic order, maximalist agendas were drawn up and a zero-sum game situation came to mark the political order in Pakistan. As state oppression increased, its external consequences also multiplied. It reinforced the reading of the Indian state that Pakistan had no faith in the peaceful resolution of differences through democratic means, and thereby hardened India's maximalist position, since New Delhi saw little chance of a peaceful resolution in East Pakistan. The dyadic version would argue that India's position resulted from its confrontation with a military regime. Had there been a democratic government in Pakistan, India might have shown greater restraint, and the issue would have taken a different turn. There would have been no military crackdown against the Awami League and the consequent civil war could have been averted. Events escalated beyond control because the military regime in Pakistan was incapable of resolving political differences in a peaceful, democratic manner. India had to intervene militarily after its attempted negotiation with the military regime had failed.

There is no overwhelming evidence clinching the case for the democratic peace theory. As against this, a standard realist reading interprets the event differently. It would argue that the Indian decision had little to do with the nature of the political regime in Pakistan, that is, whether Pakistan was democratic or non-democratic had nothing to do with the war. The dyadic version of the peace-democracy theory, however, would argue that India's position hardened primarily due to the denial of democratic aspirations and norms within Pakistan by the military regime.

Let us now shift attention to the Kargil conflict, which presents another difficult test for both the dyadic and monadic versions of the peace-democratic theory. As far as the monadic version is concerned, it presents a grave anomaly—a democratic state hatched a military plot against another democratic state, without any serious provocation. It lends credence to the view that democratic states are capable of using covert military strategies against their adversaries, independent of the political system of the latter. The Nawaz Sharif government, which was in power when the Kargil crisis erupted, apparently spared no thought for the nature of the political system in India. This puts the dyadic version of the theory under severe stress. At least in 1971, Pakistan had been a military regime. But this cannot be said of the 1999 crisis. Why did Pakistan, a democratic state in 1999, use a military strategy against the democratic Indian state, particularly after the conclusion of the Lahore Peace drive? The democratic peace theory has no answer to this.

For India, the adversary's political system was irrelevant. Having responded positively to the peace overtures of a democratic Pakistan, India found the Kargil imbroglio virtually thrust upon it. Although intelligence reports had hinted at irregular troop movements and the gathering of insurgents/mercenaries, the government allegedly downplayed the seriousness of these reports and refrained from direct action until a military imperative forced it to intervene. It is far-fetched to argue that the initial Indian reticence and moderation can be explained by the nature of the political system in Pakistan. India's forbearance and patience may have been influenced by its understanding that Nawaz Sharif's government was committed to peace, and the belief that this regime could be trusted since it was democratic in nature, but once the crisis erupted, the states decided to resolve the dispute by military means.

The institutional variant of the theory might argue that while shared democratic norms created an expectation of peaceful relations between India and Pakistan, the actual course of action was decided by institutional factors that frustrated efforts towards peace. That Kargil happened despite the democratisation of Pakistan is hardly surprising. Even in early 1990, when Benazir Bhutto was in power in Pakistan, a major crisis (with nuclear undertones) had unfolded in India–Pakistan relations, which, according to US sources, was only averted through timely American intervention. In fact, throughout the 1990s, relations between the two countries remained charged and tense, particularly after insurgency in Kashmir had peaked from 1989 onwards. Pakistani governments, despite their democratic credentials, were not deterred from adopting a strategy of low-key violence against India, which has been described as war by proxy.

There is therefore little evidence to show that democratic institutions can enable de-escalation of tensions and/or war. The civilian government in Pakistan remained hostile, and given its active support for insurgents and terrorists, the democratic governments in India had little opportunity to initiate unilateral strategies for peace. The entire period of civilian rule in Pakistan (1988–99), comprising of successive party-based civilian governments, displayed remarkable continuity in its foreign policy orientation. The issues around Kashmir and the war in Afghanistan emanated from the non-democratic phases, and continued to determine the course of Islamabad's foreign policy. The military-bureaucratic-landlord-ulema combine retained its structural dominance within Pakistan's power hierarchy. As successive civilian regimes in Pakistan actively promoted insurgency within India, a democratic Indian state extended military support to the secessionist Mukti Fauz during 1970–71. Democratic peace theory offers no convincing explanation of this anomaly.

3

The Non-Mainstream Approaches

Critical IR Theory and Postmodernist Tracks

Shibashis Chatterjee

Non-mainstream theories are a post-Cold War development in International Relations. However, they have certainly not displaced the mainstream from prominence. The bulk of American IR, even today, is decidedly realist or liberal, with rational choice and quantitative inflections constituting the preferred methodological orientation. The non-mainstream approaches are more popular in continental Europe and in Britain, largely owing to the strong lineage and popularity of social theory and political philosophy in the continent. Various nomenclatures have been used to describe these 'other' theories of the field—critical and reflectivist being the most popular epithets. We shall, however, use the term 'non-mainstream' since 'reflectivist' does not do justice to some of these alternative approaches, and the word 'critical' has distinctive connotations that are not necessarily shared by all. Non-mainstream theories share a sense of scepticism, critique, and despair vis-à-vis their mainstream counterparts.

Yet, these various approaches disagree among themselves, and do not support alternative ways of doing IR theory either. Among the great variety of such theories, some reject mainstream approaches on both epistemological and ontological grounds. Critical theory and post-modernist IR theories are excellent examples here. But theories like constructivism and norm analysis are not hostile to the epistemological underpinnings of the mainstream. So far as constructivism goes, the dominant version as formulated by Alexander Wendt is receptive to positivist methodological standards, while rejecting its ontology. James Fearon and Alexander Wendt have explained that the alleged differences between rationalism and constructivism are grossly exaggerated, that a productive and fertile middle ground exists, and that scholars would do well to avoid parochialism and rigid methodological commitments (Fearon and Wendt 2002).

Post-modernists, following their broader philosophical stance, have rejected any compromise between positivist and non-positivist approaches, and have called for a complete break from traditional ideas in the field. Of all the theories, postmodernism is most inclined to subvert the mainstream agenda when it comes to method and its philosophical underpinnings. Feminists have undoubtedly raised the most uncomfortable questions, although their own internal divisions have crept into disciplinary debates in IR, creating strange and unexpected alliances and claims of a complete retooling of the discipline. Postcolonial perspectives on IR have mostly brought major questions of history, culture, agency, and representation to bear on the discipline, claiming that practitioners across the mainstream/non-mainstream divide have demonstrated an uncritical internalisation of Orientalism, in one form or another.

Marxist and Post-Marxist Approaches

Critical theory projects have drawn from three clusters of ideas, which we shall examine before discussing the more specific renditions of critical thinking in IR theory. However, critical IR theory does not stand on its own, and is more appropriately viewed as a legacy of Marxist thought in IR. This does not mean that critical theory is exclusively Marxist in character; but if one traces the original ideas of the philosophers who have provided the central theoretical categories in IR, it becomes clear that the legacy of Marxism is central to this narrative. Therefore, we will *first* briefly discuss the broad contours of this Marxist heritage and note its various adaptations in IR. *Second*, we will discuss the three clusters of ideas in critical theory, namely Antonio Gramsci's hegemony, the ideas of the Frankfurt School, and the cosmopolitanism of Jurgen Habermas.

This will lead to a discussion of the ideas of Michael Cox and Andrew Linklater, the two most significant critical IR theorists.

It is commonly argued that Karl Marx had not written anything specifically on IR, although his works are replete with critical and incisive observations on the international affairs of his times. Marx's class-based horizontal analysis of social life differed from the segmented analysis and state-centric approach that dominates IR thinking. This was also facilitated by the abstraction and universalism that characterised much of Marx's theoretical writings. As Marx stayed away from any political organisation after the failure of the Paris Commune, and given his social and political isolation in England, the daily activities of party politics had little impact on Marx's writings in his more mature phase. This, on the one hand, facilitated the high abstraction of his theories, but on the other, deprived the theory of the critical energy of daily political activities, thereby limiting the praxiological character of Marxism as a whole. Marx believed that the nation-state was an artificial social unit not in keeping with human character, ephemeral in nature, and destined to be replaced by a global classless society—unfortunately, Marx offered no blueprint for the contours of such a society, or for its gradual evolution over time. This gave Marx a certain distance from and a resistance to IR as a theoretical enterprise, since the peculiarities of a national character and the universalism of social classes made for irreconcilable theoretical categories. All geopolitical conflicts were ultimately explained as part of the contradictions of capital.

While the European setbacks and the manifest absence of class unity among workers across the world did bring about a certain moderation in Marxist thought about international relations, Marx offered no grand theory of how capital worked in a world divided by nation-states. He—and his legatees after him—refrained from addressing the crucial puzzle of why nations form such a successful unit of human accretion, and the mysteries of scale underlying the longevity of nation-states. Later, he did acknowledge that states were vital to the changing nature of global capitalism, although he did not live long enough to study and theorise this transformation properly. In fairness to his work, he admitted that the national bourgeoisie frequently bribed the labour aristocracy, and workers occasionally overlooked their national identity. The fact that the idea of a global classless society was meaningless to the toiling multitudes in a world where people's sympathies were engaged effectively by nationalism was not lost on Marx; yet, his theory could not accommodate vertical divisions in a structural analysis of a capital that was global in nature.

Finally, two other aspects of Marx's thought complicate matters even further. Marx was committed to the Enlightenment project and believed that material science and technology had the power to rid the world of scarcity and the tyranny of nature that sought to constrain human creativity. Marx's class analysis is largely limited to the *anthropocene*, an epoch created and moulded by conscious human action. He was categorical in his denunciation of hubris and sentimentality, a fact that also accounts for his impatience with the subjective attachment to a human collective—the 'nation'—and irrationalities and prejudices of all kinds. His problem with capitalism concerned its dehumanisation, as it kept the real producers from the benefits of the enormous wealth they were creating through the class appropriation of surplus, thereby depriving labour of the fruits of their high productivity, pioneered by human achievements in modern science and technology. Marx therefore remained committed to a paradigm whereby human development was steered by science and technology, and the contradiction between the forces and relations of production was destined to destroy capitalism and usher in an epoch of classless abundance. This means that there is virtually nothing in Marx's original treatise on the perils of the anthopocene, be they ecological, moral, spiritual, or political. This introduces a certain flatness in Marx's social philosophy, visible to us in hindsight. There is not much here about the limits of an industrial society, a realisation key to the critical thinking of the Frankfurt School.

Marx's writings on the Asiatic mode of production apparently gave the impression that he was not unconditionally dismissive about colonialism. While later research has shown that Marx was averse to complicity with any form of European colonialism or territorial aggrandisement, he was brutal in his denunciation of the feudal practices of non-European Orientals. His critique was directed at the feudal mode of production that stunted growth and development and fostered many prejudicial and reprehensible social practices of the Orient, using such anomalies as ideological effects and justifications to tie the human subject to the production structures. Such a view again stems from his uncritical approach to the project of Enlightenment. In a sense, Marx could not overcome the structural limitations imposed by his own time and location. He could not rise above European provincialism in his imagination of a social order that promised to be free and universal.

There was enough of Kant in Marx to push him towards a cosmopolitan universal project based on connected human (and social) reason. That this universalism was often disrespectful of cultural differences and the genius of non-Europeans, which was borne out by much of recorded history, did not seem to matter. He was making a case for modernity and science and their impact on the social/political organisation of lives, and not for culture; nor was he deliberately obfuscating facts. Simply put, he believed that Europeans had triumphed over the Orient due to their mastery of superior science and technology, which had enabled them to conquer and subjugate the latter. Marx merely historicised European colonialism using a framework set by the cognitive categories of the Enlightenment. Much later, postmodern and postcolonial thinkers would expose the limits of this theory.

The theories of imperialism developed by J. A. Hobson, Rudolf Hilferding, Mikhail Bakunin, Rosa Luxemburg, and V. I. Lenin offer a direct approach to IR from a Marxist standpoint. While there were important and subtle differences in the theories developed by these thinkers, they broadly believed that national capital in advanced capitalist states escaped the three laws of motion of capitalism (which Marx had outlined in his *Capital*) through colonial expansion and imperialism, a phenomenon that Lenin described as monopoly capitalism or the allegedly highest stage of capitalism. This was explained by the transformation in the nature of capitalism. From an industrial, production-based process, capitalism is now driven by finance, with gigantic transnational banks and international financial houses providing the fuel for its worldwide expansion. There was a natural tendency in capital to exhaust domestic markets and produce an excess of commodities. States now came to the rescue of cartels, banks, and business houses by making available colonial territories that served as both cheap sources of raw materials and expanded or new markets and sites of mega-investments. However, the rate of growth of dominant capitalist states gradually stagnated, and new competitors came up rapidly to take their place. These new states also needed territories to escape their domestic constraints, leading to an inexorable scramble for colonial territories and ultimately forcing the states into a vortex of war over territories. Lenin described this as the war of imperialism. World

War I was one such war of imperialism, where nationalism was crafted as a mobilisational strategy to recruit workers and peasants into fighting armies in the cause of the fatherland. Lenin thought that this cataclysmic Armageddon would ultimately destroy capitalism, as the wars would enervate states and deplete resources and the corresponding capacity to buy off the labour aristocracy, and anti-colonial movements for political freedom would make it impossible for colonial powers to hold on to these possessions indefinitely.

Karl Kautsky, the Czech-Austrian Marxist theorist, spoke, in contrast, of a theory of ultra-imperialism, refuting Lenin's thesis of the destruction of global capitalism through imperial wars. He believed that imperial powers were rational enough to not destroy their assets through senseless warfare, preferring instead to collaborate and divide the booty. Kautsky's insights seem to have prevailed over Lenin's prognosis; the idea of geopolitical conflicts being induced by shifts in finance capital seemed a plausible alternative to a theory that viewed wars as either the result of rational egoistic states seeking power and security (realists), or the result of irresponsible despots using war as a diversionary tactic (liberals).

Dependency theory and the world systems theory approach emerged as the dominant left radical axes in the field. The dependency school was a distinctively local approach, inasmuch as the original contributors—such as Raul Prebisch, F. H. Cardoso, Celso Furtado, and Anibal Pinto—were Latin American structuralists who sought to offer historically grounded economic explanations of poverty and underdevelopment in Latin America. This was complemented by a more rounded and self-consciously Marxist variant, developed by scholars such as Paul A. Baran, Paul Sweezy, and Andre Gunder Frank. Walter Rodney, Clive Thomas, and Samir Amin sought to explain the underdevelopment and longstanding poverty of African states. Wallerstein and Giovanni Arrighi pioneered the world systems theory, which proffered a similar explanation of the history of the world from a structural politico-economy perspective.

Dependency theory was developed in opposition to the prescriptions of the liberal modernisation theories of economic historians like W. W. Rostow, and mainstream economists who believed that postcolonial states could easily emulate the post-World War II experience of Western European countries if they followed liberal economic policies and embraced export-led industrialisation as a model of growth. Believing that this was fundamentally erroneous and politically motivated, dependency scholars argued, against conventional Marxist accounts, that the world economy was capitalist in nature, divided into a technologically advanced core and a vast underdeveloped periphery. The real divide lay in the inability of the periphery to generate self-sustaining and autonomous technology-driven industrialisation, owing to a lack of domestic capital and insufficient technical manpower. This meant that the periphery only produced either raw materials or agricultural products, whose demand was unstable as it depended on the preference and performance of the economies of the richer core nations. Therefore, the terms of trade between the primary producer—the periphery—and the core, which exported manufactured goods, were permanently adverse for the former.

This trade asymmetry was the default position of the international political economy. The liberal prescription of export-led growth, free market policies, and economic liberalisation did not, and could not, alter this structural anomaly. Rather, this only perpetuated relations of dependency between the core and the periphery, for the economic prosperity of the core necessitated the continuous underdevelopment of the periphery (Frank 1972). Moreover, dependency was a historical process, inextricably intertwined with modern capitalist structures that needed countries to be brought together within a single trading system. Andre Gunder Frank stated:

> ... historical research demonstrates that contemporary underdevelopment is in large part the historical product of past and continuing economic and other relations between the satellite underdeveloped and the now developed metropolitan countries. Furthermore, these relations are an essential part of the capitalist system on a world scale as a whole. (ibid., 3)

Referring to the links amongst history and national and international capitalism, Susanne Bodenheimer argued, 'Latin America is today, and has been since the sixteenth century, part of an international system dominated by the now-developed nations.... Latin underdevelopment is the outcome of a particular series of relationships to the international system' (Bodenheimer 1971, 157).

World systems analysis is an umbrella term that includes a number of related but different approaches. The primary work is undoubtedly the classic three-volume study by Immanuel Wallerstein who, in the first volume, famously defined world systems theory (WST) as 'a multicultural territorial division of labor in which the production and exchange of basic goods and raw materials is necessary for the everyday life of its inhabitants' (Chase-Dunn and Grimes 1995, 389). For Wallerstein,

> A world-system is a social system, one that has boundaries, structures, member groups, rules of legitimation, and coherence. Its life is made up of the conflicting forces which hold it together by tension and tear it apart as each group seeks eternally to remould it to its advantage. It has the characteristics of an organism, in that it has a lifespan over which its characteristics change in some respects and remain stable in others.... Life within it is largely self-contained, and the dynamics of its development are largely internal. (Wallerstein 1974, 347)

Andre Gunder Frank and Barry Gills define world systems more broadly: 'The transfer or exchange of economic surplus is the fundamental criterion of a world systemic relationship. Diplomacy, alliances, and conflict are additional, and perhaps derivative, criteria of systemic interaction' (Frank and Gills 1993, 106). C. K. Chase-Dunn and T. D. Hall offer a broad definition of world systems as 'intersocietal networks in which the interactions (for example trade, warfare, intermarriage) are important for the reproduction of the internal structures of the composite units and importantly affect changes that occur in these local structures' (Chase-Dunn and Hall 1997, 855). WST is a much wider approach than dependency, but its core ideas are the same. Wallerstein drew inspiration from Ferdinand Braudel's Annales School, which insisted on the need to identify patterns of long-term (*la longue dureé*) trends, focus on the history of ecological regions rather than restricting analyses to nations and states, and utilise a comprehensive understanding of history that goes beyond the political. Additionally, he was also influenced by standard Marxist analysis of production and commodity exchanges, schemes for the reproduction of capital, and the ideas of accumulation and class struggle.

However, the central argument of WST mirrored the dependency critique of modernisation theories and the core-periphery argument that followed from it. Wallerstein emphasised the same asymmetry emerging from dichotomous technologies and adverse trade relations, the inability of the periphery to overcome its poverty and underdevelopment, continuing to remain a part of a fundamentally iniquitous system, and the central role of power hierarchies in perpetuating this inequality between the developed core and the underdeveloped periphery. As Carlos M. Vela puts it, 'Among the most important structures of the current world-system is a power hierarchy between core and periphery, in which powerful and wealthy "core" societies dominate and exploit weak and poor peripheral societies' (Martinez-Vela 2001, 4). Following the forms of economic organisation classified by Karl Polanyi in 1944, who divided them into reciprocal, redistributive, and market exchange, Wallerstein put forward a historical and spatial differentiation amongst mini-systems, mono-cultural tribal organisations based on reciprocity, world empires predicated on the principle of redistribution, and world economies that worked through the norms of market exchanges. While the latter two are both world systems comprising multiple cultures, world empires have a single political centre while the world economy consists of many independent power centres with varying capabilities. WST clearly shows why, unlike world empires, world economies would remain pluralistic in their political organisation, witnessing the cyclical rise and fall of hegemonic powers within themselves. What keeps this politically fragmented world economy together is the mode of economic organisation (capitalism), which steers the economy via market exchanges and flows of capital and labour (Goldfrank 2000).

There are major differences between Marxist–Leninist imperialism and the arguments proposed by dependency scholars, neatly summarised in Cueva, et al. (1976):

> Agustin Cueva systematically criticized Frank for abandoning Marx's notion of capitalism and equating capitalism with money economy; Rodolfo Stavenhagen for substituting a focus on exploitation and class conflict for a system of national and regional contradictions; Dos Santos for confusing the worldwide expansion of capitalism with economic growth in the periphery; Cardoso and Falleto for mixing developmental and Marxist frameworks, and Marini for differentiating classical from dependent capitalism. (Chilcote 1981, 5)

There are three major points of departure between classical Marxist–Leninist analysis and the dependency approach.

1. Unlike Marx, the dependency scholars take a monetarist view of capitalism and date it far ahead of the conventional reading;
2. Dependency scholars tend to locate surplus value in exchange circuits rather than in production processes;

3. Dependency and world systems analysts neglect class conflict, as their emphasis on external influences and linkages often detract from the domestic angularities and conflicts between labour and capital within specific historical formations. (Chilcote 1981; Munck 1981; Smith 1979)

As the world changed unexpectedly in 1991, the language of the discipline was inevitably affected. In fact, theory building in IR changed dramatically in the 1990s and beyond as familiar concepts and approaches often proved inadequate. In fact, major changes had already been underway in the social sciences; for one, the distance between the humanities and social studies was narrowing. The discursive and hermeneutic analyses popular in the humanities began to exert their influence in politics, sociology, and IR as well. The arrival of postmodern and post-structural perspectives were bound to radically alter the nature of theoretical debates, and the language of these theorists began to be accepted by a younger generation of scholars who were dissatisfied with the conventional forms of radicalism practised in the discipline.

The other major occurrence was the increasing questioning of the relevance of Marxism as an alternative theoretical standpoint. While the challenge to Marxist approaches came from expected quarters—Fukuyama, Keohane, and Mearsheimer—there was an increasing realisation that the conventional theory had been clearly overtaken both by events and our own sensibilities, and the traditional practice of dismissing new challenges or deviations could neither be sidestepped nor disregarded as a form of 'revisionism'. Rather, a new perspective was essential if the radical space had to be retained. Dependency and imperialism looked decisively outmoded to a generation that faced a different set of problems, like those related to the worsening of the climate, terrorism, population flows, and identity, or recognition-driven conflicts, which required a new vocabulary for articulation. The fracturing of the Marxist discourse, the post-structural/postmodern turn that questioned all that was taken for granted earlier, the challenges posed by feminism, and the advent of postcolonialism over a period of nearly two-and-a-half decades would change the landscape of IR theories forever. We shall discuss these new variants later in this chapter.

Critical Theory and IR

There are several inspirations for critical theory, but the ideas that have mattered most to IR scholars came from Gramsci and the Frankfurt School, especially their youngest and most prolific representative, Jurgen Habermas. While Gramsci and Lenin were inspired by a common problematic, their historical situations and organisational contexts differed radically. The central problem was explaining why the original Marxist prophecy of proletarian rebellion in advanced capitalist states had not come true. Lenin proffered a theory of monopoly capitalism and imperialism that temporarily projected all internal contradictions outwards and staved off an impending workers' rebellion. Gramsci, on the other hand, focused on the very different domestic structures prevailing in the more developed capitalist societies of western Europe, in contrast to the relatively backward settings of southern and eastern Europe. He explained this by pointing to the rule of capital by domination, achieved through brute force, in underdeveloped capitalist structures that lacked a civil society, against the consensual domination prevailing in developed capitalism, where ideas disseminated through the mediations of vibrant civil societies won the sympathies of workers, despite the economic exploitation wrought by capitalism.

In addition, political democracy and the newly introduced right of universal suffrage imbued populations with a sense of subjectivity, and led people to believe that they were not mere cogs in a system but could make a difference to the nature of the rule imposed by the political class. While there was always healthy room for scepticism and capital could become repressive if the passive ideological revolution failed, hegemony had become a collective commonsense of the masses in developed capitalist societies. Without a successful and protracted war of attrition (war of position), aimed at placing control of the ideological apparatus in the hands of the counter-hegemonic forces, there was no possibility of defeating the forces of capital. Gramsci wrote extensively on the role of intellectuals, historic blocs, and complex inter-class alliances that were refreshingly original, yet remarkably in line with the praxiological heritage of classical Marxism.

In contrast, the Frankfurt School theorised on the role of culture in modern life, particularly the rise of consumerism, which created culture industries that sought to destroy people's critical faculties or subjectivities, and mass-administered societies[1] that ultimately culminated in Nazism and fascism. The Frankfurt School comprised gifted philosophers, psychologists, and sociologists of culture, who were inspired both by Kant's idea of the centrality of freedom and Hegel's insistence on a totality of experiences. Their philosophy internalised the idea of 'immanent critique' and subjected all social ideologies to a comprehensive critique in order to liberate mankind from exploitation and subjugation. Critical theory may have been born in the crucible of Marxism, but it did not accept all its facets and objectives. Most fundamentally, it was at odds with Marxism's naturalistic conception of knowledge and its deterministic tendencies, its obsession with science and systemic knowledge, its incipient but authoritarian bureaucratisation, and its neglect of the ideas of freedom and democracy.

Yet, critical theory was primarily committed to understanding and transcending the nature of modern capitalism. As Stephen Eric Bronner argues,

> A bureaucratically administered mass society was apparently integrating all forms of resistance, obliterating genuine individuality, and generating personality structures with authoritarian predilections. Conformity was undermining autonomy. If capitalist development is connected with standardization and reification, then progress actually constitutes a form of regression. (Bronner 2017, 5)

It accepted the Marxist notions of alienation and reification as central theoretical categories, but widened their meaning and scope. It took as its primary task the explanation and transcendence of all forms of alienation and reification in modern life, and not just those that resulted from the commodification of life forms. In a sense, critical theory problematised conventional Marxism with its scientific predictions of modern Enlightenment, and the concomitant faith in the capacity of

---

[1]Modern societies, according to the Frankfurt School, are characterised by bureaucratic systems, capitalist markets, and mass media that control and standardise individuals, suppressing independent thought and self-determination. Max Horkheimer and Theodor Adorno believed that in these societies, cultural creation is standardised, transforming art, entertainment, and politics into instruments of passive compliance rather than active involvement. Powerful institutions systematically manage and shape the population, suppressing genuine resistance and individual expression.

science and technology to deliver humanity from its basic problem of scarcity.

From Theodor Adorno through Max Horkheimer and Herbert Marcuse, critical theorists disputed the blind faith in a rational solution without taking recourse to philosophical scepticism or relativism, which they rejected. Their problematisation of modernity was also the direct result of the rise of fascism, which rejected an uncritical faith in mass progressive politics and forced them to focus on the rise of authoritarian personalities and right-wing populist forces across Europe. Faced with the unprecedented carnage and atrocities perpetrated by all sides in the inter-War period, culminating in World War II, critical theorists began asking uncomfortable questions. To quote James Bohman,

> It follows from Horkheimer's definition that a critical theory is adequate only if it meets three criteria: it must be explanatory, practical, and normative, all at the same time. That is, it must explain what is wrong with current social reality, identify the actors to change it, and provide both clear norms for criticism and achievable practical goals for social transformation. (Bohman 2005, 2)

Critical theory is a deeply sensitive hermeneutic perspective that is philosophically committed to creating an open, deliberative society achieved through consensual and unconstrained communication amongst free and rational agents. Critical theorists question all authoritarian orders/structures, trace them historically, dissect the underlying justificatory discourses of such societies, and provide alternative blueprints for their eventual transformation. They are distinct from welfare liberals in their rejection of halfway measures; from conventional Marxists in their commitment to theorising the problems of capitalism as a whole and not just as an economic form; and stand apart from postmodernists in rejecting relativism and accepting the ideal of science.

The end of the Cold War and the collapse of socialism are important to this narrative. The sudden end to the Cold War dealt a major theoretical blow to all mainstream approaches, which could neither predict nor explain this cataclysmic event in satisfactory terms. This gave a fillip to alternative theoretical approaches. Non-mainstream IR theories also developed on the ruins of an earlier generation of critical approaches, most notably the dependency school and the historical materialist approaches. The collapse of socialism and the advent of new agential movements based on a plethora of identities and practices challenged the ubiquity and hegemony of class *a la* classical Marxism.

New technological breakthroughs, the massive dislocations in the environment, the transformative attributes of labour as a social category, the increasing significance of ethnicity and gender, and the multifaceted challenges of globalisation led to a transmogrification of the meaning of radicalism itself. Under these changed circumstances, it was not possible to be a radical in the conventional or orthodox sense; the radical had to be reinvented in vastly different ways. Critical theory and postmodernist interventions in IR attempted to fashion such orientations at a time when the mainstream alternative stood exposed in its inability to offer substantive explanations of events unfolding in the world at large (Brown 1997, 25–26).

Critical theory emerged from a research programme of the Frankfurt School, led primarily by Adorno and Horkheimer. The first-generation scholars of critical theory were concerned with developing a body of knowledge that would be related to, and yet distinct from, orthodox Marxism, and serve as a meta-critique of the bourgeois order, economy, polity, society, art, culture, and way of life. The second generation of critical theorists, particularly Habermas, was more directly political, writing on emancipation and social regeneration in addition to exposing the limitations of bourgeois civilisation. Habermas' central theoretical concerns with discourse analysis, ethics, and communicative action have been popular in IR theory, which has invoked these ideas to question sovereignty, territoriality, and the practices of political community at one level, and to more specific concerns related to human rights and strategies of political transformation in Europe.

But the original impulse for a critical IR theory did not come from Habermas' writings. The ideas of Robert Cox, who pioneered critical IR theory in the 1980s, were based on Gramsci's political philosophy and Marxism. Cox's celebrated distinction between problem-solving theory and critical theory builds on Gramsci's thought. While problem-solving theories take reality as a given, with fixed parameters delineating settled puzzles with built-in norms to solve them, critical theory is emancipatory, for it questions reality itself, problematises the parameters, and rejects the received puzzles and their modes of settlement. The impulse here is decidedly Marxist, minus the deterministic overtones of the classical genre (Cox and Sinclair 1996).

The Coxian perspective takes global production as the primary category of analysis and explains the relationship between revolutionary upheavals and political movements in the Third World against the backdrop of the marginalising effects of globalisation. A significant part of Cox's later writings was devoted to a social analysis of the globalisation of the means of production, multilateralism and neo-institutionalism, and emerging patterns of elite-mass relationship throughout the international system. Cox visualised the historical process as a shifting kaleidoscope of historical structures, conceived as ensembles of material capabilities, ideologies, and institutions working on various social forces, states, and the world order. These factors stood as heuristic devices, clearing the way for a proper understanding of the process of 'macro-historical changes' and an exploration of 'the further possibilities of more desirable transformation' (Haacke 1996, 272).

The affinity between Cox and Gramsci is also revealed in Cox's ideas regarding the agency of the possible transformation of global order. Cox retains his faith in the creative power of social forces to construct alternative world orders against the hegemony of global capital. Although social forces are aggregates of plural groupings, Cox privileged the working class—the force most intimately related to international production processes—as the prime mover of historical change in the face of stiff opposition from global imperialism. Cox's alternative theory is useful for its focus on social classes and modes of production, and also for its innate pragmatism. Unlike the post-structuralists, Cox did not dismiss the existence of fundamental categories such as the state. On the contrary, he provided a sophisticated social analysis of the character of the state, which made it possible to talk meaningfully about the nature and consequences of state policy throughout the world. Cox's approach is not a mechanical economic intervention in the political economy; he refrained from using historically untenable dependency categories and did not treat this global system as entirely capitalist. He incorporated the views, strategies, responses, and battles of a plurality of social forces as inter-subjective factors that function alongside international production. This allowed him sufficient flexibility to avoid the extremes of orthodox Marxist determinism on the one hand, and the relative indeterminacy of postmodernism on the other (Cox 1981, 1983).

Andrew Linklater's critical foray into IR theory remains indebted to the central philosophical categories of Jurgen Habermas (Linklater 1993,

1996, 1998). Linklater's faith in the critical promise of communicative action and discourse ethics, universal pragmatics, and the ideal speech situation led him to dwell on knowledge construction and community formation through the binaries of exclusion and inclusion, rather than on global production processes and even less on the practices of the working class. Linklater aimed to comprehend the 'changes affecting the social bond which unites members of the sovereign state and separates them from the outside world', and his primary concern is 'with the nature and future of the state as a bounded moral and political community' (1996, 287). Linklater focused on how national and international developments are weakening the bond between the state and its citizens and diluting communities in many parts of the world. Among the contributory factors, he mentions the increasing move away from the use of force by major industrial powers, which is leading to the pacification of the West. Along with this, one also witnesses the rise of movements for greater political participation from national minorities and migrant groups, who feel threatened by a rise in majoritarian identity politics. Linklater also invokes globalisation, referring to its cultural consequences, which simultaneously induce centripetal tendencies to embrace 'the cosmopolitan culture of modernity', while encouraging protest against 'the intrusion of predominantly western symbols and images'. The result of such plural efflorescence is a promise to invest in new forms of political community, something that mainstream theories are unable to explore (ibid., 292).

Linklater believes that the ethics of Habermasian discourse offers the key to the understanding and eventual emancipation of political communities from their present bounded, geopolitical forms. He recognises the problems inherent in establishing a discourse ethics through universal assertions. However, he justifies this method through procedural universalism, asserting that it creates a space for open and inclusive discussion, rather than promoting a particular vision of the good life. He elaborated this through four forms of human understanding: anthropological, strategic, Socratic, and political (Linklater 1996, 92). Political understanding involves both an appreciation of the 'plurality of moral views' to facilitate an agreement on the principles of 'exclusion and inclusion' and understanding the rules of coexistence in situations of dispute. The defining character of critical theory lies in its commitment to 'redeeming an understanding', without necessarily rejecting claims to difference. Linklater attempts to refute the critique that Habermas conflates understanding and consensus. His approach involves separating the two, with a focus on prioritising mutual understanding rather than moral consensus (ibid., 293).

Linklater's primary concern was with realising a moral/ethical and political community for mankind. To achieve this, he called for dialogue amongst realism, rationalism, Marxism, and Habermasian critical theory. Linklater remains committed to 'plural forms of praxis', which originate from an interaction of this four-pronged dialogue. In his view, the making of an ethical-political community has to await an inquiry from a critical theory perspective into 'the history of socialization of norms' and the 'practices of exclusion', in order to realise (concrete) prospects for new forms of community imminent within existing social relations, and 'the practical project of extending the community beyond the nation state' (Linklater 1996, 278).

Linklater's work is vital for several reasons. *First*, he successfully brought a number of radical concerns together by creatively drawing upon the perspectives of Marx and the Frankfurt School, particularly the philosophy of Habermas. *Second*, in the process he also expanded our understanding of human emancipation and community. Marx's transnational community was based on the eradication of class and private property. Writing in a very different context, Habermas was far more sensitive to issues of plurality, identity, and difference. Yet both Marx and Habermas were invested in a modern world where transnational communities would be built on the foundation of reason. Following in their footsteps, Linklater, too, believed that modernity and critical theory would lead to human emancipation, based on reasoned deliberation and agreement.

Linklater's great achievement lies in his reflections on the dual registers of the modern state and citizenship, the gradual overcoming of peripheral and subaltern groups, and the making of a unified discourse of citizenship coterminous with the territorial margins of the national security state on the one hand, and the moral vacuity of bounded territoriality on the other. Linklater exposes the yawning gap between our responsibilities towards our fellow citizens and those towards 'outsiders', a gap justified through a realist discourse of 'otherness' that has no correlation to any theory of morality. Realism, therefore, offers no moral theory of community at all. Critical theory is ideally situated to fill this gap. Growing vulnerabilities and risks have shown the shortcomings of national decision-making worldwide, which is largely induced by globalisation. It sees in the trans-nationalisation of material life and the increasingly global semiotics of communication the seeds of a transnational citizenry, which would expose the moral poverty of Westphalian distinctions amidst the demonstrated failings of the nation-state. While critical theory is not, by definition, anti-state, its moral language goes against the justifications offered by the national security state.

However, Linklater is also sensitive to questions of identity and difference, pluralism, and diversity, in the process bringing critical theory in line with debates in multiculturalism as well. However, he substitutes the pure Marxian imagination with the quasi-Marxist and Habermasian ontology of mainstream critical theory, which ultimately codes the categories in the language it knows: the coda and doxa of the West. The citizens, the alien, the refugee, and the stateless are all similar categories across time and place, and can be emancipated through the same processes. In this discourse of transcending 'citizens' and 'outsiders' in the quest for a rational and consensual human emancipation, histories are flattened, and people whose experiences do not fit with the West are denied their specificities. Linklater thus proposes no special theory for the postcolonial world. While this is understandable from the normative presuppositions of a critical theory that did not give up its faith in reason and modernity, as a theory of the world, it has little to offer societies which, for various reasons, are not facsimiles of the West. Postcolonial 'otherness' remains a thorn in the flesh of critical theory, just as the Orient was to Marxism in the past. While critical theory exposes the sociological naiveté and moral poverty of realism, its own democratic credentials remain contested.

IR AND POSTMODERNISM

A few aspects of postmodern thought deeply affect the discourses one comes across in IR. A closer look at a few such features is necessary to provide a backdrop to more specific discussions on themes pertinent to IR literature. Very broadly, we identify three cardinal themes: the arbitrariness and critique of modernity; the rejection of grand narratives; and reality as a construction, or the elision of boundaries of the real and the imaginary, the objective and the fictive, or reality and representation.

Postmodern thinkers consider modernity both arbitrary and incomplete. Postmodernism is a strikingly anti-Enlightenment standpoint in philosophy, articulated most forcefully by Friedrich Nietzsche, Søren Kierkegaard, and Martin Heidegger, among others. They viewed modernity as one of the several conceits of a civilisation that:

- recognised only one set of values while refuting others;
- defined knowledge as a form of cognition that was objective, classifiable, streamlined, and disciplined, thereby delegitimising any form of imagination that resisted, or was not amenable to, the sanctioned rules of objectification;
- justified modernisation as both an inevitable and normatively desirable end;
- celebrated the bureaucratisation of all aspects of social life, aimed at making it more predictable and manageable;
- upheld a form of political rationality aimed at the administration of life, which takes the populations as its subject: 'to ensure, sustain, and multiply life, to put this life in order' (Foucault 1978 [1976], 138); and
- created a form of power that 'exerts a positive influence on life, that endeavours to administer, optimize, and multiply it, subjecting it to precise controls and comprehensive regulations' (ibid., 137).

Postmodern scholars compare this modernity to a prison, seeing it as rigid and restrictive. Their argument is that it produces a predictable, homogeneous shaping of minds and bodies through broad generalisations. Such actions silence dissent and marginalise those outside its controlled norms, thereby rendering many invisible and unacknowledged. Hence, going against the high priests of modernity—rationality and science—postmodernists celebrate indeterminacy, anarchy, diffusion, decentring, and an unbounded imagination. They are critical of modernity's claims to be seeking a panacea for existential problems, as they hold modernity itself responsible for having created such problems in the first place. The fundamental trouble with science is its tendency to reduce everything to pre-set forms and standardise knowledge claims according to universal laws. Postmodernists censure the modern for its rejection of folklore and magic, its inability to see beyond its structured rules, and for having created a society characterised by a dreadful uniformity and criminalisation of the deviant. The modern is therefore anti-democratic, for it will not recognise or legitimise the 'other'.

It naturally follows that postmodernism rejects what it terms the all-encompassing tyranny of the modern, which adroitly justifies a set of knowledge claims and attendant social practices as 'normal' and 'valid', rejecting all else that does not fit such discourses. Modernity tends to set a bar, be it in the fields of philosophy or science, for social and political practices, or for the underlying norms that govern our daily lives. The bar is set in accordance with the normalised discourse that is in favour and enjoys the blessings of power, and which is seen not as a coercive mechanism of punishment but as a positive or regenerative life force. In all fairness, modernity is inconceivable without a discourse that visibilises and legitimises it. This discourse, however, is an accidental one; it has come to dominate due to its proximity to power and not because of any intrinsic worth. As Jean-François Lyotard puts it,

> I will use the term modern to designate any science that legitimates itself with reference to a metadiscourse ... making an explicit appeal to some grand narrative, such as the dialectics of Spirit, the hermeneutics of meaning, the emancipation of the rational or working subject, or the creation of wealth.... I define postmodern as incredulity toward metanarratives. (Lyotard 1984, xxiii–xxiv)

In other words, if the modern requires a commitment to a grand narrative for its existence, the postmodern exposes this dependence and shows that it is invariably achieved at the cost of silencing many micro-narratives that are either opposed to the meta-narrative or are incommensurate with it in fundamental ways. The emergence of this grand narrative is therefore purely fortuitous, and as arbitrary as it is political. It becomes visible through its complicity with power and its ability to silence the 'other' (although it fails to banish it completely). The grand narrative is therefore tenuous not only because it is accidental and arbitrary, but also because it carries the subversive other as an indeterminate possibility. This grand narrative structures modernity and gives it a voice, a sense of purpose, and direction. Yet it cannot rid itself of the subversive other, which is a necessary condition for the production of the self; the dominant meta-narrative becomes inconceivable when isolated from the ideas and discourses that it silences. In postmodern times, when technology unmoors settled realities, the tyranny of the grand narrative is finally loosened, and a genuinely polyphonic and heteronomous condition of unstructured cognition becomes a possibility.

This means that postmodernism is a radical take on modernism, rather than a simple negation of modernity. We must remember that modernism was a cultural movement against the representational idioms of the early modern imagination. In its predominant form, while recognising modernity's break from the pre-modern, it critiqued its tendency to ossify and stagnate. Especially in relation to art, it rejected the modernist insistence on realism. Art is essentially about the untamed imagination; it requires a critical distance from the real and has to be granted sufficient autonomy to deliver lasting genuine creativity. Discontinuities and breaks were as necessary in imagination as continuities and lineages. Yet modernists made a distinction between the real and its representation, claiming that in art, the latter could not slavishly follow the canons laid down by the former. The postmodernists, in contrast, deny this distinction between the real and its representation, the objective and the subjective, and reality and imagination. The simulacra are no less real than the material reality they imitate. The real and the imagined are collapsed into each other. Since postmodernism refuses to acknowledge any Archimedean vantage point to adjudicate claims of validity, whether cognitive, moral, or social, it cannot *ipso facto* recognise a separate and sanctified domain of the real or the material/ objective. It refuses to acknowledge that we can separate the real from the imagery, and that all claims to objective knowledge as existing prior to subjective imagination are merely the conceits of positivism and its progenitor, the administered societies built on an unshakable belief in science and modernity.

The Foucauldian idea of postmodernism may be viewed as a normative attempt to emancipate historical 'knowledge from all forms of human bondage and subjection, to render them capable of opposition and contest, and to operate as a mode of subversion of all received categories'. Most postmodernists reduce claims of universal truth to the moral posturing of the powerful and the privileged. The postmodernist thesis thus appears as a genealogy that lacks any conscious form of the human subject. It is difficult to represent the postmodern in IR due to its fragmented, discursive nature, and its refusal to admit the distinction between representation and reality. The anti-humanist strains of Nietzsche and Heidegger have been more influential than the writings of Kant, Hegel, and Marx. While critical theory has sought to redeem the human subject, postmodernists have gone the opposite way, doing away with the essence of the human subject altogether (Brown 1997, 26).

The postmodernist challenge has raised a number of issues. Postmodernists argue that:

- Modernity is arbitrary since the Enlightenment framework was only one of several historical possibilities, chosen due to fortuitous circumstances rather than any privileged claim to knowledge.
- Postmodernists reduce truth to a will to power or choice, since there exists no objective position from which to vindicate the truth.
- Postmodernists view existential reality as a power-laden, discursive social construction, with no sense of purpose, direction, or control.
- They consider language, conceptual frames, and paradigms to be self-fulfilling prophecies, since reality is nothing more than conventional linguistic constructions bearing multiple meanings.
- Finally, postmodernists emphasise the creation of identity as an act of power and a strategy of violation, since each identity is based on denial, all affirmations are negations, and the self is inconceivable without the other.

Postmodernists deny truth and scientific or objective knowledge, as well as its very possibility and desirability, and view theories as purely contingent and arbitrary acts of power (Vasquez 1983). In a strange yet telling paradox, the postmodern ethic of a subject-less discursive will to power unites with the realist reification of the same. Despite being the staunchest critique of the mainstream, the tragic denouement of the postmodern ethic of power in a direction similar to its dominant other is too clear to be missed.

The principal postmodernist writings in IR have come from Richard Ashley, R. B. J. Walker, Der Derian, David Campbell, and Jim George. Perhaps it is fitting to focus on the insights offered in Walker's masterpiece, *Inside/Outside: International Relations as Political Theory* (1993), which highlights the excesses and pitfalls of the postmodernist approach. Walker has located all the difficulties of IR theory in political philosophy. IR theory treats historically produced categories as given and eternal, although they do change over time. He employs postmodernism to negate this claim as well as the binary opposites that underpin all of IR theory, namely identity/difference, inside/outside, space/time, and community/anarchy. 'Inside' and 'outside' are Walker's chosen metaphors for the prevailing dichotomy of the domestic and the international, with two immutable foundations for two notions of sovereignty—the internal, which is responsive to the will and democratic in nature, and the external, which takes the form of hostility, competitiveness, and antagonism.

For Walker, postmodernity is global in scope, inaugurating a new phase in history and marked by rapid transformations and the disappearance of categories once considered eternal. Fred Halliday summarises what is missing in Walker's discourse: 'the total absence of empirical and ethical forces which may be underpinned to the ethos of post-modernity.' There is no substantive engagement of postmodern scholars with history, which paradoxically refutes their own charge against the mainstream's lack of historicity. There is some truth in Halliday's statement that the postmodern 'runs the risk of becoming the new banality, a set of assertions as unlocated and useless as vacuous generalities … that they seek to displace, and equally lacking in any conception … of how anything can be changed, of the question of agency' (Halliday 1994, 44–45).

Postmodern scholars wield theory as a subversive tool and seek to explain why certain conceptual readings, tropes, and meanings are naturalised over other interpretations and possibilities. State, sovereignty, and territory have been some of the popular ideas explored by the postmodernists. Postmodern work has also focused on the making and operations of the neoliberal world order, which requires working through several binaries. Categories like illegal migrants, insurgents, terrorists, and intelligence networks have been deconstructed to reveal how each term requires its 'other', without which the conventional understanding/s of these terms would not exist. Additionally, attention is focused on the practices of global regimes of governmentality, whereby different states are marked, classified, and watched by the reigning powers. Unlike the standard Marxist analysis of world politics, postmodernists do not subscribe to the easy determinism of global capitalism, offering instead a more richly textured and nuanced account of the various forms of domination, encounter, and resistance.

Postmodernists have found the de-territorialised and de-centred nature of global capitalism particularly amenable to their preferred meta-narratives. Identity politics across the world has also received postmodern attention. Given the postmodern scepticism of the ethical determination of political action, their analyses usually provide useful and radically different entry points to a problem. However, it is difficult to gauge the impact of postmodernism within IR. Most postmodernists loathe any disciplinary positioning and reject 'IR theory' as banal and restrictive, identifying attempts to label them as politically motivated mainstreaming. Moreover, postmodern scholars are eclectic and prone to abstraction, often invoking continental philosophers in a manner that bears no connection with international affairs. In the end, postmodernism in IR is fundamentally about double reading—exposing the hidden meanings of terms deployed by the dominant discourses as 'normal', and in the ultimate analysis, making sense of this domination in discursive and genealogical terms.

DECONSTRUCTION AND DOUBLE READING

Derridean deconstruction is a literary or textual strategy that seeks to unsettle stable concepts and break down conceptual binaries. Deconstruction exposes the hierarchical nature of conceptual oppositions and their need to hold on to their 'other' for their own stability and identity. It also reveals the tentative nature of all binaries by showing not only the dependency of opposites but also the internal differences concealed in each. In brief, deconstruction destroys the supposed neutrality of the settled structure of languages, and reveals the inevitable privileging of one term in opposition to the other (Derrida 1978, 1981).

The most conspicuous application of deconstruction is in the double reading of texts, a subversive ploy that is 'simultaneously faithful and violent' (Derrida 1981, 6). The technique unfolds by subjecting a text to dual interpretations. The initial monologist reading establishes its internal coherence or consistency, or how the text achieves stability. The second reading targets the points of instability or contradictions/oppositions, in order to break down the monologism, loosen the binds, and give voice to the silences in the initial reading. Since a text is eternally contradictory and crisis-prone, the dominant reading cannot claim privileged epistemic status. A deconstructive double reading exposes the hierarchisation and privileging that deliberately silence other (possible) interpretations of the text (Devetak 1996a, 189–90).

Given the radically unsettling potential of deconstruction, it is not surprising that that some postmodern scholars have provided novel interpretations of some of the most stable and uncontested categories in IR. Perhaps the most sensational double reading of the IR 'text' comes from Richard K. Ashley (1988), whose work was committed to undermining the hegemonic discourses prevalent in the field. Displacement of the status quo is essential so that practices might be resisted or disabled; boundaries can be questioned and transgressed; representations might be subverted, deprived of the presumption of self-evidence, and politicised and historicised; new connections may become possible among diverse cultural elements; and new ways of thinking and doing global politics might be opened up (ibid., 254).

In his dense and nuanced analysis, Ashley deconstructs the anarchy problematique through the Derridean strategy of double reading. The first reading provides the privileged interpretation that stabilises *a priori* the vision of an anarchic international system, comprised of sovereign territorial units called nation-states. The subversive reading, however, denies the fundamental anarchy/sovereignty opposition, with other binaries following from it (Chatterjee 2014, 312). The binaries of inside/outside, order/disorder, homogeneity/heterogeneity, progress/recurrence, and legitimacy/illegitimacy become possible only when the differences within sovereign states are converted into differences between them. The association of anarchy with disorder is thus conditional on a prior linking of order/community and territorial sovereignty (Griffiths 1999, 209). Ashley's double reading not only questions the natural privileging of anarchy, but also highlights the intellectual and political practices that sustain this dichotomy.[2]

[2]It must be conceded, however, that Ashley is not the only postmodernist credited with the deconstruction and subversion of the disciplinary possibility of IR. Postmodern scholars like Rob Walker, the English international society theorist Martin Wight, the critical theorist Andrew Linklater, and the constructivist John Gerard Ruggie came to similar conclusions regarding the artificiality of the dichotomy between anarchy and community, spheres of freedom and war, autonomy and necessity. The denial of ontological primacy

Rob Walker provides another significant exercise in double reading. His theoretical focus is on the concept of state sovereignty, which he considers very significant. His problematising of the state is directed at an inherent ethical contradiction. The state slides into a crisis due to its desire to monopolise human identity, political community, and legitimate authority. Situated between the community within and anarchy without, the state attempts a difficult reconciliation through the notion of sovereignty, which generalises the 'other' throughout the international system. Consequently, the most difficult problem confronting the state takes the form of a double puzzle—the need to fix the relationship between universality (community without) and particularity (community within) in two distinct spatial contexts, namely the state and political society (Walker 1993, 63–64). For Walker, sovereignty has been crucial in resolving modern binaries such as self/other, identity/difference, universality/particularity, and unity/diversity:

> As a response to the problem of proliferating autonomies in a world of dissipating hierarchies, it [sovereignty] articulates a specially modern account of political space, and does so through the resolution of three fundamental contradictions. It resolves, in brief, the relations between unity and diversity, between the internal and the external and between space and time. (ibid., 154)

Like Ashley, Walker explains the distinction between the inside and the outside, a dichotomy that results in several other antinomies with drastic consequences. The settled world of progressive, rights-bearing citizens contrasts with the violent disorder of the anarchical 'outside', a reading that inevitably privileges the community within, under the security of sovereign rule, over the anarchy without, which appears as a realm of force, violence, and compulsion (Griffiths 1999, 213–14). Walker's critique is focused on the paradigmatic dominance of rationalism, empiricism, and realism, or rather, a monological realism bereft of critical imagination.

With some exceptions, such as Walker's earlier work, *One World, Many Worlds* (1988), the post-structural positions on security, as represented by James Der Derian, David Campbell, Michael Shapiro, and Simon Dalby, resist any determination of the degree of political

---

to the territorialised nation-state is therefore not the exclusive contribution of postmodernists.

identity invested in 'the state' by an unproblematic privileging of 'the people' as a descriptive and political category. Post-structuralists contest the basic realist premise that security is a desirable condition or a good that should necessarily be striven for (Chatterjee 2014, 336). However, they do not simply reverse the hierarchical relationship between 'the people' and 'the state' embedded in the concept of national security by privileging the people; their deconstructivist method also attempts to undo the state-people dichotomy itself (Hansen 1997, 385). This may lead to a situation where the absence of an objective definition of threat makes political decisions about security more difficult, which is exactly what post-structuralism advocates and traditional security studies fears. All post-structuralists believe that security should be seen as a discursive practice rather than as a direct representation of an objectively threatening reality. Ole Waever thus understands security as a 'speech-act', because by 'saying security', a particular case is characterised as being of existential importance, requiring extraordinary measures. This concept of security reinforces, according to David Campbell, the logic of 'us-them', and is essentially defensive, protecting the status quo. Relying on the anti-methods of deconstruction, which show how dichotomies are crucial to the construction of meaning, Campbell turns the traditional understanding of security on its head by arguing that threats and insecurity do not just potentially undermine the state, but they actually constitute the state. The state only knows what it is in crude juxtaposition with the radical, threatening other. Campbell argues that states exist as states 'merely by virtue of their ability to constitute themselves as imagined communities'. Central to the process of imagination is the discourse of danger which, by telling us what to fear, also decides who we are (Campbell 1998, 191–93). Despite being labelled by critics as 'postmodern', Campbell has refrained from a similar labelling of his critical approach to security, because the term has 'become over-determined in scholarly and cultural circles'. Although he openly declares his debt to Michel Foucault and Jacques Derrida, he refutes all charges of being distanced from reality and political quietism, which accompany the mere use of a certain discursive vocabulary (Hansen 1997, 382–84).

Another author who arrives at similar conclusions is James Der Derian, who brings Nietzsche's interpretative realism and Baudrillard's hyper-realism into his genealogy of security (Der Derian 1992). He was inspired by Nietzsche's argument that, although the desire for security predominates in society, it seeks to eradicate all ambiguity, uncertainty, and paradoxes that make life worth living. These philosophical impulses are combined with Baudrillard's concept of simulation, which brings security into the 'realm of hyper-reality'. Through his inter-textual analysis, which knits together the writings of postmodern authors, public statements of presidents and government officials, and popular culture artefacts such as music, movies, and novels, Der Derian shows that security is 'highly imaginary'. It does not refer to anything real, but is part of a self-referring system perceived as more real than reality (hyper-real). He seeks to apply a post-structuralist approach to a late-modern condition of international relations that he calls 'anti-diplomacy' (ibid., viii). Anti-diplomacy represents 'a new discursive formation of statehood based on a techno-strategic triad of surveillance, terror and speed', and poses a challenge to traditional diplomatic practices (ibid., 92–118). Faced with the spasmodic immediacy of terrorism, Der Derian 'equates the terrorist's discourse with war'. Dresden, Hiroshima, Iraq, and Afghanistan testify to the ability of states in an age of total war to sanction the killing and maiming of civilians. Conversely, many terrorist groups employ the nomenclature of war. 'Security' assumes new meaning in new times when 'growing anti-diplomatic forces', such as interdependent economies and ecologies, surveillance, and media, undermine the sovereign privileges and obligations of the territorial state (ibid., 173–99). Der Derian calls the 1991 Gulf War 'the first cyber war', where technologically generated televised images (Buzan, et al. 1998, 95–97) legitimised a late-modern 'war for peace', forcing all critics of war to choose between the history of civilisation and its sanctioned destructions, neo-fascism, and a new world order.

Postmodernism and Critical Theory Debates

Critics argue that postmodern IR scholars, much like postmodernists in general, suffer from methodological vagueness, lack of objectivity, an undefined political perspective, and a tendency towards excessive relativism and value neutrality (Vasquez 1998, 217–40). While all these criticisms are powerful, their validity remains contested. The most serious of these is undoubtedly the charge of value neutrality and a deliberate silence over the choice of political position. In his work on reflexivity, Mark Neufeld voices a legitimate concern: 'There is, however, a problem. For while insisting on the politico-normative content of dominant knowledge discourses in the discipline—for example neorealism—postmodernists have been strangely reluctant to spell out, or even acknowledge, the politico-normative content of their own approach' (Neufeld 1993, 73).

Postmodernism creates its own contradiction. It states that knowledge is never neutral; all knowledge standards are power-laden and purposive. If all knowledge can be suspected of a hidden politico-normative (or power) bias, postmodernism cannot be an exception. If all knowledge positions are political positions or reflect ethico-political standards, the postmodernist stand of being simultaneously 'an emphatically political perspective' and yet one 'which refuses to privilege any partisan political line', *pace* Jim George and David Campbell (George and Campbell 1990, 281), becomes contradictory, confusing, and/or hypocritical.

Perhaps postmodern IR scholars do follow a partisan political line that manifests itself clearly in the footnotes and margins of their tracts, variously termed the *dialectical competence model* or *Ulyssesian realism* (Ashley 1984; Der Derian 1995). Der Derian explains it best:

> A realism stuck in the empirical prison of things as they really are encourages a denial and resentment towards things as they truly differ, for it is the will to reduce the other to the same and historical differences to objective laws that builds the traditionalist foundation of realism and divides the actual from the possible. Needed in its place is a *critical realism* that recognizes the tenacity of its singular reach, the instability of its antinomic foundations, and the necessity of an irreality beyond it. (Der Derian 1995, 388–89; emphasis added)

Before moving towards an analysis of reflexivity and its use in critical security studies, it is necessary to draw the line between critical theory and postmodernist perspectives in IR. Although both claim to originate in an alternative and radical paradigm, they differ on what they consider 'alternative' and 'radical'. The Hoffman–Rengger exchanges are an example (Hoffman 1987, 1988; Rengger 1988). Hoffman's celebration of critical theory as *the* alternative paradigm, capable of liberating IR from the clutches of realism-liberalism, is contested by postmodernists like Rengger on two counts. *First*, the postmodernists are conscious of their identity, and therefore their difference, vis-à-vis the critical Habermasian theory of Cox, Linklater, and Hoffman, and as a consequence, resist any attempt to subsume them under a broad critical theory banner. *Second*, and more crucially, postmodernists accuse critical theory of being insufficiently radical or subversive, and are unwilling to cut their epistemological Gordian knot with positivist Enlightenment legacy (George 1994, 185–86). The faith that critical theory reposes in elements universal to the world order and to the idea of modernity and progress disqualifies them, according to Rengger, from being genuinely anti-foundationalist and truly critical.

In response, Hoffman invoked the Habermasian defence of a nuanced and structured rationality, claiming that critical theory was 'the most self-reflective outpost of the radical tradition of the Enlightenment' (George 1994, 186; Hoffman 1987, 1988; Rengger 1988, 92). Hoffman's rebuttal of the claims of postmodernism is predictable, amounting to a dismissal of postmodernism as a depoliticised, nihilistic, detached, and dispassionate discourse: one that destroys for the sake of destruction, without proposing anything concrete as a substitute. Needless to say, the critical theory–postmodernism divide continues. Given their distinctive origins and the different ethico-political commitments underlying their positions, the divide will continue to fragment the 'other' tradition in IR that is seeking an alternative ontological as well as epistemological basis for the discipline, against the linear dominance of the rationalist-realist schools (Chatterjee 2014, 315).

REFLEXIVE THINKING ON SOUTH ASIAN SECURITY

Analysts like Ranabir Samaddar, Samir Kumar Das, and Sanjay Chaturvedi have used critical/reflexive approaches to understand South Asia's security problems. They argue that the way we pose the question is what creates the problem in the first place. We need to look deeper and ask why there is no alternative conceptualisation of what security might have meant in the subcontinent. Transforming South Asian borders into spaces of community requires one to rethink the very concept of security. As Das points out:

> Our argument is that the nation that the Indian state sought to protect and secure was or is in some fundamental historical senses divergent from the one that we were ethnically, territorially and historically

> endowed with. Securing the nation in that sense forms an inseparable part of greater nation-building exercises. (Das 2003, 54)

South Asian insecurity inheres in the constitution of the region itself. The discourse of security emerged from the territorial focus of nationalism and the division of states within a region lacking traditional borders: 'The border thus exteriorizes the interior and interiorizes the exterior' (Samaddar 1998a, 20).

The problem lies in the fact that the South Asian state system arose along with the negation of the other (past) communitarian impulse, was inexorably intertwined with the idea of modernity, muted alternative imagination(s) of space, and subverted extant communities and rival vision(s) of social organisation. The statist nationalism in South Asia turned all conflicts into state conflicts and the differences between communities into territorial differences of states. Borders provide the nation with its particularity. The state creates the nation instrumentally through territoriality and provides security for the inside by demarcating it from the outside, the other. Samaddar argues that the tension between the nation and its border is constitutive of the South Asian order itself. This peculiar valorisation of the border signifies the limits of the communitarian construction of contemporary South Asia. Any attempt to dilute the border is seen as a threat to the distinctiveness of the nation; communities must therefore be made to understand this (Samaddar 1998a).

Sanjay Chaturvedi's extensive work on borders, the diaspora, community, and critical geopolitics draw attention to reflexivity and critical otherness in South Asia. In a recent work, he theoretically links the concepts of diaspora, cultural hybridity, and nationalist imaginations—emotionally created or officially produced—and examines the constantly changing relationship between the territorialised state and 'de-territorialised identities' in the present age of globalisation and porous borders. The central assumption of this endeavour is the observation that IR theory is yet to systematically address the multifaceted phenomenon of diaspora, as well as the diverse factors and forces behind the 'transformation of historically contingent patterns of mobility and hybridity into a state of diasporic otherness' (Chaturvedi 2011).

Chaturvedi's work on Hindutva and geopolitics demonstrates how, in the fused, culturally hybrid communities of South Asia, Hindutva is essentially a religiously informed geopolitical project. It needs to be understood as a strategic project that draws on religious beliefs and cultural myths and symbols to produce imaginative geographies. Chaturvedi illustrates how the Hindutva project operates in, and is perceived by, India's immediate neighbourhood, taking up the case of Sri Lanka and the Tamil–Sinhala divide; the projection of an otherwise intensely ethno-culturally diverse society of Nepal as a Hindu state; and the reciprocation of Hindutva's hostility towards Muslims by Islamic ideologues in Pakistan in school and college textbooks. Chaturvedi calls this a 'process of trans-border othering' (Chaturvedi 2011, 292), and urges for a move towards an anti-geopolitical imagination in the culturally diverse South Asia against the 'narrow agendas of various Hindutva-type geopolitical projects' (ibid., 299).

The essential point underlying such critical scholarship is that borders in South Asia do not have a pre-colonial past, and that the histories of borders, which are viewed as natural and permanent, belong to the discourse of the state, an exercise in the nation-building project of South Asia. The subjects covered range from issues of identity formation—how states create borders to construct the categories of 'us' and 'them'—to population movements and issues of rehabilitation, victimhood, and the problem of refugees (Samaddar 2004). They challenge the mainstream realist and neoliberal accounts of borders and politics and view the state as anti-people, with a territorial and modular nationalism serving to justify and legitimise it, and with the classification of objects as the effects of power and construction of recursive binaries as essential to its existence. In contrast to claims of justice, the ethic of care is considered a legitimate moral standard to address questions of homelessness of people caught in the crossfire between irresponsible states. Is the ethic of care superior to the ethic of justice? Can the state be reformed to overcome its obsession with borders? Is modernity the ultimate problem? Can modular territorial nationalism be transgressed? While scholarship inspired by critical theory or postmodernism does not provide concrete answers to all such questions, they must be credited for having raised them in the first place.

4

Theories of IR
Constructivism and Feminism

Shibashis Chatterjee, with Moitrayee Sengupta

Theories do not grow in a vacuum. Constructivism arose at a time when mainstream IR theories, particularly realism and liberalism, appeared to have exhausted their potential and were unable to predict the sudden end to the Cold War order or offer new insights into emerging problems that could not be explained by the staple notions of power/security or wealth/commerce. As the Cold War came to a close, several new questions were raised. *First*, the conflicts immediately following the collapse of the Soviet Union inevitably involved questions of social or political identity formations, whether in Eastern Europe or in the postcolonial world. Wars fought over ethnicity and religion could not be convincingly accounted for by the familiar ideas of inter-state conflict. While these conflicts often spilled across international borders, their triggers were invariably domestic. They were unmistakably assertions of collective identity by groups that had, in most cases, lived together for decades in relative peace. Ethnic identity assertions were ultimately linked to questions of national identity and problems of secessionism in many multi-ethnic states, where the overarching national identity was unable to contain the claims of ethnic groups who often vied with each other to create sovereign homelands, breaking away violently from the earlier federal structure.

Furthermore, the question of identity had also come up strongly through debates over multiculturalism in the West, where several diasporic communities and indigenous groups began to demand a set of cultural rights that separated them from their hosts. This case for different rights was central to a politics of identity based on claims of cultural recognition, in contrast to the older politics of redistribution predicated on solidarities of class. Groups like the Asian communities or the Spanish and Caribbean people in various parts of Europe and North America articulated their demands in the language of culture; they sought their right to enjoy their distinctive culture, be it in the form of language or religion. In other words, the conflicts and struggles underway in the 1990s called for new theoretical categories that could make sense of the pivotal role that identities played in both bringing groups together and pitting some against the others.

Social constructivism therefore became an attractive theoretical alternative for it advocated taking ideational structures seriously and viewed processes of identity construction as central to its investigations. Resisting the tendency of both deterministic structuralism and unconnected individualism, social constructivism promoted the mutual constitution of both structures and practices, which was also in sync with similar trends in other social sciences. This brought it prestige and recognition outside of IR as a discipline, and many scholars found in constructivism an opportunity for alternative theoretical work that did not ask them to give up their empirical commitments. Constructivism was quick to recognise the need to steer clear of epistemic and methodological extremisms, paving the way for their acceptance within dominant institutional practices, unlike the work of postmodernists and some critical theorists, which necessitated an ontological, ideological, and methodological break from what they 'claimed' was the 'hegemony of the mainstream'. This does not mean, however, that constructivists are united as a group or that constructivism is a unified theoretical position. What this does indicate is the fact that most constructivists have found it more convenient to work in parallel with mainstream theory builders and establish a mode of communication with them that has allowed a greater space than many other schools of thought.

Constructivism takes many forms. John Ruggie, for instance, identifies three types of constructivism: neo-classical constructivism, postmodernist constructivism, and naturalistic constructivism (Ruggie 1998, 880–82). Neo-classical constructivism calls for adjusting a theory to the problem at hand, addresses intersubjectivity in speech analysis, and recognises that knowledge is dynamic and adaptation is the norm. Ruggie, Friedrich Kratochwil, Martha Finnemore, Nicholas Onuf, Peter Katzenstein, and Emanuel Adler are all neo-classical constructivists (Chatterjee 2005a, 76).

The constructivist notion of intersubjectivity valorises neither peace nor violence (Zehfuss 2002, 39–42). Communities are built on shared collective identities where unity and otherness, in-group feelings and out-group differences, both play indispensable roles. Identities both unite and pull people apart; while identities are shared, they tend to diverge in specific social settings. An identity is therefore the master variable for a constructivist, as it helps make sense of the dynamics of segregation and the politics of unification as two sides of a political process (Chatterjee 2005a, 78).

Constructivists also make a powerful case for ideas as the prime movers in world politics (Ruggie 1998, 865–69, 878–80). This constitutes a radical break from the structural realists. For Waltzian neorealism, behaviour is determined exclusively by the physical properties or material attributes of given units. While states might use ideological justifications for strategic purposes (Chatterjee 2014, 13–14), they have no causal role to play. In contrast, liberal institutionalism recognises the role of ideas. However, its functionalism and empricism ultimately make ideas derivative. In contrast, constructivists take ideas as causal; conflicts are ideational and material, intellectual as well as mechanical. Conflicts grow out of differing interpretations of facts. They are ideational in the sense of being ideologically constituted in the minds of men. For a constructivist, conflict is about the discordant or antithetical perceptions held by adversaries, and threats are always perceptual and ideational. Thus, the classification of relations—that is, who becomes a friend or a foe—depends on intersubjective interpretations, on ideas, rather than the structurally deterministic pull of anarchy. Since ideas shape the world, define actors, and set preferences, they matter equally to the myriad dimensions of security as well (Chatterjee 2014, 14).

Mainstream constructivism has three definitive characteristics.

1. Constructivists like Alexander Wendt and Adler have strongly proposed minimising the gap between rationalism and constructivism on the one hand, and realism and constructivism on the other (Chatterjee 2014, 14).

2. Constructivists have not only put forward general meta-theoretical arguments, but they have also undertaken detailed case studies that showcase the effects of norms and identities in concrete theatres.
3. Constructivism supplements the rationalist paradigm, particularly vis-à-vis the roles of constitutive norms.

The dominance of constructivism within non-mainstream approaches can be explained by its pragmatism, flexibility, and desire, particularly true of conventional constructivism, to remain in a dialogue with mainstream approaches. Their commitment to methodological plurality and recognition of the need for academic research to be predicated on methods has won them support from all quarters (ibid., 14–15).

The postmodern variety of constructivism, which derives its philosophical inspiration from the works of Nietzsche and borrows heavily from the writings of Foucault and Derrida, is more radical. It stresses the 'linguistic construction of subjects', fashions an anti-foundational epistemology, denies social science and universal truth claims, celebrates diversity, and refutes the possibility of absolute truth. Ruggie includes Walker, Der Derian, Campbell, and the feminist scholar Spike Peterson among the standard-bearers of this genre. In contrast to Ruggie, however, we adopt the conventional interpretation and exclude this group from the constructivists. They are better described as postmodern or post-structuralist scholars, who have little in common with conventional constructivist assumptions.

Ruggie's third variant is a compromise with the other two, and is grounded in the philosophical doctrine of scientific realism. Naturalistic constructivism, like its neo-classical counterpart, is committed to the idea of social science. This approach believes in a common ontology for both sciences, but argues that knowledge is essentially about knowing non-observables, and that there is a knowable world of intersubjective meaning that exists outside the mind of the scholar (Ruggie 1998, 881–82). Since Wendt's contribution to constructivism has been paradigmatic, we shall study his ideas separately.

The social world is intersubjectively constituted; it is made up of people who live in a manner they understand and relate to. The social world is predicated on the material. However, material entities become meaningful 'things' through the ideas or beliefs that people have about them (Chatterjee 2014, 15). Even military security cannot escape 'meanings'. Material capabilities assume potency once they are 'framed' into action. Weapons are inert, instruments to be wielded by people. The ideas or beliefs underlying the making, organisation, and deployment of weapons as perceived by the people subjectively configure military assets, which then assume potency in human consciousness. For the constructivist, security is not just about physical capabilities (ibid., 15–16). The material attributes defining capability are no doubt important, but more so is the understanding that people develop about these capabilities (Jackson and Sorensen 2003, 255–57).

Contrary to neorealism and neoliberalism, therefore, constructivists do not operate with set payoffs or preferences. Rather, they problematise what the mainstream takes for granted, and question how actors come to bear specific identities and interests. The mainstream regards identities as given; constructivists believe that identities are acquired, constituted, and transformed. 'Thus contra neorealism, I argued that *American* hegemony was every bit as important as American *hegemony* in shaping the post-war order' (Ruggie 1998, 863). Constructivists also differ from neoliberal institutionalists over the dynamic of choice; while neoliberals emphasise utility considerations, the constructivist enjoins identity or the definition of self as motivating such a choice. Identities are rarely fixed—they change over time, and these changes can reshape what states see as their priorities and interests. In addition, constructivists utilise the language of norms, and key constructivist thinkers have imbued normative ideas with causal potency.

Wendt defines constructivism as follows:

> Constructivism is a structural theory of the international system that makes the following core claims: (1) States are the principal units of analysis for international political theory; (2) the key structures in the state system are inter-subjective, rather than material; and (3) state identities and interests are in important parts constructed by these social structures, rather than given exogenously to the system by human nature or domestic politics. (Wendt 1994, 385)

Although Wendt's constructivism is state-centric, he does not take the state for granted. Wendt critiques neorealists and neoliberals for their inability to explain the constitutive character of international entities. They take the identities, interests, and powers of the state for granted, or, as Wendt puts it, treat them as 'ontologically primitive'. The utilitarian realist explanation of the sources of international conflict is superficial, for they see conflict as derived mechanically from anarchic structures. What they lack is a social theory of state interests, without which any proper investigation of the basis of international conflict and cooperation is impossible. Thus, anarchy produces a range of state interactions and behaviour, and a variety of social structures, depending on how states derive their interests. For states are not dull, lifeless entities; they bear a collective identity that creates basic state 'appetites', such as the drive for physical security, stability, recognition by others, and development. How states fulfil their needs, however, depends on their social identity, that is, how states define themselves in relation to others within the international system. Hence, contrary to realism, anarchy is not logically wedded to conflict and a zero-sum view of the world.

The constructivist reading of conflict is very different from the realist mode. First, as Wendt puts it: '... the deep structure of anarchy [is a] ... cultural or ideational rather than material phenomenon.' Hence, the logic of anarchy varies, and accordingly, there are different cultures of anarchy with their distinctive, concomitant roles. Wendt identifies three macro-level cultures of international politics—Hobbesian, Lockean, and Kantian—based on distinctive views of the relationship between the self and the other. The three cultures fit three distinctive roles, viz., that of enemy, rival, and friends. The upshot is that these cultures differ in terms of how a state visualises another within each one, with the possibility that these images will transform over time. States have plural social identities, some cooperative and some conflictual, depending on how they define the social situation in which they operate (Wendt 1999, Ch. 6). Wendt's fundamental contribution lies in his explanation of the variations in state interaction through a social theory of the dynamics of changing state preferences and actions.

Wendt's constructivism not only provides a useful social theory of state preferences and action, but it also supplies a dynamic model of international interaction (Ruggie 1998, 874–76). One of Wendt's most important complaints against neorealism concerns its inability to explain transformation and change. Both Wendt and Ruggie highlight the essentially static character of neorealism, claiming that its grounding in an atomistic ontology of states in anarchy makes it hostile to the idea of change. Although the payoffs under anarchy might vary and its effects might be ameliorated through cooperative strategies, neorealism does not consider any alteration of the basic structure. Neorealists err in failing to see that states do not merely perpetuate or reproduce system structures over time; they also can, and often do, transform the structure in qualitative ways.

Wendt also challenges the concept of institutions deployed by the followers of rational choice theory (both neorealists and neoliberals). The neorealists negate the role of institutions as an independent variable in international politics. Neoliberalism selectively empowers institutions, thereby altering how states strategise by modifying the costs and benefits of different approaches. Wendt, on the other hand, 'empowers' institutions, considering them capable of constituting the agents in various domains of international relations, including security.

Wendt sees the international structure as combining social relationships and material capabilities: 'Inter-subjective systemic structures consist of shared understanding, expectations, and social knowledge embedded in international institutions and threat complexes in terms of which states define some of their identities and interests' (Wendt 1992, 399). Institutions are '... a relatively stable set structure of identities and interests.... Institutions are fundamentally cognitive entities that do not exist apart from actors' ideas about how they would work.' According to Wendt, states and institutions are mutually constitutive, and so institutions are neither outside nor independent of states. They shape, regulate, and give meaning to state action, and often decide what it is to be a state; in short, they provide stable state identities. Since states and institutions act together, with each bringing about significant changes in the other, institutions can alter states' thinking and reconstitute state identities and interests at the systemic level.

Wendt's constructivism hinges ultimately on the idea of identity. The 'daily life of international politics is an ongoing process of states taking identities in relation to others, casting them into corresponding counter-identities, and playing out the result' (Wendt 1999, 21). In *Social Theory of International Politics* (1999), Wendt shows how identity is defined and how it changes via interaction. He defined identity as 'relatively stable, role-specific understandings and expectations about self' (Wendt 1992, 397). Although there is an assumption of relative stability, it does not preclude the more pressing need to understand the transformation of 'self-hood'. He believes that 'identities may be hard to change, but they are not carved in stone' (Wendt 1999, 21). The definition of identity has an impact on security practices and shapes the security environment of states. Identities provide the basis for interests; most crucially, identity determines the kind of anarchy that prevails in the international system.

How are identities constituted? To answer this, Wendt employs the principles of Anthony Giddens' structuration theory. Wendt's central contention, following Giddens, is that units do not exist independently of the structures around them; equally, those structures cannot be understood as independent of the agents, who either reproduce or transform the former. Wendt imputes a certain discursive quality to social structures, as being 'inseparable from the reasons and self-understandings' of agents. The identity of actors is determined through interactions (Zehfuss 2002, 41–42). Wendt, however, ontologically places the state before such interactions, endowing it with functions independent of the social context. Beyond this, the identity of actors becomes communicative, repeating and responding to the practices of other agents over time. This allows Wendt to refashion the binary of self and collective identity into a continuum. When states define others in exclusion of themselves, the result is a conflict based on the definition of that identity itself. When others are made a part of an actor's definition of the self, cooperation and peace become possible, being predicated again on the qualities of the definition (of identity) itself (ibid., 40).

Peter Katzenstein's work on norms, identity, and security is interesting because, unlike Wendt, he has paid the most attention to how domestic norms and identity constructs affect a state's external relations. In a sense, Katzenstein's constructivism is an inside-out perspective. His central argument is that the security environment of a state is both materially and culturally/institutionally constituted. Further, the cultural environment not only regulates behaviour across issues, it also constitutes the basic character of states, or their identity (Katzenstein 1996, 33). These two assumptions contrast with the neorealist and neoliberal understanding of security, which take actors' identities as given. Like Wendt, Katzenstein also problematises the ontological status of the actors, emphasising their socially contingent character. Third, norms and culture matter in the patterns of cooperation and conflict in international affairs, in the selection of alliances, and in the determination of neutral ground and hostile actors (ibid., 34).

Significantly, Katzenstein does not rule out the role played by material factors in the choice of security policies. Adding crucial ideational and cultural variables, he argues that conventional theories such as neorealism and neoliberalism are often unable to explain anomalies because of their neglect of cultural and ideational factors.

Katzenstein defines norms as 'collective expectations for the proper behaviour of actors with a given "identity"' (Katzenstein, et al. 1996). Norms are both 'constitutive', that is, they help define the identity of an actor, and 'regulative', in the sense of specifying the 'standards of proper behavior'. 'Thus norms either define (institute) identities in the first place ... or prescribe (regulate) behavior for already constituted identities ...' (ibid., 54).

In his summary of the contributions to the landmark volume, *The Culture of National Security* (1996), Katzenstein outlined five key functions or effects that norms have in the realm of national security. He contended that a state's cultural and institutional context significantly influences its national security priorities and, consequently, its security policies. These factors contribute to a state's identity as well. Differences in state identity lead to variations in security interests and policy choices. A state's identity impacts the overall cooperative frameworks it establishes with other states. State policies thus both sustain and transform cultural and institutional frameworks.

Katzenstein's work in general, and this volume in particular, has opened a new vista in security studies. The strength of the enterprise lies in its empirical orientation and the use of extensive and detailed case studies. It is true that the conclusions and findings of many of the essays are not convincing, and more crucially, do not rule out the possibility of rival interpretations. This underscores the necessity of creating a method to help us understand how norms specifically affect security actions. But this in no way detracts from the analytical usefulness of the approach. Katzenstein's claims that norms, culture, and identity matter to security, that actors are culturally and socially constituted, and that security is as much a matter of ideas and cultural mediation as it is a reflex of material calculations have been invaluable to the development of an alternative thinking on security.

Like Wendt and Katzenstein, Emmanuel Adler's work hinges on the role of identity. Adler was inspired by Karl Deutsch, who pioneered the concept of a pluralistic security community in the 1950s. A political community, according to Deutsch, is made up of social groups, with a process of political communication, machinery for law enforcement, and popular habits of compliance (Deutsch, et al. 1957, 3). Deutsch introduced the concept of 'security community', defining it as a group of people (or states) that have become integrated, to the point where there is a 'real assurance that the members of that community will not fight each other physically, but will settle their disputes in some other way' (ibid., 5), and differentiated between amalgamated and pluralistic security communities on the basis of their degree of integration. Amalgamated communities emerge from the formal merging of independent states, while in pluralistic communities, the legal independence of constituting member states is retained, although they share 'dependable expectations of peaceful change' (ibid., 6).

Adler defined security communities as 'socially constructed cognitive regions or community-regions', whose security and welfare frontiers coincide with the limits of shared understanding and common identities (Adler 1997, 250). Territoriality separates people and provides most of them with a definite homeland. The state becomes the basis of a citizen's unconditional allegiance. Yet states often unite for common purposes, and hence the idea of a community life coterminous with territoriality is a socially contingent one. The region, conceived as transnational space, stems from a legitimate collective imagination, bound by the mutual recognition of a shared destiny and identity. Community-regions can therefore be the most powerful destination of men.

Such community-regions are 'socially constructed', 'spatially differentiated', and transnational in nature, constituted by 'national, transnational, and international elites and institutions' (Adler 1997, 253). Adler defines such regions as 'regional systems of meanings ... not limited to a specific geographic place' (ibid.). These regions are constructed by people whose commitments go beyond sovereign territoriality, who communicate and interact freely across borders, are politically committed to working for the promotion of regional interests, and catalyse such sentiments and perspectives in their respective jurisdictions.

The identity of this construct is vital. Community-regions are physical, but Adler also describes them as 'cognitive regions or cognitive structures that help constitute the practices of their members, whose meanings, understandings, and identities help keep the region in place' (ibid., 254). Adler and Michael Barnett reworked Deutsch's idea of security community: 'Pluralistic communities, in contrast, retain the legal independence of constituting member states, but share dependable expectations of peaceful change' (Deutsch et al., 1957, 6). Deutsch's classification of amalgamated and pluralistic security communities is reproduced as loosely and tightly coupled variants, whose defining criteria, however, stemmed from the work of Wendt (trust, institutionalisation, and the culture of anarchy), rather than Deutsch.

Two other themes stand out in Adler's writings. *First*, Adler's security community is essentially meant for liberal democracies (Adler 1997, 257–60). Adler developed an interesting argument based on democracy to privilege the case for a liberal order. Totalitarian systems can create a shared understanding, but they cannot build or destroy trust. An additional element is the peaceful negotiation of conflict, in a manner that reinforces mutual trust among unknown members. While Adler admitted that security communities could thrive in other political systems, he stressed that a liberal democracy remains essential for cultivating and disseminating their foundational principles (ibid., 260).

Second, in his subsequent writings Adler did recognise the role of power behind the development and institutionalisation of security communities, although *Security Communities* (1998), co-edited with Barnett, proposed a dichotomy between force and community, and asserted that friendship represented a direct challenge to the realist imagery of power-balance (Adler and Barnett 1998, 5). Adler also noted that social reality is not merely a matter of identity and a constructed meaning. The configuration of identity and the imposition of meaning are in large measure physically determined, with material and technological resources playing a vital role (Adler 1997, 261–62). Adler's norm analysis, inherent in his idea of security community, is thus theoretically closer to Wendtian constructivism, where both material and ideational factors are given due (although not equal) weightage.

APPLYING CONSTRUCTIVISM: INDIA'S CONFLICTS WITH PAKISTAN

A constructivist reading of the India–Pakistan conflict would be qualitatively different because, in their conception, 'the deep structure of anarchy', as Wendt points out, is 'a cultural or ideational rather than material phenomenon' (Wendt 1999, 43). The logic of anarchy varies, and there are different cultures of anarchy with their distinctive concomitant roles. Wendt identifies three macro-level cultures of international politics, namely the Hobbesian, Lockean, and Kantian, based on specific images of the relationship between the self and the other. Hobbes viewed this relationship as a state of general disorder following from a lack of authority; Locke saw it as chaotic, yet containing the natural rights to life, liberty, and property, which significantly blunted its sharp edges; while Kant was invested in the idea of a loose federation of republics, which could ultimately transform the structure into something akin to a world government (for a detailed discussion, see Chatterjee [2008]).

With reference to relations between India and Pakistan, the constructivists, while not denying the enmity, would explain it as a form of cultural interpretation, and argue that policymaking elites in both countries focus on a set of norms and beliefs acquired through a long-term process of socialisation. The successful adoption of such cultural norms has led to India–Pakistan relations acquiring a certain stability, albeit one characterised by fear, hostility, and contestation.

The constructivists seek to deconstruct the 'givens' offered by the realists. It may therefore be argued that the hostility between states such as India and Pakistan is neither historical nor predetermined, and that their interests are not exogenously determined either. Their policies are constitutive of each other's images and beliefs as both are socialised into a maximalist notion of friendship, one that borders on enmity and rules out a sympathetic understanding of each other's positions, constraints, commitments, and problems. Their animosity is thus the result of a certain 'cultural' interpretation of their origins, which makes it difficult to build ties on the basis of self-reflection and toleration.

Pakistan was born from a belief in the two-nation theory, while India reposed faith in the ethos of secular nationalism. The mutual exclusivity of these belief systems resulted in each country portraying the other as a threat, and the growth of a civic nationalism that would view territorial differences in a non-essentialised cultural sense became unlikely. The logic of this postcolonial nationalism ignored all ethnic, religious, cultural, and linguistic similarities, preventing the growth of alternative models of a Lockean or Kantian kind. The rivalry between India and Pakistan can be traced back to the pre-Partition conflict between Hindu and Muslim communities in the subcontinent. After independence, this rivalry, and the binary political cultures associated with it, was so deeply enmeshed with the territorial state identity that variables like domestic regimes and the international power structure have had little to no impact on it.

Realist parameters, such as relative military spending, weapon systems, and the modernisation of the army, are inadequate when it comes to explaining the conflict, because they fail to account for the fact that neither India nor Pakistan is similarly hostile to other states in the region, including China. Realism provides no clear answers as to why they perceive each other as a threat, because the reasons behind such a perception are inter-subjectively constituted. Adversarial relations between India and Pakistan are better explained through a constructivist lens, which focuses on their incompatible notions of nationhood, while the purely realist lens focuses on the structural anarchy and asymmetrical capabilities of the two sovereign states. Constructivists caution against a simple one-dimensional reading of evidence. Materiality, after all, gathers meaning only through ideas. Hence, the India–Pakistan hostility is about conflicting political narratives of sovereignty and nationhood, and yet, these imaginations on both sides are also contested. For example, Jawaharlal Nehru, Mahatma Gandhi, and Veer Savarkar differed markedly in their understanding of India. M. A. Jinnah's notion of Pakistan did not remain unrivalled over time either. An articulation and careful reading of these differences are crucial to the constructivists. In a nutshell, constructivists concede that this bilateral dispute is real, inasmuch as it is perceived as real and threatening by the dominant political elites, and this in turn has seen to the successful dissemination and socialisation of such images in the public consciousness. As a result, there has been a perpetuation of the cycle of mistrust and a weakening of their ties.

POSTCOLONIAL IR THEORY?

The problem with theorising in IR is that the theories are mostly based on Western ideas, experiences, and practices, with narrow cognitive horizons. Hence, some scholars have argued that even those marginalised under the existing power relations continue to perpetuate the same system of dominance. A. Acharya and Barry Buzan sought to explain this apparently contradictory trend in their celebrated *Non-Western International Relations Theory* (2010). They sought a non-Western IR theory that is not self-consciously predicated upon the assumptions of Western IR. Thoroughly metropolitan in nature, Western IR emerged through the dominant power's interactions with the non-Western world. While realism was not unknown in the non-Western world, it developed primarily as a Western—or, more specifically, American—theory, under conditions that did not exist in most other parts of the world. The neat binary of inside and outside was a Western construct that held little relevance for non-Western states. In the postcolonial world, most conflicts were on issues of domestic political control, ethnicity, and community. Security was less a matter of guarding borders against external predation and more about securing them against internal threats. Malnutrition, poverty, and deadly diseases took more lives than inter-state wars. States and regimes were poorly demarcated, and elites considered holding on to power more important than guaranteeing the security of citizens. Identity was pivotal to violence in the postcolonial world, and as a result, neither realism nor liberalism could offer satisfactory accounts of violence. The non-West was made an uncritical part of a standard analytical drawing board, where grand theories held sway. There was little realisation of the fact that the non-Western world had a different genealogy that required sufficient analytical space. Without a proper historicisation of the postcolonial world, it is impossible to explain their violence.

Developing a non-Western Asian approach to international relations, primarily driven by the rise of Asian powers, may not lead to a completely new paradigm. This will only turn Asia into a proxy for the non-West, comprising powers that can successfully rival the dominance of the West. The literature on major or rising powers bears testimony to this. The real promise of a postcolonial IR lies in a different route. The logic of power and wealth would create Asian adaptations of realism and liberalism, with minor inflections. Robert Cox's dictum, 'theory is always for someone and for some purpose', will be faithfully followed by Asian thinkers, who would create their own theories for the state. Western IR theory will therefore serve the purpose of rising Asian powers, as it had done for their Western counterparts. As Ching-Chang Chen puts it,

> While realism, liberalism, and (the pluralist wing of) the English School may indeed speak for the West and in the interest of sustaining

> its power, prosperity, and influence, the 'solution' is not that Asian states should also have an interest in 'indigenous' IR theory that speaks for them and their interests, which would only reproduce the very hegemonic logic of dominance which Robert Cox himself has warned against. (Chen 2011, 4)

Amitava Acharya and Barry Buzan, whose work on non-Western theories has assumed canonical status, found IR theory Western-centric, insensitive to world history and the different experiences of non-Western worlds. Their work sought to redress that 'imbalance' by bringing various Asian experiences, cultures, and history into the domain of IR theory. They offered five possible explanations for the absence of non-Western IR:

1. Western IR theories are right.
2. They have become hegemonic.
3. Non-Western theories are either marginal or concealed.
4. The material and normative structures discourage non-Western IR.
5. Given the early lead taken by Western IR theories, it is tough for non-Western theory to catch up. (Acharya and Buzan 2010, 16–21)

The real challenge lies in creating a body of theory based on the current historical sociology of non-Western states. This exercise would not only provide a new ontological vantage point, but would also help scholars understand how non-Western experiences and ideas were vital to the making of Western IR over time. The West knew that the 'international' was created not at the theoretical expense of the non-West, but rather, 'through' it. It is this dialectical process that needs to be studied, instead of reproducing the sterile binary of West and East as oppositional entities.

Postcolonial theories seek to identify what needs to be problematised in the discipline's interrogation of the non-Western world: the conceptual histories of the nation-state, nationalism, sovereignty, territoriality, security, and identity. The basic argument is this: we need to historicise the meaning/s of the state and nation, the imagination of political community, and the constitution of territorial units in a pre-existing landscape of multiple identities to make sense of the nature and causes of violence and conflict in the non-Western world. In most non-Western societies, colonialism destroyed much of the earlier constitutive idioms and practices, and the idea of the sovereign territorial state and nationalism came to dominate the public and political imagination in these societies, thereby completing the process of globalising the Westphalian project. As a result, the non-Western world witnessed, in one form or another, the inevitable clash between two dynamics, one based on culture and civilisation that historically delineated regions as space/s of communication and meaning, and the other a more modern idea of territorialised, sovereign nationhood, thriving on principles of exclusivity, differentiation, and loyalty. Much of the conflict in the non-Western world remains caught in this bind, poised precariously in the interactions of two radically different dynamics that are equally active in defining their existential realities. As modernity reinforced the nation-state's territorial claims to power, the difference in culture and territory opened up scope for conflict within and between states, an understanding of which requires a sustained engagement with historical processes and cultural anthropology that had remained outside the normal bounds of academic IR. Many of these conflicts are sustained by fragile and precarious elites, who find such conflict invaluable in perpetuating their illegitimate rule over restive and demanding populations. The categories of refugees and internally displaced persons (IDPs), insurgents, revolutionaries, and mercenaries will not fit within the regular parameters of IR discourses; they hint at a distinctive ontology that calls for a radical departure from the received heritage.

The postcolonial articulation of sovereignty created the ultimate paradox for elites, who realised immediately the artificiality of their constructs, the historical anomaly involved in this model of the nation-state, and hence invested entirely in the idea of territoriality, which went beyond mere physical land and was instead a terrain of political legitimacy for the new state. Borders became exclusionary and non-negotiable, and if the space outside was disorderly and dangerous, it became the *raison d'être* for disciplining the inside. Mounting a defence against any challenge to the legitimacy of the state-led nation-building project sought to create the trinity of one land-state-people. Whether the state has been predatory or not remains debatable. But the argument that the state's foreign policy was not merely about realising international or global purposes but was also the forging of the national project in peripheral regions remains a sound one.

The common basis for conflict in the global South remains internal or domestic, arising out of distributional inequalities or problems of recognition. The conflation of regime sustenance with the stability of the state, the reification of territoriality and sovereignty, the absolute rights of states as the sole legal representatives of national societies at international forums, and the increasingly state-centric institutionalisation of an international law that strengthens the inviolability of borders—the introduction of humanitarian law in recent years notwithstanding—have all led to strange forms of asymmetric statism in the non-Western world. Long-lasting civil conflicts, often involving international actors, have been substantially fuelled by these and other elements. The deep tensions between historical realities and artificially imposed Western concepts of sovereignty, frequently contested by grassroots ethnic identities, are the primary cause of this. Unresolved questions of identity within artificial and rigid state borders compound such conflicts. No conventional paradigm of academic IR, including the constructivist engagement with identity discourses, has been able to explain such disputes clearly, given its self-consciously Western genealogy. Hence, what needs to be problematised in the non-Western world is the domestic, for its international relations in general and the discourses of conflict in particular remain firmly rooted in the historical creation of its interior.

Postcolonial theory is the best point of entry to interrogate the non-Western. IR therefore must interrogate the 'postcolonial' to gain a proper understanding of the non-Western world, as a precondition to explaining its conflicts. Knowledge of the postcolonial can be problematic; it can either signify a period of time, which begins after the end of colonialism and the formal transfer of political power to the colony, or might refer to orientation, a structure of feeling or even a form of subjectivity, which transcends the colonial in the ideational and existential senses of the term. In this second reading, political freedom is only one condition of the postcolonial; more crucial is the 'real' snapping of ties with colonial power in all dimensions of life. Both these readings are partially correct. Till date, most IR scholarship has sought to understand the non-Western world through meta-narratives of the expansion of modernity, capitalism, or international society, all of which originate in the West. What is lost in these narratives is the central and constitutive role of colonialism, subjugation, and empire-building in the making and unmaking of the subjectivities of people who underwent tumultuous experiences throughout the non-Western world.

The meaning of 'postcolonial' is therefore critical to this field. Sanjay Seth brilliantly summed up what is at stake here:

> The 'post' in postcolonialism, let it be noted, is not a periodisation that signals the beginning of an era where colonialism is part of the past; on the contrary, it signifies the claim that conquest, colonialism and empire are not a footnote or episode in a larger story, such as that of capitalism, modernity or the expansion of international society, but are in fact a central part of that story and are constitutive of it. The 'post' does not mark the period after the colonial era, but rather the effects of this era in shaping the world that is ours. This world was not born out of the West having an impact upon and 'awakening' a dormant non-West, but out of both of these being constituted in the course of multifarious (unequal, hierarchical and usually coercive) exchanges, such that neither was left untouched. (Seth 2011, 174)

There is scope to debate if non-Western ontology can be sufficiently understood by holding on to Western knowledge systems and cognitive categories. Most postcolonial IR scholars have argued that unless Western mental habits are relinquished, no fundamental epistemic break will be possible. The postcolonial world cannot be understood as a mirror reflection of its Western counterpart. There is, however, a need to guard against excesses. The trap of Orientalism is too well-known to merit repeating. Mainstream IR's overall neglect of history and its manifest Western bias do call attention to the need to critique the silences, show why its historical accounts are partial and discriminatory, and clear the path to building histories of the postcolonial world that recognise subaltern agencies and complex political realities that defy generalisation. Whether this requires a fundamentally different knowledge system is debatable. Claims of pristine experiences and unique cultures often degenerate into nativist ethnocentrism, and even if one grants the uniqueness of the past, given the onset of modernity and the arrival of modern forms of politics that radically broke from that past, the terrain of postcolonial politics, both domestic and international, has been fundamentally altered. We will therefore argue that the constitution of the international is a dialectical process in which elements of Western and non-Western experiences cannot be organically separated as distinctive epistemic strands (Chatterjee 2014, 21–22).

FEMINIST INTERNATIONAL RELATIONS THEORY[1]

Theories are stories. Storytelling is an art of interpretation through which we understand the world around us. In fact, IR developed as a theoretical discipline in the inter-War years to understand why the world was in the grips of unprecedented hostility following World War I, and why another war seemed inescapable (Burchill and Linklater 2005, 6). Since then, its energies have been directed towards diagnosing war and preparing diverse prescriptions for stability, cooperation, and peace. Questioning the ontological and epistemological concerns of this primary subject and the ways of studying it, feminist theories of international relations have played two key roles since the 1980s: revisiting old diagnoses of wars and building new prescriptions to avert them. They ask a fundamental question: Must the discipline continue to study states alone? And additionally, must the discipline continue to study states through the same old methods?

As a young researcher, Ann Tickner, one of the first scholars in the discipline to set up feminist IR as a field of inquiry, found few women studying issues of national or international security (Tickner 1992). Not only did academic and policy spaces represent women poorly, but the discipline also left out questions of basic needs, fundamental rights, and human security in favour of studying inter-state competition. When the discipline turned to the use of scientific methods in the 1960s, political reality was classified into three levels of analysis by Kenneth Waltz (1959)—the system of states, the state, and the individual (notably termed 'man')—to study the underlying structural causes of war. The constitution of states, the evolution of nations, and relationships of power within states began receiving less attention in explanations of inter-state competition than the distribution of power and forging of alliances outside and among them. States were viewed as unitary actors, defined only by their relative capabilities; their unique identity and constitution did not matter in distinguishing their foreign policies (Tickner 2001, 45). Accordingly, the discipline concentrated on the study of conflicts using only one of three levels of analysis—the system of states—while

[1]This section has been written by Moitrayee Sengupta, a RUSA Fellow and former Nippon-Sasakawa Trust (SYLFF) Fellow, Jadavpur University, who is presently a research fellow at the Department of International Relations in Jadavpur University, Kolkata.

ignoring the need to understand violence within states and in the social relations of individuals (ibid., 63; Parashar, et al. 2018, 6).

Feminist approaches to IR, along with constructivism, normative theory, historical sociology, post-structuralism, critical theory, and postcolonial theory, began looking inside states for answers to the old problems of the discipline. Using gender as a central conceptual category, feminists revised the traditional gender-blind interpretations of global politics. Revisiting old accounts of security, conflict, and cooperation, they introduced gender-based causal variables to study them. They introduced a new ontology or new objects of political research into the discipline by not only studying states or relations among them from the top, but also social relations between and the identities of people making up the states from the bottom. Their agenda has not been one of theorising on the system of states, but has focused on an emancipatory politics that reveals hitherto unquestioned sources of power and the inequality embedded in it. Other than conceptual research, feminist approaches to IR have pursued empirical knowledge on gendered dimensions in international conflicts as well. They also constitute a normative project that aims to remedy gender inequality in the study and practice of international security (Sjoberg 2010, 4).

This section develops through several parts. *First*, developments in feminist approaches to IR are traced, and their central research questions and the uniqueness of their research programme are discussed. Their choice of ontology, or approaches to the study of political reality, epistemology, and research methodologies are explained. The *second* section describes the feminist research programme in greater detail, outlining varied concerns on issues of power, peace, war, violence, and security. The *final* section anchors the feminist research programme in South Asia and discusses why scholars believe that global norms and institutions that promote gender equality have not been implemented effectively yet in the region's conflict settings.

The Feminist Research Programme in IR and its Concerns

At the first conference on feminist IR in 1988, scholars asked: Where are the women in the discipline? (Halliday 1988). In fact, IR opened itself up to feminist perspectives only at the end of the 1980s, when a series of conferences was organised and books were written, creating a theoretical and empirical space for the sub-field to emerge (Wibben 2004). In particular, three conferences—one at the London School of Economics in 1988, a second at the University of South Carolina in 1989, and a third at Wellesley College in 1990—set the stage for studying global politics through a gender lens.

In wanting to locate women and their perspectives in the discipline, the process has not been one of simply 'adding women' and 'stirring them in' (Harding 1986). The aim has been to transform how international political reality can be studied by uncovering the gendered nature of the traditional subjects of study in the discipline, such as power, war, security, and peace. Other than alternative 'ways of knowing', feminists are also interested in alternative 'ways of being' (Peterson 1992a). Feminism is a political project that seeks to transform the world into a better place by removing inequalities of gender.

Gender is a set of socially constructed identities that are attributed to people because of their biological sex, but with no scientific justification for it. This means that gender is a system of symbolic meanings that creates social hierarchies based on perceived associations with masculinity and femininity (Sjoberg 2009, 187). Characteristics typically associated with masculinity or the socially constructed identity of being men hold greater social value than those typically associated with femininity. For example, men and women are described in universal dichotomies, such as rational *versus* emotional, inhabitants of the public sphere *versus* those of the private sphere, strong *versus* weak, objective *versus* subjective, and protector *versus* dependent (Tickner 1988). The existence of these gender dichotomies or binaries devalues women as human beings; their right to a life of equal worth is denied through cycles of structural and sexual violence. Feminist approaches to IR therefore claim that gender plays a role not only in the private lives of women, where they are sexually violated, economically marginalised, and socially undervalued, but also in how they remain trapped in the private sphere and are unable to access legitimate political power in the public sphere. They particularly study how the state, through narratives of security, peace, and war, creates a myth of protection to legitimise its power over its populations (Tickner 1992, 2001).

It is important to situate gender in what feminists study vis-à-vis global politics, why they study it, and how they study it (Ackerly, et al. 2005). The objectives of feminist research are essentially normative.

Gender is a transformative category, not because one can do away with it once it is analysed and studied, but because once it is understood, its impact on all levels of social and political life can be potentially transformed (True 2005). Feminist research is guided by the normative aim of eliminating gender hierarchies. This guides the epistemological concerns of feminist scholars—what concerns knowledge—and is tied to their ontological concerns or what constitutes political and social reality. They claim that knowledge, instead of being value-neutral, objective, and abstract, is always contextual, contingent, and political (Keller 1985). They argue that all objective knowledge is actually subjective knowledge, which uses the guise of neutrality to hide the underlying relations and interests of power. For example, feminists point to the traditional preoccupation of the discipline with the security-seeking behaviour of great powers as a biased and non-neutral enterprise, one that benefits the interests of the political elite of these countries. They claim that knowledge must instead be emancipatory, and plant their ontological anchor in studying relations of power in the world from the points of view of marginalised people. They identify gendered language, meaning, and symbols in the discourses of states and policies of security, which are ignored in mainstream research problems.

These epistemological and ontological concerns inform feminist methodologies of research in the discipline. There is no one single feminist methodology, but multiple ones joined together by their concern with 'which research questions get asked and why'; 'the goal of designing research that is useful to women (and also to men) and is both less biased and more universal than conventional research'; 'the centrality of questions of reflexivity and the subjectivity of the researcher'; and 'a commitment to knowledge as emancipation' (Tickner 2005, 22). Feminist methods coincide temporally as well as substantively with the post-positivist turn of the discipline around the end of the Cold War (Tickner 2001). Feminism, along with other post-positivist approaches to IR such as critical theory, post-structuralism, and historical sociology, highlights the limitations of social scientific methods in studying international politics. Scholars emphasise that no object of research is exogenous to its social and historical constitution, and that political reality is constituted by norms, values, beliefs, and practices, and cannot be studied in intellectual abstraction. Whereas social scientific methods rely on the ontological centrality of the state and make use of causality, hypothesis testing, and replicability to study it, feminists claim that in order to highlight and transform social injustices, it is not useful to separate theories from the real world or from the normative project of the theorist (Tickner 2005). Feminists use theory as a critique and an everyday practice, instead of treating it as an objective tool whose function is only to analyse the world in order to manage it more efficiently (Zalewski 1996).

The feminist research programme of the discipline is unique in the diversity of approaches that it accommodates. While the use of a gender lens denies that social and political reality is ontologically prior to our conception of it, feminists also study how they can work with the state to promote feminist agendas of equality, security, and justice, which can function in the interest of all citizens, particularly women and other marginalised individuals (Tickner 2018, 27). In this sense, feminism studies the role of gender in state policies and world politics, accepts the ontological centrality of the state, and tries to incorporate gender-sensitive policies and gender-balancing reforms in institutions of political, social, and security governance. For example, the UN Action on Conflict-Related Sexual Violence instituted in 2009 works with member-states, women's rights organisations, non-governmental organisations (NGOs), and other departments and agencies within the United Nations (UN) system to prevent the perpetration of sexual and gender-based violence as a weapon of war. Feminist work in international security can be separated into 'feminist Security Studies' and 'feminist security studies' (Cohn 2011), or 'feminist takes on traditional war theorising' and 'feminist war theorising' (Sjoberg 2019). In feminist Security Studies or feminist takes on traditional war theorising, scholars view war theorising and security studies as a pre-set field of inquiry through gendered lenses. Feminist security studies or feminist war theorising, on the other hand, goes beyond traditional war theorising to study the effective timing and scope of conflicts. According to them, war is an episodic expression of violence which has no discrete beginning or end. They study women's lived experiences of wars as well as their protracted impacts on the everyday life of people living in conflict settings (ibid.). These multidimensional and multi-level approaches of the feminist research programme are discussed in the following section.

The Gender-Security Continuum

A key aim of feminists studying international relations is to understand how issues of gender constitute theories, policies, and the practice of international security. Feminists contend that gender affects not only how security is viewed, but also how it is practised. For instance, scholars participating in one of the first gender and IR conferences at Wellesley College in 1990 discussed how gendered constructions of the state-society relationship affect both IR theory and practice (see Peterson 1992b). Two years earlier, at the 1988 *Millennium: Journal of International Studies* conference at the London School of Economics, scholars argued that international politics has been traditionally viewed as a man's world, and this reinforces the under-representation of women in high ranks of political and military office where security is practised. In their view, the discipline suffered from a 'masculine perspective' (Tickner 1988), because theories on power, peace, security, and war reflected the monopoly of men in both the public and the private sphere (Elshtain 1988). Few women found interest in the study of security, leaving the field depleted of alternative perspectives. But if international theory had failed to theorise gender, feminist theory too had till then failed to theorise international relations (Brown 1988, 461). There was only one solution to this problem—since the way in which political reality is described has an effect on the way power and security are practised, new perspectives with a gender lens could lead to new ways of constituting power and implementing security (Tickner 1988, 434).

Gendering Power

In the foundational text of the discipline, *Politics Among Nations*, Hans Morgenthau (1948, 3–18) outlined six principles of political realism. Political realism, premised on assumptions of human nature, presents itself both as an explanation and a toolkit of action for foreign policy decision-makers. Morgenthau finds states, like men, to be driven by *animus dominandi*, or an insatiable lust for power and domination over others. Power is described as the control of man over man, and when extrapolated to the state, the national power of a state increases with the domination and control of other states. He abstracts politics as an autonomous sphere of action separate from other spheres of life, such as economics or ethics, and 'political man' from other aspects of human nature such as morality or religion. Moreover, unless the international realm is tackled rationally, objectively, and unemotionally, national interest, defined in terms of power, cannot be realised. Feminist IR theorists point out that political realism takes a partial view of human nature in terms of the 'political man', and can only offer a limited understanding of power. Power can be understood multidimensionally and not just as a means of domination. Feminists concentrate on cooperative and constructive elements of power; in order to arrive at a full understanding of how power works in the world, both elements of cooperation and conflict intrinsic to the concept ought to be included (Tickner 1988).

Realist ideas of power as antagonistic provide a blinkered perspective. Feminists point to a more expansive view of power, which is not destructive but mutually enabling and empowering (ibid.). The difference can easily be recognised if one thinks of the French word *pouvoir*. As a noun, *pouvoir* translates into power, while as a verb, it implies positive capabilities or to have possibilities for action. In feminist theories of power, the notion of power as domination over the weak or the deviant is replaced with that which is empowering and can effect constructive change and fulfil capacities. Nancy Hartsock (1983) describes a feminist view of power to imply strength, energy, force, and ability, which differs starkly from masculinist ideas of the same, as domination, control, and subjugation. Hartsock's feminist standpoint, analogous to a Marxist standpoint in favour of the proletariat, views social reality from the position of women who have lived different lives from men because of the sexual division of labour in society. Women's experience of domestic labour leads them to focus on elements of community, cooperation, and connection, while men are socialised to develop their gender identity through separation, individuation, and opposition. She develops her concept of feminist power as empowerment from Hannah Arendt's separation of power from the instrumentalism of violence, so as to denote the human ability to act in concert with one another (Arendt 1967).

Similarly, Dorothy Emmett (1954, 12–14) describes power as an omnibus concept, two key ways of understanding which are in terms of causal efficacy and creative energy. While both can produce change, there is a stark difference between the latter, which stimulates activity, when compared to the former, which can only manipulate and coerce action. This is also reflected in Mary Parker Follett's (1934) distinction between power-over and power-with as constituting coercive and coactive action. Coactive power resembles feminist theories of power as empowerment by implying the capacity to make things happen effectively, in which people can grow in collaboration (Emmett 1954, 9).

Gendering Peace

The traditional view of power as destructive is rooted in a partial analysis of human nature. Gender, being a social construction of identity, pervades the depiction of the 'political man' as amoral, rational, objective, and unemotional. All of these qualities can be understood as traditionally masculine abilities, in the sense that they are socially and culturally associated with the identity of men. That is why Morgenthau's portrayal of human nature, which forms the logical basis of political realism, can only account for 'masculine' attributes and do not impart a complete understanding of it (Tickner 1988). Radical and psychoanalytic feminists interested in object-relations theory, which discusses the socialisation of gender identities from early childhood, emphasise the need to account for 'feminine' attributes of human nature as powerful resources for conflict resolution and peace (Tickner 2001, 15). According to them, women are socialised into becoming mothers and care-givers and therefore possess the skills and qualities necessary for peace-making in the public domain. Mothering practices involve love, nurturance, and training to meet the three important demands of childcare—the preservation, growth, and social acceptability of their children. Violence and maternal work are mutually contradictory phenomena, for the latter is fundamentally non-violent action. These nourishing attributes of human nature that are constituted by maternal thinking translate into strategies for building peace that require similar qualities of resilient cheerfulness, a grasping of truth that is caring, and a tolerance of ambiguity and ambivalence (Ruddick 1989, 219–22).

Other than distinct ways of thinking and acting attributed to the identity of being a mother, studies in moral development psychology showed how men and women view social reality differently because of different experiences of identity formation—those of separation and individuation, and attachment and connection. While men are inclined to pursue an ethic of justice that proceeds from a premise of equality and objective fairness, women pursue an ethic of care based on the premise of non-violence and empathy (Gilligan 1982, 174). A person's moral orientation is not only based on impartial and universal accounts of justice, but is also equally a function of caring action and responsibility that is felt by the situated self, or a person contextualised and embedded in their ties with friends, relations, and family (Blum 1988). A full account of human nature must therefore incorporate both elements of 'masculine' fairness and 'feminine' care (Gilligan 1982, 174). Moreover, violence among states in the public sphere is an expression of the violence of the patriarchal system in the private sphere. It is argued that feminine values of caring, cooperation, and mutuality can help to address this by becoming instruments for instituting peace, and shifting the focus of security from state subjects to human subjects in the international realm (Reardon 1985).

However, scholars of feminist IR also point out that the division between 'masculine' amoral politics and 'feminine' morality, or that between public and private life, leads to the perpetuation of inequalities of gender in both spheres. The essentialisation of masculine identity as objective, universal, rational, unemotional, autonomous, and violent, and that of feminine identity as subjective, situated, emotional, connected, and peaceful is ultimately an unhelpful differentiation (Tickner 2001, 58–61). Human nature is not biologically determined, but varies with social and cultural representations. Hierarchies of gender are ultimately fostered by the dichotomisation of gender identities; women can be both peaceful and war-like, cognitive and affective. In fact, through centuries of discourse on war and peace, women have been portrayed as both divine and harmonious, like the Greek goddess of peace, Eirene, or the Roman goddess Pax, as well as demonised as a *force majeure* that wreaks havoc in the orderly lives of men as the goddess of fortune (Elshtain 1988, 444). The portrayal of women as essentially pacific lends power to the patriarchal value system of gender binaries and reinforces their subjugation.

Gendering War and Violence

Feminists view global politics, including the meanings, causes, experiences, and consequences of wars, through a gender lens. They claim that it is gender inequality that produces war, and war that produces gender inequality (Sjoberg 2013, 108–34). This means that war-making and fighting and gender hierarchies reinforce each other. Gender dichotomies constitute state narratives or states' justifications for fighting wars when they invoke the honour, protection, and security of women as reasons for engaging in conflict (Tickner 1992, 2001). The myth of the protective state and its national warriors as the guardians of women and children shatters when the actual experiences of war reveal sexual and gender-based violence as constituting military strategy. In a span of a few years, about 60,000 women were raped during the Bosnian war and between 100,000 and 250,000 women were raped during the Rwandan genocide. In 1993 and 1994, the International Criminal Tribunal for the Former Yugoslavia (ICTY) and Rwanda (ICTR) included wartime sexual violence against civilian populations as a war crime and a crime against humanity. Rape committed during wars becomes a military tool to terrorise populations, teach lessons, or destroy communities and commit ethnic cleansing by changing the ethnic identity of the next generation of children through the systemic forced impregnation of civilian women. Rape, along with instances of sexual slavery, forced prostitution, forced pregnancy, forced abortion, enforced sterilisation, forced marriage, or any other form of sexual violence that may be perpetrated against women, men, girls, or boys in situations of conflict, falls under a category known as conflict-related sexual violence (CSRV) (United Nations 2009). A mandate for action on sexual violence in situations of conflict was adopted through Security Council Resolution 1888 by the UN in 2009.

In feminist theories of war, states employ hegemonic masculine images and narratives of paternal protection to generate popular validation for engaging in conflict and coercion against other states or armed groups, often for reasons that have little to do with human security and more to do with regime security of the political class, or for gaining strategic advantages for the state (Maruska 2010). The consequences and outcomes of wars are felt unequally along gendered lines, not only because conflict-related sexual violence is used as a tactic of warfare and terrorism, but also because the material impacts of conflicts are felt more severely by women than men. A diminished availability of food, water, shelter, household goods, medical care, education, and jobs in conflict-affected regions impacts women more due to their pre-existing higher levels of relative poverty and subordination in their families and communities (Sjoberg 2013; True 2012). Departing from a narrow episodic view of war in mainstream war discourses, feminists argue that wars begin long before the first shot is fired and end long after the ceasefire is signed (Sjoberg 2013). Wars are deeply pervasive and endure for a longer period of time than the actual incidence of conflict by fomenting structural inequalities, such as gender-based violence, marginalisation, and impoverishment.

A gendered approach to international politics similarly does away with the epistemological tool of 'the levels of analysis' used by neorealists to explain international conflict (Parashar, et al. 2018; Peterson and True 1998; Sjoberg 2013; Sylvester 1994; Tickner 1992, 2001; True 2005). Neorealism, the dominant research programme in the discipline (Vasquez 1983), shows how wars occur because of the structural feature of anarchy, which is the undeterred security-seeking behaviour of states due to the absence of a governing authority in the international realm. In simple terms, they contend that wars happen because there is no robust mechanism to prevent them. Anarchy is a structural component, belonging to the third level of analysis of world politics. Neorealists refuse to grant any overwhelming role to the internal constitution of the national state (the second level of analysis) or the capacities of the individual political leader (the first level of analysis) in explanations of international conflict. Feminists contend that like anarchy, gender hierarchy is also a structural feature of international politics, which also constitutes the identities of states, their relative positions, and interactions (Sjoberg 2013). Violence—including armed conflicts between states—which runs across all three levels is intrinsically connected to gender norms such as the social construction of violent masculinities (True 2012). This also means that the violence in wars or the application of lethal force on the battlefield is essentially interconnected with the insecurity and violation of human rights inside states, institutions, communities, and families. Feminists study violence with the help of analytical 'layers' across the household, community, state, and international realm, and through several 'forms' of manifestation such as physical, structural, and symbolic violence (True and Tanyag 2019, 16–21). Physical violence or conflict-related sexual violence in wartime is only a limited sample of the violence that women and children face when compared to their everyday experiences of violence, insecurity, indignity, and inequality.

Gendering Security

Gender is central to any analyses of international security in three ways:

- It is important conceptually because it helps to uncover the gendered structure of international politics;
- It is important analytically because it helps in analysing the causes of international practices, processes, and policies, and predicting their outcomes;
- It is important normatively in inspiring projects of transformation and positive change (Sjoberg 2009).

As we saw above, feminists expand traditional understandings of what counts as a security issue. In their view, wartime violence is interconnected with structural violence across all levels of analyses. By linking the gendered constitution and consequences of violence at the local level to violence in armed conflicts, they claim that the personal is not only political but also international, and the international is personal (Enloe 2000). They shift the subject of security from the state to the people, particularly to those who are marginalised and oppressed due to gender subordination and political marginality (Sjoberg 2009, 207).

As previous sections have shown, feminists argue that practices of security are also gendered. They search for alternative policies that can promote gender inequality. They draw attention to how conflicts affect men and women differently by studying gendered marginalisation in post-conflict societies, and to the way conflict-related sexual violence is used as a tactic of national warfare and terrorism. It is largely due to feminist work on the need for women's protection during conflicts that issues of gender began to be included in global security policies. For example, the Women, Peace, and Security (WPS) Agenda was instituted through UN Security Council Resolution 1325 in 2000 to prevent violence, protect women's rights in times of conflict, and enable their participation in peace-building processes. But feminists also argue that the mandate of women's protection in the WPS Agenda enjoys greater institutional commitment than women's equal participation in peace and security governance or the prevention of conflict and violence. This reveals how gender dichotomies play out in even institutional contexts (George, et al. 2019). Similarly, in another major step, 183 UN member states at the Beijing Platform for Action in 1995 instituted gender mainstreaming as a global strategy for achieving gender equality by ensuring the equal representation of women in public and private organisations and policies. But feminists also argue that gender mainstreaming reforms do not include LGBTQIA persons, nor does it address the gender hierarchy embedded in social structures (Hudson and Huber 2019).

Feminist security studies point to the use of gendered language in states' narratives of war (see Peterson 1992b; Tickner 1992), peace-making (see Whitworth 2004), and soldiering (see Enloe 2000; Golan 1997). Feminists claim that the foreign policy choices of states are gendered because they are based on ideas of masculinity and virility over other states (see Maruska 2010; Peterson 1999). They find defence experts using de-humanised and abstract 'technostrategic' language in discourses of nuclear security, impassive to the prospect of hundreds and thousands of people dying as a consequence (see Cohn 1987). In fact, scholars also claim that the omission of gender issues from mainstream security studies and policies does not make them gender-neutral or unproblematic; rather, it makes them gender-biased and gender-blind (Sjoberg 2009). Feminist approaches therefore broaden the meaning of security as well as its subject of reference. They look into gender-based causal variables of violence, analyse gendered language in security discourses, and seek to translate empirical and conceptual research into security policies and practices.

From the Global to the Regional and Local: Gendered Violence in South Asia

The UN Security Council Resolution 1325, which instituted the WPS Agenda in 2000, has three important pillars: prevention of gender-based violence during conflicts, protection of the human rights of women and girls in conflict contexts, and ensuring women's participation in conflict resolution and peace-building measures (George, et al. 2019). A fourth pillar, that of the prosecution of gender-based crimes, was added to the WPS Agenda following the adoption of UN Security Council Resolutions 1820, 1888, 1889, and 1960 (Singh 2017, 233). Fifteen years later, in *A Global Study on the Implementation of the United Nations Security Council Resolution 1325*, it was reiterated that all forms of violence against women increase in situations of conflict. Women's fundamental rights to food, health, sanitation, education, and livelihood are exploited, their rights to land and productive assets denied, their political rights violated, and they suffer from increased vulnerability to sexual violence (UN Women 2015). The study also acknowledged that if the Agenda's normative goals of rights, equality, and justice are to be realised, they would have to be diffused into local, national, and regional settings (Singh 2017).

Two years after the 2015 study, in a special issue of the *Journal of Asian Security and International Affairs*, feminist researchers similarly pointed out that although there was sufficient academic attention on the conceptualisation and global implementation of the WPS Agenda, studies on the implementation of the Agenda in specific local or national contexts were rare. They pointed to the need to identify local variables that facilitate or inhibit the implementation of the Agenda's normative framework in specific conflict contexts (ibid., 223). For instance, in the context of South Asia, there existed three gender-based variables that inhibited the localisation of the Agenda (ibid., 223–25). *First*, conflicts continued long after the formal termination of war, and could not be readily differentiated from post-conflict settings. For example, even after the civil war ended in Sri Lanka in 2009, the state continued to use securitisation and militarisation as a policy, especially in the violence-prone areas of the country, thereby affecting the everyday lives of people. Securitisation refers to the discursive practices deployed by political and military elites to articulate threat or insecurity in order to serve some specific strategic and political ends. Militarisation refers to the deployment of militaries and military infrastructure to fulfil those securitising practices. In post-conflict Sri Lanka, military security is so high that it blurs the line between conflict and post-conflict settings. In 2014, there was at least one soldier deployed for every six civilians. Other than rising defence budgets and heavy militarisation, soldiers also took over banal functions of civilian life, such as 'building roads, selling vegetables, running hotels, offering whale-watching tours, and renovating cricket stadiums' (ibid., 226). Most of these security measures were instituted during the civil war years, and have remained in place even after its formal resolution. Similar state practices of militarisation and securitisation also feature in Kashmir in India and the Chittagong Hill Tracts in Bangladesh (ibid., 232). In fact, South Asia is a region that is rife with internal conflicts, insurgencies, and the perpetration of acts of terrorism. Borders between states, particularly between India and China and India and Pakistan, also witness interspersed, often protracted, conflict.

The *second* variable interdicting the diffusion of the WPS Agenda is the need to study gender-specific consequences of conflicts, along with attending to the intersecting identities of class, caste, race, religion, and ethnicity. To continue with the example of post-war Sri Lanka, experiences of women differ according to their ethnic, religious, marital, and political identities. The post-conflict experiences of women who head households differ along religious and ethnic lines—based on whether they are Tamil and Muslim—and their marital identity as widowed and separated. War widows and ex-women LTTE (Liberation Tigers of Tamil Eelam, a Tamil organisation based in northeastern Sri Lanka, which was militarily defeated in 2009) combatants also suffer the consequences of conflict differently, long after the formal ceasefire has been drawn. The author contends that although the central analytical category of gender must be preserved, the different life experiences of women from those of men, and crucially, among themselves, must be equally incorporated in local implementations of the WPS Agenda (Singh 2017).

Third, while the Agenda views women as both agents and victims of violence, women in South Asia are often located in between (Singh 2017). For example, research on the experiences of Nepalese women combatants who were part of the Maoist conflict in Nepal depicts this problem very well (Luna, et al. 2017). During the conflict period, women combatants could access positions of leadership and power within the organisational structure of the Maoist political party that were earlier reserved for men. Non-combatant women, on the other hand, were driven deeper into their homes during the civil war. They often had to take up full responsibilities of their households if their husbands died, migrated, or went missing during the war. After the war, the positions of ex-combatant and non-combatant women were reversed. Due to the failure of government-aided reintegration of women ex-combatants into society, the lack of formal education, and little opportunity for employment, these women were compelled to return to their pre-conflict traditional roles of housework and depend on their husbands for material sustenance. Non-combatant women, on the other hand, began farming and selling their produce in local markets, set up small businesses like restaurants and tailoring shops, and found jobs in NGOs and financial organisations (ibid., 191). Even in instances where women participate as agents in armed conflicts, they remain vulnerable to structural inequalities of gender.

At the end, it is essential to underscore that most feminist analyses of world politics begin from the hypothesis, 'secure states often contain insecure women' (Sjoberg 2009, 198). They claim, albeit from different ontological, epistemological, or methodological positions (as we have seen above), that the security of states does not automatically translate into the security of its populations, particularly women, girls, and LGBTQIA persons, who have traditionally been viewed and treated as less valuable than men. Men are also undervalued and violated when they fail to live up to idealised, hegemonic, and unitary ascriptions of masculinity (Higate 2019). Feminists contend that gender binaries pervade the public realm as much as they do the private realm. States employ gendered hierarchies in their discourses of foreign policy, national security, war-making, peace-building, and securitising practices. They study both direct and structural violence across the traditional levels of analyses in the discipline—the international system, national states, and individual human beings embedded in social relations and identities. Their investigation of violence takes on a transformative agenda—to build a world that is safer, better, and peaceful for everyone. Feminists differ on how to think about peace. While some contend that women are inherently pacific and can bring about positive change as peace-builders in societies transitioning from conflict, others claim that the essentialisation of women as peaceful reifies hierarchies of gender. Still others argue that peace is elusive because conflict-related violence is pervasive, and can endure for a long period of time after physical violence ends. It is the normativity, plurality, diversity, and internal conversations of multiple feminisms in IR that distinguishes their research programme from the others.

CONCLUSION

Theories are meant to clarify reality, to make sense of a great mass of events that apparently share no connections or meanings. The enterprise of theory in social sciences is suspect, for there are major divides regarding the meaning and purpose of theory. Critical theory makes one abiding contribution: it shows clearly the distinction between problem-solving theories that take the world as 'given' and critical theories that question that very 'given-ness'. Theories, in other words, are not innocent cognitive artefacts; rather, they are conscious tools that serve specific purposes. Game theory, to take an example, is a problem-solving tool. The relational logic amongst playoffs is crucial here. The agent looks at the matrices bearing playoffs and decides the optimal outcome. Critical theory, in contrast, will problematise the playoffs and ask why different outcomes cannot be entertained at all.

There is another way to contrast theories in IR. The traditional view takes theory as a patterned generalisation that explains an effect by locating specific causes. Mainstream theories are therefore causal and empirical in nature and emphasise the need for an empirical validation of propositions. Such validation requires standard statistical procedures and, following new advances in experimental economics, even laboratory tests are recommended. In simple terms, theory in this enterprise can only be scientific, and the mission for theoretical knowledge seems to be to find the truth. Against such scientific theories with a causal cast are hermeneutic theories that emphasise the plurality of meanings, the discursiveness of social texts, and the intersubjective nature of all knowledge.

Chapters 4 and 5 have surveyed some of the alternative theoretical perspectives to political realism and liberal theories in IR. Since IR evolved during the inter-War period in the West as a systematic study that sought answers to the problem of war, its birth was overlaid by security considerations. While this preoccupation with military security, war, and peace continues to dominate the field even today, concerns about the political economy and the complex interplay of commerce and defence have assumed greater importance over the years, and IR as a discipline has done much to expand the subject of security, both in depth and in scope. The post-Cold War period has added concerns of globalisation and of identity/community. Marginal voices—of women, refugees, and those working for the environment—have subsequently become more important, and can be heard even in the most conservative settings of the discipline.

The real change has been the fashioning of a range of alternative perspectives within IR theory, including critical, postmodern, and post-structuralist theories, constructivism, feminism of different shades, historical sociology, and postcolonial and environmental perspectives. This proliferation has had a positive effect—it has considerably relaxed the grip that mainstream theories had over the field. These approaches have questioned the narrow disciplinary foundations of academic IR, a welcome development for a discipline marked by conservatism and orthodoxy. This is not to argue that the conventional approaches are useless, or that the new theories are unblemished. A student of contemporary IR has to delve into this theoretical diversity as a precondition to learning the discipline.

5

Power, Polarity, and National Security

Anindya Jyoti Majumdar

The main units of international relations are the states, and the impact, role, and dynamism of a state are determined by the extent of power that a state commands. A powerful state behaves differently from a weak state. As international politics is influenced heavily by power relations, major powers often set the rules of the game. Power, which is never static, may grow or decline, and world history has been witness to the rise and fall of many great powers. In the process, a balance is sought to be established, and balance-of-power mechanisms often manifest themselves in world politics. Power equations also create polarity in the international system, which in turn influences the patterns of international politics. All states, however, are mired in a perpetual quest for an elusive security, and different ways and means have been formulated over time to understand and achieve that security. This chapter explains the concepts of power, polarity, and security impacting the patterns of international relations.

The Concept of Power

Power can be regarded as an attribute of a nation-state, and as a measurable unit in terms of the state's economic output or military strength. Different states possess varying levels of power, which results in a hierarchy: states are arranged on the basis of their ability to influence events and the patterns of relations among them. Very broadly, we find major powers, middle powers, and small powers in the international community, where the ability of each state varies according to the sum of power it commands. States that are exceptionally powerful or ahead of others earn the epithet of 'superpower' or even 'mega-power', and provide security to many other states. Max Weber identified power as the ability to exercise one's will over others, while for Hans Morgenthau, power comprises anything that establishes and maintains the control that one entity exercises over another. Robert Dahl stated that power is the ability to shift the probability of outcomes. In international relations, power denotes the aggregate of the strength and capabilities of a state, applied to protect and promote its national interests and goals.

In international politics, power is viewed as a relationship between two political actors, where one actor has the ability to control or influence the actions of the other. Power cannot exist in a vacuum; the power of one is always measured in comparison to others, allowing for dynamic power relationships. Since the power of an actor can grow or decline over time, power relations are temporary and fragile. Realists consider power the necessary currency that can buy values such as peace, security, prosperity, and progress, and therefore power is viewed as the means to an end. It appears, then, that power becomes the primary means to promote and protect any objective of the state, and since greater power would secure more objectives, power becomes an end in itself. For those who believe that a state's main objective is survival and that power purchases security, the continuous augmentation of power itself becomes a goal of state policy.

According to realists like Morgenthau, power can be seen to have three predominant forms.

1. **Force**. Coercion and explicit threats through the use of military and economic instruments, aimed at changing the course of events.
2. **Influence**. The use of persuasion to maintain or alter the behaviour or policy of a particular state in a manner that suits the preferences of another.
3. **Authority**. A state voluntarily complies with the directives or preferences of another because of the perceptions it holds vis-à-vis the other. This element is more in tune with what Joseph Nye calls 'soft power', where the form of influence includes

> non-political affinities. Hard power involves a specific country commanding and coercing others to do its bidding. Soft power is the ability to attract and co-opt other countries into wanting the same outcomes. While the former is based on coercion and payments, the latter relies on culture, political values, and foreign policies guided by normative principles.

Since power is now categorised as 'hard power' and 'soft power', it is obvious that a country would rely on one more than the other depending on the power resources available to them. The dividing line between the two categories is, however, not clear. A good image and unqualified prestige are rare for a state in the international system, and unless backed by hard power, mere soft power cannot substantially alter the outcome of events, even though it enhances the acceptability of the actor and its views. Hence, scholars focus more on the smart power of a state, which is another name for the comprehensive national strength of a state. National power combines all forms of power—hard/soft, intertwined with military, economic, and cultural elements. In the contemporary period, power also rests in the ability to establish in the international arena which state is a part of a problem and which can be part of the solution, and then act accordingly.

Almost anything that contributes to a state's ability to influence the outcome of events and the behaviour of other states can be considered an element of power of that state. However, a distinction is usually made between the tangible and intangible elements of power.

Tangible elements are the material indicators of power—territory, population or demographic composition, agricultural capacity, natural resources and industrial capacity, the extent of technological advancement, and military strength and mobility. Although the size of a territory, its strategic location and geographical significance, and the availability of fertile lands contribute to a state's power, mere size will not suffice if the other elements of power are trivial. Not all big states are powerful states, and landlocked countries are especially handicapped.

Similarly, citizens who are healthy, skilled, unified, and loyal can contribute to national power. Mere numbers will not help; in fact, over-population might become a liability rather than an asset in the face of a scarcity of resources, general backwardness, and lack of opportunities for upward mobility. Agricultural productivity ensures the ability to feed the population, with both production and distribution being important.

In the same manner, a state endowed with natural resources like fossil fuels, precious metals, and minerals is at an advantage compared to a state that has little or no natural resources. However, the state must also have the ability to extract and process natural resources on its own; a weak state with precious natural resources is in danger of interference by major powers, thereby undermining its security. The levels of industrial capacity and application of sophisticated technology also contribute to the power of a state. Finally, the military strength of a state, that is, its ability to support and sustain operations on land, sea, and air, and the weapons it possesses—in both qualitative and quantitative terms—determine its relative power compared to other states.

Intangible elements are difficult to measure and are open to subjective interpretations. Factors such as leadership and the personality of leaders, bureaucratic efficiency, societal cohesiveness, reputation and image, international connections and networking—all contribute to national power in varying degrees and in myriad ways. The national power of a state is the combination of all these as perceived (or misperceived) by others, and together with the tangible elements, they define the ability of a state. When states decide to demonstrate their capabilities in visible or perceptible forms, it eventually results in a projection of power.

Not all states of the world enjoy all the elements of power equally, and therefore, despite the cherished principle of the sovereign equality of all nations, states differ in their abilities. Moreover, one or the other element of power can acquire importance at different points in time and in different situations. States do, in pursuit of their interests, seek to increase their power. This endless quest for power often allows for the emergence of new and powerful actors in the global arena, altering the existing power relations.

BALANCE OF POWER

An asymmetrical distribution of power makes weaker states vulnerable to the designs of the powerful. A state that enjoys a preponderance of power can become a threat to the others. 'Balance of power' is an age-old concept that seeks to establish an equilibrium in the distribution of power among international actors. It is viewed as a mechanism to regulate the behaviour of states through an equal distribution of power among the contending parties. Perfect equilibrium is a myth, however, since states have shown a tendency to group and regroup in select formations and alliances, to ensure that the apparent weakness of a nation does not tempt an aggressor to attack or exploit those vulnerabilities. Such arrangements are often imperfect; but as long as states remain the basic units of the international political process, their patterns of behaviour will be influenced by the need to ensure balance.

The chief function of the balance of power is to protect a state's independence from the threat of domination, but peace may emerge as a byproduct of this process. Regional powers could arrive at a regional balance among themselves. A state could take on the role of a 'balancer', that is, a powerful state can side with a less powerful state when the latter is threatened by another powerful state. However, an unbiased and unprejudiced balancer is difficult to find.

The prerequisites for a balance of power are not hard to imagine. Balance of power requires multiple sovereign actors, who are unequal in terms of power distribution, engaged in continuous competition over scarce resources with no centralised authority exercising control over them. States follow different techniques, and Morgenthau points to the age-old method of 'divide and rule', whereby states seek to weaken the opposition by keeping them divided. Annexation and partition of territories as a part of compensation is another method to maintain a balance of power among the major powers, and armaments serve as yet another tactic, whereby states develop and procure arms in order to augment their strength and maintain a balance. The most prominent is the formation of a coalition of states against a common threat, and as Morgenthau observes, alliances are a necessary function of the balance of power operating within a multiple state system.

The major powers interested in maintaining a power status quo can proceed to bring about a balance. Two periods highlight the successful operation of balance of power; the first began from the Treaty of Westphalia (1648) and continued till the French Revolution of 1789, a period in which major wars were averted by the aristocracies. While Napoleon Bonaparte's adventurist campaigns disturbed the pattern, balance of power was again established by the European powers in the Congress of Vienna in 1815, as Napoleon's army was defeated. This period continued until 1914 when World War I broke out. It is said that the greater part of the twentieth century reeled under exclusivist and contending political ideologies—Fascism, Nazism, capitalism, and communism—creating an unsuitable environment for the balance of power to operate. Classical considerations were overridden by ideology.

The benefits of balance of power include the stability it introduces in relations, its restraining effect on state behaviour, and the protection it offers to the vulnerable against domination. However, criticisms abound, and one line of argument maintains that there is no way of measuring relative power to see whether it is evenly distributed. Measurement is at best an estimate or a guess, and is by nature subjective. Moreover, all distribution of power is temporary, unstable, and inconstant. Others argue that balance of power actually increases the possibilities of conflict among adversaries, rather than averting conflicts between states.

During the Cold War, balance of power took a new form. In Winston Churchill's words, a 'balance of terror' replaced the classical balance of power, drawing its strength from the assumption that if the adversary could maintain sufficient nuclear weapons, ready to be delivered within a short span of time and capable of causing unlimited damage—it is immaterial who initiates the war—then the rational choice would be to carefully avoid the use of such weapons that could result in mutually assured destruction. This is also the essence of nuclear deterrence. While many debated on the actual number and types of nuclear weapons necessary to maintain a balance, the two superpowers acquired thousands of warheads and thereby achieved overkill capacity, that is, they had many more than was actually necessary. John Lewis Gaddis (2007) observed that nuclear weapons have changed the nature of warfare, the meaning of self-reliance, and the commitments of allies; they make irrelevant the balance of military forces as deterrence is achieved through the ability 'to get only a few nuclear weapons through'. Balance often is not a simple numerical balance of 50:50, but rather a match of combat capabilities in terms of the total impact a country may have at the levels of contact between two adversaries.

However, balance is dynamic and fragile, and is hence sought to be repeatedly re-established at higher levels, with massive economic costs. As a consequence, some scholars argue that balance of power contributes to the arms race. One has to consider that the quest for balance itself takes the form of a latent war, and it actually becomes a quest for superiority. Any party that finds it difficult to keep pace with the relentless race to improve offensive/defensive weapons and forces eventually capitulates. Its economy comes under a heavy strain and its military strength crumbles under pressure in the absence of adequate economic provisions for its civilian needs and defence spending. During the Cold War, the North Atlantic Treaty Organization (NATO) and the Warsaw Pact were involved in an intense race for an improvement of weapons and forces to issue counter-challenges through symmetrical military measures. As the Pact came under severe economic pressure that undermined its strength, it lost the race and was dissolved. Most Warsaw Pact members eventually became members of NATO, which comprehensively won the Cold War without firing a single shot at the adversary.

The concept of a global balance of power remains undefined and ambiguous. In contemporary times, this idea is based on a nascent multipolar system. Predictability and the rigid Cold War model have shaped our attitude towards a bipolar model of balance, but it seems that a diffused balance is already in place among the major powers. Three of the major actors can be easily identified: the US, Russia, and China. There are also powers like Germany in the European Union and countries like India, Japan, and Brazil in the Global South. The basic idea behind a global diffused balance is not a power equilibrium—military and economic—but a recognition that these major powers gain nothing from an armed conflict among themselves. Their economic relations are deeply connected and prudence dictates that they avoid direct confrontations and not destabilise the world at large. In this loose multipolar model, however, there remain grey areas, open to limited contests and manoeuvring, especially if one takes a final showdown as inevitable in the long run. This makes the contemporary global balance fragile because, by continuously redrawing the lines, the United States, Russia, and China will leave little space for other states to remain neutral.

Balance of power is applied in different forms in different regions. The United States used the term 'rebalancing' in 2012 with a clear focus on a rising China and the trans-Pacific region. China shares her borders with Russia and states in East Asia, Southeast Asia, South Asia, and Central Asia. No other state in Asia has such a vast expanse and access to both land and sea routes. These geopolitical considerations make both Asia and the Indo-Pacific oceanic zone the theatre of rebalancing approaches. This necessitates a shift from a trans-Atlantic to a trans-Pacific balance for the US and its allies, although the trans-Atlantic balance is firmly kept in place to meet any possible challenges emanating from Russia in Europe. Such anticipatory moves are displayed by states that are apprehensive of the intentions of rising powers, and are usually accompanied by an increase in cooperation among them. A rising China thus compels the United States to focus on a rebalancing in the South China Sea, and on greater coordination and closeness among the United States, India, Japan, and Australia, which form the Quad. The leading Asian countries, which have also made substantive economic progress, are in the game because of the traditional geopolitical considerations of balance of power.

POLARITY

The hierarchical power relations among states lead to a polarity in international relations. As patterns of international politics and most geopolitical interactions revolve around one or more power centres, these centres are regarded as the poles, and attract the lesser powers towards themselves. A strong and leading state—or group of states—can emerge as a power centre, with their corresponding rival power centres or poles. This may create a division among the states veering towards one or the other power centre. When a single leading state with no comparable challenger emerges as the most powerful nation, the structure of international relations tends to become unipolar. When two such states who are competitors and adversaries emerge along with their allies, the pattern becomes bipolar. When a number of more or less evenly matched powerful states emerge in the international arena, the structure takes the form of a multipolar arrangement.

A unipolar world indicates the preponderance of a single powerful state that can act as the hegemon, exercising a restraining effect upon the other states and thereby able to establish peace or stability on its own terms. Such a state exerts direct or indirect control over other states, pushing them to follow basic rules and cooperate with one another. A unipolar system thrives when other states are either unable or unwilling to challenge the dominance of the leading state. However, while stability is theoretically possible under a unipolar system, the hegemon, in the pursuit of its own interests, can injure the interests of other states, and consequently those aggrieved states may look for ways to reduce its dominance. A preponderance of power enjoyed by one state is often viewed as a threat, and a tendency to establish a balance is inherent in any unipolar system.

The Cold War rivalry between the two superpowers—the US and the Soviet Union—provides the best example of a bipolar world. After World War II, the United States emerged as the most powerful state in the world, even as the erstwhile European colonial masters lost their power and glory. However, the Soviet Union soon emerged as a rival power centre and Europe was divided between the Western Bloc and the Eastern Bloc, each with its own military alliances; and contending political ideologies further exacerbated the divide. The Cold War rivalry extended to other parts of the world as well, and almost every local issue was viewed in global terms—as part of the contest between the two superpowers. In a bipolar system, each pole deliberately adopted policies aimed at injuring the interests of the other. A reaction to this bipolar world came from a group of developing countries attempting to stay away from the power rivalry, and took the form of the Non-Aligned Movement. The bipolar system came to an end with the end of the Cold War and the disintegration of the Soviet Union.

The bipolar system established a stable pattern in the international arena as the big powers, despite provocations aplenty, managed to avert direct military confrontations. However, the stability during the Cold War also resulted from the big powers' awareness of the existence of nuclear weapons in each others' arsenals and the fear of complete destruction as a consequence of a possible nuclear exchange. A bipolar system does not offer flexibility, and the lesser powers in both rival camps have little option but to remain within the fold. Flexibility of this sort is possible when a number of powerful states, rather than merely one or two actors, dominate international politics. In a multipolar system, no state can dominate too many others without coming in conflict with the other poles. This system appears to suit the smaller powers as no power here is big enough to take over the role of hegemon. Some would argue that the application of the balance-of-power principle is most effective in a multipolar system. Others would say that any system with several major powers would be prone to greater contests between national interests, and would consequently face deliberate or inadvertent conflict.

Debates range on whether the contemporary world is unipolar, bipolar, or multipolar in nature. As the established bipolar system collapsed after the end of the Cold War, a unipolar and then a semblance of a multipolar world emerged for a brief period in the 1990s. The European Union emerged as a possible new power, along with China and Japan. Gradually, the United States sought to assert itself in international politics, propagating a new world order through its promotion of democracy and regime change. It led a War on Terror along with a coalition of willing partners, and no other state seemed able or willing to challenge the US, despite clear disagreement with its policies. It soon became impossible to formulate policies without taking into consideration the economic clout and military reach of the US, and as a result, the world appeared unipolar in the first decade of the twenty-first century. However, with an economic slowdown at home and its military intervention in Iraq backfiring, the view that the US was a declining power gained popularity.

Meanwhile, China's impressive economic progress, subsequent modernisation of its military, and growing assertiveness in its neighbouring regions contributed to the apprehension that China seeks a unipolar Asia and a bipolar world. However, this is still a transitional period and it is premature to judge the structure of the world in terms of polarity. The twenty-first century remains somewhat unipolar in essence with the United States yet to be matched by any other power, although the emergence of other poles are anticipated. It may be said that the world today is predominantly unipolar, with manifest multipolar tendencies.

NATIONAL SECURITY

Security is defined as freedom from risk and danger. Does it mean the absence of threat in a given environment or a zone of peace and stability? Even if the objective is to achieve freedom from all threats and dangers, is such a state of being even attainable? Since many threats and challenges are based on subjective interpretations (or misinterpretations) of the actors, security can also be a state of mind, and hence would depend on the attitude of the actors involved. With the meaning of security being broadened and the increasing securitisation of human existence, along with the emergence of security challenges, security has become a way of life. In this sense, security is elusive, and as a result, any security discourse can take the form of an insecurity discourse, focusing on threats, challenges, and vulnerabilities. Security scenarios often reflect a matrix of complex relations among actors, where challenges from the environment emanate in waves and threats issue from the very nature of the relationships among the actors, creating and reinforcing an environment that requires constant management, and the reduction and elimination of such challenges through the application of special skills and capabilities. In this sense, security is defined as a constant application of skills to respond to and cope with both anticipated and unforeseen challenges to the established order. In the conventional sense, security may be understood as national military security, where threat or the use of force and instruments of cooperation are combined to protect and promote survival and a good life. The focus is primarily on measures to delay, manage, or prevent a crisis (which may fail occasionally), and not on a deliberate and substantial remodelling of the system.

Historically, the ruling regime of a territorial nation-state has been the primary actor in ensuring national security. In effect, conventional security is the security of the state and, by extension, that of the people of the state. The state has the primary duty to protect the lives and property of its citizens from external attacks, establish internal stability, and promote law and order. If a state fails to do so, it loses its legitimacy. The dominant approach in IR—realism—upholds the primacy of the state in ensuring security. It takes a conflict of interest among states as inevitable, and believes that the purpose of statecraft is national survival in a hostile environment.

Structural realists argue that in the absence of a central enforcing authority, a situation of anarchy prevails where states need to resort to self-help to survive and flourish. This leads to the constant augmentation and accretion of national power through strategic alliances. International institutions prescribing the rules of behaviour are essentially platforms for power struggles, and states cannot entrust the task of protection to international security organisations. Since the maximisation of power is usually the national goal, stability will result from maintaining a balance of power. Moral principles apparently interfere with the pursuit of national advantage.

Hence, traditional security considerations have always been associated with the state. Here, security would mean freedom from fear and any threat to a state's political and economic survival and national values. A state is responsible for securing its territorial integrity, political independence, way of life, people, and economic assets from external attacks. Since complete freedom from threat is difficult to achieve, national security is ensured through appropriate protective measures, including the accumulation of military power through armaments and alliance-formation. Often, however, this may lead to an arms race among adversaries and to a security dilemma, that is, a situation where a state's arming for defence provokes other states to arm themselves in response, with the result that the national security of all actors involved decline in proportion to the increase in armaments.

The quest for national security is a quest for comprehensive national strength. Military power, in terms of weapons and weapon systems, might not be enough to influence international politics unless it is backed up by viable economic support. In the same manner, mere economic affluence without the requisite military power may fall short of influencing a successful outcome of events. A state with both military power and economic clout can boast of comprehensive national strength. Moreover, as noted earlier, a judicious combination of hard and soft power generates smart power, which is necessary for national security.

Although challenges have been posed by the liberal, constructivist, and critical approaches, with their focus on transitional relations and regimes, economic ties, cooperation and interdependence among states, the role of norms, taboos, and culture, and the ethical and human concern for people, realist approaches have dominated the conventional understanding of security. Scholars like Barry Buzan brand national security as a politically powerful but 'weakly conceptualized, ambiguously defined' concept, which offers political and military elites the scope to generate strategies to maximise their power. Even in the contemporary era, realist prescriptions remain relevant and important for at least two reasons:

1. All other approaches draw partial sustenance from their efforts to criticise and be different from the mainstream realist security discourse, but often fail to specify the structural set-up necessary for a different type of international order; and
2. Major powers have a tendency to subscribe to the basic tenets of security in its conventional sense.

It may be argued that realism suits the major powers, inspires the mid-level powers to follow in the footsteps of the major powers, and places the small powers at the receiving end. While the West views the rest of the world as mired in anarchy, a different angle depicts the world as a power hierarchy. In fact, most states respond to the demands of security through certain set patterns established by the major powers in the existing system. These major powers set the rules of the game and the agenda at major international meetings (where they prioritise issues according to their preference), and any international regime is dependent on their support. The middle and small powers have to respond to and adjust their policies according to the policies and decisions of the major powers. National security priorities for the middle-level and small states are necessarily different from those of the key actors, determined as they are by cultural context and objective conditions, as well as the rules imposed on them by the major powers.

However, as wars between states become increasingly lethal, destructive, and expensive, non-conventional issues of global concern are gradually taking centre-stage. Intra-state conflicts are becoming more important, as is the misuse of power by officials of the state. This development took place in the post-Cold War political flux, and witnessed the growth of non-state actors capable of seriously challenging the authority of the state.

Security goals are perceived and constructed in order to provide the best support to the survival and prosperity of the state. There are three broad categories of security:

1. Core territorial security: This refers to the measures that ensure a state's existence as a viable unit on the world map. Intra-state conflicts over territorial possessions can be regarded as a struggle of proto-states to establish a separate state identity.
2. Core interest security: This refers to both long-term and short-term priorities thrown up through the process of securitisation.
3. Core value security: This refers to the protection of predominant political beliefs, convictions, and cultural practices, where strength is derived from the opposition to other beliefs, convictions, and practices. National security considerations often have to make adjustments in the face of traditional and non-traditional challenges.

Non-Traditional Security

Much has been said about the distinction between traditional and non-traditional security issues. It is said that national security measures are ill-equipped to tackle the present-day challenges of climate change, displacement and forced migration, and international terrorism, which call for multilateral actions that presuppose a certain degree of cooperation among states. Further, while national security accepts the state as the main unit of analysis, it prioritises state interest rather than individual interest. It has been argued that a secure state, militarily powerful enough to defend its borders, does not necessarily mean secure citizens if the state itself becomes a threat to the freedom and rights of its own people. Great games of power politics become irrelevant as security becomes enmeshed in the everyday lives of people. Hence, human security, incorporating as it does varied dimensions of human life and concern, receives wider currency. Intra-state conflicts are more frequent than inter-state conflicts, and national security is therefore viewed as inadequate, although not obsolete. Intra-state conflicts may, however, reflect a competition among potential proto-states, and under their combined pressure, the parent state can disintegrate.

Although it is true that in the contemporary world, security is no longer confined to the consequences of power struggles among states, given the various new challenges of a non-traditional nature that have emerged, many so-called non-traditional security issues can be seen to be intertwined with traditional concerns. The power struggle continues, coercive measures just short of war are employed to ensure a national advantage, and the powerful continue to decide the agenda of world politics (including non-traditional security issues) and prescribe the rules of the game.

Security, in the ultimate analysis, is indivisible, with various integral elements (such as traditional and non-traditional security, state security, and human security) amalgamated into one comprehensive idea. There is no contradiction between traditional and non-traditional security, and one cannot legitimately exist without the other. If a militarily powerful and secure state neglects issues of human security, it will undermine the legitimacy of the state and pave the way for threats from within that, in the long run, will prove detrimental to its existence. Likewise, human security cannot be protected in a state that is insecure and vulnerable, susceptible to pressure from and interference by external agencies. A secure state with good governance can best ensure human security. What is important is the comprehensive national strength of a human collective within a secure geographical area, which has the ability to combine acts of contestation and cooperation and is capable of responding to the dynamic and multidimensional aspects of security.

Security can only change its form and not its nature. It has prismatic elements; for example, the displacement of people, leading to forced migration, is essentially an issue of human security—such forced migration to another state and the settlement of those forced to migrate as refugees create tensions within the host community, which may take the form of non-traditional security concerns. The subsequent political unrest might be orchestrated and exploited by an external third party, and may become a national security problem. Any security issue can have various repercussions and require attention on multiple fronts. Non-traditional security issues also require the support or active involvement of state agencies, with all other civil society organisations working to make the state aware of its obligations, priorities, and responsibilities. Since conflict, competition, and cooperation offer a wide range of options, there cannot be a set response to challenges that emanate from within the system, and hence unpredictability ensues. Uncertainties lead to apprehensions, which in turn contribute to insecurity.

Cooperative and Collective Security

National security aspirations can lead to an arms race, a preponderance of power, with one state dominating affairs while the others experience relative vulnerability, and attempts to establish a balance of power by states which perceive threats in a power hierarchy, but are not capable of dealing independently with their security vulnerabilities. States can pursue different methods of protecting themselves and promoting security, using two major models.

Cooperative Security

When states cooperate with each other through assurances and confidence-building measures, recognising each other's legitimate security needs in order to build an environment of mutual trust, the process is viewed as 'cooperative security'. The focus is on a high level of non-institutionalised collaboration in order to settle disputes and reduce differences through the use of compromise and not force. States that apply these techniques constitute a security community, as the parties remain alert to the needs of fellow members and contribute to common benefits enjoyed by all.

Cooperative security usually takes place within a geographically defined region where the states are more or less similar in terms of their power. There may even be multiple states with similar abilities who cancel out each other's propensity to dominate. A common historical experience, similar levels of economic development, similar political ideologies and culture, similar forms of administration, and common goals help to foster cooperative security. Any response to conflict, especially in an era of uncertainty, will follow different patterns of conflict prevention, conflict management, conflict reduction, and finally, conflict resolution. A comprehensive security approach (including non-traditional security issues) is the preferred option, based on political and security cooperation, confidence-building measures, preventive diplomacy, and constructive engagement geared towards promoting stability in the region.

The Association for Southeast Asian Nations (ASEAN) provides a good example of cooperative security, indicating an attempt on the part of states to understand security in multilateral terms without compromising on national interest. Members seek to manage, nurture, and construct measures for peace and stability, eschewing control and contestation and resisting possible threats. Norms and principles evolve to create mechanisms of conflict management derived from shared knowledge and state practices. Attempts to expand such dialogue and consensus-building to a zone that spreads beyond Southeast Asia, while sustaining the Southeast Asian region at its core, have led to the development of a platform for avoiding conflict through consultation and dialogue—the ASEAN Regional Forum (ARF). However, as it goes beyond the core region of Southeast Asia and covers multiple unique security complexes (for example, the South Asian security complex), the efficacy of the ARF is diminished.

Collective Security

The collective security model, which stems from the idea of collective defence arrangements, provides a regulatory mechanism for ensuring stability in international politics. Such an arrangement establishes internal peace and secures each member from external attack by providing a united response. Extended on a global scale, collective security calls for a voluntary system of regulation where the parties to the arrangement refrain from the use of military force as an instrument of state policy. Parties are also collectively responsible for the maintenance of international peace and security. An act of aggression by one state against another is regarded as an attack against all, and all other states can collectively impose punitive measures—military or economic sanctions—upon the aggressor. However, although the first such experiment, put in place after World War I—the League of Nations—failed, the key actors once again tried to build on the model after World War II, and the United Nations Organization (UNO) came into being.

The United Nations is based on the principle of collective security. Member states agree to settle their disputes by peaceful means and refrain from the threat or use of force against the territorial integrity or political independence of any state, or in any manner inconsistent with the purposes of the United Nations. However, it is the Security Council of the United Nations that is responsible for investigating any dispute to determine whether it is likely to endanger international peace and security. The Council can recommend appropriate procedures or methods of adjustment and measures for the pacific settlement of disputes. Further, it can determine the existence of any threat to peace, breach of peace, or act of aggression, and decide on the punitive measures to be taken using air, sea, or land forces. All members of the United Nations undertake to make available to the Security Council their armed forces, assistance, and facilities.

The collective security model is not constituted merely of punitive measures against an aggressor, but includes other means that contribute to the maintenance of international peace and security, including the peaceful settlement of disputes, disarmament and arms control, preventive diplomacy aimed at peace-making, and the use of military means geared towards peacekeeping and subsequent peace-building. Certain practical problems plague the collective security model, which include the special status of the great powers and selective engagement.

Common Security

It is often emphasised that no individual, group, or nation can be secure without all other individuals, groups, and nations being secure at the same time. No country can achieve security on the basis of unilateral decisions, because security depends upon the actions and reactions of adversaries and has to be achieved collectively. Common security is a non-violent approach. It foresees no enemies at all, and so goes beyond the need to secure oneself against enemies; however, there is a long way to go before the idea is materialised.

Historically, international security mechanisms have always been dependent on the major powers of the day. For obvious reasons, small powers cannot impose penalties upon major powers who violate the rules. As a result, the big powers are the ones that are primarily responsible for maintaining international peace and security, albeit on their preferred terms. The Security Council has five permanent members (China, France, Russia, the US, and the UK) who enjoy veto power, that is, the power to annul a decision made by all the others. (Reforms to reflect the reality of the contemporary power hierarchy are pending.) This elevated status accorded to the big powers hampers the functioning of the Security Council, since the big powers tend to focus on the differences among them and pursue their own interests. During the Cold War, US–Soviet Union rivalry, which resulted in the frequent use of the veto by one or the other state, severely curtailed the functioning of the Security Council and the mechanism of collective security suffered. Both superpowers actively protected their allies and protégés, preventing any punitive measure from being implemented against them.

The Security Council has also not concerned itself uniformly with every dispute. While some conflicts have attracted the immediate attention of the Council, in others, the international community delayed appropriate action. For example, the chaos in Kosovo in former Yugoslavia provoked a prompt reaction, but the United Nations was accused of immoral inaction during the genocides in Darfur and Rwanda, where millions were massacred. It is not surprising that while the United Nations is credited with huge successes in the fields of sustainable human development, it has never been viewed as very effective when it comes to maintaining international peace and security, or even as a useful platform for resolving international disputes.

6

National Interest and Foreign Policy

Anindya Jyoti Majumdar

In the international system, sovereign independent states interact with one another. While each state has its own set of objectives and strives to achieve them by pursuing policies in the international arena, the goals and techniques are influenced by situational and operational necessities. States ordinarily compete with one another on a broad spectrum, oscillating between two extreme possibilities of conflict and cooperation as they respond to the demands of the day. States cannot live in isolation and connectivity increases interdependence. Hence, taking into consideration both internal and external variables, states formulate and execute foreign policy in conformity with their national interests. At the same time, certain shared ethical values in human societies that have universal appeal across borders may also influence the foreign policies of states. This chapter explores the concept of national interest and then proceeds to discuss the objectives, techniques, and determinants of foreign policy.

National Interest

National interest comprises the goals that states pursue to maximise what is best for the people and the country, as perceived at a given point in time. Broadly, a state should promote the internal welfare of its citizens, including economic development and prosperity, and protect political independence and territorial integrity against external aggression. Further, a state may also seek to preserve the values and ways of life of its people. This may mean competing with other states to gain power, position, and prestige through a process that combines elements of both cooperation and conflict.

National interest includes priority goals and peripheral goals, permanent and variable interests, and general and specific ends. Following Joseph Frankel, the term 'national interest' may be used for aspirational goals as well as operational policies. The term could be explanatory and polemical, as one explains, justifies, or disapproves of foreign policy measures.

However, while frequently used, the term 'national interest' may hold different meanings for different people. Some scholars equate the aspirations and dreams of a nation with national interest, but according to Hans Morgenthau, the proponent of the realist school, the residual meaning inherent in the concept of national interest is survival. In other words, the minimum requirements of states seem to be the protection of their physical, political, and cultural identity against encroachment by other states. Policies pursued by the state should be logically compatible with these basic and primary considerations. Since power ensures the achievement of objectives, Morgenthau equates national interest with the pursuit of power. He perceives that policies must be guided by national interest rather than by moralistic, legalistic, or ideological criteria. This view is, however, debatable as national interest cannot be merely mechanical; the interest itself is influenced often by the moralistic or ideological positions adopted by the state. Morgenthau offers a prescription to policymakers, but history is witness to the fact that many of the policies adopted by states have been guided by ideational and ideological zeal masquerading as the promotion of national interest. However, it can be pointed out that national interest can also be promoted under the garb of ideology and with reference to near-universal values. The rivalry between the two superpowers—the USA and the Soviet Union—during the Cold War period is a fascinating case study in this context.

With regard to scope and range, Morgenthau states that a country's national interest should be proportionate to its capabilities. A legitimate exercise of state power should not take the form of arrogance. Rationality and prudence provide the ability to assess one's own needs and aspirations while carefully balancing them against the needs and aspirations of others. Since the international system is neither naturally harmonious nor conflict-ridden, possibilities of a clash of interest between states can be reduced by a prudent adjustment of interests through diplomatic action.

Today, no country can afford to pursue its own welfare in a manner that reduces its competitor's security and welfare, and chauvinism and intense nationalism can be counter-productive in defining national interests. Global challenges and common concerns may induce states to seek greater unity and cooperation in order to pursue human interests and a common good. However, states adopt a common policy only after intense bargaining, which is often based on competitive national interests.

National interest does not belong to a group, class, or elite establishment. Although the decisions are taken by a few powerful people at the helm of government affairs, national interest is a compromise between conflicting political interests within the country and the outcome of domestic politics. It is the product of constant internal political competition within the state, even though the government is ultimately responsible for defining and implementing policies oriented towards the national interest.

Three aspects mark the idea of national interest:

1. National interest is the primary justification for state action. It is obvious that theoretically, each policy that the government pursues is for the good of the people and the country, aimed at maintaining or increasing benefits and reducing the probability of harm. Under this basic consideration, the government may decide what the people need (which may or may not be what the people want), and the policies are modified and altered according to the support or opposition extended by internal political constituencies or external actors. With the exception of a few vital issues like survival and economic development, what constitutes the national interest of a specific country can be a matter of interpretation by different groups.
2. A demonstrable national advantage must ensue from policies oriented towards the national interest. While 'advantage' and 'benefit' are relative terms, there has to be a sense of comfort at the popular level with the consequences of the policies pursued by the state. Any loss or disadvantage as a result of a policy is readily

interpreted as working against the national interest. While, under normal circumstances, there will always be detractors and critics of government policies (as well as supporters), and the government will always make strenuous efforts to point out the benefits of those policies, a visible advantage is what is implied by the term 'national interest'.

3. While national interest remains constant on the core issues, it could be flexible in terms of its priorities and techniques. As mentioned earlier, there are certain core or vital issues like survival (hence, security) and increasing standards of living (hence, development and prosperity), which everyone is in agreement with. However, the formulation of strategies to achieve these core goals involves matching the ways (measures to be adopted) and the means (available capabilities) with the ends (the objectives). For example, the nature of a threat to survival can differ in different countries: it could be a military threat in one country, economic challenges in another, and serious environmental hazards in others. In each case, the priorities and consequent policies would differ.

It should be mentioned that authoritarian governments care little for procedural niceties and the substantive issues of any policy are prioritised. On the contrary, in democracies, debates around and people's participation in what constitutes the public good and collective interest may dilute the substance of the policy considerably. Certain assumptions may follow: whereas authoritarian states can respond swiftly to an emerging situation, democracies may take time to formulate their response; in other words, authoritarian governments (with little consideration for public opinion) can decide and act quickly, while democracies have to first debate the situation (unless it is an emergency) and come to a widely acceptable solution, and, depending on the composition of the administration and the support the top echelon enjoys, the probability of the policy being modified with time is also high.

In contemporary times of intense connectivity and interdependence among states, an aggressive pursuit of one's own national interest with little concern for the legitimate national interest of fellow states is self-defeating. Indeed, certain global challenges can be best tackled by collective efforts, and here, national interest converges with the global interest. In other words, a common good, like the prevention of hazardous climate change or protection of the environment, can turn into a national interest. However, this is not to say that vital national interests will be readily sacrificed by states in order to achieve the global interest on all occasions.

FOREIGN POLICY

Foreign policy goes beyond the jurisdiction of a single state and is directed towards other states. Today, a state encounters not only other sovereign, independent states arrayed in a power hierarchy, but also various non-state actors. Nevertheless, primary foreign policy objectives are determined by the vital national interests of the state. Most scholars agree on four basic objectives of foreign policy. As listed by K. J. Holsti, these are: (*i*) security of the state; (*ii*) economic development and prosperity of the state; (*iii*) autonomy or freedom in decision-making; and (*iv*) status and prestige in the international arena (which might act as soft power in favour of the state). States, depending on their capabilities and needs, would have their own priorities to immediately pursue, but these basic objectives are in fact prioritised in terms of their importance.

A state has to first exist on the map as a recognisable separate entity before it strives to achieve any goal. To secure itself against external challenges, especially threats to its sovereignty, independence, and territorial integrity, the state adopts various measures. Ranging from alliance formation, regional security arrangements, and bilateral treaties to general measures aimed at creating a stable environment of durable peace, security in its many forms is a primary condition for a state's existence, and therefore often becomes its first priority. However, states also seek to usher in better standards of living for their people and then maintain those standards. Hence, economic development remains a crucial goal for underdeveloped and developing states, while the developed ones strive for prosperity. One may say that physical existence and some sort of economic development are possible under the patronage of a big power, but such a situation severely limits the freedom of the state to take its own decisions. Meaningful statehood requires autonomy, whereby only the people of that state can determine their destiny. As these three objectives are fulfilled, the state, through its success in achieving perceptible advancements, can seek to earn the prestige that will enable it to play a bigger role in international politics. In the process of achieving the primary objectives, there may appear a plethora of secondary objectives that are of an immediate, intermediate, short-term, and long-term nature, and different issues may require tactical responses. However, all these sub-goals are linked to the primary objectives.

TECHNIQUES OF FOREIGN POLICY

While foreign policy formulation is influenced predominantly by perceived national interests, the execution of foreign policy requires certain techniques. Strategies and tactics become parts of foreign policy. While diplomacy is by far the single most effective means to pursue foreign policy, propaganda and coercive means can also be viewed as corollary instruments of foreign policy execution.

Diplomacy

Diplomacy presupposes the use of communication and negotiation for official transactions between states and other international entities, which help to manage international relations. Such communication, which usually involves bargaining and persuasion, cannot be casual or frivolous, and necessitates the application of intelligence and tact. Diplomacy is moreover perceived as a complex skill aimed at achieving the objectives of foreign policy.

The age-old practice of diplomacy has evolved over the years, and contemporary diplomatic structure is codified by international law. With time, the tasks of the diplomats have also changed. Earlier, diplomats were the only available channel of communication between states, and their reports from distant lands, comprising information and analyses of the challenges and opportunities in the countries of their posting, were the only reliable basis for formulating policies and shaping bilateral relations. With the huge improvement in transport and communication technology, diplomats have lost some of their prominence. However, although information can now be obtained very easily and very fast from multiple sources in this interconnected world, especially through the electronic media, a diplomat's report remains useful for an assessment of the issue at hand.

Box 6.1: Functions of a Diplomat

The major functions of a professional diplomat can be categorised as:

1. Representing the sending state in the receiving state;
2. Negotiating on behalf of the sending state with the receiving state;
3. Collecting useful information and reporting back to the home state;
4. Protecting the interests of the home state and its people in the receiving state; and
5. Providing consular services.

A diplomat represents their home country in the country of their posting and acts as a bridge between the two. As mentioned earlier, even though the revolution in information technology has reduced the value of the report in terms of information, the assessment and insight provided by the diplomat on various aspects remains invaluable. The position has a symbolic value as the diplomat attends ceremonial, official, and social occasions and functions, but the political substance of their activities stems from the fact that through interactions, they seek to promote the interests and image of the home country in a foreign land. Contacts with leading politicians, bureaucrats, businessmen and entrepreneurs, intellectuals, the military, and journalists can be leveraged to obtain information, influence opinion, and promote the home country.

While direct communication between heads of states is possible today through hotlines and special emissaries can be sent by the leader of one state to another, the bulk of the negotiation is still carried on by professional diplomats. With their knowledge of the local mood and positions on a particular issue, the diplomat can successfully communicate between states. Tensions and disputes are usually sought to be diffused at this level and the groundwork prepared for mutually beneficial and collaborative initiatives. Often, a collaborative project is announced in principle by the heads of states when they meet; it then becomes the task of diplomats of both countries to negotiate the details of the project for implementation. Likewise, diplomats may also negotiate an agreement over an issue by reducing differences of opinion, enabling heads of states to announce projects of collaboration on their next visits or meetings on an international platform.

The diplomat has the added responsibility of assessing the power, abilities, and aspirations of the receiving state, in comparison to the home state. A diplomatic report has the ability to steer the direction of foreign policy.

In a foreign land, a country's embassy also protects the interests of citizens from the home country. Any national in trouble in a foreign land, whether as a visitor or a resident, may contact their country's embassy for help. The embassy also issues visas and provides other consular services as required.

The task of diplomacy is carried out by career diplomats who are led by the Ambassador (in the member-countries of the Commonwealth of Nations, they are called High Commissioners) stationed in the embassy (or the High Commission) in the receiving state. The diplomat performs all necessary functions of communication and enjoys immunity or special protections as codified in the Vienna Convention of 1961 in order to carry out their usual duties. They can be declared a *persona non grata*, that is, an undesirable person, and be asked to leave if their activities are interpreted as detrimental to the interests of the receiving state.

It is usually in times of emergency and significant political events that the heads of states or high dignitaries have personally met with one another. Over time, diplomatic interactions have taken new forms, mostly due to the improvement in transport and communication technologies, which have made it possible for the heads of governments and ministers to travel swiftly to distant lands on brief visits. This has resulted in the practice of Summit Diplomacy, where the heads of state, ministers, and officials from different countries can meet, air their respective views, issue a communiqué, and disperse. Such meetings can decide future paths of collaboration. While Summit Diplomacy is not an entirely new practice, the frequency of such multilateral summit meetings has increased with the growth of international and regional inter-governmental organisations. Heads of state may even rely on personal diplomacy and interpersonal relations in resolving an issue. Foreign trips can be used to present their own ideas and visions, attract investments, and seek security ties. With their emissaries working for them, leaders can also depend on their personal charisma and contacts and thereby create a form of personal diplomacy.

Multilateral issues require the participation of several countries and issues of regional or global interest call for a diplomacy through conferences. The codification of international law (the Hague Conferences of 1899 and 1907), which has shaped an international economic system (the Bretton Woods Conference of 1944, out of which emerged the International Monetary Fund [IMF] and the World Bank) and established a world organisation (for example, the San Francisco Conference of 1945, where the Charter of the United Nations was approved) are some examples of diplomacy through conferences. The practice is prevalent with regard to issues of global concern, such as disarmament, climate change, or sustainable development. On international platforms, global issues are discussed often in a manner similar to parliamentary debates. The United Nations General Assembly, for example, passes resolutions on common concerns after much debate and discussion. This form of activity is termed 'parliamentary diplomacy'.

Of late, another form of diplomatic activity has come to the fore. Branded 'public diplomacy', its content remains ambiguous; on the one hand, it aims to improve public relations and thereby propagate the ideas and visions of a state to the general public, at home and abroad, and ensures feedback on the policies as well. On the other hand, it involves greater people-to-people contact and the use of civil society groups to further state interests. This non-official channel of communication between select groups across borders is also known as Track-II diplomacy, Track-I being the conventional official form. Feedback and suggestions from these groups allow governments to explore further avenues of cooperation. However, public diplomacy works as a corollary to conventional forms, and has limited independent application.

Although career diplomats are no longer sole agents in the execution of foreign policy, they remain indispensable in the contemporary system. Other forms of diplomacy can only add to conventional ways, but cannot replace them. Diplomacy may be further characterised by adding a prefix like 'economic', 'nuclear', or 'climate', to denote either the subject matter or the specific tool of influence. Economic diplomacy, for example, may simply mean negotiation over aid, trade, investment, and/or issues relating to quotas and tariffs, but it may also suggest how economic measures—both supportive and coercive—can be successfully used to promote state interests.

The old diplomatic practices of the European aristocratic class had, until the late nineteenth century, led to many secret pacts and understandings. There was an apprehension that adverse public reaction would undermine an otherwise beneficial arrangement, and secret pacts also contained an element of surprise and shock for a potential common enemy. Practitioners of secret diplomacy believed that statecraft included dimensions that ought to be kept outside the purview of common people, in their own interest. This pattern was gradually replaced in the twentieth century as democratic ideas began to spread, and administrations became more responsive to their citizens. Secret pacts began to be looked down upon and demands for open diplomacy increased. Secret diplomacy was contrary to the principles of democracy, and hence an open diplomacy was advocated.

Open diplomacy conforms to US President Woodrow Wilson's famous dictum, 'open covenants of peace, openly arrived at'; however, it is not as open as one may surmise. While the treaty provisions are made public as the conclusion of a treaty requires ratification in the national Parliaments of the concerned states, the conduct of diplomacy, especially when dealing with sensitive issues, is difficult under the public glare. The process of bargaining involves concessions and compromises, and open negotiations may compel diplomats to take rigid positions inimical to negotiation. Even in open platforms like the United Nations, where a form of parliamentary diplomacy takes place, back-channel negotiations thrive among smaller groups. Open diplomacy therefore follows the principle of open covenants, secretly arrived at, that is, the negotiation is often conducted behind closed doors, but the end result is made available to the public.

Propaganda

Governments have always identified particular groups, classes, and/or communities in foreign countries as legitimate targets in order to promote state interests. Propaganda is a process by which a communicator seeks to persuade the target population to accept a particular point of view and act in a manner that suits the preferences of the former. Propaganda has been used widely to influence the attitude and behaviour of people in foreign countries, in order to sway them in the propagandist's favour. As public opinion grew in importance and governments became responsive to the public mood, states began to develop favourable public opinions among foreign nationals in the hope of effecting a similar change in the attitude of foreign governments. With the growth of civil society and social media, propaganda or image-engineering takes precedence. Hence, governments pay special attention to image-building, using embassies to arrange seminars and exhibitions, as well as cultural and educational exchange programmes; using the electronic and print media and publications targeted specifically at foreign nationals; and through contacts with local communicators. Propaganda is legitimate as long as it aims to raise the image of the propagandist. However, propaganda can become combative, offensive, and aggressive, especially among rival states. Exaggerated fabrications and false accusations mark the techniques of negative propaganda, which can include prophecies of doom supported by unauthenticated data and forged documents, used to incite rebellion and political instability in a target state. Hence, states are involved in counter-propaganda as well.

In order to garner support for a particular policy, states find it easy to justify their actions if a receptive ground has already been prepared through the use of propaganda. The repeated use of symbols and metaphors may create and impose a new identity on a group of people or on particular states. Target groups or states are tagged with a particular label, such as 'axis of evil' or 'rogue states', which is then popularised not only through government documents but also through the constant use of those terms in academic and diplomatic circles. During the Cold War period, both the US and the Soviet Union made active use of propaganda, as each sought to retain the moral and ideological high ground over the other and ensure the loyalty of their respective people.

Coercive Means and Sanctions

Despite the contention that military strength is primarily a wartime requirement, meant for the protection of a country, it is undeniable that the projection of hard power in the form of military strength increases the probability of success for a foreign policy. In *On War* (1832), Carl von Clausewitz asserted that 'war is a mere continuation of policy by other means', and that it is a rational instrument of national policy. Although the comity of nations has over the years tried to make aggressive wars obsolete, international politics has always been controlled by the great powers, which decide its agenda and prioritise the issues of the day. Any international regime, be it a human rights regime or that of nuclear non-proliferation, depends on the support of the great powers to be effective. In the contemporary world order, ruled by a hierarchy of power, big powers decide and smaller states respond, and then adjust their behaviour accordingly. The maintenance of international peace and security has always been the primary responsibility of the big powers, and this allows them to be discriminatory, as the decisions taken mostly suit their own preferences. However, military strength is often a consequence of economic abilities, and hence requires constant economic support in order to retain its efficacy.

The military plays a vital role in the formulation and execution of foreign policy, not only in a state where a military junta is in power, but also in authoritarian administrations and countries where the civilian administration is weak and unstable. It can be presumed that under such circumstances, there will be a tendency to favour military solutions for political problems. However, in democracies, too, the military-industrial complex plays a major role in the formulation and execution of foreign policy, given their access to and influence over men in high positions. Indeed, the very presence of a powerful military boosts foreign policy execution.

Coercive means may take the form of economic sanctions upon states that have violated international rules and norms. These sanctions can be imposed by the United Nations or a major power, aimed at pressuring the target state to rectify its actions. For example, North Korea and Iran have often come under international sanctions for pursuing nuclear weapons programmes, resulting in restrictions upon their international trade and other economic activities. As opposed to coercive means, 'soft power' is the ability of a country to attract and co-opt, through non-political affinities such as cultural similarities, skilfully employed to persuade other countries to seek the same outcomes. Persuasion plays an equally significant role as coercion in international relations. However, an effective use of soft power may require the backing of hard power. Diplomacy combines both elements in bargaining, as and when necessary.

Determinants of Foreign Policy

The 'state' is an abstract entity. The policies of a state are adopted by individuals. The task is to figure out the strategy, on the basis of the resources and capabilities available, in order to achieve the objectives of foreign policy. Certain factors condition the formulation of foreign policy. It is obvious that a state has to respond to its environment and the challenges or opportunities that emanate from this environment. State policies have to take into consideration the constraints and leeway offered by the international environment, which comprises organisations like the United Nations and its many specialised agencies; international regimes like nuclear non-proliferation; and the foreign policy choices of fellow states.

An important determinant is the geographical nature of the state itself, that is, its territorial extent, its location, its natural resources, and its topography—all the physical features that give the state its distinctiveness. Although the primary foreign policy objectives of a state that is big in size and rich in resources would perhaps be similar to a state that is smaller and poorer in resources, their policy measures would differ. They may have similar ends, but they will adopt different means, based on the difference in their assets. However, no stretch of land or waterway is inherently strategic; it becomes so when such an identity is imposed upon it by external actors, whose interests are greatly affected by those very geographical features. Geography determines the neighbourhood and proximity to other states, and may breed disputes if common resources like river water are to be shared. On the other hand, aspects of regionalism and regional cooperation are often influenced by the composition of the group, which again is often the result of geographical proximity.

Another determinant of foreign policy is the profile of the material assets that contribute to the state's abilities. The level of economic growth influences foreign policy choices, as does the standard of technological advancement. Likewise, military strength contributes to the power and resultant influence of the state.

At the level of ideas, tradition and heritage can have an impact on foreign policy formulation. States often stand for certain values and their unique ways of life. Religion and culture can impact foreign policymaking. However, while political ideology can be a driving force for foreign policy formulation, ideology may be used to justify actions, even when the real motive remains the perceived national interest.

The making of foreign policy is essentially a political act, mostly influenced by political actors. In authoritarian systems, the legislative body merely endorses the policies initiated by the executive. However, in democracies, the political structure of the state normally assigns the legislative body some control over foreign policy through the power to debate, discuss, and make budgetary allocations for activities related to foreign policy. Public opinion is also considered a determinant of foreign policy. It might be unstructured and unclear and not the organised, cohesive opinion of all people, instead being the opinion of a section of people or a group. Public opinion is shaped and expressed by political parties, interest groups, lobbyists, and the media, but the final call is taken by the executive. When a vital decision comes up for referendum and public opinion is divided, the majority decision is carried out. Britain's exit from the European Union—Brexit—was the result of such a referendum.

Interest groups and lobbyists continue to influence policymakers through sustained efforts, and many international NGOs like Red Cross and Amnesty International are credited with successfully persuading states to conclude important treaties. The Geneva Conventions of 1949 that apply humanitarian laws during armed conflicts or the Convention against Torture have resulted from the activities of these NGOs. We often hear about the role played by the Israel lobby or the India caucus in the United States. Their task is to influence the administration to adopt policies that are pro-Israel or pro-India in nature.

However, the most important foreign policy determinant is the political leadership. In most cases, the main thrust of foreign policy comes from the top leadership, which might include the head of the government as well as the foreign minister. It is only when the top leadership is either ill-equipped or uninterested in foreign policymaking that the task is assumed by the foreign office bureaucracy. Leadership initiatives depend on the extent of support enjoyed by the leader in the government. If the government is formed by a coalition of different political parties, then the decisions of the government might depend on the domestic compulsions of appeasing a coalition partner, while foreign policy considerations take a backseat. During the UPA-I administration, the left parties withdrew support as Prime Minister Manmohan Singh went ahead with the nuclear deal with the United States, and during the UPA-II administration, regional parties influenced the decisions of the Central government with regard to relations with Sri Lanka and Bangladesh.

Foreign policymaking is a complex process based on a cost-benefit analysis, and a rational choice is made from alternate courses of action. However, there is scope for intuitive moves and tactical shifts. Despite stated ideological positions, in reality pragmatism guides the state to frame methods and techniques to attain and accomplish goals oriented towards the national interest.

7

FROM WORLD WAR I TO WORLD WAR II

Causes and Consequences

Anindya Jyoti Majumdar, with Souryadeep Sen

In the first half of the twentieth century, two devastating wars ravaged the world. In many ways, the two long-drawn conflicts not only shaped the fate of the European states and their colonies, but also touched the lives of people worldwide. Changed geographical boundaries, fluctuating power equations, and the rise of exclusivist political ideologies together impacted the patterns of international politics as practised during that time. The European powers held their sway over global politics, and intense competition among them and the resultant alliance formations eventually led to the two great wars of the last century. This chapter explains the causes and consequences of these wars, with special reference to the revolutionary changes in Russia and the rise of Fascism and Nazism in Italy and Germany, respectively, in the inter-war period.

WORLD WAR I (1914–18)

In 1867, the Austro-Hungarian Empire came into being as Austria and Hungary agreed to a compromise and accepted a union of two equal states under a common monarch. The Emperor of Austria was also the King of Hungary. While the states enjoyed much liberty with regard to their respective domestic jurisdictions, foreign and military policies were under joint supervision. Austria-Hungary became the major power of the day, spreading over a large territory in Central Europe. By 1878, Bosnia and Herzegovina had come under its occupation, and was fully annexed in 1908. This unilateral act led to much protest and impaired relations with the two neighbouring states of Serbia and Russia. Serbian nationalists soon started a movement in Bosnia to break off from Austria and join Serbia.

Archduke Franz Ferdinand was the heir to the throne of the Austro-Hungarian Empire. While on an official trip to the Bosnian capital Sarajevo to inspect the imperial armed forces, he and his wife Sophia were assassinated on 28 June 1914 by a 19-year-old Bosnian Serb nationalist. Austria-Hungary held Serbia responsible for the act and wanted to punish Serbia for the alleged promotion of nationalist movements in areas under its jurisdiction. But at the same time, they were concerned about the possible response of another major power, Russia, a known supporter of Serbia. Austria-Hungary sought the support of its ally, Germany, and their armies began mobilising. Meanwhile, France agreed to extend support to Serbia against Austria-Hungary.

An ultimatum was issued to Serbia on 23 July, demanding the fulfilment of certain conditions. The demands were partially rejected, especially the provision that called for allowing the operation of Austrian police within Serbian territory, and on 28 July Austria-Hungary declared war on Serbia. What was essentially a dispute between Austria-Hungary and Serbia soon took the form of a global war as major European powers and their allies became involved. The war eventually spread to other parts of the world as the colonies and imperial territories of European states were sucked into the war as well. Unrestricted war activities harmed the interests of even the neutral states; for example, German submarine attacks on US merchant vessels led the United States, a neutral state so far, to declare war on Germany in April 1917. The conflict—known in history as World War I—continued for four years, until 1918, and resulted in millions of deaths, of both combatants and civilians.

While the assassination of Archduke Ferdinand is considered the immediate cause of World War I, the complexities of the Great War cannot be sufficiently explained by the disputes between the two original antagonists. At a popular level, the main reasons for World War I are often abbreviated as MAIN, indicating the crucial roles played by Militarism, Alliances, Imperialism, and Nationalism. In fact, a shifting balance of power based on industrial output and armaments, alliance politics, geopolitical aspirations, and national cohesion influenced relations among the major European states. To quote Paul Kennedy, '... there existed in governing elites, military circles and imperialist organization a prevailing view of the world order which stressed struggle, change, competition, the use of force, and the organization of national resources to enhance state power' (Kennedy 2017, 252).

New nations had also arisen. By 1871, the unification of Italy and Germany from clusters of smaller entities that merged through conflicts marked the rise of two powerful states, which continued to expand their military strength by developing naval fleets and modern armies. Germany made huge advancements and by the sheer speed and extent of its explosive growth in industrial, commercial, and military terms, due largely in part to a naval fleet that was second only to England's, it soon became almost the most powerful state at the centre of the old European state system (Kennedy 2017, 270). Germany's rise threatened the other great powers. In fact, the Franco-Prussian war of 1870–71 led to the defeat of France, and the united German states under the leadership of Prussia formed the German Empire, with Prussian King Wilhelm I as the emperor. While Chancellor Bismarck took care to play down Germany's ambitions, after he was removed from his position by young Kaiser Wilhelm II, Germany, under the new ruler and his advisers, prepared for the inevitable confrontations with other powers. A mutual suspicion led to all major powers moving towards greater militarism by the turn of the nineteenth century.

Along with growth in military capabilities, the powers also looked for alliances and secret guarantees of support in times of war. A triple alliance was formed by Germany, Austria-Hungary, and Italy in 1882. The triple entente took shape by 1907, and comprised Russia, France, and the United Kingdom, based on the Franco-Russian Alliance (1894), France-UK Entente Cordiale (1904), and the Anglo-Russian entente (1907). The Franco-Japanese Treaty (1907) ensured that another rising power—Japan—would be ranged on the side of France and its allies. An alliance was ratified between the German Empire and the Ottoman Empire in August 1914. Mutual defence arrangements pulled the states into conflicts; Italy, however, was unpredictable, and eventually moved towards the Anglo-French combination. The triple entente parties (Russia, France, and the United Kingdom) entered World War I as the Allied Powers (later joined by Japan, Italy, and the United States) against the Central Powers—Germany and Austria-Hungary and their supporters, including the Ottoman Empire, which entered the war by attacking the Russian coast in October 1914.

The late nineteenth and early twentieth centuries witnessed the West European powers, Russia, and Japan acquiring overseas territories and extending their control throughout the world, especially in Africa and Asia. The exploitation of the raw materials and valuable resources of these subjugated territories was necessary for the sustained growth of the major powers. Consequently, the competition to acquire imperial territories and the aspirations of imperial expansion led them into conflicts and disputes in Europe and other parts of the world. Geopolitical advantages were sought and new territories thus acquired strategic significance. Known as the New Imperialism, this process saw large parts of Africa and Asia being conquered and occupied mostly by the European powers. The scramble for Africa—almost all of Africa was occupied by and divided amongst the European powers between 1870 and 1914—was a result of heightened colonial activity. These areas became theatres of conflict and helped to spread the war.

Nationalist chauvinism on the part of states further worsened relations among them. Each state, in a fit of nationalist passion, refused to negotiate and accommodate the legitimate interests of competitors. Collective egotism laced with pride and over-confidence, along with hatred for the other, created an intoxicating atmosphere, leading the states eventually into conflict. At the same time, many areas in Europe under the yoke of empires were seeking freedom and self-determination. In fact, even though the assassination of Archduke Ferdinand served as the catalyst for the Great War, it had been in the making for several years.

A number of intermeshed variables had therefore instigated World War I, and a deadly conflict ensued among the major powers of the day. On 4 August 1914, Germany entered neutral Belgium in order to invade France. The French and British forces stopped the invading German army in the First Battle of Marne in September, but both sides dug into their respective trenches and a war of attrition followed on the Western Front. On the Eastern Front, Russia made repeated attempts, but failed to break the German resistance. In 1917, a revolution in Russia overthrew Czar Nicholas II and Russia agreed to an armistice with the Central Powers. Austria-Hungary, with the support of Germany, defeated Italy in 1917.

An attack by the Allied Powers against the Ottoman Turks failed in 1915, leading to a retreat of Allied forces in 1916. Serbia resisted the invasion bids of Austria-Hungary in 1914, but capitulated in 1915 when German and Austrian forces overran the Balkans. Serbia was ultimately liberated by the Allied Powers in November 1918. As mentioned earlier, German submarine attacks brought the United States into the war, on the side of the Allied Powers. The tables were soon turned as the Allied Powers took back Italian land, stalled the Ottoman Turks, and successfully defeated a fresh German offensive in the Second Battle of Marne in 1918, launching counter-offensive operations. The long-drawn, devastating war took its toll on both the Austro-Hungarian Empire and the Ottoman Empire as their economic and military strength dwindled, and both faced opposition from nationalist movements within. In October 1918, the Ottoman Turks signed a treaty with the Allied Powers, and in early November, Austria-Hungary and Germany reached an armistice and World War I came to an end.

THE CONSEQUENCES

A war fought on such a great scale brought with it death and destruction and ruined most of the economies involved. The United States was an exception, perhaps because of its geographical distance from the theatres of war and its late entry into the action; it actually emerged stronger than the others. For years after the war, the European countries faced inflation, unemployment, and economic instability, while their bridges, roads, and railway lines had to be repaired and rebuilt. A flu pandemic with a high mortality rate that began in early 1918—dubbed the Spanish Flu—also killed millions. Early reports were censored in the interests of the war, which only aggravated the situation, and the pandemic spread rapidly with the war movements. It is also argued that the virus hit the Central Powers harder before spreading to the Allied Powers, helping the Allies in their war efforts in 1918. As millions of young men either engaged or perished in the war, women came forward to replace them as the workforce in public life, which led to a transformation in social attitudes towards women in general and in the rights accorded to them in particular.

The War led to a few profound political changes. The world map was redrawn and new countries emerged out of the old empires. Austria and Hungary were separated, and Poland, Czechoslovakia, and Yugoslavia were three prominent new states carved out of the erstwhile empires. In the Middle East, countries came under British and French control, and what was left of the Ottoman Empire became Turkey. Along with the major powers, their allies too benefitted from the post-war arrangements. For instance, Australia acquired control of German New Guinea; New Zealand got Samoa; and Belgium acquired the African territory of Ruanda-Urundi from the German Empire. Japan secured the West Pacific and Indian Ocean region during the war, captured several island colonies of Germany, and expanded its influence in China.

As the empires collapsed, new political ideas gained acceptance. In many countries, republican governments came into being as the monarchs were forced to abdicate their thrones. As Germany established the Weimar Republic, the dissolution of the Austro-Hungarian Empire spawned the separate republics of Austria and Hungary. The division and occupation of the Ottoman Empire by the Allies led to the Turkish National Movement, and a Republic of Turkey came into being in 1923 under the leadership of Kemal Pasha.

The Treaty of Versailles, signed in Paris on 28 June 1919, codified the peace terms. It took away German colonies and compelled Germany to give up its claims over certain areas in Europe; forced Germany to pay £6.6 billion in reparation; and demilitarised the country by imposing substantial limitations upon the German military in terms of arms and equipment. The harsh provisions of the Treaty actually fuelled ultra-nationalist sentiments in Germany, and soon the Treaty of Versailles began to be counted as one of the reasons that instigated World War II.

A part of the Treaty of Versailles was the adoption of the Covenant of the League of Nations. One line of thinking advocated the limitation of armaments and proposed consultations among the states to diminish the possibility of further wars. In January 1918, President Woodrow Wilson of the United States put forward his Fourteen Points containing his vision for the post-war world. A general association of nations that would mediate international disputes was thus propounded, and the League was formally established on 10 January 1920. It was reasonably successful in non-political activities, providing labour laws that adhered to basic standards, international transit rules, refugee care, and child welfare, but failed miserably in maintaining international peace and security. Within two decades, the world witnessed a deadlier military conflict when World War II erupted in 1939.

THE BOLSHEVIK REVOLUTION IN RUSSIA

A revolution is an abrupt and fundamental change in political power, engendered by an active revolt of the masses against an existing government or system of property relations in a violent or non-violent manner. The success of a revolution depends upon the intelligence and active participation of its leadership, without which it soon degenerates into a chaotic rebellion with no determinate political or social objectives. In the Marxist canon, political revolution can be distinguished from social revolution, insofar as the former involves merely an alteration of the form of government—like the French Revolution of 1789—while in the latter, old property relations are fundamentally challenged and altered, like in the Russian Revolution of 1917.

It can be argued that the Russian Revolution of 1917 became successful not only because of the crises in Russian society and its economy, but also because of the presence of active and ideologically driven factions of the Russian Social Democratic Labour Party (RSDLP, formed in Minsk in 1898), which united under the leadership of Vladimir Ilyich Ulyanov, aka Lenin. The Bolshevik (or majority) and Menshevik (or minority) factions articulated the grievances of the people and provided them with leadership during the revolution's volatile years. Lenin was its chief ideologue, having altered Marx's original maxim that a successful social revolution is a proletarian revolution. For Lenin, in tune with Russia's erstwhile industrial backwardness and dependence upon agriculture, the social revolution promised to engender a revolutionary dictatorship of the proletariat and peasants, before the state withered away after the achievement of communist utopia.

We will first discuss the political and socioeconomic background of the 1917 revolution, then enumerate events in Russia from 1917–18 onwards, and finally provide a survey of the problems facing revolutionary Russia, until Lenin's untimely demise in 1924. Already at the beginning of the twentieth century, Russia was mired in various troubles. Tsar Nicholas II (1894–1917) ruled with an iron fist, but failed to deal with his empire's political and economic problems. Under him, the Russians were defeated in the Russo-Japanese War (1904–05) and, coupled with the hapless condition of the masses, revolutionary sentiments were on the rise, forcing the Tsar to acquiesce to the October Manifesto (granting an elected Parliament or Duma). The ineffectiveness of the Duma and further civil unrest, along with humiliations suffered during World War I, culminated in two revolutions in 1917: the February Revolution, which dethroned the Tsar and created a provisional government; and the October Revolution by the Bolshevik or Leninist wing of the RSDLP, which, through its clamour for 'all power' to the Soviets or elected government councils, created the world's first socialist country.

The Years Leading Up to the 1917 Revolution

The reign of Tsar Nicholas II survived the 1905 revolution for a number of reasons:

- The lack of professional revolutionaries and experienced leaders who could guide the rebellion;
- The Tsar's conciliatory tone and compromises vis-à-vis the October Manifesto;
- Russia's economic improvement in 1906 and the Tsar's 1908 proclamation, promising to achieve universal education in Russia within ten years; and
- Consequent to these changes, the RSDLP's going on the back foot, perpetually suffering from a dearth of funds, internal rivalries, and leadership issues, as most of their ideologues were in exile.

On the other hand, the reasons behind Tsar Nicholas II's fall were even starker:

- He reneged on most of his promises vis-à-vis substantive socio-political and economic changes in Russia;
- The regime failed to implement land reforms;
- Despite the government's outreach towards industrial workers, they struck work intermittently under the influence of revolutionary parties;
- The Bolshevik and Menshevik factions of the RSDLP attempted to reclaim lost ground, preaching the maxims of scientific

socialism to the impecunious masses through their revolutionary newspaper *Iskra* (The Spark);

- The royal family's interminable scandals and controversies, such as those involving the infamous self-professed 'holy man', Grigori Rasputin; and
- The most damning of the Russian Empire's problems was its humiliation in World War I.

Historians agree that Russian failures in World War I made the impending revolution inevitable. The war revealed the backwardness and corruption of the Russian state machinery. To make matters worse, Tsar Nicholas II committed the fatal error of appointing himself Supreme Commander by circumventing the senior leaders of the armed forces. By 1916, political and economic leaders in Russia were ready to sacrifice the dysfunctional Tsar to avoid a worse revolution that threatened to obliterate the existing social structure.

The February and October Revolutions

In 1917, the first revolution began on 23 February (or 8 March outside Russia, since Russians were still using the old Julian calendar that was thirteen days behind the Gregorian calendar used in the rest of Europe) as a result of the bread riots in Petrograd. The rioters were joined by striking factory workers, and when the Tsar ordered the use of force to end the demonstrations, some of the troops refused to fire on unarmed crowds, ultimately inciting the entire Petrograd garrison to mutiny. The uncontrollable mob seized public buildings, police stations, and arsenals, and when Nicholas II still refused to grant a constitutional monarchy, instead sending more troops to quell the rebellion, the Duma and senior leaders of the army were convinced that his time was up. The Tsar eventually abdicated when factions of the RSDLP, along with the socialists and a few republicans, tightened the noose around the monarchists in what has come to be known as the bourgeois-democratic revolution in Russia. With the Tsar's abdication, the Russian monarchy came to an end. The Duma, already weakened by repeated Tsarist interventions, struggled to take control, and the people's aspirations for a democratic republic with an elected Parliament only got as far as the institution of a liberal provisional government. In July 1917, Alexander Kerensky, a socialist, became the prime minister. However, within months the provisional government was overthrown, this time by the Bolsheviks. One should not forget that World War I was still raging at this time.

The foremost reason behind the provisional government's failure was the requirement that it share power with the Petrograd Soviet—an elected committee of workers' representatives that attempted to rule the city. As the Soviet had the support of the soldiers, the provisional government could not rely on their support in case of an uprising. The government also delayed elections to the Constituent Assembly under the pretext of Russia's involvement in World War I. Meanwhile, to foment further confusion within Russia—especially once the provisional government's failures had become clear to its external enemies—Germany allowed Lenin to travel back to his motherland. After his return in April 1917, Lenin directly took on the provisional government, attacking its failures to implement land reforms, control inflation, and negotiate Russia's exit from the attritional world war. In his *April Theses* (1917), he urged the Bolsheviks to withdraw their support from the government and agitate instead for bestowing all land on the peasants, giving workers control of the factories, and for food to be made available at cheaper prices. The provisional government, which was also at loggerheads with the Bolsheviks, accused Lenin of being a German spy. In July and August, the government attempted to forcibly silence the Bolsheviks' anti-war propaganda and their demand to hand all power over to the Soviets. But public opinion swung against the war and in favour of the Bolsheviks, the only party to openly support a separate peace with Germany.

Although the term 'Bolshevik' means 'majority', the group was actually in a minority in the country as a whole, winning in October 1917 a majority only insofar as the crucial Moscow and Petrograd Soviets were concerned. With that majority, Lenin took the crucial decision to seize power. He was supported by Leon Trotsky and Joseph Stalin (who was later to expel Trotsky from not only the party but also the country, and subsequently would successfully plot his assassination). Since Lenin was again forced underground, Trotsky, Stalin, and Yakov Sverdlov led the masses, the Bolshevik Red Guards, and troops loyal to the Petrograd Soviet on the night of 25–26 October to assume control of important government buildings and storm the Winter Palace. Ministers of the provisional government—except Kerensky, who managed to escape—were arrested and the government overthrown in an almost bloodless coup. Tsar Nicholas II and his Romanov family were assassinated on

17 July 1918, and with the Mensheviks and Social Revolutionaries walking out of the Second Congress of Soviets, Lenin and the Bolsheviks were free to set up a new Soviet government called the Council of People's Commissars, or *Sovnarkom*. However, huge problems awaited the minority government.

The Revolution after October 1917

The Bolsheviks now had to gain a majority in elected councils throughout the country, negotiate a separate peace with Germany, and finally, salvage the already shattered economy while simultaneously delivering on their promises of land for the peasants and factories for the workers.

The first problem was dealt with swiftly, albeit undemocratically. After nationalising all land, banks, large factories, and mines, legitimising workers' control over factories, cancelling all debts incurred by the tsarist and provisional governments, and granting the right to self-determination to every nationality, Lenin was certain that the entire population would vote for the Bolsheviks. The Bolsheviks also set up a new security police force—the Extraordinary Commission for Combating Sabotage and Counter-Revolution or *Cheka*. Lenin allowed elections, and to his consternation, the Bolsheviks won only 175 seats out of 700, while the Social Revolutionaries won 370. Lenin used the Red Guards to dispense with the Constituent Assembly—justifying his actions as the highest form of democracy, since the Bolsheviks were the only party who had knowledge of the aspirations of workers, whom no other elected body could represent. Thereafter, the *Sovnarkom* replaced the Constituent Assembly, and the resentment that resulted from this imperiousness led to the civil war.

The solution to the second problem adversely impacted Russian morale. Trotsky tried in vain to persuade the Germans to moderate their demands in lieu of an armistice. What the Treaty of Versailles would later become for the Germans, the Treaty of Brest-Litovsk became for the Russians in March 1918. Russia lost Poland and the East European territories, along with Ukraine, Georgia, and Finland. It also lost a third of its farmlands, a third of its population, two-thirds of its coal mines, and half of its heavy industries. This reinforced Bolshevik anti-incumbency, especially given Lenin's insensitivity towards such heavy losses. Lenin, as a firm believer in permanent revolution, was hopeful that when the Soviet experiment succeeded, the rest of Europe would encounter a domino effect, that is, European countries would become communist one after another. Since Russian agents would lead and successfully foment revolution in the rest of Europe, that domino effect would reintegrate the lost territories with the motherland. However, after Brest-Litovsk, a civil war in Russia became inevitable.

The Bolsheviks dealt simultaneously with external and internal enemies. While Brest-Litovsk took Russia out of the war, internally the Bolsheviks were resorting to large-scale violence to silence their detractors. Lenin ordered the 'liquidation' of *kulak*s or the well-off peasants, accusing them of hoarding foodgrains, which in turn caused shortages and inflation. Moreover, the Social Revolutionaries were undermining Brest-Litovsk, and embarked on a campaign of terror that elicited a violent response. Although Lenin widened Marx's understanding of proletarian revolution by including the peasantry in the state-in-transition, he overestimated the impact that the October Revolution had on European states. These states showed not the remotest sympathy towards the nascent socialist state, nor did they attempt to follow its path. Counter-revolutionary forces challenged the Bolsheviks, from both inside and outside. The Red Army, now under the leadership of Commissar Trotsky, was compelled to unleash the 'Red Terror', especially after a failed assassination attempt on Lenin. Thousands of people deemed counter-revolutionary by the Bolsheviks were either arrested or executed—including the former Tsar and his family. Diseases raged and many in the countryside who opposed the Bolsheviks were deliberately starved to death. Finally, the White Army, or those loyal to the Romanovs and the aristocracy, gathered international support from Russia's former World War I allies to put an end to the Red Terror.

The ensuing civil war (1917–22) in Russia was fought between the Whites—which included ex-tsarist officers, Mensheviks, and Social Revolutionaries—and the Red Army under Trotsky, who ran the campaign from his mobile headquarters in an armour-plated train. The masses, who did not want to restore the monarchy but to ensure democratic transition in Russia, joined in the war. But power flows not from sentiments but from discipline, propaganda, and the barrel of the gun. Despite international support, and even after the end of World War I, the Whites lost decisively. As their supporters withdrew, the White Army was surrounded and slaughtered. In 1920, Polish and

French troops invaded Ukraine, and by the Treaty of Riga (1920) parts of it, along with White Russia, were ceded to the victors. Eight million people died in the civil war, including those targeted by the Reds and Whites, those killed in anti-Semitic pogroms, and those who died from starvation and epidemics.

The civil war ushered in irreversible changes in Soviet life. The Whites were branded as comprador bourgeoisie or those who collaborated with foreign capitalists for their own gain. To deal with them, Lenin had instituted war communism, or a series of decrees for economic centralisation, which later had disastrous effects. The Bolsheviks portrayed themselves as nationalist forces fighting against foreigners. Politically, the regime became even more repressive and militarised—factionalism was banned in 1921 in the name of democratic centralism, and one-third of the old guards were 'purged' for opposing Lenin's policies. The 'Politburo' or executive committee of the Bolshevik party came to rule in the name of the party and the people.

And yet, at the height of the civil war, Lenin instituted the capitalist-leaning New Economic Policy (NEP) to bring about a bourgeois-democratic revolution in Russia. Various Bolshevik old guards were opposed to this. Thus, complexity and confusion were the perennial hallmarks of Soviet communism. Lenin tried to justify his measures by arguing in 1919 that socialism cannot be achieved in a backward culture, which had to be changed by educating the masses. Under NEP, peasants were allowed to keep their surplus produce after taxation, private trade was resumed, and some small industries were restored to private ownership. Foreign investment was encouraged to rejuvenate the Russian economy. However, NEP was a temporary compromise; Lenin believed that when workers were in the majority and proletarian culture could flourish, the Bolshevik Party would act as their vanguard and seize control of all means of production for the common enjoyment. Lenin's dream was cut short by his untimely death in early 1924. At the time of his death, the revolutionary dictatorship of the proletariat and peasants was nowhere in evidence, the only legitimate political party was that of the Bolsheviks, and it was up to Stalin, who assumed power by mercilessly circumventing the old guards, and his theory of 'socialism in one country' to build the world's first communist state in his own image—which sometimes mirrored, sometimes contradicted, and often surpassed his predecessors in ideology, as well as in cruelty.

The Rise and Fall of Fascism in Italy

The political ideology of fascism emerged first in Italy at around the same time that Lenin's Red Army was grappling with Russia's multiple problems. Eventually, fascism exerted considerable influence in European politics. Fascism is based on the repudiation and persecution of opposing political forces, and advocates an ideologically driven political life involving unflinching reverence towards the leader. This 'cult of personality' is the hallmark of fascism, in which the political leader is deliberately presented to the people as a great person, worthy of reverence, public admiration, and continuous mass support, even in the face of stark failures. Its mechanisms and benefits for modern times were first identified by Benito Mussolini, the founder of Italy's National Fascist Party (NFP). Mussolini's methods to put in place a personality cult influenced various dictators and their respective regimes: from Stalin in the Soviet Union, Adolf Hitler in Germany, and Francisco Franco in Spain, to more contemporary regimes like Romania under Nicolae Ceaușescu.

The basic difference between Soviet communism and Italian fascism was ideological: the former leant towards the left, while the latter subscribed to an extreme right-wing totalitarianism. However, both exploited the personality cult to great initial success. Soviet communism succeeded by portraying the infallibility of Stalin, under whose watch the worst forms of political violence were justified in the name of economic development. Similarly, Italian fascism began and ended with the personality cult built around Mussolini; however, it had failed even before the country was destroyed by its participation in World War II. The meaning of fascism and the context in which it arose will be discussed here, along with the impact it had on Italian political life. We shall finally study the role played by Italian fascism in the origins of World War II as its most terrible contribution to European affairs, one that ultimately led to its violent condemnation and abrupt demise.

The unification of Italy in 1870 did not bring about lasting peace and economic development. Its involvement in World War I adversely affected its economy and the Treaty of Versailles prevented it from accruing financial gains commensurate with its war efforts. After the failure of five successive governments, Mussolini, then a former socialist politician and journalist, launched the NFP in 1921, winning only thirty-five seats in the elections. However, Mussolini and his 50,000 Black Shirts (a fascist paramilitary group) marched on Rome, compelling the sympathetic King Victor Emmanuel III to invite him to form the government in October 1922. Mussolini's regime was far from totalitarian, as he lacked the courage to overthrow either the King or the Pope in Rome, eventually signing the Lateran Treaty in 1929. By this treaty, Mussolini recognised Vatican City as a sovereign state, paid the Pope a large sum of money as compensation for all his losses, accepted the Catholic faith as the official state religion, made religious instruction compulsory in all schools, and left the Church free to continue its spiritual mission without interference from the government. In return, the Pope promised not to interfere in politics. Bridging the rift between Church and State has been historically interpreted as Mussolini's most durable and noteworthy achievement. His foreign policy was also initially successful.

However, his 'corporate state' remained pro-rich, employing tools of propaganda to elicit the support of workers, even as the fascist party grew rich from the handsome donations made by industrialists. The inadequacies of this arrangement were revealed after Mussolini made the fatal mistake of joining World War II in support of Germany, despite knowing that Italy was neither militarily nor financially prepared for another war. After the British and American forces invaded Italy, Mussolini was deposed and arrested in July 1943. He was rescued by German forces from Gran Sasso d'Italia, and installed as a puppet ruler in northern Italy under German protection. During the final months of the war, he was captured by communist *partisans* and executed by a firing squad. His body was taken to Milan and strung up by the feet in a public display, an ignominious end to his twenty years of rule.

Fascism: Meaning and Background

Unlike communism, fascism was a practice that lacked a coherent theory. All theoretical criticism of fascism emerged after the fascists were overthrown; hence, its theoretical defence was practically absent. The word *fasces* meant a bundle of rods with a protruding axe, which symbolised the authority and power of the ancient Roman consuls. Before assuming power, the fascists were opposed to the monarchy, the Church, and big businesses. Fascism, as perceived and practised by

Mussolini, hinged on authoritarianism, single-party dominance, ultra-nationalism, economic autarky, militarism, and an extensive use of modern propaganda devices. It succeeded because of the disillusionment, frustration, and poverty of Italian citizens, who had not only been robbed of their rights by a succession of corrupt governments, but also faced mass extortion and injustice at the hands of the mafia. After the failure of sporadic attempts by leftist groups to launch a communist revolution, Mussolini began to attract widespread support because of his promise to provide strong leadership and effective governance. He became the hero for those who sought to prevent Italy from turning into another Russia. The rise of the fascists was aided by the lack of a united opposition and the sympathetic attitude of the King, and not least by Mussolini's ability to win popular support by portraying himself as a strong and decisive leader.

Mussolini in Power

At first, Mussolini was merely the prime minister of a coalition government, in which only four out of twelve ministers were fascist. His Black Shirts were legitimised as the National State Voluntary Militia (MVSN). After the promulgation of the Acerbo Law (1923),[1] election rules were changed to suit the needs of the fascists. Mass rigging and violence resulted in their re-election, this time with an overwhelming majority. With firm control over the state machinery, Mussolini began to de-legitimise every other political party. Along with persecuting the opposition, his regime enacted further changes to the Constitution, in order to make his position immune to challenges. Mussolini assumed the title of *Il Duce* or The Leader, the dictator of Italy.

Propaganda and censorship were extensively used to promote the Mussolini cult and to curb dissent. Education and employment policies became more centralised. The 'corporate state' became the hallmark of

---

[1]The Acerbo Law was an Italian electoral law proposed by Baron Giacomo Acerbo and passed by the Italian Parliament in November 1923. The purpose was to give Mussolini's fascist party a majority of deputies. The law was used only in the 1924 general election, which was the last competitive election held in Italy until 1946. See https://dbpedia.org/page/Acerbo_Law (accessed April 2025).

the fascist system. Mussolini claimed that it was designed to promote cooperation between employers and workers, and put an end to class warfare. Unions controlled by the fascists had the sole right to negotiate for the workers. Both unions and employers' associations were organised into corporations, and were expected to work together to settle disputes over pay and working conditions. Strikes and lockouts were disallowed. Workers were compensated for their loss of freedom, but only to some extent.

The common factor in Mussolini's domestic and foreign policies happened to be his disposition towards races. His government was not particularly racist to begin with, demonstrating only a mild form of discrimination towards the people in Italy's African territories—Abyssinia or modern-day Ethiopia, Libya, Eritrea, and Somalia. However, after joining the Rome–Berlin Axis in 1937, Mussolini quickly began to emulate Hitler's blatant anti-Semitism for tactical benefits. The two countries united quickly under the common banner of fascism.

Mussolini's foreign policy before World War II was a mixture of adventurism and caution. In 1923, Italy was involved in the Corfu incident[2] and occupied Fiume. Under fascist rule, Italy attended the Locarno Conference in 1925 and cultivated friendly relations with Greece, Hungary, and Albania. Mussolini's regime shared a special relationship with Britain, and he even agreed to mediate between Hitler and Winston Churchill when the latter's forces were surrounded in Dunkirk during World War II. Italy was the second country (after Britain) to recognise the Soviet Union, and even sent forces to its frontier with Austria to protect it from Nazi invasion.

After joining the Axis Powers, Italy's foreign policy became more bellicose. Despite its involvement in the Abyssinian crisis since 1935—winning it decisively despite facing the League of Nations' economic sanctions—Mussolini sought more visible successes. Italy sent troops

---

[2]The Corfu incident of 1923 refers to a brief occupation of the Greek island of Corfu by Italian forces. In August 1923, Italians who were part of an international boundary delegation were murdered on Greek soil, leading Mussolini to order a naval bombardment of Corfu. After the Greeks appealed to the League of Nations, the Italians were ordered to evacuate, but Greece was forced to pay Italy an indemnity. See https://www.britannica.com/event/Corfu-incident (accessed April 2025).

and aid to Franco's regime during the Spanish Civil War (1936–39). Understanding that the French and the British were averse to war, Mussolini began offering support to Hitler's Germany. The Rome–Berlin Axis was followed by the Anti-Comintern Pact (1937), in which Italy, Germany, and Japan pledged themselves to unite against Bolshevism. Italy's participation in the Munich Agreement of 1938 greatly increased Mussolini's international prestige. However, with his ego satisfied, he ended up invading Albania, his long-term vassal state. Carried away by these successes, Mussolini hammered another nail in his coffin by signing the Pact of Steel (1939) with Germany, promising the latter full military support in case of war. Under the influence of Hitler, Mussolini consented to the Charter of Race (1938), which declared that Jews, Africans, and Arabs belonged to inferior races. Although this policy did not become popular among the general public, with the Pope being strongly opposed to it as well, Mussolini refused to renege, arguing instead that all Jews must be expelled from Europe. It was clear that by the beginning of World War II, he was fast becoming a sad caricature of Hitler (even though the latter had publicly acknowledged Mussolini as his mentor after becoming the German Chancellor).

The Decline of Italian Fascism

It must be emphasised that the Mussolini regime's acute militarism, and his lust for power and visible military glory, led to its downfall. The regime had shown initial promise: industrialism was encouraged; infrastructure developed; the lira underwent positive revaluation; land reforms were instituted by undermining the mafia; agricultural production increased under the 'battle for wheat' initiative; and birth rates revived with fewer work hours and more opportunities for leisure activities. However, the cardinal problems of the Italian economy remained virtually untouched. These included its perennial shortage of raw materials; the decline of pasture and arable lands after the 'battle for wheat' programme reserved these for cereal production; and finally, the lira's high rate of exchange, which inhibited Italian exports after the Great Depression of 1929. Mussolini's regime did nothing to prevent its citizens from becoming destitute. Its ultra-rightist policies also prevented social welfare, with no stable unemployment policy even during the Depression years.

Joining World War II was the immediate cause of Italian fascism's downfall. Although Mussolini continued to enjoy the support of the traditional elites—including the King and the Pope—and was hailed as infallible by the media, his decision to enter the war on Germany's side eventually became a costly mistake. The majority of Italians were averse to this. Italy also lacked the military equipment necessary to commit to a protracted war. Moreover, after the bombing of Pearl Harbour in 1941, he made a second fatal mistake by declaring war on the United States, a move which alienated him from bankers and industrialists dependent upon economic transactions with America. As for the general public, Mussolini had failed to convert them to his aims of European war and conquest. All the propaganda about reviving the glories of ancient Rome had failed to arouse any fighting spirit or military enthusiasm among people already suffering from penury. Mussolini grew increasingly insecure, physically unwell, and mentally unstable by the end of the war: many fascist leaders themselves realised the lunacy of trying to continue the war, but Mussolini refused to make peace because that would have meant deserting Hitler. Eventually, the Fascist Grand Council turned against Mussolini, and the King dismissed him. Many revisionist historians have tried to absolve Mussolini of his sins, often portraying him as an inspirational leader and orator. But his end in a Milan square reinforces his image as a man whose rabid ideology almost brought Italy and the rest of Europe to the brink of total destruction.

The Rise and Fall of Nazism in Germany

Nazism, or National Socialism, emerged in Germany as a variant of fascism with the transformation of the German Workers' Party (DAP) into the National Socialist German Workers' Party (NSDAP) in 1920. The Nazi Party emerged from the nationalist, racist, and populist para-militarism of the German Freikorps, which persecuted the country's communists after World War I. Under its founder Anton Drexler, and later Adolf Hitler, then an ex-lance corporal of the Bavarian Army, the party became an instrument for promoting *völkisch* nationalism, involving the racial persecution of Jews and other so-called 'non-Aryan' races. The addition of 'socialism' to its title was a mere gimmick, meant to lure workers away from the truly socialist parties. Nazism was a reaction against the failures of Germany in World War I, its humiliation at the hands of the victors in Versailles, and its pathetic economic and military condition after the war. Akin to Mussolini, Hitler effectively cultivated his own personality cult, promoting himself as the only person worthy of rebuilding his country into a virile and opulent *reich* ('realm' or 'state') that would endure for millennia. Although Hitler's regime could boast of tangible successes before World War II, its militarism and racism soon led to its destruction, along with that of Germany, the rest of Europe, and other parts of the world. Its domestic policy was based on the propagation of Aryan superiority and exclusivity, totalitarianism, autarky, and a marked hostility towards socialism. In the international sphere as well, the Nazi regime exuded belligerence, militarism, and exclusivity, committing some of the worst brutalities in recorded history, all in the name of racial purity and the struggle for resources and living space.

Hitler and his Nazis came to power by effectively exploiting the weaknesses of the Weimar Republic (1919–33) and by promising an alternative that would enable Germany to regain its former glory. The Treaty of Versailles of 1919 had already crushed Germany under the weight of reparations. It lost 10 per cent of its territory, all its overseas colonies, almost 13 per cent of its population, 16 per cent of its coal, and 48 per cent of its iron industries. It was also forced to limit its armed forces to a bare minimum, in the hope that this would disable it from launching another world war. The Nazis used extensive propaganda to educate the masses about the harsh terms of the treaty. Hitler's personality cult became the pivot on which Nazism revolved, as during the entire period he was projected as the leader, *Der Führer*, who could rebuild the country and avenge its humiliation. We shall now discuss the background to the Hitler phenomenon, followed by his rise to power and the domestic and foreign policies of the Nazis until the beginning of World War II.

Weimer Germany: The Launching Pad of the Nazis

From its inception, the Weimar Republic was mired in socio-political and economic problems. In 1919, Germany was on the verge of bankruptcy following the enormous reparations and war debts that it was required to pay. Hyperinflation was rampant and the value of the Papiermark fell rapidly.[3] To make matters worse, Germany lost its most important industrial belt, the Ruhr, to the French in 1923. Germans began to live off American loans equivalent to £40 million, granted by the Dawes Plan of 1924, which aimed to ease Germany's economic burdens by adjusting the terms of reparation payments. This, however, was discontinued after the Great Depression of 1929. In Germany, Chancellor Brüning's government reduced social services and unemployment benefits, rendering huge masses of Germans homeless and destitute. On the political front, the Weimar government failed to recognise the democratic aspirations of the masses, and the political parties had very little experience of operating democratically. The government could also not contain the massive outbreaks of violence organised regularly by the Nazis and their followers. The Spartacist uprising (a communist coup) was crushed with the help of the Freikorps, and the rightist Kapp Putsch (1920) and Beer-Hall Putsch (1923) were failed attempts by the Nazis to seize power. Hitler was sentenced to imprisonment, during which time he wrote his autobiography-cum-manifesto, *Mein Kampf* (1925), underlining his ideology and vision for Germany. After Hitler's release, his private army, the *Sturmabteilung* or SA, the Brown Shirts, regularly clashed with the communists and government forces, and used intimidation, extortion, and methods of torture to realise its cherished dream of installing Hitler as the Chancellor. The SA later gave rise to the *Schutzstaffel* or the SS, Hitler's terrifying paramilitary force.

But it was not entirely intimidation that brought the Nazis to power in 1933. They were democratically elected, and this fact still inspires awe and disbelief amongst political experts and historians. How was it that an entire nation was hoodwinked into believing that a regime so brutal, discriminatory, and intolerant would re-establish German glory? This question has no single answer. In reality, the Germans were enamoured of Hitler's charisma and audacity. The Nazis provided an alternative to the corruption, decadence, and weakness of successive governments until 1933. Recent archival scholarship has also revealed that some

[3]The currency of the Weimar Republic, till 1923, was the Papiermark. Due to hyper-inflation, it was replaced by the Rentenmark in 1923, and then by the Reichsmark in 1924. The Deutschemark became the official currency of West Germany from 1948 until 1990, and later of unified Germany from 1990 until the adoption of the Euro in 2002.

sections of Germans were supportive of Hitler's race theory, as well as his marked intolerance and authoritarianism. There is no doubt that the rise of Hitler and the Nazis, fostered by the economic crisis, was one of the most important causes of the downfall of the Weimar Republic: in the elections of July 1932, with the number of unemployed standing at over six million, the Nazis became the largest single party, winning 230 seats out of 608.

For Hitler and his Nazis, National Socialism was an ideology or an action-related set of principles, which gradually became a way of life dedicated to the rebirth of the nation. It was more totalitarian in organisation and practice than Italian fascism and equally militaristic: every facet of personal and political life was to be organised on a military footing. The race theory was cardinal to Nazism. Through such exclusivism, the Nazis promised national unity, prosperity, and full employment, not least, to avenge the country's humiliation at Versailles.

Although the Nazis won the 1932 elections, President Hindenburg refused to invite Hitler to form the government, considering him an uncouth political upstart. In the end, it was political intrigue that brought the Nazis to power. A small clique of right-wing politicians, armed with support from the *Reichswehr* (the Weimar army), decided to bring Hitler into a coalition government with the Nationalists. As Chancellor of the coalition government, he insisted on another general election in the hope of winning a substantial majority for the Nazis. The election of March 1933 encountered massive violence: Hitler's SA and SS attempted, this time with the help of the police, to whip up a Nazi majority. The Reichstag fire, an alleged conspiracy by the Nazis (which they blamed on the communists), enabled Hitler to manipulate nationalist sentiments in his favour. However, the Nazis failed to win majority seats and remained dependent upon other right-wing nationalists. The threat of a communist uprising gave Hitler enough space to persuade the ailing President Hindenburg into signing an emergency legislation aimed at giving Hitler sweeping powers as Chancellor. This came to be known as the Enabling Law (1933), which became the legal basis of the Nazi regime: Hitler could now introduce laws without the approval of the Reichstag for the next four years, could ignore the constitution, and could sign agreements with foreign countries. The Weimar Republic came to an end after this swift legislation.

National Socialism in Power

After the Enabling Law was put in place, Hitler began sidelining the Chancellery and establishing a Nazi police state. The policy of *Gleichshaltung* or 'enforced coordination' turned Germany into a police state that subscribed to a virulent form of fascism and anti-Semitism. The country began to be run by Hitler's Gestapo or secret police; a single-party political system was created; civil services were purged of Jews, who were then systematically divested of their businesses, homes, and dignity; trade unions were abolished and replaced by the Nazi Labour Front; education and entertainment were closely monitored by the Minister of Propaganda, Joseph Goebbels, and his staff; religion was state-controlled; and autarky was prioritised. The police, aided by the SS and the Gestapo, worked to prevent all open opposition to the regime. The law courts were not impartial: the so-called 'enemies of the state' rarely received a fair trial, and the concentration camps introduced by Hitler in 1933 were fast filling up. Before 1939, some of the main concentration camps were Dachau near Munich, Buchenwald near Weimar, and Sachsenhausen near Berlin. They contained Jews, homosexuals, and political prisoners: the communists, Social Democrats, Catholic priests, and Protestant pastors.

By 1935, Hitler's anti-Semitic paranoia led him to claim that there was a global Jewish/communist plot to wrest political control from his regime. He gave legal status to the ongoing persecution through the Nuremberg Laws of 1935, which deprived Jews of their German citizenship, forbade them to marry non-Jews to preserve the purity of the Aryan race, and ruled that even a person with only one Jewish grandparent must be classed as a Jew. The laws led inexorably to *Kristallnacht* or the 'Night of Broken Glass' in November 1938, when a vicious attack on Jewish synagogues and other Jewish properties throughout the whole country was carried out by a coalition of the Gestapo, the SS, and SA. Even in the midst of World War II, Nazi Germany was not deterred from carrying out the 'Final Solution' or the mass extermination of Jews, both within the country and in its occupied territories. The Holocaust, as this came to be known, claimed the lives of six million Jews and five million non-Jewish victims in the most systematic and shocking pogrom the world has ever witnessed.

Nazism until World War II

There were two broad reasons for Hitler managing to lead his country into a global catastrophe like World War II: *first*, his regime successfully curbed dissent and intimidated his detractors; and *second*, his domestic and foreign policies until the war broke out in 1939 were relatively successful, thereby garnering huge support from the German masses. Nazism's innate militarism and its cherished desire to create a strong German military presence in the world, coupled with its zest to avenge the country's shame in Versailles, impelled Hitler to order a massive rearmament drive. The terms of the Versailles Treaty were disparaged, and this drive ensured that Germany reached full employment within a few years. It is true that Hitler genuinely tried to make life better for the average German: unemployment was eliminated in Nazi Germany; agricultural self-sufficiency was achieved; workers benefitted from government schemes and recorded increased productivity; German industrialists and businessmen were supportive of the regime's policies vis-à-vis communists; and, most importantly for Hitler, the *Reichswehr* began to treat him as their messiah, especially after the Röhm Putsch or the 'Night of the Long Knives' in 1934. In this purge, Hitler used the SS to execute Ernst Rohm and his SA, who were gradually becoming critical of his regime and were seeking admission into the *Reichswehr*. This move wiped out all opposition to Hitler within the Nazi Party.

However, critics have claimed that it was Hitler's domestic policies that gave rise to his bellicose foreign policy, which was initially very successful. His idea of the *Lebensraum* or the 'struggle for German living space' involved not only the emptying of Jewish apartments throughout Germany, but also served as a prelude to the invasions of Eastern Europe. This policy, coupled with marked hatred for the Jews, Poles, Slavs, and Russians, meant that Hitler was only waiting to invade these countries once his economy and weapons production were stabilised. However, the policy of war-preparedness was also unsuccessful; Hitler had not anticipated that the British and the French would declare war on Germany after he invaded Poland with guarantees from the Soviet Union vide the secret Nazi-Soviet Non-Aggression Pact of 1939. Concomitant with an increased focus on rearmament, there were shortages of food and other necessities, while an increase in wages entailed longer working hours.

In the foreign policy domain, Hitler successfully destroyed the Stresa Front by first signing a naval agreement with Britain, then by recapturing the Ruhr from the French, and finally, by pressuring Mussolini's Italy into joining the Rome–Berlin Axis in 1937. Although *Anschluss* (Nazi plans to integrate Austria with Germany) failed, Hitler was able to breach the Versailles Treaty by reintroducing conscription, a move which elicited no response from the British and the French. It was clear by now that Hitler would exploit his enemies' policy of appeasement. He launched a successful propaganda campaign in Sudetenland and annexed parts of Czechoslovakia in the process. This led to the Munich Conference (1938), which legitimised the annexation in the hope that Hitler would refrain from further aggression. However, Britain and France received a rude shock when Hitler—despite continuous pressure from their governments—invaded Lithuania and Poland, after demanding the return of Danzig and a road and railway across the corridor linking East Prussia with the rest of Germany. This led to World War II, as Britain and France upheld their commitments to Poland and declared war on Germany. The war claimed the lives of seventy-five million people, and became the most tangible and long-lasting bequest of the racist, militarist, and intolerant Nazi regime to Europe and the rest of the world.

WORLD WAR II (1939–45)

The evolution of international politics in the interwar period, as influenced by the economic constraints of the day and authoritarian nationalist chauvinism, was a perilous mix, leading to inevitable confrontations. Although Germany under Adolf Hitler was held primarily responsible for the second great conflict of the century, a number of other factors contributed to the clash among the major powers of the day.

The Great Depression of 1929 led to the collapse of international trade as barriers were erected to protect local industries. Banks failed and economies shrank with the falling prices and demand, leading to unemployment and homelessness. It is said that World War I created the economic disruptions that brought in the Great Depression, and the Depression in its turn led to World War II as it allowed the rise of the Nazi Party under Hitler on its promise of revitalisation. Access to raw materials and resources became necessary at this point, and while the other major European powers had their colonies, Japan, Germany, and Italy sought to annex territories to compensate for their lack of resources.

The Treaty of Versailles, signed at the end of World War I, itself carried the seeds of future conflict in its attempt to constrain Germany into a state of insignificance. Overturning the Treaty became the national goal for Germany under authoritarian rule. The surrender of all German colonies as mandated by the League of Nations, the return of Alsace-Lorraine to France, the cession of other territories, strict demilitarisation and reparation provisions imposed upon Germany—in short, the treaty provisions were harsh enough to sustain peace for a long time. Germany always regarded the treaty as unfair, and it was only a matter of time before it tried to gain back the power it had enjoyed before World War I.

Germany increasingly viewed itself as a young, energetic state destined to grow into a great empire. Karl Haushofer, a noted author on geopolitics, believed that after World War I, Germany was spatially restricted and struggled badly as the available area it was allowed was not enough to sustain the German population. His ideas are dispersed in his writings and lectures, but he is mostly credited with the concept of the *Lebensraum* (living space), which was later included in Hitler's autobiography. The plot suggested that Germany had to acquire more living space by vastly expanding its territory. This idea of living space was echoed by Hitler, who emphasised that an adequately large space ensured freedom of existence for a nation, and promised that Germany would become a world power one day. This meant occupying areas of German interest and bringing them under one flag, including the territories lost after World War I, in order to establish a civilisation in its best and purest form. As previously discussed, this racist overtone of the regime was responsible for the atrocities committed on people and the massacre of 'the impure' in concentration camps during the war.

The rise of militaristic totalitarianism brought like-minded states closer. In the 1930s, Japan invaded Manchuria (1931) and Italy seized Ethiopia (1935–36), and by 1936–37 the Rome–Berlin axis had turned into the coalition of the Axis Powers of Japan, Germany, and Italy. German aggression on Austria in March 1938, on Sudetenland in October 1938, and Czechoslovakia in March 1939 and Italy's annexation of Albania in April 1939 went effectively unopposed by the other major powers.

If, on the one hand, the rise of militarism is regarded as a vital cause of World War II, the policy of appeasement adopted by the major powers at the time was equally responsible. In the Munich Agreement of 1938, the United Kingdom and France allowed Germany to annex Sudetenland, much to the disappointment of Czechoslovakia. Anxious to avoid a military confrontation with Germany, the UK and France advised Czechoslovakia to submit to the prescribed annexations. In August 1939, Germany signed a non-aggression pact with the Soviet Union under Stalin, who sought to broker peaceful terms with Germany, and this allowed Germany to overrun Poland without opposition. The pact was, however, nullified when Germany invaded the Soviet Union in 1941.

Finally, almost all the major peace efforts—the Washington Conference of 1921, which sought to limit competition among the great powers in naval warships; the Locarno Conference of 1925 for territorial settlements; and the Kellogg-Briand Pact of 1928 that renounced war as a state policy—failed. Due to a lack of effective enforcement mechanisms, none of the commendable intentions declared in the conferences could materialise. A glaring example of this failure was the League of Nations, which was established in 1920 to primarily bring about disarmament and prevent further wars, and ensure collective security and a peaceful settlement of disputes. The League operated on the principle of unanimity in a fractious world, and disagreements among members prevented it from applying sanctions on the nations charged with aggression. Members-states also deserted the League whenever convenient to avoid its strictures or escape being censured. The League came to an end with the onset of World War II.

In September 1939, Germany invaded Poland. Committing themselves to protecting Poland, the British and the French declared war on Germany. The Soviets invaded Poland as well, and the country came under the occupation of both Germany and the Soviet Union. In 1940, Germany moved towards Denmark and Norway and attacked France. Italy entered the war and the conflict began to spread to the colonies in Asia and Africa. Greece was invaded, as was Yugoslavia. While the Soviets established control over the Baltic states, in 1941 Germany invaded Soviet Union and overran these areas. In December, Japan bombed Pearl Harbour and brought the United States into the war. Thereafter, the war between the Axis and the Allied Powers (comprising the UK, France, the US, and the Soviet Union) raged across Europe, Asia, and Africa. The Allies invaded Italy in late 1943 and by mid-1944, Rome had come under their control. Subsequently, the Allied troops liberated Paris. New offensives were launched against Germany and in May 1945, Germany surrendered to the Allied Powers. In August 1945, the United States dropped atomic bombs on the Japanese cities of Hiroshima and Nagasaki, forcing Japan to surrender as well.

Contrary to the popular conception that war begins with border clashes and then gradually escalates, the German lightning war (*blitzkrieg*) began with massive offensive operations by the Nazis. Quick and deep penetration through coordinated tank attacks, a motorised artillery and infantry along with an air force, and the speed and superiority of German firepower took everyone by surprise. *Blitzkrieg* accounts for Germany's initial successes, but the overall balance was heavily in favour of the combined strength and resources of the Allied Powers, leading to the ultimate surrender of Germany.

The Consequences

Millions of people lost their lives and were displaced in the course of the war, and many countries were devastated. The Allied Powers instituted War Crime Tribunals to punish the people responsible for launching this aggressive war and for the atrocities committed on civilians. The Nuremberg and Tokyo trials handed out punishments to those found guilty. Germany was divided into two: western Germany came under the occupation of the US, UK, and France, while eastern Germany remained under the Red Army. Subsequently, two sovereign states—East Germany and West Germany—emerged. However, the war led to far-reaching changes that transformed the configurations of global politics.

World War II brought to an end the European dominance of international politics, since the major European states were all too weak to exercise control over global geopolitics. The vacuum that was created was filled by two powerful states, the US and the Soviet Union. European states soon became either dependent on, or subservient to, these two superpowers. An era of intense competition soon began between the two superpowers, as they sought to expand their respective spheres of influence. Europe was soon divided, as military alliances were formed under the leadership of both powerful nations. In the absence of a direct military clash, the hostile relationship between the two became known as the 'Cold War', which continued for almost forty-five years until the disintegration of the Soviet Union.

The end of World War II not only heralded the end of dictatorships in Italy and Germany, but with the fall of fascism and Nazism as political ideologies, also left the field open for a contest between communism as advocated by the Soviet Union and capitalism in the form of the liberal democracy propagated by the United States. This ideological contest was an essential component of the Cold War.

As the war weakened the European colonial masters, it became easier for their colonies to assert their self-determination and seek eventual independence. The process of decolonisation that began gave birth to a number of independent states in Asia and Africa, which were mostly backward and underdeveloped. Together known as the 'Third World', these newly independent states sought to build their national identity and added a new dimension to international politics.

The lessons learnt from the failure of the League of Nations had equipped the states to develop a better world organisation for peace. This took the form of the United Nations, which was established in October 1945. The principle of unanimity was discarded in favour of majority decisions, and special care was taken to make the United Nations the hub of international cooperation, with universal membership and collective obligations.

However, the period of the Cold War was not free from tension, conflict, and power politics. With the introduction of nuclear weapons in 1945, the fear of global annihilation loomed large, and with time, new issues of development and security emerged that gave the post-war decades a distinct form and identity.

8

Conflicts and Crises in International Relations

Anindya Jyoti Majumdar

Two devastating World Wars in the twentieth century provided the impetus for meaningful international cooperation to avoid any recurrence of such massive armed conflicts in the future. The Charter of the United Nations, established at the end of World War II, emphasised the peaceful settlement of disputes among nation-states. However, conflicts and crises frequently occurred in subsequent decades, although the nature and patterns of armed conflict changed over time. As World War II came to an end in 1945, the dominance of the European colonial masters, who had suffered badly during the war, over international politics had weakened. The end of European dominance created a power vacuum. Two rival superpowers, the United States and the Soviet Union, emerged in its place and aspired for a leadership role, seeking to expand their power and influence over the world.

Since the two competitors were apprehensive of each other's intensions and were guided by opposing exclusivist political ideologies—capitalism and socialism—their rivalry took the form of a hostile relationship. Obviously, the fear of a possible nuclear war that could result in the mutual destruction of both parties restricted both states, and the United Nations Organization (UNO), despite its limitations, exercised to a certain extent a moral force upon the war-mongering. Nevertheless, the post-World War II period was marked by a hostile relationship between the two superpowers, and in the absence of a direct military clash between the two, came to be known as the

Cold War. This adversarial relationship led each state to adopt measures that could potentially injure the interests of the other, in an attempt to contain the influence of the rival while striving to increase its own hold on global affairs.

THE GENESIS OF THE COLD WAR

As World War II drew to an end, differences developed between the two principal victors over the fate of some of the countries liberated during the war. Soviet Premier Joseph Stalin sought to establish a Soviet sphere of influence by installing friendly communist regimes in Eastern Europe, in order to secure itself against any potential threat from European powers in the future. This process, however, ended up posing a threat to the countries in West Europe. Throughout 1946–47, the mutual distrust increased and the West European states, apprehensive of a probable Soviet invasion, began depending on the United States for security. In 1946, in Fulton, Missouri, Winston Churchill, the former British Prime Minister, remarked that an 'iron curtain' had descended across Europe, effectively dividing it into two blocs.

George F. Kennan, a diplomat in the US Embassy in Moscow, assessed the motivations behind Soviet behaviour and sent a long telegram to Washington in February 1946. He observed that a sense of insecurity could trigger an aggressive Soviet foreign policy, and the US response should be a long-term, patient, yet firm and vigilant containment of Russian expansionist tendencies. Kennan's ideas were published anonymously in *Foreign Affairs* as an article titled 'The Sources of Soviet Conduct'. The article was merely signed 'X', and became popular as the 'X Article' that propounded the policy of containment of the Soviet Union. This was made official as President Harry Truman, in March 1947, committed the United States to the support of 'free peoples' who were resisting attempted subjugation (ostensibly by the Soviets). From then onwards, the US became the champion of democracy worldwide, supporting any movement anywhere against the Soviets. The Truman Doctrine was followed by the Marshall Plan in June 1947, which aimed to rebuild the heavily damaged economies of Europe. These were viewed as efforts to curtail Soviet influence in Europe.

In 1949, the North Atlantic Treaty Organization (NATO), a military alliance, was formed, which crystallised security links between North

America and West Europe. In fact, by this time the idea of containing Soviet expansionism had become the cornerstone of US foreign policy. The early 1950s saw a number of alliances being formed: the ANZUS (Australia, New Zealand and United States Security Treaty) in 1951; the South East Asian Treaty Organization (SEATO 1954–77); and the Central Treaty Organization (CENTO 1955–79).

It is interesting to note that in November 1946, a long telegram arrived in Washington from Moscow, sent by Soviet Ambassador Nicolai Novikov. Novikov observed that the American foreign policy reflected the imperialist tendency of American monopolistic capitalism, which sought world supremacy. This provided a justification to the Soviet policy of opposing US economic imperialism in order to promote international revolution and world communism. Fearing American designs to destabilise the Soviet Union, the Stalin regime became increasingly repressive within the Soviet Union and tightened its control over Eastern Europe. It pressured East European countries to reject the Marshall Plan and launched an Economic Recovery Programme. In 1947, the Molotov Plan was announced, to offer aid to Communist countries. In 1955, the Warsaw Treaty Organization, popularly known as the Warsaw Pact, came into being, formalising the military alliance between the Soviet Union and its East European partners.

The genesis of the Cold War has been interpreted from different perspectives. Pro-American interpretations consider it a consequence of Soviet expansionism. Pro-Soviet explanations, on the other hand, find fault with US economic imperialism, which believes that an America-dominated world order is necessary for its continued economic expansion. Geopolitical writings view the relationship as a phase in the perpetual contest between continental and maritime powers. Those who explain it as a tussle between exclusivist ideologies observe that the Cold War actually began in 1917 when Tsarist Russia turned Communist; it took the US a long time to even recognise this. They also state that both parties suffered from a mirror image syndrome, that is, they viewed others as the opposites of their own selves, and responded in a similar manner that only fuelled the rivalry. In truth, a combination of factors shaped the Cold War, central to which was the power transition after World War II and the perception of mutual threat, which propelled the two superpowers into a global competition in order to protect and promote their own interests. While the contest was mainly over accumulating power, ideology was used to justify their policies. The constant effort to carve out separate zones of influence and seek allies created an increasingly divided world, led by two superpowers and their respective partners. Some newly-independent postcolonial nations, however, chose to remain non-aligned.

The Cold War saw the emergence of serious issues, the responses to which not only influenced trends in bilateral relations, but also substantially impacted the patterns of international politics. A few examples will help us understand these patterns and how the Cold War evolved.

THE DECADES OF CONFLICTS

Post-World War II politics led to the demarcation and delineation of separate spheres of influence. However, several points of friction remained, and the fate of Germany presented the first real crisis after World War II. Germany was occupied by the Red Army on the eastern side and Allied forces on the west. For administrative purposes, Germany was divided into zones, but it was to be treated as a single unit economically. The American, British, and French zones were fused into one, and parliamentary democracy was promoted in the west with commensurate economic assistance. These measures disturbed the Soviet plan to turn Germany into a weak communist state and extract huge reparations. When a new currency, the Deutschmark, was introduced in the western part, the Soviet Union blockaded Berlin in protest in 1948.

Berlin—the capital of Germany—was also divided into different administrative sectors, and was viewed as an enclave within the eastern part of Germany under Soviet occupation. The presence of Western officials within its zone was a matter of discomfort for the Soviets. With the objective of ousting them and integrating Berlin into the occupied zone, the Soviets cut road and rail routes and halted the supply of gas and electricity to the western sector of Berlin. A threat of force being used by either side was ever present, but none of the powers was willing to initiate an armed conflict. Ultimately, the Western powers resorted to airlifting provisions—food and fuel—to West Berlin. After 318 days (July 1948–May 1949), the Soviet Union relented and lifted the blockade. However, Germany was permanently divided. West Germany became the German Federal Republic, while the Soviet Union retained its hold over the German Democratic Republic in East Germany. West Germany joining NATO in 1955 was one of the factors behind the Soviet Union forming a military alliance, the Warsaw Pact, with its satellite states in Eastern Europe, which included East Germany. Berlin, too, remained divided, and in 1961 a wall was erected along the line of division by the Soviet Union to stop migrants from both the East and the West using Berlin as a gateway. It was only at the end of the Cold War that Germany was united again, and the dismantling of the Berlin Wall by the people in 1989 heralded a new beginning.

The Cold War took a new turn and went beyond Europe when China became a communist state in 1949. Post-World War II settlements were complicated further with the rise of new actors. After Japan's surrender in 1945, the United Nations assumed administrative responsibility and directed the Soviet Union to administer the northern half of Korea and the United States to administer the southern half. After Japan's withdrawal, the Korean peninsula was divided at the 38th parallel by the superpowers as a temporary arrangement, and a unified government was to be established. As it happened, a communist government was formed in North Korea while South Korea joined the so-called 'free world'. In the late 1940s, the superpowers mostly withdrew their forces and each government—in the North and the South—claimed to be the only legitimate government of Korea.

In June 1950, North Korea attacked South Korea in an attempt at a forced reunification. The US sent immediate naval and air support for South Korea, along with a UN resolution to repel the aggression. With this support, South Korea had almost overrun the North when communist China joined the war, driving the advancing forces out of North Korea. Military operations finally ended in a stalemate at the 38th parallel in 1951, and an armistice was negotiated and signed in 1953. Korea has remained divided ever since. In North Korea, however, the regime became increasingly authoritarian, with dynastic rulers growing into larger-than-life figures and exercising tight control over the state and its people. The present leader, Kim Jong Un, is better known for his propensity to flaunt nuclear weapons and issue threats to South Korea and its allies, the US and Japan, threatening war and instability in the region.

By the mid-1950s, US–Soviet relations seemed to be improving as the new Premier of the Soviet Union, Nikita Khrushchev, and US President Eisenhower brought a little warmth into their relations. However, they retained a tight hold on their lesser allies and steadfastly protected their respective spheres of influence. The process of decolonisation gave birth to a number of independent states, most of which chose to remain non-aligned. However, instead of maintaining true impartiality, many of these new nations showed an inclination towards either the Soviet Union or the US, which competed for their support. The new nations saw this as an opportunity to turn to a superpower to protect their own interests.

From 1954, under Gamal Nasser, Egypt experienced a distinct rejuvenation of Arab pride and called for a Middle East free from Western powers and Israel. A disapproving US retaliated by stopping funds for the Aswan Dam project on the Nile. Nasser turned to the Soviet Union, and an arms agreement followed. Emboldened, Nasser nationalised the Suez Canal in 1956. The Suez Canal links the Red Sea in the Indian Ocean with the Mediterranean Sea through Egypt, forming an important strategic waterway between Asia and Europe. This Canal had been under British control since 1887, and the nationalisation came as an affront to the West. In response, the United Kingdom and France, along with Israel—which was antagonistic towards Egypt after Nasser's anti-Israel rhetoric, and sought to exploit the opportunity that presented itself—attacked and defeated Egypt. This attack was condemned by developing countries as yet another colonial conspiracy, and the Soviet Union quickly moved to capitalise on this anti-West feeling. However, the United Nations negotiated a truce and ensured the withdrawal of the attacking forces. Egypt remained in control of the Suez Canal. The war achieved little and Arab-Israeli confrontations continued, culminating in the Six Day War in June 1967 in which Israel defeated the combined forces of Egypt, Syria, and Jordan and wrested control of the Gaza Strip from Egypt and the Jordanian area west of the Jordan river (commonly known as the West Bank territory), parts that now constitute the State of Palestine.

Although the Soviet Union acquired nuclear weapons in 1949, it did not have the requisite delivery vehicle to launch a nuclear attack on US territory. As it developed its space programme and, in 1957, launched the satellite *Sputnik* into orbit, it established its missile capability in the eyes of the world; this meant that the US was no longer a nuclear monopoly. However, while the Soviets needed long-range Inter-Continental Ballistic Missiles (ICBMs) to reach US territory, by 1960, the US had installed Intermediate Range Ballistic Missiles (IRBMs) in Turkey, Italy, and the United Kingdom, targeting the Soviet Union.

The IRBMs required less flight time to reach their targets. Communist Cuba allowed the Soviets to rectify this missile gap by installing nuclear missiles in Cuban territory.

In 1959, Fidel Castro seized power in Cuba, overthrowing the American-supported administration of General Batista, and accepted Soviet military protection in 1960. The rise of a communist state within 90 miles of the American mainland led to much consternation in the US. In 1961, the US Central Intelligence Agency (CIA) engineered the Bay of Pigs invasion into Cuba to dethrone Castro; however, this ended in a disaster for the invaders. In October 1962, a US reconnaissance aircraft took a photograph of a missile launching pad armed with a missile in Cuba, and what followed came to be known as the Cuban Missile Crisis.

As the matter came to the notice of US President John F. Kennedy, he took the call to quarantine Cuba and issued an ultimatum to the Soviet Union to cease further installations and withdraw, or else face adverse consequences. After a few nerve-wracking days when a nuclear war appeared imminent, Khrushchev relented and agreed to dismantle the missile sites on the assurance that the US would not attack Cuba and would withdraw its own missiles from Turkey.

The Cuban Missile Crisis led to the realisation that an all-out war involving nuclear weapons would result in mutually assured destruction, and must therefore be avoided. The relationship of nuclear deterrence was thereby firmly established. It was an adversarial relationship in which the fear of extreme damage as a result of a nuclear exchange prevented either party from initiating the first nuclear strike. The crisis was in a way instrumental in establishing a working relationship between the superpowers. In the years to come, they worked together to prevent the spread of nuclear weapons beyond the five permanent members of the UN Security Council and established the Nuclear Non-Proliferation Treaty (NPT) in 1968. This outcome disappointed Premier Mao of China, who disapproved of Khrushchev surrendering to American demands. However, the recognition of the principle of mutual coexistence led to a relaxation of tension between the superpowers in the 1970s, known as the period of détente in the history of the Cold War. Both superpowers had their own troubles to tackle in the 1960s, and sought to reduce the intensity of their rivalry.

In the late 1960s, the United States entered the war in Vietnam, which proved to be its undoing. Vietnam was a part of the French colony of Indochina, which had been under Japanese occupation during World

War II. As Japan was defeated in the War, France sought to reassert control over the area, but the French forces were defeated in a war of liberation led by Ho Chi Minh in 1954 at Dien Bien Phu. The negotiation that followed in Geneva divided Indochina into four countries: Cambodia, Laos, North Vietnam, and South Vietnam, divided at the 17th parallel. North Vietnam established a communist government under Ho Chi Minh, and the South became a client state of the United States that allowed successive rulers to follow repressive policies to quell any attempt to unify the two parts. South Vietnam's rebels began a guerrilla war for unification that was supported openly by the North, which the Americans viewed as yet another example of communist expansion, to be resisted by the free people.

In 1965, President Lyndon Johnson sent American troops to Vietnam, using as a pretext the Gulf of Tonkin incident in which a US naval ship was allegedly attacked by the North Vietnamese, and America's war against Vietnamese nationalism began. A war of attrition raged through the 1960s and the American forces experienced a series of debacles on unknown terrain. As more and more American soldiers lost their lives, public sentiment in America turned against the war, and several anti-war rallies were held. The United States, under President Richard Nixon, who came to power in 1969, looked for ways to extricate itself from the war. The war not only resulted in huge American casualties, but was also an enormous drain on the American economy. Nixon wanted to 'Vietnamize' the war through a gradual withdrawal of American troops and a huge supply of military provisions to the South Vietnam army. The war also resulted in distancing the Third World countries further and disrupting American relations with its allies. The United States had to ask the two communist countries of Soviet Union and China to exercise their influence and persuade North Vietnam to negotiate peace. Although intermittent peace talks began in 1969, the war continued through the early 1970s. The US exit from the war came in 1973 and in 1975, the South Vietnamese army was defeated by the North, and a united Vietnam came into being.

The Vietnam War resulted in a staggering number of Vietnamese casualties—from both the North and the South—and created an incalculable number of refugees. The immense physical destruction resulted in very low agricultural productivity. Soon Vietnam, facing serious economic constraints and with little assistance from the West, turned to the Soviet Union for aid and thereby strained its relations with

China, which had by the early 1970s detached from the Soviet Union and developed better relations with the United States.

In 1949, communist China had become a natural ally of the Soviet Union. However, after the death of Stalin in 1953, Mao Zedong saw himself as the rightful leader of world communism and developed serious differences with Khrushchev as the latter consolidated his position in the Soviet Union in 1956. The Soviet Union preferred a subservient ally and not a competitor, and Mao's criticism of Khrushchev and his policies led to animosity between the two communist states. The Soviet Union withdrew the promised economic and technical assistance to China and refused support during the India–China war of 1962. It also did not like China's growing influence over Albania and Mongolia, two of its erstwhile protégés. In the late 1960s, Mao's cultural revolution in China focussed on true communism, degrading 'Soviet revisionism' and 'socialist imperialism', and finally in 1969, Soviet and Chinese forces clashed over the control of several disputed islands along the Ussuri River. The estrangement of the two nations was now complete. On the other hand, the US warmed up to China and in 1972, President Nixon visited China, signifying a US–China rapprochement.

From Cold War to Détente, and the New Cold War

The 1970s saw a relaxation of tensions between the two superpowers. This period was known as *détente* in US–Soviet relations. By this time, the superpowers had agreed to a nuclear parity, acknowledging that a nuclear war would result in mutually assured destruction. Arms control was therefore given prominence and strategic (nuclear) arms limitation treaties (SALT I and SALT II, in 1972 and 1979, respectively) were negotiated, which imposed a ceiling on the number of missile launchers. The prohibition on the Anti-Ballistic Missile Defence (ABM) Treaty, along with the Prevention of Nuclear War Agreement (1973), were other important arms control measures.

West Germany, under Chancellor Willy Brandt, made overtures to the two countries in the early 1970s, which came to be known as eastern politics (*Ostpolitik*), and concluded non-aggression treaties with the Soviet Union, Poland, and East Germany. Such developments created a congenial environment for the Helsinki Process, which began with the 1975 Conference on Security and Cooperation in Europe (CSCE), and culminated in the Helsinki Final Act agreement. Emphasising that no European state border would be violated or altered by force, the conference *inter alia* encouraged trade and tourism between the Western and Eastern sectors of Europe, and allowed the movement of people among European states across the blocs.

However, the exchange of weapons and economic assistance between the superpowers and their respective allies beyond Europe continued, and the Soviets managed to gain an advantage in Angola, Somalia, and Mozambique. In 1979, the Soviet-supported Sandinistas came to power in Nicaragua, and the US intensified its support to the Contra rebels. However, that same year saw two other incidents that pushed the United States to take remedial measures, thereby disrupting the pattern of peaceful coexistence. The early years of the 1980s were marked by the New Cold War; the *détente*, as it appears, was short-lived.

Until almost the end of the 1970s, Iran, under the rule of Reza Shah Pahlavi, was close to the United States. The Shah was considered a friend of the United States in West Asia, who looked after American interests in the region. However, Iran was teetering on the brink of a civil war. In January 1979, the Shah fled the country and the exiled religious leader Ayatollah Khomeini returned to Iran in February. He had already proclaimed Western civilisation as antithetical to Islam, and denounced the Shah as the servant of evil. Under the Ayatollah, the radicals fought and subdued all opposing forces, including the secular and the left political outfits, and ran a harsh anti-US campaign that culminated in the taking of fifty-two hostages in the US Embassy in Tehran. While the hostages were freed after 444 days of captivity, the crisis affected US–Iran relations adversely. An Islamic government was formed in Iran, a new Constitution based on Islamic laws was introduced, and a new oppositional force to the West was established in the form of a militant Islam. It was only after Khomeini's death in 1989 that Iran gradually started accommodating to international circumstances, although the tussle between the reformers and the hardliners continues to influence its domestic politics and foreign policy. Relations between Iran and the US have remained bitter ever since.

In recent years, Iran's nuclear ambitions have become a matter of concern for the international community. After years of diplomatic negotiation and bargaining, the US and other world powers reached an agreement with Iran in 2015, known as the Iran Nuclear Deal, under which Iran acquiesced to a number of restrictions along with a comprehensive inspections regime in order to ensure a peaceful nuclear programme. During Donald Trump's first term as President, the deal was abrogated by the US as relations between the two countries worsened further. In 2025, the US and Iran were once again involved in a nuclear negotiation. However, with the attack by Israel on Iran's military bases and the Natanz nuclear facility in 2025, the chances of a negotiated agreement have reduced drastically.

In December 1979, the Soviet Union sent its forces to Afghanistan, invited by, and in support of, a Marxist regime. In the 1970s, Afghanistan went through political turmoil and the Soviet Union suspected that the new incumbent Hafizullah Amin, who had forcibly replaced the pro-Soviet Nur Mohammed Taraki, might turn to the US for support. Soviet forces overthrew Amin and installed Barbak Karmal in his place. The reforms initiated by Taraki and followed by Amin and Karmal enraged not only the landowners and the clergy, but also a large number of citizens who remained traditional in their attitude and practices, especially with regard to the opening of co-educational schools and the removal of the veil for women. These measures also challenged the zealously guarded authority of local chieftains in areas far from Kabul.

The United States viewed the invasion as a demonstration of the Soviet ambition to establish access to the Indian Ocean, thereby altering existing geopolitical patterns. Pakistan was viewed as a small obstacle, and India had been a close friend of the Soviet Union since 1971. This came as an affront to the US, especially after the Islamic Revolution in Iran. Towards the end of the 1970s, dissatisfaction with the 'incompetent leadership' prevailed in the US, with neo-conservatives and disgruntled bureaucrats increasingly viewing *détente* as a deluded measure. Cold War maxims were resurrected with greater vigour under the presidency of Ronald Reagan from 1980, sparking off the New Cold War.

President Reagan led a vitriolic campaign against the Soviet Union and initiated armament programmes, the most popular among which was a multilayered, space-based defence system known as the Strategic Defence Initiative or the 'Star Wars' programme. The US grew increasingly active and interfering. In its effort to remove Soviet forces from Afghanistan, the US ironically lent its support to the *mujahideen* or Islamic fundamentalists, who were ready to fight communism in the name of Islam. Pakistan, as a US ally, became a frontline state in this war and was instrumental in creating committed bands of *jihadi*s known as the Taliban, who emerged as a prominent force in the mid-1990s. With the help of Saudi Arabia, foreign *jihadi*s entered Afghanistan to fight against the Soviets.

FALL OF THE SOVIET UNION

As the US under President Reagan regained dominance over international politics in the early 1980s, the Soviet Union suffered from a weak leadership. The deaths of successive heads of state—Leonid Brezhnev, followed by Yuri Andropov and Konstantin Chernenko—hindered a Soviet counter-response. In 1985, Mikhail Gorbachev came to power in the Soviet Union and initiated a restructuring programme, popularly known as *perestroika*, to be brought about in a milieu of openness or *glasnost*. By this time, the Soviet economy had stagnated and industrial production was low. Dissident movements began in Ukraine and Lithuania, and a stiff arms race and foreign commitments were eroding the state's resources. In an attempt to gain a period of relative peace with the US, lower unnecessary defence spending, and gain access to Western technology and capital imports, Gorbachev began to announce unilateral arms cuts, a withdrawal of Soviet forces, and reduce his foreign commitments. While Gorbachev became immensely popular with an international audience as a promoter of global peace, *glasnost* led to open debate and criticism of the Soviet regime, and it became clear that Soviet forces would no longer be used to suppress rebellion and dissent. In 1989, he removed his forces from Afghanistan, leaving the Najibullah administration to defend itself. In 1996, the regime was overthrown and a Taliban government was established in Kabul.

The United States entered into negotiations from a position of strength. The Soviet Union found it difficult to keep pace with the huge armaments programmes of President Reagan, and at a summit meeting between the two leaders in 1985 in Geneva, both agreed that a nuclear war would be futile and should never be fought. In 1987, the Intermediate-range Nuclear Forces (INF) Treaty was signed between the two. Meanwhile, people's desire for change had gathered miraculous momentum throughout Eastern Europe. In 1989, people broke down the Berlin Wall—the symbol of the Cold War divide—and in 1990, the two German halves were officially reunited. With the fall of the Berlin Wall, the Cold War collapsed. Communist governments in Eastern Europe were mostly deposed. Non-communist governments came to power in Poland and Hungary; in Romania, a civil war broke out in an attempt to overthrow the communist regime; Yugoslavia imploded in 1991 and disintegrated into several entities, creating a new crisis in Europe; and Czechoslovakia broke into two republics in 1993.

In 1990, the Conventional Forces Treaty was signed between two rival alliances—the NATO and the Warsaw Pact—to impose equal ceilings on key conventional armaments essential for conducting surprise attacks or large-scale offensives. Soon after, the Warsaw Pact was wound up, paving the way for the expansion of NATO into the erstwhile Soviet sphere of influence. In 1991, the Soviet Union itself disintegrated; it survived for a while as a Commonwealth of Independent States until finally, the constituent republics became independent countries. Erstwhile countries of the Eastern Bloc, like Poland, Hungary, the Czech Republic, Slovakia, Romania, Bulgaria, Albania, Croatia, and Slovenia, became members of NATO, as did the erstwhile Soviet provinces of Estonia, Latvia, and Lithuania. Nuclear arms control gained momentum as cuts in strategic arsenal took place through the Strategic Arms Reduction Talks (or the START process) between the US and the successor state of the Soviet Union—Russia.

THE POST-COLD WAR WORLD POWER CENTRES

With the fall of the Soviet Union, the United States remained the only superpower in international politics. The new world order that took shape after the end of the Cold War appeared unipolar, with the US as the only unchallenged mega-power. The political ideology of liberal democracy came to be viewed as the political philosophy that had defeated not only Nazism and Fascism, but also Communism as competitive political narratives. Forces of globalisation based on a free market economy were championed as the forerunners of a borderless, integrated, and interconnected world. Liberal democracy as a political ideology and a free market economy seemed the only options after the fall of communism in the Soviet Union. As Francis Fukuyama observed in *End of History and the Last Man* (1992), liberal democracy marks the end point of mankind's ideological evolution and the final form of government. In the 1990s, it was perceived that a world order dominated by the West, which would, in turn, be led by the US, would make the twenty-first century an American century. However, the US soon became embroiled in a War on Terror after the 2001 Al Qaeda attacks in New York, and over the years, the American century was challenged by the rise of China and the resurgence of Russia. Moreover, multiple actors, including the European Union and aspiring middle powers like India and Brazil, introduced multipolar tendencies in the world system.

The post-Cold War period has not been free from conflict and contestation. The spate of people's uprisings in the former Soviet republics in the early 2000s came to be known collectively as the 'Colour Revolutions'. As people took to the streets in massive peaceful protests against corrupt or authoritarian governments and non-violent pro-democracy demonstrations for good governance escalated, the governments succumbed to the pressure and made way for changes. The movements had not been guided by political parties and, in many cases, were not led by a specific political personality. In the absence of a party flag, demonstrators used ribbons or flowers of a specific colour as a symbol for identifying fellow protesters; hence the term 'colour revolution'. Social media played a significant role in ensuring contact and coordination among the people.

A series of such uprisings took place in the erstwhile Soviet Republics, and soon spread to other regions as well. Georgia (Rose Revolution, 2003), Ukraine (Orange Revolution, 2004), and Kyrgyzstan (Tulip Revolution, 2005), where people's movements led to political change, may have encouraged the Cedar Revolution in Lebanon in 2004 against the presence of Syrian forces and the Blue Revolution in Kuwait in 2005 over suffrage for women. In 2010, the Jasmine Revolution took place in Tunisia, forcing President Ben Ali to leave the country under pressure, and in 2011, the Lotus Revolution in Egypt dethroned the authoritarian regime of President Hosni Mubarak. By this time, developments in the Arab world had acquired a new sobriquet—'Arab Spring'. However, the protests increasingly grew violent, and the movement in Libya to depose the dictatorial Colonel Gaddafi involved armed clashes, with support from a coalition led by the United States.

As the spirit of the colour revolutions—spontaneous people's uprisings for good governance—influenced many, a movement to 'Occupy Wall Street' began in the US (but fizzled out soon enough). Scholars soon began to suspect that America's programme to promote democracy was behind such movements. Agencies like USAID, Freedom House, and the National Endowment for Democracy were perceived as instrumental in training youth in the basic tenets of democracy—the rule of law, an impartial electoral process, independent media—inspiring them to start revolutions for effective regime change. While diplomatic pressure through a 'top-down' approach can achieve change, these were 'bottom-up' approaches, with educated youth aspiring to a democratic transition. This unnerved China and Russia, who favoured the principle of 'regime security' as against 'regime change', and viewed these movements as a 'new form of warfare' and a 'soft coup'. Certain 'corrective' measures were prescribed, which included detecting and blocking global financial flows to local NGOs and involving the youth in 'nation-building' activities. In his second term, President Trump substantially reduced the activities of USAID.

In 1990, as the Cold War drew to a close, Iraq, under President Saddam Hussein, invaded Kuwait in a blatant act of aggression that sparked international condemnation. While the US had maintained close relations with Iraq and supported it during the Iran–Iraq war, this was also when the US was advocating a new world order, in which it would play the global policeman. Armed with a United Nations Security Council mandate, the US led a coalition force and the subsequent 1991 Gulf War compelled Iraq to withdraw from Kuwait. However, President George H. W. Bush's declared objective of removing Saddam Hussein from power was not achieved; that task was left to his son, President George W. Bush, who overthrew Hussein in 2002. This action led to a series of unfortunate events that posed serious challenges for the US as well as for the international community.

The invasion of Iraq in 2002 took place on spurious grounds; charges were fabricated about Iraq possessing dangerous chemical and biological weapons that could kill several million people. The United Nations and most major powers sought to avoid a military confrontation, with only the United Kingdom supporting the US position. The US led a coalition of willing states into Iraq. Hussein's administration was toppled, the old order undone, and the army and police were disbanded. What followed was near-anarchy as vast stores of weapons and explosives were looted by the people and violence escalated, contributing to the formation of resistance groups against the foreign occupiers. Attempts to reconstruct the economy failed as political stability eluded Iraq even after power was transferred to an Iraqi government. The resistance, increasingly led by Sunni Islamist militants, began attracting jihadists from foreign lands. When news of the systematic torture that prisoners in Abu Ghraib prison near Baghdad had suffered at the hands of American troops broke, the situation worsened further.

From this turmoil emerged the Islamic State of Iraq and Syria (ISIS)—rebranded from the al-Qaida in Iraq—which propagated an Islamic Caliphate free of the corrupting influence of the West. ISIS adopted conventional military tactics and seized entire cities, brutally massacring and beheading prisoners and enemies and committing atrocities on women in the process. In 2014, it named Abu Bakr al-Baghdadi as its Caliph. It made successful use of social media to spread propaganda, attract young foreign fighters, and instigate lone-wolf attacks. The war that raged between the ISIS and Syrian and Iraqi forces, with the involvement of extra-regional powers, created millions of refugees, who sought shelter in Europe in yet another chapter in human tragedy. Over time, the ISIS lost control; however, it had encouraged the formation of splinter groups in other countries by then.

As the US gradually withdrew its forces from several parts of the world, a shift in power appeared to be taking place from the West to the East. The 'Rise of Asia' theory has inspired people to visualise the twenty-first century as an Asian century. With the end of the Cold War, China appeared to challenge America's pre-eminence in international affairs. Subsequent debates and discussions in the US with regard to a suitable policy towards China bestowed the country with a near-superpower status. China is the fastest-growing economy in the world and has a huge impact on the global economy. Along with its economic clout, its modern military, authoritarian political set-up, and pragmatic, self-focused policies have drawn much attention in the contemporary era.

A 'Rising China' located at the core of continental-maritime Asia shares its borders with four of five Asian regions (the East, Southeast, South, and Central Asia), and is not very far from the fifth region (West Asia). Border disputes and the hegemonic territorial claims of China may thus result in recurrent conflicts in many Asian regions. In East Asia, Japan is China's major competitor; despite economic interdependence, areas of tension remain. The issue of the sovereignty of the Senkaku Islands is not fully settled yet, and Japan's close relations with Taiwan also irks China. After regaining Macau and Hong Kong, China viewed the integration of the renegade province of Taiwan as the logical next step. While the international community has refrained from according independent status to Taiwan, the US remains committed to Taiwan's security and Chinese attempts to effect a forced integration could be resisted. In Southeast Asia, smaller neighbours are resisting China's territorial claims. China claims sovereignty over its 'historic waters', where oil-rich islands are scattered across the South China Sea. They have laid claim to the entire Spratly and Paracel Islands archipelago, created artificial islands out of submerged reefs and built infrastructure on these islands that can sustain military operations, and declared an air defence zone in the region. While states like Vietnam, the Philippines, and Malaysia have disputed Chinese claims, the US and others have declared freedom of navigation in the area. The presence of US warships in the region has frequently provoked reactions from China. The US follows a policy of 'rebalancing' with greater cooperation from its allies and friends over a vast theatre that has come to be known as the 'Indo-Pacific Region', where the dynamics of both the Indian Ocean and the Pacific Ocean regions converge.

In 2020, when the world was reeling under the COVID-19 pandemic, China was involved in conflicts in the South China Sea, sinking Vietnamese and Malaysian boats, sending gunboats to Japanese islands, flying into Taiwanese airspace, and engaging in a stand-off with India at the Line of Actual Control (LAC). Viewed in this context, it can be said that China has a strategy of leaving out the main enemy, instead hitting those they believe are 'accessories' when they find themselves unable to confront the main targets (Balachandran 2020). China's primary rival is the United States. The trade war between the two and the gunboat diplomacy in the South China Sea have worsened relations further, with US allies now becoming targets of the Chinese. However, Xi Jinping's vision of China as a superpower is being challenged as well. Chinese intentions and designs are being distrusted the world over, and charges of a cover-up and lack of transparency with regard to the COVID-19 pandemic were openly levelled against it. This, however, has only served to make China more aggressive and assertive. China appears to be following the prescriptions laid down by the master strategist of the fifth century BCE, Sun Tzu, who advised an attack on the enemy's strategy, followed by attacks on their allies and finally their soldiers. US Secretary of State Mike Pompeo was of the opinion that President Xi was testing the world to see if anyone would stand up to China's threats and bullying, and that the US should take this seriously.

India, another rising power in South Asia, has faced challenges in its bilateral relations with China. The entire length of the Sino-Indian border is under dispute; interpretations of the notional LAC vary on both sides, and transgressions occur frequently. China's claim over the entire state of Arunachal Pradesh; irritation over the Tibetan government-in-exile, which has been given refuge in India; the presence of its troops in the Gilgit-Baltistan region of Pakistan-occupied Jammu and Kashmir (POJK); its refusal to allow India membership in the Nuclear Suppliers' Group (NSG); and the support it extends to Pakistan as well as the proposed China–Pakistan Economic Corridor that runs through POJK are all indicative of a troubled relationship. However, China remains a prominent trade partner, although India's exports to China are much lower in volume than its imports. Both meet frequently on the platforms of the BRICS or SCO (Shanghai Cooperation Organization), and both realise the dangers of destabilising a system that offers them enough benefits. However, trouble occasionally rears its head, and one such face-off took place in 2017 at the Doklam Plateau, near the tri-country junction of India, Bhutan, and China. While there have been attempts to re-establish mutually beneficial relations through informal summit meetings in subsequent years, termed the Wuhan Spirit and Chennai Connect, in 2020 the countries clashed again at the LAC, resulting in casualties on both sides. However, a hegemonic China's territorial ambitions may have provoked the formation of a joint platform led by the US, India, Japan, and Australia, known as the QUAD—or, as China describes it, the Asian version of NATO—to promote increasing coordination among them.

Throughout the 1990s, Russia was in a state of turmoil, looking to rebuild itself and regain its lost status in the world arena. At home, rapid privatisation, financial crisis, social unrest, and leadership chaos under the maverick Boris Yeltsin made Russia vulnerable until Vladimir Putin came to power in 2000. There was an anti-West nationalist upsurge as Putin consolidated his position, and as the West sought to brand his style as authoritarian, Russia strengthened its ties with China. On the basis of its energy and arms exports and through assertive state intervention, Putin gradually brought in stability and sought to stop the expansion of NATO in Russia's neighbourhood. In 2008, Russia was involved in a five-day war with Georgia, after which it seized the separatist territories of Abkhazia and South Ossetia, recognising them as independent states. In 2014, Russia annexed the Crimean Peninsula from Ukraine. This act of occupying the territory of a neighbouring state by force rekindled apprehensions that Russia might seek to expand its territorial reach, but a more plausible explanation can be found in Russia's insecurity at the relentless expansion of NATO. This led to the Russian invasion of Ukraine in 2022, and the war continues in 2025 with Russia occupying about 20 per cent of Ukrainian land despite economic sanctions and appeals from other states to stop the war. Russia has also shown a keen interest in supporting its allies and joined the battle in Syria in 2015 to strengthen Bashar al-Assad's regime, striking against the rebels and concluding a deal in 2017 to maintain an airbase in Syria for half-a-century. However, the Assad regime fell to the rebels in December 2024.

The European Union has emerged as a strong power bloc after the Maastricht Treaty, signed in 1992, laid the foundation for the Union. The journey from the European Economic Community to the Union, with a common currency and citizenship, indicated a highly effective institutionalised functional integration. Aiming towards a common foreign and security policy, the idea of 'Fortress Europe' caught the imagination of the people, and the Union was regarded as a potential power centre. However, the national perspectives of major states remain dominant on important policy issues. In recent years, the EU has been troubled by economic distress in some member states, debt crisis, and policies concerning the sheltering of refugees from Iraq and Syria. On 31 January 2020, the United Kingdom left the European Union following a referendum that took place in 2016. Known as 'Brexit', this move raised questions about the EU's future as a viable, powerful bloc in international politics.

Post-Cold War Politics

Certain simple assumptions are usually made about conflicts and crises in the post-Cold War era. China is viewed as a system-supporter since it has participated in and derived much benefit from existing world economic arrangements. However, it is at the same time seen also as a potential system-challenger, in terms of bringing about a change in the prevailing power equations. The re-emergence of Russia and its close ties with China are also a concern for the West. The retreat of the US would facilitate an expansion of China's influence, which is why the US is seeking to bring dependable allies into the power game. The mid-level powers, too, will continue to play a balancing game to avoid inadvertent conflicts and increase the possibilities of cooperation over issues of common concern.

In the 1990s, the understanding of international relations began to be marked by anxiety. Despite its victory in the Cold War, the West soon found its power and influence diminishing over the rest of the world. New powers emerged, and new challenges ranging from climate change to international terrorism engulfed the world as a whole. The concentration of power was shifting to new actors located predominantly in Asia, a phenomenon known as the 'Rise of the East', prompting some scholars to prophesy that the twenty-first century would be an Asian century. In between the American century and the Asian century, we saw the emergence of an interconnected multipolar world.

Many issues have drawn our attention in the post-Cold War era: international terrorism, climate change, human displacement and migration, health hazards and pandemics, and human rights violations. Regional disputes involving long-drawn enmities, like the Israel–Palestine conflict, need to be resolved. Yet the world order continues to rely on state-based hierarchical power equations, and regional disputes and political minefields are all too prevalent in the contemporary world.

With the increase in national power, new areas of interest emerge and expand. States become enmeshed in a web of agreements, and seek to resolve disputes through peaceful cooperation. These arrangements can either be accommodative, or attempt to unobtrusively contain the expansionist tendencies of rising powers. They do not, however, hamper the upward mobility of states. Since the contemporary world order is in a state of flux, the major actors explore various means to increase and expand their power, prestige, and influence. Competition is inevitable, and conflicts and crises may recur in international politics.

Contemporary great power politics resembles the pre-World War II period, with economic hardships, emerging powers, charismatic leaders, aggressive nationalist stances, and a stockpiling of arms. While dictatorial interventionist policies might not be that easy, confrontations cannot be ruled out. Eighty years after World War II, the world has changed drastically, and another major war is unviable for several reasons. The presence of nuclear weapons and the fear of extensive devastation continue to restrain states; however, even without the threat of nuclear weapons, a conventional war would be harsh, not only in terms of the huge loss of economic and human resources, but also because rebuilding the economy will be well-nigh impossible after such a calamity. Unfortunately, the great powers continue to explore the possibilities of a limited war through the application of technology—in the form of cyber-warfare, for example. Any such action on the part of one state will impact all others; Germany, by starting World War II, had brought down the European imperial powers, allowing the US and USSR to emerge as superpowers. While the great powers today take recourse to preventive diplomacy to avoid such a situation, limited warfare always remains a possibility.

9

Prevention of War and Nuclear Weapons Proliferation

Anindya Jyoti Majumdar

World politics is replete with armed conflicts among states. Clashes of interest occur frequently and war among or within states is not an uncommon phenomenon. Force and other instruments of coercion have been an important component of state policy, used by the major powers to influence and reshape existing power equations. Since ancient times, the rise and fall of great powers have usually been accompanied by great wars, and the projection of military power has been key to maintaining dominance over others. In the absence of a central authority with a commanding power over sovereign and independent states, major powers have often taken up the responsibility of maintaining a semblance of order in the international system by using force to punish an aggressor, protect treaty provisions, maintain the balance of power, and establish new rules. In the process, however, many weak and small states have been victimised, especially when a major power, motivated by an urge to expand its influence or establish control over larger territories, has launched aggressive wars. As a result, the boundaries of states have frequently changed, small states have been merged with bigger entities, and new states have emerged. Periods of peace have often been disturbed by wars that broke out at regular intervals.

With time, as new weapons and technologies developed, war became increasingly destructive and lethal. Two World Wars in the twentieth century and the advent of nuclear weapons generated a renewed quest for lasting and durable peace. While international organisations like the United Nations were established with the primary purpose of maintaining international peace and security, innovative conflict-avoidance and confidence-building measures have been advocated among adversaries. Nevertheless, armed conflicts have been taking place in one part of the world or another. After the end of the Cold War, the possibility of war between the major powers receded significantly, but new arenas of conflict have emerged and intra-state armed conflicts are a prominent feature of the contemporary world.

In this chapter, we explain the conception and forms of war and armed conflicts, as also the various methods adopted over time to prevent war. Major methods include the renunciation of war by the states, peaceful ways of settling international disputes and resolving conflicts, and confidence-building measures. The emergence and spread of nuclear weapons pose a grave threat to human existence, and the challenges of nuclear proliferation have been increasing by the day. Reducing the threat posed by the proliferation of nuclear weapons is a matter of crucial importance. This chapter explores the challenges posed by the spread of nuclear weapons and the efficacy and limitations of disarmament and arms control as measures to prevent nuclear proliferation.

War and Armed Conflicts

By 'war', we generally understand a violent armed conflict between adversaries where either of the contesting parties tries to impose a military defeat on the other. It is a pattern of purposive, organised violence undertaken by one group against another at different levels, both among states or within states. Adhering to conventional legal tradition, L. Oppenheim believes that war is a contention between two or more states through their armed forces, the ultimate aim being to overpower each other and impose such conditions of peace as the victor pleases (Freedman 2012, 19). It is viewed as a perennial feature of human history. As Carl von Clausewitz tells us in his famous treatise, *On War* (1832), war is a mere continuation of policy by other means; an act of violence intended to compel our opponents to accept our will. However, with time, traditional concepts of war have changed significantly as total wars have become increasingly lethal, destructive, and more expensive, offering very little benefit in return. Conflicts limited in scope and intensity have become frequent instead. At different points in time, the nature of war has been influenced by the purpose and stakes involved in the venture—ranging from mere occupation of territories or control over strategically important areas and access to and control over resources, to identity issues that led states to support people in other states with similar religions, ideologies, or ethnicities.

Before the emergence of a total war, the term 'limited war' was used to denote European battles of the late eighteenth century, in which the armies were smaller in size and battles were fought to achieve limited political and dynastic aims. The common people were not directly impacted by such wars. Many such wars were fought across the world and rulers were overthrown in different states, and although such wars brought in their wake massacre, plunder, and arson, the scale of hostility was limited.

A total war involves a near-total mobilisation of the resources of a state in the war effort. Whenever the volume of destructive force deployed in a war is increased over time, the common people (or non-combatants) are directly affected, as weapons are used indiscriminately without distinguishing between military and non-military targets, such as civilian lives and private property. The outcome is either complete victory or a complete defeat of one or the other contesting party. War is no longer confined to the armed forces; its impact extends to non-combatant civilians as well, who are involved in war preparation, suffer from economic measures taken against them, from aerial bombardment by the enemy, or from the use of nuclear weapons. The practice of total war was best reflected in the two World Wars. As the economic costs of conducting such a war, and then of post-war reconstruction, are huge and the risk of complete destruction looms large, states often prefer limited hostilities to fulfil their limited objectives and avoid a total war, which usually gains its own momentum and goes out of control over time.

In recent times, we have witnessed frequent recourse to conflicts that are in fact limited hostilities, and very often, these are undeclared wars as well. If the principal objective is to avoid a total war, the goal of complete military victory in the traditional sense has to be sacrificed in favour of limited military gains. In the contemporary period, therefore, limited wars are more in vogue. Hostilities are limited with respect to the area of operation, in terms of the volume of force and types of weapons deployed, and with respect to the targets engaged. A conscious effort is made to exercise deliberate control over the spread of war. The 1999 Kargil War between India and Pakistan was a limited, undeclared war. Pakistan's objective was to push the Line of Control (LoC) deeper into India, and thereby gain a strategic advantage. India, however, pushed the infiltrators back onto the other side of the LoC. Both parties were reluctant to turn the conflict into an all-out war, and the international community played an active role to ensure an early end to hostilities.

With significant improvements in the technology used in warfare, new dimensions and theatres of conflict are opening up. The application of sophisticated technological tools on a grand scale may bring in the simultaneous transformation of armaments, strategy, organisation, and political-military relationships, a phenomenon that has been termed a revolution in military affairs (RMA). It denotes the technological excellence of the militarily powerful state with its access to secure, accurate, real-time, all-weather information systems and unmanned, long-range, and highly lethal weapons designed to achieve precision kills. The possibility of military activity in space cannot be dismissed, especially when satellites play such a major role in surveillance and the command and control system of a state, and hence can become military targets during armed conflicts. Similarly, we hear about cyberwars in which unauthorised access to computer resources, leading to a denial of services and data theft, might make way for the execution of bigger military plans. However, not many states enjoy such technological prowess and despite future apocalyptic scenarios, these issues are yet to occupy centre-stage in mainstream international relations.

In certain cases, the difference in the technological levels of two opposing parties leads to an asymmetric war; the US forces' engagement in operations against the Taliban in Afghanistan exemplify such a mode of war. In such cases, because of the disparity in power between the opposing parties, the tactics and strategies adopted by each differ significantly. While the powerful seeks to eliminate resistance in a decisive clash, the weaker party often resorts to unconventional weapons (like improvised explosive devices) and irregular methods (like suicide bombing), leading to a hybrid form of warfare.

Intra-state Conflicts and Civil War

Within a state, grievances against the ruling regime can give birth to conflicts. Organised groups can resort to an intense armed contest aimed at gaining control of the state apparatus and its administrative machinery. Violent conflict can take place between the ruling regime and forces loyal to it on the one hand and those seeking to dislodge the regime on the other. The opposing group could be insurgents or rebels, forming a militia against the state's coercive machineries. Apart from popular uprisings against an unpopular ruling regime, conflicts may also occur between ethnic groups, religious communities, or among groups subscribing to different political ideologies. As a result, internal rebellion, secessionist revolts, ethno-nationalist conflicts, and a power struggle among groups armed with weapons can trigger violent domestic conflicts.

Driven by a sense of relative deprivation and alienated from mainstream political life, some people may take up arms against the ruling regime and engage in intermittent low-intensity conflicts with the state police and the army. Intense, sustained, and widespread insurgency can instigate a civil war, unless it is effectively put down by the state. On the other hand, desperate regimes can exploit ethnic differences, adopt a deliberate policy of discrimination, and instigate violence in order to divide people and enable a substantial number of people to rally behind them. The Hutu-Tutsi genocidal massacre in Rwanda and Burundi is a case in point. Domestic conflicts usually lead to serious human rights violations.

In intra-state conflicts, heavy civilian casualties may occur over a sustained period of time, during which established conventions codifying the laws of war are not followed. Such conflicts often result in high numbers of internally displaced persons and refugees. Each party tries to mobilise loyalties and assumes a moral high ground, and child soldiers, improvised weapons, and unconventional methods become recurrent features. Intra-state conflicts are sometimes aided by external actors who support the party of their choice diplomatically, logistically, and militarily. The international community or groups of states may also intervene to influence the outcome to their advantage. Intra-state conflicts, although categorised at times as non-international armed conflicts, rarely remain within domestic jurisdictions, and inter-state relations are often affected in a significant way. The conflicts in former

Yugoslavia, Afghanistan, Iraq, Syria, and Sri Lanka provide ample evidence of these patterns.

Prevention of Armed Conflicts: Renouncing War

The experience of devastating wars led the international community to attempt to exercise control over such conflicts in the future. After World War I (1914–18), the League of Nations was formed and half-hearted measures were adopted to renounce war. The members of the League were required to seek a peaceful settlement to their disputes before resorting to war. It did not, however, prohibit the states from exercising their customary right to wage war. The League was unsuccessful in preventing World War II (1939–45).

Outside the League, an important attempt was made to prevent war. This was known as the General Treaty for the Renunciation of War or the Paris Peace Pact of 1928. The signatories condemned any recourse to war as a solution to international controversies, and renounced war as an instrument of national policy in their relations with one another. They also agreed to seek a peaceful solution to all disputes or conflicts. Nevertheless, the treaty had many shortcomings: war was permitted in self-defence, as a measure of collective action, and between the signatories of the Pact and non-signatories. There was also no provision in the treaty for an authoritative agency that would determine breach of obligations on the part of the signatories, and a lack of agreement about 'what constitutes war' and the 'use of force short of war' left the treaty provisions open to varied interpretations, as suited to the preferences of the signatory states.

These arrangements failed to prevent World War II. At the end of this devastating conflict, however, war was increasingly being understood as not a legitimate prerogative of a state but as a breakdown in the system. Little wonder, then, that various peaceful methods of dispute settlement were propagated and recognised in the United Nations Charter, which came into being immediately after the war. Members of the UN have the obligation to settle disputes peacefully and not use force in their relations with one another. The states that do get involved in armed conflict (which is not included in the collective action mandated by the UN) try to camouflage their war through the use of euphemisms such as 'campaigns', 'missions', and 'peacekeeping' operations, to avoid legal complications.

PEACEFUL SETTLEMENT OF INTERNATIONAL DISPUTES

The international system comprises sovereign, independent states. In their ongoing relations with one another, states can choose between two dominant modes of interaction: close cooperation or intense conflict. It is advisable to establish a working relationship and opt for a peaceful yet competitive relationship. A middle path between these two options would be the perfect arrangement, but in the international system, the interests of one state often goes against those of another, and disagreement ensues.

States may disagree on points of fact (for example, two neighbours can lay claim over a stretch of territory if the boundary lines between them are contested or not clearly marked) or on the interpretation of rules, norms, and the law or provisions of a treaty. Each side contests the other's viewpoint and the resultant claims on the rights they seek to enjoy. If the contesting parties perceive such disagreement as a clash of incompatible interests, it may turn into a dispute that can range from minor, temporary, low-intensity frictions to a prolonged, long-lasting, high-intensity contest. Since these disputes are quite common and frequent, and often disturb and endanger international peace and security, the basic objectives of international law include developing peaceful methods to resolve such conflicts.

Article 33, paragraph 1 of the UN Charter stipulates:

> The parties to any dispute, the continuance of which is likely to endanger the maintenance of international peace and security, shall first of all seek a solution by negotiation, enquiry, mediation, conciliation, arbitration, judicial settlement, resort to regional agencies or arrangement, or other peaceful means of their own choice.[1]

Of these, arbitration and judicial settlement are legal techniques that involve a third party, which hears the case and issues binding decisions,

[1]See https://www.un.org/en/about-us/un-charter/full-text#:~:text=The%20parties%20to%20any%20dispute,or%20other%20peaceful%20means%20of (accessed May 2025).

whereas the other methods are diplomatic in nature. Arbitration, a very old method of settling disputes, is a process whereby the disputing parties refer the dispute to certain persons of their own choice, who then seek a legal settlement. The decision of the arbitrators—known as the award—is binding upon the parties. When the disputing parties opt for an *ad hoc* tribunal, they decide these matters on the basis of an arbitration agreement. International law relating to arbitration was codified in the 1899 Hague Convention. In later years, it also established a Permanent Court of Arbitration (PCA).

International disputes are settled by a court of law through a judicial settlement. At present, we have the International Court of Justice (ICJ), a successor of the Permanent Court of International Justice (PCIJ) under the League of Nations. When the League was dissolved, so was the PCIJ, and the ICJ took its place. It began its work in the same city (The Hague), the same place (the Peace Palace), and in the same hall. The Statute of the ICJ, which is an integral part of the UN Charter, is also based on the Statute of the PCIJ. It appears that the framers of both the League and the UN preferred judicial settlement to all other peaceful means.

The ICJ is the chief judicial organ of the UN. All members of the UN are *ipso facto* parties to the Statute. The Court is constituted of fifteen judges in a manner that represents all the principal forms of civilisation and principal legal systems. All decisions of the Court are based on a majority opinion. The President of the Court is empowered with a casting vote in the case of a tie. If the Court includes on the bench a judge who belongs to a nation that is one of the parties to a dispute, the other party can elect a judge of their own to sit on the bench on an *ad hoc* basis. According to Article 59 of the Statute, the decisions of the ICJ are binding upon the parties, but only with respect to that particular dispute. A judgment of the Court is final, and without appeal.

The ICJ's jurisdiction has always been a matter of interpretation. By jurisdiction, we mean the power and authority of the Court to render a binding decision on the substance and merits of a case. The jurisdiction of the Court is of two types: contentious and advisory. Of these, contentious jurisdiction can be further divided into voluntary jurisdiction and compulsory jurisdiction, based on an optional clause. The Court has yet another type of jurisdiction, known as transferred jurisdiction, which it inherited from the PCIJ. For example, if there is a dispute concerning the interpretation of a treaty that is still in force, but had been concluded during the time of the League, in the absence of the

PCIJ today, the ICJ has the jurisdiction (transferred from the PCIJ) to resolve any disputes regarding the treaty.

According to Article 36, paragraph 1, the jurisdiction of the Court covers all cases submitted to it voluntarily by the parties. The Court cannot compel the states to submit a case, but if the parties refer a case to it, jurisdiction belongs to the Court and its decision therefore becomes binding upon the parties. Article 36(2) is known as the optional clause, by which a state can confer compulsory jurisdiction upon the Court by making a declaration with respect to any other state that also accepts similar obligations. Article 36(3) states that such declarations can be made unconditionally, or on condition of reciprocity, or for a certain period of time. Therefore, states often make conditional declarations with several reservations, thereby effectively curtailing the Court's jurisdiction. This type of compulsory jurisdiction has often been criticised as being a misnomer; it requires the consent of the states and is therefore not compulsory at all.

The General Assembly, the Security Council, and other organs and agencies of the UN authorised by the General Assembly may request the ICJ for an advisory opinion on a legal question. The Court contributes to the progressive development of international law, clarifies the grey areas, and tries to establish a rule of law in inter-state relations. However, all too often the Court is sidestepped. States have a tendency to settle their disputes by diplomatic methods, rather than by legal methods.

Disputes can be resolved through negotiation. It is a less formal method and can proceed through both structured and unstructured channels. Negotiations can be arranged and carried out by career diplomats, political leaders (in the form of summit diplomacy), or through special missions or special envoys. Indeed, states are constantly engaged in negotiation over one issue or the other, which include attempts to resolve disputes as well. When states are unable to resolve a dispute through bilateral negotiation, or because of the serious nature of the dispute, they are in no position to initiate negotiation, and a third party—a state, or an international organisation, or an important individual (for example, the UN Secretary-General or a Head of State)—may offer its *good offices* for creating a conducive environment that will enable negotiation. Here, the third party may put forward some general suggestions, but it will not take part in the actual negotiation. France offered its good offices to the United States and North Vietnam to end the Vietnam War. When the third party not only offers its services but also actively participates in the negotiation to resolve the dispute, the process is called 'mediation'. The mediator seeks to reconcile the opposing claims. However, it is difficult to draw a clear line between good offices and mediation as the third party's involvement may go beyond simple logistical services; it may also indulge in behind-the-scenes diplomacy without taking active part in the formal dialogue.

Instead of a mediator, a group or a committee of impartial states/ persons can investigate the facts of a dispute and provide a report in which the members recommend proposals for settlement. This process is known as 'conciliation'. The recommended proposals, however, are not binding upon the parties. Along with an objective assessment of the situation, the sensitivity and susceptibilities of the states are also taken into account. The 1899 and 1907 Hague Conventions made provisions for a Conciliation Commission. Parties may set up specific Conciliation Commissions as well. Another method, 'enquiry', is often used as a subsidiary process along with other methods. It simply means an investigation into the facts of a dispute, which might contribute to resolving a problem. Enquiry missions are often set up to look into boundary disputes. Secrecy is often maintained over the proceedings, while the states pursue diplomatic methods to avoid the problems associated with a rigid public stance.

Under Article 2 of the Charter, member-states of the UN have resolved to settle their disputes peacefully. Accordingly, Articles 33–38 of Chapter VII of the UN Charter have provisions for the peaceful settlement of international disputes. The General Assembly and Security Council can make recommendations for peaceful settlement. The Council can investigate any dispute to determine whether it is likely to endanger international peace and security, and recommend appropriate methods and procedures for adjustment. It cannot, however, investigate disputes involving matters that fall within the domestic jurisdiction of any state. If the states fail to resolve their disputes peacefully, they are required to refer the dispute to the Security Council; but recourse to the Council is regarded as a last resort, only after primary methods of settlement have failed. All legal disputes are referred to the ICJ as a rule, and the ICJ functions as the chief judicial organ of the UN, seeking peaceful solutions through judicial settlement. The Secretary General can be instrumental in resolving disputes through mediation or by offering their good offices. Upon authorisation, he can send observers and fact-finding missions.

There are compulsive methods of settling international disputes as well, where a disputing state uses a certain degree of force or compulsion to make the other party accept their terms of settlement. Of these methods, intervention is a controversial technique, as it can be perceived as dictatorial interference by one state in the affairs of another, or by a third state in disputes between two parties—diplomatically or militarily—to resolve a political difference on terms laid down by the intervening state. Intervention goes against the targeted state's right to sovereignty, territorial integrity, and political independence, and hence international law prohibits intervention.

There are only two valid grounds of intervention:

- Self-defence. However, no aggressive attack can be launched on the grounds of self-defence. An armed attack must occur first to justify the use of force in response.
- Collective intervention by the UN, either to check an act of aggression that endangers international peace and security or to protect human rights in a state, but only if the matter is connected with the maintenance of international peace and security. The Charter does not authorise any state to intervene in the affairs of another on humanitarian grounds, and it appears that pre-emptive strikes are illegal under any circumstances.

However, in the case of rampant human rights violations in a state where the administration is either incapable or unwilling to protect its citizens, a humanitarian intervention might take place with the mandate of the UN. Debates have ensued on whether states have the right to violate the sovereignty of another citing human rights abuses, and the more acceptable argument is that the international community has a Responsibility to Protect (R2P), and that the principle of sovereignty can be ignored when a state fails to perform its primary duty to protect its citizens.

Under Chapter VII of the UN Charter, the Security Council can take enforcement actions against an act of aggression. It can call for a complete or partial interruption of economic relations and other means of communication, and the severance of diplomatic relations with the offending state (Article 41). If these measures prove inadequate, the Security Council can take action through air, sea, and land forces, including demonstrations, blockades, and other operations (Article 42).

CONFLICT RESOLUTION AND CONFIDENCE-BUILDING

Any competition that ensues in the effort to accumulate power and ensure relative economic gains leads not only to a clash of interests, but may also result in sustained adversarial relations among states. Difference in perception and disagreement on issues of vital interest can lead to hostility, and eventually to conflict. However, conflicts can take many forms—from low-intensity violence to war—either involving several states or within states. Solutions follow a similar pattern, depending on the circumstances and causes of a particular conflict.

A solution can take the form of compromise through bargaining, where each contestant realises the futility of conflict and, in the interests of peace, stability, and development, agrees to make concessions. Solutions can come in the form of altered perceptions, that is, a shift from a unilateral perception of security to cooperative security. The simple logic underlying this is: war is not desirable, but comprehensive peace is not feasible either. The best options then are adopting measures to prevent conflict, managing conflict situations, reducing the frequency and intensity of conflict, and finally, resolving a conflict. The role of the intellect is prioritised over instinctive actions, and the fear of the form that future conflict might take, as well as of the impact it might have, works as a restraint and serves to stimulate cooperation.

Conflict resolution entails the application of methods and processes to ensure the peaceful cessation of a conflict, with parties agreeing to refrain from using arms against one another. *Conflict avoidance* and *confidence building* are two important steps towards conflict resolution. Conflict avoidance measures (in the form of unilateral or bilateral declarations of ceasefire/non-aggression/non-interference) prepare the platform for effective confidence-building measures (CBMs). These measures are aimed at ensuring that adversaries do not launch sudden disabling military strikes, and instead adopt procedures and methods that corroborate their declared intentions, such as flag meetings at the border, advance notice of military exercises and movements of forces, and prior information about weapons tests. Viewed thus, CBMs are essentially military in nature.

However, non-military CBMs also contribute to the overall betterment of relations between two adversaries. They may include any positive move towards constructing working relationships free of conflict among the adversaries. Communication links, mutually beneficial economic relations, people-to-people contacts and cultural exchanges, connectivity—all contribute to improving relations between adversaries. This theory emerged from the 1975 Helsinki process in Europe, which improved relations between the Eastern and Western blocs during the Cold War, and these methods were then sought to be applied in other regional theatres. A CBM process in a regional theatre, however, must begin with the willing cooperation of the regional members; otherwise, CBMs can become yet another instrument of diplomatic offensives aimed at gaining a propaganda advantage, where CBM proposals are made with the knowledge that the proposal would either not be accepted by the other party, or, even if accepted, would not make much of a difference to existing power equations or prevailing situations.

A study of the CBMs that mark India–Pakistan relations exemplifies the point. While they did acknowledge the important role of CBMs, their progress in negotiating CBMs was painfully slow in the midst of their verbal tirades against each other. After a phase of intense hostility that halts all normal relations, CBMs become necessary to bring relations back on track. Bus links, rail links, and sporting or cultural links are either suspended or re-instituted depending on the level of bilateral animosity, and rarely do CBMs help to substantially alter these behavioural patterns. The CBM agreements between India and China, too, eventually failed to maintain peace on the borders.

Many would argue that CBMs (especially non-military CBMs) are not very effective in improving relations among adversaries; they might work under specific circumstances, and not in others. Some would even argue that 'they are least effective when they are most needed and most effective when they are least needed'. In other words, non-military CBMs are instituted and maintained when relations are good, but in times of conflict, all communication channels, and economic and cultural ties, are the first to be snapped.

CHALLENGES OF NUCLEAR PROLIFERATION

Weapons of mass destruction (WMDs) are those weapons whose use blurs the sacrosanct distinction between military targets and non-military (civilian) lives and property, the lethal effect of which never remains limited to combat areas. There is another way of defining a WMD, based purely on the type of elements present in the weapon: chemical, biological, and nuclear. Little wonder, then, that most serious efforts at arms control have been directed towards restraining the production, stockpiling, and use of WMDs. While we have a Biological Weapons Convention (1972) and a Chemical Weapons Convention (1993) that prohibit the use of such weapons by the signatories, there is no such convention on the use of nuclear weapons.

War among states with the uncontrolled use of nuclear weapons will be catastrophic, and may well mean the end of civilisation. The first atom bombs were used by the USA in a non-nuclear situation (in August 1945 on the cities of Hiroshima and Nagasaki in Japan), that is, there was no possibility of retaliation in kind. Today, the scenario is different and a nuclear war will be cause for anxiety for not only the parties to the war, but also for humankind in general. Preventing the use of such weapons is therefore a common concern.

However, when both adversaries possess nuclear weapons, a relationship of deterrence comes into being. Deterrence draws its strength from the assumption that if adversaries can maintain a sufficient stock of nuclear weapons, ready to be delivered within a short span of time and with the potential to cause unacceptable damage—it is immaterial who initiates the war—then the rational option would be to carefully avoid the use of nuclear weapons, as that would result in 'mutually assured destruction'. Hence, deterrence is viewed primarily as a relationship between or among adversaries, where the fear of damage caused by a nuclear exchange prevents either party from striking first. It also depends on a state's ability to survive the first attack and retain the capacity to launch a retaliatory second strike. During the Cold War, deterrence relied on the balance or parity of strategic nuclear weapons between the USA and the Soviet Union. However, to establish regional deterrence (such as that between India and Pakistan), it is not necessary to have hundreds of warheads to ensure a balance; deterrence is achieved from the ability to strike the adversary with only a few nuclear weapons guaranteed to cause 'unacceptable damage'.

Deterrence presumes that one's adversary will always behave rationally. Deterrence, however, is mostly instinctive, and based on the survival instinct. While it appears to be a rational option among states, deterrence has no utility when terrorist strikes are involved. Nuclear weapons are weapons of a last resort, and the very stability of nuclear weapons at the top allows for freedom of action at the lower levels. Assuming that nuclear weapons would not be used in small armed clashes or low-intensity conflicts, adversaries might be tempted to test each other through shadow wars, proxy wars, and other sub-tactical activities like supporting infiltration, often under the safety of the so-called 'nuclear shield'. However, there remains the risk of a low-intensity conflict snowballing into a full-scale war, a situation that deterrence seeks to prevent. At any rate, nuclear weapons do not help to reduce conventional military expenditure, as conventional weapons and forces are being continuously improved and increased to raise the threshold of nuclear warfare.

One line of reasoning states that we have not experienced a world war after 1945 because of the presence of deterrence among the major powers, and this can work just as well among regional adversaries, too. Neorealists argue that war has become less likely as the costs of war rise in relation to possible gains. While some of them visualise a world populated by many nuclear-weapons states, others consider the idea of nuclear weapons spreading among states frightening. Most, however, would support a regime of non-proliferation. Between the two extremes of elaborate nuclear war preparedness on the one hand and a total abolition of nuclear weapons on the other, a middle path advocates a nuclear balance with the adversary. In effect, pending nuclear disarmament, the consensus is to settle for a 'minimum deterrence' for nuclear-weapons states and 'non-proliferation' for the non-nuclear states.

In the interests of national security, every state arranges for armed forces and procures weapons to repulse possible invasions. Armament, or the procuring of arms, is thus a legitimate exercise. However, in an attempt to ensure adequate preparedness and outdo the adversary, states continue to increase the number and quality of their weapons and forces, thereby entering into a competition known as the arms race. An arms race does not necessarily indicate any imperialist or hegemonic ambitions on the part of the parties involved; it often gathers its own momentum, irrespective of state policy. Any action of procuring/producing arms is sought to be replicated by the adversary. The three main branches of the armed forces—Army, Navy, and Air Force—compete among themselves for a greater share of the defence budget of a country, leading to a net increase in the stock of weapons in a state. Driven by the motive of earning profits and boosting sales, firms engaged in the production of arms and military equipment try to influence states to buy their products. As science progresses, newer and more sophisticated weapons are created, tempting states and instigating a new arms race with qualitatively superior weapons and weapon systems.

An uncontrolled arms race introduces tension and instability in relations among states. Many well-meaning people consider the arms race to be at the root of many evils. They believe it is a waste of economic and human resources, for the money spent on arms could be better utilised for the development of useful infrastructure. Moreover, weapon tests lead to environmental damage, and from an ethical standpoint, we do not have the right to make the world a dangerous place for future generations.

Nuclear weapons remain important as the big powers continue to rely on them. It is still the ultimate weapon when it comes to the protection of the national interest or survival, and the acquisition of nuclear weapons also warns potential adversaries of the high costs and risks of possible attacks. Nations that lack military alliances are more inclined to think in these terms. Inferior conventional weapons and forces can be compensated with the acquisition of nuclear weapons. The acquisition of nuclear weapons also appears to be a rational move, in terms of countering nuclear blackmail. A state should have the ability to retaliate in kind when facing a nuclear threat, a consideration that prompts states to go nuclear. While such weapons arguably do not enhance international prestige and status, states that have acquired nuclear weapons, or have shown a proclivity towards them, have sought to justify their actions on the grounds of national security. While these considerations may trigger a possible spread of nuclear weapons, efforts have been made to prevent proliferation through arms control.

DISARMAMENT AND ARMS CONTROL

The term 'disarmament' (as opposed to 'armament') connotes the idea of a reduction or complete abolition of arms. In its absolute sense, disarmament implies the complete abolition of all weapons and weapon systems, and the disestablishment of all armed forces. This is called 'total disarmament' or 'general and comprehensive disarmament': general, because it covers all states, and comprehensive, because it covers all weapons and forces. On the face of it, the idea of a general and comprehensive disarmament seems utopian and idealistic. A practical approach would entail the abolition of a particular type of weapon or a reduction in the number of existing weapons (especially if armament is taken as an increase in numbers and improvement in the quality of arms), which is better described as partial disarmament. The distinguishing feature of disarmament is abolition or reduction.

Weaker powers are prone to emphasising disarmament, not in the primary interest of global peace but to minimise the existing gaps between themselves and powerful states. By the same logic, powerful states resolutely oppose any arrangement that will (in their perception) lower them to the level of other states. The inadequacies of the disarmament approach and the resultant frustration paved the way for another approach in the 1950s—the idea of arms control. Broadly, arms control denotes all measures involving weapons and weapon systems, and aims to minimise the possibility of unintentional war. Should war break out, arms control then serves to minimise the cost and damage of war. Arms control has been adopted by many states as the goal of state policy. Apart from the abolition or reduction of arms, the arms control process includes limitations, prohibitions, or restrictions on all experiments, production, or use of particular weapons.

A major aim of arms control is the creation of stability, where both parties are evenly matched and the result of war is thereby uncertain. To create such a situation, arms control advocates can even support the increase of arms in certain cases. This is where it differs from the disarmament process: advocates of disarmament would never support an increase in arms under any circumstances. The basic objective of arms control is to curb those factors that induce or tempt states to go to war. For example, arms control advocates believe in nuclear deterrence, while disarmament advocates do not. However, arms control seeks to establish a balance by settling for a lower level of armaments as far as practicable at less cost, through a process of continuous negotiation and management. Reductions are pursued insofar as they do not threaten stability, as a stable balance is regarded as an effective device for maintaining peace. If the adversaries can agree on what constitutes the minimum requirements for a stable military balance, then the process becomes easier. Thus, arms control may include the reduction and elimination of particular types of weapons, but its approach differs markedly from that of disarmament. As a goal of state policy, arms control can be used to maintain a status quo, the dominance of a few over the majority, and negotiations (especially regarding verification) can be exploited to derive political mileage through propaganda. Under such circumstances, considerations of balance and stability may take a back seat.

To prevent the spread of nuclear weapons, different measures have been adopted by the international community. One way is to collectively impose geographical restrictions on the spread of nuclear weapons in an area hitherto free of them. The Antarctic Treaty (1959), followed by the Outer Space Treaty (1967) and the Seabed Treaty (1969), prevent the spread of nuclear weapons to these areas. Similarly, states in a particular geographical region can come together to declare that region free from nuclear weapons. In Nuclear Weapons Free Zones (NWFZ), member countries commit to not manufacturing, acquiring, testing, or possessing nuclear weapons, although they may use nuclear energy for peaceful purposes. There are many NWFZs in the world today: in Latin America and the Caribbean (Tlatelolco Treaty, 1967), in the South Pacific (Rarotonga Treaty, 1985), in Southeast Asia (Bangkok Treaty, 1995), in Africa (Pelindaba Treaty, 1996), and in Central Asia (2006). Mongolia has declared itself a single-country NWFZ.

Another way is to prohibit tests that facilitate the development of nuclear weapons. It began with the Partial/Limited Test Ban Treaty of 1963, which prohibited physical nuclear tests in the air, on the surface, and under the sea. This Treaty did not prohibit underground tests, however, and in 1996 the Comprehensive Test Ban Treaty (CTBT) banned underground tests as well. Although computer simulations and laboratory experiments were possible, the CTBT was opposed by countries like India who wanted to retain their right to conduct tests.

The most important step was taken through the Nuclear Non-Proliferation Treaty (NPT) of 1968, which came into force in 1970 for twenty-five years, and was extended indefinitely in 1995. The NPT divides the world into two categories—Nuclear Weapon States (NWS) and Non-Nuclear Weapon States (NNWS)—with the former agreeing to not help the latter acquire nuclear weapons, and the latter in its turn expecting help with their civilian nuclear programmes. Only states that acquired nuclear weapons capability before the NPT came into being are officially recognised as NWS (and these are also the five permanent members of the UN Security Council): the US, Russia, the UK, France, and China. All other signatories were branded as NNWS, with no right to acquire nuclear weapons. Certain states—India, Pakistan, and Israel—remained outside the ambit of the NPT, and as they acquired nuclear weapons capability, came to be known as non-NPT NWS.

While many other aspirants have been either forced or persuaded to embrace NPT, North Korea, another *de facto* nuclear-weapons state, continues, even in the face of sanctions imposed by the international community, to defy the non-proliferation regime and projects its nuclear power regularly. US President Donald Trump tried, unsuccessfully, to bring North Korea back to the non-proliferation mainstream. Iran has been suspected of having a clandestine nuclear weapons programme, despite a deal with the major powers promising to shun the path of nuclearisation.

Regimes thus created are stable but not sacrosanct. They depend on the support of the existing powers and willing participation of the signatory states. Such a regime can be challenged by clandestine activities of non-compliant actors too. There are specific arrangements to reduce possibilities of violation of treaty provisions and exercise control over supplies of materials and technologies necessary for spread of such weapons. For export control, certain international bodies have been instituted, like the NPT Exporter's Committee (Zangger Committee, 1970), Nuclear Suppliers Group (1974), and the Missile Technology Control Regime (1987). These are attempts to stop the proliferation of WMDs and the necessary delivery vehicles. However, such regimes may also accommodate recalcitrant states into it. The India–US nuclear deal paved the way for the greater participation of India in nuclear commerce, even though India is not a signatory to the NPT.

While multilateral efforts are made to stop horizontal proliferation, bilateral measures have been adopted by the two most powerful nuclear weapons states: the U.S. and the erstwhile Soviet Union/Russia to gradually reduce and limit deployed strategic nuclear forces under the Strategic Arms Reductions Talks or the START process. It is to be noted that despite all attempts to condemn and eliminate nuclear weapons, campaigns by international NGOs like ICAN (International Campaign to Abolish Nuclear Weapons), and occasional pronouncements of good intentions by statesmen, major states are hardly ready to give up the option, citing the supreme national interest of the state. Arms control becomes synonymous with non-proliferation in the contemporary era; the spirit is to ensure that no further spread takes place while states who possess nuclear weapons behave responsibly.

However, all the treaties and agreements are among states and therefore they are applicable to states as parties. A terrorist organisation will have scant regard for any such treaty and therefore a terrorist threat of WMD use cannot be tackled by an arms control treaty alone. Of necessity, measures must go beyond mere arms control. Circumvention of treaty provisions does not mean that the treaty is flawed but that the parties to the treaty lack integrity. Arrangements that are instituted to cut off supply lines of WMD materials to terrorist groups need to be reinforced further. In this context, the Proliferation Security Initiative has come up, which is an arrangement of willing partners led by the United States that aims to interdict shipments of suspected WMD materials to apparently hostile destinations.

In the contemporary era, when the very idea of security has undergone quite a change, many of the common concerns with inherent global dimensions have become parts of national security considerations. For example, climate change and environmental degradation is a global security threat that calls for concerted and collaborative actions towards sustainable development. On the other hand, depletion of natural resources like fossil fuel and fresh water can instigate a new bout of rivalry among states in the form of resource war. With global warming, the melting of ice sheets, and the rise in sea levels submerging low-lying areas, the possibility of state collapse under pressure from refugees is real. While states are compelled to cooperate to tackle common challenges, in order to prepare itself for the worst-case scenario, a state might still use force to ensure near-exclusive control and access over resources or to ensure spatial exclusion to keep unwanted refugees at bay. The possibility of conflicts and use of force therefore continue to exist despite a shift in security priorities and various measures adopted to prevent war and the proliferation of weapons.

10

Sub-State Nationalism and International Intervention

Sulagna Maitra

Introduction

Sub-state nationalism and international intervention are difficult topics in International Relations as they challenge state sovereignty and territorial integrity—the two cardinal principles that, even in this era of global politics, form the basis of relations among nations. To complicate matters further, there is no single sequential path for sub-state nationalism and no universally agreed-upon doctrine on international intervention. This makes it hard to objectively determine international responses to sub-state nationalist movements. For example, should the European Union intervene and support Catalonia's declaration of independence to uphold the principle of self-determination, or should it defend the territorial and constitutional integrity of its member state, Spain? Is it any easier to devise an international response when sub-state nationalist conflicts cause complex humanitarian emergencies and forced displacement such as in Syria, which in turn can jeopardise the stability and security of a region? These are some of the questions that this chapter will dwell upon and try to answer by looking towards contemporary international policy and practice.

Despite difficulties and challenges, the question of sub-national movements in IR has been unavoidable. Writing in the immediate aftermath of the Cold War, Schechterman (1991) eloquently stated that the agenda of the earlier dismantling of empires[1] remains incomplete and inconclusive in numerous parts of the world, such as the Middle East, Central and Eastern Europe, the Western and Southwest Pacific, and most of sub-Saharan Africa. Examples of dissent and expressions of the aspirations of political movements and their impact on international relations and regional politics are not too difficult to find throughout history, and indeed in contemporary international relations. For example, the impact of political and militant movements in Kashmir in Indo–Pak–China relations, the ongoing crisis in Arunachal Pradesh and its role in shaping Indo–China relations, the suppression of Rohingyas and the global outcry against Nobel Peace Prize winner Aung San Suu Kyi, and the political movements in Scotland, Northern Ireland, and Wales within the United Kingdom are just some of the cases in point. Thus, scholars like Bernard Schechterman have called for a refocus on this often overlooked factor in international politics (Schechterman 1991, 4–17).

In recent years, the COVID-19 pandemic saw the coinage of 'vaccine nationalism', the idea that states want access to vaccines for their populations first, rather than to participate in global efforts towards equitable access. This parochialism was especially manifest in Europe, where nationalist undercurrents that have been growing in strength found new outlets through health security. The UK, which left the European Union on 31 January 2020, forged ahead with a national strategy to ensure vaccine supplies, entering into contracts with pharmaceutical companies such as AstraZeneca early on (Greer, et al. 2021). The European Union, on the other hand, was criticised for a vaccine procurement process that was slower and more bureaucratic. Tensions reached a climax early in 2021 when the European Commission slapped export controls on vaccines, aimed particularly at AstraZeneca, which placed British contracts ahead of European deliveries. The move fuelled allegations of protectionism and further poisoned post-Brexit relations between Brussels and London.

---

[1] Such as the Ottoman, Austro-Hungarian, and German Empires after World War I and the British, French, and Japanese Empires after World War II.

This escalation of 'vaccine nationalism' was about more than just logistics—it reflected and further shaped the spread of nationalist rhetoric and policy throughout the continent. Populist parties in Eastern Europe, in countries like Hungary, Poland, and Italy, used the pandemic to stigmatise the EU and recapture the national sovereignty narrative (Schwiening and McKee 2021). Meanwhile, in the UK, Eurosceptic voices argued that the country's more rapid vaccine deployment was proof that Brexit had been the right decision. So the political implications of the vaccine became wrapped up with broader issues of identity, authority, and the legitimacy of supranational institutions. The pandemic exposed rifts in European integration and showed how crises can inflame nationalist instincts, undercutting efforts to work together even as the global moment calls urgently for such cooperation.

Outside Europe, 'vaccine nationalism' followed a global pattern, a result of the underlying geopolitical rivalries and imbalances in the world order. In the United States, the Trump administration authorised 'Operation Warp Speed', committing billions of dollars to domestic vaccine development and production and securing early claims on millions of doses, long before the global COVAX initiative materialised. Countries like India and China, in turn, practised 'vaccine diplomacy', deploying bilateral vaccine donations and exports to bolster regional influence and soft power (Fidler 2021). India, via the Serum Institute of India, initially became the largest supplier to the COVAX facility. However, it had to halt exports in 2021 due to domestic surges in COVID-19 cases, which left it and dozens of countries in the Global South without supplies. China exported millions of doses of its Sinopharm and Sinovac vaccines to Latin America, Africa, and Southeast Asia, casting itself as a benevolent global player, even as doubts lingered over their effectiveness.

These patterns revealed striking inequalities between the vaccine haves and have-nots, as high-income countries at one point had possession of more than 80 per cent of the global supply. In contrast, many African countries had vaccinated less than 2 per cent of their population. In this respect, 'vaccine nationalism' was not just emotionally loaded patriotism or domestic politics, but became a proxy for wider contests over global hierarchy, trust, and the moral legitimacy of international institutions.

Nationalism and Sub-Nationalist Movements

Nations as Imagined Communities

Benedict Anderson (1983) famously described a nation as an *imagined community.* According to him, 'It is imagined because the members of even the smallest nation never know most of their fellow members, meet them, or even hear of them. Yet in the minds of each lives the image of their communion' (ibid., 15). In fact, he adds that 'all communities larger than primordial villages of face-to-face contact (and perhaps even these) are imagined' (ibid.).

Thus, the concept of nation is distinct from the definition of state, which is:

> [A] form of human association distinguished from other social groups by its purpose, the establishment of order and security; its methods, the laws and their enforcement; its territory, the area of jurisdiction or geographic boundaries; and finally by its sovereignty. The state consists, most broadly, of the agreement of the individuals on the means whereby disputes are settled in the form of laws. (Encyclopaedia Britannica 2017c)

John Breuilly (2011, 388) conceptualises nationalism as the 'idea that membership of the nation provides the overriding focus of political identity and loyalty, which in turn demands national self-determination .... a nation refers to a whole society occupying a specific territory'. Nationalism can thus be defined as ideology, as politics, and as sentiment (ibid., 399). Anderson (2013) explains that even though the nation is not a physical object, nationalism is very real. This can be seen in terms of how people are moved by national symbols such as songs, flags, and war memorials; the emotions that people feel towards their nation are very real. There is a strong association between nationalism and death, in the sense that people feel compelled by nationalistic fervour to give up their lives and the lives of their children and grandchildren for the sake of people or communities whom they may personally not know.

Similarly, citizens of a nation are always aware of the sacrifices made earlier by individuals in order to secure their nation and future. Nationalism also generates a sense of simultaneity—different people doing the same things at the same time, such as watching the 9 o'clock news or a cricket match. For Anderson, this shared consciousness and sense of simultaneity lie at the heart of nationalism (Anderson 2012). Breuilly (2011) concedes that it is difficult to define nationalism and a nation. He cites the example of Turkish nationalists who claim the Kurds in Turkey as Turkish, a view rejected by the Kurdish nationalists. Speaking on contemporary forms of nationalism, Anderson (2013) cautions against an increasingly dangerous trend: 'There is this growing feeling that English is something you have in your blood and not where you live or pay your taxes.' He believes that such people are not nationalists but racists, or those who have retreated into a sense of ethnic identity and not a nationalist one (ibid.). Eric Hobsbawm (1992, 9) contends that 'the word "nation" is today used so widely and imprecisely that the use of the vocabulary of nationalism today may mean very little indeed'. According to Breuilly (2011), it is helpful to understand nationalism in its two aspects—civic and ethnic. Civic nationalism refers to commitment to a state and its values. Ethnic nationalism, on the other hand, is commitment to a group of people with (imagined) common descent, where the nation precedes the state.

Nations as Artificial Constructions

Commenting on nation-states and their formation, Noam Chomsky (2015) termed nations 'artificial constructs', which were almost always established through violence. Nation-states force people from diverse cultures, religions, languages, and ethnicities into a single entity. It is not easy to mould people from diverse backgrounds into a single national culture and model of social commitment, service, and state power, and the effort it takes is evident in the history of the establishment of national boundaries, which has often been a very violent process (ibid.). According to Chomsky, Europe was the most savage place in the world for centuries, during the period when the nation-state system was coming into being. Peace came to Europe only after World War II, when its leaders realised that another such war could wipe everything out (ibid.). Indeed, historian John Merriman (2009) believes that, given the multitude of nationalist and sub-nationalist claims that emerged in the early twentieth century, one should ideally be investigating how major empires like the Austro-Hungarian or the Russian had survived for so long, instead of dwelling on the reasons for their collapse.

It is important to remember that nation-states are a relatively recent phenomenon, and that the formation of nation-states around the world is an ongoing process. Breuilly (2011, 388) has traced the evolution of nation-states since the 1500s. His estimation of the number of nation-states is based on historical judgement and the membership of the League of Nations and of the United Nations. According to Breuilly, in the 1500s there were only two nations—England and France. This number grew to thirty in the 1900s, including Belgium, Germany, Italy, Serbia, Romania, Greece, Brazil, Argentina, Japan, and Canada. Today, there are 193 UN member states (United Nations n.d.[d]). In this regard, 1960 represents a special year, as this was when the UN admitted seventeen new countries (bringing the total membership to ninety-nine), most of which had recently gained independence from decades of colonialism. This represented the largest increase in a single year since the organisation's founding (United Nations n.d.[e]). The struggle for self-determination, however, is far from over, as there are several groups around the world still fighting for recognition as nation-states, including regions like Palestine, Taiwan, Kosovo, Tibet, Northern Cyprus, and Catalonia.

It is important to recognise the fluidity of the conceptualisation of a nation and nationalist thought (Chatterjee 2013). Tracing the evolution of the Indian freedom movement, Partha Chatterjee comments on how, in its early moments, the movement was an extremely elite project. Mahatma Gandhi's contribution marked a departure from this project as he transformed it into a mass movement. Jawaharlal Nehru subsequently constructed a state ideology from this mass project (ibid.). Chatterjee believes that it is important to locate these internal fissures, departures, and manoeuvres in nationalist thought, and not view them as seamless narratives, a view that tends to dominate popular perceptions.

Sub-State Nationalism

According to Subrata Mitra (2012), sub-national movements signify cultural nationalism in a territorial space (*a homeland*), which its advocates strongly believe is legitimately theirs. This is not much different from a nationalist ideology that attaches huge importance to self-determination. As such, the argument for movements based on cultural or ethnic nationalism is not difficult to understand. Just as a person cannot develop their personality if they are not allowed to act freely, a nation cannot prosper when dominated by another country or community (Miller 2008). Sub-nationalist movements typically draw support from people who have an affinity for a particular language, religion, ethnicity, or region, or who share a deep sense of collective grievance. Such movements challenge the fixed character of nation-states and gather force when the leading initiators succeed in attracting sympathetic support from the 'imagined community' that corresponds to the cultural catchment (Mitra 2012). The current system privileges existing state actors to a great extent, and any attempt to channel claims of self-determination are often met with resistance from existing nation-states and international organisations (Moore 2004). Thus, ethno-nationalist conflicts are often labelled in contemporary literature as ethnic/communal violence, ignoring or trivialising the nationalist fervour within such movements (Cederman and Wucherpfenning 2017). Contemporary global politics is dealing with several such conflicts, in places like Syria, Ukraine, Afghanistan, China, and South Sudan.

The causes of such conflicts may be understood in two broad ways:

1. Through the perception of foreign rule and denial of self-determination; and
2. Horizontal inequality (or the perception thereof) (ibid.).

Both lead to evaluations of injustices meted out historically and blame the groups in power. Typically, in a vicious cycle of events, open challenges to governments from sub-nationalist groups yield a repressive response from government agencies, usually in the name of securitisation. This in turn reinforces the felt grievances and alienation of the community seeking freedom from cultural and political domination. Mitra (2012) has identified an ideal five-stage cycle in sub-nationalist movements:

Stage 1. When a few highly motivated leaders (who are willing to sacrifice themselves) seek to mobilise the 'imagined community' that underpins the conceptualisation of their nation. At this stage the movement is more of a cultural initiative than a social or political project.

Stage 2. If stage 1 is successful, the movement gains momentum as a social and political project and a semblance of organisation begins to appear. Organisation is important as it lends the movement credibility and sustains momentum.

Stage 3. The movement enters the third stage when it becomes a contender for political recognition and power.

Stage 4. In the fourth stage, the movement transforms itself into an organisation (for example, a political party) with mass support, which is engaged in governance and power sharing.

Stage 5. The movement finally enters the fifth stage when the sub-national struggle is almost a memory, and the office-holding leaders work towards creating norms and institutions for their imagined community.

When Should Sub-Nationalists Break Away?

Scholars like David Miller (2008, 541) see certain practical challenges in extending the notion of self-determination to all sub-nationalist movements, and in the operationalisation of such movements. *First*, nearly all nation-states today (except for a handful, like Iceland) contain ethnic minorities. Political decisions are supposed to express the common will. However, in real life, political decisions usually represent the voice of the majority, and all too often serve the interests of the elite. *Second*, in a globalised and interconnected world, the political decisions of a nation are always constrained by the international political and economic milieu and power equations. Thus, the idea of self-determination may be a myth.

So the question remains: Under what circumstances are minorities justified in breaking away and forming a state of their own? Miller (2008, 541–42) identifies three broad traditions in political theory to answer this question. The *first* school of thought, championed by scholars like Allen Buchanan, posits that secession is justifiable only when minority rights are being violated by the state, and/or the territory has been seized through illegitimate means. Under this view, secession is justified only as a remedy for injustice. A *second* and contrasting view, upheld by scholars like Harry Beran, argues that any population group with a majority is entitled to secede from the state it currently belongs to, so long as it is prepared to respect the minorities within its own territory and offer them equivalent rights. In this view, secession is more of an individual right with no intrinsic connection with nationalism. A middle ground is presented by a *third* view of secession: the nationalist view, which claims that breaking away is justified insofar as it promotes national self-determination for everyone, that is, takes into account the demands of secessionists, the claims of those who would be left behind in the old state, and the concerns of minority communities in the newly seceded territory. In this view, secession always creates winners and losers—culturally, economically, and politically—and the optimal solution is the one that comes closest to giving each nation an equal opportunity for self-determination.

Existing nation-states can respond to sub-state nationalism in two mutually non-exclusive ways. The *first* option is to redraw their political boundaries along nationalist or ethnic lines and devolve power to local authorities. Here, it is important to remember that nationalists are focussed on self-determination for all, and therefore it is a mistake to believe that secessionist movements encourage a free-for-all anarchy whereby territories are sub-divided into smaller and smaller nations. The *second* option is to embark on a nation-building project to weave multiple ethnicities and communities into a single nation. Most nations today are multi-ethnic and embody a civic and ethnic conceptualisation of the nation-state. The nation-building exercise thus has to be constructed carefully so as to not impose a homogeneous culture on all members of the imagined community; instead, it should broaden the cultural and socio-political imagination of the nation, such that all members feel that they are part of the community.

INTERNATIONAL INTERVENTION AND SUB-STATE NATIONALISM

As mentioned earlier, international intervention in sub-state nationalism sits uneasily within international relations as it challenges state sovereignty. Scholars and policymakers have drawn on several philosophies and devised international doctrines like the Responsibility to Protect (R2P) in order to objectively determine the international response to sub-state nationalism.

Just War Tradition and International Intervention

There is a very long just war tradition in international relations, spanning more than 2,000 years, influenced by religious teachings and thinkers like Cicero, St. Augustine, Hugo Grotius, and Immanuel Kant. Both humanitarians and international policymakers have often drawn on the rich political philosophy of the just war tradition to inform debates on international intervention in sub-state nationalist movements. A just war is determined on the basis of an assessment of the motives behind the intervention (*jus ad bellum*), the methods used in the war (*jus in bello*), and the post-conflict policies pursued by the intervening actors (*jus post bellum*) (Hehir 2010). The criteria for *jus ad bellum* are:

1. Those seeking to intervene must be motivated by just intentions rather than expediency.
2. Force must be used only to correct or prevent grave injustice.
3. The anticipated benefits of the use of force must outweigh the injustice being addressed.
4. Force should only be used as a last resort after all peaceful means of resolving a conflict have been exhausted.
5. Force may be used only if there is a strong likelihood of success.
6. The right to use force is reserved only for recognised public authorities.
7. Finally, resort to force must be publicly declared and justified.

The criteria for *jus in bello* are:

1. Discrimination: Force should be applied only against aggressors and never against non-combatants.
2. Proportionality: There should be minimal force employed and the force should be proportionate to the original aggression.
3. Just conduct: All national and international laws governing the use of force must be obeyed during the military action.

Jus post bellum calls for:

1. Just peace: The final settlement should be publicly declared, reasonable, and fair.
2. Proportionality: The aim of the settlement should be to confirm the rights that were initially violated.
3. Discrimination: The settlement should distinguish between the leaders, the army, and the civilians of the party held responsible for the violence.
4. Responsibility: Aggressors on both sides should be held accountable and punished in a fair manner.
5. Compensation: Innocent victims on all sides must be compensated for their losses. (Hehir 2010)

Approaches to Intervention in International Law and Policy

It is important to understand state-centric biases in the contemporary international system if there is to be any hope of channelling secessionist sub-national movements into a peaceful, perhaps even non-secessionist, direction (Moore 2004). There are currently two broad views in international law—the Westphalian sovereignty model and the UN intervention model. The dominant Westphalian view argues that the co-existence of nations is based on an allocation of jurisdictional authority, which should be respected under all circumstances. Secessionist movements are internal matters and should be dealt with by the states themselves. The Westphalian model considers state sovereignty absolute and asserts that international law should at all times be cognisant of this cardinal principle. It is important to respect state sovereignty so as to maintain order in international relations.

In contemporary international relations, the roles and responsibilities of states vis-à-vis their own citizens and citizens of other countries are clearly laid out in customary and international law, as well as in the UN Charter. The state functions as the provider and protector for its own citizens, implements international conventions, and is the primary entity responsible for human security, disaster prevention and mitigation, and conflict resolution. The jurisdiction of governments differs in accordance with the nature of the political system—the federal system, unitary system, etc. For citizens of other countries, the role of the states is to ensure the practice and promotion of the principles enshrined in international treaties and laws. The UN Charter upholds that the sovereignty, territorial integrity, and national unity of states must be respected in accordance with the Charter of the United Nations. Any international assistance should be provided with the consent of the affected country, and in principle, should follow an appeal from that country. The affected state plays the primary role in the initiation, organisation, coordination, and implementation of response within its territory. The most fundamental responsibility when a disaster or emergency occurs is for the affected state to take action to initiate, organise, coordinate, and implement its response within its territory. It also encourages the countries bordering it to work closely together and, as far as possible, do everything within their territories to ensure that international assistance is transmitted efficiently.

The minimalist view of international intervention is challenged by solidarists in international law, who argue that the international community reserves the right to intervene whenever common global values such as peace, self-determination, human rights, etc., are endangered by the actions of an existing state or sub-nationalist movement. This solidarist interpretation of international law is also championed by sub-nationalists, who argue that *first*, the principle of state sovereignty is not absolute, and *second*, sovereignty and self-determination should be applied to all national groups (Moore 2004). For solidarists, cases like the Rwandan genocide, the Syrian conflict, and conflicts in Haiti and Kosovo were incidents that warranted a proactive international response in order to protect humanity. To facilitate the transportation of international aid, neighbouring states are encouraged to collaborate closely with affected countries in international relief operations.

Chapters VI and VII of the United Nations Charter deal with the Pacific Settlement of Disputes (Articles 31–38) and Action with Respect to Threats to the Peace, Breaches of the Peace, and Acts of Aggression (Articles 39–51), respectively (United Nations n.d.[b]). International interventions for peacekeeping and peace-building are usually undertaken vide these two provisions. Chapter VI endorses a traditional approach to peaceful conflict resolution by employing methods such as negotiation, mediation, and confidence-building measures. Chapter VII, on the other hand, mandates UN peacekeepers to enforce peace with the authorisation of the UN Security Council. It is important to note that this authorisation is vital if operations to enforce peace are to be considered legal. However, several nations, including permanent members of the UN Security Council, have acted without such authorisation, which has in turn undermined the credibility of the UN-led global governance system and its management of such conflicts. In 1999, the United States, France, and Britain sent forces into Kosovo without a Security Council resolution since Russia and China were opposed to this. Similarly, Britain and the US invaded Iraq in 2003 without a UN mandate. Russia too acted without UN authorisation when it sent troops into Georgia in 2008 (Whiting 2013).

EVOLUTION OF INTERNATIONAL INTERVENTION

The nature of international intervention has evolved since World War II. When UN peacekeeping operations began in 1948, the blue helmets, as the peacekeepers are widely known, were mostly focused on Chapter VI missions, that is, maintaining peace lines and facilitating conflict resolution through negotiations. There were no mandates for civilian protection, or gender or human rights. They primarily focussed on inter-state conflicts. Due to the principles of sovereignty and non-intervention, the UN avoided interfering in countries' internal affairs. However, the end of the Cold War saw a significant rise in several types of intra-state conflicts, such as sub-nationalist movements, internationalised intra-state conflicts, conflicts between non-state actors, and state-based internal conflicts[2] (UCDP n.d.). With these new conflicts, the UN found itself confronting complex humanitarian crises, state as aggressors violating the life and liberty of their own people, and civilians and international actors becoming deliberate targets in protracted low-intensity conflicts. This gave rise to calls for peace enforcement.

The next major development came in 2005 when the UN, at its World Summit, espoused R2P, stating that if states could not, or would not, protect their civilians and there were massive and systematic violations of human rights and/or denial of humanitarian access, the United Nations could intervene under Chapters VI and VII (Whiting 2013). In early 2009, UN Secretary-General Ban Ki-Moon released an annual report exploring the full range of the operationalisation of the R2P (ICRtoP 2017). Since then, an annual report on R2P has been released every year, and the General Assembly informally discusses and debates all progress. The thinking on the doctrine of R2P has evolved over the years. States no longer question the existence of or the need for R2P, but focus on how best to operationalise it (ICRtoP 2017; Whiting 2013).

Over the years, especially since the end of the Cold War, there has been an increase in peace enforcement missions under Chapter VII as compared with peacekeeping missions under Chapter VI. Further, these missions have moved from pure military functions to what is known as comprehensive or joint missions, which bring together a host of peace-building, humanitarian, and development professionals to enforce peace,

[2]For a full description of the different types of conflicts, see the Uppsala Conflict Data Program (UCDP), at https://ucdp.uu.se/ (accessed May 2025).

build state structures, and initiate a nation-building project. This is a much more comprehensive, intensive, and protracted intervention than the initial intervention-reconstruction-withdrawal (IRW) approach (Ramsbotham, et al. 2016).

Theoretical Perspectives on International Intervention

Finally, it is important to interrogate the motive, method, and efficacy of international interventions from the standpoint of IR theory. This section summarises some recent perspectives on international interventions and doctrines like R2P (Baylis, et al. 2014; Hehir 2010; Holzgrefe and Keohane 2003).

Realists are in general cautious about international interventions for several reasons. They believe that states are engaged in a struggle for power in the international arena to secure their survival. Their primary moral duty is to secure and provide for their citizens. Thus, in the international arena, states have to act strategically and not morally, which may at times entail supporting 'perpetrators' of violence. Further, there is no universal moral code or moral authority. In its absence, international interventions, even those carried out on humanitarian grounds, will be viewed as hegemonic and violent undertakings by the dominant groups. Besides, the sovereignty of states is inviolable. International interventions, however, are inherently disruptive. Finally, the effective decisions taken by states are always with strategic concerns in mind, and not moral compulsions. This keeps the goals of intervention focused and achievable. International interventions taken with humanitarian compulsions or the responsibility to protect in mind inevitably lead to total war because of their inherently expansive goals and moral fervour.

The liberal or institutional perspective posits that persons and states face a dilemma between individual freedom and societal benefit. The rational choice for states is cooperation, and not conflict. These notions allow for international cooperation on moral questions. Further, the Western capitalist system and liberal democracy form the best possible political-economic system, and one can trust contemporary international regimes, as they are progressive in nature. It follows, therefore, that the spread of liberal ideas (including humanitarian interventions) is a part of this progressive transformation. States and their leaders are justified in being concerned for citizens of other nations who are in need, and are not required to hide behind realist calculations. According to the liberal perspective, international interventions are justified when (*i*) a state is composed of two or more communities, one of which is engaged in a struggle for independence; (*ii*) as a counter-intervention when boundaries have been crossed; and (*iii*) in the event of gross human rights violations. However, this perspective does acknowledge the need for an unbiased and strong international institutional system that is not solely reliant on powerful countries like the US for its efficacy.

Constructivists view international interventions as a way of perpetuating the existing power hierarchy by encouraging institutional isomorphism and reinforcing the notion of 'us', the saviours *vs.* 'them', the far-away victims. According to them, developments in international relations since the end of World War II have seen a deepening of the sense of an international community with its norms and codes of behaviour, and a state's identity is increasingly tied into this sense of international community. This has led to states gravitating towards particular models of behaviour and organisation in order to gain greater legitimacy. However, this institutional isomorphism only reinforces the existing power imbalances instead of rectifying them.

Finally, critical theorists, like the realists, also believe that states do not act morally in world politics. However, unlike the realists, critical theorists, drawing on Marxist analysis, view states as the culmination of an institutional arrangement to perpetuate existing social inequities. They are more likely to use the inviolability of sovereignty as an excuse for inaction. So they believe it unlikely that states will be concerned about human suffering in other nation-states. When international interventions do take place, they mask the ulterior motives of power and capitalism in the post-Cold War era, with little means of international control. Critical theorists thus espouse intra-class solidarity and an international class struggle that transcends national borders as a catalyst for world politics, so as to rectify the inherent injustices. To them, violence and war are an inherent and inevitable part of international interventions.

11

States, Ethnic Conflicts, and International Relations

Shibashis Chatterjee

This chapter discusses in detail two of the most fundamental concepts in International Relations: the state and ethnicity. While each is conceptually examined in its distinct theoretical capacity, the linkages between the two will unfold as the chapter progresses. The state has been the dominant paradigm as well as the primary framework of analysis in IR. While states have been traversing the complexities of the Westphalian and post-Westphalian orders and regularising transactional interactions through the myriad models of international cooperation and the process of globalisation, the rules of the game are yet to find universal predictability and stability. The norms and procedures aimed at responding to transnational challenges are evolving, and hence mechanisms of global governance cannot always be effective. On the other hand, a range of ethnic conflicts that challenge the legitimacy of the state as well as of national security and question the nature of a national society perversely entrenches the indispensable role of the state, which they then both manage and manipulate. This chapter studies such conflicts in South Asia, Africa, and Yugoslavia.

The State

Several assumptions undergird the primacy of the state in IR.

- *First*, the state is a relatively autonomous unit of analysis and not a figment of imagination.
- *Second*, the meaning of 'state' is quintessentially relational: the state is an amalgam of social formations with clear control and coordinates among the constituent classes, although it is not an organisation exclusively of class relations. The class character of a state determines the particular form it takes. In conceptual terms, the state is an organisation with structural power. It is a distinct mode of spatial articulation; a cultural definition of the articulated space (the emotive bond of nationalism); and provides a technological basis to a culturally defined area.
- *Third*, the international system is structurally distinct from the state, with many other actors who are equally relevant to international relations.

The autonomy of the state is limited by the international political economy, which integrates states (in varying degrees) within a global system of production and exchange along capitalist lines, as well as by ethnocultural factors that divide most states.

The Traditional State

As a discipline, IR is principally located in the state, which was conceived as a form of public authority. The importance placed on official authority, with the state as its sole legitimate bearer, is due to the discipline's commitment to traditional security concerns, especially military and political security. While realists have predictably taken the lead in this reification of the state, other scholars have also conceded that the state performs functions pertinent to the transaction of international life, paramount among which is security. The situation has changed in the past two decades in particular, with new structures of global governance emerging in many spheres. It is therefore imperative to explain the rise of private authority in global governance. In conjugation, we have witnessed the ascension of an amorphous body called global civil society, which poses a challenge to both global governance and the state.

However, this in no way signifies the death of the traditional state. The modern state has adjusted remarkably with changing global trends, reinventing itself on many fronts. The story of global governance and civil society is therefore not a direct battle against the state; rather, it comprises complex interactions among non-state actors, global institutions, and states.

The Meaning and Role of the Traditional State

Realists like Michael Mastanduno, Robert W. Lake, and John Ikenberry believe that the state dominates the international system, and recognises no authority higher than itself. States are loath to share sovereignty, the power that makes them stand apart and over all other groups and associations in society. *Second*, realists view states as competitive entities, which naturally flows from their basis in an anarchic system that forces them to become self-reliant. *Third*, realists view the state as coherent and purposeful, pursuing the material well-being of its population and building power.

Classical realists do make oblique references to state-society relations, but leave the relationship under-theorised. In fact, realists tend not to discuss the internal dimensions of the state; more critically, they take the nation to be coterminous with the state. Classical realists like Hans Morgenthau recognised the need for autonomy among state officials so they could build power and generate wealth by designing proper foreign policies. They also hint at the need for state officials to draw upon social resources and control the economy for strategic reasons. Morgenthau also thought that state officials could project national power across state borders by deftly cultivating public opinion, educating citizens, and strengthening the institutions of authority.

Most realists agree that state and society are not the same, and recognise the significance of domestic politics in the successful pursuit of foreign policy goals. However, realists take the concept of 'national interest' as a given and do not investigate further to see how political systems produce such interests. They neither explain the relation between state and society nor tell us how states mobilise and extract the resources needed for foreign relations.

The modern state is an organisation that has sovereign territoriality. Political realism has always found it convenient to trace the principle of sovereignty back to the alleged anarchic environment itself, and explain it as a norm that transforms the Hobbesian universe of mistrust and relative power calculation into a weak form of social cooperation. This depiction of sovereignty, however, is conceptually inadequate. The post-Westphalian system of modern European nation-states came into being and matured alongside the triumph of modernity. It brought in its wake Eurocentric ideas of anarchy, uncertainty and mutual distrust, individualism, and the discourse of private rights (especially the right to property), which crafted sovereignty after the image of the eternal egoist, marking off his domain of autonomous reason and knowledge.

Externally, the state not only provides security at the borders, but it also secures a feeling of national specificity. Nationalism is a tricky business, and most often, the state creates a form of national consciousness rather than nations marking their states. Further, the efficient performance of security does not accord legitimacy to the state; rather, it is the culturally determined sanctity of the border that carries the life of the state. Border-making is thus more valuable to the state than guarding those borders. The internal mechanisms of legitimating the state are organically linked to its external purposes. As the sole guarantor of security to its population, unless the state guarantees external security, it will lack any basis for democratic legitimacy. Historically, this process has enabled state elites to manage internal conflicts by engaging in warfare with neighbouring states. The hard façade of the state became the precondition for a just internal polity that, over centuries, bestowed democratic rights, liberty, equality, and justice on its citizens. This outside/inside distinction has been cardinal to the power exercised by the modern state, and the security-centric reading of international relations was its natural corollary.

The Critique of the State

IR scholars working with an outside-inside view of the nation-state had routinely expressed serious reservations about its functional capacity as well as normative desirability since the end of World War II. The early sceptics who doubted the continued relevance of the state as the chosen unit of analysis in IR were the functionalists (Haas 1958, 1961, 1964; Mitrany 1966). They believed that the apparent trends in functional cooperation, although limited to Europe, and the unprecedented proliferation of issues in the agenda of international relations were capable of bringing about new patterns of spatial integration in Western Europe. Although Mitrany and Haas put up a brave front against a counter-assault from the realist orthodoxy, by the mid-1960s political trends in Western Europe had begun to limit the appeal of the functionalist imagination severely.

As the number and strength of permanent organisations predicated upon extra-territorial allegiances continued to grow, there was no indication that the nation-state was ready to abdicate the centre-stage of history to its extra-territorial competition. The proponents of change found it tough to counter the pervasive centrality of the state. For example, Karl Deutsch's notion of 'political community', indicating mutual expectations regarding the non-use of arms, worked through the security dynamics of the nation-state (Deutsch 1957). Neo-functionalism grudgingly recognised that the nation-state had come to stay in Europe, and despite the many attractions of economic, social, and political integration, states were loath to part with their sovereign rights.

International relations became increasingly complex over time, with widening contracts among non-state actors, the emergence of large transnational companies in the sphere of international business, and revolutionary developments in the field of communications. These dramatically reduced the global space and called for an integration of the international political economy, and as a result, the pervasive authority of the state became vulnerable and intellectually suspect. Raymond Vernon's elegant metaphor, 'sovereignty at bay', captured the changing mood succinctly. Large multinational companies had not only been independent of the regulations of particular states, but they also inaugurated a new era of hitherto unrecognised extra-territorial allegiances. In a later work, Vernon explicitly voiced his dissatisfaction with the role played by national authorities in curbing the unencumbered functioning of major transnational companies (Vernon 1971, 1991).

Following Mitrany, Haas, Vernon, and others, pluralists and interdependency scholars—notably Robert Keohane and Joseph Nye—continued to amass evidence that challenged the state's universal claim to authority. In their authoritative *Power and Interdependence: World Politics in Transition* (1977), Keohane and Nye developed the concept of 'complex interdependence', which questioned the unidimensional realist worship of power and security *qua* nation-states. To the conventional realist prescription of inter-state ties, Keohane and Nye added 'transnational' and 'trans-governmental' relations, disaggregated the complex agenda of international relations into 'multiple issues', and denied the necessity of military forces in domains marked by complex interdependence. Although Keohane and Nye were careful about specifying the limited applicability of their concepts, and weakened their case by juxtaposing realist and complex interdependency conditions, their empirical findings contributed to eroding the credibility of the state in managing non-military issues of everyday life (Keohane and Nye 1971, 1977).

Pluralists like Graham T. Allison had meanwhile shown that the realist insistence on black-boxing states was empirically and theoretically unacceptable, as all states were in essence complex condensates of social relations, governed by myriad interests with varied degrees of success (Allison 1971; Allison and Zelikow 1999). The state was thus a complex organisation in relation to the wider society, with which it was in constant communication. The domestic basis of foreign policy was therefore a crucial aspect of decision-making that IR scholars conveniently chose to forget. James Rosenau's work on linkage politics had also emphasised the need to bring the domestic and the international together (Rosenau 1969). Robert Putnam's classic two-level game of conflict resolution also came to similar conclusions (Putnam 1988). On the whole, a number of scholars of comparative politics argued against the realist claim that the international and the domestic were separate, showing that the two were inextricably intertwined in real life.

By the end of the 1970s, however, the paradigm of pluralism, along with its scepticism regarding the viability of the state, was strongly rebutted by neorealists, who refuted evidence of autonomous behaviour on the part of transnational firms. To Kenneth Waltz, for example, these companies were mere economic agents of their parent states. Without the steady support granted to them (which included, in extreme cases, the assurance of intervention by armed forces) by their respective parent states, and without the cooperation of the receiving states, these companies would be unable to play their penetrative role in international business (Waltz 1979).

The spirited realist riposte to pluralist and dependency critiques temporarily succeeded in overcoming the academic crisis of the state, following the proliferation of non-state actors, growing functional linkages, sectoral integration in selected areas of the international economy, and the innate dynamics of complex interdependence. However, as power politics temporarily calmed following the dismantling of Cold War institutions, values, and practices by a reformist Soviet Union, the realist version of the nation-state again appeared vulnerable, impotent, and academically indefensible. It was now attacked from several quarters: the new anti-statists comprised corporate theoreticians with considerable business stakes in globalisation and liberalisation, on the one hand, and radical post-positivists, for whom the authority, centrality, and universality of the state seemed entitled and self-indulgent, on the other. They were joined by neo-Marxists and critical theorists like Robert Cox, who did not deny the relevance of the nation-state, but considered it appended to a hegemonic international political economy. Cox explained that a compromise had been sought in fashioning a 'liberal institutionalism'—a convenient halfway home between the contrasting centripetal and centrifugal forces of state power and globalisation, respectively (Cox 1981, 1987).

For post-positivists, the principal target is the knowledge-constituting practices underpinning the modern nation-state. Richard Ashley's 'untying of the sovereign state', and his dismissal of sovereignty as a practice of closure, traced the fallacies of the nation-state ultimately to the realm of consciousness of modern humans, whose capricious quest to master the discourse of Western modernity called for the authoritative intervention of the nation-state to clear the path for an autonomous accumulation of knowledge.

Finally, some scholars have identified the real threat to the survival of the nation-state as originating from within. Perhaps the most comprehensive account of a probable decay-from-within view of the state has come from James N. Rosenau (1990, 1995, 1997). Rosenau's main concern is the 'vulnerability' of the state to the '... growing density of population, expanding complexity of the organized segments of society, the globalization of national economies, the relentless pressure of technological innovation, the challenge of subgroups intent on achieving greater autonomy, and the endless array of other intractable problems' (Rosenau 1997, 74). Due to the worldwide assertion of subgroup identities and the emergence of a new criterion of performance for legitimacy, the authority of non-performing states has become increasingly shaky. In this situation, which has rendered states vulnerable and impotent, Rosenau anticipated the gradual crystallisation of a multi-centric world, where transnational and sub-national actors would rise, causing states to fragment from within.

THE STATE UNDER GLOBALISATION

The increasingly dominant role played by financial capital, both at the national and international levels, has gradually eroded the original autonomous capacity of the state to realise its objectives through a planned implementation of policies. As Robert Gilpin clearly pointed out, the post-World War II financial situation has been marked by three fundamental shifts (Gilpin 1981). The *first* concerned the rise of the Euro currency market that weakened political control over international finance considerably. The *second* shift related to the problems of Third World debt in general, and Latin American indebtedness in particular, which culminated in a reassertion of IMF–World Bank influence throughout Third World economies. And *third*, the trajectory of the international financial system took an unprecedented turn when Japan replaced the US as the world's foremost financial power. The period that saw the world's monetary and financial systems, once dominated by the dollar, being underwritten by Japanese capital, was appropriately termed the era of globalisation of financial capital (ibid.).

The same trends were accentuated over time with the steady growth of the fluidity of global finance. Scholars are divided over how to depict this transformation, with some believing that a radically different financial and trading order has come to stay, and that the world economy is no longer regulated authoritatively by the state. For sceptics, this global economic transformation relates more to redefining such functions, following certain structural adjustment policies, than to the creation of any new centre of authority in place of the state. Others believe that the power of the state to plan, implement, and control a set of economic policies in order to fulfil desired objectives seems to have diminished in the wake of the growing mobility of international finance; however, this has neither prevented the state from extending its control to new areas of economic management nor rendered it a purely reflexive category, at the mercy of more vibrant corporate actors.

To understand the nature of the challenges posed to the predominance of the state, it is imperative to study certain key areas of the contemporary global political economy. The first relates to productive processes in general. Here, one may identify a gradual shift from the formalism of Fordist principles of economic organisation to an 'economics of flexibility'. Big manufacturing industries have increasingly lost out to complex assemblage plants within intricate supply chains.

Such a restructuring has orchestrated international production at the global level, and has largely freed global business functions from political regulations. These new production processes are controlled by private companies located mostly in Western capitalist states, which use a growing but organisationally precarious labour force divided along lines of ethnicity, culture, and religion, thereby undermining the bargaining power of international labour movements throughout the world. Further, the diffusion of global production has led to a somewhat unprecedented disharmony between international labour and capital (Stubbs and Underhill 1994).

However, in the new millennium, with the rise of China and India as major economic players, a number of Chinese and Indian companies have come to rival the American and European business conglomerates. Thus, the nature of global investment flows is far more complex now. Investments occur at both ends, and while Western multinationals do business in Third World states, the leading business houses of China, Japan, South Korea, and India also invest liberally in Western economies, in sectors that are profitable. The relation between manufacturing and services has assumed vast complexities and states find it difficult to pursue coherent policies vis-à-vis private businesses in these areas.

The *second* crucial area of change concerns the role of global finance. The post-War period saw the recovery and subsequent resurgence of the world capitalist order, which has successfully extended its hegemony, both through its specific institutions (such as the IMF and the World Bank) and its policies across the globe. Also, the great upsurge in neoliberal economic policies and the gradual integration of much of the hitherto reclusive Third World economies through the twin process of liberalisation (or structural adjustment) and globalisation of productive systems has created a new integrated globalised economy ruled by financial capital. However, the most mobile and dominant capital today is not productive but speculative in nature, controlled and manipulated by global rentier interests, inaugurating an era aptly described by Susan Strange as 'casino capitalism' (Strange 1986). Riding the crest of an amazing information revolution, which has provided global finance with a nearly 'unregulated and electronically connected twenty-four hour network', speculative capital has severely undermined the notion of sovereign territoriality in the sphere of political economy. Moreover, states are increasingly surrendering before neoliberal demands and facilitating whatever they can to retain private capital. This dichotomy between production and finance is a serious malaise, causing seasonal unemployment, intermittent spells of recession, and an overall decline in world industrial output.

The growth of speculative finance has eroded the economic power base of the state. It is the dynamics of global finance rather than the exercise of free choice of sovereignty that decides the outcomes of major global economic decisions. The increasing volatility in global money markets has had catastrophic consequences since 2007, with the sub-prime crisis tearing apart the private real estate and banking markets in the absence of good regulatory devices. The crisis exposed a series of hoary deals by unscrupulous investors, who bet against the housing market in collusion with key government and banking officials. Europe was mired in a different crisis that occurred at the same time, which arose from the difficulties faced by economies that were unable to make any worthwhile profit, and yet had welfare responsibilities requiring high levels of spending. In some states like Greece, Spain, and Italy, the national banks were unable to underwrite the finances and the European Central Bank, led by Germany, refused to bail them out. The economic crisis gradually turned political in states like Greece, where a few left-wing political parties captured power.[1]

There has been a decline in the bargaining power of organised labour vis-à-vis capital. While the number and variety of jobs has indeed gone up worldwide, much of this job creation has taken place in brief spurts, and is temporary or seasonal in nature. Temporary workers find it difficult to unionise, and states that have withdrawn from most spheres of the economy find little political logic in supporting the politics of labour. One reason for this decline is the growing discrepancy between the mobility of capital and the relative immobility of unskilled

[1]The Coalition of the Radical Left, popularly called SYRIZA, came to power in Greece in a populist coalition with Independent Greeks (ANEL) in January 2015. While the maximalist government had refused to bow before the harsh bailout terms set by the EU, when Prime Minister Alexis Tsipras and the SYRIZA government acceded to the third Memorandum of the European Union on Greece's debt, the government collapsed, with twenty-five ultra-hardliners deciding to quit. Tsipras dissolved the government and went to fresh polls. The SYRIZA-led New Democracy won the elections, winning 145 seats. The Greece story reveals the constant vacillation between state and financial institutions, an uneasy political stalemate whose future remains uncertain.

or semi-skilled labour, juxtaposed, ironically, by the hyper-mobility of highly skilled workers in knowledge and information-based service sectors of the globalised economy.

Transnational firms have emerged as the most powerful catalyst in this gradual but steady marginalisation of organised labour in the postcolonial world. The sociological consequence is the emergence of a polarised class structure, with highly skilled functional elites at one end and the functionally superfluous, marginal, and impoverished people at the other (Apter 1987). The emergence of a specialised technical and functional elite has been instrumental in forging a hegemony of international capital, by making alliances amongst professionals across national boundaries and developing functional networks between varied neoliberal cosmopolitan interests. The gradual decline in the organisational strength of international labour affects the state in three ways.

- *First*, it implies the retreat of virtually every form of state intervention, giving rise to a new ideological climate marked by the aggressive optimism of capital and the equally pervasive defeatism of labour.
- *Second*, this downward mobility of workers is directly responsible for much of contemporary migration—a phenomenon that has been at the heart of demographic challenges in many European states. With the decline in class ideologies and the growing appeal of radical religious doctrines, a section of this floating population is now available for, and engaged in, violent activities in their host societies. The relative weakening of class and upsurge in identity politics have paradoxically increased the surveillance and punitive powers of the modern state, often compromising democratic principles and human rights.
- *Third*, it has confused the upwardly mobile classes, along with intellectuals and professionals, who constitute a new historic bloc in contemporary global capitalism.

The state is not a silent spectator in this massive restructuring and transformation of the international political economy. While it has lost several levers of economic control and management, it has gained in other areas. The political economy of the contemporary global order is pervaded by institutions of the state. From crisis management to fiscal disciplining, the state's economic policies remain a crucially relevant parameter of the globalisation of finance and production structures.

ETHNICITY

Most texts on IR argue that ethnic conflicts have gained a new lease of life after the Cold War. While this statement is empirically true, in the postcolonial world ethnicity had always been a pivotal anchor of conflict, both between and within states. Academic IR, however, has made few sustained forays into the subject, although IR scholars have shown an interest in explaining the transnational effects of ethnic conflicts. Ethnicity is important for the sovereignty of states, rather than for competitive struggles between sovereignties. Ethnic conflicts become a security concern when they involve competing claims to sovereignty. All multi-ethnic states face varying degrees of ethnic problems, some threatening the security of territorial configurations from within, while others are successfully negotiated or managed by the state. Therefore, it is the territoriality/identity bind that is central to the agenda of ethnicity-security research. Territorial nationalism and ethnicity come in conflict—although they do not necessarily pose a security threat to the state—because their constitutive principles are often contradictory. The dialectics of these two apparently different modes of articulation of identity—territorial/national and ethnic (self)-definition/mobilisation—is responsible for ethnic conflicts across the world.

Ethnicity, Security, and Political Violence

Mainstream literature in IR usually privileges the safety considerations of states and defines security primarily in inter-state terms. Political realism, still the dominant paradigm in IR, postulates a primal anarchy in which states are exposed to high levels of mutual threat, emanating from an unhindered freedom of action. Unlike the domestic situation, where a universal sovereign can be constituted, the international system remains anarchic in the absence of a central regulatory authority. The original realist conception of power and security did not focus on the internal dynamics of security, since its epistemic domain comprised the external relations of states. Soon, however, the artificiality, if not outright impossibility, of such a watertight compartmentalisation became clear, and considerations of internal security were made legitimate pursuits of security experts. This became even more decisive with the realisation that states have their own agendas against communities and individuals, which can take the form of a social and political-cum-military threat. The result has been an expansion in the ambit of security, without, however, ignoring the central realist assumption, that is, international security, of and for the nation-state. The idea of societal security—as distinct from state security—remained unexplored in IR, with the exception of a marginal and dissenting group of scholars who, working with modified socialist assumptions, pioneered theories of dependency and world systems and defined security in economic and systemic terms.

Ethnicity is a fundamental component of security. Variations in the definitions of ethnicity and security, however, have significant ramifications for both. If the sanctity of the territorial boundaries of existing nation-states is an absolute precondition for nation-state security, then ethnicity, as an invariant of ethnic identity mobilisation by a particular section of the political elite for political or sociocultural benefits, will constitute a threat, especially if such mobilisation aims to transform the existing territorial boundaries of the nation-states (Phadnis 1990, 16). From the perspective of community, problems of national security *qua* ethnicity are problems of the state, for it is the inescapable tendency towards domination in the ideology of territorial nationalism, which 'marginalized, disciplined, and punish(ed.) recalcitrant communities', that can sustain a 'system of interest representation, a framework for group representation, and a system of institutionalization so that the bureaucratic-authoritarian regime can consolidate its hold as well as forge extensive constituencies for its rule' (Samaddar 1998b, 108, 112). Security for the state therefore often demands the deliberate subversion of communities, turning ethnicity into something that produces and reproduces state militancy through time.

Such blanket prioritisation of communities poses problems, however, especially when one attempts to link ethnicity with societal security. Planning security based on the dominant ideology of nationalism is deeply flawed, and often leads to intense ethnic counter-mobilisations. These movements aim to mimic the 'territorial exclusivism' embedded in the marginalising power of territorial nationalism. To criticise such a strategy is not to believe that, left to themselves, the communities, conceivably in a state of ethnic mobilisation, would achieve security for themselves. Although these communities have suffered the consequences of a politics of nationalism, following the articulation and then institutionalisation of territorially demarcated nation-states, it is difficult to believe that ethnic groups had faced no problems of security, order, and competitive equilibrium prior to the making of a world order comprising nation-states. The relationship between the nation-state and ethnic communities is complex. Any theoretical framework that overemphasises the claims of one over the other must concede that their interaction is primarily shaped and sustained through the mediations of intricate power relations. While this can be imaginative and possessed of a subtle elegance, its contribution to an essential understanding of security cannot be granted automatically.

ETHNICITY AND SECURITY IN DIFFERENT CONTEXTS

In international politics, the study of how ethnicity impacts security calls for several presuppositions. *First*, the security concerns of multi-ethnic states are real, and not necessarily contrived. *Second*, ethnicity would constitute a security threat if a particular ethnic component dominates the allocation of scarce resources and significant positions of power within a state. If ethnic groups that are victimised or discriminated against have ethnic affiliations with other bordering states, the nature of conflict (and hence the issue of security) will not only be domestic, but will also assume inter-state dimensions. *Third*, subjective awareness of a series of experiences is crucial to the formation of ethnic identity. The range of demands and the intensity of a group's commitment to pursuing these generate its relative sense of security vis-à-vis other groups. *Fourth*, communities share a common worldview comprising intersubjective symbols, notions, customs, and dialogue, which generates a spectrum of conflict and cooperation that has crucial salience for group stability and security.

In poly-ethnic states, the security needs of both the state and ethnic groups often diverge, leading to conflicts. The inherent fluidity of the national imagination means that conflict is caused not only by a dissonance between the territorial national form and the ethnic view of national boundaries, but also pits one group against the other as patterns of social stratification and culture come in conflict (Hoetink 1975). This means that these boundaries may shift at random, and hence the politics of boundary-making is itself a source of violence in many postcolonial societies. *Fifth*, it indicates that securitised ethnic identities reify the state as the institution within which resides the political national identity that often compels community ties to follow the territorial logic of the state (Chatterjee and Maitra 2020, 112–14).

Understanding 'Ethnic Group'

It naturally follows that one's understanding of the concept of 'ethnic group' is key to a proper assessment of the relationship between ethnicity and security. An exclusively objectivist or cultural-anthropological conception of ethnicity is not useful in a study of the linkages between ethnicity and security. Fredrik Barth defined ethnic group solidarity as being based on certain recognised characteristics, which create a distinct cultural world that can be sustained through social practices (Barth 1969, 9–38). In this sense, the formation of ethnic groups depends on the use of ethnic categories and interactions as proposed by leading actors of the group. The stability of a plural society, or a stable system of inter-ethnic relations, therefore requires recognised rules of interaction along the boundaries of groups. The extent to which such recognised rules are weakened, threatening to displace the boundaries, will inform the measure of insecurity for the political unit.

Ethnic Group Insecurities

In such a situation, vulnerability may take two distinct forms. *First*, if the contestation over rules becomes intense enough to threaten the internal solidarity of an ethnic group, ethnic violence engendered by this sense of displacement and insecurity will target rival ethnic groups, even where the weakening of the rules is not deliberate. If, on the other hand, the intrinsic cultural identity of the group is threatened through 'peace-making' overtures to the ethnic character of the state as a whole, the group will invariably threaten the ethnic security of the latter. In this battle over boundaries, groups are often targeted both by custodians of the state, who seek to preserve its ethnic core, and separate communities who feel insecure as their distinct identities come under an existential threat. Whenever the state or a group mobilises its supporters, ethnic boundaries tend to get militarised (Chatterjee and Maitra 2020, 114).

The Dynamic Role of the State

The more pronounced the violent arm of the state, the greater its insecurity vis-à-vis forces of ethnicity. In situations where ethnic groups lock horns independent of the nation-state, problems related to security and political and social order will be grave even during the initial phase of such struggles. If one hypothetically grants the possibility that the nation-state, undecided on which contending group to support, will prefer to remain uninvolved, the resolution of such conflicts will be left to the regulatory mechanisms of the ethnic groups themselves. This will presumably involve attempts to redefine boundaries, alter the significance of old social and cultural symbols, and evolve new identities capable of creating a cooperative inter-ethnic threshold.

The road to such a resolution could well be tortuous and bloody, given the re-negotiation of intra- and inter-community power relationships, involving indicators such as the economic status of groups, their demographic growth, and the incidence of cultural and territorial boundary-crossing. Holding on to the cultural and somatic attributes of ethnic groups is vital to both their perception of difference from other groups and their internal cohesion. Where territories have been ascribed with cultural or sentimental significance, which are transmitted down to new generations, there can be no resolution in the case of transgression by 'others'. If ethnic identity is based on a sense of 'otherness', this feeling of exclusion is not necessarily created by the nation-state alone. If communities find themselves unable to settle their differences without resorting to ethnic violence, the state will retain the moral authority to be consulted in such disputes, and may be required to intervene and mediate in such conflicts.

The question, however, is: Can the state make available such powers of mediation? The history of state-ethnic group relations suggests that the state intervenes successfully in favour of a community only after it has insulated itself sufficiently from the ideology of territorial nationalism, and considers the community a partner in seeking a solution to group disputes. Such a bifurcation between the identity of the nation-state and the ideology of territorial nationalism may sound strange to those who define the state by territoriality alone. However, it seems that the nation-state is about more than just territory; otherwise, the enduring presence of such a widespread political structure would be difficult to explain. The state may resist aspersions of territorial nationalism if it consciously articulates a set of performance criteria attached to the legitimacy of political rule itself (Mitra 1997, 17–49). Moreover, even as the nation-state disciplines communities, the communities together can work to build that same nation-state. This mutual relationship provides the communitarian foundation for the political legitimacy of the nation-state, and is vital for stable state-ethnicity relations.

Ethnicity and Governance

In a modernising and developing society, ethnicity remains enmeshed with problems of governance. Ethnicity, in this sense, poses ideological and cultural challenges to orderly management from the outside. The governance of a society will reflect the dominant interests of powerful groups; it will at times be unable to sufficiently broaden the scope for political participation for members of all groups along lines of fair, politically regulated competition; and it might even allow the blurring of boundaries and responsibilities for purposes of better governance. In such a situation, the conflicting interests of the state, responsible for providing territorial governance, and those of secessionist ethnic groups will continue to generate insecurity, both for the state and for the groups themselves.

Security in Multiethnic Societies

Multiethnic societies are often torn apart by ethnic violence because we reduce the complex dynamics of state-community relations to simplistic views of ethnic groups. These communities now exist within political structures defined by sovereign territoriality, which affect all boundaries, both political and social.

A nation-state is composed of a variety of geographical imaginations. The vitality of such cognitive views may not, however, be reflected in creative or transformative projects of spatial rearticulation. The social transformations underlying multiethnic societies do carry the power to destroy the nation-state, but only if the nation-state has lost all significance as a geographical or territorial construct, according to the normative criteria defining social reality.

ETHNIC IDENTITY AND THE COPENHAGEN SCHOOL

The long-standing neglect of ethnicity in IR has been partially repaired by the Copenhagen school, pioneered by Barry Buzan, Ole Waever, and others, who argue for a dual understanding of security, one that combines state security, predicated upon sovereignty, and societal security, which is concerned with identity. As Waever, et al. argued: 'At its most basic, social identity is what enables the word "we" to be used as a way to collectively identify the "thing" to be secured' (Waever, et al. 1993, 17). Societal security is crucial because security is not exclusively a matter for the state. The definitions of identity that matter for security originate from society itself. The Copenhagen school thus follows a constructivist agenda vis-à-vis ethnic identity formation. They point out that what is being constructed are not just state identities, but the whole range of actors who have to be secured, and the nature of the threats involved must also be created in the process. In ethnonational conflicts, for example, what is usually securitised is an 'ideal'. Hence, such conflicts cannot be reduced to physical elements alone, but require the deployment of a strong constructivist strategy, one that sufficiently explains the constitution (or creation) of the given political objects and the way in which different identities are developed. Since the nature of any threat depends on where identity is anchored, it is the understanding of identity that is pivotal to the security of the object.

Myron Weiner's Theoretical Construct

The security of sociocultural identity in the face of a cross-border movement of *outsiders*, or the security of the identity of a refugee-receiving state when faced with a tide of migration, is a central theme in this new genre of research. Myron Weiner's work is crucial here (Weiner 1992–93). Weiner uses a flexible research strategy that combines materialist (realist) and ideational (constructivist/societal security) elements. His central concern is analysing how definitions of threat thresholds are determined across settings, and how such limits change as a result of the policies and practices of different states.

Weiner has advanced a security/stability framework for the study of international migration that focuses on state policies on emigration and immigration, as shaped by concerns over internal stability and security. He contrasts his framework with that of international political economy, on the basis of structural factors like economic inequality, labour and capital market conditions, and levels of technology. Weiner's analysis proceeds from a constructivist position: 'Security is a social construct with different meanings in different societies' (Weiner 1992–93, 195). His chief concern is with explaining why and when migration flows and population movements are considered a 'threat' by receiving states. His analysis highlights the limits of explanations based on a materialist or economics framework, for neither 'economic absorptive capacity' nor the raw volume of refugee immigration can explain the riddle. This underscores the inevitability of identity-based explanations, not against material trends but in association with them. Hence, a resource-poor or economically stagnant state would feel 'threatened' by a population influx under most circumstances, and move to securitise immigration automatically.

For a relatively resourceful state, however, the nature of identity would matter in the perception of threat. Take the example of the dispute between India and Bangladesh on the refugee issue. India's economic position attracts migrants from Bangladesh. But the enumeration or naming of such migrants has changed over time. In 1971, Muslim Bengalis were designated refugees, but by 1991–92 they had become 'infiltrators'. Again, Bangladeshi migration to West Bengal is understood differently from their migration to other Northeastern states. The moment in time when demography transforms into an existential issue, and is thereby securitised, is shaped by social and political issues.

Ethnicity is a key determinant of identity. Weiner shows a close correspondence between a state's ethnic homogeneity and the perception of immigration as a security threat on the one hand, and a weak correlation between ethnic heterogeneity and the securitisation of migration on the other. But he also warns against any absolutisation of ethnic categories. Ethnic affinity matters in the construction of a threat from migration, but such an affinity is also a *social construct*, subject to evolution and change. Social norms are fluid; hence, the definition of who is welcome and who is not is a variable and not a constant.

Ethnicity and Societal Security

From the perspective of societal security, ethnic conflicts pose serious security threats not because they weaken the state, but because such conflicts entail gross violations of human rights. In most cases, such violations take the form of violence against different group members, and the killing of innocent victims like women, children, and the elderly by extremist groups. It also includes action by state security forces, sporadic mob formation, the rape of women, arson, loot, appropriation of private properties, and spatial dislocation and internal displacement of groups. The protection of human rights involves the freedom to escape physical violence and trauma, and an effective articulation of this right may necessitate a 'natural right of migration' for affected communities. If migration is a natural right, necessary to protect the fundamental human rights of threatened groups, then such a precondition will automatically run counter to the demands of state security. For not only is the sanctity of borders the key element in territoriality, but the free movement of people, regardless of international borders, would also leave states vulnerable from within by significantly altering their regional demographic patterns, exhausting their scarce resources, and inviting complex third-party involvement in the crisis. If a state is unable or unwilling to protect a community, and its neighbour state adamant in its right to refuse entry to the threatened people, then there can be no hope for societal security for the concerned group.

State Security vs. Societal Security

State security violates societal security not merely through the deployment of armed forces or the unleashing of state terror, but because the ideologues of state security are often unable to concede to group demands. To view the state as the supreme arbitrator of inter-ethnic conflict is to believe that the 'state' will, one day, provide an appropriate resolution for these disputes. Such a perspective is, by definition, hostile to any claim of ethnic distinction, or to any identity resisting being taken over by the state, lest the granting of a minor concession leads to a chain reaction, thereby undermining territorial security.

In societies marked by significant wealth and income disparities, where economic divides are exacerbated by ethnic differences, members of ethnic groups become increasingly aware of their distinct identity in relation to others within the state. Consequently, they are more inclined to identify with the symbols of their own community than with the more distant symbols of the state. The more the state denies this, the more the group feels alienated; they fear that their cultural symbols are in danger of being appropriated by the authoritative pronouncements of the monolithic state. The smaller groups are especially insecure, fearing that every aspect of their existence will be penetrated and consumed by the state. The problem is that, in South Asia, existing state ideologies are not predicated upon cultural rights. As a result, people whose lives are defined by cultural rights remain perennially insecure.

Consociationalism

Ethnic cleavages are invariably politicised in most societies, with no easy solution to such conflicts. In some societies, the boundaries of ethnicity and class largely coincide, making the political management of such conflicts easier when compared to communities where disparities make the prospect of alliances across ethnic and class frontiers exceedingly complex. Many polyethnic states in Scandinavia, Africa, and Malaysia have preferred consociational democracy to open, competitive democracy for reasons of internal security, order, and social harmony. According to renowned consociational theorist Arend Lijphart, 'consociational democracy means government by elite cartel designed to turn a democracy with a fragmented political culture into a stable democracy' (Lijphart 2008, 31). Consociationalism has laid the foundation for a complex contractual power sharing, delineating distinct patterns of inter-elite and mass elite relationships.

Malaysia is an excellent example. From its inception as an independent state, it is mostly mono-ethnic political formations that have dominated the Malaysian political system, and attempts to create multiethnic political parties catering to multiethnic audiences have all been unsuccessful. Consociationalism has succeeded in Malaysia because the elites have recognised the necessity of cooperation by striking a balance of power among rival ethnic groups, although in practice, this balance has always meant the political dominance of the United Malays National Organisation (UMNO) party within the ruling inter-ethnic coalition. In other words, UMNO leaders have asserted the claims of the Malay indigene to stand over other communities, and openly proclaimed 'Malay dominance' (*Ketuanon Melayu*) in the 'land of the Malays' (*Tenah Melayu*). This political structure has not only secured Malay ethnic dominance within a growing economy, but it has also brought stability and order to a racially divided society. By incorporating other ethnic parties into the ruling Barisan coalition, it has enabled rival ethnic elites to actively protect their communal interests. As a result, UMNO's approach to community-based power-sharing has become a viable model for political stability and inter-ethnic harmony. The Barisan Nasional was dealt a severe political blow in the 2008 general elections when it lost more than one-third of the parliamentary seats to Pakatan Rakyat, a loose alliance of opposition parties, which also captured a few state governments. A closer look at the coalition, however, suggests that it too is modelled along consociational lines.

Box 11.1: Consociationalism in Malaysia

The success of consociationalism depends on four factors that are readily available in Malaysia.

1. The Malaysian political elite has shown an ability to accommodate the divergent interests and demands of various racial groups, namely the ethnic Malays, the immigrant Chinese, and the Indians.
2. This success is explained by the ability of ethnic elites to transcend their respective races and join in a collective effort with rival ethnic groups.
3. This inter-ethnic compromise has resulted from an overarching consensus to guarantee stability and order above all else.
4. Finally, the success of the consociational model results from the belief, shared by elites across the board, that unmanageable chaos, instability, and anarchy will emerge from political fragmentation unless ethnic disturbances are neutralised.

State and Ethnic Conflicts in South Asia

An ethnic movement can be termed secessionist if the nation-state is viewed as an 'external agency' by the struggling ethnic group. This has been the case with the Naga, United Liberation Front of Asom (ULFA), and Kashmiri militants in India, the Liberation Tigers of Tamil Eelam (LTTE) in Sri Lanka, and the Mohajirs in Pakistan, although the intensity of these movements and their claims to secede from their parent state varied considerably due to differences in the capability and political unity of the ethnic groups, the availability of arms and foreign support, and their ideological character. There are ethnic movements that are more accommodative in nature and target the nation-state for special concessions, benefits, and autonomy. They remain accommodative as long as the state remains receptive to their demands and makes the necessary concessions. Demands for the creation of Jharkhand, Gorkhaland, and Uttarakhand within India, and the demands of the Nepalese of Bhutanese origin in Bhutan and the Baluch and Pashtun peoples in Pakistan for greater autonomy within a looser federal structure, are examples of controlled ethnic mobilisation. There are no criteria for determining when an ethnic movement can be termed 'secessionist' and when it can be called 'controlled' or 'accommodative'. A racially discriminatory policy of distribution of resources and opportunities may turn accommodation into radical, even secessionist, demands. The LTTE in Sri Lanka and the Muttahida Qaumi Movement (MQM) in Pakistan are key examples.

Secessionism may also emerge from the failure of development strategies, or from the state's apathy in prioritising the development of neglected areas. Ethnic disturbances in Northeast India (whether openly secessionist or otherwise) are classic examples. Ethnic mobilisation agsinst the state can also result from the political process itself, when competing local ethnic leaders fail to meet the increasing demands of their precariously defined constituencies, or when concessions made by an ethnic elite to the state, either through negotiations or a reduction in the intensity of insurgency and militancy, are viewed as capitulation, leading to a dangerous escalation of militancy and inexorably pushing one of the groups to make open secessionist claims. The rise in prominence of the LTTE in Sri Lanka as the most powerful and popular instrument of Tamil consciousness by a gradual process of emasculation, marginalisation, and open extermination of more liberal Tamil democratic forces perhaps serves as the best example here.

Impact of State Policies

Much of the ethnic turmoil in contemporary South Asia is the result of state policies. The discourse of territorial nationalism is peculiarly incapable of legitimising the right to difference of peoples, communities, and ethnic groups. Territorial nationalism generates a binary opposition by encouraging homogenisation and disciplining the differences that often develop along ethnic lines. The state divides ethnic communities through racially discriminatory distributive policies. A good example is the issue of admission by ethnicity in Sri Lankan universities, a perennial bone of contention between the Tamils and the indigenous Sinhalese. The Government of Pakistan's policy of assigning regional quotas for entry into the Federal Civil Service was responsible for ethnic turmoil in the urban areas of Sindh, with Karachi being ravaged by armed conflicts.

The state creates ethnic constituencies by adopting political policies or supporting political narratives that fuel conflict. This was the case, for example, in East Pakistan, with the Government of Pakistan refusing to consider the numerical majority of the Bengali Muslim community a condition for their political representation. This led Sheikh Mujibur Rahman to launch the language movement in the 1970s, which ultimately catalysed the mass movement for the sovereign state of Bangladesh. The policies of the Indian state—or, to put it more aptly, the electoral calculations of political parties—have also fuelled ethnic unrest in many parts of India. Indira Gandhi, for example, encouraged the militant Sikh leader Sant Jarnail Singh Bhindranwale to exploit ethnic Sikh sentiments to oust the moderate Akali leadership from power in Punjab. As Bhindranwale's appetite for power grew, he sought to transform the collective Sikh identity into a militant and anti-Indian Khalistani identity that soon demanded secession from the state of India. The Indian state has also found it difficult to politically restrain identity politics in many Northeastern states, which remain subject to cycles of insurgency and counter-insurgency with no lasting solution in sight. The conflicts in Assam, Nagaland, Mizoram, and Manipur have distinct ethnic roots. The Indian state's politics of federal accommodation have had varying success in finding a durable solution to this scourge. Ethnic groups have also tended to swing between demands of autonomy and outright secession. The successful Assamese youth movement of the late 1970s found it impossible to stabilise the 'politics of ethnicity' in Assam once it came to power after 1985, and surrendered the initiative to the more radical anti-state organisation, the ULFA.

While the state does not create social identities, it does prioritise them. This prioritisation reflects the dominant interests of the state and not those of the communities, which, in South Asia, often cut across sovereign state boundaries. States find it virtually impossible to deal with the challenges of ethnic identity assertion because it refuses to admit the legitimate right of social communities to organise alternative spaces or entertain new geopolitical visions. Whether communities are even capable of developing such alternative spaces is an altogether different issue. The fact remains that the unique socio-historical experience of state-building in South Asia has turned communities into purely mechanical categories, dependent on nation-states for the sustenance of their life-forms, resources, and opportunities for development. The banal forms of discipline imposed by states upon ethnic communities have often turned the latter against the former, and much of the ethnicisation of South Asian politics is a natural corollary to the near unitary control exercised by the state.

Box 11.2: Cases of Intra-ethnic Conflict

South Asia is rife with ethnic conflicts, which often divide communities as well. Disputes between Nagas and Kukis, among Kukis, Mizos, and Paites, between Chakmas, Hajongs, Tibetans, and the indigenous Arunachalese, between Bodos and Santhals, between the Baluchis and Pathans, among the multi-tribal Baluch community, among the heterogeneous Naga tribes, between Mizos and Riangs, are all examples of disputes between communities divided by ethnicity, either from within or against each other. At times, ethnic groups have allowed larger collective identities to supervene in inter-ethnic clashes in service of a joint struggle against the authority of an 'alien' state. Thus, while diverse Naga groups like the Angamis, Aos, Semas, Konyaks, and Tangkhuls are often engaged in inter-tribal conflicts, they have nevertheless successfully projected a pan-Naga collective identity against common enemies like the 'Indian state', or the Kukis in Manipur. The Baluch community of Pakistan remains embroiled in deep inter-tribal feuds, which have not been transcended by a larger collective Baluch identity, except in times of crises.

Armed Militias and Ethnic Conflicts in Africa

Africa has been home to some of the world's deadliest and most protracted ethnic conflicts, created primarily by artificially drawn colonial borders across historically mobile and deterritorialised tribal populations. The duration and intensity of some of the ethnopolitical conflicts in Africa stem from the brutal domination of a few ethnic communities, which consistently provoked violent opposition from alienated and exploited ethnic groups. The latter resorted to armed political struggle to further their demands for political inclusion and representation in administrative processes. The state often resisted such attempts to broaden the political base, responding with brutality and violence, and triggering in the process violent backlashes in the form of armed resistance movements.

Georg Sørensen (2001) offers a compelling theoretical explanation that brings together the domestic and international dimensions of the problem. Sørensen argues that postcolonial states moved through a long process of decolonisation that gradually institutionalised the post-1945 international order. This order was based on the sovereign equality of states and the inviolability of borders. As a result, great powers became the guarantors of postcolonial boundaries, in the most minimalist legal sense of the term. Several developments occurred in this context. Many of the postcolonial states lacked ethnic homogeneity and were captured by dominant groups. State and regime security were thus equated in many cases, and ethnic leaders came to dominate political systems in several postcolonial African nations. Their commitment lay in creating security for their ethnic cohorts rather than establishing stable states. This naturally fuelled ethnic discontent amongst dominated groups, who often took recourse to violence. As ethnic affiliations cut across international borders, these conflicts frequently involved neighbouring states. What is instructive is that, as borders were secured under international norms, ethnic elites freely squandered resources on domestic political feuds. Their detractors were caught in the same bind. Security dilemmas in classical West European nations had yielded strong states.[2] But post-

---

[2]In classic European terms, the security dilemma describes how a state's attempts to enhance its security (for example, military build-up or alliances) are viewed as threatening by other states. Consequently, other states build up their military strength, thus decreasing the first state's security. Ironically,

World War II international norms had put an end to such dilemmas for postcolonial states. The Hobbesian anarchy thus did not need to be displaced, and authority and legitimacy did not need to coincide in such states. The result was national security issues between conflicting ethnic groups, each of which had a high stake in monopolising political power so they could deny political participation and economic leverage to other groups. In this way, ethnopolitical conflicts have been both the outcome and indirect cause of the economic and political crisis in Africa. This also explains the central role of ethnicity in many conflicts in Africa, which have resulted in protracted violence over decades.

The ethnic Somalis in the Ogaden and parts of Ethiopia, in Djibouti, and in the Northern Frontier of Kenya wanted to unite with Somalia, giving rise to a significant ethnic conflict in postcolonial Africa. Similar demands were made by the Ewe-speaking people of Togo for a reunion with their ethnic community in Ghana. But communities also went to war in order to control the state. The ethnic Baganda in Uganda wanted to recover lost territory and status and build a Baganda nation within Uganda, which was violently opposed by other groups and went against the Ugandan political authority as well. In Ethiopia, the three major ethnic minority groups, the Oromo, Somali, and Tigray, made secessionist demands against the dominant Amhara ethnic group, under the banner of the Oromo Liberation Front (OLF) and the Tigrayan Peoples Liberation Force (TPLF). Biafra in Nigeria and the South Kasai in Zaire are further examples of inter-ethnic conflicts, involving territorial and secessionist claims that degenerated into civil wars. Nigeria has witnessed violent demands by ethnic minority groups for a greater share of government largesse; having failed, they resorted to violent rebellion, as evidenced by the Tiv Riots in the 1960s and uprisings in the oil-rich Niger Delta since the 1990s.

---

self-defence measures can trigger a dangerous spiral of mistrust and escalating arms races, thus increasing the risk of war, as the security dilemma illustrates. This pattern of insecurity can heighten tensions and even lead to conflict, unintentionally escalating to war. This dilemma was strikingly evident in the pre-World War I era, where the competitive military expansion of European powers created a climate ripe for large-scale conflict. West European states used the security dilemma to wage wars against neighbours, which strengthened the states internally.

Rwandan Conflict

The most devastating ethnic conflict in postcolonial Africa, however, took place in Rwanda. In 1994, Rwanda's population of seven million comprised three ethnic groups: the Hutu (approximately 85 per cent), Tutsi (14 per cent), and Twa (1 per cent). While the Hutus were the dominant group, the Tutsis had controlled the political process for a long time. In the early 1990s, Hutu extremists within Rwanda's political elite blamed the entire Tutsi population for the country's increasing social, economic, and political troubles. Tutsi civilians were targeted for supporting a Tutsi-dominated rebel group, the Rwandan Patriotic Front (RPF). Habyarimana, the then President, used state propaganda and patronage to divide the communities further. Myth and memories of past atrocities of Tutsi rule were invoked to galvanise the Hutus against the Tutsis, successfully breeding resentment, fear, and hatred. The death of President Habyarimana in a plane crash was widely blamed on a Tutsi conspiracy. Violence erupted immediately, and Hutu militias went on a rampage to destroy the entire Tutsi civilian population. High-profile political leaders were assassinated. In the weeks following 6 April 1994, 800,000 men, women, and children died in the Rwandan genocide. Thousands of Hutus also lost their lives for opposing the ethnic cleansing of the Tutsi people. The civil war and genocide came to an end when the Tutsi-dominated rebel group, the RPF, defeated the Hutu perpetrator regime and a new regime under President Paul Kagame took charge. The RPF, it may be noted, had carried out guerilla warfare against the Hutu regime from across Uganda and Congo, thereby internationalising the ethnic conflict even further.

The international community played a negligible role in this massive human tragedy that claimed more lives than any conflict had since World War II. Rwanda's neighbouring countries were flooded with refugees who led miserable lives in makeshift camps. The Western world did not do enough to either prevent the tragedy or ameliorate its consequences. Policymakers in France, Belgium, and the United States, and at the United Nations, were aware of the preparations for massive slaughter, but did not act against it. Although acutely aware of Tutsi vulnerability, Western leaders refused to recognise the genocide, and did not de-recognise the Hutu government for days. There was no planned operation and no significant investment in a much-needed humanitarian intervention. When sanity returned, the worst of the carnage was over.

Sudan

Sudan has been ravaged by domestic conflicts that have roots in a neighbourhood marked by endless turmoil. The Darfur crisis has raged since early 2000, when the Sudan Liberation Movement (SLA) and the Justice and Equality Movement (JEM) launched a full-scale rebellion against the Sudanese government, in response to mass killings, rampant economic deprivation, and marginalisation. The conflict assumed an ethnic character as armed militias were formed by settled tribes like the Fur and the Zaghawa, which were foiled by the state through policies that openly aided the formation of armed bands out of roving tribes like the Rizeigat and the Misseriya, who were quickly won over with land deals and armed protection. The government-aided Janjaweed militias were deliberately defined along Arab lines, even though in Sudan, inter-ethnic intermarriages made a mockery of racial distinctions. The various factions of the SLA fought a bitter war with the Janjaweed militias, leading to an appalling loss of over three million lives and the displacement of countless others. While the UN-sponsored peacekeeping mission, following the Darfur Peace Agreement of 2006 signed between the rebel leader Suliman Arcua Minnawi and Omar al-Bashir, the President of Sudan, initially appeared to promise a resolution, by 2010 the rebels had defected, accusing the state military of betrayal and plunging the country back into violence. Although international interlocutors remain in talks, there is little hope of any settlement, as the rebels have closed ranks against a renewed state offensive.

Democratic Republic of Congo

Two wars in the eastern provinces of the Democratic Republic of Congo (DRC) between 1996 and 1997, and then from 1998 to 2003, involved over forty militias and nine neighbouring states. DRC's tragedy is not uncommon in Africa, involving the cruel cohabitation of abundant natural resources and crippling poverty. The enormous natural bounty of the state, which has the world's richest diamond mines amidst other sources of mineral wealth, not only divided its ethnic groups but also lured looters from the neighbourhood. War and domestic conflicts have claimed over five million lives and displaced countless people, and horrific acts of crime have been perpetrated against women and children. The country was systematically pillaged. Despite the presence of the world's largest UN peacekeeping force, which has operated in DRC for over fifteen years, the nation remains in a state of war. Internal and international wars in DRC have claimed massive casualties and pushed the country to the lowest position in terms of per capita income in the world. The Rwandan-backed FDLR, a Hutu militia; the factions supported mainly by Uganda, called the M23, who lead the new charges; and various local splinter groups called the Mai Mai have continued to wreak havoc in DRC, fighting to control key diamond fields and other mines. International attention, apart from the apparently massive UN budgets to support the peace troopers, has been anaemic, and, expectedly perhaps, the great powers have shown little interest in becoming actively involved. In spite of the scale of the human tragedy involved, the global media, too, has largely abandoned DRC's cause, leaving it only to a handful of NGOs and civil society groups to provide succour.

The Disintegration of Yugoslavia

However, Africa is not exceptional so far as ethnic violence is concerned. There is no peculiar primordial or tribal bellicosity at work here; the best example of that comes from the violent breakup of the Yugoslavian Republic in the 1990s. By 1992, ethnic nationalism had seriously conspired against the Yugoslav Federation and replaced communism as the dominant force in the Balkans. Slovenia, and then Croatia, left the federation, but generated a conflict with Serbia in the process. The war in Croatia was particularly violent and led to hundreds of thousands of refugees, seriously undermining peace in Europe for the first time since the end of World War II. By 1992, civil war had erupted in Bosnia, which had followed Croatia and Slovenia in declaring independence. The Bosnian Serbs, however, were determined to remain within Yugoslavia and help build a greater Serbia. Violent conflict ensued between Muslims and Serbs, eventually bringing in the Croats, who had plans for a greater Croatia. While the US-brokered Dayton Agreement did lead to a settlement in 1995, violence did not cease altogether for many more years.

In 1998, ethnic violence erupted in Kosovo, where the Kosovo Liberation Army, supported by the majority ethnic Albanians, challenged Serbian rule. The international community supported greater autonomy for Kosovo, but rejected claims of independence. Serbian bellicosity, however, did not subside. Threats of military action by the West culminated in the launching of NATO air strikes against Yugoslavia in March 1999, leading to massive Serbian losses in terms of infrastructure and facilities. Within a decade-and-a-half of the death of Marshall Tito, the creator of the Yugoslav federation, the country had completely disintegrated, succumbing to chauvinistic ethnic nationalism that resulted in a massive human tragedy at the very heart of Europe. This ethnic fragmentation engendered a looser union called simply Serbia and Montenegro, with Croatia, Slovenia, Bosnia-Herzegovina, and Macedonia emerging as independent states.

Ethnic conflicts remain alive in many post-Soviet Republics, with Russia and Ukraine having gone to war over Crimea and tussles in the North Caucasus region between Russia and Chechnya having led to numerous deaths. The increasingly authoritarian tendencies of Russian President Vladimir Putin and deteriorating relations between Russia and the West are ominous portents insofar as ethnic tensions are concerned. A number of post-Soviet states have large Russian populations that are being increasingly viewed with suspicion by the more nationalist political forces. The massive refugee dislocations following the crisis related to ISIS in Syria and Iraq, which partly flow into Europe, the economic downturn in many European states, and the controversies surrounding Britain's decision to quit the European Union (EU) have led to the increasing visibility of ultra-nationalist outfits in the continent, and ethnic and religious divides have sharpened considerably in the recent past. While not all of these have the potential to snowball into protracted ethnic conflict and war, political violence along ethnic lines cannot be dismissed in many parts of Europe. The influx of East Europeans has long been a source of tension in states like Italy, and terrorist strikes linked with ISIS and other radical religious groups have aggravated the situation further.

Conclusion

Ethnicity remains a critical factor in world politics. While in many developed countries multiculturalism, federalism, and the politics of autonomy have dampened ethnic demands considerably, in other parts of the world loyalties have continued to be divided along ethnic lines. Since most states are multiethnic and the cartography of borders does not coincide with that of ethnic demographics, the possibility of ethnic conflict remains alive in international politics. But ethnic violence is more a problem within states than it is between states. This is both because of the sanctity of borders and the inability of ethnic elites to sustain war-like conflicts.

Moreover, globalisation has also contributed to encouraging population movements in many parts of the world. Demographic patterns of many migrant-receiving societies are changing, opening up issues of both debate and conflict over the distribution of resources and recognition of differences. Multiculturalism has thus become a vital aspect of many societies, although there is no agreement about what it means and the consequences that might arise from it. On the whole, the debate continues amongst liberals who want a cosmopolitan framework predicated upon liberal values, soft communitarians claiming the protection of cultural rights, and hard fundamentalists bent on defining life according to their preferred view of culture, understood either along religious or ethnic lines.

12

Globalisation and World Politics

Shibashis Chatterjee

Introduction

Globalisation has changed our lives fundamentally, a fact we need to come to terms with, both academically and in our everyday lives. International Relations (IR) has been profoundly transformed in the past two decades by the process of globalisation. Many now seem to prefer global politics over IR since the state-centric image of the latter appears ill-at-ease with the transnational character of contemporary world affairs. Globalisation has problematised all the common pillars of IR, be it the centrality of the nation-state as the basic unit of the discipline; the meaning/s of border, sovereignty, and territoriality; the significance of flows, processes, and means of communication across frontiers; the role of actors other than the state; the massive rise in the significance of liberal-capitalist financial systems; the fundamentals of the global political economy; and the nature of a host of other hitherto defining signposts of the international order.

Globalisation thus provides one of the overarching contexts of contemporary world politics that impacts virtually all domains of life—power politics, trade, development, media, fashion, entertainment, sports, and the nuts and bolts of our mundane consciousness. It is also ideologically divisive, with virulent detractors and blind enthusiasts describing it in radically different ways. Some see it as globally empowering, disseminating ideas of accountable governance, disciplined authority, and democratic circulation of power, and reducing distances of all kinds. Others see a grand imperial conspiracy, causing serious democratic deficit within states and disproportionately empowering global financial magnates and oligarchs at the expense of civil society organisations and the underclasses. Likewise, there are claims and counter-claims regarding the wealth or poverty engendered by globalisation. While these divergent readings are a part of the discourse on globalisation, what remains uncontested is the fact that it has fundamentally altered the dynamics of world politics. We will now attempt to make sense of these divisive narratives and track how globalisation affects our daily lives.

DEBATES ON MEANINGS AND SCOPE

Globalisation has spawned an enormous range of literature. There are four broad areas of contention.

1. A debate regarding the novelty of globalisation. Against the more popular claim that globalisation is an unprecedented development, a number of historians state that while globalisation is certainly new, it is far from novel.
2. There is a fierce debate regarding its economic and social benefits. The champions of globalisation, who belong to the neoliberal or free-market schools of thought, unhesitatingly celebrate the virtues of the newly globalised world, calculated in terms of the aggregate benefits accruing to people. Sceptics and critics from either the left or centre-left have denounced globalisation as anti-poor, accusing it of having increased the gap between the rich and the underprivileged.
3. The third debate concerns political issues. Scholars are divided over the political effects of globalisation on the state, sovereignty, and territoriality, with some arguing that globalisation undermines these categories, while others emphasise the opposite.
4. The fourth debate is over its cultural consequences, with liberals urging that a cosmopolitan culture is increasingly uniting the globe, even as critics highlight the disruptive, volatile assertions of local cultures against the threat of Western cultural imperialism.

This chapter will study some of these perspectives and suggest possible frontiers of research opened up by globalisation.

Understanding Globalisation

Globalisation defies any simple definition. It is best understood as a multi-pronged process characterised by an extension of social, political, and economic activities all over the world, irrespective of political boundaries, so that an incident in one area invariably impacts the lives, decisions, and patterns of activities undertaken by others in distant locales. It also connotes an unprecedented intensification and deepening of interconnections across all spheres of social existence, whether economic or environmental, benign or harmful, in thought or action. Globalisation, moreover, is also about the massive increase in the speed at which these interconnections, be they material or ideational, concrete or symbolic exchanges, spread throughout the world. The result of this extension in connectivity, speed, and velocity of movements is the novel enmeshing of the local and the global. In fact, globalisation seems to dilute the very distinction between the two; the local and the global slide into one another, ushering in a new age of time and space compression unknown to human history. Thus, most commentators see globalisation not as a process of simple connectivity; in the words of Anthony McGrew, it is: 'A process involving a fundamental shift or transformation in the spatial scale of human social organization that links distant communities and expands the reach of power relations across regions and continents' (1997, 63).

Impact of Globalisation

Globalisation is widely claimed as universal. As is well-known within social science academia, globalisation has both strong partisans and detractors, with the former arguing that it has qualitatively altered global politics, while the latter espouse the no-change thesis (Held and McGrew 2000; Kofman and Young 1996). Globalisation complicates problems of national development by facilitating the flight of capital across territories. It forces rapid technological adjustments upon all states, failure to comply with which adversely affects the interests of those states. It urges flexibility in financial institutions and frameworks to enable states to adjust rapidly to changes in global capital flows. It integrates markets of various kinds, and thereby interlocks economic systems. In nearly every domain of collective existence, it compromises the control of sovereign territoriality, indicating the increasing obsolescence of the state. Votaries of globalisation believe that the days of the sovereign state are numbered, although they are unclear about what is to take its place.

Globalisation also entails a revolutionary transformation in information technology that reduces distance dramatically and redefines the contours of the workplace. Physical distances collapse and space becomes more mobile. There is a multiplicity of spaces at various levels, with no clear hierarchy or significance of a particular conception of space. Globalisation also manifests in the sphere of culture (Featherstone 1990). It involves the universalisation of a particular cultural form—Western culture—across the globe, leading to intense cultural conflict between the global and the local in parts of the world. Those with a positive outlook on globalisation often ignore the potential for cultural resistance that emanates from identity clashes between the West and the non-Western regions. Critics remain unconvinced and relate the recrudescence of recent identity politics to the cultural uniformity imposed by globalisation. However, despite arguments concerning different aspects of globalisation, most scholars across the social sciences accept the inevitability of the phenomenon and urge existing states to adapt to it to the best of their ability. Strong supporters of globalisation, however, are sceptical about such an adaptation, believing instead that globalisation disrupts the contemporary international order, making it impossible to return to the days of confident nation-states.

Information Technology and Globalisation

Many scholars have defined globalisation in terms of the unprecedented developments in information and communication technology. According to this view, it is technology that creates the prospect of a global village, of establishing ties across states and connecting far-off places, and gives people the material means to imagine a shared life-world comprising both risks and possibilities. According to Ankie Hoogvelt, this new global consciousness manifests through the dispersal of economic processes and production patterns, or the accelerated movement of capital flows across borders, or by generating 'a global market discipline' through the intrusions of international media. Without the revolutionary developments in digitised technology, the 'global consciousness' of 'shared phenomenal worlds' would not have been born, and as a result, none of these critical changes could have occurred in history (Hoogvelt 1997, cited in Randall and Theobald 1998, 246).

GLOBALISATION AND HISTORY

The fascinating historical research of scholars like Charles Bayly and A. G. Hopkins, among many others, has contributed significantly to creating what is known as 'global history'. These historians have indicated that global history could date back to the eighteenth century, a perspective that does not deny the uniqueness of the present phase of globalisation, but points to continuities while highlighting the significance of larger trends or patterns as a precondition to understanding the events of the present. 'Global history points to broader connections and probes the assumptions that lie behind the narratives which regional historians construct' (Bayly 2004, 469).

Archaic and Modern Globalisation

Bayly mentions the terms 'archaic' and 'modern' globalisation and shows how the two converge and diverge. In terms of ideology, modern globalisation comprises nationalism, capitalism, democracy, and consumerism. Archaic globalisation, in contrast, has three linked ideologies: 'the notion of cosmic kinship; universal religion and humoural understandings of the body and the land'. Bayly concludes:

> Already in the period 1750–1850, features of proto-globalization based on the supremacy of market driven, profit maximizing forces emanating from Euro-American capitalism and the nation states were apparent.... However, agents of archaic globalization were slowly subordinated to these forces rather than being wiped out by them. Modern and post-colonial globalization was built on and was in turn modified by these earlier social promotions, contributing

> to the persistence of long continuities of form even under modern capitalism. (Bayly 2002, 50)

Bayly cites economic competition, multi-centric origins of ideological production, and the new imperialism of the late nineteenth century as pointing to the 'multiple and interconnected origins of global change' (Bayly 2004, 471–72).

Historical Roots of Globalisation

The globalising tendencies of the late nineteenth century have led a number of historians and social scientists to question the novelty of the phenomenon. According to A. G. Hopkins, the late nineteenth century was marked by two distinctive changes: '… the shift from state mercantilism to open, free trading policies, and the development of far-reaching improvements in technology. Structural adjustment, as it would be called today, opened up economic potential as a world scale technological innovation enabled it to be realized' (Hopkins 2002, 28). The debate concerning commodity exports and capital investment from developed Western states reached levels that would be equalled again only in the late 1980s. Economic convergence across vast areas of the world, reflected in the equalising of prices, also took place around this time. Measured by innovations in the transport sector or through labour mobility, the period between 1895 and 1914 is often compared to the globalised modern world. This nineteenth-century globalisation, however, did not threaten the state. Rather, it led to the beginning of a genuine international system that saw the hegemony of the nation-state as the chief organisational frame of life.

> If it is accepted that expansion (through free trade), imperialism (which could be informal), and empire (which was a constitutional entity), between them, comprised a process of globalization, then the globalization of the 19th century was not only consistent with the existence of the nation state but reinforced it too. (ibid., 30)

GLOBALISATION AND POLITICS

Political economists have mostly analysed the impact that globalisation has had on domestic politics. Many scholars focus on Peter Gourevitch's pioneering work (1978) on how changes in international factors are transmitted to domestic life. As trends in the international political economy change, they impact the livelihood prospects of both producers and workers, although this may take different forms. If the impact is large enough, politicians get involved, and build and mobilise coalitions of affected interests within the economy. This resembles a transmission belt that builds upon changes in the pay structures of the stakeholders involved. Some groups are invariably more affected than others by globalisation, and across states, the fate of similar interest groups would often vary. Thus, if profit and jobs are involved in substantial measure, both capitalists and workers would oppose the easy entry of low-priced products into their state. However, the trade-off may often work differently. Capitalists can benefit easily from increased investment opportunities across states, while workers find their bargaining position seriously compromised due to the greater mobility of capital flows across national borders. These trends can be seen across continents and states. Globalisation coincided with the collapse of the Soviet-styled planned economies, and thus at the entry level, the political appeal of pro-labour policies were far less. This facilitated the crafting of pro-capital coalitions of domestic interest under the careful aegis of politicians groomed by big business houses, seen in most economies of the world. While it is too early to conclude that globalisation has necessarily produced liberal, pro-reform politics everywhere, this seemed to be the general political trend that emerged over the years.

State Sovereignty and Economic Interdependence

Globalisation has meant that domestic politics now needs to adjust to the complex intermeshing of global and domestic economic processes. In the past, states enjoyed a capacity for what Suzanne Berger describes as 'macro-economic sovereignty' (Berger 2000). What this means is that, in the post-World War II international political economy, relatively stronger states 'were able to use interest rates, the exchange rate, and the supply of money as levers of control in their economies' (ibid., 53). However, with free capital flows and the ushering in of a WTO-based free trading order, the older controls lost their efficacy. This has meant that the state cannot easily stop the entry of foreign capital and goods or use macroeconomic tools such as regulating interest and exchange rates to rein in economic problems that threaten to spiral out of control. Globalisation has lessened the time available to states to adjust to global economic trends that have a considerable bearing upon the domestic economy and polity. All states have become wary of this challenge, and compete to keep open their borders lest productive investment opportunities are lost to others. Instead of focussing mainly on domestic economic policies, countries now emphasise appearing attractive to investors, preferring to welcome global investment rather than hinder it.

Some scholars suggest that globalisation reduces tax liabilities on business while increasing those upon labour (Przeworski and Wallerstein 1988), but others find no evidence of such unfair distribution of the tax burden (Swank 2002). Globalisation leads to different possibilities with varied consequences. For many states, it makes available global sources of funds, a positive move as the inflow of global capital is likely to generate more economic activities and create new jobs. However, the remarkably short gestation period of investment and capital flows tend to complicate strong domestic industrialisation, as capitalists are constantly seeking outlets that maximise their returns on investment. The state-aided model of economic prosperity of the post-World War II era has fallen victim to globalisation. Economic miracles like Japan and South Korea would therefore not work under globalisation.

How does this work out politically? There are no easy answers; the fact is that the nature of the modern economy has also changed fundamentally. Supply chains and assemblages are now integral to any economy. If local producers dovetail well with global investors, innovate, and learn to adapt to fast-changing technologies, pro-globalisation politicians can ramp up effective coalitions in favour of global capital flows. If these are missing, and local producers are orphaned by big multinationals, protectionist coalitions can become stronger, although, given the challenges that states face in getting their macroeconomic parameters right, the possibility of long-term resistance politics is rather weak.

Globalisation and the Welfare State

The real political challenge unleashed by globalisation concerns the welfare state. Again, academic findings differ; many analysts have argued that given the state's loss of economic sovereignty, the slide in its tax base, and the increasing complications in the fiscal health of the economy, the state's capacity for social-sector spending has taken a backseat (Pierson 1994; Rodrik 1997). This view predicts a collapse in labour wages, the withering away of labour regulations, and the steady whittling down of social welfare schemes over time under the impact of rapid financial regulation. Their detractors, however, stress the greater resilience and capacity for adaptation on the part of states that will safeguard against any precipitous slide in social provisioning. The politics of the welfare state is a mixed one. Pro-welfare politicians are often opposed to financial market liberalisation as it strengthens the capacity of capitalists to swiftly relocate a business to low-wage destinations, abandoning large sections of the workforce to grave economic uncertainties and crisis. Others are more cautious and willing to enter issue-based coalitions, depending on how globalisation impacts a range of interests. At a certain level, democratic politics requires the support of the masses. Hence, no matter how compulsive the demands of labour deregulation and financial market liberalisation, political buffers are created to absorb economic shocks under globalisation. The more organised the politics in a state, the greater is the effect of such insulation. However, empirical trends suggest that in many developing countries, organised labour finds it difficult to stand up to mediations of global capital, and political elites often shy away from protecting weaker interests, fearing a greater economic backlash if capital escapes their borders.

Global Identities vs. National Identity

A new global ethic that disputes the identification of political good with the 'nation' has inspired a genre of globalist thinkers to visualise alternative futures. They point out, *first*, the essentially contested character of national identity; the different meanings that people attach to such identity; and the fluid, constructed nature of these categories. Political identity is therefore never unitary in character. As McGrew and Held argue,

> … contemporary reflective political agents, subject to an extraordinary diversity of information and communication, can be influenced by images, concepts and lifestyles and ideas from well beyond their immediate communities and can come to identify with groupings

beyond their borders—ethnic, religious, social and political. (Held and McGrew 2000, 33)

Second, the rationalisation of a unitary national identity is misplaced since individuals identify with diverse political communities simultaneously. People can participate in transnational social movements and mobilise on behalf of their local communities without necessarily violating their political commitments to the state. The erosion of the state's capacity to deliver political goods is strengthening transnational networks and local forms, and thereby creating new organisational structures across the globe. Add to this the hollowing out of the state due to a decline in sovereignty and autonomy in deciding the fate of national communities, which are increasingly influenced and conditioned by global developments and are caught in the webs of global and regional governance. These make it exceedingly difficult for states to perform their conventional duties of citizenship or sustain the universal structures of rights (ibid., 33–34). Globalisation has therefore altered the meanings of fundamental categories of the Westphalian order—territoriality, sovereignty, and the state (Ashley 1987, 1988; Biersteker 2002; Falk 1999; Harvey 1989; Held 1995; Hirst 2000; Krasner 1999; Murphy and Nelson 2001; Ruggie 1993; Sassen 1996; Scholte 1993).

State and Statehood: Realities and Perspectives

States have become increasingly marginal in the provision of global public goods, be it regulative, distributive, or redistributive. The economic capacity of states has either shifted towards globalised financial markets or other private institutions modelled on the principle of market competition, and their capacity to mobilise resources as a precondition to providing effective security or guaranteeing domestic stability and peace has also decreased. Hence, states can no longer decide their agenda on their own terms (Cerny 1996). Since the quality of states' performance of their critical functions—authority and economic well-being, in the broadest sense of the terms—is the chief determinant of the intensity of emotive attachment of the people, a decline in the former is destined to translate into an erosion of the latter. A good example of this view comes from Richard Falk: 'I think we are living at a time when states are losing their organizational advantage in the provision of public goods, with the revealing exception of security … conceived in the narrowly artificial terms of military/police activities' (Falk 1999, 41). Again, '… all states, no matter how militarily potent and economically formidable, have become to a significant degree "quasi-states" while "real states", if these persist at all, are a hopelessly endangered species of political animal whose reality is subject to various forms of doubt' (ibid., 43).

Contrary to such an account, Paul Hirst states that if globalisation has denied the state a number of vital economic powers, it has also helped to regenerate others, which explains the continued relevance of the state for a range of globalised economic activities (Hirst 2000, 185). Moreover, successful globalisation demands good governance, which is closely connected to the successful exercise of authority and implies a legitimate polity. Sceptics believe that the identity of the state is not fixed, and its history is not universal or unilinear. Depending on the circumstances, the state proved superior to other organisations, for varying reasons. Hence, the impact of globalisation on the idea of the state as a form of public culture can only be variable and indeterminate.

Globalisation appears to have undermined the regulative, distributive, and redistributive powers of the state, which has in turn complicated its role as the dispenser of security and authority. Less powerful nations often find it difficult to cultivate loyalty among their population. Nonetheless, globalisation remains unconcerned with this situation. Several states continue to be characterised by decreased economic leverage, a strongly authoritarian state, and mass allegiance to state power.

Retreat of the State

There has been a gradual evolution in the 'meaning' of the state at the global level, in a shift away from the Weberian model of the state towards a neoliberal variant (Biersteker 2002, 159). The state became gradually entrenched over three decades after 1945, with substantial economic interventionism and a rise in security apparatuses in response to the geopolitical imperatives of the Cold War. This gave way to a move towards de-concentration and withdrawal, partly as a result of the cessation of Cold War hostilities, but more due to the centrifugal forces of globalisation that made obsolete all statist control of the national economy.

Globalisation gave rise to two distinctive tendencies:

1. The massive extension of the project of liberal capitalism across different parts of the world, particularly in Eastern and Central Europe, which had been under socialist rule during the Cold War.
2. Globalisation also coincided with a series of spectacular collapses of postcolonial developmental projects, most specifically in Africa, leading to the rise of failed states that could neither provide security to its citizens against myriad threats, both conventional and unconventional, nor provide effective governance through traditional welfare means.

The combined result of this is an apparent retreat of the state, or at least a redefinition of the state in a conscious shift away from a Weberian understanding towards a more symbolic plane (Biersteker 2002, 160). The state today is not entirely superfluous, but its legitimacy is deeply contested, its authority fragmented and challenged by a host of extra-territorial or sub-state categories, its allocative powers decisively compromised due to its inability to discipline the forces of globalisation, and its military function has become incongruent in a world no longer trapped in the geopolitical abyss of balances and counter-balances.

Space and Networks of Globalisation

Space was fast losing relevance in the context of the new sovereignty of time. In fact, technology has created a multiplicity of spacing(s), where the transaction of different commodities paid scant attention to the settled cartography of borders (Ashley 1987; Harvey 1989). Globalisation has breached the divide between the inside and the outside, and territorial forces have not been strong enough to prevent this massive transformation (Walker 1993). The control of networks and flows has become more important than the territorial or hierarchical control of space (Biersteker 2002, 165–66).

Transformation of the Idea of Sovereignty

Together with territoriality, the meaning of sovereignty has also undergone changes under the impact of globalisation. The classical meaning of sovereignty, as undisputed control over physical territory, is no longer significant. Recognition has now become cardinal to sovereignty, and this recognition is no longer a function of the demonstrated physical control of territory, but hinges more on a prescribed threshold of democratisation and human rights. Transparency and accountability are now more vital to a recognition of sovereignty than physical control, thereby delinking sovereignty and coercive authority. The European Union and the United States *recognised* the states of Croatia and Slovenia not on the ground of physical or military control of their territory, but because of their commitment to endorse liberal democratic practices along with the Western agenda of human rights (Biersteker 2002, 162–63).

Stephen Krasner has offered a powerful counter to this transformation thesis, describing the practice of sovereignty as 'organized hypocrisy'. He shows that there never was a Westphalian model of states; in practice, states deviated from the norms and practices underlying such a system, openly flouting them to further their national interest. In its classical sense, therefore, sovereignty never connoted an uninterrupted control of space. If that criterion was to be stringently applied, then very few states could be classed as sovereign. Intervention has been the norm of the international system. If one takes sovereign to mean the unconstrained capacity for self-determination and autonomous action, then most states were not sovereign entities. States still need to be in physical control of their territories to formalise any form of government or create a framework for human rights (Krasner 1999).

Climate Change Three other political effects of globalisation need to be engaged with. The *first* refers to the new-found global consciousness towards the environment, particularly the scientific evidence pointing to global climate change and the need to counter environmental degradation across the world. Although there was no global consensus amongst the developed and developing states, either at the UN-sponsored Earth Summit in Rio in 1992 or at the 2009 Copenhagen Summit, there was no denying that political leaders around the world considered the matter a grave global challenge that demanded immediate collective action, regardless of any policy consensus on the finer points of implementation.

Much has happened in climate action since the 2009 Copenhagen Summit. The 2015 Paris Agreement stands out as a pivotal moment, when nearly every country joined forces to combat global warming. Subsequent years brought revised climate pledges from countries, but these efforts have largely fallen short. Despite the growth of renewable energy and widespread net-zero pledges, global emissions remain stubbornly high. Public pressure and climate activism, meanwhile, have ratcheted up, causing both governments and corporations to take the crisis more seriously.

Governance The *second* issue refers to the huge expansion in governance structures at the regional, international, and global levels, involving both state and non-state actors and cutting across diverse issues. Once again, the question is not how effective these institutions are; their mere existence implies a new global awareness concerning the structuring of modalities of governance through and beyond nation-states. These institutions highlight the simple fact that increasingly, problems are becoming global, and so their solution demands appropriate global responses as well. Global governance does not imply seamless entities, but reflects asymmetries and power differences between the developed and developing worlds. There is also a growing realisation that states cannot rely on exclusivist sovereign responses in many domains of modern life. Although there has been no discernible movement towards a world government, there is an increasing global governance of issues.

Social Movements The *third* effect relates to class formation. Globalisation has ushered in a variety of social movements and created anti-globalisation rainbow coalitions that innovatively use information and communication facilities to interconnect, share, and organise their struggles. Environmental groups or the greens, the LGBTQIA community demanding recognition of their right to difference, indigenous groups and ethnic communities asking for social and cultural space, groups crusading for human rights against oppressive states, and various women's activists have been empowered by globalisation to express their demands more effectively and vociferously. There are also solidarity movements for beleaguered labour suffering the alienating consequences of globalisation, although they remain weak. As opposed to this, globalisation has created a new political class of entrepreneurs who define their national interests in terms of the needs of global capital, and orients values and practices that strengthen the rights of capital against those of others.

GLOBALISATION AND CULTURE

While the positive and/or negative economic consequences of globalisation can be debated and political effects can be seen as either far-reaching or exaggerated, it can never be depicted as politically neutral. While access to global connectivity, markets, and culture is more open now than earlier, the process of enabling access and the agencies that put these in place are ideologically configured by the meta-context of Western imperialism. Global culture is thus imperial in character and context, disseminating subtle forms of hegemony that function in accordance with the familiar codes of the classical triad of imperialism, modernity, and capital. The culture of globalisation is therefore conditional on the imperial structures of power that use Western cultural forms to unite the world in the interests of the ruling ideas of capitalism and modernity, acquiring new forms through the information revolution of the new epoch.

Impact on the Local

The second aspect complicating the linear narratives of globalisation emphasises its nature as a transcultural process, the dialectic of dominant cultural forms, and their practices. Here, the response of the local becomes critical. The technological innovations of the global era are theoretically open to all; local communities have instant access to techniques with which to craft new strategies of representation and organisation, and thereby influence global systems. Globalisation, as both a context and a process, is empowering for marginalised groups, which can now stand up against the oppressive practices of their parochial cultures by invoking global values, symbols, and representations.

But what does this actually connote in practice? Do the strategies and representational dynamics of culture make for an increasingly homogenised world? Perhaps not. As Mike Featherstone, et al. point out, 'in the most minimalist sense can we speak of a global society or a global culture', as our conception of both society and culture cannot be separated from the process of nation-state formation (1995, 2). Stuart Hall feels that global culture is manifest in a mass culture: 'The new kind of globalization is not English, it is American. In cultural terms, the new kind of globalization has to do with a new form of global mass culture' (Hall 1997, 27). A significant representation is provided by Anthony D. Smith. He finds global culture 'eclectic', 'a pastiche of cultural motifs and styles, underpinned by a universal scientific and a technical discourse'. However, an understanding of global forces relies on local perspectives and contexts. In Smith's words, 'Standardized, commercialized mass communities will nevertheless draw for their contents upon the revival of traditional, folk or national motifs and styles in fashions, furnishings, music and the arts, lifted out of their original contexts and aesthetized' (Smith 2000, 239). In a similar vein, Arjun Appadurai, criticising the singular emphasis placed on homogenisation, which draws upon the dual terms of 'Americanization' and 'commoditization', reminds us that

> [A]t least as rapidly [as] forces from metropolises are brought into new societies, they tend to become indigenized in one way or the other way: this is true of music and housing styles as much as it is true of science and terrorism, spectacles and constitutions. (Appadurai 1990, 295)

Roland Robertson offers a similar perspective when he says that the growth of fundamentalism across the world should not be viewed as being against the forces of globalisation, but must be addressed dialectically and regarded as the effect of globalisation on native responses (Robertson 1992).

Some scholars believe that cultural and economic globalisation feed on each other, united by the logic of consumerism and the market. Leslie Sklair notes:

> The ideological cultural project of global capitalism is to persuade people to consume above their own perceived needs in order to perpetuate the accumulation of capital for private profit, in other words, to ensure that the global capitalist system goes on forever. The culture-ideology of consumerism proclaims, literally, that the meaning

> of life is to be found in the things we possess. To consume, therefore, is to be fully alive, and to remain fully alive we must continuously consume. (Sklair 1991, 41)

Global Culture and its Meanings

Like the global economy and global polity, global culture has varied meanings. It means different things to different people. It connotes the effective global dissemination of images and representations of ideas, practices, and political symbols, and their apparently easy accessibility throughout the world. People can now appreciate 'other cultures' and access them easily. This, however, does not lead to cultural homogenisation. The vast majority of people remain embedded and situated in their familiar local cultures and contexts most of the time. But the local has to adjust to the global; they mediate the global through their native prisms. The idea of a global culture articulated in Western idioms circulates more freely now. Several societies have experienced the securitisation of culture, with regimes using cultural threats and isolation to maintain power. Xenophobic societies have become increasingly rare in a globalised world, but states can remain aloof if they choose and virtually every state regulates the dissemination of global culture to some extent. The technology of the new world makes it impossible to isolate oneself completely. In states as different as China or Iran, dissenting individuals have been emboldened by the new global culture, which stresses freedom and human rights. People's imagination has been broadened by the cultural dynamics of globalisation, creating new opportunities and fears, domination, and empowerment in different societies. Neither homogeneity nor heterogeneity can explain the global cultural flaws. As stated earlier, the global and the local share a symbiotic relationship, and it is politics that decides the balance.

Conclusion

The multifaceted debates on globalisation have turned the attention of scholars to new frontiers of research, which had hitherto remained outside the purview of the more established and settled academic disciplines. Globalisation has profoundly altered the logic of disciplines by questioning the efficacy of existing cognitive boundaries, which they believe are out of sync with reality. No social science discipline can ignore the international and the global, no matter how local its interests and preoccupations. All disciplines are potentially global now; if this is not reflected adequately in the academic structures of conventional universities, inertia is to blame, together with the long-established institutional dynamics in higher education across the world. The tendency towards greater openness and dialogue cannot be reversed.

What Lies Ahead

Globalisation continues to attract the interest of economists and sociologists, whether from the left or right, positivist or non-positivist, optimists or sceptics. With new trends underway in the world economy, new challenges, too, are on the rise. Attention now needs to be riveted on the global management of global flows and governance, particularly the possibilities of crafting innovative structures that would neither attempt to bypass the state, nor remain hostage to the archaic model of sovereignty. Grey zones and complex interstices need the attention they deserve.

Last but not least, for multicultural and polyethnic societies like India, globalisation opens a series of critical puzzles. The dynamic of globalisation and geopolitics, the impact of globality on India's power projection capacities, and discourses on rights, citizenship, culture, and political legitimacy are all ineluctably problematised by global networks and flows. Writing a global history of South Asia is perhaps the most exciting challenge before social scientists today.

OVERVIEW OF THE IMPACT ON SOUTH ASIA

In purely economic terms, the impacts of globalisation have varied in South Asia. South Asia remains a poorly connected space despite globalisation, and this is certainly attributed to its political difficulties, pivoting mainly around the India–Pakistan conflict that impacts all aspects of life in much of the subcontinent. India is ahead of other states in the region on every indicator of economic growth, although Sri Lanka has always fared better in terms of average per capita income and human development indicators. To be fair, economic liberalisation has promoted growth in virtually all South Asian states, although its social impact remains varied and contested. While globalisation has created more unconventional jobs, it has snatched away many conventional ones, and strengthened the interests of capital over those of organised labour. Political parties in South Asia have adapted to these changes with varying degrees of efficiency. The politics of the left has changed substantially in the process. Most mainstream left parties have accepted globalisation as inevitable and organised against its inequities, while a few have gone underground.

On the whole, spectacular reforms have not worked here. In India, particularly, reform by stealth has been preferred to big bang changes. A politics of caution, graft, and balance has come to prevail. While poverty has come down in all states, the gap between the classes has grown, and the idea of economic inequality as a precondition for high growth has become politically acceptable. Economically, South Asia remains a paradoxical space. Its urban life, particularly in Indian megacities, follows the logic of global capitalism, reflected in urban planning, extant industrial and service patterns, new technological frontiers, and a certain fluidity in the aesthetics of everyday life. The West looms large upon both the economic and cultural horizons of our upwardly mobile cities. Villages and towns have been undeniably globalised as well, even though the nature of the economic, political, and cultural intrusions remains distinct. Overall, globalisation has turned us into contested locales and fluid societies, and while several older barriers to mobility have given way to the forces of electronic communication, a host of new walls have come up. This trend holds across other South Asian states as well.

It is difficult to find any correspondence between globalisation and political trends in South Asia. Proponents of globalisation might draw inspiration from the events unfolding in India from 1990 onwards, but a closer scrutiny reveals no evident causal connection between the dynamics of globalisation on the one hand and, say, the nature and prevalence of domestic violence in India or elsewhere in the subcontinent on the other. It is wrong to argue that globalisation ushers in a brand of liberal politics that affects major political configurations and conflicts. A closer look at India shows continuing violence over territoriality (Kashmir), separatism (in Kashmir and the Northeastern states), issues related to governance and social justice (ultra-left insurgency in over ten states and riots/violence in north India), communal divides (Hindu/Muslim riots), and demands for autonomy (which have led to a number of new states being carved out of existing ones).

The Indian Context

It is also true that the nature of the state in India has undergone a change under globalisation. It has laid aside its intrusive welfare role and moved in the direction of neoliberalism. Globalisation has greatly increased the intensity and extent of urbanisation, and engendered complex social dislocations in response. The liberal, Western, consumerist, and cosmopolitan culture of globalisation can be seen in India's leading cities, reflected in the modes of popular representation in media and entertainment. Globalisation has also unleashed a great developmental debate, with the country's intelligentsia divided on its relative merits and demerits. And yet the state has become more xenophobic, and there is little domestic support for a new politics of regionalism, which might redefine South Asia in ways that are more consistent with the demands of globalisation. There is some political questioning of territoriality or sovereignty, particularly in the virtual space. Recently, the concepts of nation and nationalism, especially regarding citizenship, cultural identity, and the interpretation of history, have been the subject of much discussion in India. No mainstream political party ever questions the national borders, or doubts the need for security and border control.

While the state has undoubtedly become more contested and fragmented, there is no alternative imagination of a political community that transcends the framework of the nation-state. Sub-national communities in the Kashmir Valley or in parts of Manipur and Nagaland in India's Northeast have become more globalised in actively demanding an autonomous homeland, independent of the existing state. But their imagination follows the territorial metaphor of the nation-state and their struggles are essentially against what they consider the illegitimate vanities of the Indian state. In the end, globalisation has not altered the basic framework of politics in South Asia. Territoriality, sovereignty, national security, and surveillance continue to dominate the political cartography of the subcontinent.

13

The International Political Economy

Sulagna Maitra

Introduction

Political economy is the branch of social science that studies the relationship between individuals and society as well as between the state and markets (*Encyclopædia Britannica* 2021). International Political Economy or IPE seeks to understand the evolution of world affairs by investigating how international politics and economics are intertwined (Phillips 2020). Like International Relations, IPE is also concerned with the question of power. More specifically, it focuses on the relationship between power and wealth. One of the earliest definitions of IPE was offered by Professor Susan Strange, the first woman professor and chair at the London School of Economics. Professor Strange opined that IPE should concern itself with the relationship between 'states and markets' (Strange 1988). Subsequently, however, this approach was found to be too restrictive and scholars like John Ravenhill (2014) observed that IPE is about the 'interrelationship between public and private power in the allocation of scarce resources'.

It is important to note at this stage that IPE is a rich and diverse field that builds on theoretical perspectives drawn from IR, political economy, political science, sociology, and other related disciplines (Phillips 2020). This chapter presents a brief overview of the key features of contemporary global political economy. It begins with the emergence of the field of IPE and the various approaches used to study it. It then traces the evolution of the international political economy through the ages to understand the forces that shaped the current global economic system. Finally, the chapter concludes by highlighting some of the challenges facing contemporary IPE.

Why Study International Political Economy?

Globalisation has changed the world economy profoundly over the past few decades. Contemporary politics is now intrinsically linked with economic production. The study of IPE gained prominence within IR after World War II. With its focus on the 'interplay of economics and politics in world affairs' (Woods 2014), IPE was instrumental in explaining the complex relationship between post-war socioeconomic reconstruction, peacebuilding, and the emergence of new stakeholders in international politics. The reconstruction of Japan and Europe was made possible with massive economic loans from the United States, which in turn interlinked these economies. The emergence of the USSR presented an alternative socialist model of political economy where, unlike in the capitalist model of the US, the state controlled the commanding heights of the economy. Imperial empires weakened by World War II crumbled and several independent nations emerged between the 1940s–1960s. Quite a few of these new countries in Asia, Africa, and Latin America were wary of superpower politics and lobbied for a new international economic order that would address their development and peacebuilding challenges. Global leaders came together to establish international cooperative institutions, such as the United Nations and its specialised agencies, regional organisations, the International Monetary Fund (IMF), and the World Bank to ensure that global political and economic transactions promoted peace instead of conflict. These institutions, together with new actors such as transnational corporations, non-governmental organisations, and civil society networks, increasingly played an important role in politics. International relations was no longer the exclusive domain of states and their militaries locked in a struggle for power.

Simultaneously, the international economy also underwent significant changes. Traditional trade relations based on the exchange of manufactured goods (mainly from the developed North) in return for raw materials (from the global South) were replaced by a growing intra-industry trade. This increased interdependence between economies eventually led to the emergence of the European Common Market, which represented an unprecedented level of cooperative institutionalism amongst former enemies. At the opposite end of the spectrum, OPEC (Organization of the Petroleum Exporting Countries) countries drastically increased the price of petroleum and precipitated the economic crisis of the 1970s, thereby exposing the vulnerability of nation-states to non-military threats. As Martin Carnoy (1997, 4–5) stated, globalisation

> represents a profound shift of economic time and space, from the local and national into the global arena … production is less and less conducted in one location or even one country. Capital and labour and knowledge are increasingly conceived of in global terms … capital flows have expanded in speed and volume.

Even this short recap of past global events makes clear that it is almost impossible to understand international politics and society without grasping the developments in global political economy, that is, the interaction between public and private wealth and power. The next section briefly describes the main approaches to IPE and its key tenets. However, it is important to mention at this stage that IPE has many rich theoretical traditions, and there is no one particular methodology or perspective that can be considered dominant (Phillips 2020).

Scope of IPE: Main Themes, Theoretical Approaches, and Dichotomies

As a field of study, IPE is broadly located within IR and can be distinguished from both international politics and economics. The economic component of IPE renders it distinct from other fields in IR, while the international focus of IPE sets it apart from the traditional field of economics. As mentioned earlier, IPE borrows heavily from other fields, such as security studies, economics, law, history, politics, and sociology. It has been the site for the development of the neo-institutional approach to international regimes. Seminal works by scholars such as Robert Keohane, Robert Gilpin, and Joseph Nye helped to establish the field of IPE. Keohane and Nye's book *Power and Interdependence* (1977) played a key role in establishing IPE as a sub-discipline of IR.

The origin of IPE as a scholarly tradition is, however, disputed. Some believe that it emerged as a distinct field of study only in the 1970s in order to explain the developments in post-war international relations. They point to the works of Albert Hirschman (see Hirschman 1958, 1967, 1970), Jacob Viner,[1] and Charles Kindleberger[2] as evidence of the relatively recent origins of IPE. Others assert that IPE merely re-emerged during the 1960s–1970s; its origins can be traced way back to the classical traditions of the 1800s. They point to the works of classical economists like Adam Smith, J. S. Mill, and David Ricardo, institutional theorists of social change such as Karl Marx and Emile Durkheim, and institutional economists and anthropologists like Thorstein Veblen and Karl Polanyi to substantiate their claims.

KEY THEMES IN IPE

Given its (re)emergence in the post-war context, IPE was preoccupied with finding ways to restore collaboration among key actors in the global economy in its initial period. Scholars seldom pondered over normative discussions, focusing instead on the conditions that would facilitate collaboration among states and regimes. Several lines of enquiry emerged, which remain at the centre of IPE, and which scholars such as John Ravenhill (2010, 544) and Michael Veseth (2001) have conflated into various prominent themes.

International monetary relations among states was by far the *most dominant* line of enquiry among most students of IPE. While some scholars argued for the US as the dominant power to play a more responsible role in the global economy (Strange 1976), others focussed

[1]Jacob Viner, a Canadian economist, is often regarded as an influential member of the Chicago School and was famously an intellectual opponent of John Keynes' position during the Great Depression. Viner's work, *Studies in the Theory of International Trade* (1937) remains one of best-regarded works in the field.

[2]Charles Kindleberger was an economic historian and is best known for the hegemonic stability theory. His book, *Manias, Panics, and Crashes* (1978), regained relevance after the dotcom bubble burst in the early 2000s.

on the role of regimes and international institutions as a catalyst for sustained economic cooperation (Ravenhill 2010, 544). Veseth (2001, 5) stated,

> [M]uch of the work on the IPE of international trade has been … an attempt to bring economic factors into the study of International Relations by taking economic security concerns and economic foreign policy tools into consideration. This process has also produced a counter flow—bringing political factors into the analysis of international economics.

As the Cold War decades progressed, the global economy had to constantly cope with political phenomena such as the emergence of newly independent countries, demands for systemic changes from the global South, an increase in complex political emergencies, and the wars in the Middle East. Thus, IPE scholars turned their attention to the differentiated capacities of mainly industrialised economies to deal with these changes and the challenges of stagflation,[3] which may be described as the *second* major theme within IPE. These studies also necessitated collaborations with academics from sister fields such as comparative politics and sociology. These collaborations produced seminal works such as *The Political Economy of Inflation* (Hirsch and Goldthorpe 1978) and *The Politics of Inflation and Economic Stagnation* (Lindberg, et al. 1985), which approached IPE from a multidisciplinary perspective and looked beyond a select few states.

The *third* major theme is international finance, that is, the analysis of exchange rate policies, foreign exchange systems, international capital movements, and the institutions to which they relate. These present the third set of issues analysed by IPE scholars (Veseth 2001, 6). This includes the political implications of economic institutions such as the Bretton Woods system, or the economic and political significance of a single regional currency such as the Euro.

A *fourth* line of enquiry relates to the study of economic instruments such as sanctions as an effective tool in international diplomacy and foreign policy. The 1973 Arab-Israeli War, the Soviet invasion of Afghanistan (1979), and sanctions against the South African

---

[3]Persistent inflation combined with stagnant consumer demand and relatively high unemployment (Merriam-Webster 2017).

government by the British Commonwealth nations were the main catalysts of such studies.

The *fifth* theme concerned itself with global North–South relations amidst attempts to establish a New International Economic Order (NIEO), the success of the OPEC countries, and an increase in South–South cooperation. Scholars were especially keen to identify the conditions under which regimes from the North and the South could collaborate to overcome common problems in the global economy. This branch of study has been linked with development economics, and scholars in this field eventually established links with Marxist and critical theories such as dependency theory.

Other areas of interest in IPE have been the study of individual non-state actors such as multinational corporations (MNCs) and transnational enterprises (TNEs). Walzenbach (2016, 1) believes that the major approaches in the field of IPE have largely focussed on international systems perspectives. As a result, non-elite actors and ordinary individuals have often been neglected. However, this is changing fast as states increasingly intensify their relations with MNCs and other non-state actors. Several scholars now prefer the term 'global political economy' to 'international political economy' so as to emphasise the plurality of actors within the system: 'The nature and impact of globalization is a subject of profound debate within IPE' (Woods 2014, 252). The term has been employed to capture the effects of several drivers of change, including internationalisation, technological revolution leading to deterritorialisation, and liberalisation (ibid., 253). The global expansion and diversification of production, finance, and market structures have a cause-and-effect relationship with politics, business, culture, technology, the environment, population movements, tourism, and social identity relations (Veseth 2001, 12).

THEORETICAL APPROACHES TO INTERNATIONAL POLITICAL ECONOMY

Ngaire Woods (2014, 249–52) groups the theoretical approaches to the study of IPE into traditional and new perspectives. Ravenhill (2010, 547–49) classifies the approaches based on their central problematique, that is, hegemonic stability and the role of international regimes. The liberal,

Marxist, and mercantilist/statist approaches, also known as traditional approaches, were concerned with hegemonic stability, which 'combined realism with arguments on the logic of collective action' (ibid., 545).

Mercantilist Approach

The mercantilist approach extended the logic of inter-state competition to the global economy (Woods 2014, 250). Mercantilism is based on the idea that economic prowess equals political power in international relations. The more wealth a country has, the more it is able to invest in building an army, consolidating administration, etc. Thus, according to the mercantilists, it was incumbent upon each nation-state to seek maximum economic wealth and profit in the international arena. They believed that economic and political order would be achieved through balance of power or hegemony.

The Liberal School

Borrowing from scholars like Adam Smith and David Ricardo, the liberal school posited that the world economy could potentially become a 'global market' with free movement of trade, capital, and labour, which in turn would shape government and economic policies. Economic and political order 'would be achieved by the invisible hand of competition in the global market-place' (Woods 2014, 250).

The Marxist Tradition

The Marxist tradition viewed global economy as an arena for competition among the bourgeoisie and the proletariat, who were in constant conflict with each other. The capitalists, viewed as the oppressors in Marxist analysis, owned the means of production, that is, trade and industry. The proletariat or the working class were the oppressed, who provided the labour within the capitalist system and were exploited by the bourgeoisie for further profit. The 'Marxist approach' is an overarching term used for several variants of the Marxist and critical theoretical traditions that not only analysed conflict between social classes, but also extended this analogy to interpret global North–South relations.

Dependency and world systems theorists described the global capitalist system as comprising of a small 'core' of industrialised, developed countries whose very survival (and supply of raw materials) depended upon the large majority of developing, poor countries in the 'periphery'. According to them, 'the global capitalist order within which these societies have emerged is, after all, a global capitalist order that reflects the interests of those who own the means of production [namely the industrialised core]' (Woods 2014, 249).

The newer approaches to IPE concern themselves with the role of international regimes and how they affect the prospects of collaboration between nation-states (Ravenhill 2010, 545). Rational choice theorists explain that the outcomes of IPE are a result of the utility and power maximising choices made by international actors within the frames of particular incentives and institutional constraints (Woods 2014, 251). Institutionalists also draw on rational choice, but reach a different conclusion. According to them, states collaborate to create international institutions, and then delegate power to them in order to maximise utility and power within the constraints of the global market economy. Social constructivists focus their attention on the way governments and other non-state actors operate within IPE, and highlight the role played by identities, beliefs, traditions, and values (ibid.). Feminist approaches to IPE focus on how the power, structures, interests, and ideas underpinning the global economy are fundamentally gendered in their nature and consequences (Phillips 2020).

Finally, it is important to briefly consider some of the dichotomies that have emerged. The most common discussion in this regard has been how IPE has evolved in the US as compared to the rest of the world. Usually, scholars distinguish between the American or the dominant approach to IPE and the British or European approach to IPE. The American school has also been variously described as rationalist, mainstream, hegemonic, and orthodox (Ravenhill 2010, 547). IPE is a significant branch of IR in the US, with a large number of scholars professing to belong to this field of study. The American school has adopted a positivist, hard-science approach to IPE, and focuses mainly on the role of the sovereign state (Cohen 2014). The alternative to this school, the British school, is variously known as reflectivist, radical, progressive, heterodox, and non-hegemonic (Ravenhill 2010, 547). This school is more normative in its approach, and its scholars tend to be critical of established orthodoxies and are more engaged with social and ethical issues, in an attempt to identify and redress injustice (Cohen 2014, 51). Ravenhill (2010, 547–48), however, considers this dichotomy unhelpful, preferring to view them as two extremities on a spectrum that contains a whole range of approaches in the middle.

Another growing body of literature, often marginalised in mainstream discussions, comprises perspectives from the so-called 'Third World' on IPE and globalisation. According to this perspective, contemporary IPE has not only facilitated globalisation, but the model itself has also become more globalised as it is embraced by or imposed upon the developing countries. Third World perspectives dwell upon the consequences of contemporary IPE and globalisation policies on developing countries, including the progressive marginalisation of social groups, erosion of citizen's rights, perpetuation of external dependencies and vulnerabilities, poverty traps and inequities, even as governance systems in these countries continue to morph into models that mirror global institutions and glorify the international market systems (Haque 2002, 117).

International Political Economy through the Ages

This section is divided into three parts: the global economy pre-World War I, the economy during the inter-War period, and the post-War global political economy. Together, they map the key trends in international trade, finance, and development of international regimes and institutions in response to key political events.

The Global Economy Pre-World War I

The contemporary global economy has its origins in late-fifteenth to sixteenth-century Europe. This period is also known as the era of mercantilism, that is, economic nationalism for the purpose of building a wealthy and powerful state (LaHaye 2008). Specifically, national wealth was measured in terms of gold and silver bullions, and it is therefore often remarked that bullionism lies at the heart of mercantilism (*The Economist* 2013). An increase in bullions generated by trade surpluses or through the annexation of territories allowed kingdoms to increase their military strength and extend their markets (Ravenhill 2014, 8). Mercantilism had important consequences for the global political economy. *First*, the economic rationale of mercantilism led to the consolidation of regional feudal centres of power into powerful, competitive nation-states in the sixteenth century (*The Concise Encyclopedia of Economics* 2008). These powerful kingdoms of Western Europe in turn strove to maximise their net exports in order to increase their national prosperity and power (*The Economist* 2013; Ravenhill 2014, 8).

Second, the governments of these states and their mercantile classes worked hand-in-hand to increase the nation's wealth. The government enacted policies to protect the mercantile class from foreign traders and competition, while the latter paid taxes and levies to support the government and maintain a robust army and administrative system (Ravenhill 2014). This collusion in turn fuelled the industrial revolution and the shipping industry, and led to the emergence of a strong, full-time navy and a professional army (*The Concise Encyclopedia of Economics* 2008). Thus, the foundations of the modern nation-state and market economy were laid in this period. Mercantilism also fuelled imperialist ambitions in Western economies, and eventually led to the creation of a Eurocentric world economy with the colonies as suppliers of raw materials and Europe as the source of luxury goods. The Netherlands, Britain, Portugal, France, and Spain were the dominant powers of the time. This period saw more military and trade conflicts between nation-states than any other period in history (ibid.). The purpose of these conflicts was to prevent an enemy state from gaining in the trade wars. For example, during the Napoleonic Wars, while governments did not prevent their foes from importing food, they blocked the enemy's ability to export goods, thereby draining the latter's gold reserves (*The Economist* 2013).

Third, the nation-states introduced policies to block enemy states from free trade. For instance, Spain and Portugal focussed on establishing a strong shipping industry to bring in gold and silver from the New World, while France increased port duties for foreign vessels entering the French ports (*The Concise Encyclopedia of Economics* 2008). Britain undertook several domestic reforms and used policies like the Navigation Act (1651–1849) to restrict the ability of other states to trade with Britain and its colonies (*The Economist* 2013). Ravenhill (2014, 8) observes, however, that mercantilism did not increase the overall global wealth, and per capita incomes, too, did not differ significantly from the previous eight centuries.

While protectionism remained an important economic doctrine until the inter-War period, governments were not effective in curbing smuggling and other violations In fact, Britain, one of the countries that gained the most during this period, had removed the last traces of the mercantile era by the 1860s (*The Concise Encyclopedia of Economics* 2008). The Industrial Revolution (1760–1840) in Britain brought about a seismic change in international and domestic economies. Its main features were economic, technological, and cultural (*Encyclopædia Britannica* 2017). The introduction of steam power and refrigeration revolutionised transportation, both internally and internationally (Ravenhill 2014). Advances in technology, transportation, and communication led to the invention of power looms, the steam locomotive, the internal combustion engine, electricity, the automobile, airplane, telegraph, and the radio, and the utilisation of iron and steel on an industrial scale (*Encyclopædia Britannica* 2017).

As the world began to 'shrink' with improvements in transportation and communication, the value of global exports grew ten-fold between 1820 and 1870 (Ravenhill 2014). However, this pattern of trade did not change much until 1945. The powerful Western European economies dominated the scene with the export of manufactured goods, while the rest of the world provided the raw materials. USA and Japan climbed onto the bandwagon around the twentieth century. England's dominance as a manufacturing and financial power and the emergence of the USA as a major agricultural exporter (especially cotton) provoked the other European powers to resume their protectionist policies and arms race—which eventually led to World War I (*The Concise Encyclopedia of Economics* 2008). Improvements in transportation and communication also facilitated the movement of people and capital, especially in the second half of the nineteenth century. Ravenhill (2014, 9) estimates that between 1820 and 1913, approximately 26 million people migrated from Europe to the US, Canada, Australia, New Zealand, Argentina, and Brazil. Approximately five million Indians under British rule travelled to other parts of the Empire, namely Myanmar, Sri Lanka, Malaya, and various parts of Africa. In terms of capital, Ravenhill estimates that by 1913, UK, France, and Germany had a total investment of $33 billion abroad.

The rudiments of an international financial system began to appear in the early nineteenth century when major economies such as Britain, the US, and Germany fixed the value of their national currency in terms of gold. By 1910, most countries of the world had 'monometallic monetary systems', with gold alone as the standard of currency value, which helped to remove all difficulties in trading with both gold and silver (Lewis 2013).

> The great contribution of the gold standard to facilitating international commerce was that economic agents generally did not have to worry about foreign exchange risks: the possibility that the value of the currency of a foreign country would change vis-à-vis their domestic currency and thus, for example reduce the value of their foreign investment. (Ravenhill 2014, 11)

It is important to note that this confidence in the gold standard was based on the commitments made by individual governments, and was not guaranteed by any international financial institution.

The latter half of the nineteenth century was characterised by an expansion in trade, supported by a network of bilateral trade treaties (WTO 2007). This began in 1860 with the Cobden–Chevalier Treaty between Britain and France. This treaty introduced the principle of Most Favoured Nation (MFN), which 'led to a free trade epidemic that infected the European continent and led to a swift break with centuries of protection' (Lampe 2010).

> Bilaterally agreed reciprocal tariff reductions, together with the application of the unconditional most favoured-nation (MFN) clause contained in the treaties, led to historically low tariff levels, in particular for agricultural products. This period of largely unfettered trade across Europe lasted for nearly two decades up to 1879, faltering gradually thereafter and collapsing with World War I. (WTO 2007)

Contrary to what the name seems to indicate, the MFN principle is the cornerstone of non-discrimination in international trade (Ravenhill 2014). Basically, it means that a state is obliged to grant the partner with whom it has an agreement an equivalent or better treatment in trade transactions than to others. This principle is included in Article 1 of the GATT agreement, which stipulates that all World Trade Organization (WTO) members should treat fellow signatories as MFNs (WTO 2017).

The Global Economy during the Inter-War Period

World War I dealt a devastating blow to liberal free trade in Europe and created havoc in the global political economy. International private commercial transactions were replaced by government controls as all outputs were dedicated to supporting the war efforts (WTO 2007). The War ended an era of economic interdependence and openness in international trade among leading industrial countries (McGrew 2014). Foreign exchange controls, high tariff levels, and restrictions and prohibitions on import and export dominated the economic policy of all major powers (WTO 2007). Economic reconstruction after the War was complicated when the victorious Allied forces demanded that Germany pay reparations for its aggression. Further, Britain and her partners needed to repay wartime borrowings to the US (Ravenhill 2014). US President Woodrow Wilson had, in the meantime, declared in his Fourteen Point Programme for the post-War period, which stated that all economic barriers should be removed (as far as possible) and equality of trade conditions among all nations (which consented to the peace) should be established (WTO 2007).

Ravenhill (2014, 11) opines that although the collapse of international trade in the 1930s was the dominant story of that era, the most fundamental problem of the period was the inability of states to construct a viable international financial system. The gold standard system broke down with the advent of World War I, and the misalignment of currency exchange rates created problems of economic adjustment in the 1920s. The League of Nations was overwhelmed, and in spite of its initial success in the early 1920s with regard to reconstruction packages, it was unable to contain the political and economic disarray of the inter-War period. The United States had emerged as the most powerful economy in the world; however, it was reluctant to play a political role commensurate to its economic prowess. The global economy was in recession as a result of high tariffs, speculative attacks on currencies, collapse of the gold standard, and eventually, the Wall Street collapse of 1929.

The Global Economy after 1945

The global political economy post 1945 was qualitatively different from the previous era in several fundamental ways. *First*, the states made a commitment to embedded liberalism (Ruggie 1982), that is, allowing for the opening up of the domestic economy to restore international trade on the one hand, and maintaining a commitment towards full employment on the other. Essentially, this principle of embedding liberal economic policy within a domestic economic and political agenda was an acknowledgement of the fact that international economic collaboration was a bargain, which depended, in the end, upon domestic political consensus (Ravenhill 2014).

The *second* distinguishing feature of post-War IPE was the commitment of nation-states to the multilateralism enshrined in the founding of the Bretton Woods multilateral financial institutions. The Bretton Woods system created an international basis for exchanging one currency for another (Stephey 2008). Forty-four governments were represented at the United Nations Monetary and Financial Conference (1944), held in the village of Bretton Woods, New Hampshire, USA. The purpose of the conference was to bring together governments and their economic advisors to chart the future of the post-war international political economy (Ravenhill 2014). The member states, in an effort to free international trade and fund post-war reconstruction, agreed to peg their currencies to the US dollar. The American politicians in turn assured global leaders of the dependability of the dollar by tying $1 to 35 oz. of bullion (Stephey 2008). The conference also established two major institutions to assist in the management of this new financial arrangement, namely the International Monetary Fund (IMF) and the World Bank.

The primary purpose of the IMF is to ensure the stability of the international monetary system—the system of exchange rates and international payments that enables countries (and their citizens) to transact with each other. The Fund's mandate was updated in 2012 to include all macroeconomic and financial-sector issues that have a bearing on global stability (IMF n.d.[a]). The International Bank for Reconstruction and Development, commonly referred to as the World Bank, was originally set up to provide loans to rebuild countries devastated by World War II. Over time, the Bank's focus shifted from reconstruction to development, with a heavy emphasis on infrastructure such as dams, electrical grids, irrigation systems, and roads (The World Bank n.d.[b]). The International Finance Corporation was established in 1956 and the International Development Association in 1960. The

IFC enabled the Bank to lend to private companies and financial institutions in developing countries. The International Development Association helped to place greater emphasis on the poorest countries, with the result that a steady shift toward the eradication of poverty was to become the Bank Group's primary goal (ibid.).

These international institutions, created in the aftermath of World War II, were designed to facilitate cooperation in the world economy. The onset of the Cold War, however, delayed their development. The 1970s, especially, were marked by a lack of international economic cooperation among the developed nations, which floated their own exchange rates and indulged in a new form of economic protectionism. The developing countries, which constitute approximately 70 per cent of the world's population, were also increasingly frustrated with the global economy, and taking advantage of their majority in the General Assembly, passed a resolution for a New International Economic Order via the United Nations (1974). The main objective of this resolution was to rectify the unequal share of resources and development of the dependent economies that had been established as a result of mercantilist and capitalist economic policies (Akinsanya and Davies 1984).

After the tumultuous 1970s, IPE faced its next major crisis in the 1990s with the dissolution of the former USSR and the Asian financial crisis of 1997. The countries emerging from the USSR faced economic stagnation, even regression, and a drop in their annual GDP (World Bank 2017). Most of them had a painful, and often violent, transition to liberal democracy and economic restructuring. The Asian financial crisis shocked the world and exposed the vulnerabilities of the emerging Southeast Asian economies that had blindly bought into the Washington Consensus.[4] A localised currency and financial crisis in Thailand soon spread to neighbouring Southeast Asian countries, and by 1998 the contagion had affected Russia and Latin America and stock markets

---

[4]The Washington Consensus refers to a set of economic policy recommendations for developing countries, and Latin America in particular, which became popular during the 1980s. The term 'Washington Consensus' usually refers to the agreement between the IMF, World Bank, and US Department of the Treasury on those policy recommendations. All shared the view, typically labelled neoliberal, that the operation of the free market and reduction of state involvement were crucial to development in the global South (*Encyclopaedia Britannica* 2017).

in New York and Tokyo had crashed (PBS 2014). Joseph Stiglitz (2002, 86) stated:

> [T]he result of the policies enforced by Washington Consensus have not been encouraging: for most countries embracing its tenets development has been slow, and where growth has occurred, the benefits have not been shared equally; crises have been mismanaged; the transition from communism to a market economy has been a disappointment.

In 2008, the world economy faced another meltdown, this time originating in the US: 'The 2008 recession highlighted the tensions between states and markets, the challenges of globalization, shifting global power, and the role of institutions in the global economy' (Ravenhill 2–14, 243).

However, the international political economy did register significant advances in the post-War era. *First*, it saw an unprecedented level of economic growth when compared to any other period in history. From the end of World War II until the 1970s, the global economy registered a growth of 5 per cent per annum (Ravenhill 2014, 15). This was later adjusted to a growth of approximately 3 per cent per annum after the 1970s oil crisis and stagflation and the collapse of major economies in Latin America and Africa. Similarly, global trade also grew at around 8 per cent per annum. There has been an expansion in terms of merchandise, and trade in goods as well as services (such as banking). This has been facilitated by the growth in ICT and reduction in the cost of transportation. International competition has also increased, although the US remains the dominant economy in the world. Trade barriers have declined since World War II as a result of negotiations through multilateral institutions. For example, in most industrialised economies, tariff barriers came down from 40 per cent during the War to just 6 per cent (Gilpin 2001). The World Economic Outlook published by the IMF (n.d.[b]) projected that global output will grow by 3.5 per cent in 2017 and 3.6 per cent in 2018.[5] Inflation is also set

---

[5]The World Economic Outlook of the IMF for 2025 states:

> After enduring a prolonged and unprecedented series of shocks, the global economy appeared to have stabilized, with steady yet underwhelming growth rates. However, the landscape has changed as governments around the world reorder policy priorities and uncertainties have climbed to new highs. Forecasts

to decline in both advanced economies and emerging economies such as BRICS countries. Investment capital has also increased dramatically since the 1990s, from US$ 1.5 trillion to US$ 5.1 trillion in 2016 (ibid.). However, the World Economic Outlook Report identifies several risks to global growth, such as political instability, high policy uncertainty in certain countries (especially triggered by events such as Brexit), and the negative consequences of inward-looking policies and geopolitical risks, such as the return of American isolationism, the rise of conservatives across Europe, instability in the Middle East, etc.

A major factor in this overall growth of the economy was the role played by transnational enterprises or multinational corporations. It is estimated that by 2009, there were 82,000 MNCs with 810,000 subsidiaries worldwide, which generated wealth worth 10 per cent of the global annual GDP (Ravenhill 2014, 15). Their increased participation in the global economy and the close links they share with the state have not only increased diversity and complexity in IPE, but have also permanently altered the nature of global trade and manufacturing. For example, international trade has shifted from the exchange of finished goods to the exchange of parts of a product (for instance, the component parts of a car) across national borders. This is because an MNC operates via multiple countries, based on tax incentives, relation with political regimes, proximity to markets, labour costs, etc. Until 2013, it was estimated that TNCs commanded a two-third share of global trade (Ravenhill 2014, 15–16).

A final distinguishing feature of the contemporary political economy is the mainstreaming of the development agenda and the increasingly salient role played by NGOs and humanitarian actors. These NGOs and civil society groups have had a significant impact on lobbying for environmental, developmental, and humanitarian issues within the high politics of IPE. Newly emerging economies from the global South, such as the Gulf countries and BRICS and ASEAN nations, are also collectively lobbying for a more equitable global economic and political system. Even though much of global capital and trade is still

---

for global growth have been revised markedly down compared with the January 2025 World Economic Outlook (WEO) Update, reflecting effective tariff rates at levels not seen in a century and a highly unpredictable environment. Global headline inflation is expected to decline at a slightly slower pace than what was expected in January.

concentrated in the West, the shift in the political economy since the 2000s is clearly visible, with particular focus on the role of China in international trade, finance, and development assistance.

CONCLUSION

This chapter has provided a snapshot of contemporary IPE, focussing on the key approaches to its study and highlighting the central features of the global economy. IPE represents an ever expanding and increasingly important field of study within IR. Each of the points raised above may be studied in depth, although such an exercise is beyond the scope of this chapter. However, it is important to note that IPE has also been criticised for its narrow focus in terms of processes such as international trade and finance, and actors such as the state and, more recently, international institutions and MNCs. In terms of the global economy, several scholars have identified the high costs of globalisation, such as income inequality between nations, chronic unemployment, environmental degradation, and destruction of national economies through unrestricted financial flows. These negative consequences have led to anti-globalisation movements and economic isolationism, which are at odds with contemporary international relations and global politics. The world is poised on the brink of seismic changes in international political economy and global politics. With increasing diversity, scope, and complexity within IPE, the need for systematic rigorous analyses and normative discussions has become more important.

14

Regionalism in World Politics

Sulagna Maitra

Introduction

'Ours is a world of regions,' claims Peter Katzenstein (2005, 1). The term 'region' denotes a distinguishable geographical area within a larger territory. Typically, a region can be located within a state or transcend national boundaries. Regionalism may therefore be understood as the umbrella term for various forms of cooperation and/or integration between nation-states across the world. This chapter limits itself to a discussion on regionalism in the international context.

States in a geographical area have always come together on an *ad hoc* basis to leverage political, economic, and strategic benefits in international politics. Yet regionalism became part of the International Relations lexicon only after World War II. Prior to that, few regional groupings existed in the form of international associations.[1] International politics in this period was extremely Eurocentric, and focussed on ideas of universal or global governance. The failure of the League of Nations had brought into question the liberal notion of collective security and global governance through a supranational agency. Early drafts of the UN Charter from the Dumbarton Oaks Conference (1944) acknowledged the role of regional agencies as the first port of call for resolving peace

[1]The General Postal Union and the International Law Association are two examples of early forms of regional associations.

and security issues (Fawcett and Hurrell 1995, 12–13). After World War II, as the newly formed United Nations lay paralysed due to Cold War politics, a number of regional agencies such as NATO, the Warsaw Pact, SEATO, and OAS emerged to serve the agendas of superpower geopolitics. In the post-Cold War phase, there was a dramatic increase in the number and diversity of regional organisations. This phenomenon is often referred to as 'New Regionalism' (Hurrell 1995). In fact, some went so far as to say that regional organisations were the 'crown jewels of world politics' (He 2020).

Several factors facilitated the emergence of New Regionalism. *First*, the end of the Cold War meant that states were no longer encumbered by superpower geopolitics. This made it possible to imagine new cooperative frameworks based on shared interests. *Second*, economic integration and globalisation in the 1990s, coupled with uncertainty over existing multilateral trading arrangements, incentivised regional cooperation, especially for smaller nations like those in Southeast Asia, to enable them to exercise greater leverage on the international stage. *Finally*, the success of political experiments like the European Union, NAFTA, and ASEAN served as catalysts for New Regionalism.

There is no doubt that regionalism is a pervasive feature of contemporary international relations (Best and Christiansen 2014). Currently, there are some 659 regional trade agreements, of which 445 are in force (WTO 2017). Similarly, there has been a significant increase in regional peacekeeping missions, especially since the end of the Cold War (Williams 2016). Scholars such as Edward Best and Thomas Christiansen (2014, 402) have stated that 'regionalism has in the last decades become one of the forces challenging the traditional centrality of states in international relations'. Andrej Krickovic (2015, 557) posits that emerging powers such as Brazil, China, India, and Russia have assumed leadership roles at regional levels to provide financial stability and deal with recent global financial crises. However, due to regional compulsions, these countries have had a mixed record in dealing with other issues, such as non-traditional security threats, climate change, and the proliferation of weapons of mass destruction. Regionalism has also progressed at varied paces in different regions. While Europe and East and Southeast Asia have made good progress in regional cooperation, regions such as South Asia, the Americas, and parts of Africa have not been as successful.

Further, certain dramatic events from 2016–17 showed that a more cautious approach is warranted to understand regionalism and its role in international politics. The departure of the United Kingdom from the European Union (or Brexit, as it is called), US President Donald Trump's 'America First' policy, and the rise of right-wing nationalist parties in Europe and parts of Asia and Latin America have served to undermine some of the oldest regional projects, such as the EU and NATO. Irrespective of the fate of various regional arrangements, there is no doubt that contemporary global governance is multilayered, complex, and multifaceted, comprising global, regional, transregional, and local entities (Krickovic 2015, 574). Regional organisations are now permanent, and can serve as vehicles for a more inclusive and legitimate global governance system. Further, scholars, especially those from Asia, claim that doomsday predictions about regionalism being in peril may be Eurocentric in origin, and ignores the efforts of countries like China to foster regionalism (He 2020; Hoshiro 2019). They assert that while much attention has been paid to organisations like the EU and ASEAN, different brands of regionalism proffered by countries like China, Australia, Brazil, India, South Africa, and other emerging players have been largely ignored. This leads to a skewed notion of the relevance of regionalism in international politics, a pitfall in analysis that must be avoided at all costs.

In this context, this chapter will dwell on the evolution of regionalism in world politics, explore the different theoretical perspectives on regionalism, present the different types of regionalism, and finally highlight the various forms of regional organisations in different parts of the world.

MEANING AND SCOPE OF REGIONALISM

At the outset, it should be stated that understanding regionalism in world politics poses a challenge due to ambiguity in the meaning of the word 'region', as well as the huge diversity in the types and forms of regional organisation.

As explained above, a *region* may be understood as 'a distinguishable part of some larger geographical area' (Best and Christiansen 2014, 402). The word 'region' can denote both territories within a state (for example, Northwest Pakistan) and a particular region of the world, including several nation-states (for example, South Asia). Joseph Nye conceptualises an international region as 'a limited number of states linked together by a geographical relationship and by a degree of mutual interdependence'. *Regionalism*, according to him, is the 'formation of interstate groupings on the basis of regions' (Nye 1995, 11).

The terms 'regionalisation' and 'regionalism' are inextricably linked and can often lead to confusion. A useful analysis of the distinction between the terms can be found in the work of Hiroyuki Hoshiro. The scholar explains that,

> Regionalization is defined as an increase in the cross-border flow of capital, goods, ideas, and people within a specific geographical area. Regionalization can be called a spontaneous, bottom-up process in that its core players are firms or individuals and it develops through societally driven processes deriving from markets, private trade, and investment flows, none of which is strictly controlled by governments.... In contrast, regionalism is defined as a political will (hence ism is attached as a suffix) to create a formal arrangement among states on a geographically restricted basis. (Hoshiro 2019, 200)

Regionalism is a multidimensional concept. There really is no limit to the areas in which states can choose to cooperate. Generally, regional agreements cover social, economic, political, and/or security aspects. Regionalism may take the form of interdependence, cooperation, and/or integration. *Interdependence* includes social, economic, political, and even strategic interdependence, accompanied by a growing common interest, shared identity, and heightened awareness about the region. This growth of interdependence and a shared identity may occur 'organically' through market-led processes, or it may be shepherded by the states for strategic reasons. Regional *cooperation*, as the name suggests, refers to individual states cooperating on a specific issue or sector, which can be economic or political, or related to energy, transport, etc. Regional *integration* refers to the process by which states create a shared space, by removing obstacles to interaction and establishing a set of norms specific for that regional space. Best and Christiansen (2014, 403) have concluded that while it is important to recognise that cooperation and integration involve distinct choices, one must be wary of overemphasising the distinction. Drawing examples from regional organisations, including the European Union, they demonstrate that all such entities combine both processes.

History of Regionalism

Before proceeding further, we shall briefly look at the evolution of regionalism and identify its key determinants over the decades. For analytical convenience, the phases have been divided into the following chronological order: (*i*) Early Regionalism in World Politics (until the end of World War II); (*ii*) Regionalism during the Cold War Period; (*iii*) Post-Cold War or New Regionalism.

Early Regionalism (Until World War II)

One of the earliest examples of regional organisations is the Inter-American Defense System, created in 1942 in the aftermath of the Pearl Harbour incident. It is the world's oldest organisation for regional security (IADB 2017). However, the IADS is a notable exception. The nineteenth century saw the rise of numerous public and private associations, such as the General Postal Union (1874) and the International Law Association (1873). Several Eurocentric international organisations emerged during this period, although they were by no means the regional organisations that we know today. Scholars have concluded that in this period, the concept of regional organisations or regionalism was at odds with the prevalent notions of collective security and global governance, as epitomised by entities such as the League of Nations. The two World Wars and other intermittent political and economic upheavals of the time did sow the seeds of regionalism. The old European order was shattered and the world was divided into two competing blocs that sought to increase their influence. Simultaneously, newly independent countries around the world became increasingly assertive and conscious of their own regional dynamics.

Regionalism During the Cold War

The Cold War incapacitated international organisations such as the UN, preventing them from playing a constructive role in international politics, economy, and security. Realpolitik replaced the idealist utopia of global governance and collective security. In the early years of the Cold War, selective security pacts such as NATO, the Warsaw Pact, the Rio Pact, SEATO, and CENTO mushroomed to alleviate the security concerns of nations and extend the influence of the two superpowers—the US and USSR. Organisations such as the Arab League and the African Union emerged as part of the 'pan' movement to create solidarity among member nations. However, these organisations also fell victim to Cold War geopolitics, and failed to effectively unify its diverse membership base.

The period from the end of the 1960s to the 1970s is often known for the first wave of regionalism. During this time, two major regionalist movements arose to 'challenge' the Cold War bloc politics. The *first* attempted to foster regional integration for functional reasons, such as economic benefits. The European free trade and common market initiatives were followed by proposals for NAFTA, PAFTA, and LAFTA.[2] These initiatives prompted scholars to declare the period as an era of regionalism. However, few of these initiatives were successful. The *second* 'challenge' to East–West bloc politics came from the newly independent countries of the global South, which organised themselves into the Non-Aligned Movement or NAM. The development of a broad coalition of countries of the South generated interest in Third World regionalism and organisations such as ASEAN, ECOWAS, CARICOM, and OPEC.

The 1980s saw a heightening of Cold War tensions, which gave rise to serious attempts to foster regional security. The South African Development Coordination Conference, the Gulf Cooperation Council, and SAARC emerged to deal with the insecurities of the 'Second Cold War'. The end of the 1980s, towards the end of the Cold War, also saw dramatic changes in Eastern Europe and a broadening of scope of the European Community. These changes set in motion a new era of regionalism that was far more ambitious than its previous generation.

New Regionalism (Post-Cold War Developments)

There were several catalysts for the New Regionalism that emerged after the end of the Cold War, once the constraints of bipolar geopolitics had been lifted and the antagonism eased between the two blocs. This paved the way for a new attitude towards international cooperation and a renewed focus on regionalism. One significant feature of this new

[2]The North American Free Trade Agreement; the Pan-Arab Free Trade Area; and the Latin American Free Trade Association.

attitude was that regional organisations and international cooperation were no longer considered antithetical to each other. Rather, regionalism was conceived like a 'halfway house between the nation-state and a world not ready to become one' (Wilcox 1965). In fact, UN Secretary-General Boutros-Boutros Ghali's 1992 report, *An Agenda for Peace,* spoke of how regional organisations in Europe, Africa, the Americas, and Asia were sharing a greater burden.

Decentralisation of the international system and the emergence of a multipolar world provided regional organisations with a greater scope to contribute towards economic benefits and collective security. Traditional regional organisations in the West, such as the European Union and NATO, consolidated themselves and even expanded their memberships. Further, the former superpowers, USA and Russia, also pursued an active policy of engaging in regional initiatives. For developing countries, regionalism became a powerful tool in international politics to assert greater independence, avoid marginalisation, and ensure economic and political security in a highly volatile post-Cold War era.

The decision of the European Community to initiate a single market by the end of 1992 had strong repercussions around the globe. *First*, it reinvigorated the idea of the European Community, then comprising twelve members, and warned the remaining countries about a 'fortress Europe'. This briefly prompted countries such as the US to abandon multilateralism and pursue regionalism. The Arab Maghreb Union, the Andean Pact, Mercosur, ASEAN, and CARICOM all committed to a common market, at least on paper.

Global trends, such as changes in the global political economy, shifts in the balance of economic power, and an increase in outward-oriented policies in many developing countries, also facilitated regionalism. Many countries saw regionalism as an effective answer to unbridled globalisation and uncertainty over the Uruguay round of the General Agreement on Tariffs and Trade (GATT) talks. Scholars have commented that contemporary economic activity is concentrated around four poles: the European Union, North America, Asia, and the Pacific Rim (Held and McGrew 2000).

The end of the Cold War and the display of greater assertiveness by developing countries also saw the end of the broad Third World coalition. Disparity in economic and political development as well as the inherent diversity among the countries meant that sub-regional groupings and functional regional coalitions had become far more effective than a single platform such as NAM (even though it continues to exist).

Political and economic liberalisation and democratisation have been conducive to promoting regionalism. In some cases, such as in Eastern Europe, political and economic restructuring were crucial to their accession to the European Union. In other places, such as Africa and the Middle East, an absence of strong institutions and lack of political stability have hampered the growth of regionalism.

Analysing the proliferation of regional organisations at the time, Nye (1971) suggested two major categories of regionalism: (*i*) micro-economic organisations such as ECOWAS, the EEC, and the Gulf Cooperation Council, which economically integrated states from a region through formal regional structures; and (*ii*) macro-regional political organisations such as the African Union, the Organization of American States, and the European Union, which were primarily political organisations concerned with controlling conflicts. Andrew Hurrell (1995, 332) provided four additional characteristics to describe regionalism in the post-Cold War era:

1. The emergence of North–South regionalism through organisations such as NAFTA.
2. The wide variation in the level of institutionalisation within the new regional organisations. According to him, new regional organisations have consciously avoided traditional bureaucratic structures such as may be found in the EU model.
3. Contemporary regional organisations are dynamic and multidimensional, that is, they do not necessarily draw a line between economic and political regionalism.
4. Many parts of the world are experiencing an increased regional consciousness, which may or may not transform into regional organisations.

While scholars like Hurrell and Louise Fawcett (1995) have identified these determinants as the key driving forces, others like Richard Falk (2003, 64) warn against an over-emphasis on the dismantling of Cold War politics as a catalyst for the new regionalism. There was probably a tendency among the scientific community to exaggerate the discontinuation of Cold War geopolitics while underplaying the evolutionary factors of change that facilitated, and sometimes even necessitated, the growth of regionalism. Factors such as technological innovation, the emergence of networked global communities, and the realisation among states that issues such as climate change and weapons of mass destruction need to be tackled collectively made the growth of regional organisations not only possible, but also necessary (Falk 2003).

Challenges to regionalism and regional organisations continue to emerge in contemporary world politics, especially since the events of 11 September 2001. However, despite these challenges, regionalism has survived and even strengthened in some parts like East Asia, while the Westphalian model of the state has been increasingly strained due to globalisation and the rise of extremism. A cursory survey of contemporary regional organisations suggests the presence of several 'brands' of regionalism, with new actors and agendas. For example, China's approach to a state-centric regionalism in East and Southeast Asia is mainly driven by a strategic interest in the regions (He 2020). Similarly, non-state actors such as multinational corporations and powerful global civil society networks are likely to become key allies, and in some cases, even members of regional initiatives.[3] While it is impossible to capture all the shades of regionalism within a single framework, efforts are underway to study regionalisation and the emergence of regional organisations systematically. Chronologically, the pluralism of regional initiatives have led some scholars to describe the current phase as 'multilateralism 2.0', where regional organisations vary greatly in terms of their composition, purpose, and operations (Langenhove 2010). Falk (2003), on the other hand, analyses regional organisations as *positive* or *negative* on the basis of their purpose and influence. Positive initiatives are those with 'desired' or cooperative objectives and outcomes, such as the reduction of political violence, attainment of economic well-being, and promotion of human rights (for example, the European Union). Negative initiatives are those that seek to contain the adverse impacts of international affairs, such as anarchy, empire building by states, the negative outcomes of globalism, etc.

It will now be useful to consider the various theoretical perspectives on regionalism to gain a deeper understanding of the phenomenon.

---

[3]For example, the UN Trust Fund on Human Security, led by Japan, is a global initiative comprising state and non-state actors. While this initiative is not limited to any specific region, it may be argued that it is only a matter of time before such multilateral initiatives play a key role in shaping world politics.

Theoretical Perspectives on Regionalism

Analysing regionalism through different theoretical lenses is a challenging task, because it is difficult to capture all aspects of this highly complex phenomenon. One approach studies the evolution of regionalism through early (1950s and 1970s) and more recent debates. The relevant theories pertaining to the early debates are federalism, functionalism, and neo-functionalism (Söderbaum 2012). The more recent theoretical debates are informed by variants of institutionalism, security complex theory, and constructivist approaches, all of which try to capture the multidimensionality and pluralism of contemporary regionalism (ibid.; Söderbaum and Shaw 2003). Hurrell (1995) presents three broad categories of theoretical perspectives: (*i*) systemic theories; (*ii*) regionalism and interdependence; and (*iii*) domestic level theories. For analytical convenience, this section adapts Hurrell's typology to discuss the various theoretical perspectives on regionalism.

The first group of theories to be discussed is *systemic theories*, which focusses on the international system within which the regional arrangements are embedded. Adopting this theoretical lens helps us understand the impact of broader political and economic structures and outside forces on the functioning of regional organisations. Systemic theories include the neorealist perspective and theories of structural interdependence and globalisation.

Neorealist Perspective on Regionalism

For neorealists, regionalism represents the politics of alliance formation, usually in response to external systemic challenges. As such, there is no difference between economic and political regionalism. Neorealists emphasise the pressures of power politics as well as mercantilist economic competition as the key drivers of regionalism. Thus, they point to systemic factors such as the end of the Cold War, the dramatic political and economic shifts in Europe, the disintegration of the USSR, the Marshall Plan, and US encouragement as key drivers of European integration. Economic regional organisations such as APEC and NAFTA were created by the US to gain leverage against Japan and the EU in the neo-mercantilist game. According to neorealists, regionalism serves as a powerful tool for weaker nations, allowing them to increase their bargaining power and reduce outside intervention. However, they maintain that the success of these regional and sub-regional groupings is contingent upon the policies of major powers.

An under-theorised aspect of neorealism is the relationship between hegemony and cooperation. So far, studies have noted four different relationships:

- *First*, regional groupings may emerge in response to the existence of a hegemon. For example, ASEAN was created to counter Vietnam and China, SADCC against South Africa, Mercosur against the United States, and the Gulf Cooperation Council against Iran.
- *Second*, regional organisations may create institutions to curb the free hand given to powerful member nations. For example, the European Union and NAFTA both have highly evolved institutions aimed at restricting powerful nations such as Germany and the United States, respectively.
- *Third*, in the event of a huge power differential, regional organisations can benefit weaker nations both materially and strategically by formally aligning them with a regional hegemon. However, scholars such as Krickovic (2015) note that sometimes this may result in dominant states being averse to regional initiatives, as they are seen as a drain on the latter's resources. He believes that India's reluctance vis-à-vis SAARC is partly due to this reason.
- *Fourth*, the hegemon may become actively involved in the regional organisation as a 'core state' to further its dominant position.

Neorealist perspectives, while insightful in understanding the external geopolitical drivers of regionalism, suffer from several deficiencies. There is little focus on regionalisation or regional economic integration, since these are to be determined by larger international economic factors. Determinants of regionalism at the domestic level are also ignored, as neorealists remain preoccupied with global strategic factors. They are also unable to explain the nature and characteristics of institutions within regional organisations. Finally, there is little weight given to regional self-awareness.

Interdependence, Globalisation, and Regionalism

Globalisation has emerged as the most important theme of the post-Cold War era. While rarely articulated as a theory, globalisation has brought in certain fundamental changes in the international system. These are: (*i*) a dramatic increase in the intensity and depth of economic interdependence; (*ii*) a revolution in information and technology, enabling the easy diffusion of ideas and knowledge; (*iii*) unprecedented awareness and recognition of global problems, such as human rights, climate change, and a consciousness of a common humanity; and finally (*iv*) societal interdependence, created as a result of the changes mentioned above.

While globalisation is not always conducive to regionalism, it has acted as a stimulus for the latter in certain cases. States believe that regional collaboration is key to addressing shared global challenges. States may fear marginalisation in global organisations, and at the same time be incapable of dealing with global issues on their own. A shared history, culture, and convergence of political, economic, and security interests make regional organisations a viable tool to effectively minimise vulnerability in the international arena. Regionalism is the crucial level at which to reconcile the integrative political and market forces on the one hand, and the divisive trends towards fission and fragmentation on the other. Finally, many 'global' issues can have practical and powerful regional responses. For example, even though the problem of environmental refugees is technically a global issue, it is far more effective to deal with it at the regional level.

Regionalism and Interdependence

There is a cluster of theories that speak of a close link between regional interdependence and the growth of regionalism.

Neo-functionalism[4] emphasises the role of interest groups, professional associations, and labour unions who are in a position to form transnational coalitions in order to push their regional agenda.

[4]Ernst B. Haas is considered the father of neo-functionalism. For a detailed analysis of Haas' contribution and neo-functionalism see Schmitter (2005).

With its roots in democratic pluralism and taking off from the work of David Truman and Robert Dahl, this theory proffers that a government can be disaggregated into its component group actors (Hooghe and Marks 2019). Unlike realists, who view state interests as a composite whole, neo-functionalists see state interest as an outcome of complex interactions among interest groups. Thus, they posit that rising interdependence among non-state actors is the key driver of regional integration, and will ultimately lead to the creation of supranational institutions. Thus, while regional integration begins with cooperation on common technical, non-controversial issues, it eventually *spills over* into high politics. This also sets in motion a process of institution-building, which will in turn create its own self-sustaining dynamics. Eventually, loyalties will shift from state entities to these newly created institutions. Neo-functionalists have often been criticised for their overwhelming concern with European integration. However, these scholars believed that the European integration project would ultimately spill over to other regions of the world.

Neoliberal Institutionalism Neoliberal institutionalists analyse the resurgence of regionalism from the following perspectives:

1. Increasing interdependence has given rise to a demand for international cooperation. Institutions are thus created to seek collective solutions to common problems and enhance welfare.
2. Institutionalists believe in the primary role played by the state, and also do not consider themselves an impediment to regional cooperation.
3. Institutionalist theorists focus on how strategic calculations may give rise to cooperative regional solutions. The emergence of regional security regimes such as ARF and CSCE are examples of powerful alliance formation.

Constructivism These theories focus on cognitive regionalism, that is, a regional awareness, shared identity, and a sense of belonging to a particular regional community. Constructivists emphasise a sustained sense of community, high trust levels, and cognitive interdependence as key factors in maintaining regional cohesion. Instead of focussing exclusively on material incentives, this group of theories highlights the power of shared knowledge, ideational forces, normative and institutional structures, and identities and interests in understanding the emergence and sustenance of regional communities.

Domestic-Level Theories

This cluster emphasises the role of shared domestic attributes such as ethnicity, religion, culture, history, the consciousness of a common heritage, and compatibility of political and economic values. Scholars have identified three ways in which domestic factors may be related to contemporary regionalism:

1. Regionalism is generally seen to thrive in spaces with strong, or at least relatively stable, states, such as Europe, Latin America, Southeast Asia, and Southern Africa. Political instability, civil war, economic stagnation, and an erosion of the social fabric often create disintegration and anarchy in fragile states, which impedes the growth of regionalism.
2. The relationship between democracy and regionalism is complex and understudied. In some cases, such as Eastern Europe and Latin America, democratisation played a major role in regional integration. Yet, in other regional experiments, such as ASEAN, several member countries have rejected a homogeneous, Western-style democratic political system.
3. Finally, convergence theories seek to converge the common domestic policy preferences of individual states with regional economic integration. Thus, the growth of regionalism is not about a 'beyond-state' utopia, but is instead built around sheltering and protecting a particular domestic economic, social, and political project.

Synthesising the different theoretical perspectives, Best and Christiansen (2014) have chosen to explain the dynamics of regionalism in three ways:

1. The management of independence, that is, the need of newly independent states to determine their relationship with the former colonial powers and other powerful states.
2. The management of interdependence, which refers to state-led initiatives for peace, security, and economic cooperation in order to collectively manage regional issues.

3. The management of internationalisation, that is, regionalism as a response to a multilateral international system and forces of globalisation.

A second theory of regionalism emphasises the interdependencies between regions and sub-regions, instead of studying external (international) or internal (domestic) drivers. It believes that regional organisations do not exist in isolation from each other; rather, models of regional cooperation and integration spread across the globe. There is thus a diffusion of institutional models and policies (Risse 2016).

Tanja Borzel (2016) critiqued the dominant theories of regionalism as being biased in favour of state actors and formal institution-building processes. New regionalism and non-Western approaches, on the other hand, focus on the role of non-state actors. Instead of replacing mainstream theories, Borzel posits governance as the central analytical concept to counter the formal institutional and state bias in prevalent theories. She believes that governance confers equal status upon state and non-state actors, and thus provides a useful framework to systematically compare the varieties of regionalism across time and space.

REGIONAL COOPERATION IN A GLOBAL CONTEXT: SELECT CASES

Regionalism is measured in terms of 'social cohesiveness (ethnicity, race, language, religion, culture, history, consciousness of common heritage), economic cohesiveness (trade patterns, economic complementarity), political cohesiveness (regime type, ideology) and organizational cohesiveness (existence of formal regional institutions)' (Hurrell 1995, 333). Every region has their own unique experience of regionalism, depending on the impact of global 'external' factors, domestic drivers, and the level of diffusion from other regional institutions. This section presents excerpts from the official documents of some main regional organisations in order to understand their membership, objectives, and policies. The list of organisations discussed below is by no means exhaustive; it is only meant to be illustrative of the different types of regional organisations found across the globe (Best and Christiansen 2014, 405).

Regional Integration of Europe: A Timeline of the European Union

Best and Christiansen (2014, 411) characterise regionalism in Europe as a 'gradual process of integration leading to the emergence of the European Union. It was initially a purely West European creation between the original six-member states, born of the desire for reconciliation between France and Germany in a context of ambitious federalist plans.' Today, the EU is a unique economic and political union of twenty-eight European countries, which together cover much of the continent (EU n.d.). What began as a purely economic union has evolved into an organisation spanning policy areas ranging from climate change, environment, and health to external relations and security, justice, and migration, reflected in the change in nomenclature from European Economic Community (EEC) to European Union (EU) in 1993. The EU has delivered more than half-a-century of peace, stability, and prosperity, helped raise living standards, and launched a single European currency: the Euro. In 2012, the EU was awarded the Nobel Peace Prize for advancing the causes of peace, reconciliation, democracy, and human rights in Europe. People can now travel freely throughout most of the continent since border controls have been abolished between EU countries. It has also become much easier to live, work, and travel abroad in Europe. The single or 'internal' market is the EU's main economic engine, enabling the free movement of most goods, services, money, and people. Another key objective is the development of this huge resource in areas such as energy, knowledge, and capital markets, to ensure the maximum benefit for Europeans.

The EU is based on the rule of law: everything it does is founded on treaties, and voluntarily and democratically agreed upon by its member countries. The EU is also governed by the principle of representative democracy, with citizens directly represented at the Union level in the European Parliament and member states represented in the European Council and the Council of the EU.

Regionalism in Asia

In Asia, regionalism has followed different patterns. Asia as a whole is too big and did not have a unified regional experience. The major regional initiatives in Asia include: the South Asian Association of Regional Cooperation (1985), Association of Southeast Asian Nations (1967), Gulf Cooperation Council (1981), Shanghai Cooperation Organization (2001), and Economic Cooperation Organization (1985). Some of these initiatives are discussed below.

The South Asian Association of Regional Cooperation (SAARC) was set up in 1985 and comprises seven members: India, Bangladesh, Pakistan, Nepal, Bhutan, Sri Lanka, and the Maldives. Later, Afghanistan joined the organisation as well. The objectives of SAARC were set out in a declaration by the foreign ministers of member states in New Delhi in 1983, which is also known as the Delhi Declaration:

> [T]o promote the welfare of the peoples of South Asia and to improve their quality of life; to accelerate economic growth, social progress and cultural development in the region and to provide all individuals the opportunity to live in dignity and to realize their full potentials; to promote and strengthen collective self-reliance among the countries of South Asia; to contribute to mutual trust, understanding and appreciation of one another's problems; to promote active collaboration and mutual assistance in the economic, social, cultural, technical and scientific fields; to strengthen cooperation with other developing countries; to strengthen cooperation among themselves in international forums on matters of common interests; and to cooperate with international and regional organizations with similar aims and purposes. Decisions at all levels are to be taken on the basis of unanimity; and bilateral and contentious issues are excluded from the deliberations of the Association. (SAARC 2009)

The motto of the **Association of Southeast Asian Nations (ASEAN)** is: 'One Vision, One Identity, One Community'. Ironically, Southeast Asia is not a homogeneous region with a clearly demarcated territory, shared history, or political system. The term emerged in international relations parlance to denote the areas south of China that were occupied by Japan during World War II (Best and Christiansen 2014, 408). Decolonisation and Cold War rivalries facilitated the emergence of common interests in Southeast Asia (Mukherjee and Mukherjee 2008). ASEAN was established in 1967 by Indonesia, Malaysia, the Philippines, Singapore, and Thailand via the Bangkok Declaration. Brunei Darussalam joined on 7 January 1984, Vietnam on 28 July 1995, Lao PDR and Myanmar on 23 July 1997, and Cambodia on 30 April 1999, making up what is today the ten member-states of ASEAN.

The aims and purposes of ASEAN are:

> To accelerate economic growth, social progress, and cultural development in the region through joint endeavours in the spirit of equality and partnership in order to build a strong foundation for a prosperous and peaceful community of Southeast Asian nations; to promote regional peace and stability through abiding respect for justice and the rule of law in the relationship among countries of the region and adherence to the principles of the United Nations Charter; to promote active collaboration and mutual assistance on matters of common interest in economic, social, cultural, technical, scientific, and administrative fields; to provide assistance to each other in the form of training and research facilities in the educational, professional, technical, and administrative spheres; to collaborate more effectively for the greater utilisation of their agriculture and industries, the expansion of their trade—including the study of problems of international commodity trade—the improvement of their transport and communications facilities, and raising the living standards of their peoples; to promote Southeast Asian studies; and to maintain close and beneficial cooperation with existing international and regional organisations with similar aims and purposes, and explore all avenues for even closer cooperation among themselves. (ASEAN 2017)

The functions of ASEAN are conducted through eleven permanent and six *ad hoc* committees, which handle issues such as food, agriculture, tourism, transportation, sociocultural affairs, science and technology, mass media, and commerce and finance. Scholars such as Anja Jetschke and Philomena Murray (2012) have critically analysed the diffusion of EU-style institutions, in particular the EU's Committee of Permanent Representatives, within the economic integration process in ASEAN.

The **Gulf Cooperation Council (GCC)** is a political and economic alliance of six Middle Eastern countries—Saudi Arabia, Kuwait, the United Arab Emirates, Qatar, Bahrain, and Oman. It was established in 1981 to achieve a closer union between the energy-rich Gulf countries. Western analysts originally attributed its foundation to security concerns, which have always plagued the Gulf monarchies, but the founding charter focussed more on issues of social and cultural cohesion, environmental and scientific coordination, and economic cooperation (Sikimic 2015).

The **Shanghai Cooperation Organization (SCO)** is a permanent intergovernmental international organisation created on 15 June 2001 in Shanghai, China by the Republic of Kazakhstan, the People's Republic of China, the Kyrgyz Republic, the Russian Federation, the Republic of Tajikistan, and the Republic of Uzbekistan. It was preceded by the Shanghai Five mechanism. The SCO's main goals are:

> [S]trengthening mutual trust and neighbourliness among the member states; promoting effective cooperation in politics, trade, the economy, research, technology, and culture, as well as in education, energy, transport, tourism, environmental protection, and other areas; making joint efforts to maintain and ensure peace, security, and stability in the region; and moving towards the establishment of a democratic, fair, and rational new international political and economic order. (The SCO n.d.)

The **Economic Cooperation Organization (ECO)** is an intergovernmental regional organisation established in 1985 by Iran, Pakistan, and Turkey for the purpose of promoting economic, technical, and cultural cooperation among the member states. On 28 November 1992, the ECO was expanded to include seven new members, namely the Islamic Republic of Afghanistan, Republic of Azerbaijan, Republic of Kazakhstan, Kyrgyz Republic, Republic of Tajikistan, Turkmenistan, and Republic of Uzbekistan. This date is observed as the ECO Day. ECO member states have been collaborating to accelerate their pace of regional development through common endeavours. Besides shared cultural and historic affinities, they have been utilising existing infrastructural and business links to further fortify their resolve to translate their hopes and aspirations into a tangible reality. ECO has embarked on several projects in priority sectors, including energy, trade, transportation, agriculture, and drug control (ECO 2017).

Regionalism in the Americas

There are several—even competing—regional organisations in the Americas. The most notable ones are discussed below.

The **Organization of American States (OAS)** came into being in 1948 with the signing of the Charter of the OAS in Bogotá, Colombia, which entered into force in December 1951. The OAS is the world's oldest regional organisation, dating back to the First International Conference of American States held in Washington, D.C. from October 1889 to April 1890. That meeting approved the establishment of the International Union of American Republics, and the stage was set for the weaving of a web of provisions and institutions that came to be known as the inter-American system, the oldest international institutional system (OAS n.d.). The OAS comprises thirty-five independent states of the Americas and constitutes the main political, juridical, and social governmental forum in the hemisphere. In addition, it has granted permanent observer status to sixty-nine states, as well as to the European Union (EU). The OAS uses a four-pronged approach to effectively implement its primary purposes, based on its main pillars: democracy, human rights, security, and development.

The **North American Free Trade Agreement (NAFTA)** is a comprehensive trade agreement that sets the rules of trade and investment between Canada, the United States, and Mexico. Since the agreement entered into force on 1 January 1994, NAFTA has systematically eliminated most tariff and non-tariff barriers to free trade and investment among the three concerned countries.

However, President Donald Trump's 2025 Presidency saw a resurgence of aggressive trade protectionism, a stark contrast to the regional economic integration promised by NAFTA and the USMCA (United States-Mexico-Canada Agreement). Using the excuses of immigration and the trafficking of fentanyl to justify the measures, Trump slapped wide-ranging tariffs on goods from Canada and Mexico, with International Emergency Economic Powers Act (IEEPA, a 1977 US federal law) providing the authority. Most goods from these countries were subject to a 25 per cent tariff, while Canadian energy exports were subject to a 10 per cent tariff, which was implemented on 26 February 2025 (Viser, et al. 2025). Products covered under the USMCA were initially exempt from the order; however, in April 2025, this temporary exemption became permanent, resulting in uncertainty and volatility in cross-border supply chains. In a swift response, Canada enacted retaliatory tariffs against US goods.

For his part, Trump announced an expanded regime of tariffs in April 2025, in what his administration called 'Liberation Day', which began with a universal 10 per cent tariff on virtually all imports, followed by more fulsome country-specific increases, which focussed on major trading partners (Harithas, et al. 2025). The unveiling of 35 per cent tariffs on Canadian imports and 30 per cent on those from Mexico and the EU on 1 August 2025, contingent on new bilateral agreements, concluded the tactic (Bacon 2025; Sweney and O'Carroll 2025). A federal court subsequently deemed the 'Liberation Day' tariffs unconstitutional under IEEPA, but those decisions did not apply to the emergency tariffs on Canada and Mexico. These actions were antithetical to the values of free trade and predictability that NAFTA and USMCA had sought to promote, causing significant uncertainty in the North American economic calculus.

The **Andean Community (CAN)**, established in 2012, is a trade bloc of four countries: Bolivia, Colombia, Ecuador, and Peru. Chile, Argentina, Brazil, Paraguay, and Uruguay are associate members, while Panama, Mexico, and Spain are observers. The regional integration in Andean countries began with the signing of the Cartagena Agreement (by Bolivia, Chile, Colombia, Ecuador, and Peru) in 1969, thereby leading to the Andean Pact with the objective of creating a Customs Union and a Common Market (Government of India 2013). Venezuela joined the Pact in 1973 but withdrew in 2006 after Colombia and Peru signed Free Trade Agreements with the USA. Chile withdrew in 1976, claiming economic incompatibilities. In 1993, four members (with the exception of Peru, which was temporarily suspended) established a free trade zone. In 1995, the members adopted a Common External Tariff. In 1996, the Protocol of Trujillo renamed the Pact the Andean Community. It also converted the Board of the Cartagena Agreement into a General Secretariat based in Lima, Peru, with both technical and political functions, thus giving a new political direction to the integration process. In 2001, the Andean Passport was created, enabling citizens of member states to travel between the countries without a visa. In 2005, the integration of Latin American and Caribbean regions was prioritised in the agenda of the Andean Community. In 2006, the Andean Free Trade Area became fully operational after the incorporation of Peru (MEA, Government of India 2013).

The **Southern Common Market Agreement (Mercosur)** is an economic and political bloc comprising Argentina, Brazil, Paraguay, Uruguay, and Venezuela. Created in 1991 as Argentina and Brazil sought to improve their diplomatic and economic relations, the bloc saw a five-fold increase in regional trade in the 1990s. Together with the Andean Community, Mercosur represents the largest trading bloc in South America (MEA, Government of India 2013). However, many experts believe that Mercosur has failed to live up to its ambitions, and trade within the group has fallen relative to its members' total trade in the past twenty years. The political and economic crisis in Venezuela, which joined the group in 2012, has revealed fractures within the organisation.

Members have threatened to suspend Caracas for failing to comply with the rules on trade and democracy (Council on Foreign Relations 2024).

Other regional organisations in the Americas are: the Central American Integration System, Central American Common Market, Caribbean Community, Union of South American Nations, Community of Latin American and Caribbean States, and Latin American Integration Association. 'The 21st century has witnessed a change of era in Latin American regional governance projects as they explicitly or implicitly seek to reduce the influence of countries north of the Rio Grande in political, economic and social processes and outcomes in the region' (Bertucci 2015).

Regionalism in Africa

The African continent has witnessed a proliferation of regional initiatives in the last few decades. Notable among them are the African Union, Arab Maghreb Union, Community of Sahel-Saharan States, Economic Community of West African States, West African Economic and Monetary Union, Central African Monetary and Economic Community, Economic Community of the Great Lakes Countries, Economic Community of Central African States, East African Community, Common Market for Eastern and Southern Africa, Intergovernmental Authority for Development, Southern African Customs Union, and the Southern African Development Community.

The African Union (AU) was established in 1999 by the heads of state and government of the Organisation of African Unity *vide* the Sirte Declaration to accelerate the process of integration in the continent, so as to enable it to play its rightful role in the global economy while addressing multifaceted social, economic, and political problems that have been compounded by certain negative aspects of globalisation. The AU was preceded by the OAU, whose main objectives were to rid the continent of the remaining vestiges of colonisation and apartheid; promote unity and solidarity among African states; coordinate and intensify cooperation for development; safeguard the sovereignty and territorial integrity of member states; and promote international cooperation within the framework of the United Nations (African Union n.d.).

The **Economic Community of West African States (ECOWAS)** was established on 28 May 1975 via the Treaty of Lagos. The members are Benin, Burkina Faso, Cape Verde, Cote d' Ivoire, The Gambia, Ghana, Guinea, Guinea Bissau, Liberia, Mali, Niger, Nigeria, Sierra Leone, Senegal, and Togo. Its mandate is to promote economic integration in all fields of activity in the member states. ECOWAS was set up to foster the ideal of collective self-sufficiency, and as a trading union, it is also meant to create a single large trading bloc through economic cooperation. Integrated economic activities as envisaged in the area revolve around, but are not limited to, industry, transport, telecommunications, energy, agriculture, natural resources, commerce, monetary and financial issues, and social and cultural matters. Today, the organisation is one of the pillars of the African community, and is acknowledged globally as a successful regional body (ECOWAS n.d.).

Conclusion

This chapter has shown that regionalism is truly a global phenomenon. The twenty-first century has seen a growth in regional initiatives, especially in Asia, Latin America, and Africa. As the West, especially Europe and North America, grapple with seismic political changes, emerging economies such as Brazil, China, India, and Russia are increasingly assuming leadership roles at various regional forums. Similarly, regions such as Latin America, Southeast Asia, and South Asia have seen a greater assertion among smaller powers and a move towards an increasing democratisation of regional organisations. The old schisms between globalisation, collective security, and regionalism, while not fully resolved, have been replaced by a more cooperative arrangement, whereby regional organisations are viewed as an integral part of the global political and economic system. In academia, scholars have proposed a more constructivist approach to studying regionalism and are looking at concepts such as governance as new units of analysis. However, several areas, such as the relationship between democracy and regionalism, diffusion theories on the proliferation of regional institutions, and the role of smaller nations in regionalism, remain under-theorised. The political and economic developments of the twenty-first century promise to provide a new lease of life to studies on regionalism, and offer a more nuanced understanding of regional experiments across the globe.

15

Culture, Identity, Technology, and the International Order

Shibashis Chatterjee

This chapter discusses the role of culture, identity, and technology in IR by looking at a few contrasting images. The role of culture and identity has become exceedingly important to international relations for a variety of reasons. *First*, the end of the Cold War, the disintegration of the Soviet Union, and the decline of Soviet-style Communist systems across eastern and southern European states led to a resurgence of culture and identity conflicts in many parts of the world, and academic IR could no longer turn a blind eye to it. The rise of constructivism as one of the most popular IR theories also reinforced this trend. Samuel Huntington's clash of civilisations thesis, despite its problems, cast an immediate spell upon the discipline. The violent break-up of the Yugoslav federation and the wars among Serbs, Croats, Bosnians, and Kosovars could not be explained without invoking culture and identity. The conflicts in Russia, Azerbaijan, Armenia, and Chechnya, among others, were similarly over claims of identity and nationalism. In the same vein, class or distribution issues could not adequately explain the conflicts in Rwanda, Somalia, and Sudan. They were deeply intertwined with issues of recognition.

The terrorist attacks in New York on 11 September 2001 and their immediate aftermath brought wars that were fought against 'terrorists' and their supporters, who invoked the language of *jihadi* Islam against perceived distortions in culture and values caused by Westernisation and globalisation. As the new millennium rolled on, it witnessed a rise in the politics of nationalism, and right-wing cultural nationalists have either become politically significant or have come to power in several states across the world. Their authoritarianism calls for approaches that recognise the validity of culture and identity as independent explanatory variables.

The politics of identity, nationalism, and culture has emerged as a global force because of the incredible developments in science and information technology, which have metamorphosed global communications. Speed has emerged as central to global politics and nations blessed with technological superiority have maintained their stranglehold over world politics. Science and technology have long been the key to unlocking the power potential and capabilities of states since the Enlightenment. Colonialism and imperial conquests would have been impossible without the technological marvels of the Europeans. However, with postcolonial states coming into their own and gaining in prominence, the competition for control over technology has intensified further. The powers of science and technology are now married to the politics of identity; from right-wing nationalism closing its doors to radical forces trying to knock them down, culture and identity are what fire world politics at present, and its energies, speed, and powers of dissemination are determined by the process of scientific enterprise. This chapter is an attempt to come to terms with these forces.

IR and Culture: A Problematic Relationship

IR's default position on culture, across theories and genres, is underdeveloped and disappointing. Following Christian Reus-Smit (2019), we can identify several reasons for this. *First*, the use of culture is largely instrumental. Analysts across schools seek to explain when and how culture fuels conflict, and how this can be managed. There is little interest in tracking culture independently. *Second*, culture is viewed either as homogeneous, thereby crushing its innate divergences and varieties, as demonstrated so richly in other disciplines such as anthropology or world history, or it has been relegated to disciplinary margins because of its untamed diversity, which renders 'scientific' analysis impossible. The dominance of materialism further accentuates this neglect. Realists and rationalists have either rejected culture and identity or accepted them with reservations, thereby trivialising their significance and relevance. Realists have recently come to recognise that culture matters, but this recognition presupposes a prior hegemony of Western civilisational values. With the rise of the non-Western world, realists bemoan the loss of this cultural meaning and, on that ground, dismiss the role of culture as a 'serviceable idea' in world politics. Rationalists admit to the relevance of culture, which enables states to overcome problems of coordination by helping them map shared meanings, norms, and values. Yet, culture is reduced to a mere idiom of communication. Rationalists work when a shared script is available; if the norms are divergent, communication is impossible, and culture's role in coordination is thereby denied (ibid.).

Reus-Smit states that constructivists invest in culture and norms and recognise their causality. However, even though they finesse the divergences, a degree of functionalism seems inescapable in their treatment, whether it applies to norm diffusion or conceptions of order. Underlying the English School's perspective on states and international systems are cultural assumptions. The argument is double-edged: *first*, it considers international society the guarantee for states that survive in anarchy, conduct regular business, seek security without overstretching their resources, and practise civility on the whole. Yet, and this is the *second* argument, international society functions only when there is a common culture that binds members. Martin Wright, perhaps the best proponent of this argument, complained that with decolonisation, the shared bond was ineluctably lost. Since then, international society has thinned out, and now solely legitimates an order of sovereign units, and the possibility of a robust international order that agreed normatively on underlying fundamental cultural norms was lost forever. As postcolonial IR theorists have shown, this argument is both logically fallacious and culturally imperialistic. Yet, crucially, IR scholarship has done little to present an alternative account of culture and identity that would be neither parochial nor functionalist (Reus-Smit 2019).

Culture matters to us in many ways. It is indispensable to our identities and notions of selfhood. Culture is also critically important in the selection and dissemination of certain values and the resistance to several others. It matters in how we relate to people in distant places, located across considerable distances. As earlier chapters in this volume have shown, the modern understanding of the 'international' and its attendant categories have cultural moorings. If IR largely remained a Eurocentric or Western field of study, then the role of culture in its constitution cannot be exaggerated. Race is a cultural construct of immense affect and temporality. Racism and supremacist attitudes have radically changed the nature of world politics. The colonial practices that brought the world closer were deeply racist and disparaging of native populations. The expansion of Nazism was also a nefarious racial project, aimed at Aryan domination over all other people. Imperial Japan often justified its wars in cultural terms. In the post-1945 period, Africa fought as much against colonial rule as against the racial domination of European settlers. Nelson Mandela's historic struggle to emancipate South Africa created an archetypal moment in a post-racist order. However, racism, like sexism, is as much institutional-structural as it is agential-cultural. Hence, the death of overtly racist institutions and practices does not automatically connote an end in racist attitudes to life. Race remains as much a cleavage in the domestic domain as it does in the international.

However, culture is not merely about difference and domination, discrimination and negativity. It is also a tool of foreign policy and helps to build bridges. All states deploy their cultural resources to develop friendly ties and build a positive image of their societies and people. While cultural diplomacy is a burgeoning field in today's global politics, tracing the natural tendency of culture to escape all artificial boundaries of life, it is hardly new. Explorers, traders, travellers, artists, and educationists have travelled freely in the past, carrying their own heritage and traditions, and bringing back stories from afar. Artists and performers are the living embodiments of cultural diplomacy as they interact with different cultures and experiment in various idioms of shared meanings. Some analysts cast their net wider and claim all interactions in the various fields of art, music, literature, the sciences, sports, and even business exchanges, as integral to cultural diplomacy. In this wider sense, cultural diplomacy includes an exchange of ideas and sharing of values, traditions, heritage, and symbols that bring people together and contribute to all-round prosperity. Its practitioners can be formal public servants and diplomats, representatives of civil society, business and other functional groups, or even individuals in their private capacities.

A couple of problematic aspects hide behind these seemingly innocuous practices. *First*, cultural diplomacy can be practised to both advance national interests and goals and to bring people across the world together. The soft-power version of cultural diplomacy is very different from the cultural diffusion that civic societal groups engage in, and crucially, these may often contradict each other. Culture can be arrogated by states and wielded as an element of national power. *Second*, cultural interactions have assumed a whole new meaning in a digitised world, where the rapidly expanding technologies of social media and communication produce convergences and challenges, and induce opportunities and crises of meaning. While a globalised world seeks common cultural resources to enable a meaningful and sustainable heterologue among vastly dissimilar peoples, the search for uniformity attracts an inevitable atavistic backlash in many parts of the culture.

However, students of IR need to engage with the scholarly literature generated in the field over the past thirty years in order to offer sound estimates of how culture works in global politics. Conventional IR scholarship provides an excellent opportunity to assess the most conflicted readings of the global order. The role of culture in the foreign policy of states remains a contested matter in IR theory. Culture is not a new phenomenon in IR, nor is its use monolithic. There are at least four areas where cultural explanations have made significant contributions in recent times: the construction of worldviews, the issue of cultural diversity, culture as sources of conflict and cooperation, and the idea of cultural internationalism. There has also been a deluge of contributions on identity and norms that bear an organic link with 'culture' as defined in a broad sense. Yosef Lapid's excellent metaphor, 'Culture's Ship', captures the story perfectly (Lapid and Kratochwil 1996). The ship of culture comes to, stays at, and leaves the shores of IR, only to return again. The off-loaded baggage remains behind and seldom gets the attention it deserves. Some prosper, others perish, and still others undergo metamorphoses. The restitution of culture is therefore neither spectacular nor unprecedented in the history of the discipline.

Yet, culture's ship has found a more hospitable port in recent times, especially since the end of the Cold War. The new world order could not be materially cast; it needed to be understood in ideational terms, but not in terms of the ideology of the familiar. The new discourse of identity and intersubjectivity pervading the social sciences soon influenced IR theory. The language of the discourses of power and security thus had to be reconfigured. 'Culture' became the catch-all label that united a disparate group of scholars, whose origins lay in diverse sources and who were inspired by different considerations, and yet all of whom celebrated this new culturalist paradigm in the discipline.

Between cultural internationalism and culture war lay a spectrum of possibilities, captured and highlighted by a large body of scholars. Of these, three strands became particularly significant. The *first* concerned the use of culture, norms, and identity in the foreign policy discourses of states, cutting across diverse issues and straddling many domains. The *second* manifested most dramatically in the work of Samuel P. Huntington, who sought to create a new culturalist paradigm that could account for all leading conflicts of the contemporary world, which he described through the evocative phrase 'the clash of civilizations'. The *third* involved the mapping of the cultural consequences of globalisation, most notably the battles of identity politics and the dilemmas of multiculturalism in plural societies. The application of norms to security issues is one of the exciting theoretical developments of the past two decades in security studies. In a broad sense, norm analysis is located within the constructivist paradigm, and several scholars have expressed their affinity with the use of constructivism in security affairs.

Norms have been used variously by security analysts, but four approaches deserve special mention. The most dominant approach in rule analysis remains that of Peter Katzenstein and his team, who have published extensive surveys on the role of norms, identity, and culture in different dimensions of national security (Katzenstein, et al. 1996). A second tendency has been to use norms to flesh out the theoretical implications of security communities in constructive mode(s). The works of Emmanuel Adler and Amitava Acharya deserve special mention in this genre (Acharya 1999; Adler 1997; Adler and Barnett 1998). The third is the strategic culture approach, best reflected in the writings of Alistair Johnston (Johnston 1995, 1998).

Cultural Security Studies

Some scholars have sought to explain security and foreign policy choices through cultural explanations. Can IR deliver a stronger cultural moment? Or is there a built-in dynamic within the discipline itself that is status-quoist, given to appropriation(s) and co-option/s of radical tendencies? Michael C. Desch denied the cultural thesis and argued that these new cultural theories are only useful as supplements to realist theories (Duffield, et al. 1999, 156–80). Desch's essay met with protests from scholars like Theo Farrell, John S. Duffield, and Richard Price, among others, who had invoked cultural arguments to explain several cases that realism apparently had no answer for. Farrell claimed, in contradistinction to Desch, that culturalists outperform realists on the theories of balance of threat, security dilemma, and democratic peace (ibid., 166–68).

Farrell and others have unfortunately been outwitted by their detractors, who make several claims. To begin with, the theory of the balance of threat, as formulated by Stephen Walt, is *not* a cultural theory; it is predicated on material factors upon which it raises a theory of intentions. The key to the security dilemma is not intentions, but how material factors make motives quite irrelevant in threat assessment. As for the theory of democratic peace, the corroboration is often not direct, the hypotheses are too localised and limited, and their operationalisation insufficient to lend credence to the theory's universal appeal. Therefore, in a significant number of cases where democratic nations do not become involved in conflict, it is not clear whether this is an outcome of their democratic ethos or due to the lack of any noteworthy conflict of national interest. The lack of concrete statistical correlation obscures the truly explanatory variable, hindering any refutation of realist critiques.

John Duffield argues that the post-war security policies of Germany and Japan cannot be explained by conventional realist theories and require culturalist explanations. His primary contention is that neither Germany nor Japan had behaved like great powers after the collapse of the Soviet Union and the dissolution of the bipolar Cold War international structure. Both states have remained peaceful and stayed away from large weaponisation programmes, despite having the financial capacity to support such a drive. Duffield claims that this relative pacifism emanates from their particular strategic cultures (Duffield, et al. 1999, 156–60). However, as Desch shows, this offers a rather weak challenge to realism, which is capable of explaining the behaviour of both Germany and Japan in realist terms.

Desch sees an apparent divergence in the military postures of Germany and Japan. Germany agreed to 'reduce its standing military forces, lower its defence spending, and to limit its use of force to operations such as peacekeeping in Bosnia' because its 'primary threat—the Soviet Union—has disintegrated' (Desch 1998, 175). In Bosnia, the Germans decided to pass the buck to NATO and the United States, in conformity with realist expectations. In contrast, being located in a threat environment that is far more hostile and severe than Germany's, Japan, its peace rhetoric notwithstanding, 'has adopted a more assertive national security policy' (ibid., 176). Had Germany become aggressive and Japan turned benign, relative to their respective threat settings, the realists could have been accused of having failed to explain such behaviour. Germany is peaceful because Europe has become a far safer continent after the Soviet demise. Japan, on the other hand, follows a more assertive foreign policy because the Asia-Pacific continues to remain tense, particularly with lower US military commitments, a steep decline in the Russian naval reach, and a steady increase in China's maritime power. How did realism get it wrong, then?

Richard Price advanced a normative or culturalist argument to explain why biological and chemical weapons had been used only in a select number of cases. At the core of his argument is the issue of identity. Chemical and biological weapons were considered uncivilised because of the manner in which they killed and unleashed devastation, and so its use could only be contemplated against savage adversaries. Price believes that this explains the restraint shown by their possessors (Duffield, et al. 1998, 169–72). Desch's counter is again remarkably direct. He argues that in all the case studies used by Price, the adversary lacked a convincing deterrent or retaliatory capacity, or, as during the US war in Vietnam, there was a convincing military justification for the use of such weapons. Hence, chemical weapons have been used in cases where the targets did not have the material or the military means to resist such use, and have never been used where a deterrence relationship existed. Again, if realist explanations are to be countered, we need to show abstention from the use of such weapons despite the possibility of their use, even where the victim lacks a deterrent capacity.

The wording of the questions posed, combined with how culturalists uniquely interpret these puzzles, ensures their appropriation into some form of a realist perspective, despite their feeble resistance to such reductionism. In the cases discussed so far, realist explanations do seem unassailable in terms of the realist assumptions. Briefly put, if states remain the paradigmatic unit of IR, if foreign policy is reified in restrictive terms, if national interest remains central to policymaking, then the cultural baggage assembled from diverse sources will continue to supplement, and not supplant, the realist discourses. The research on identity, culture, and security therefore does not constitute a moment of cultural departure in the history of the discipline.

Researchers who have argued for a third path between realist determinism and more culturally articulated positions have failed to deliver. Take Alexander Wendt's canonical text on social constructivism, which claimed a causal role for identity against materialist explanations of international behaviour. Social constructivism is fraught with internal tensions. Its epistemology is both causal and interpretive, while the ontology reifies mainstream categories through a subtle reconstitution of the realist imagination. Nayeem Inayatullah and David Blaney (1996) have correctly criticised Wendt's inability to extend social theory critique far enough. Yosef Lapid agrees with Inayatullah and Blaney's criticism that Wendt had not sufficiently addressed the role of culture in international relations theory (Lapid and Kratochwil 1996, 13–14).

Identity and Huntington's Clash of Civilisations

Perhaps the most pessimistic interpretation of the present world order comes from Samuel P. Huntington's geo-cultural thesis, which states that global conflicts will be increasingly civilisational in character. Huntington predicts the coming of a new age of conflicts/wars among eight distinct civilisations. The 'clash of civilisations' remains one of the most debated, commented upon, and controversial essays in recent times. In this section, we discuss the major themes of Huntington's work and test the validity of his arguments.[1]

[1]The cultural imagination of the global order need not be confined to the Huntingtonian thesis of civilisational clashes. In fact, Huntington's definition of civilisation in cultural terms is extremely parochial. More significantly, it attempts to map a certain kind of world, in which civilisations are sustained by an internal structure of power, and coexist in geopolitical relationships with each other. Contrast this with the work of Akira Iriye, who used the term 'cultural

Writing on the nature of crises before the international order came into being, Huntington dismissed both ideology and economic factors as the primary sources of conflict in the new world.

> The great divisions among humankind and the dominating source of conflict will be cultural. Nation states will remain the most powerful actors in world affairs, but the principal conflicts of global politics will occur between nations and groups of different civilizations. The clash of civilizations will be the battle lines of the future. (Huntington 1993, 22)

Huntington's central thesis is that cultural identities, which he terms 'civilizational' at the broadest level, will condition the patterns of cooperation, conflict, communication, and fragmentation in the post-Cold War international system. He classifies global civilisations into seven basic types—Western, Sinic (Chinese), Japanese, Hindu, Islamic, Orthodox, and Latin American—holding the possibility of a further variation in the shape of the African civilisation (Huntington 1996).[2]

internationalism' to refer to the motivation and achievements of 'individuals and groups of people from different lands that sought to develop an alternative community of notions and people's on the basis of their cultural interchanges and that ... their efforts have significantly altered the world community...' (Iriye 1997, 2). Nevertheless, a closer reading shows that the optimism of cultural internationalism emanates from an essentially liberal, cosmopolitan vision, the chief dimensions of which were seen in the second image of the global order.

[2]The book argues that current global politics is uniquely multipolar and multi-civilisational. Many major states across non-Western civilisations were fiercely modern and vehemently anti-Western in their cultural choice. At present, the West is declining in relative importance, both in its economic and strategic strength. The demographic explosion of Islamic states is posing a challenge to all non-Islamic states. It chronicles the emergence of a civilisation-based world order, where societies sharing cultural values were seen as cooperating with each other. In this world of civilisational divides, cultural renegades are missing. It strongly urges the United States, the custodian of Western culture, to reaffirm its Western identity and lead the West against numerous non-Western challenges. The West needed to recognise the distinctiveness of their civilisation by surrendering the vision of cultural universalism (Westernisation as modernisation). Huntington prognosticates an intense inter-civilisation clash based on incommensurate cultural identities.

Of the various themes put forth by Huntington, three deserve particular attention. Huntington's fulminations, misgivings, and concerns about Islam stand out from the rest of his argument. He asks why, at the dawn of the new century, Muslims outnumbered members of any other civilisation in their involvement in intra-group violence. He suggests six possible causes, three historical and general, and three more recent ones. The first is the familiar argument that Islam is by birth a militant faith: 'The Koran and other statements of Muslim beliefs contain few prohibitions on violence and a concept of nonviolence is absent from Muslim doctrine and practice' (Huntington 1996, 263). The second reason, a natural corollary of the first, points to Islam's history of expansion *qua* an aggressive, coercive, and enforced policy of proselytisation. Unlike most other religions, Islam was spread by the sword. The third reason behind the Muslim–non-Muslim clash lay in the 'indigestibility' of Islam. 'Even more than Christianity, Islam is an absolutist faith. It merges religion and politics and draws a sharp line between those in the Dar al-Islam and those in the Dar al-harb' (ibid., 264).

To these, Huntington adds three more factors. The *first* argues that Muslims are the victims of a Western imperialism that targets Islam's material weakness, and is led by the West's own anti-Muslim prejudice. The violence of Muslims thus becomes the armed resistance of the victim, the torn, and the undignified. The *second* argument explains the instability of Islam as emanating from the absence of a dominant leader. The *third* and final cause is attributed to a demographic explosion in Muslim societies, which resulted in an army of youth in the age group between fifteen and thirty, who form a natural source of violence and instability throughout the world (ibid., 264–65).

The next major contention put forward by Huntington is about the volatility and intensity of fault-line wars, the paradigmatic case being the disintegration of Yugoslavia in general and the devastation of Bosnia in particular.

> In fault line wars, each side has incentives not only to emphasize its own civilizational identity but also that of the other side. In its local war, it sees itself not just fighting another local ethnic group but fighting another civilization. The threat is thus magnified and enhanced by the resources of a major civilization, and defeat has consequences not just for itself, but for all of its own civilization. (Huntington 1996, 270)

Referring to the war in the former Yugoslavia, Huntington commented:

> In the early shapes of the Yugoslav breakup … the leading actors in Western civilization rallied behind their coreligionists. Boris Yeltsin's government, on the other hand, attempted to pursue a middle course that would be sympathetic to the orthodox Serbs … Islamic governments and groups … castigated the West for not coming to the defense of the Bosnians. (Huntington 1993, 37)

Huntington also used the case studies of the 1991 Iraq War and the war between Armenia and Azerbaijan (1992–93) to reinforce his theme. He found a clear civilisational contrast in the responses to the Gulf War between the people of West Asia (including some of their leaders), who hailed Saddam Hussein as a great hero standing against the Western bully, on the one hand, and the reactions of the West on the other. In the battle between Armenia and Azerbaijan, too, Huntington identified the role of civilisation in the division between the supporters of Islam (with Turkey supporting Azerbaijan) on the one hand and the supporters of orthodox Christianity (Russians coming to the aid of Armenia) on the other. Huntington contrasted this with intra-civilisation problem(s), like the clash between Russia and Ukraine, which, despite its intensity and seriousness, remained non-violent (Huntington 1993, 35–38).

Huntington's chief concern was to forcefully argue the 'West *versus* the rest' thesis, in which he saw the Confucian–Islamic connection as the most serious threat. The new-found civilisational consciousness of non-Western states created a sharp divide between the two. The non-Western countries were either isolationist, or had joined the West for aid and protection, or were contemplating a balance with the West through various means.[3] Interestingly, Huntington drew a contrast between the old arms race policy, where each party developed its own capabilities to match the other, and the new Islamic–Confucian alliance against the

---

[3]Huntington's conclusion is emphatic: 'The central axis of world politics in the future is likely to be … the conflict between "the West and the Rest" and "the responses of non-Western civilizations to Western power and values"' (Huntington 1993, 41). Commenting on the Confucian-Islamic anti-Western strategy, he stated: 'A Confucian-Islamic military connection has … come into being, designed to promote acquisition by its members of the weapons and weapons technologies needed to counter the military power of the West' (ibid., 47).

West. While the former was playing a conventional game, the latter was relying on non-proliferation and self-reduction strategies.[4]

In all fairness, the crisis of the West thesis is not the sole monopoly of Huntington. Scholars like Farid Zakaria, Kishore Mahbubani, and R. D. Kaplan, among others, have also indicated an anti-Western cultural turn in world politics. In fact, Kaplan's own pessimistic reading of an evolving conflict-prone international system, which is replacing the more balanced bipolar one, or John Mearsheimer's aggressive realism, which predicts an intense geopolitical rivalry in Europe and East Asia, are not very different from Huntington's predictions (Kaplan 1994; Mearsheimer 2001). But neither Kaplan nor Mearsheimer share Huntington's belief in civilisations as the moving structural force behind this dark, pessimistic anarchy. In this sense, Huntington's thesis is indeed unique (Chatterjee and Maitra 2020, 110).

Realists have refuted the cultural paradigm in international politics. However, they have offered no explanation for domestic conflicts, particularly ethnic violence, which constitutes perhaps the most constant source of violence in today's world, leading to millions of deaths across the globe. It is true that once ethnic conflicts are externalised, realism tends to subsume them under standard state-based conflicts of power. It is also true that much of the ethnic violence in the Third World was configured by the logic of Cold War bipolar politics. Yet most ethnic conflicts involve identities and differences, concepts that are alien to pristine realism.[5]

---

[4]There are various shortcomings in Huntington's work. Robert Bartley, amongst others, argued that the greatest potential for conflict was *within*, rather than *between*, civilisations. Fouad Ajami refuted Huntington's conflation of civilisations and states, and his tendency to collapse the second into the first, and saw Huntington's work as a mischievous rallying point for the American right wing. The whole enterprise seemed convoluted, bereft of either the depth of scholarship necessary to compare the cultural essence of civilisations, or the theoretical flexibility to capture the nuances of categories such as 'civilisation' and 'culture' (Ajami 1993; Bartley 1993; Kirkpatrick, et al. 1993; Weeks 1993).

[5]Although scholars like Barry Posen and Van Evera have sought to fill this lacuna in realist thought, there is no questioning of the making of national or sub-national identities in these tracts (Posen 1993; Van Evera 1994). Realism also cannot explain the long-observed peace between democratic states. Most crucially, realism has failed to offer a theoretical explanation of terrorism, the one phenomenon that has triggered Western/US intransigence in recent times.

Terrorism cannot be called a structural property of the anarchic system. It is also not a state-based phenomenon, although particular states do support, nurture, and export terrorist groups for ulterior ends. Terrorist groups are not necessarily rational or purposive in their method and action. Hence, the fight against terrorism is an elusive war against an invisible foe, and cannot be convincingly won by traditional means. As a result, the statist response, a compulsive articulation for the realist, does not provide an appropriate punitive or corrective policy for the menace of terrorism. Realists might still partially salvage their case by arguing that terrorists become powerful only in the shelter of the state. Huntington's clash of civilisations thesis, despite its oversimplifications and inherent crudity, became appealing in the post-9/11 world as a useful frame of reference to describe the contours of the new global (dis)order. US President George H. W. Bush's talk of the 'axis of evil' and 'crusades', Italian Prime Minister Silvio Berlusconi's reference to the threat posed to Christianity from hostile Islamic forces, and the increasing use of religious/communal metaphors by leaders of a host of nations cutting across faiths seemed to emphasise Huntington's thesis, particularly his prediction that a macrocosmic conflict between Islam and other religions would lead to great wars. To what extent are today's conflicts cultural? Is the US conscious of any civilisational role? Are anti-Western states responding and acting in culturally explicit terms (Sussex 2004, 28–50)?

Huntington claims that the international system is changing from one where nations cooperate, compete, and even battle in their pursuit of material interests to one where states are defining their identities and interests along cultural/civilisational lines. Therefore, the war on terrorism is primarily a cultural battle between the Christian West and Islamic civilisation. It is a fact that Osama bin Laden and his terrorist organisation, the Al Qaeda, portrayed their conflict in these terms. It can also not be denied that ruling elites in Islamic states around the world are critical of Western cultural imperialism in general and the celebration of hedonism in particular. Take the victory celebrations and processions of youths across the Islamic world, where several of them protest against the illegitimacy and gross inefficiency of the ruling regimes, whose survival is nearly exclusively guaranteed by American hegemony in the region. In contrast to the public, the reaction of ruling elites all over the Muslim world was sober and cautious. If identities and interests are determined by culture, such reticence in the face of military invasions makes no sense at all.

Although President Bush did indulge in quasi-religious propaganda immediately after the tragedy of 9/11, he was quick to recant and refrained from invoking religio-cultural metaphors while putting together a global coalition against terrorism. A careful perusal of the papers and documents related to the Project for the New American Century (PNAC), the philosophical/intellectual fountainhead of the Bush administration, shows *no confirmation* of the clash of civilisations thesis. It is true that some members associated with the PNAC have occasionally paid lip service to Huntington's theory.[6] And yet the PNAC vision, while certainly about domination, is *not* about *cultural* domination. It is about establishing 'Pax Americana' across the globe and transforming the United States, the sole remaining superpower, into a planetary empire primarily through military means. Realising the PNAC vision might require the surgical excision of a vast number of Islamic states in the Middle East and North Africa, but the list also includes North Korea and China. The mention of China and North Korea as 'rogue' states suggests that the exclusions are not defined solely by culture.

For the culture/civilisation paradigm to make sense, one needs a definition of culture that is separate from either culture as ideology or culture as power renditions of the concept (Chatterjee and Maitra 2020, 110). Despite Huntington's claim that the clash of civilisations may actually be conflicts between cultural identities, many of his examples are unconvincing. For one, analyses based on power differentials often do a better job of explaining many of these conflicts. Huntington does not convincingly demonstrate that states have been caught in a civilisational crisis. Moreover, if relations between states were decided by either cultural similarity or dissimilarity, then there can be no convincing explanation for the cordial ties between the US and Southeast and East Asia, or Russia's disputes with neighbours who are culturally similar, or the endless crises in West Asia. Throughout the world, empirical

---

[6]The most prominent among them has been Norman Podoretz, a noted Jewish conservative who, after specifying a long list of states and regimes that 'richly deserve to be overthrown and replaced', declared that this action was about 'the long-overdue internal reform and modernization of Islam' (quoted in Pitt 2003, 3).

evidence on the correlation between cultural identity and violence has been conflicted.

Military alliances across the world in the past thirty years also contradict the clash of civilisation thesis. China and Pakistan possibly represent one of the world's strongest military and economic partnerships, despite having no religious or cultural factors in common. If religion was pivotal in shaping alliances, the world should have witnessed co-religionists lining up in support of the warring parties in the Iraq Wars of 1990 and 2003, or the war against the Taliban in Afghanistan in 2001. These wars saw a variety of coalition partners, but they were certainly not arranged along religious or civilisational lines. A standard realist explanation is certainly more acceptable here (Sussex 2004, 35). There is ample evidence to show that while China and Russia did not approve of the US military expeditions in 1990, 2001, and 2003, they refrained from any confrontation. Again, there was no religion or civilisation-based coalitions at play in the international military action against the ISIS. The problems of alienation and economic inequality spawned by globalisation, along with the waves of refugee migration from West Asia and North Africa to Europe, have led the West to become politically divided as never before in recent decades. Political tussles between right-wing populist forces and liberals cannot be explained by religious or cultural factors. While the fear of losing jobs to outsiders does provoke backlash and fuel right-wing extremism, the targets are both East Europeans and Muslims migrants, and therefore Huntington's claims do not seem convincing enough.

Further, Huntington appears to gloss over the distinction between the use of cultural identities for domestic political consolidation and mobilisation and the use of macro-cultural resources in international politics. Huntington misses a simple fact about identity—identities are always plural and attempts to streamline and mainstream identity are usually fraught. In contrast, Huntington freezes identities and oversimplifies interests. Seeking the misplaced comfort of clarity and parsimony, he sacrifices the ambiguities, trade-offs, and nuances of civilisations (Chatterjee 2005b, 5502). Moreover, Huntington's reading of the past is narrow and discriminatory. He neglects the fact that zones of mixed cultures have always been prone to interpretive disputes over symbolic meanings and deliberately exaggerates episodes of conflict, even though these mixed zones have witnessed more periods of peaceful coexistence than outright or exclusivist hostilities.

Huntington's work represents perhaps the most grotesque perversion of the cultural paradigm in IR. It is essentially a cruder version of *machtpolitik*, with a manifest ethnocentric bias towards the inherent superiority of Western culture, and taking the form of postcolonial narratives, it offers a masculine and intensely provocative counter-attack on the genre of writings initially popularised by Edward Said's *Orientalism*. Huntington's cultural thesis is overtly functionalist; it is doubtful if his argument can even claim to be a cultural explanation of world affairs. He disregards the idea of culture as an independent variable and views its role as fatalistic or wholly determinate. This defeats the idea of using a cultural explanation for world affairs, since culture is made entirely subordinate to the conflictual tendencies inherent in nation-states operating in an anarchic environment. Huntington simply ethnicises realism by ignoring the diversity and plurality of cultural identities across the world. Here, he does realism a disservice, because realism did offer an agnostic and secular reading of conflicts. Huntington's use of identity politics is bereft of the nuances and complexities that are part of cultural politics. It is both theoretically and normatively incapable of interrogating the role of culture in world affairs.

LIBERAL IR THEORY AND CULTURE

As an example of a liberal take on culture, Francis Fukuyama's end of history thesis reveals a misplaced philosophical arrogance while completely dismissing the problem of culture as a valid theoretical concern. In his work *The End of History and the Last Man* (1992), Fukuyama does attempt to correct this neglect and falls back largely on Friedrich Hegel, via Alexandre Kojeve, to state that claims of recognition cannot be banished by an ideology of material development, consumerism, and wealth. Yet, the narrative is largely dismissive of cultural difference, reading them as an unsettled problem of the past, a part of history unqualified for inclusion in post-history, which Fukuyama triumphantly claims is what liberalism has ushered into the developed world. From the rise of ethno-nationalism and religious extremism to nativism, Confucianism, and white supremacist politics, culture and identity have become the dominant narrative of our times.

Identity politics has returned with a vengeance on the global scene and cultural nationalism is, empirically speaking, the dominant 'ism' of the contemporary world.

Liberals have responded in two ways to this turn of events. *First*, a group of liberals have argued that identity politics is backward and progressive liberalism must counter it by rallying powerfully behind the idea of the rights-bearing person who refuses to be defined in parochial, closed, and static cultural terms. *Second*, many liberals have sought to reconcile with identity claims within liberalism through the various arguments of multiculturalism that address cultural diversity, either through group rights or cultural *laissez faire* (or some combination of both). Yet, these are essentially arguments meant to adjudicate the cultural question within states, and liberals have done precious little in theoretical terms to extend this project globally, notwithstanding the works of Thomas Pogge and Kimberly Hutchings, among others.

However, the liberal articulation of the problem we face in cultural terms is important. It is sensitive to the role that technology plays in disseminating cultural norms and images across the world with breathtaking speed, the manifest dialogues and reciprocal relations among cultures, the evolution of cultural identity, and the need to identify a language or a moral standard that might help societies resolve their ethical problems in the event of a clash of cultures. While most liberals have given up the attempt to build a culture-neutral universal theory that would gravitate towards a pluralism of values, the need to find answers to the conundrum of culture clash remains a central concern. Although liberal IR theories may not have shed light on the cultural predicament of humans, they continue to grapple with the problem. Most liberals have eschewed arguments of liberal hegemony and veer now towards more democratic ways of seeking multicultural solutions to the vexed claims and counter-claims of collective identities.

Let us now return to Fukuyama. Several analysts and commentators of world politics predicted an era of unprecedented peace and global prosperity as the benefits of a triumphant liberalism spread across states. However, the most dramatic prophecy came from Francis Fukuyama, a Japanese social scientist settled in the United States. Fukuyama's work is singled out for two reasons. *First*, it represents the most optimistic variant of scholarship within the liberal paradigm, one that sought to link issues of war and security with democracy and the market. *Second*, and more importantly, Fukuyama's work stands out for its philosophical sophistication, no matter how controversial his ideas and regardless of the arbitrary nature of his intellectual borrowings. Fukuyama's work therefore complements that of the peace-democracy brigade, although it also highlights the limitations of applying this connection in underdeveloped regions of the world.

Fukuyama's provocative essay, 'The End of History', boldly declared the demise of socialism as the final obstacle to the ultimate victory of liberal capitalist democracy. He posited this as the ultimate achievement of history's predetermined progress towards liberal ideals and free markets. These ideas were subsequently developed further in a comprehensive work of philosophy and sociology that set the tone for one of the most important debates of the post-Cold War era (Fukuyama 1989, 3–18; 1992). With the defeat of communism and the collapse of the Soviet Union, the victory of liberal democracy and capitalism was complete. Liberalism thus vanquished all challenges and achieved the goals of security, liberty, and democratic equality, their mutual tensions notwithstanding. Fukuyama's work ingeniously combines the thought of both Plato and Hegel, and can be justified on both material and moral-ideational terms. We will look into these claims, as they were framed in ideational-cultural discourses, more closely.

Fukuyama built on Hegel's teleological philosophy, mediated by the liberal readings of Kojeve. In simple terms, Fukuyama argued that the end of the Cold War also signalled the end of grand ideological battles. Liberal democracy had finally prevailed over its ideological rivals—fascism and communism/socialism—in a triumph of freedom over totalitarian organisations. Fascism was defeated in the course of World War II. The challenge posed by socialism, however, was far more pervasive and difficult. But even state socialism ultimately crumbled as it failed to keep pace with the unprecedented developments of the capitalist world. The end of the Cold War was the result of an implosion of the communist project in the East. This was what Fukuyama considered the end of history, a time when grand ideological battles become obsolete and liberalism ws left with no rivals. The end of history, Fukuyama argued, was not universal since some pockets of the developing world remained mired in historical conflicts over atavistic ideologies like nationalism and fundamentalism. Yet the trend, even in the developing world, was to hitch their wagon to the liberal West.

Whether in authoritarian Asian states like South Korea or Singapore, or in East European states freed from Soviet control, the winds of change were irreversible. Markets, democracy, and freedom were the bricks and mortars of the liberal millennium, and ultimately, the functional need to survive in a highly competitive global market built on innovation and mobility would trump the residues of social backwardness across the world.[7]

In the developed world of post-history, states would continue to direct their attention and resources towards security. But inter-state competition would be limited to economic issues as military confrontation and doctrinal hostility would have become a thing of the past. International relations of the developed world would therefore be conducted within innovative, collaborative frameworks based on the calculation of absolute gains. Sectarian violence and parochial sub-nationalism(s) would continue to burden history without compromising 'the deep configurations of time'. One cannot criticise Fukuyama for having predicted an end to all conflicts and mutual rivalries. His primary contention was that fundamental conflicts would not recur in post-history since all the main rival paradigms of liberal capitalism had been defeated (Anderson 1992, 281–85, 331–41).

We have come a long way since Fukuyama wrote his liberal *fin de siècle*. Two developments have been particularly galling. *First*, the history of the postcolonial world has taken its revenge on the post-history of its Western counterpart. The catastrophic events of the 9/11 terrorist attacks in the heart of the United States devastated the calm of a triumphal liberalism. *Second*, as the world went into the severest recession since the Great Depression of 1929, the economic or material claims of liberal prosperity came apart dramatically. While the advocates of neoliberal orthodoxy had been able to silence their detractors for a long time, these cataclysmic events had to be responded to. In the words of Eliane Glaser,

> Over the last three years, however, in a slow reaction to the 2008 bank bailouts, cracks have started to appear. Global Occupy protests and demonstrations against austerity have led many commentators on the left … to wonder whether history is on the march once again. 'What is

[7]Fukuyama's path-breaking article came out in 1989 and his book followed in 1992. He came up with a spirited reply to his critics in a thoughtful article in 1995. For an excellent analysis, see Elliott (2008).

> going on?' asks Badiou. 'The continuation, at all costs, of a weary world? A salutary crisis of that world, racked by its victorious expansion? The end of that world? The advent of a different world?' He tentatively regards the uprisings of 2011 as game-changing, with the potential to usher in a new political order. For Milne, likewise, developments such as the failure of the US to 'democratise' Iraq and Afghanistan, the financial crash and the flowering of socialism in Latin America demonstrate the 'passing of the unipolar moment'. (Glaser 2014)

The collapse of an upbeat liberalism has led a number of scholars to describe the post-2003 international order as an 'empire'. 'Empire' has become a much-debated idea in IR discourses. It is not just a geopolitical and geoeconomic term; it is, in fact, deeply cultural. Tarak Barkawi and Mark Laffey argue,

> Empire most often denotes a distinct type of political entity and imperialism a policy of foreign conquest and rule. Understood in such a way the concept has limited purchase on contemporary world politics. However, in our view, the empire concept … points the way to a more adequate theorisation of the 'international' as a distinct space of social interaction—a space within which processes of mutual constitution are productive of the entities which populate the international system. (Barkawi and Laffey 2002, 111)

Michael Hardt and Antonio Negri believe that sovereignty has changed under pressure from capitalist globalisation—from a modern to a postmodern form, engendering a new global form of rule termed as 'empire' (Negri and Hardt 2000). World power is primarily predicated on capitalism and Western cultural hegemony, which produces a constant churning. 'The realisation of that power requires the remaking of modern sovereignty, which is a sovereignty of borders and limits' (Barkawi and Laffey 2002, 117). The American domination of the international order is certainly unique and defies historical parallels or lazy generalisations. Americans have displayed a profound sense of cultural 'exceptionalism' that has sought to separate them from the classical European colonialists. Alexis de Tocqueville first used the term 'American exceptionalism' during his maiden trip to America in 1831, a term he defined not by shared ethnicity or history, but by a set of common beliefs. While the role of the US in the international order hinges on this idea, the meaning and consequences of this conviction remain deeply contested. What is not in doubt, however, is that American culture is the fountainhead of the modern project of globalisation, which is both economic and cultural. Perhaps 'American Empire' is the wrong term, connoting as it does the coming of age of a hyper-real modernity where culture and economy are fused in unprecedented ways. If old empires ruled their colonies by invoking the idea of a benevolent despotism predicated largely on industrial modernity, the American domination of the contemporary international order is justified on the promise of democracy, liberty, and global justice.

TECHNOLOGICAL DIMENSION

Technology, the State and Global Communication

Charles Weiss (2005, 297) points out that science and technology do not stand on their own but are social processes susceptible to the forces of politics, economics, and social change. Science and technology are in themselves distinct sources of power and influence, and affect policymaking in a variety of ways. The debates on climate change and much of modern political economy are ultimately to do with questions of science and technology, their social or political interpretations, the regional distribution of knowledge-based capacities, and the trajectories of influence that such capacities generate. Hence, science and technology are politically vectored into instruments of statecraft, and advanced industrial powers invest massively in cutting-edge technologies, for both market considerations of selling the high-quality consumer goods that are vital to their profits and to retain political, military, or strategic influence, since military power is largely predicated on control over precision-guided technologies, artificial intelligence, information systems, and miniaturisation.

Ivan V. Danilin argues that the growing influence of artificial intelligence and information technology is directly relevant to traditional diplomacy and foreign policy, as speed is pivotal in the swift and targeted dissemination of influence (Danilin 2018). Whether states that possess more lethal technologies can unsettle the given distribution of power remains an open question.

Weiss finds that technology has changed the science of war-making. This could be seen with each major development in weapons technology, such as the discovery of the fighter jet, missiles, and most dramatically, the advent of nuclear weapons. These developments affect the pattern or distribution of manufacturing, services, and markets; direct competition for control over spheres like space technology; and also affect the overall capacity of states and regions to invest in scientific and technological research, infrastructure development, calibrated risk-taking in new frontiers of technology, and social adjustment to the use of new technologies in everyday life. In fact, modern power is largely a function of the innovative capacities of nations, more so than the conventional measures of the past (Weiss 2005, 297–98).

This is not to suggest that science and technology have unmediated access to power. These are social processes whose use is politically decided by national elites, and they tend to corroborate or reinforce the existing fault-lines. Science and technology have no independent existence: from decisions about investment and budgetary allocations to the nature of technologies, politics looms large in every aspect. While technological breakthroughs may be autonomous, their development, significance, use, and trajectories are deeply political. Foreign policy goals often play a critical role in how states decide on technological issues. India's recent conflict with China was instrumental in New Delhi's decision to embrace self-sufficiency in manufacturing, particularly in the domains of defence and security, which would have a critical effect on industrialisation and technology-development processes. Israel's progress in energy conservation and dry farming technologies have resulted from its political isolation and unremitting conflict with its neighbours. America's open-door policy, inviting the best of scientific minds and technical talents in the world, paved the way for its technological dominance, which was in turn critical to its becoming the world's most dominant power since the end of World War II. China's decision to make unprecedented investments in frontier technologies like 5G was motivated primarily by its desire to emerge as the next superpower. Similarly, the European Union's crusade for cleaner and greener technology has led to it becoming a powerhouse of modern technologies in alternative energy production.

There is no denying the definite technological basis of the existing nation-state system. If technological systems change rapidly, the nation-state system has to respond to it. The technological foundation of each era resulted in different social structures. The monarchical empire was historically supported by primitive technologies (a few isolated exceptions notwithstanding), while the technology of the Industrial Revolution—the railways, post and telegraph, and the early transmission systems—was a major factor behind the emergence of the modern nation-state and the imperialism of colonial powers. Digital technology revolutionised communications, which in turn complicated the technological basis of the post-Westphalian inter-state system (McLuhan and Powers 1989).

Technology is always bound up with questions of knowledge and power. Colonialism brought about the modern integration of the world in ways that were unknown in the past. Colonial penetration produced a complex set of trends that resist standardisation. However, in most colonial societies, political resistance to the domination of the 'White Man' involved a recognition of the material superiority of the West, and the resulting commitment to emulate modern Western science, technology, and institutions. Modernity engendered ideologies of modernisation and development as the most efficient panacea to the material impoverishment of the newly independent states. The objectivist, positivist outlook and values of Western modernity advanced the cause of technological development throughout the world. The social use of technology, however, had always been ideologically biased and guided by certain ethnocentric assumptions, inherent to which were notions of exclusion/inclusion and subjugation/liberation. As in the past, it seems that the battle-lines of the future will be determined, *inter alia*, by the technological fault-lines of the international system, and the way the modes of social communication and culture activate and energise these existing fault-lines (Sola Pool 1990).

The strategic impact of this information and communication revolution on the long-term viability of the nation-state is difficult to predict. Marshall McLuhan, the celebrated media and communication theorist, has cogently explained how the human conception of space is gradually changing from 'linear and visual' to 'acoustic and simultaneous' in the electronic age: 'The present electronic age, in its inescapable evocation of simultaneity, presents the first serious threat to the 2500-year dominance of the left hemisphere' (McLuhan and McLuhan n.d.). Electronic technology is an immensely powerful and instantaneous carrier of cultural forms. The impact of informatics-powered social media and cyberspace is profound, as they are a constitutive medium of human thought and feeling, generating new modes of meaning and new worlds of the mind.

While cyber technologies create a borderless world, there is a price to be paid for these technological benefits. The world of international communication, information, and media is thus not a free world, predicated on the norms of an egalitarian democracy. This world, like every other, is underpinned by Western knowledge practices and controlled by developed capitalist states. Communication theorists like McLuhan believe that political boundaries have become technologically redundant, and may usher in a process of vertical integration via communication technology. The penetration of information and satellite technology, whether military or civilian, is so intrusive and pervasive today that it transgresses the territorial boundaries of nation-states with little resistance. This has opened up possibilities of redefining space by means of modern technology. Digital technology and social media have created new forms of politics that threaten to bypass state controls.

Whether one studies the Arab Spring or the Shahbagh Movement in Dhaka, the impact of digitised communication in the virtual space, instigating political mobilisation and protests, is unmistakable. And yet these examples drive home the limits of modern technology. Connectivity galvanises political movements and creates ingenious networks of solidarity across spatial boundaries. However, political battles are fought in actual societies, on streets and by-lanes amidst real social forces and often against oppressive states. No amount of global solidarity expressed in the virtual space can win political battles. The denouement of the Arab Spring is a case in point. While protesters made initial political gains in a number of states, the outcome ultimately resulted from what the global powers were doing on the 'ground', and how the state responded to the challenge.

The COVID-19 pandemic showed that science and technology do not only direct power and influence in world affairs, but are also vital ingredients in collaborative efforts between governments, states, and businesses, politics, the economy, and educational institutions, and regional bodies and non-governmental organisations. The picture is, however, a mixed one. The pandemic initially led to frenzied nationalistic responses, with states attempting to control the available medical resources and infrastructure, which were woefully inadequate in tackling the enormity of the crisis. The WHO and the ECOSOC, among others, highlighted the urgency of multi-level collaboration and coordination of aid and research, even as the major powers remained committed to their own citizens. The world did witness significant medical cooperation during the crisis, and the vaccine research and breakthroughs that took place could not have been possible without international cooperation. Yet such collaborations could not overcome the limits set by major global conflicts, particularly that between China and the US, which considerably retarded the progress that could have otherwise been achieved by scientists in their fight against the COVID-19 virus. This once again demonstrates that, *first*, science and technology are social processes, and *second*, the crucial influence that international politics exert on scientific collaboration even in the face of an existential crisis.

Cyber technology transgresses borders, yet the same technology is often appropriated and used effectively by states to advance their national security. Cyber cells exist in all key states across the world; their weapons are their computers, just as the security personnel have their guns. They protect states against both virtual and real threats. Even in our present electronic age, national communication policies have not lost their relevance. If the globalisation of finance, resources, and jobs is inspired, coordinated, and controlled by intrusive, border-jumping information technologies, conventional and non-conventional security issues are also largely fought and managed in cyberspace. The state is very much a part of this game, as is a set of new non-state actors.

Conclusion

This chapter has shown how the prevalent cultural readings of the international order and its technological basis are mostly harsh and divisive, with scant regard for the freedom and rights of the vast majority across the world. This is not normatively justifiable from the vantage point of an ethic of resistance, one that is pertinent to the ontology of the poorer states of the world. Radical alternatives are theoretically possible, but are less likely to work at present. The weaker states have, on the whole, abstained from a politics of resistance. This anomaly can be explained by the absence of a politics of emancipation, one that can challenge the normative vacuity of the power/culture image(s) of the contemporary world. However, while one aspect of this new cultural politics is divisive and conflictive, there are other channels of cultural collaboration throughout the world, and so we cannot conclude pessimistically that identity and culture in world politics are mere adjuncts to wars between and within states. Cultures are neither unique nor homogeneous, and modern technologies that transgress borders allow cultural communication to happen all across the world. Cultures and identities evolve over time; yet the malleability of cultural flows that modern technology now permits makes the guardians of culture nervous, and attempts to reinforce their identity generates a politics of difference both within and between states, with violent repercussions.

In other words, cultural imageries are neither negative nor positive. How culture and identity play out in world politics depends on the nature of societies and their heritage, their dominant ideologies and view of culture, and the cleavages that criss-cross social orders. Academic IR was long silent on culture and identity. The past thirty years have, however, set the record right.

16

Global Governance, Global Civil Society, and NGOs in International Relations

Shibashis Chatterjee and Sulagna Maitra

This chapter discusses the concept of global governance and its limitations. Governance is indispensable to all institutions, regardless of level or scale of operations. It requires some form of authority since decisions need to be successfully implemented, services rendered in an orderly manner, contracts signed between parties properly honoured, violators identified and dealt with effectively, and a modicum of continuity established in the transaction of different activities. Governance is, however, possible without coercion, as the daily business of most economic and civil societal associations would seem to suggest. However, in case of flagrant violations of established rules and conventions, some recourse to course correction is required, like the abrogation of membership for a repeat offender. This type of governance is possible without a sovereign authority that uses force to uphold legally binding rules. However, such institutions usually flourish in close-knit communities that display moderate to high levels of mutual trust (Deutsch 1957; Haas 1958, 1964; Haas 1992; Mitrany 1966). Globalisation has undeniably resuscitated the idea of global governance since the unprecedented proximity of states and businesses, non-governmental organisations and civil society associations, the increasingly digitised nature of economic transactions, and the remarkable increase in the role of information in everyday life require institutions, rules, and practices commensurate with these tasks.

Even as states regularise transactional interactions through the myriad models of international cooperation thrown up by globalisation, the rules of the game are evolving and prediction and stability remain critical challenges. With increasing globalisation, the need for appropriate institutions and governance structures became crucial. As economies, societies, and polities became variously intermeshed, their transactions became complex and national institutions often found themselves ill-equipped to respond to new issues. States were both attracted to globalisation and feared its uneven consequences. The management of the system assumed grave importance as new economies of scale began operating at the local, state, inter-state, regional, trans-regional, international, and global levels. This led to a sovereignty paradox: while states were unable to shield their economies from transactions, they refused to compromise on their sovereign rights. Governing the multifaceted interactions across various sectors required innovative approaches, as most states were wary of supranational institutions and thus rejected shared sovereignty. Postcolonial states feared a return of imperialism through the back door. Weaker economies were critical of the dominance exerted by stronger ones through formal institutions. New areas like environment and information technology needed regulation, but there were no precedents to build upon. Soon, non-state actors emerged on the scene and laid claim to status and power alongside sovereign nation-states. Norms and procedures detailing the response to such transnational challenges had to be set up in this complex context, and thus the mechanisms of global governance could not always be effective. This chapter will also delve into the various meanings, aspects, and politics of the idea of global civil society, both in relation to the deficiencies of the nation-state and the practices of global governance.

GLOBAL GOVERNANCE

While there is no world government as yet, the modern communication revolution has meant an increased movement of various kinds of commodities and services across both the physical and virtual space, with unbelievable speed and under reasonable security. This involves surveillance and regulatory frameworks, norms and standards, and a range of compliance instruments—in short, the various institutions and practices of global governance, with no international legislature or executive bodies backed by a supra-state authority. This qualifies as a governance that involves a quasi-authoritative allocation of values. How does this happen? The answer '... lies in global governance. It is the sum of laws, norms, policies, and institutions that define, constitute, and mediate relations between citizens, societies, markets, and states in the international system—the wielders and objects of the exercise of international public power' (Thakur and Weiss 2015, 27). Global governance is understood as:

> ... the ways in which global affairs are managed. As there is no global government, global governance typically involves a range of actors including states, as well as regional and international organizations. However, a single organization may nominally be given the lead role on an issue, for example the World Trade Organization in world trade affairs. Thus global governance is thought to be an international process of consensus-forming which generates guidelines and agreements that affect national governments and international corporations. Examples of such consensus would include WHO policies on health issues. (World Health Organization n.d.)

Critique of Global Governance

Criticisms have been levied against the idea of global governance. For example, the World Health Organization (WHO) states that three primary gaps exist: the *jurisdictional gap* between areas that need management and the absence of an authority performing these tasks; the *incentive gap* between the need and motivation for international cooperation across national borders; and the *participation gap* between the actions of states and civil society groups in advancing governance without frontiers. It is argued, however, that globalisation is narrowing the last two gaps, although insufficient authority structures continue to bedevil global governance. Again, the rapid spread of technology and social media is encouraging global social movements to cohere around specific nodal functions, for example, over a range of health issues as a response to pandemics (World Health Organization n.d.).

Ramesh Thakur and Thomas G. Weiss mention (2015) five particular 'gaps' in global governance: knowledge gaps; normative gaps; policy gaps; institutional gaps; and compliance gaps.

To understand global problems and organise for their eventual elimination, we need knowledge. Information and scientific knowledge are therefore indispensable for global governance. Experience enables us to have the resources that allow us to see the problem that needs solving. Normative gaps follow knowledge gaps. Addressing the issue logically demands developing appropriate norms. While norms are usually formed within societies, international organisations such as the United Nations also play a role. Norms 'matter because people—citizens as well as politicians and officials—care about what others think of them' (ibid., 32). Thus, individuals, organisations, and groups need to set norms on various issues, be they economic trade, environmental issues, or human rights, in order to enable the agencies of global governance to address them.

Norms, however, will not automatically translate into policies. Strategies involve 'the articulated and linked set of governing principles and goals, and the agreed programs of action to implement those principles and achieve those goals' (Thakur and Weiss 2015, 33). Global governance requires complex forms of policymaking involving states, civil society groups, and international organisations, and the relationship among these varied elements is not necessarily smooth. Further, policies may be purely *ad hoc*, and good governance will only ensue once we design institutions for specific purposes. Thus, when speaking of environmental rights abuses, an institutional gap can be seen in the absence of mechanisms that can operationalise the existing body of environmental law. Where war crimes or human rights are concerned, institutions are again necessary. Before it was finally set up, nations spent a long time debating the creation of an International Criminal Court that can try war crimes globally, so that convicted actors are held accountable for their offences. Despite most states agreeing to set up the body, there has been no real progress. Organisations like the United Nations High Commissioner for Refugees (UNHCR) exist to look into refugee issues, while the Office of the Commission for Human Rights or the Human Rights Council is meant to promote human rights globally. However, nation-states are not prepared to empower these bodies sufficiently as states themselves are usually the perpetrators of large-scale violence and crimes against humanity.

Finally, the main problem remains the persistence of 'compliance gaps'. We witness commonly that '[r]ecalcitrant or fragile actors may be unwilling or unable to implement agreed-upon elements of international policy, for example, a ban on commercial whaling, the acquisition of proliferation-sensitive nuclear technology and material, or the cross-border movement of terrorist material and personnel' (Thakur and Weiss 2015, 36). Further, it is difficult to enforce penalties on violators, since global governance lacks a global army. Hence, enforcement actions against powerful violators are virtually absent. If strong states violate the accepted standards of human rights, something that Russia, the United States, or the People's Republic of China, among others, have often done in recent times, there is no record of any enforcement action taken against them.

Global Social Movements

Global governance is associated with the creation of a neoliberal international order dominated by the interests of Western capitalist states, particularly the US. Global crises such as rising economic inequality, volatile financial markets, and devastating climate change illustrate the deficits of a world economic order controlled mostly by transnational corporations, wealthy states, and other elites. As the impacts of such crises have intensified, they have generated a new wave of protests across the world. This new surge of resistance is predicated upon transnational activism and new experimental tactics propelling pro-democracy movements around the world. Global civil society is 'the sphere of ideas, values, institutions, organisations, networks, and individuals located between the family, the state, and the market', which operate across borders and beyond the confines of national politics and economics (Anheier, et al. 2001, 17; Ikenberry 2003). The neoliberal economic order has met with repeated resistance from global civil society groups, from the Seattle WTO protests in 1999 to the Toronto G20 protests in 2010, which question the agendas and class interests of the nation-states that subscribe to the global international trading order (Koon-hong 2014). These movements question the accountability of states and the historical bloc, and build opportunities for global governance in the 'absence of global government' (Riazati 2006). Transnational activism since the end of the Cold War, including United Nations world conferences and those directed at World Trade Organization (WTO) meetings, created temporary coalitions of groups that came together with various agendas and overlapping concerns. Global summits and UN meetings have traditionally provided focal points for activists working across borders on a diverse array of issues. Such movements have used these platforms to shape the radical discourses of human rights and ecological sustainability, thereby challenging the norms of territorial sovereignty.

Meanings of Global Social Movements

The age of global transformation has witnessed the ascendance of a global civil society as an independent frame of reference vis-à-vis a state-based international order. The idea of a global civil society emanated from various overlapping streams of concern. There is wide variation in the definition of global social movements. Scholars like Arturo Escobar (2001, 2) see social movements as 'sources of alternatives, hopes, and theories of how the world can be made differently'. Somewhat analogously, Pierre Bourdieu asserted that there can be no change in the functioning of global economic systems and dominant institutions without powerful social movements (Bourdieu 2003). Alain Touraine (1985, 773), on the other hand, argued that '[s]ocial movements are not positive or negative agents of history, of modernization, or of the liberalization of humanity. They act in a given type of social production and organization.'

Broadly speaking, some scholars see these movements as issuing from the organisational and political opportunities created by structural changes in the contemporary world, and for them, the sole merit of these groups lies in their achievement of concrete goals. Others view global social movements as a conglomerate of class conflicts and identity politics, with complex claims of recognition and redistribution built into them (Ghimire 2005). These are therefore rainbow coalitions accommodative of a wide range of groups, which come together to oppose contemporary structures of domination and injustices of various kinds. Global social movements are therefore understood as both ideological and interest-driven, and there is little agreement about the dynamics that undergird these groups.

Following John Keane, one can identify seven such dynamics at work.

1. Revival of the old language of civil society, especially in Central and Eastern European theatres.
2. A growing realisation of the revolutionary effects of the new satellite and computer-mediated technologies.
3. The new awareness, stimulated by peace and ecological movements, of individuals as members of a fragile and potentially self-destructive environment.
4. The disintegration of Soviet-style socialist systems, implying a new global political order.
5. The worldwide growth of neoliberal and capital market economics.
6. The growing disillusionment with the developmental tragedy of many postcolonial states.
7. A growing concern about the multiple dangers posed by the breakdown of the existing global order. (Keane 2001)

There is little agreement among scholars about what global civil society means. There is a general consensus that the concept refers to the need for a new social, political, and economic arrangement at the global level, given the tectonic shifts that have taken place. They also agree that global civil society should be separated from governmental institutions and organisations at the international level. Beyond this, however, scholars diverge. A number of experts see in the idea of global civil society a way of understanding the complex social relationships at the global level, built over time. Other scholars take it as a guide to formulating a political strategy. A third group of analysts sees it as a normative ideal. A brief discussion of these three viewpoints is necessary as a prelude to identifying the boundaries of the concept.

Usages of 'Global Civil Society'

The *first* usage of the term is formal in nature, and identifies key institutions, actors, and events, and profiles their evolution. Analysts focus on the various social developments that affect the nature of global political developments. The *second* view recommends a strategic and political use for the concept, where it serves as a standard for the attainment of desirable ends. The creation of any locale is ultimately a political question. New actors need to surmount institutional constraints in their search for opportunities, and social groups and other agents need to evolve strategies, mindful of the costs and benefits, vis-à-vis the state or authority structures. This approach, however, does not probe the underlying normative assumptions of these groups.

Finally, global civil society is also a normative ideal. Normative factors can, *first*, map the ethical appropriateness of agencies and actors against the norms of sovereignty. At stake is the morality of global civil society relative to the state. *Second*, the concept of global civil society functions as a justificatory ideal to highlight social reality. Mary Kaldor argues that the term has three uses: it refers to the varied social movements that came to dominate the political imagination of the post-Soviet world; the global institutions and Western governments used the term to convey the specificity of the West—it was seen as a mechanism by which to introduce market reform and parliamentary democracy. Kaldor calls this the 'neoliberal version'. The final version contrasts the Western model of civil society based on individualism with the more collective or social ethos of the East. This version, which Kaldor describes as 'post-modern', argues that new religions and ethnic movements that grew dramatically in the 1990s must also be included as a part of global civil society (Kaldor 2003).

Transnational activists build their appeal on expertise, moral influence, and a claim to political legitimacy. Peter Haas's project on epistemic communities, which showed how scientist-activists come to wield influence in policymaking on the strength of their scientific and technological expertise in the modern world, is widely recognised as a major point of departure in this field (Haas 1992). There is enough evidence to show that scientist-activists had gained access to and influence over prominent political leaders even during the Cold War. Rationalists and constructivists differ on the role of the epistemic community. Rationalists describe scientists as instruments, used by politicians to further their preferred policies. Norm analysts, in contrast, contend that scientists often offer uncomfortable wisdom, and exercise considerable influence on many aspects of policy. This authority stems from the social legitimacy offered to experts who possess scientific and reliable knowledge. If the social capital attached to their expertise is weak or absent, the role of the scientific community in disseminating knowledge is also insignificant.

Influence of Human Rights Activists

Human rights activists derive legitimacy from their reputation as impartial experts, or as neutral third parties whose information and assessment can be trusted. The appeal of human rights groups often hinges on the fact that their role is above 'politics'. In contexts where political actors are viewed with suspicion, international human rights activists consciously trade on political neutrality. However, in states where domestic political forces enjoy legitimacy, international organisations find it difficult to convince people about the importance of their roles. Even where local political actors are morally bankrupt, states are reluctant to allow an international audit of their human rights record. Nonetheless, human rights activists have successfully exerted influence in cases where domestic political forces are neither trusted nor powerful enough to ignore public disaffection over their poor performance. This explains the acceptance and success of organisations like Amnesty International or Human Rights Watch.

Moral authority thus emerges as a key factor. Decision-makers and/or citizens choose to trust human rights groups not only because of their expertise or ability to provide reliable and objective knowledge, but also because of the morality underpinning their actions. In other words, the legitimacy of human rights actors does not depend on their expertise and neutrality alone; rather, the issue of human rights is quintessentially political. In conservative societies, political groups in power dismiss campaigns for women's rights as tools of Western cultural imperialism. Demands for democratic reforms are also stalled on similar grounds. The debate around Asian values is a familiar illustration. Authoritarian political attitudes coupled with traditional values often masquerade as anti-imperialism. Moreover, moral principles always empower some sections more than others. Antonio Gramsci's path-breaking work on hegemony has shown how the ideational power of civil society was more efficient than the brute material power of the state in creating a leadership of the ruling social groups. Louis Althusser showed how the ideological state apparatus moulded subjectivity. Similarly, Robert Cox and Stephen Gill have demonstrated how international historic blocs legitimise certain ideas while denying moral and political acceptability to many, mostly radical, alternatives. The contemporary manufactured global consensus on liberal economic policies and open trading systems are examples of the working of such historic blocs.

Elements of Global Civil Society

First, not all non-statist phenomena fall under the ambit of global civil society. One would therefore need to exclude organisations like the UN or the EU, as these are statist in constitutive and operational terms, and are modelled on the bureaucratic apparatus of the government. *Second*, terrorist organisations and groups that either seek to create new states or take control of existing ones do not qualify either. *Third*, global civil society has a complex relationship with market-based institutions. Global civil society is an ensemble of groups, agencies, and even powerful individuals and business houses with diverse economic interests, not all of which are motivated by considerations of profit. Different groups bring in different interests and concerns: there are groups that seek to liberalise the rules undergirding trade and investment, and stand for efficient governance structures. There are also radical groups that question the legitimacy of the existing neoliberal order and work to transform it (Kaldor 2003).

The economic groups comprising global civil society are invariably motivated by social and even political concerns that the state and market have failed to address adequately. Viewed in this way, global civil society refers to a dynamic non-governmental system of interconnected socioeconomic institutions that straddle the whole world and impact diverse global processes. Global civil society has no regular structure; it is fluid and amorphous, consisting of groups, institutions, and agencies with different motives, purposes, and commitments. It remains committed to the values of civility, democratic accountability, and decentralisation. Global civil society usually consists of women's movements, environmental groups, anti-nuclear fronts, consumer forums, and a range of groups and organisations fighting for human rights or mobilising on localised issues like education and health, along with different cultural movements.

Character of Global Civil Society

Three other broad features tie the concept of global civil society: its non-governmental character, the idea of civility, and the meaning of 'global'. *First*, global civil society refers to agents and processes that are not a formal part of the state or government, although these structures often target, interact with, fight, or resist the state. *Second*, global civil society upholds the idea of civility, showing respect to and accepting 'strangers'—to some extent. Civility is a cultural concept, and different civilisations have a varied understanding of the term. Complications arise when one sees that the so-called global norms of civility are Western in inspiration and exert hegemony over local understandings. Culture is neither general nor unique. Moreover, as citizens of a global society, we require norms and standards through which to reach out to each other using a range of complex modes of interaction.

The rules of global hospitality or civility and global civil society can be seen as a space inhabited by various overlapping standards of civility, which does not, however, mean that it is entirely free of conflict. Global civil society may protect racketeers, gangsters, war criminals, arms traders, and terrorists, who misuse the freedom available therein for networking purposes. But despite these imperfections, social campaign networks mobilise against such violence and criminality and aim to repair the torn fabric of society. They resist harmful prejudices, exert pressure on states to undertake legal reforms and policies that reinforce civility, and oppose the violence of groups that misuse the space of global civil society. Therefore, despite the possibilities of abuse, there is ample evidence to show that global civil society can work as a crusader for civility, fairness, and non-violence. Insofar as these actors reject violence and violence-prone institutions, they reassert the essence of global civil society as an ensemble of non-governmental and therefore non-coercive institutions (civilian), which tends to have non-violent (public) effects (Kaldor 2003).

Third, we need to consider what is specifically meant by the term 'global'. The term has several usages: *One*, global civil society comprises groups that forge strategic links across borders, with a view to challenging the nation-state as the exclusive locus of democratic action and loyalty. States are criticised for their failure to build social capital and trust. Global civil society groups seek new forms of democracy and social mediation on a global scale.

Two, the belief that NGOs are perennially opposed to the state is false. Cooperation is particularly crucial at the level of international organisations, where many NGOs are formal consultants, and states often entrust them with various tasks. Such NGOs are thus a part of the formalised processes and institutions of global governance. Through their participation in international organisations, NGOs are often effective in pressuring states to adhere to democratic norms and uphold human rights. This successful negotiation with states complicates the understanding of global civil society as being inherently made up of non-governmental bodies. However, this is a contradiction only inasmuch as these international groups, NGOs, and the movements accorded formal consultative status by international organisations do not, *ipso facto*, become statist in their composition, methods, and actions. It can even pave the way for the performance of creative roles by global civil society in many areas of global governance.

Three, civil society is increasingly global not only because groups forge strategic linkages across national borders, but also because of the nature of the issues around which these institutions and actors come together. Struggles over health, the predicament of refugees, homelessness, water, ecology, and urban problems indicate the complex structures and processes that have a global reach. *Finally*, despite their universal character, these bodies remain remarkably diverse. This robust diversity complicates the idea of the state as understood as the legitimate source of violence, since legitimacy is mediated by the ideational frameworks of the governed. The parameters of legal authority are increasingly predicated upon the successful completion of a range of functions deemed crucial by a global and thickly diverse citizenry (Kaldor 2003).

Limitations of Global Civil Society

While the idea of global civil society is admirable, it calls for caution, both theoretically and in practice. In terms of theory, the tendency to advocate for a vibrant global civil society as a panacea to many contemporary challenges is suspect for a number of reasons. *First*, the idea of a global civil society is largely a Western concern. In fact, the category is often far removed from the common problems facing the postcolonial world, particularly countries ravaged by endemic religious violence. There are also no agreed-upon norms of representation—of either global civil society or global governance—and issues of global accountability therefore hang in the balance. Institutions of global governance are particularly afflicted by this problem, as are civil society groups (Koon-hong 2014).

Second, nation-states are still loath to subject themselves to supranational authority. In matters considered 'sensitive' by powerful states, global governance surrenders before claims of national sovereignty. States tend to resist global initiatives in what they consider 'internal disputes'. China's attitude towards the recent verdict of the International Court of Justice (ICJ) over its claims in the South China Sea is a case in point. American recalcitrance vis-à-vis global institutions of climate change and the International Criminal Court are also examples of what strong states do when confronted with the claims of global governance, especially if these are viewed as going against a parochial national interest.

Third, global democracy requires civil society groups, which in turn call for democratisation. While cosmopolitan democracy may be a desirable world standard, this is far from being a global trend. Moreover, states like China and Russia seem averse to notions of democracy and civil society, and might move even further away from global groups if such criteria are insisted upon.

Finally, the optimistic views of scholars such as Mary Kaldor are challenged by David Chandler, whose work highlights how this optimism undermines the traditional realist separation of the internal and external affairs of the state. As nation-states are increasingly marked by democratic deficits, any hope of progress and morality seems to now lie with the international agencies of global civil society. The problematic concepts of a progressive domestic order and a chaotic international state system are not improved by the new trend of relying entirely on global civil society (Chandler 2004).

A couple of these criticisms need careful scrutiny. The authority of transnational civil society actors undoubtedly hinges on transparency. Often, their legitimacy derives from their ability to speak for affected communities in the Global South and represent marginal domestic constituencies in institutionalised political processes. Existing political institutions often seek to bolster their own legitimacy by criticising civil society activists for being 'unrepresentative', when it is their own lack of transparency and arrogance that demands transnational scrutiny in the first place. Since governments or international organisations like the IMF have been proven to be unreliable custodians of the public interest, transnational civil society seems the only alternative for citizens seeking to fight for their cause.

Transnational activists are also seen as challenging the power and processes of the state. Two observations can be advanced here: one has to discover, empirically, whether transnational activists are actually challenging the authority of the state; and where they are shown to rival the state, questions of under-representation must arise if they are seen to usurp legitimate political authority through undemocratic means. As civil society pushes for more democratic and transparent authoritarian regimes, global activists may act in ways that challenge the existing political order and the principle of non-interference. Nevertheless, such governments often lack popular support. Instead of a confrontational model that pits the state against global civil society, we need to bring states and transnational activists together in a complex, multilayered relationship. Given the power and ubiquity of the state, the best that global civil society can do is inform and persuade governments and businesses fairly, and adopt, modify, or abandon certain policies or agendas. The world is witnessing a serious reconfiguring of state-society relations, which simultaneously empower the state in some areas while strengthening civil society in others.

Anti-Globalisation Movement

Global social movements have worked actively on many issues and in diverse fields. Of these, the most sustained has been transnational protest movements, traditionally called the 'anti-globalisation' movement—and, more recently, 'alter-globalisation' movements—that united diverse social forces with multiple and sometimes contradictory agendas (Ghimire 2005). They have been active at international conferences or summits and during the annual regional and international gatherings of the World Social Forum (WSF), also known as the Porto Alegre Forum. These groups use such spaces to advance their social and political claims. Bernard Cassen (2004), one of the architects of the WSF movement, described it as the 'globalization of alternative globalization', while Susan George (2002, 111), another key figure spearheading the movement, complained that 'the label "anti-globalisation" is at best a contradiction, at worst a slander'.

Social movements have both negative and positive agendas. Their primary role is to critique the exploitative dimensions of global economic and political systems that function through powerful institutions, such as the IMF, the World Bank, the Group of Eight Industrialised Countries (G8), the World Trade Organization, and various regional trade bodies and agreements such as the North American Free Trade Agreement (NAFTA). On a positive note, they defend the cause of global justice and public goods, demand a refurbished role for the state, and support the cause of a new globalisation from below, which can allow the poor and marginalised classes to enjoy the benefits of modern science and technology (Ghimire 2005). While such movements are part of the natural terrain of left parties throughout the world, global social movements have over time achieved wider political acceptability, particularly after the banking crisis that triggered the deep global recession of 2007–09.

Conclusion

Ideas such as global civil society, global governance, and global commons have fundamentally challenged the terms of reference of the academic discipline of IR. Conventional IR theories have contributed little to clarifying these concepts, for two main reasons: the idea of space and the sociology of interactions. As a discipline, IR is based on the reality of the nation-state and the prioritisation of territoriality. Within mainstream approaches, there is little questioning of the given parameters of our political life. Radical theories, on the other hand, question the binary of inside/outside that serves as the central assumption of the discipline, and seek to drastically redefine the subject through a fundamental transformation of the idea of space. IR now needs to actively interrogate the dynamics of global governance and global civil society, which are no longer peripheral categories in world politics. We require richly textured empirical analyses of the agencies, institutes, and practices of global civil society, which will problematise the received wisdom of IR as a statist subject of enquiry.

It is also commonplace to concede that, of all the social sciences, IR is the one that most conspicuously lacks a firm sociological foundation. IR therefore requires a sense of the world and of humanity as complex and vulnerable totalities. The discipline operates either through the ontology of a humanity divided by national allegiances or imagines its utopian other in the notion of global community. The lack of a sociological perspective within the discipline has limited its capacity to engage meaningfully with the diversity of the global community. Consequently, it does not adequately examine the idea of a unified political system. It fails to appreciate a model of society that is in conflict, that is neither spontaneously self-regulating nor self-reproducing. IR thus fails to interrogate the innate character of global civil society as a sociological phenomenon. Global civil society builds on a shared natural sociability among citizens and humans, something that IR refuses to recognise. Unless IR takes historical sociology seriously, it will continue to find categories like global civil society mystifying, and will be unable to contribute to a better understanding of a changing world.

17

Climate Change

Sulagna Maitra

Introduction

Climate change 'refers to any long-term change in Earth's climate, or in the climate of a region or city. This includes warming, cooling and changes besides temperature' (NASA 2016). The twenty-first century world is slowly coming to terms with climate change. Adapting to and coping with climate change will involve seismic changes in living conditions and contemporary patterns of energy use. Not surprisingly, this has made climate change a mainstream political issue, to be discussed at G8 summits and other high-level political meetings (Giddens 2008; Vogler 2014). Climate change is thus different from other environmental issues such as the conservation of natural resources and pollution, which have frequently been relegated to the domain of 'low politics' in international relations. In spite of the mounting evidence on the causes and consequences of climate change, both the science and the politics of it have been plagued by controversy and problems surrounding collective action. The year 2015 marked a watershed moment in climate change and disaster risk reduction governance as world leaders made significant agreements to establish specific targets and global regimes to reduce vulnerability to climate change and environmental disasters. This chapter will present a brief overview of climate change and disaster risk reduction governance, and outline some of the key challenges to collective action.

Understanding climate change and its governance requires, at a minimum, a grasp of a range of scientific claims about the earth's complex climate system; an overview of policy discourses on climate politics at the international level; and an understanding of the cultural and social contexts and worldviews on climate change that shape individual action and media coverage.

For the most part, climate change, like many other environmental issues, had been conceptualised and articulated in 'narrowly technical and reductionist terms' (Demeritt 2001). It was regarded as a 'scientific object' of study, which meant that much of the knowledge remained in the domain of research and the information that was available in the public domain was technocratic and difficult for the public to understand and rally behind. The fact that there was not, until recently, any agreement on the science of climate change served as a further cause for political apathy. However, with an increase in climate-related disasters, the availability of satellite data that can measure changes in the earth's atmosphere and on its surface, mass mobilisation, especially among the youth, and improvements in climate change modelling, climate change is now largely accepted as one of the most pressing challenges facing humanity in the twenty-first century. It may be safely stated that, globally, public awareness and mobilisation (even polarisation) on the issue of climate change has gained serious momentum, catapulting climate change to the top of the global political agenda.

We shall now introduce a brief timeline of the key events[1] and actors in relation to climate change governance, in order to chronologically introduce the developments that have taken place in science and international governance on climate change and related issues.

Evolution of Climate Governance: Historical Timeline

The history of the human impact on climate change can be studied from the early eighteenth century, with the invention of the steam engine and the subsequent Industrial Revolution. The Industrial Revolution introduced fundamental changes in society and altered the human

[1] The timeline has been created on the basis of numerous sources. However, the main source is Black (2015).

relationship with nature forever. Notable among these changes were the use of coal on an industrial scale, advancements in transportation, and improvements in healthcare. Soon, the world's population crossed the one-billion mark and automobiles began to be commercially produced. Around the same time, scientists in Europe discovered the greenhouse effect, that is, the natural ability of the atmosphere to absorb and retain non-luminous heat radiated from the earth. They discovered that the presence of water vapour and even tiny concentrations of carbon dioxide in the atmosphere could lead to greenhouse warming. Swedish chemist Svante Arrhenius claimed that the large-scale burning of coal could enhance the earth's natural greenhouse effect, but along with other scientists, considered this mostly beneficial.

By the 1930s, the human population numbered two billion and carbon emissions from fossil fuels had crossed 1 billion tonnes per year. Advancement in technology, especially the use of computers in the 1950s, made possible the systematic study of changes in the earth's climate. Systematic analyses were soon made of temperatures, the absorption of greenhouse gases by the earth's atmosphere and the oceans, and the level of carbon dioxide in the atmosphere. Studies found that temperatures had been rising globally, coinciding with an increase in the concentration of carbon dioxide in the atmosphere. This led to suggestions of a possible correlation between the two. However, at the time, meteorologists dismissed such claims. It was soon found that seawater does not absorb the excess CO_2 produced by humans, as had previously been assumed. This in turn implied that any impact of the greenhouse effect would have to be borne by the planet's inhabitants. Amidst increasing concern over the Earth's deteriorating climate, a US President's Advisory Committee (1965) deemed climate change a 'matter of real concern'.

Shortly after, in 1972, the first UN Environment Conference was held in Stockholm, culminating in the launch of the United Nations Environment Programme (UNEP). The Conference, however, failed to recognise climate change as a major issue, focussing instead on chemical pollution, atomic bomb testing, and whaling. In 1975, American scientist Wallace Broecker published an article entitled 'Climate Change: Are We on the Brink of a Pronounced Global Warming?' in the popular journal *Science*, which helped to provoke discussions on global warming in the public domain.

Around the same time, in the early 1970s, scholars in the US University of California, Irvine, began studying the harmful impact of chlorofluorocarbons (CFCs) on the earth's ozone layer. Representatives of the aerosol and halocarbon industries bitterly opposed this study, even lodging an official complaint with the university to discredit and stop the dissemination of the study findings. However, the findings were later corroborated by the US National Academy of Sciences (NAS), and funding was made available to continue the research. In 1985, British Antarctic Survey scientists speculated on the correlation between an increase in CFCs in the atmosphere and the abnormally low ozone concentrations. This eventually led to the term 'ozone hole' being coined, creating a sense of urgency amongst the participating nations in the Vienna Convention of 1985, who sought to establish regulations on ozone depleting substances. Merely eighteen months after the discovery of the ozone hole, the Montreal Protocol (1987) restricted the use of chemicals considered harmful to the ozone layer. Even though this Protocol was not drawn up with climate change in mind, scholars agree that it was more effective than the Kyoto Protocol in limiting greenhouse gas emissions (GHGs) (Vogler 2014). The CFC industry, especially in the United States, continued to oppose legislations limiting their use, arguing before the US Congress that the scientific evidence was not conclusive enough to warrant such restrictions.

Amidst controversy and uncertainty regarding the science of GHG emissions and their impact on the planet, the World Metereological Organization (WMO) and UNEP established the Intergovernmental Panel for Climate Change (IPCC) in 1998. In an unprecedented move, the Panel brought together most of the world's climate change scientists to assess the evidence on climate change, its impact and future risks, and options for adaptation and mitigation. IPCC has three main working groups, on climate science, its impacts, and socioeconomic dimensions. Government officials supervise its work, helping to ensure that the report's claims are written carefully and cautiously to reflect a consensus. The IPCC has produced six comprehensive Assessment Reports (ARs) on climate change, the latest of which was published in 2023.

Concern about the Earth's deteriorating climate grew from the end of the 1980s. Carbon emissions from the fossil fuel industry reached 6 billion tonnes per year, and the human population crossed five billion by the end of the 1980s. The first IPCC report, published in

1990, concluded that temperatures had risen by 0.3–0.6° Celsius over the last century and human activities were adding to GHGs, leading to global warming. In 1992, twenty years after the first conference was held on the environment, the United Nations convened a Conference on Environment and Development, better known as the Earth Summit, in Rio de Janeiro. Its purpose was to help governments rethink economic development and find ways to halt the destruction of irreplaceable natural resources and combat the increasing pollution. The Summit did not only mobilise governments, but also involved people from all walks of life to convince the political leadership to adopt a climate-sensitive approach to economic development. Governments agreed on a United Nations Framework Convention on Climate Change (UNFCCC) with the objective of 'stabilization of greenhouse gas concentrations in the atmosphere at a level that would prevent dangerous anthropogenic interference with the climate system' (Grantham Research Institute on Climate Change and the Environment 2022). Developed countries agreed to revert their emissions to 1900 levels. The Conference of Parties (COP) was established as the supreme decision-making body of the Convention to review its implementation as well as any other legal instruments related to it. All states that are party to the Convention are represented in the COP, and usually meet every year. A key responsibility of COP is reviewing the national communications and emission inventories submitted by parties to assess the efficacy of the measures taken.

The Earth Summit was significant in that it influenced all subsequent UN conferences that examined the relationship between human rights, population, social development, women, human settlement, and sustainable development (United Nations 1997). Further, the concept of eco-efficiency as a guiding principle for businesses and governments reverberated around the world through the over 10,000 journalists present at the conference. Over the years, the UNFCCC has become a universal treaty, with 190 signatories.

The IPCC's second report in 1995 mentioned a 'discernible human influence' on the Earth's climate. This was the first statement at the global level that unequivocally deemed human actions as responsible for climate change. In 1997, the Kyoto Protocol (COP3) was signed under the aegis of the UNFCCC, which declared that the high levels of GHGs in the atmosphere was a direct result of 150 years of industrial activity.

Thus, the industrialised developed countries are principally responsible for contemporary global warming. Accordingly, the Protocol introduced the principle of 'common but differentiated responsibilities', which placed a heavier burden on developed nations to cut GHG emissions. On average, developed nations were required to cut emissions by 5.2 per cent from a 1990 baseline by 2012. Specific national targets were set under the principle of differentiated responsibility; for example, the USA had to cut emissions by 7 per cent and the EU by 8 per cent. On the other hand, Australia and Iceland could increase their emissions by 8 and 10 per cent, respectively (UNFCCC 2014a). The Kyoto Protocol set up a complex mechanism of emission trading and offsetting arrangements (Joint Implementation and the Clean Development Mechanism [CDM]), which was expected to help countries to achieve their targets.

The division between developed and developing countries created by the principle of differentiated responsibilities stymied collective action on the reduction of emissions (Moore 2014). Developing countries argued that cutting emissions without any viable alternative technology would effectively mean halting their economic development and measures to reduce poverty. This would be grossly unfair, given that most developing countries had already suffered under imperialism and had contributed very little to global warming in the nineteenth and twentieth centuries. Further, per capita emissions in most developing countries were much lower compared to developed nations. On the other hand, developed countries, especially the US, argued that without the participation of large emerging economies like India and China, the exercise of cutting emissions would be rendered meaningless. The US Congress declared its intention to not ratify the Protocol, and in 2001 President George Bush formally withdrew America from the Kyoto process. By 2012, the EU was the only major signatory committed to the Protocol.

Extreme weather events and scientific research in the late 1990s and early 2000s brought to light further evidence of climate change. In 1998, strong El Nino conditions combined with global warming produced the warmest year on record. That year, the average global temperature increased by 0.52°C over the 1961–90 mean. In March 1999, Michael Mann, Raymond Bradley and Malcolm Hughes' study produced the controversial 'hockey stick' graph, which indicated how unusual the modern-day temperature rise in the northern hemisphere is in comparison to the last 1,000 years. The same year, IPCC's third Assessment Report (AR3) found 'new and stronger evidence' showing that humanity's emissions of GHGs were the main cause of global warming. In 2006, the Stern Review on the Economics of Climate Change[2] concluded that climate change could damage global GDP by up to 20 per cent if left unchecked; however, curbing it would cost about 1 per cent of the global GDP. This review remains one of the most influential studies on climate change. The Fourth Assessment Report (AR4) of 2007 found a greater than 90 per cent likelihood of human emissions of GHGs being responsible for modern-day climate change.

In 2007, IPCC and US Vice-President Al Gore received the Nobel Prize for Peace, 'for their efforts to build up and disseminate greater knowledge about man-made climate change, and to lay the foundations for the measures that are needed to counteract such change'. That same year, governments under the aegis of the UN agreed to a two-year 'Bali Roadmap' to establish a new global treaty by 2009. Accordingly, 192 global leaders met in Copenhagen in 2009 for the Climate Summit (COP 15). Unfortunately, all expectations were belied as the Conference ended up merely 'taking note' of a three-page non-binding political agreement—the Copenhagen Accord—which was hammered out by twenty-eight heads of states in the last twenty-four hours of extended negotiations (Backstrand and Lovbrand 2016). Meanwhile, by 2009, China had overtaken the US as the world's biggest emitter of GHGs,[3] CO_2 concentrations had risen from 315 ppm (1958) to 380 ppm (2008), and carbon emissions from fossil fuels had crossed 8 billion tonnes per year. By 2013, CO_2 concentrations had reportedly crossed 400 ppm. The 2013 IPCC report (AR5) concluded with 95 per cent certainty that humans have been the 'dominant cause' of global warming since the 1950s.

Scholars of IR (Backstrand and Lovbrand 2016) have often regarded the 'Copenhagen failure' as signalling the end of UN-led mega-multilateralism and the rise of a more fragmented and decentralised

[2]The Stern Review on the Economics of Climate Change was published in October 2006 by economist Lord Nicholas Stern, Head of the UK Government Economic Service and now Chair of both the ESRC Centre for Climate Change Economics and Policy and the Grantham Research Institute on Climate Change and the Environment at the London School of Economics and Political Science.

[3]However, the US still has a significant lead in terms of per capita emissions.

climate policy architecture. This altered geo-political climate context has been variously characterised as anarchic, complex, and polycentric. However, climate politics is not just plagued by chaos and conflict; rather, a novel political structure has emerged, which has seen partnerships between the public and private sectors, states, and sub-state and non-state actors. The dichotomy between developed and developing nations has been replaced with new political coalitions between 'major economies' and 'major emitters' across the Global North and South (ibid.)

After the disappointment in Copenhagen, expectations around the 2010 UNFCCC Summit in Cancun (COP16), Mexico were low. However, this conference drew almost 12,000 participants, including over 5,000 government officials, 5,400 representatives from the UN, intergovernmental bodies, and NGOs, and approximately 1,200 accredited members of the media (UNFCCC 2014b). The meeting created the basis for a comprehensive and far-reaching international response to reduce carbon emissions and build a system that would make all countries accountable to each other for these reductions. Governments committed to a maximum temperature rise of 2°C above pre-industrial levels, and agreed to consider lowering that to 1.5° in the near future. Further, the innovation, development, and spread of new climate-friendly technologies were to be made operational by 2012. A Green Climate Fund was established to provide financing to projects, programmes, policies, and other activities in developing countries via thematic funding windows. Developed countries also affirmed their commitment to implementing the 'Fast Start Finance'. Finally, a Cancun Adaptation Framework was established to promote the implementation of a stronger cohesive action on adaptation. The Cancun Summit signalled a strong commitment to creating a low-carbon economy. In reality, however, the pledges put forward by governments totalled only 60 per cent of the emission reductions needed to have a 50 per cent chance of keeping the rise in temperatures below the 2° Celsius goal (ibid.). The Conference also failed to resolve the uncertainty surrounding the fate of the international carbon market and the future of the Kyoto Protocol.

In December 2015, at COP21, also known as the Paris climate conference, 195 countries[4] adopted the first ever universal, legally

---

[4]At the time of writing, seventy-five countries, including India and China, had ratified the Paris Agreement and it was set to enter into force on 4 November

binding global climate agreement. The agreement was seen as a bridge between current policies and climate neutrality before the end of the twenty-first century. It set out a global action plan to avoid dangerous climate change by limiting global warming to well below 2°C. The Paris Agreement requires all parties to propose 'nationally determined contributions' (NDCs) and report regularly on their emissions and on implementation efforts. Building on the UNFCCC, the Paris Agreement charted a new course in global climate effort by bringing together all nations for a common cause: to combat climate change. The Agreement also provides enhanced support to developing countries to facilitate the adaptation and mitigation of climate change.

The year 2015 was significant in demonstrating 'joined up thinking' between global regimes, with the United Nations and its agencies at the heart of this neoliberal move. Significantly, the other major achievement of the year was the agreement on the Sustainable Development Goals,[5] which declared 'Climate Action' one of its key action areas. As Goal 13, Climate Action[6] set ambitious targets for the global community (UNDP 2020):

- Strengthen resilience and adaptive capacity towards climate-related hazards and natural disasters in all countries;
- Integrate climate change measures into national policies, strategies, and planning;
- Improve education, awareness-raising, and human and institutional capacity on climate change mitigation, adaptation, impact reduction, and early warning;
- Implement the commitment undertaken by developed countries to the UNFCCC. The goal is to mobilise jointly $100 billion

---

2016. Today, 195 parties (194 states plus the European Union) have joined the Paris Agreement. However, the US, under President Donald Trump, has exited the Agreement.

[5]The Sustainable Development Goals (SDGs), also known as the Global Goals, were adopted by all United Nations member states in 2015 as a universal call to action to end poverty, protect the planet, and ensure that all people enjoy peace and prosperity by 2030. The seventeen SDGs are integrated—that is, they recognise that action in one area will affect outcomes in others, and that development must balance social, economic, and environmental sustainability.

[6]Take urgent action to combat climate change and its impacts.

annually by 2020 to address the needs of developing countries in the context of meaningful actions towards mitigation and transparency on implementation, and operationalise the Green Climate Fund through its capitalisation;

- Promote mechanisms for raising the capacity for effective climate change-related planning and management in the least developed and small island developing states. This will include a focus on women, youth, and local and marginalised communities.

According to the UNDP (2020), GHG emissions are currently 50 per cent higher than they were in the 1990s. In order to limit global warming to 1.5°C, global net CO_2 emissions must drop by 45 per cent between 2010 and 2030, and reach net zero around 2050. Their estimate suggests that bold climate action could create up to 18 million new jobs in the energy sector by 2030 and deliver economic benefits of up to $26 trillion.

In 2015, the United Nations Office for Disaster Risk Reduction successfully created the Sendai Framework for Disaster Risk Reduction 2015–2030.[7] The Framework outlines seven clear targets and four priorities for action to reduce the existing disaster risks and prevent new ones: (*i*) Understanding disaster risk; (*ii*) Strengthening disaster risk governance; (*iii*) Investing in disaster reduction for resilience; and (*iv*) Enhancing disaster preparedness for effective response, and to 'Build Back Better' through recovery, rehabilitation, and reconstruction (UNDRR 2020).

Taken together, the Sustainable Development Goals, the Paris Climate Agreement, and the Sendai Framework provide a clear mandate for increased coherence in the approaches of states towards climate change and disaster risk reduction (OECD 2020).

After the policy successes of 2015, climate politics met with a few obstacles, especially with major countries such as the United States rescinding on previous agreements. However, in some ways, the blatant scepticism about and inaction on climate change from political leaders served as the catalyst for an unprecedented global movement on climate action, spearheaded largely by the youth and with social media playing

[7]The Framework was adopted at the Third UN World Conference on Disaster Risk Reduction in Sendai, Japan, on 18 March 2015.

a key role. While the impact this movement will have on concrete policy targets is yet to be seen, it undoubtedly made climate change a household topic of discussion. *Second*, the movement was the living embodiment of climate *action* (as described in the SDGs), a change from its passive predecessors that called for efforts to 'ensure environmental sustainability' (Millennium Development Goals).

The election of Joe Biden as the forty-sixth US President in 2020 briefly infused optimism regarding America's cooperation in meeting climate change targets. His decision to rejoin the Paris Climate Agreement on the very first day that he took office (20 January 2021) signalled that his administration would take the issue seriously. Significant climate-sensitive policies were enacted during the Biden era: a pledge to achieve net-zero emissions by 2050; an active re-engagement with international climate diplomacy, including hosting a Leaders' Climate Summit and taking a proactive role in COP26; and instituting the Inflation Reduction Act in 2022, which included historic investments in clean energy, electric vehicles, and carbon capture, making it one of the most expansive climate legislations in the country's history.

However, US climate diplomacy has once again suffered a setback with the election of Donald Trump as the forty-seventh President. As President Biden's successor, critic, and political opponent, he walked back most of the measures initiated during the previous regime. USA withdrew from the Paris Agreement once again, and the 'Big Beautiful Bill' (2025) recently signed into law measures that would repeal spending on initiatives to reduce emissions; repeal tax credits for climate-friendly energy technologies such as wind, solar, and electric vehicles; and provide opportunities to exploit America's fossil fuels (The White House 2025). Several think-tanks and universities have provided varying estimates of the impact of these latest measures, but all the models unequivocally predict that repealing the Biden-era policies and encouraging the use of fossil fuels will wipe out almost a third of the progress made in reducing US emissions over the past twenty years.

In yet another significant development, China's Premier Xi Jinping has announced that the country will aim to hit peak emissions by 2030 and for carbon neutrality by 2060 (McGrath 2020). China's commitment to the long-term goal of carbon neutrality came as a welcome surprise at the UN General Assembly meeting in September 2020, marking a departure from its previous political stance (ibid.). The importance of engaging China[8] and the United States in climate action cooperation cannot be overstated.

COP26 was held in October–November 2021 in Glasgow, Scotland under the shadow of a worldwide COVID-19 pandemic, and threw up both surprises and controversies. COP26 will perhaps be mostly remembered for the 'phase-out, phase-down coal controversy'. The International Energy Agency stated that one of the most critical factors in staying within the 1.5°C rise in global temperature will be a sharp decline in the use of coal (often branded as one of the dirtiest fossil fuels). According to estimates, at least 40 per cent of the world's 8,500 coal-fired power plants will have to shut down to achieve this target. In a bitter fight in Glasgow, China and India joined ranks, insisting that the term be changed to '*phase-down*' from the original 'phase-out' in the final agreement. While India was criticised for 'betraying' vulnerable nations, it should be noted that the phrase 'phase-down' had already been used for coal in a bilateral agreement between the US and China.

Aside from this controversy, COP26 made significant strides in climate policy. They came up with a roadmap for swifter revisions of Nationally Determined Contributions (NDCs), committed to phasing down unabated coal consumption and phasing out inefficient fossil fuel subsidies (significantly, this was the first time since the Kyoto Protocol in 1997 that the final COP agreement made a direct reference to phasing out fossil fuels), and promised to increase climate financing to $500 billion over the next five years and double the proportion of climate financing meant for adaptation.

UN Secretary General Antonio Guterres described the outcomes of COP27, held in Sharm el-Sheikh, Egypt, thus: 'COP27 concludes with much homework and little time' (UNFCCC 2022). The most significant achievement of this meeting was the establishment of the 'loss and damage fund' for vulnerable countries hit by recurring floods, droughts, and other climate disasters. The second major development was the clear intention to move towards implementation, with the UN Climate Change Executive Secretary declaring, 'Paris gave us the agreement and Katowice and Glasgow gave us a plan, Sharm el-Sheikh shifts us

---

[8]China is the world's biggest source of carbon dioxide, responsible for around 28 per cent of global emissions.

to implementation' (ibid.). This included holding businesses and other sectors accountable for their commitment to climate mitigation.

In 2023, the Dubai COP28 initially made headlines for the wrong reasons when UAE nominated Sultan al-Jaber, veteran technocrat and CEO of Abu Dhabi National Oil Company, to preside over the Conference. However, COP28 remains a milestone in climate governance as it marked the first '*global stocktake*', that is, a systematic process by which countries and stakeholders measured their progress in achieving the goals of the Paris Climate Agreement. Unsurprisingly, the stocktake revealed that, at the current rate of GHG emissions, we will certainly not be able to restrict global warming to 1.5°C. Dubai sought to continue efforts to phase out fossil fuels, operationalise the loss and damage fund, and enhance global efforts to strengthen resilience. Focusing on implementation, the meeting introduced some unprecedented efforts, such as linking climate action with nature conservation, ramping up innovative practical climate solutions, and laying the groundwork for an enhanced transparency framework.

It is clear that significant progress has been made, especially in the twenty-first century, on climate change governance. Neil Carter (2010) has identified three main factors that contributed to climate change's ascent into 'high politics', with support from major economies like the US, UK, India, China, and the EU.

1. After decades of controversy and resistance, the political elite has finally accepted the scientific message on climate change and its far-reaching consequences for the earth's environment.
2. The Stern Review (2007) clearly established that the costs of inaction will increase rapidly if mitigation efforts are delayed, and these costs can go up to 5 per cent of the global GDP each year.
3. Public opinion has tilted in favour of action on climate change, and governments can no longer be seen as not taking measures to mitigate its impacts.

Additionally, the issue of climate change has been securitised by many governments, including the US. In April 2007, CNA Corporation, a think-tank funded by the US Navy, released a report on climate change and national security that concluded, 'Climate change can act as a threat multiplier for instability in some of the most volatile regions of the world, and it presents significant national security challenges for the United

States.' That same month, the UN Security Council, at the behest of the UK government, held the first ever debate on the potential impact of climate change on peace and security. While the rise of illiberal regimes in Europe and Donald Trump's 'America First' doctrine may be seen as barriers to climate negotiations, the increasing instances of wildfires, hurricanes, floods, and droughts have made climate change a household topic for discussion and debate.

Extrapolating from research on communication, it may be concluded that these debates are held along the following fault-lines. Climate leaders and activists tend to argue that climate change is an inescapable reality of our times, and therefore investing in climate mitigation and adaptation is crucial to securing the Earth's future. Further, such investments will boost economies and foster interest in new clean technology. Taking an environmental justice perspective, the leaders advocate a fairer and more equitable system with special assistance for the most vulnerable entities. In contrast, the more ethnocentric climate 'deniers' frame their arguments more negatively. Pointing to job losses in traditional fuel-powered factories and mass migration, they deem 'climate politics' a ploy to thwart economic growth and competitive advantage.

The next section will summarise the impact of climate change on environmental disasters.

CLIMATE CHANGE AND ITS IMPACT

One can identify two groups in the community of scientists investigating climate change: believers and sceptics. Some go further and introduce a six-fold division along the believer-sceptic spectrum: the alarmed, the concerned, the cautious, the disengaged, the doubtful, and the dismissive Leiserowitz, et al. 2009a, b). The believers posit that human activities, such as burning fossil fuels, deforestation, and raising livestock, add to the natural greenhouse[9] effect by trapping more energy and increasing

[9]The greenhouse effect refers to the process by which the earth maintains its warmth as its atmosphere traps the infrared radiation emitting from the earth's surface. The earth's surface absorbs heat from sunlight and gives off energy in the form of infrared radiation. Carbon dioxide, methane, and other gases present in the atmosphere help trap this radiation to maintain the earth's warm climate. An increase in the level of these GHGs in the atmosphere causes the

the temperature (BBC 2025; Carter 2010). It is important to note that the IPCC and UNFCCC have slightly different definitions of climate change, which is reflected in their approach to the issue. IPCC defines climate change as '*any change in climate over time, whether due to natural variability or as a result of human activity*' (IPCC 2007a). This definition is very much in line with the Panel's consensus approach to the science of climate change. The UNFCCC, however, defines climate change in terms of alterations in the composition of the global atmosphere, that can be either directly or indirectly attributed to human activity, and *in addition* to the natural climate variability observed over comparable time periods.

Since the Industrial Revolution began in 1750, CO_2 levels have risen by more than 30 per cent and methane levels by more than 140 per cent. The concentration of CO_2 in the atmosphere is now higher than at any time in at least 800,000 years (BBC 2025). Records dating back to the nineteenth century show that the earth's temperature has risen by 0.8°C in the last 100 years, and about 0.6°C of this warming occurred in the past three decades (ibid.). Satellite observations since the 1990s reveal that sea levels have been rising at an approximate rate of 3mm per year (IPCC 2007b). Further, they estimate that global sea levels are going to rise at an increased rate (4mm per year), compared to 1961–2003. The three main factors in the rise in sea levels are the thermal expansion of seawater,[10] melting of glaciers, and the retreat of polar ice caps. Satellite data shows a dramatic reduction in regional ice cover. Since 1979, the Arctic sea-ice extent has been decreasing at about 3–4 per cent every decade (NSIDC 2016). Records from September 2012 show that the Arctic sea extent had receded to 3.41 million km^2, 44 per cent below the

---

earth's temperature to rise by trapping greater heat. Carbon dioxide (CO_2) and other GHGs can persist in the atmosphere for a long time. The earth's natural reservoirs, such as oceans, can only absorb so much CO_2. Everyday human activities such as agriculture, industrial production, and natural processes such as volcanic eruptions add to the level of GHGs in the atmosphere. This level affects the world as a whole as these gases become globally mixed. Thus, even though some countries produce, or historically have produced, more GHGs than others, global warming affects everyone and requires global action (United States Environmental Protection Agency 2016).

[10] As the sea water warms up, the molecules become less densely packed, causing an increase in the volume of the ocean.

1981–2010 average, and 16 per cent below the last average recorded in 2007 (ibid.).

> Every year since 2007 has seen more than 10 million square kilometers of seasonal ice melt, reflecting both a transition towards thinner winter ice that melts out more easily in summer as well as changes in the Arctic climate that foster more ice melt each year. (Stroeve 2015)

The Greenland Ice Sheet has also experienced record melting in recent years. Estimates say that it is losing 110 million Olympic-sized swimming pools worth of water each year (Abraham 2016). If the entire 2.8 million km^3 sheet were to melt, it would raise sea levels by 6m (BBC 2025). Most of Antarctica, however, is yet to feel the impact of global warming. According to the National Snow and Ice Data Center (2016), while there are no clear patterns visible for East Antarctica, a large area of West Antarctica is losing mass. Contrary to these findings (which are also supported by the IPCC), NASA (2015) has observed small ice gains in East Antarctica and the interiors of West Antarctica. However, Jay Zwally, a glaciologist with NASA, observed,

> If the losses of the Antarctic Peninsula and parts of West Antarctica continue to increase at the same rate they've been increasing for the last two decades, the losses will catch up with the long-term gain in East Antarctica in 20 or 30 years—I don't think there will be enough snowfall increase to offset these losses. (NASA 2015)

The climate sceptics, on the other hand, talk about a *pause in global warming.* Some commentators have argued that since 1998, there has been no significant global warming in spite of an increase in carbon dioxide in the Earth's atmosphere. While there is no general consensus on the exact causes of this *pause,* scientists have offered various reasons, such as a variation in the Sun's energy output, greater storage of heat in the oceans, and a decline in atmospheric vapours. Climate sceptics point to this pause and the uncertainties and variabilities in the science as proof of the fallibility of climate change models. This claim, however, has been rejected by a growing number of scientists, who believe that the so-called hiatus in global warming is just one component in a complex climate system. Global mean surface temperature is just one of many indicators of global warming. Other indicators, such as melting ice, changes in plant and animal life, and the number and intensity of climate events, continue to indicate the reality of climate change. A study has called into question the claim that there has been a 'pause' in global warming (Rajaratnam, et al. 2015). In general, the 2013 IPCC assessment had indicated that the rise in global surface temperature would likely exceed 1.5°C by the end of the twenty-first century, relative to 1850. Thus, if drastic measures are not taken, we will be facing crises such as food shortages, flooding, reduced access to drinking water, and millions of environmental refugees (Carter 2010).

Over the past two decades, natural disasters have caused an average of 68,000 deaths and affected 218 million people every year. Studies also show that there are 341 climate-related disasters each year, which now account for 80 per cent of all calamities and contribute to massive economic losses and displacement (CRED 2015). In 2015 alone, an estimated 89 million people were affected by disasters caused by natural hazards (GHA 2016). This included large-scale sudden onset disasters such as the Nepal earthquake along with several small-scale disasters. During 1994 and 2013, 43 per cent of all disasters were the result of floods, which affected nearly 2.5 billion people. In the past ten years, 1.7 billion people have been adversely affected by disasters, and economic losses in major disasters amounted to $1.4 trillion (UNDRR 2015). Droughts affected nearly one billion people (25 per cent of the global total) between 1994 and 2013 (CRED 2015) and while it accounted for only 5 per cent of all environmental disasters, it was heavily concentrated in lower-income nations (ibid.). Nearly 41 per cent of droughts in this period took place in African countries. In terms of absolute numbers, USA and China were the most affected by disasters between 1994 and 2013, possibly due to the sheer size of their landmass, population, and population density. Asia had the highest number of people affected by natural disasters, with 3.3 billion people affected in China and India alone (ibid.). The number of people affected has, however, fallen from one in twenty-three to one in thirty-nine over the 1994–2013 period.

It is clear that the impact of climate change is differentiated and has introduced new divisions in the world. Developing nations, with their limited infrastructure and major habitations along the coast, are the most vulnerable (Vogler 2014). Developed countries such as the Netherlands are better equipped to deal with these risks (Carter 2010). While scientists do not attribute a single weather event like Hurricane Katrina to climate change, they assert that climate change increases the likelihood of such extreme weather events (Busby 2007).

The statistics above reflect the high price that climate change is extracting from the environment and the people. In comparison, climate governance seems to be moving at a sluggish pace, marginalising a large number of climate-affected people. Scholars explain that political action on climate change has been impeded by the 'tragedy of commons', that is, while only certain section continue to exploit fossil fuels and pollute the global atmospheric commons to the maximum extent, the costs of climate change are shared by all (Carter 2010). This decreases the incentive to take purposive action until all the concerned actors come on board. Carter (2010) and Volger (2014) explain that:

1. Developing countries argue that most of the *allowable 'carbon space'* has already been utilised by the historic emissions of the old industrialised economies, because of which the latter should continue to take the lead in cutting emissions.
2. The newly industrialising nations, at the behest of the IMF and the World Bank, have followed the path of the developed countries, placing a higher premium on growth than on environmental protection. This has endangered several developing countries, who have fewer capacities to cope with the consequences of climate change. For example, ozone levels in Mexico City exceed the standards set by the WHO 300 days in a year. China's economic boom, based on the use of coal and fuel-inefficient technologies, has created unprecedented health hazards for its population. For example, sixteen of the twenty cities around the world with the worst air pollution are in China, which contributes to half-a-million premature deaths every year from diseases related to air pollution, and estimates suggest that 50,000 newborn babies die of fatal lung damage (Green and Luehrmann 2007)
3. Structural adjustment programs (SAPs) that promote exports intensify the pressures on land and other resources. The deforestation and desertification associated with the overexploitation of the environment have only grown with neoliberal economic reforms. Globalisation is directly connected to environmental devastation; for example, SAPs urge countries to increase their growth rates by increasing productivity, which in turn is often defined by an opening up of untouched areas and exploitation of resources. During the early 1990s, all sixteen

debtor nations were linked to significant deforestation, and the leading non-Western debtors were among the ten worst worldwide.

4. Per capita emissions still vary widely among the Northern and Southern economies, which makes treating them on an equal footing unjust and politically unacceptable.
5. It is sometimes difficult to ascribe responsibility for emissions in a globalised, economically interdependent world. For example, much of the current Chinese emissions are a direct result of the transfer of production from the US and Europe; so who, then, is actually responsible?
6. If some countries jointly agree to make expensive cuts, then others who do not enjoy the environmental benefits of such cuts without having to pay for them. This is known as the 'free-rider problem'.

So who should bear the burden of combating 'dangerous' climate change (Caney 2010)? This question of 'burden-sharing'[11] has sharply divided the international community. This fierce debate is centred around three principles of burden-sharing:

- *Polluter Pays Principle:* This holds that the burden of how much an entity has to pay should be predicated on the quantum of their emissions. While this is a plausible approach because it emphasises responsibility, as scholars like Shue (2014) have pointed out, it unfairly penalises the historically disadvantaged developing countries, which are currently seeking to develop their economies, and consequently have high carbon emission rates. Critics also argue that this approach 'punishes' agents for emissions that they were unaware of, since the technology did not exist at the time. They also question how polluters who are no longer active or alive can be asked to pay.
- *Beneficiary Pays Principle:* This posits that agents should pay to the extent that they have benefitted from the emission of GHGs. Most of the criticism levelled at the Polluter Pays Principle also applies to the Beneficiary Pays Principle. It does not take into account

[11] A well-rounded and detailed discussion on climate justice can be found in The Stanford Encyclopedia of Philosophy.

the benefits accrued by past generations or how to determine who benefits from what, and by how much. Finally, critics argue that the term 'benefits' is itself misleading. People living in poor countries may emit GHGs to achieve a basic minimum standard of living, and yet be burdened with payments because these are deemed 'benefits'.

- *Ability to Pay Principle:* Finally, this principle proposes to distribute the costs of climate change based on an agent's ability to pay, that is, the greater the ability to pay, the greater the responsibility for shouldering the costs. The obvious problem with this approach is that, to a certain extent, it divorces payment from the so-called 'benefits' of GHG emissions. This principle is similar to the idea that the wealthy in society have a responsibility to provide assistance to the poor, or the Gandhian philosophy of trusteeship.

The Paris Agreement of 2015 marked a step forward in consolidating burden-sharing, including market-based approaches such as carbon pricing. Articles 6.2–6.5 of the Agreement suggest mechanisms for cooperation on carbon pricing across jurisdictions, along with a robust accountability mechanism to increase transparency (UNFCCC 2020). While the efficacy of these mechanisms is yet to be determined, it is clear that negotiations on the burden-sharing of carbon emissions will occupy a key space in international politics in the medium to long-term.

MAPPING DISCOURSES IN CLIMATE CHANGE ACTION: CHALLENGES TO COLLECTIVE ACTION

While the science wars on climate change still inform and heavily influence climate politics, an exclusive focus on this can obscure important issues. Indeed, there is a tendency within the environmental political discourse to underestimate the ideological and social theoretical underpinnings of the environmental debate (Manno 2004). Ironically, a framing of climate change based on scientific consensus—as a global humanitarian cause that flows logically from science—is just another side of the same coin, as it ignores the myriad discourses within climate politics.

With the global climate change regime finally taking shape in the present century, studies in international relations and global politics have begun to incorporate discourses on the politics of climate change. Scholars such as Backstrand and Lovbrand (2016) and Jorgensen and Corry (2016) study the range of works in IR that offer typologies of different diplomatic stances and argue that the most popular approaches to the politics of climate change do not distinguish between rival positions on policy and governance, focussing on the believers vs. deniers dichotomy instead. However, as the contours of a climate politology begin to be discerned, authors across disciplines are mapping out multiple climate-political positions, each focussing on a different question and pointing to a different referent[12] (Jorgensen and Corry 2016). Their survey of the politics of climate change yields the following categories.

It is important to remember that these categories are analytical constructs and subject to empirical findings. In practice, there is a considerable overlap between them, and they are by no means exclusive. Further, the positions of various actors are contingent upon social, political, economic, and historical factors at any given point in time. As the social reality changes, actors tend to rearticulate and reposition themselves within the climate politics discourse. For example, under George Bush, the US was sceptical of climate change and withdrew from the Kyoto Protocol. However, under the Obama administration, it pledged to 'engage vigorously' with the world on climate change. Jorgensen and Corry (2016) point to an analytical overlap between the categories as well; for example, grassroots civic environmentalism may be similar to the green radical, expansive sustainability, or limits discourses. The green governmental position could include tenets of both expansive environmentalism and mainstream sustainability. Further, hierarchy, egalitarianism, and competitive individualism also overlap at times with green governmentality, civic environmentalism, and eco-modernisation, respectively (ibid.). Finally, Backstrand and Lovbrand (2016) warn that discourses are rarely complete or coherent. Rather than focussing on political opposition or the intersections of discourses, analysts should pay close empirical attention to the many

[12]For example, media framings of attitudes to climate change, policy discourses, varying logics and codes, and different worldviews on climate change.

Table 17.1: Typologies of Climate Change

Ideal Types in Climate Politics	**Sceptics** Global warming is just one of the terrors of the modern age	**Radicals** Focus only on the risks of climate change and the worst-case scenarios	**Mainstream** Epitomised by the IPCC: the middle ground, consensus-based approach	
Discourses on Climate Governance	**Mainstream Sustainability** Accepts the current economic order and seeks to prevent pollution while engaging in economic development	**Expansive Sustainability** Accepts the current economic order. Climate politics is oriented towards human development	**Limits** Emphasises the need to stay within social and natural boundaries	**Green Radicalism** Challenges the current economic and political orders
Discourses on Climate Governance	**Green Governmentality** Advocates for a multilateral climate regime negotiated under the auspices of the UN and involving a science-based monitoring of the global climate system	**Eco-Modernisation** A liberal economic framework relying on the initiative and creativity of individual rational actors to work towards the lowest-cost solutions to climate-related problems	**Civic Environ-mentalism** Relies on the third sector or civil society for climate action instead of the market or the state. This group may be further sub-divided into radicals and reformists	
System Codes and Social Spheres	**Society, Religion, and Culture** Truths/untruths, information/disinformation, ideological beliefs	**Politics** Power/non-power, governed/governor	**Economy** To pay, or not to pay	**Media** Information/lack of information.
Cultures or Worldviews	**Egalitarianism** Climate change is a result of profilgacy, capitalist competition, and overconsumption in an unequal world	**Hierarchist** Climate change is a result of lack of central control and planning—a global tragedy of commons	**Individualists** Climate change in general means business as usual, as any 'top-down' governance would fail	

fractures, mutations, and minor transformations that are frequently missed in the zeal to generalise and systematise.

INTERNATIONAL RELATIONS AND CLIMATE POLITICS

Maximilian Terhalle and Joanna Depledge (2013, 572) stated: 'the complex politics of climate change cannot be properly understood without reference to deeper geopolitical trends in the wider international system'. Exploring the resurgence of great power politics, most notably between the United States and China, with the help of IR theory, these scholars argue that contemporary international politics 'is witnessing a meshing of non-Western world views into a ground that is traditionally embedded in most IR mindsets as Western, universal, and without competitors'. Inherent assumptions and biases are preventing IR theorists from recognising the importance of distinct (but not universal) worldviews, which is in turn limiting their analysis of climate action politics (ibid., 583).

International Relations is generally concerned with the social realm in world politics, in which anarchy and the need to maintain order take precedence over morality and the desire to achieve global justice (Falkner 2019). Several scholars have recently commented on and carried out empirical studies to establish that IR experts and political scientists have paid scant attention to climate change (Keohane 2015; Pereira 2017). This is due to the limitations within conventional disciplinary structures that do not allow IR to address the multidimensionality and complexity of global environmental issues (Pereira 2017).

Critics have identified several failings of IR as a discipline to explain its inability to comprehensively analyse some of the most pressing challenges of the twenty-first century, such as climate change. *First*, scholars point to the insularity of IR, claiming that most theorists prefer to remain close to the mother discipline of Political Science instead of opting for more transdisciplinary approaches (Buzan and Little 2001) This makes it difficult for IR theories and approaches to fully capture a complex global phenomenon like climate change. *Second*, IR's tendency to borrow conceptual frameworks from the natural sciences (for example, a closed system) precludes it from analysing complex, layered, and interconnected open systems. *Third*, IR's grandiose ambition to focus on 'top-level' issues prevents it from discussing subjects like climate change in a meaningful and realistic way (Pereira 2017). Thus, there is a need for greater innovation and intellectual freedom in IR theory, methods, and approaches in order to comprehensively analyse issues such as climate justice and offer critical insights to policymakers.

18

Terrorism and Counter-Terrorism

Anindya Jyoti Majumdar

Violence in different forms and measures, arising out of hostility between groups, has always been a key element of political life. Ruling regimes often resort to coercion to ensure conformity and submission, and a retaliatory response is always a possibility. In an asymmetric distribution of power, the groups opposing the ruling regime are in a position of relative disadvantage. Terrorism has been regarded as a political tool that includes the use of indiscriminate violence as a strategy, used by a weaker party against a powerful adversary.

Terrorism is usually characterised by attacks on soft targets, that is, unarmed, innocent civilians, with the intention of spreading terror and panic and thereby informing a larger target audience about the ideas, objectives, and demands of the terrorist group. Terrorism uses violence to pressurise the opponent in order to achieve a political goal. Rebels and insurgents—who organise themselves into militias to counter the coercive machineries of the state—may also indulge in occasional terrorist acts. Terrorist methods may even be applied during freedom movements against colonial rule or alien occupation.

This chapter explains the concept of terrorism and its evolution into what is now regarded as international terrorism, which has its own distinguishing features. It will discuss how terrorism is increasingly becoming enmeshed with violent extremism. It will also talk about the response of the global community to the challenges of terrorism, including the 'war on terror' and its repercussions.

The Concept of Terrorism

Differing political perceptions have prevented states from presenting a widely acceptable definition of terrorism at the international level. Guided by parochial interests that manipulate one group against another, states refrain from committing to binding regulations. The sponsorship of terrorism as an instrument of foreign policy holds many attractions. The costs are low and benefits high; if the action fails, the terrorists can be easily and plausibly disavowed. In fact, the absence of an acceptable definition allows states the freedom to define what terrorism is according to their domestic laws, and adopt the necessary counter-measures. The US military defines terrorism as: 'The calculated use of unlawful violence or the threat of unlawful violence to inculcate fear; intended to coerce or to intimidate governments or societies in the pursuit of goals that are generally political, religious or ideological' (quoted in Mockaitis 2012, 17).

This definition is by no means complete. Some consider terrorism to be a war of attrition, which can over time corrode the resistance of opponents and compel them to negotiate. Distinctions must, however, be made between acts of terrorism and rebellion and insurgency (although there are overlaps between the two). The primary motivation for both groups is to draw attention to their demands. While terrorists attack undefended non-military targets, attacks against the military and police forces through unconventional methods, such as suicide bombers and assassinations, are not ruled out. Terrorism supplements a bigger political struggle, but the very nature of a terrorist act—the killing of innocents—distinguishes it from other forms of legitimate resistance. With the global recognition of the need to protect human rights and uphold human security, terrorism has lost validity as a politically expedient device. Although terrorism has by itself never succeeded in bringing about revolutionary changes in power, terrorist activities remain frequent and numerous.

Defining terrorism has become increasingly problematic as the term has acquired revolutionary connotations over the years, coming to be regarded as the tool of the 'oppressed' against an 'oppressor' with superior resources and strength. In contrast to common criminals, terrorist violence is motivated by a 'cause', and not personal and selfish reasons. Terrorism is a political weapon insofar as it creates and exploits fear through violent acts in the pursuit of political change. However, despite the liberal usage of the term, the varying connotations associated with it, and the tendency of groups to combine terrorism with other modes of political action, one common refrain stands out: acts of terrorism, whatever their motivation, always kill and injure innocent non-combatants. This lone element distinguishes an act of terrorism from a freedom struggle, insurgency, or other legitimate modes of political resistance involving the use of force.

Statements such as 'one man's terrorist is another man's freedom fighter' seek to override the natural human aversion for terrorists and their techniques. Such beliefs imbue terrorist propaganda with far more credibility than it deserves, while legitimising terrorist acts. The argument ignores the fact that terrorist violence violates the human rights of innocent civilians. Interestingly, this element is not clearly highlighted in even attempts to define international terrorism. Terrorism is still defined as the perpetration of unlawful and intentional acts by any means that cause death and injury to any person or serious damage to public and private property, infrastructural facilities, transportation systems, etc., aimed at intimidating a population or compelling a government or an international organisation to do the terrorists' bidding. Such a broad definition allows states to brand most violent acts of opposition groups as terrorist acts.

Therefore ruling regimes now tend to brand almost any act of violence by rebels, insurgents, or secessionists as acts of terrorism and adopt punitive counter-measures, which often injure innocent civilians. This, in turn, transforms the terrorists into perceived freedom fighters. Even if we consider people's right to self-determination, there are various other methods of protest and resistance, ranging from peaceful non-cooperation or civil disobedience movements, to guerrilla warfare and insurgency. In their truest sense, none of these methods would advocate deliberate attacks on innocent persons or soft targets, but would be directed against the state and the coercive machineries at its command. In short, a clear line is drawn and maintained between combatants and non-combatants. Terrorism blurs this distinction by initiating deliberate attacks on non-combatants, who are punished for their seeming alignment with the ruling regime or for offering tacit consent to state policies. However, even if the innocence of non-combatants is in doubt, this in no way justifies the criminal act of murdering citizens.

EVOLUTION OF TERRORISM

The use of violence has been a constant feature of political processes and acts of terrorism have been employed to gain political power and advantage from ancient times. History is replete with frequent assassinations of political personalities and members of target groups, with only the method of assassination, the weapons used, and the degree of impact changing with time. Ruling regimes have developed various mechanisms to protect themselves against terrorist acts, while terrorist groups, in their turn, seek to make full use of the technology accessible to them. Often, the success of a terrorist attack depends on the innovative application of available means. Terrorist acts have evolved through the ages: from the use of daggers and knives to firearms, from the kidnapping of individuals to hijacking passenger aeroplanes, from planting bombs and lobbing grenades to suicide bomb attacks, from driving a truck full of explosives into target areas to using hijacked passenger aeroplanes as destructive missiles. The use of weapons of mass destruction cannot be ruled out either. Scholars agree that terrorism is not a static phenomenon but has evolved with regularity, keeping pace with changing political environments and advancement in technologies. Terrorist groups frequently use innovative measures as states eventually become aware of and familiar with the methods and techniques implemented by particular groups, and the consequent counter-measures adopted by the target state compel terrorists to search for even more novel tactics.

Often, terrorism becomes a relatively easy method through which to gain *de facto* prominence and worth, bringing greater attention to the group's agenda. Faced with the powerful coercive machinery deployed by a state or a group of states, terrorist groups may find the use of indiscriminate force much more effective than a direct clash or long-drawn and often futile negotiation politics, which they have little chance of winning. When other powerful states support terrorist groups with financial and logistic help, encouraging them to carry on proxy confrontations with an enemy state on their behalf, terrorism thrives. Deprivation, poverty, and lack of opportunities for upward mobility, along with general underdevelopment, may ensure a steady supply of cadres. Localised confrontations spread when state adversaries seek to injure the interests of enemy states by providing clandestine assistance to such groups. However, terrorism does not result exclusively from a lack of economic, social, political, and cultural protection, nor is it solely a rebellion against attempts by a dominant segment within a state to enforce a common identity, overriding pluralism in the process. It is also not the result of state competition for power, which creates and nurtures terrorism to achieve parochial ends. Terrorism is a lethal combination of all these, and more. Hence, predominant liberal explanations that seek to portray terrorism as emanating from a sense of grievance against economic or political deprivation, or conservative explanations that view terrorism as a form of sectarian resistance against systems of unified rules, remain inadequate.

Many of the existing democratic political systems allow the articulation of demands to varying degrees, but these cannot always redress the multifaceted grievances of all the people. Dissent, protest, and resistance to the ruling regime are crucial, and while the government has a duty to respond, inept handling can further worsen the situation. However, the legitimacy of a demand is often determined by political exigencies, and the validity and justification of a protest and the consequent use of force are often judged by the outcome of such actions. Acts of terrorism are no exception. One successful act may encourage another, and over the years, a terrorist group may acquire legitimacy as it dons the image of freedom fighters engaged in a war of attrition with an apparently dictatorial power. However, except under extraordinary circumstances, terrorism is often unable to ensure the effective redistribution of power by itself.

Many conventional terrorist groups have put forward their respective political agendas in different parts of the world, all of which are mainly aimed at challenging the authority of the existing ruling regime. Not all such groups are equally active at the same time, and they range from purely political and ethno-nationalist movements to those that challenge the predominant cultural values of a state. Depending on the objectives, nature, and composition of terrorist groups, attempts have been made to classify terrorism under broad heads like ethnic terrorism, religious terrorism, political terrorism, etc. However, terrorism is essentially political, whether it is the Provisional Irish Republican Army seeking to remove British forces from Northern Ireland and unify the country, or the Basque Fatherland and Liberty, which sought to create an independent homeland in Spain's Basque Region, or Hezbollah, which seeks to establish an Islamic Republic in Lebanon, or Hamas in Palestine, all of these groups have used terrorism as essentially a political weapon against the powerful ruling regimes of the land.

The traditional understanding changed in the early twenty-first century as the new phenomenon of international terrorism emerged, necessitating a shift in analysis. With the emergence of groups like Al Qaeda, terrorism, it is said, has come of age and is now greatly influencing the process of international politics. The traditional form of terrorism persists, however, and it is important to note that all these groups cannot be treated in an identical manner—even though, in the era following the communication revolution, mutually beneficial links are often established among different groups worldwide. It is therefore pertinent to categorise terrorism in the twenty-first century into two dominant streams:

1. Groups that are clearly political and localised in nature, with immediate regional goals (which may include religious connotations in some cases).
2. Groups that are essentially global in nature with strong cultural connotations, aimed primarily at punishing adversaries for their beliefs, values, and consequent policies.

A third category is represented by cult groups obsessed with the impending apocalypse, who indulge in acts of terrorism to bring about death and destruction and hasten the end of the world. For example, the Aum Shinrikyo cult in Japan believed that the turn of the century would see the total destruction of the world, which would be survived by only the spiritually enlightened. They reportedly used chemical and biological agents to experiment with weapons of mass destruction. The infamous Sarin gas attack in the Tokyo subway in 1995 led to the cult members being arrested. Yet another category can be represented by the extreme right in the West, which opposes the transformation of their nations into multicultural, multi-racial, plural societies with the migration of people who come mainly from developing states. Hate crimes are usually directed against randomly selected targets. Groups propagating ideas of a 'race war' often suffer from organisational limitations, as well as ideological and personality differences within the groups themselves. These acts are usually viewed as a problem of law enforcement within the domestic jurisdiction of the state, and law and order machineries are capable of tackling this menace through surveillance and arrests of the ringleaders. Administrations are usually concerned about such acts of domestic terrorism, and the domestic polity of states have been evolving and countering the destructive tendencies of these small groups.

One may argue that states themselves can indulge in terrorist violence under the ploy of deterring the violence of non-state actors. Countermeasures adopted by states often provoke retaliatory terrorism, instigating stricter countermeasures in turn. A state experiencing terrorism is tempted to use its coercive machinery to eradicate all terrorists, and often adopts extreme measures to eliminate the threat they pose. Fearing that attempts to negotiate with and/or accommodate the demands of terrorists might be construed as weakness and vulnerability, states usually opt for coercion over political negotiation. If the murder of innocents in terrorists attacks is condemnable, so too are the charges of custody deaths, fake 'encounters', and untraced victims levied against states. States can also take recourse to terrorist violence in order to frighten and intimidate their own people. Unpopular authoritarian regimes can resort to terrorist methods to crush opposition and coerce people to follow their dictates. Such acts are categorised as *state terrorism*. Unlike terrorists, however, the state is usually silent about the violent methods it applies, and avoids taking responsibility for its actions, even though successful operations using violent methods (comprising selective assassinations or special missions) against known adversaries of the state are viewed as legitimate exercises to maintain national security.

Over time, terrorism has become a useful tool in the hands of states willing to sponsor particular groups in a proxy war with their adversaries. Groups are financed, and provided with training, weapons, and supplies to challenge the adversary from within. *State-sponsored terrorism* and proxy wars go hand-in-hand in an era where full-fledged armed conflict between states is becoming increasingly irrelevant, given the costs of a total war. In such circumstances, terrorism can be used as a sub-tactical method of warfare against the enemy. The 'nuclear shield' logic is allegedly said to be an element in the Pakistani policy vis-à-vis India, which assumes that Pakistan can continue to provide support to militants against India, safe in the knowledge that a retaliatory Indian invasion is unlikely, given the fear of a possible nuclear response from Pakistan. This logic is not all that sound, since India has undertaken surgical strikes in response to Pakistan-sponsored terrorist attacks within the country. Nevertheless, low-intensity sub-tactical warfare continues in veiled forms, under the umbrella of nuclear deterrence. Ordinarily, terrorism is linked to specific regional situations. As inter-state conflicts induce states to sponsor terrorism and encourage the networking of terrorist groups across borders, the security of the region as a whole deteriorates.

THE NEW INTERNATIONAL TERRORISM

The 11 September 2001 attacks on the twin towers of the World Trade Center in New York in the United States introduced a new phase in the discourse on terrorism. At the end of the Cold War, when the world tended towards unipolarity and the supremacy of US hegemony was re-established, the 9/11 incident dealt a blow to plans of an impending American century. Terrorism became truly transnational—even global—with this one strike. Scholars have distinguished the 'new terrorism' from traditional patterns, highlighting its worldwide networks, greater destructiveness and lethality, the use of unconventional weapons, and willingness to punish the target rather than merely seeking publicity for and drawing attention to the terrorists' cause. Viewed thus, the new terrorism is only different in its scale, rather than in its essential nature. Its worldwide networks have resulted from the global interconnectedness made possible by rapid improvements in communication and information technology. With new areas and new means of operation, new forms of terrorism have appeared: for example, attempts to disrupt the communication network and information flow and breach the security of the state constitute cyber-terrorism, which may range from unauthorised access to computer resources, web-hacking and defacement to denial of service, data theft, and disruption of social activities.

This 'new terrorism' is also branded an Islamist jihad against Western dominance in general and American supremacy in particular and the policies they pursue, which impact the political, economic, and cultural values in Islamic states. Samuel Huntington's famed thesis of the impending clash of civilisations (Huntington 1996) led many to believe that the events of 9/11 provided a blueprint for future world politics. However, a band of religious fanatics and extremists do not represent a 'civilisation', and arguing that an Islamist monolith exists without taking into consideration the fractured identities and differences within the so-called monolith—the Shia–Sunni divide, for instance—is a little fantastical.

One important dimension of this new terrorism is 'super-terrorism' (or 'mega-terrorism' and 'macro-terrorism'), that is, the possible use of unconventional weapons—more specifically, weapons of mass destruction, chemical, biological, and nuclear. There is also the likelihood of future catastrophic terrorist attacks using such dangerous weapons. While the desire to inflict greater injuries may encourage terrorist groups to seek unconventional means, there are obvious technological limitations to both acquisition and deployment. But states remain apprehensive of the threat of catastrophic terrorism, which might go beyond their effective control. This also alerts them to the need for collaboration; international terrorism has made it clear that while non-state actors are establishing links among themselves, individual states often fail to act in unison to meet the challenges they pose.

Over time, changes have become noticeable in the patterns of terrorist activities. The rise of the Sunni-Arab territorial militia in parts of Iraq and Syria, whose political goal is to establish an Islamist Caliphate in West Asia and beyond, is a case in point. The Islamic State of Iraq and al-Sham (Greater Syria) or ISIS has its origins in Al Qaeda in Iraq, although the two groups officially broke away as ISIS gathered strength while Al Qaeda declined steadily. The ISIS, predominantly active in Iraq and Syria, launched brutal and indiscriminate attacks on civilians, non-Muslims, and Shiites, and used terrorist techniques of mass murder, suicide bombings, and publicised beheadings of non-combatants. In face of contest over control of land areas, the group used civilians as human shields in times of military operations.

Popular resentment against foreign interference, a sense of victimhood and lost glory, and grievances against the perceived injustices perpetrated by ruling regimes led the alienated Sunni-Arab radicals on a path of vengeance. Plans for a 'regime change' through the use of force, ostensibly to usher in democracy, went out of control, as the 2003 invasion of Iraq showed, and a contest between 'regime change' (as advocated by the US) and 'regime security' (as advocated by China and Russia) can degenerate into widespread instability and chaos, as Syria under President Assad portrayed. The rise of ISIS was facilitated by the policies of the major powers of the day. While the Islamic State fought its battles in Iraq and Syria, it indulged in terrorist acts across the world, inspiring radicalised Muslims to operate on its behalf. These radicalised people, many of them the youth, left their home countries to join the ISIS and ally themselves to its ideals. Some returned, only to launch terrorist attacks at home, in countries as far removed as France and Bangladesh. However, ISIS collapsed in 2019 due to military defeats. As turmoil continued, with various splinter groups active in the region, in December 2024, a militant group called Hayat Tahrir al-Sham was instrumental in taking over power in Syria, leading to the fall of the Bashar al-Assad regime.

Regionally prominent terrorist groups have also emerged, such as the Islamic State in West Africa, better known as Boko Haram, and splinter groups like al-Shabaab in East Africa. Moreover, the idea of a holy war against 'non-believers' inspires some individuals, termed as 'lone wolves', to sacrifice their lives for the 'cause', taking countless lives and damaging property across the world in the process. Such sporadic attacks also affect state policies, as states arm themselves with laws that often impinge on civil liberty.

Today, defining terrorism has become even more controversial and confusing as the boundaries blur between terrorism and other forms of political violence. Traditional understandings of terrorism had always focussed on the nature of the act, with the perpetrator being labelled a terrorist. However, the recent tendency to distinguish between dissidents, freedom fighters, special operation agents, even 'good' versus 'bad' terrorists, necessarily focusses on the identity of the perpetrator; the nature of the act becomes immaterial, with some actors even being legitimised. As a result, states can be very selective in the particular act of political violence or group they choose to label as terrorist/terrorism. What makes it more difficult to determine acts of terrorism is the fact that now, insurgent groups are increasingly applying terror techniques by killing civilians while terrorist groups are attacking both soft and hard targets. Throughout the world, terrorism has evolved and expanded, and we are now experiencing a phase of 'violent extremism'.

THE GLOBAL 'WAR ON TERROR'

Despite their differences, most states share a common interest: protecting themselves from the threats posed by non-state actors. Under ordinary circumstances, even those states that use terrorists to further their own interests would never allow them to acquire the kind of power that might be turned against itself. The world over, the counter-terrorism measures initiated have also given rise to differing perceptions with regard to the application of such policies, as states frequently disagree on the measures to be adopted and on the role that a particular nation will play. In essence, the contemporary era signifies constant fear and anticipation of terrorist attacks, combined with unrelenting preparations to guard against such extreme possibilities. However, while it is imperative that the international community develop a united front against all forms of terrorism, it should also distinguish between transnational and regional terrorist activities in order to develop suitable policies to counter such acts.

A state suffering from the menace of terrorism deploys coercive machineries and adopts extreme measures to eliminate all threats. Violence begets violence. In many regions of the world, poverty and lack of opportunities for upward mobility create deprivation, which, in combination with indoctrination, turns into violence against the ruling regime and other communities. Poverty and deprivation ensure a steady supply of fighters, some of whom might be lured by material benefits while others may be guided by a new hallowed identity and thoughts of martyrdom. Counter-terrorism measures bolster animosity against the hostile ruling regime. However, following the principle of the 'carrot and the stick', special economic packages are announced at regular intervals, apparently to exacerbate divisions between the terrorists and the common people, in specific regions. In the process, the violence fluctuates and becomes a long-drawn affair, often with no realistic end in sight.

Especially after the 11 September attacks in New York, most states have put certain measures in place. These include the suppression of all finances meant for terrorist groups, freezing the funds, financial assets, and economic resources of declared or known terrorists, terrorist groups, and their associates, surveillance and information exchange with regard to suspected agents, and the practice of quiet diplomacy, at times through informal channels, to enable a common understanding of the necessity for collaboration. There are bilateral and multilateral, regional and global mechanisms in place to ensure coordination in such activities.

However, not all mechanisms are equally effective. The European Union's counter-terrorism strategy, based on prevention, protection, pursuit, and response, is a better approach compared to the intention of SAARC countries to strengthen the legal regime against terrorism by implementing international conventions related to combating terrorism. Even the success of the United Nation's Global Counter-Terrorism Strategy, as adopted by the General Assembly in 2006, would always be dependent on the willing participation of nations. Resolution 1267 of the United Nations Security Council, adopted in 1999, established a sanctions regime to cover declared terrorists and terrorist entities. Nations are required to adopt measures against such individuals and entities, monitored by an international team. However, political exigencies often inform the policies adopted by states in designating terrorists: India, for example, had been steadily campaigning to have the chief of Jaish-e-Muhammad and alleged mastermind of several cross-border attacks, Masood Azhar, declared an internationally recognised terrorist, but China had stymied all such attempts for years before eventually agreeing to concur with the other nations in 2019.

Indeed, there is no dearth of international conventions and protocols with regard to the suppression of international terrorist and other criminal acts, ranging from the unlawful seizure of aircraft, taking of hostages, and crimes against internationally protected persons, to the protection of nuclear material, safety of civil aviation and maritime navigation, and suppression of terrorist bombings, financing of terrorism, and transnational organised crime (including trafficking in persons and illicit traffic in narcotics). The success of all such conventions will depend on the willing participation of most states in formulating a joint organised response to terrorism in all its forms and manifestations. Only when terrorism is accepted as a global phenomenon that needs to be tackled globally will such efforts be successful. Despite the intermittent challenges they pose, terrorists can still be used as pawns by the major states, and both terrorism and counter-terrorism can be used as excuses to consolidate state power, both domestically and beyond their borders.

Terrorism, like almost all other issues in international relations, lends itself to tactful bargaining among states. While it is impractical to expect all states to rally round a common programme of counter-terrorism, a consensus among the leading states on how to conduct the war on terror is necessary. It is true that the responsibility for maintaining international peace and security rests largely on the prevailing major powers, and relations among the top states encourage or discourage the operational manoeuvres of other states in the system.

After the 11 September attacks, the US unleashed a military retaliation. They fought a war in Afghanistan, removed the Taliban, and installed a friendly regime in its place. Thus began the era of the 'war on terror'. Although the US sought international support, the doctrine of pre-emptive strikes and regime change in the fight against international terrorism was put in place almost unilaterally by the George H. W. Bush administration, and did not receive any overwhelming support from the international community. On the one hand, this reinforces the belief that the war on terror launched by the US and its allies is deeply enmeshed in attempts to consolidate global power and control over resources. On the other, it might have created a security environment in which terror and extreme violence have become tools of political, social, and economic change, leading to an endless cycle of intermittent retaliatory terrorist acts and counter-measures. Many scholars consider the war on terror a futile exercise in resolving the problem of terrorism.

> Few would fail to notice the growing common ground between the perpetrators of 9/11 and the official response to it called 'the war on terror'. Both sides deny the possibility of a middle ground, calling for a war to the finish. Both rally forces in the name of justice but understand justice as revenge. If the perpetrators of 9/11 refuse to distinguish between official America and the American people, target and victim, 'the war on terror' has proceeded by dishing out collective punishment, with callous disregard for either 'collateral damage' or legitimate grievances. Both practices are likely to nurture the spirit of revenge.... (Mamdani 2004, 230)

Under these circumstances, other major powers have grown apprehensive of the utility and long-term impact of US schemes. Most of the states would have been willingly involved had there been a consensus on international collaboration through the multilateral platform of the United Nations. However, like many other crucial issues of international politics, this is also characterised by intense debate and controversy. The definition of terrorism and identity of terrorists are issues that divide, rather than unite, the world.

The possibility of terrorists using unconventional weapons also demands international cooperation and coordinated activities to suppress the black market in radioactive material and the clandestine transportation of arms and sensitive weapons. The US has introduced the proliferation security initiative, a flexible arrangement of willing states with the aim of interdicting the shipment of sensitive materials.

This policy, which supports the non-proliferation regime, also impacts the clandestine proliferation of weapons of mass destruction. The war on terror has fallouts that influence global power equations as well.

Most established groups with professed political aims that have taken recourse to terrorist acts in the past do not really need terrorism to draw attention to their cause. The terrorist activities were undertaken to reassert the existence of the cause and recruit people who would carry it forward. Today, terrorism generates a sense of loss through cross-currents of irrational violence, and consequently begets hatred. The new terrorists use terrorism to ensure long-term political impacts: to create divisions among communities, to disturb peace processes, or to generate suspicions among neighbours.

The attacks of 11 September and the consequent US-led war on terror have led to a tendency to view international terrorism and counter-terrorism as a clash of religious ideologies. During the Iraq war, the world was unsure of the legitimacy and efficacy of US actions. But in 2014, when the US sought a global coalition to defeat the Islamic State, a large number of states promised support to a long-term, multi-pronged strategy that intended not only to wipe out IS operational bases through airstrikes and ground sweeps, but also aimed to ideologically delegitimise ISIS. They supported effective governance in Iraq, checked the inflow of foreign fighters and financial support to the IS, and provided humanitarian aid to the general population. Russia and Iran, despite not being formal coalition partners, joined in to allegedly protect the Assad regime from the challenge posed by ISIS in Syria.

FORMS OF TERRORISM IN SOUTH ASIA

In South Asia, the particular pattern that terrorism follows within a country is seen to conform to the historical traits unique to that country. One such type is the formation of territorial militias and, finally, establishing control over the state. For example, despite attempts to keep them away, the Taliban has once again acquired power in Afghanistan and is running the state government. Russia was the first country to formally recognise the Taliban as the legitimate government of Afghanistan. Many other states carry on regular interactions with this government. Historically, the Afghan state has never held sovereign monopoly over its entire territory, as self-governing tribal and agrarian social formations retained their autonomy, paying only nominal or symbolic allegiance to a central authority. During the late 1970s, when the Mujahideen fought the occupying Soviet forces, Pakistan promoted the militant clerics and Islamist groups, thereby undermining the influence of tribal elites. The former legitimised their rule in the name of Islam, enforcing it through armed militants.

In 1996, the Taliban took over Kabul and established a government under Mullah Omar. This was overthrown by the coalition led by the US in 2001. History is witness to the dramatic chain of events in Afghanistan: the beginning of the war on terror after 9/11, the fall of the Taliban, the Bonn Agreement to establish a government in Kabul, the attempts at state-building, the resurgence of the Taliban and informal peace talks as the Taliban opened offices in Dubai and Qatar, and finally, the capture of Kabul by the Taliban once again in August 2021 following the withdrawal of the US and its allied forces. State-building in Afghanistan has always been a difficult task, but attempts have been made nevertheless. India was involved in this task along with the previous Afghan government, contributing to infrastructure development and providing essential services to the people. This created goodwill among Afghans for India. Subsequently, India developed decent relations with the new Taliban regime as well.

The Taliban also grappled with a leadership problem. Between the two main parties exercising control over their respective areas are ungoverned spaces, which serve as secure zones for all other Islamist groups, including Al Qaeda and the Islamic State. In the absence of normal economic avenues and opportunities, smuggling, drug trafficking, and trade in small arms have become lucrative business. The huge task of state building is almost insurmountable but attempts have to be made nevertheless. Many countries, including India, are involved in this task along with the Afghan government.

Pakistan has become known for terrorism in South Asia, as the Directorate of Inter-Services Intelligence (ISI) of the army in Pakistan has often used terrorism as an instrument of its security policy. Pakistan's security policy is controlled by its army, whose aims are:

1. To exercise control over Afghan politics.
2. To keep India in check through a constant war of attrition.
3. To create unrest, particularly in the state of Jammu and Kashmir (which is at present a Union Territory in India).

To meet these goals, terrorism has become a useful tool. Pakistan's close links with groups like Laskar-e-Toiba and Jaish-e-Muhammad ensure that terrorism is confined to non-state actors, along with being a sub-tactical instrument of warfare to achieve state interests.

On the other hand, the Pakistan army is at war with the Tehreek-e-Taliban Pakistan, a group that operates within the country and yet opposes the establishment, as well as with the Baloch nationalists. Pakistan seems to have become a victim of its own design. It has developed, supported, and promoted terrorism, and uses it as a state policy. However, it no longer enjoys control over all the groups. In fact, in recent years Pakistan has suffered from several devastating terrorist attacks, which has led to the realisation that terrorism perhaps poses a greater threat than India. The civilian governments, especially, are becoming increasingly aware of the worsening internal security prospects and missed economic opportunities. However, recent terrorist attacks on the Uri military base and at Pulwama, as well as the murder of innocent tourists in Pahalgam in 2025 provoked retaliatory surgical and air strikes from India, leading to a deterioration in the already shaky India–Pakistan relations. Given the enormous distrust between the two nations, it is difficult to foresee any substantial positive change in the near future.

Since its inception, Bangladesh has been struggling with two equally dominant yet contradictory strains of identity, both of which are products of its brief history. The spirit of 1971—a moderate Islamic Bengali nationalism—was in sharp contrast to the spirit of 1947, which gave rise to a state based on religion and had a greater affinity with an orthodox pan-Islamic brotherhood. It is among this section of people that the Jamaat found its support. While the Harkat ul Jihadi Islami and Jamatul Mujahideen Bangladesh took extreme positions, the Jamaat too has had its own role to play. Sheikh Hasina, as the protagonist of the spirit of 1971, had spearheaded the unfinished business of the liberation war by punishing the Razakars (people who collaborated with the Pakistan Army in 1971 and committed atrocities on Bangladeshis). In August 2024, however, the Sheikh Hasina government was overthrown and she fled to India. The interim government that replaced the previous regime reversed many policies of the Hasina administration; a number of militants were released from jail and radicalism resurfaced in Bangladesh. The present government is now seeking to try and punish Sheikh Hasina for her alleged administrative excesses.

Sri Lanka experienced an intense civil war from 1983 onwards, between the dominant Sinhala and the Tamils, led by the Liberation Tigers of Tamil Elam (LTTE). The LTTE was finally defeated by the Sri Lankan military in May 2009, thus ending a conflict that had raged for twenty-six years. The LTTE, created along the lines of a militia, had its suicide and bomb squads trained to assassinate political leaders and even innocent non-combatants at times. The Sri Lankan military operations, too, were accused of massive human rights violations. The principle of 'an eye for an eye' is reciprocal; the violation of established rules by one party releases the other from any obligation to abide by them.

Historically, India, the land of diversity, has experienced diverse sources and types of political conflict. Determined to tackle violent extremism in any form, India has established various Acts aimed at preventing 'unlawful activities' and has banned several groups associated with violence, especially those with external links. The Indian approach exemplifies the attitude of states in general: in the absence of a universally accepted definition of terrorism, a state is free to define a terrorist/terrorism based on its own interests and the exigencies of a situation.

This discussion has provided a picture of the varied faces of terrorism in South Asia. Terrorist activities lead to an atmosphere of suspicion and distrust both within and beyond states, which is further worsened by propaganda and the recruitment activities of terrorist groups. Countermeasures and state excesses increase the presence of sympathisers, lone wolves, sleeper cells, and dormant modules who act on their own. Terrorist groups usually establish linkages beyond borders, making terrorism a truly global phenomenon. One may, therefore, conclude that terrorism in South Asia is blurring boundaries and becoming enmeshed in widespread violent extremism. As it merges with the domestic politics of a state, it also conforms to the historical traits unique to that particular state. The impact it has is different, depending on each state's political evolution, and consequently, the response also varies; hence, it is difficult to fashion a common ground for meaningful cooperation among all states in South Asia. (This explains why the SAARC Convention on Suppression of Terrorism, 1987 was a non-starter.) However, bilateral and limited multilateral actions based on common interests cannot entirely be ruled out. In fact, what is true about South Asia is also true about the world in general.

Twenty-first century world politics operates on flexible, issue-based coalitions of states, rather than concerted global efforts. All the major powers of the day share a common concern for preventing terrorist acts in their respective homelands. States are perforce compelled to share information, coordinate backroom activities, and foster a general understanding of the rules of the game, even though they are yet to agree on a definition of terrorism and its categories, or on a grand strategy to fight the menace.

Nevertheless, terrorism has increasingly become a global scourge, which, like organised crime syndicates, persists through its links with the illegal trade in narcotics, small arms, and other transnational crimes. Terrorism is also emerging as a new avenue of employment. Along with fighters committed to a cause, groups are now hiring surrogate terrorists who are lured by money. Political or ideological justifications have always underlined terrorist acts. In this process, the victims, increasingly, have been human rights and individual freedom, which are now under constant threat and subjected to state surveillance.[1]

[1]Some of the themes expanded in this chapter have been drawn from Majumdar (2003, 46–57; 2009, 75–87).

19

Displacement and Forced Migration

Anindya Jyoti Majumdar

There are more people moving across borders today than at any other time in history. Nearly 272 million people lived in a country other than their own in 2019. Human movement has also become easier with the development of communications and the high levels of interconnectedness in the contemporary world. According to the International Organization for Migration, a migrant can be defined as

> [A]ny person who is moving or has moved across an international border or within a State away from his/her habitual place of residence, regardless of:
>
> - the person's legal status
> - whether the movement is voluntary or involuntary
> - what the causes for the movement are
> - what the length of the stay is. (United Nations n.d.[f])

However, voluntary migration is not an all-encompassing, uniform phenomenon. There are varying reasons for such widespread movement. In some cases, the possibility of better economic opportunities fuels human movement, while in others, the threat to life and liberty forces people to embark on journeys to unseen lands. Forced migration involves the involuntary forced movement of people as a result of conflict, developmental projects, or natural or human-made disasters.

Interestingly, human history is replete with conflicts or disasters that sparked immeasurable catastrophes and weakened the capacity of large swathes of people to cope with the ensuing violence and destruction. Often termed 'humanitarian' crises, these developments threatened the very existence and safety of the people concerned and reverberated across the international system. In the twentieth century, the issue of forced migration dominated high politics and national and international security concerns, especially in the aftermath of World War II and during the Cold War, while the powers-that-be sought ways to deal with it. During the Cold War, the quest to support and protect forced migrants stemmed from ideological and political reasons based on the rivalry between the United States and the Soviet Union and their geopolitical interests. There are numerous examples of people from the Soviet Union, its satellite states such as Hungary and Czechoslovakia, and Cuba taking refuge in liberal, democratic Western countries.

With the end of the Cold War and the fall of the Soviet bloc, the international refugee regime faced an uncertain future in the absence of any ideologically-driven goal to offer protection to migrants. This made movement difficult, especially given the unpredictable participation of the major powers and the weakness of the regime itself. Therefore, the international community adopted different approaches while dealing with humanitarian crises in countries such as Somalia, Bosnia, Croatia, Kosovo, Rwanda, among others, after the fall of the Berlin Wall in 1989. International responses to such crises were often moulded by the national prerogatives of major powers, concerns over the cultural and demographic identity of receiving countries, and the ability to provide for the migrant communities.

Towards the end of the twentieth century, the invasion of Iraq by the US-led coalition of the willing, the civil war in Syria, and the subsequent rise of the Islamic State of Iraq and Syria (ISIS) created havoc in the two countries. Faced with chaos, mayhem, and brutal violence, many citizens fled, seeking refuge in other states. As the waves of refugees from Iraq and Syria entered neighbouring states and Europe, often undertaking perilous journeys across the Mediterranean and the Aegean Sea in small boats, the international community faced a serious and complex challenge in accommodating the victims. Forced migration once again became an international issue, bringing to the fore the tussle between the protection of basic human rights and the security of the state. The post-Cold War period was also marked by a large number of internal conflicts in South Asia, where the Sri Lankan civil war and the continued turmoil in Afghanistan uprooted millions from their homes.

The plight of the displaced people and the process of forced migration have created complex emergencies. This chapter will discuss the broad dimensions and types of human migration and the reasons underlying the phenomenon, and will explore how states and organisations responded to ameliorate the plight of the millions displaced, while also examining the mutual relationship between international relations and migration. The chapter will also study the predicament of women and child refugees, who remain peculiarly vulnerable to crime and exploitation in the different conflict-prone zones of the world. It will end by discussing the contemporary refugee crisis, focusing on the host country in particular.

Human Movements and Forced Migration

Mobility has been an essential part of human development. From ancient times, people have been crossing frontiers, and the history of human civilisations provides evidence that territorial conquests, economic links, or cultural expansion have all depended on human movement. Those people who remained static grew parochial in nature, and soon faced the onslaught of expansionist civilisations. Over the ages, the evolution of the cultures, habits, and customs of ethnic groups has been influenced by the human tendency to seek opportunities beyond their familiar geographical regions.

The emergence of the nation-state, with its sacrosanct political borders, in relatively recent times sought to restrict the movement of people, and maintain homogeneity by keeping out all outsiders. But even though the flow of inter-state human movement has been halted partially, the firmly imposed political boundaries have been unable to curb human movement, which, compelled by the lure of better opportunities or the need to seek refuge from adverse living conditions, violence, or conflicts, continued unabated. The nation-state and its sacrosanct borders were incapable of resolving the issue satisfactorily.

The states, however, control the flow of movement and migration through visa regimes, which issue permission and allow people to move across borders. Depending on the policies of the states, different categories of people are allowed to enter, and all movement is monitored, controlled, and documented. Sometimes, however, individuals and groups might cross national borders in search of a better life or to save themselves from life-threatening situations without the proper documents. Under compulsion, migration can assume various forms, ranging from infiltration to mass exodus. The lure of gain and fear of loss are the two predominant motivational pull-and-push factors in migration.

The promise of economic security, better employment prospects, and enhanced living standards compels individuals to migrate from their countries of origin. The movement of resourceful, highly-skilled people from the Global South to the more advanced economies of the West is a prime example of such migration. These ideas take deeper root in countries that lack opportunities and prospects of employment. Such a move signifies a movement out of localised traps of misery towards a globalised world of possibilities. The presence of networks—family or kinship connections—also acts as a motivational factor in migration.

More importantly, migration is often promoted as meeting the demands of a few receiving countries, especially in terms of resource generation and economic growth. In the nineteenth and twentieth centuries, countries such as Australia and New Zealand promoted migration in order to make up for their lack of human resources. Today, the emigration policies of countries such as Canada, which invite applications for citizenship from diverse individuals, mirror these developments.

However, the biggest reasons for human movement are the *fear* of loss—of life and honour—and *actual* loss of viable means of living and property, which force individuals and groups to leave their places of habitual residence. Colossal natural calamities, sustained ethnic and religious conflicts, devastating wars and intense violence may force people to migrate and seek shelter in neighbouring lands. Myron Weiner states that inter-state wars, ethnic conflicts, non-ethnic civil conflicts, and flights from repressive, authoritarian, and revolutionary regimes can lead to a mass refugee exodus: 'Refugee flows can be the result of conflict between states or by populations in war against their colonial rulers. Refugees may be consequences of drought, flood, famine and environmental disasters' (Weiner 1996, 9).

While the scope of human movement is normally unlimited within a state, intra-state movements also have the potential to disturb group homogeneity within a defined geographical space, unless that space was originally multicultural and multiethnic. Diverse reasons, such as a history of enmity and violence between communities, or ethnic rivalries, or the rise of non-state actors seeking to persecute minorities, can trigger forced migration within a state, as people leave an affected region and seek shelter in some other, safer region. In the post-Cold War era, especially, internal—rather than inter-state—conflict has exacerbated forced migration.

Human movement and forced migration have been categorised in several ways. Article 1 of the 1951 UN Convention Relating to the Status of the Refugees and its 1967 Protocol define a refugee as a person who,

> owing to well-founded fear of being persecuted for reasons of race, religion, nationality, membership of a particular social group or political opinion, is outside the country of [their] nationality and is unable or, owing to such fear, is unwilling to avail [themself] of the protection of that country; or who, not having a nationality and being outside the country of [their] former habitual residence, is unable or, owing to such fear, is unwilling to return to it.

The Organization of African Unity Convention relating to African refugees (1969) added 'generalized violence' as another ground for refugee status. Another classification, 'asylum seekers', includes people whose claims to refugee status remain undecided, even though they might have moved beyond the international borders of their countries. As decisions on such claims are based on the political interests of concerned countries, asylum seekers often find themselves living in a limbo, while recognition of their status remains pending. In cases of forced migration within the boundaries of a country, where a person has not crossed international borders, the concerned person is categorised as an internally displaced person (IDP).

Large-scale development activities can also uproot communities, who might be forced to migrate in the absence of proper and effective rehabilitation programmes. In official parlance, such groups are known as 'development displacees'. There are also environmental and disaster displacees, which include people forced to move due to environmental hazards such as desertification or deforestation, or natural or human-made disasters, respectively.

Two major issues emerge out of the phenomenon of forced migration: *first*, it is pertinent to secure the basic human rights of the victims of forced migration, and *second*, it is equally important to secure the internal stability of the host state in cases of refugee influx.

MIGRATION AND INTERNATIONAL RESPONSE

Although the international community took up the issue of refugees under the League of Nations, it gained serious momentum only after World War II. Initial attempts were made to tackle the massive refugee crisis in the last years of World War II. They led to the formation of the United Nations Relief and Reconstruction Agency, which functioned from 1944–47. However, with the beginning of the Cold War, there was a need to create a more robust architecture. In 1947, the International Refugee Organization was created to address the problem of refugees in Europe, but it was terminated after the General Assembly of the United Nations created the Office of the United Nations High Commissioner for Refugees (UNHCR), which had the responsibility of providing international protection for refugees, in 1950. The United Nations Convention on the Status of Refugees followed in 1951.

Once granted the status of refugee, a person is entitled to a series of rights. Under the 1951 Convention, states have an obligation to not forcibly send refugees back to their country of origin, which is known as the principle of non-refoulement. However, refugees can be resettled in third countries or voluntary repatriation can be encouraged if conditions in the country of origin improve. Protection must be extended to all categories of refugees without discrimination, and they are to be accorded standard treatment in relation to their right to work, access to healthcare and education, family integration, freedom of movement, and personal freedom with regard to religious and cultural practices. In reality, however, host states impose many restrictions on refugees. The implementation of the legal rights of refugees depends on the will of the host states, many of which believe that the economic, social, and political costs of refugee protection are very high.

A country that hosts and assists a large number of refugees may face certain problems. In many cases, the host countries have limited resources, and in developing countries, especially, where many of their own citizens face abject poverty, the ability of host countries to extend hospitality to outsiders remains a matter of debate. Given their limited resources, the assistance and support they can provide are inadequate. Many countries face persistent socioeconomic problems marked by unemployment and poverty. Under such circumstances, refugees are viewed as an additional burden on these limited resources, a pressure on the infrastructure, and as unwelcome competitors in the job market.

Additionally, the responses of sovereign states to migration are largely shaped by foreign policy priorities and national interests. While states are often bound by international obligations and treaty expectations to accept refugees and provide protection, the realpolitik around humanitarian crises and the subsequent responses of countries are directed by realism. The question of who can or cannot enter is viewed through the prism of national security. Normally, governments led by nationalists or populists often use security as a prime excuse for not opening their doors to migrants or refugees. The idea of defending one's borders and resources or a specific definition of identity becomes paramount. In contemporary times, there is the added apprehension of terrorists sneaking in under the guise of refugees.

In recent years, the growing populist tendencies in the United States or several European countries, especially vis-à-vis the Syrian refugee crisis, have highlighted this trend. Anti-refugee sentiment is spurred by anxieties over cultural disintegration or loss of control of resources, along with fears of a rise in crimes such as smuggling and drugs and arms trafficking. There have been movements against migration in the past as well, for example, the anti-Semitic drives in nineteenth-century Britain and the Nativist movements in the US in the 1920s. On the other hand, when migration is promoted on the basis of religious or ethnic affinity, or a shared identity and values, such security risks are often ignored. The privileges of free entry accorded to Hindus from Pakistan and Bangladesh in India, to Jews from across the world in Israel, and the opening of borders to *pieds-noirs*[1] from Algeria by France are prime examples.

The political economy of international migration also shapes the responses of major powers in significant ways. In a growing number of countries, highly-skilled professionals—in the form of brain labour—have been welcomed, especially to steer the revenue-generating service industries. This trend has become a norm in a globalised world where countries like the United States have become the top destinations for students from India and China. On the other hand, there has also been

[1]The *pieds-noirs* (literally, 'black feet') are an ethno-cultural group of people of French and other European descent who were born in Algeria during the period of French colonial rule from 1830–1962. Many of them left for France after Algeria gained independence in 1962.

a continued export of manual labour from India to countries in the Middle East, which serve to sustain its varied economy.

However, countries often face multiple issues while promoting economic migration. The host country may need to allay its citizens' fears of job losses or potential threat of unemployment. Moreover, the problem of illegal immigrants, especially with regard to the extension of their visas or stay permits for financial reasons, at times compels countries to respond to the migration question in a harsh manner. As a result, domestic immigration laws and policies often have international repercussions. For example, the high numbers of illegal immigrants from Asian countries like India, Pakistan, and Bangladesh in the US and UK have become major irritants in bilateral relations.

In an international system where countries are increasingly looking inward, there has been a growing clamour for international financial assistance for building domestic infrastructure along with aid for refugees, so that both the refugees and the local host community can benefit. The creation of programmes that benefit both the refugees and the local community would mean that refugees would no longer be viewed as burdens; on the contrary, the host community would welcome their presence, especially if the international assistance provided leads to greater developmental work. However, financial assistance always falls short of the actual requirements, and the host community derives little to no benefit from the presence of the refugees. With 'donor fatigue' and the rise in intra-state conflicts in the post-Cold War world, states are more interested in containing mass refugee movements.

This attitude is reflected in the international support for the right of refugees to return (to their own country). In the case of Palestinian refugees, this principle upholds the inalienable right of Palestinians to return to their homeland; this, however, is opposed implacably by Israel, which views it as a ploy to destroy the Jewish state. Interestingly, the right to return might also uphold the refugee's inalienable claim to protection from their national government, thereby encouraging the refugee to return voluntarily to their homeland (which otherwise goes against the principle of non-refoulment). In effect, while this will reduce the number of refugees, it will increase the number of IDPs. In 1998, the 'UN Guiding Principles on Internal Displacement', meant to address the specific needs of IDPs worldwide, was submitted to the Commission of Human Rights. There is no international institutional system in place for the protection of IDPs, and the UN Guiding Principles emphasise that national authorities have the primary duty and responsibility to provide protection and humanitarian assistance to IDPs within their jurisdiction (Principle 3[1]).

Complex humanitarian emergencies call for international humanitarian assistance, and may, in certain cases, make way for humanitarian intervention by other states, especially when the national government is either unable or unwilling to provide protection to its citizens. Forced migration is often associated with rampant human rights violations. Since the notion of 'in-country protection' has gained ground, taking the form of 'safety zones' and 'safe havens' within the state—to prevent mass exodus to other countries—some use of force and intervention has become necessary. This in turn has created a controversy in international politics as the sovereignty of the target state and its domestic jurisdiction is violated. Nevertheless, under the principle of the Responsibility to Protect (or R2P), the international community can initiate measures overriding the target state's objections.

In 2016, the United Nations General Assembly adopted the New York Declaration for Refugees and Migrants that reaffirmed faith in the international refugee regime and sought to protect people on the move in 2016. Consequently, two global compacts—the Global Compact on Refugees and the Global Compact on Safe, Orderly and Regular Migration—were adopted in 2018 by member states to uphold the protection of international refugees and migrants as a shared responsibility, and aid countries affected by such movement. While these are welcome developments in the face of the massive Middle East crisis, these compacts simply reiterate fundamental themes, such as the need for international cooperation in times of disaster and the upholding of state sovereignty in dealing with such issues.

Vulnerable Communities during Forced Migration

In this section, we will focus on the problems faced by two particularly vulnerable communities—women and children—in complex humanitarian crises. While the international refugee regime and the overarching human rights framework provide for the protection of all individuals, the intricate issues faced by these groups require a more concerted response from both international organisations and national governments. In most cases, political issues and the limitations of international statutes limit credible intervention in conflict situations.

Women Refugees

Women face unimaginable difficulties while trying to flee persecution in their countries of origin. The range of problems that refugee women face include physical and sexual violence, such as rape, sexual exploitation, forced impregnation, forced abortions, trafficking, sexual slavery, and prostitution, from fellow refugees, from officials in receiving countries who are supposed to offer protection, from non-state actors engaged in conflict in their countries of origin, and/or from humanitarian aid providers. Women also face the risks of forced abduction, forced recruitment, and abandonment during such conflicts. Women and children are the most vulnerable of all populations in such fraught situations. Often, the violence perpetrated against women is part of a calculated policy of aggression or serves as an instrument of war, to terrorise communities or 'show them their place'.

Across the world, women make up at least half the total number of refugees. In 2015, following the massive humanitarian crises in the Middle East, more than one million men and women sought refuge in Western Europe. By 2016, the number of women and children moving across borders far outnumbered the men in the region. The issue of women's protection and related themes have been absent in the discourses on refugees since World War II. While the 1951 Refugee Convention and its 1967 Protocol provided the overarching framework for the protection of all individuals, they largely accounted for individuals purportedly fleeing the totalitarian regimes of the Communist bloc. Article I of the Refugee Convention includes the possibility of persecution on the basis of race, religion, nationality, membership of a particular social group, and/or political opinion. Gender-based persecution in international conflict or civil wars was, however, not considered. This was also before questions of gender equality and women's rights became a dominant theme in international relations.

In fact, women's issues and the gender dimension of all crises became part of mainstream discourse only in the 1980s, when transnational networks of women's organisations put pressure on the

UNHCR to pursue these topics (Freedman 2010). The realisation of the plight of women worldwide and related issues of violence were first seen in the work of the UN General Assembly in the Convention on the Elimination of All Forms of Discrimination against Women (CEDAW) in 1979. Highlighted as an international bill of rights for women, the Convention sought to tackle discrimination, defined as

> ... any distinction, exclusion or restriction made on the basis of sex which has the effect or purpose of impairing or nullifying the recognition, enjoyment or exercise by women, irrespective of their marital status, on a basis of equality of men and women, of human rights and fundamental freedoms in the political, economic, social, cultural, civil or any other field. (United Nations 1979)

Moreover, during this time, several advocacy groups and arms of the international refugee regime, such as the Women's Commission for Refugee Women and Children, were developed worldwide, which steered the conversation on these issues.

Following these developments and the 1985 World Conference on Women in Nairobi, the UNHCR responded through a series of policy documents—'Policy on Refugee Women' in 1990, 'Guidelines on the Protection of Refugee Women' in 1991, and 'Sexual Violence against Refugees: Guidelines on Prevention and Response' in 1995. These guidelines sought to aid refugee assistance in spaces of conflict and identify the concerns that affected women in particular in such contexts. The policies also sought to include refugee women in the decision-making and planning process for refugee protection. In addition, the UNHCR and other international agencies have also upheld the practice of gender mainstreaming as an effective tool to bring about gender equality in its policies. The UN focusses not only on women and girls, but also tries to inculcate a gender perspective in each of its institutions, highlighting systematic changes in the conduct of men and boys as well.

The UNHCR listed its five commitments to refugee women in 2001, which included:

1. The membership and participation of women and girls in decision-making;
2. Individual registration and documentation as a fundamental practice to ensure the exercise of their basic rights;
3. The gendered management and distribution of food and non-food items in conflict situations;

4. The introduction of vocational and technical training to women to further their employment opportunities and empower them economically;
5. Prioritising the focus on sexual and gender-based violence.

Over the years, there have been multiple declarations and strategies to tackle the problem. The 1993 'Declaration on the Elimination of Violence Against Women' made it obligatory for states to take on the responsibility to protect women, including refugees. In 2008, the UNHCR also developed the *Handbook for the Protection of Women and Girls*, which compiled a list of principles and practices for ensuring gender equality, ways to identify the risks to women and girls, and devised a set of adequate responses and international and regional legal frameworks for the protection of women. The UNHCR's *Action against Sexual- and Gender-Based Violence: An Updated Strategy* (2011) sought to protect victims by working on three areas: data collection and analysis to identify and map the existing risks of sexual and gender-based violence (SGBV); devise effective counters, invest in the capacity building and expertise of UNHCR staff dealing with SGBV, and also allocate sufficient resources; and increase cooperation between different UN agencies, international organisations, and government and non-governmental bodies.

Even then, there have been instances of mass rapes, used as an instrument of war in theatres of conflict such as Bosnia, Uganda, Myanmar, and Congo. More recently, Rohingya women from Myanmar and Yezidi women from Iraq have been coerced into sexual slavery or subjected to sexual violence due to their ethnic and religious identities. In refugee-hit countries such as Lebanon, Syrian refugee women have been compelled into forced prostitution or 'survival sex' to ensure their basic existence. The UNHCR faces multiple challenges, such as inadequate finding, limited access to women and children in conflict situations, a lack of coordination between agencies, and the political pressure to focus on issues considered more urgent, such as food, shelter, or medical care. Moreover, a male perspective predominates in decision-making, which often overlooks the most basic issues faced by women, such as the absence of any documents in their own names or the availability of sanitary products. Most importantly, the ability to take the necessary steps to protect women hinges largely on the cooperation of countries where conflicts originate as well as the receiving countries and other major powers and international organisations. All too often, the politics of extending selective protection acts as one of the biggest obstacles to ensuring the safety of refugee women.

Child Refugees

At times, the security of children is threatened in even 'normal' societies. This is exacerbated in refugee situations. Refugee children are often subject to military attacks, forcibly drafted into military or paramilitary forces and other groups, including enforced labour camps, abducted, physically and/or sexually harassed and exploited, and grossly discriminated against. The security and liberty of refugee children are never guaranteed, and they are usually abandoned, neglected, and subjected to inhumane detention for years. In this section, we will limit our analysis to the problem of child soldiers and international law. We begin by taking cognisance of the limited scope of international humanitarian law in conflicts involving child soldiers, focus on the role of the UNHCR in ensuring the safety of refugee children-turned-warriors, and finally link the problem of child soldiers with the safety and liberty of children as guaranteed under the United Nations Convention on the Rights of the Child (CRC).

No rule in the Geneva Conventions of 1949 or Additional Protocol 1 of 1977 prohibits explicitly the transformation of a child into a combatant. Instead, limitations are placed on the authorities to control this recruitment process. Article 77(2) of Protocol 1 imposes limitations on the freedom to recruit children. Critics, however, have rightly pointed to the insufficiencies of the Protocol, and stressed the need for the adoption of a mandatory formulation that would compel parties to take 'all necessary measures' to prevent child participation in wars. Let us now scrutinise Article 7(2) of Additional Protocol 1, which states:

> The parties to the conflict shall take all feasible measures in order that children who have not obtained the age of fifteen years do not take a direct part in hostilities and, in particular, they shall refrain from recruiting them into their armed forces. In recruiting among persons who have attained the age of fifteen years but who have not attained the age of eighteen years, the parties to the conflict shall endeavour to give priority to those who are oldest.

A careful reading of the wording of the Article is necessary here. The first key word is 'recruit', which is vital to all international and non-international armed conflicts. According to one interpretation, the word 'covers both compulsory and voluntary enrolment, which means that the parties must also refrain from enrolling children under the age of fifteen years of age who volunteer to join the armed forces' (Dutli 1990, 424). This means that the prohibition on recruiting children below the age of fifteen is not restricted to compulsory enrolment policies that go against the will of the children. It also effectively prohibits 'voluntary recruitment', that is, cases where children have been sufficiently indoctrinated into the cult of terror to allow them to choose to join armed groups. The underlying idea is to drive home the point that such indoctrinations are motivated by arbitrary considerations, and run counter to the rights guaranteed to children under the CRC.

Parties to the conflict are required to take 'all feasible measures' to ensure that children below the age of fifteen 'do not take a direct part in hostilities'. Legally speaking, 'feasible' connotes that which is capable of being done. This means that anything that comes under the jurisdiction and control of a party is, *prima facie*, capable of being done. This raises difficulties: for example, it may be feasible for fighting units to adopt a policy of non-recruitment of children. But this does not automatically mean that they will actually adhere to this, or that it will be implemented at all levels. Complexities multiply when forces are dispersed among a population, and where the minors are unusually enthusiastic about participation. The situation is made more difficult when the state remains deliberately neutral to the recruitment of children, or where the existing legal facilities available to the child cannot be used for various reasons. What, then, comprises the protection of the law in such cases?

Apart from Protocol 1 of the Geneva Convention, the legal protection of child soldiers, refugee or otherwise, depends on the interpretation of the relevant Articles of the CRC. Particularly relevant is Article 37, which states that children should not be '... subjected to torture or other cruel, inhuman or degrading treatment or punishment'. Articles 32, 33, 34, 36, and 38 reiterate the need to protect children from economic, sexual, military, and all other forms of exploitation. When these provisions are related to Article 77(2)(c) of Protocol 1, it becomes clear that parties to any conflict are obliged to refrain from the recruitment of children under fifteen into their own forces. Here, 'feasibility' refers to the competence or authority of the parties concerned, and is wide enough to prohibit recruitments under the age of fifteen. It is clear, therefore, that where prohibition cannot be made mandatory, any responsibility arising out of the failure to comply to rules attaches directly to the parties concerned, regardless of any excuse or defence offered.

The formal immunity of children from recruitment and involvement is stronger in the situations of civil war anticipated in Additional Protocol II. Key here is Article 4(3)(c), which provides that 'children who have not attained the age of fifteen years shall neither be recruited in the armed forces or groups nor allowed to take part in hostilities'. The Protocol clearly spells out two distinct obligations of conduct (recruitment and participation in hostilities) and the voluntary and involuntary participation of children below fifteen is prohibited *stricto sensu*. From a strictly legal perspective, however, the Protocol has crucial limitations. Most importantly, it formally binds parties only where the state has ratified the treaty, or where the conflicting party possesses the strength to make 'a valid unilateral declaration of intent to respect the rules of international humanitarian law'. The contradictions and complexities inherent in Protocol II were made clear in many treaties of civil war, especially in the Philippines and El Salvador, where the governments and insurgents expressed their willingness to accept the provisions of Protocol II, but in practice, continued to recruit youth under eighteen into their armed forces and enlisted children in great numbers in paramilitary forces and opposition groups.

It should be noted that the child has long been entitled to both 'General Protection' and 'Special Protections' in a large number of international instruments. The idea is to safeguard the child as a protected person, so that they are 'fully prepared to live an individual life in society, and brought up in the spirit of the ideals proclaimed in the Charter of the United Nations…', as the Preamble to the 1989 CRC envisions. The Fourth Geneva Convention contained important provisions benefitting or protecting children, both as civilians and in their own right. Article 3 deems child soldiers who have surrendered arms or been incapacitated due to sickness, injury, detention, etc., as non-participants, to whom protection should be extended accordingly. Specific protection clauses under the Fourth Geneva Convention obliged states to grant free assistance to children below fifteen [Article 23], required that occupying powers facilitate the proper functioning of institutions for the care of children in occupied territories [Article 50(1)], and reminded states to arrange for food for interned children [Article 81(3)]. The 1977 Additional Protocols expressly confirmed the special protection due to children, with Article 71 of Protocol II confirming the obligation to provide children with the needed care and aid, with special reference to education, family reunion, limitations on recruitment, and temporary evacuation.

The most comprehensive protection to the child, however, comes from the CRC, which embraces the whole spectrum of children's rights with the aim of integrating children within a regime of rights oriented towards individual development and self-fulfilment. Article 38 declares unequivocally that 'State Parties *shall refrain* from recruiting any person who has not attained the age of fifteen years into their armed forces'. Obviously, as we have pointed out, all such provisions will have to be evaluated against existing ground realities; it is not uncommon, for instance, to find children enlisted in the armed forces in Afghanistan, El Salvador, Sri Lanka, Bosnia, Somalia, Ethiopia, Rwanda, Burundi, the Philippines, Nicaragua, Morocco, and Tunisia. The law can function only to the extent that political systems allow it to function, and laws relating to child protection are no exception. Moreover, the problem of the child soldier is a vast discourse, including the demobilisation of child soldiers, child psychology and ecology, detention under international humanitarian law, state programmes and policy interventions, the education and training of ex-combatants, modalities of evacuation, etc.

We will now move on to our concerns about refugee children. While the recruitment of children under the age of fifteen into the armed forces is a violation of international humanitarian law, that law does not discriminate between citizens and refugee children. The primary obligation of states is to ensure that children below fifteen do not 'take a direct part in hostilities'. Article 77 of Additional Protocol I, Article 4 of Protocol II, and Article 38 of the CRC consider 'direct participation' a violation, regardless of whether the child volunteered or was conscripted, whether the conflict was international or a civil war, or whether the forces in question belonged to the government or the opposition. These categories have complicated the legal regulation of the problem of child soldiers. And yet, no specific measures have been included for refugee children, who are often conscripted into existing combatant forces.

Military service is a serious issue for many refugee children and youth. They turn to arms because of a need for physical protection, food, and other care, or out of commitment to a cause (which they may not understand, and yet internalise), social pressure, memories of torture, a desire for revenge, psychological imbalance resulting from unbearable stress, or even pure adventurism. Refugee girls and young women are often deliberately used as volunteers: they serve as messengers, transmit arms, or even work as direct soldiers (as in the case of the LTTE in Sri Lanka).

The onus of protecting the child refugee has primarily fallen on the institutional interventions of the UNHCR. The UNHCR advocates that no refugee, adult, adolescent, or child should be conscripted. Refugees cannot be forced into military service in a country that offers them asylum because that violates their neutral status. As military activities are incompatible with refugee status (in law), any adult taking active part in armed hostilities *ipso facto* loses the UNHCR's protection. The only exception applies to children who take up arms, even if they do so voluntarily, for as minors, they cannot be held responsible for their actions. In 1987, the UNHCR placed the problem of refugee children, especially the practice of forcible recruitment, on the agenda of its Executive Committee. In its report, the Committee condemned forced recruitment and the exposure of refugee children to physical violence, and any other violation of their basic rights. In August 1988, the UNHCR issued Guidelines on Refugee Children, which confirmed its commitment to ensuring that the liberty and safety of refugee children were properly defended. More significantly, it pledged 'to assume direct responsibility in many situations for protecting the safety and liberty of refugee children'. Despite this, however, there has been a marked increase in such recruitment in Africa, Latin America, and Asia, exposing both the inadequacies of the available legal safeguards and the ineffectiveness of the UNHCR in persuading states to extend CRC standards to all children, refugee or otherwise, and invoke the additional Protocols to stop the menace of child recruitment across the world.

Refugee children are particularly vulnerable to threats to physical security because they lack the support of the authorities, have insufficient documents proving their identity, and suffer the effects of the dissolution of their traditional family, clan, and community structures. This is despite the universal principle which states that the personal security of the refugees, particularly refugee children, is an essential element of international protection. Refugees are to be considered an integral part of international civil society, even though their territorial status may remain indeterminate. This indeterminacy should not lead to their exploitation, especially not their forceful conscription into armed bands. Children are in fact in need of maximum protection, and the UNHCR is the only international agency (apart from certain non-governmental organisations and philanthropic associations that work with refugees) which can address the legal predicament of refugee children who are forcefully conscripted into the armed forces. Yet the UNHCR, by its own admission, is a social and humanitarian organisation, with an '*entirely non-political*' mandate. The irony here is that the transformation of refugee children into mercenaries is essentially a political problem, which has to be resolved through political means. Unless accompanied by concrete political prescriptions, the malady of refugee child soldiers can never be resolved through international law alone. Given that, any further refinement of the Additional Protocols can do little to ameliorate the plight of the child soldier.

THE CONTEMPORARY HOST-COUNTRY PREDICAMENT

The twenty-first century has witnessed several mass refugee movements and the consequent humanitarian crises. Currently, more than 79 million people around the world have been forced to leave their homes. A staggering one-third of this population includes refugees. Despite the evolution of the international refugee regime and the attempts of major powers to contain conflicts within their national borders, the international system is facing its greatest refugee crisis since the end of World War II. The problem has affected countries across Europe and Asia, with thousands of refugees and asylum seekers turning up on their shores, after being forced to flee violent conflicts or persecution.

It is also necessary to understand how this issue has played out in the current century. In most instances, we see that despite the presence of international laws, host countries and the international system have failed to respond adequately to the humanitarian crises afflicting the world.

Several states in South Asia have witnessed cross-border population movements. South Asian states are not party to the 1951 UN Convention

Relating to the Status of Refugees. They have no regional convention or domestic legislation guiding their refugee policy either. Hence, the treatment meted out has varied for different categories, or been implemented differently by different states. Security considerations are uppermost in the formulation and implementation of refugee policy in South Asia.

In countries like India, cross-border movements have adversely affected bilateral relations. In fact, the magnitude of the 1971 refugee influx from then East Pakistan led to the war between India and Pakistan, and the subsequent emergence of Bangladesh. While India has hosted refugees from Tibet, Myanmar, Sri Lanka, Bangladesh, and Bhutan, there is now a growing disinterest in, and vocal opposition to, the further entry of refugees among domestic constituents. Demographic changes and ethnic competition, which have led to internal political instability, have caused a gradual change in India's outlook on refugees. The assassination of Indian Prime Minister Rajiv Gandhi in 1991 by the Sri Lankan LTTE resulted in a gradual erosion of sympathy for Tamil refugees from Sri Lanka. There has been intense political turmoil in India's Northeast over the presence of 'foreigners', and humanitarian interests have had to take a backseat in favour of state interests. This shift in attitude is evident in India's current handling of the Rohingya refugee crisis. From taking a sympathetic approach to the crisis in Myanmar in 2012 and providing for the rehabilitation of refugees to counter China's influence in its neighbourhood, India has now framed the Rohingya crisis within a security perspective, shutting its doors to incoming refugees while highlighting the threat of terrorism within its borders.

The Rohingya crisis has become a major issue in South Asia, affecting Bangladesh the most. With a long history of ethnic and religious discrimination, the Rohingyas represent a minority in the Rakhine state of western Myanmar. The anti-Muslim campaign in the region dates back to before the formation of the Union. The military junta has engaged in violent campaigns against the minority Rohingyas over the years, especially in 1978 and 1991, triggering the forced migration of the persecuted community to neighbouring Bangladesh. More importantly, with the citizenship law of 1982, the Rohingyas have been stripped of their rights and privileges as Burmese nationals (Rusconi 2023).

However, since 2011–12, local ethnic groups among the Rohingyas have begun pushing back violently. Foremost among them has been the Arakan Rohingyas Salvation Army, which led attacks on the majority community as well as the national army. This resulted in a massive majoritarian retaliation from the national army and Arakan and Buddhist monks, triggering the most severe phase of the crisis in the region. Amidst allegations of ethnic cleansing and unlawful killings, including rape and other forms of sexual violence directed at women and children, roughly 624,000 Rohingyas have left Myanmar in the last few years (International Crisis Group 2017).

Bangladesh has borne the brunt of this upheaval. Over the years, Bangladesh has opened up its borders to Rohingyas, due to a variety of reasons that include religious affinity and its own history of violent persecution at the hands of Pakistan. Many of the Rohingyas have moved to countries in Southeast Asia, such as Malaysia, Thailand, and Indonesia, where sporadic instances of refoulement—when several boats carrying Rohingya refugees were turned away by the marine forces of these countries—led to international condemnation.

However, since 2015, Bangladesh has been turning away the increasing numbers of migrants, attempting instead to foster a regional settlement of the issue. The large refugee population has created widespread social, financial, and environmental difficulties for Bangladesh, and the previously sympathetic citizens are now gradually viewing the newcomers with hostility. There have been growing insecurities over land, rising crime and unemployment, and a lowering of wages due to the availability of cheap labour. In 2017, the Bangladesh government signed a repatriation agreement with Myanmar, signalling their intention to not host refugees for an indefinite period of time. However, the crisis continues unabated, given that neither international organisations nor major powers has been able to alter the conditions in Myanmar. While the major powers have condemned the situation and initiated soft sanctions against military leaders in Myanmar, not much has changed on the ground. Many states, including Bangladesh, have been seeking a solution that will allow the Rohingyas to return to their homeland, but the majority Buddhists are against this, and the Rohingyas themselves fear higher levels of persecution if they return.

In contemporary times, the humanitarian crisis in the Middle East, especially since 2011 following the Syrian conflict, has had a debilitating impact on both the region and the world. Since the outbreak of the conflict, more than five million Syrians have been forced to leave their country, while another six million have been internally displaced.

The Syrian civil war began after a pro-democracy movement erupted in March 2011, seeking to oust the government of President Bashar al-Assad. The regime retaliated with force, and the country soon descended into a spiral of violence and chaos. The civil war assumed a sectarian character, with the country's majority Sunni population pitting itself against the President's minority Shia Alawite sect. The conflict was exacerbated when the major powers joined the war—Iran and Russia sided with Assad while Sunni-majority countries such as Turkey, Saudi Arabia, Qatar, and Jordan, along with the US, the UK, and France, allied with the rebels. The refugee crisis worsened with the rise of the Islamic State, which fought rebels and other terrorist organisations alike to establish control over vast swathes of land in Iraq and Syria.

While roughly 10 per cent of the refugees made their way to countries in Europe, the forced migration from Syria mostly affected countries such as Lebanon, Jordan, and Turkey, which became the first countries of asylum. In most of these, the constant tide of incoming refugees led to changes in domestic policies on migration, along with massive political turmoil.

Patterns of transnational movement in the region, for commercial and economic purposes, had allowed the free movement of Syrians across Lebanese and Jordanian markets for decades. However, since the refugee crisis peaked in the region, Lebanon has suspended the right to access of Syrians to their labour markets from 2014. Jordan also implemented restrictive entry regulations, disallowing the easy movement of Syrians into their country. Neither country is a signatory to the 1951 Refugee Convention, and both feared disruptions in their demographic identity and threats of sectarian violence if the balance was disrupted. Moreover, the growing pressures on economic and financial resources and infrastructure, a decline in their ability to deliver key services, and growing levels of poverty further pushed Lebanon and Jordan into a defensive position vis-à-vis the incoming refugees. The European Union, on its part, signed a deal with Turkey in 2016 to restrict the flow of refugees into the continent, and several countries such as Serbia, Slovenia, and Austria have closed their borders to refugees. As a result, Syrian refugees have been left in the lurch, heavily dependent on international humanitarian assistance.

Forced migration and displacement remain a challenge for the international community. While the need for compassion and an understanding of the displaced persons' plight and immediate assistance and respect for their human rights are undeniable, not all states are capable of effectively tackling the mass influx of refugees. Hence, states take different approaches to the issue of forced migration and implement differing protective policies towards the refugees, which in turn affects the quality of assistance offered. Syrian refugees seeking shelter in European countries were met with hostility and border control in Balkan states, even as Germany extended an open-door policy to them. These problems cannot be solved by international law alone. While economic development, good governance, and the promotion of human rights may create a regime that can prevent displacement and forced migration, the refugee-generating states have failed to adhere to such norms and are themselves responsible for forced population movements.

20

Human Security

Sulagna Maitra

Introduction

Human security is commonly understood as 'protecting the vital core of all human lives in ways that enhance human freedoms and human fulfilment' (Human Security Unit 2009). The concept is a heuristic tool for a people-centred, whole systems approach to peace and sustainable development. While not an entirely new concept, the human security approach gained momentum in the early 1990s when it was championed by development economists under the aegis of the UNDP Human Development Report (HDP) (Acharya 2014). The altered security environment of the post-Cold War era necessitated a broadening of the notion of security, from 'arms to human development' (UNDP 2014). The significance of this development for international policymaking cannot be overstated. The Cold War period had mostly been dominated by traditional security thinking, which was preoccupied with protecting the nation-state.[1] In contrast, the human security approach viewed both security studies and development through a new lens (Kaldor 2007). Traditionally, security policies focussed on threats posed to states and on military capabilities. Economic aid, humanitarian interventions,

[1] Doctrines such as Mutually Assured Destruction (MAD) and the Domino Theory contributed significantly towards asserting state dominance within the framework of bloc politics.

and development were considered entirely separate, and as the remit of development economics and peace-building. This truncated approach not only ignored the interdependence between the three fields, but was also incapable of assessing how the lack of development could exacerbate insecurities, and vice-versa (ibid.; see also Gomez and Gasper 2013).

The human security approach broadened the scope of security analysis and policy from territorial security to the security of the people, thus allowing for a wide range of new opportunities to tackle contemporary threats in an integrated manner (Gomez and Gasper 2013). Thus, complex, interrelated security threats, both old and new, such as chronic poverty, ethnic violence, human trafficking, climate change, pandemics, international terrorism, and sudden economic fluctuations that are transnational in character and transcend traditional notions of security can be comprehensively dealt with under this approach (Human Security Unit 2009). In the post-Cold War era, several factors necessitated a reconsideration of approaches to conflict, poverty, and state security, and served as catalysts for the emergence of the human security approach. According to Alkire (2003), these factors may be described in three broad categories:

1. Empirical changes in the nature of security threats;
2. Analytical progress in understanding the interconnections among various security threats;
3. Institutional changes, both within security structures and at national and international levels.

These factors will be discussed in greater detail later in the chapter. Critics, however, believe that the human security approach is too broad to provide a suitable framework of analysis (Acharya 2014). Others challenge the newness of the concept and argue that its emphasis on non-traditional elements of security are mirrored in the notion of 'comprehensive security' (Acharya 2001). Scholars like Chandler (2012) note that there is a tendency for broad human security approaches to be sidelined by more focussed doctrines such as the 'responsibility to protect' (R2P), military intervention, and resilience.

This chapter discusses the factors that led to the rise of the human security approach, its analytical dimensions, key principles, and linkages with other policy frameworks such as state security, human rights, human development, humanitarian intervention, and peace-building.

Before proceeding further, however, it is important to compare traditional security with human security in order to appreciate their complementarity as well as inherent differences. Security is a multivocal word that lends itself to ambiguity, both in its scope and definition (Rubenstein 2017). Traditional notions of security stem from realist and neorealist paradigms, which believe that states need to protect their territorial integrity, autonomy, and domestic political order in an anarchic international system (Lahiry 2020). Thus, it encompasses various forms of 'power-based' actions against real or perceived threats and/or interests—diplomatic, economic, and strategic (Rubenstein 2017). The main assumption here is that the nation-state is the primary actor, whose main concern is the protection of citizens and territorial integrity. In contrast, the concept of human security holds within itself the notion of a global society, thereby de-emphasising (but by no means negating) the role of the state. In this approach, security is redefined as the *security of the basic needs of individuals.* Thus, human security is people-centred while traditional or state security is centred round the nation-state. Human security also offers a broader multidimensional vision of security, which includes environmental, personal, community, economic, and other aspects, as opposed to the narrower traditional definition of security.[2]

HUMAN SECURITY: EVOLUTION AND CRITICAL VOICES

The concept of human security has evolved organically in response to the changing geopolitical environment and threats, progress in institutional cooperation, and global governance and analytical advances. In fact, it is important to note that the idea of human security has always existed, even before it came into vogue in the 1990s. Indeed, as early as June 1945, the US Secretary of State, reporting to his government about the San Francisco Conference,[3] said:

---

[2]Often described as *hard security*, that is, strategic, economic, and diplomatic.

[3]Forty-six nations, including the four sponsors, were originally invited to the San Francisco Conference: nations which had declared war on Germany and Japan and had subscribed to the United Nations Declaration (United Nations n.d.[a], [d]).

> The battle of peace has to be fought on two fronts. The first is the security front where victory spells freedom from fear. The second is the economic and social front where victory means freedom from want. Only victory on both fronts can assure the world of an enduring peace. (Stettinius Jr. 1945)

Acharya (2001, 444) points out that while most understandings of human security trace it back to the 1994 Human Development Report, the roots of the concept can be found in the debates on the disarmament-development nexus that took place during the Cold War. The United Nations International Conference on the Relationship Between Disarmament and Development (August–September 1987) acknowledged the interconnectedness between freedom from fear and freedom from want by stating that 'disarmament and development are two pillars on which enduring international peace and security can be built' (United Nations 1987, 1). It further stated:

> Security is an overriding priority for all nations. It is also fundamental for both disarmament and development. Security consists of not only military, but also political, economic, social, humanitarian and human rights and ecological aspects. Enhanced security can, on the one hand, create conditions conducive to disarmament and, on the other, provide the environment and confidence for the successful pursuit of development. (ibid., 3)

Thus, the Conference report broadened the definition of security and linked it squarely to national security and development. Several other independent works, such as the Brandt Commission (1980),[4] the

[4]The Brandt Commission was formally known as the Independent Commission on International Development Issues. It was formed and headed by former German Chancellor Willy Brandt in 1977 at the behest of the President of the World Bank. The Commission comprised of eighteen distinguished politicians and economists from the Global North and South, excluding the Communist bloc. It examined the consequences of changes in international relations and the world economy on less developed countries, with a focus on trade, financial, and monetary issues, as well as problems of food and energy supply (ODI 1980).

Brundtland Report,[5] and the Commission on Global Governance,[6] also helped shift the focus of security analysis from national and state security to security for the people. This is why some scholars, especially from Asia, have questioned the apparent 'newness' of the human security concept, arguing that the focus on a broad range of non-military threats is already part of the long-held framework of comprehensive security (Acharya 2001, 443). Closely related to the concept of human security is the idea of multilateral cooperative security. Both comprehensive and cooperative security have strong Asian roots, especially in Japan and Southeast Asia, and governments in this region often consider them more suitable, contextualised alternatives to the human security policy framework.

Developing countries in Asia are often wary of human security, especially its emphasis on freedom from fear and want. They view it as a liberal Western ploy to impose its values and institutions on non-Western societies (ibid.), preferring the terms 'comprehensive' or 'cooperative' security instead, with their strong Asian roots (Acharya 2014).

The suspicion and unease surrounding human security stems from the important differences in the way the term is conceptualised and operationalised. These different interpretations and the policy emphasis of key actors are described below.

[5]The Brundtland Report is also known as 'Our Common Future: Report of the World Commission on Environment and Development'. The Commission was constituted of twenty-three experts from twenty-two different countries, and was chaired by former Norwegian Prime Minister Gro Harlem Brundtland. The report was presented to the UN in April 1987 and laid the foundation for sustainable development by defining development as a phenomenon that meets the needs of the present without compromising the ability of future generations to meet their own needs (*Down to Earth* 2012).

[6]The Commission on Global Governance was established in 1992. An international commission, it comprised twenty-eight individuals who suggested new ways in which the international community might cooperate to further the agenda of global security (Encyclopaedia Britannica 2013).

CANADA'S APPROACH TO HUMAN SECURITY: AXWORTHY DOCTRINE

A major pillar of the foreign policy strategy of Canada during the 1990s and the early 2000s was the promotion of human security. The country has dedicated funding allocations in its budget and employed explicit human security terminology in its foreign policy doctrine to champion its version of the human security framework (Alkire 2003, 21; Bernard Jr. 2006, 233). Much of the energy behind this foreign policy strategy can be credited to Canada's Minister for Foreign Affairs (1996–2000) Lloyd Axworthy (hence the name 'Axworthy Doctrine'). For Axworthy,

> [H]uman security means safety for people from both violent and non-violent threats.… The litmus test for determining if it is useful to frame an issue in human security terms is the degree to which the safety of people is at risk.... State security and human security are mutually supportive. Building an effective, democratic state that values its own people and protects minorities is a central strategy for promoting human security. (Ross 2001, 76–77)

Thus, the Canadian government criticised the 1994 UNDP Human Development Report for focusing too much on threats associated with underdevelopment, at the expense of 'human insecurity resulting from violent conflict' (Acharya 2001, 445; Ross 2001, 76).

The Canadian approach to human security is distinct, especially when compared to the Asian variations. *First*, Axworthy distinguished between human development measures such as access to reliable employment, education, etc., and human security measures such as protection from crime and violence and threats to human rights (Ross 2001, 76). Canada believed that in its basic form, human security meant freedom from fear (Alkire 2003, 21). 'On the agenda were issues like protecting civilians in armed conflict, reforming sanctions regimes to mitigate negative humanitarian outcomes, bolstering the rights of women in places like Afghanistan, and the necessity of humanitarian intervention to protect against future Rwanda or Srebrenica' (Axworthy 2001). To this end, the Canadian government championed the 'Responsibility to Protect' doctrine by establishing the International Commission on Intervention and State Sovereignty in December 2001 (United Nations n.d.[a]). The Commission published a study on the controversial question: When, if ever, is it appropriate for states to take collective, coercive (even military) action in order to protect civilians within another state that is unable or unwilling to protect its own citizens? This study referred repeatedly to the notion of human security while exploring the responsibilities of the international community of states to protect its own citizens, as well as those in other states.

Second, Axworthy believed that the underlying principles of human security are enshrined in the International Committee of the Red Cross, the Geneva Conventions, the United Nations Charter, and the Universal Declaration of Human Rights (Acharya 2001, 445). It followed, therefore, that human security is neither an alien nor a new concept, but something that has always been at the heart of international cooperation.

Third, the Canadian government advocated more targeted attention to issues such as landmines, the unchecked proliferation of small arms, and inadequate protection for children during armed conflict (Ross 2001, 76). In fact, Canada took on a leadership role at the Ottawa Convention,[7] which sought to stop the production of and destroy stockpiles of anti-personnel landmines in signatory countries. Peace-building was an essential pillar of human security. To this end, Canada viewed NGOs with a proven track record of promoting the human security of people as essential partners (ibid.)

Norway's approach to human security is similar to Canada's, in that it prioritises freedom from fear (Alkire 2003, 21). Both nations have argued that the concept of human security adds the greatest value when it complements existing international agendas on the promotion of national security, human rights, and human development. To this end, Norway and Canada founded the Human Security Network (1999), an association of twelve countries who have set themselves the task of promoting human security as a feature of national and international policies, in particular within the United Nations and in cooperation with academia and civil society (UNISDR 2016).

---

[7]The full name is Convention on the Prohibition of the Use, Stockpiling, Production and Transfer of Anti-Personnel Mines and on Their Destruction, 18 September 1997.

ASIAN ROOTS OF HUMAN SECURITY

Human security has very strong roots in Asia. As has been acknowledged, the UNDP 'Human Development Report' of 1994 was the result of the scholarship of Pakistani economist Mahbub ul Haq (Acharya 2001, 444, 2014, 449). Haq outlined a proposal for a human security policy framework that would seek:

1. *Developmentally*: sustainability, equity of opportunities, and global justice through a major restructuring of the world's income, consumption, and lifestyle patterns.
2. *Militarily*: reducing arms expenditure, stopping arms transfers, eliminating arms export subsidies, restraining employment in defence industries, and converting military aid to economic aid.
3. *North-South restructuring*: removal of trade barriers and equitable access to global markets for poor countries, financial compensation from rich countries for bad economic conduct, and environmental and economic damages and controls.
4. *Institutionally*: restructuring of global governance institutions like the World Bank, the IMF, and the UN, with greater focus on economic development, democratisation, and devolution of power, and a resuscitated veto-less Economic Security Council that would be the highest decision-making authority 'to deal with all issues confronting humanity'.
5. The evolution of a *global civil society*, with grassroots-level participation. (Bajpai 2000)

Haq's proposal for altering the security paradigm was far-reaching, and focussed equally on global restructuring, justice, and freedom from fear and freedom from want.

Asian governments have tended to adopt a needs-oriented human security approach that is more conducive to preserving the regime status quo (Acharya 2001, 448). The Japanese government, for example, emphasises that it *does not prioritise* freedom from fear over freedom from want, but holds them as dual objectives of human security (Alkire 2003, 21). Many countries in Asia and the Pacific have opted for this broader conceptualisation of human security, which is akin to comprehensive security with a limited focus on human rights and humanitarian intervention. Acharya (2001, 448) states that the human needs aspect of human security became particularly significant in the aftermath of the economic crises which drastically increased poverty levels, undermined social and political stability, and exacerbated ethnic and inter-state tensions. These crises also underscored the need for social safety nets to protect vulnerable populations as well as states during an economic downturn.

Another important aspect of the Asian understanding of human security is its emphasis on contextualising the human security approach to ensure cultural appropriateness. Governments in Asia argue that the East's traditional understanding of the cultural and political specificities of security should be taken into account while operationalising human security in these contexts. Further, these governments argue for a non-selective implementation of human rights, that is, political rights should be favoured over economic and social rights while advocating human rights. Taken together, the Eastern understanding of human security is quite distinct from the Canadian version, which, with its emphasis on freedom from fear, is viewed as the Western/liberal version of the concept.

However, Acharya (2001, 448) and Bajpai (2000, 35) warn us against a preoccupation with the differences between these conceptualisations for, *first*, a comparison between the two approaches shows that the similarities outweigh the differences, and *second*, there are equally significant familial differences within the 'Eastern' and 'Western' approaches to human security.

At this point, it is imperative to note some of the significant contributions that Asia has made to human security. Former Japanese Prime Minister Keizō Obuchi was one of the chief architects of the Japanese conceptualisation of human security. While Asia was recovering from a catastrophic financial crisis, as the then Foreign Minister of Japan, Obuchi opined that 'human beings should be able to lead lives of creativity, without having their survival threatened or their dignity impaired' (Obuchi 1998). He thus squarely rooted the concept of human security at the individual level, rather than pinning it at the state level. Years later, Nobel Laureate Amartya Sen built on Obuchi's conceptualisation and highlighted the contemporary challenges to (*a*) security of survival, that is, health, peace, and tolerance; (*b*) daily life and quality of living; (*c*) information and ecology; and (*d*) dignity, equity, and solidarity (Sen 2000). Sen called upon global institutions and states to go beyond current financial and monetary structures to create a comprehensive development framework that would provide avenues to further strengthen human security. He regarded the United Nations as central to this enterprise (ibid.).

Japan continues to champion this notion of human security by advocating for a 'human-centred 21st Century' (Ministry of Foreign Affairs of Japan 2009). Along with several bilateral and multilateral initiatives at the regional and global levels, the Japanese government helped establish the Friends of Human Security group in 2006 following the World Summit Outcome 2005. This group has made major contributions to mainstreaming human security and has more than eighty-six countries and sixteen organisations as members. Similarly, in March 1999, Japan delivered on Prime Minister Obuchi's commitment to establish The Trust Fund for Human Security under the aegis of the United Nations with an initial endowment of ¥500 million. Japan's contribution to this Fund has grown steadily, exceeding ¥39 billion in the mid-2000s. The Trust Fund is thus well placed to achieve its objectives of realising human security while applying the protection and empowerment approaches (ibid.).

As a final note, we need to mention Mahatma Gandhi's holistic notion of security. Gandhi saw security as a natural corollary of peace and development. According to his teachings, human relations are common across communities and the individual is part of a global society. It would be fallacious to separate the different notions of security. Instead, Gandhi proposed an interwoven conceptualisation of security, wherein all discrimination on the basis of race, gender, and caste can be eradicated through global education and international peace-building. Development and peace were as crucial to individual security as they are to state security. Thus, Gandhi's security strategy in international affairs may be understood in terms of three concentric circles, starting with the *immediate sphere* (neighbours) and extending outwards to the *middle sphere* (other developing countries and regions such as Latin America), and then finally onwards to the *outer sphere* (developed countries) (Gangal n.d.).

Having discussed the meaning, scope, and interpretations of human security, we can now explore the linkages between human security and related approaches such as human rights, development, and humanitarian intervention.

POST-COLD WAR CATALYSTS OF HUMAN SECURITY APPROACH

The 1994 UNDP 'Human Development Report' noted that the post-Cold War global society was characterised by

> unprecedented human progress and unspeakable human misery, of humanity's advance on several fronts mixed with humanity's retreat on several others, of a breath-taking globalization of prosperity side by side with a depressing globalization of poverty. As is so common in human affairs, nothing is simple and nothing is settled for ever. The progress should reassure humankind about its capacity to engineer change, and the present scale of human deprivation should continue to challenge humankind to design a much better world order.

Thus, not only are security threats persistent (and in some cases, unprecedented), but the opportunities to counter these threats have also increased due to advances in science and technology. Human insecurities today are thus largely the function of a mismatch between security threats and appropriate response mechanisms (Alkire 2003). These security challenges and opportunities are presented below.

Empirically Observable Changes

Empirically observable changes include the rising threats and opportunities that constitute the landscape of human insecurity. Several global events—both during and after the Cold War—served as catalysts for the emergence of the human security approach. To begin with, civilians became the direct targets in post-Cold War conflicts, most of which were intra-state. Civilian casualties increased from 5 per cent in the early 1900s to about 90 per cent towards the end of the twentieth century (Kaldor 1999; UNDP 1998). Not everyone accepts this percentage, however, and the number of deaths caused by contemporary conflicts remains contested (Roberts 2010). However, there is little disagreement over the fact that the nature of conflicts changed after the Cold War, and in the 'new wars', belligerent parties used extremist politics of fear and hatred, mobilising the people and eventually leading to mass expulsions, genocide, and intimidation (Kaldor 2007). According to the Uppsala Conflict Database (2016), which mapped the number of battle-related deaths[8] by type of conflict for the period 1989–2015, the number of deaths spiked in the immediate aftermath of the Cold War and has increased in recent years, and the number of deaths from intra-state or internationalised intra-state conflicts is higher than from inter-state conflicts.

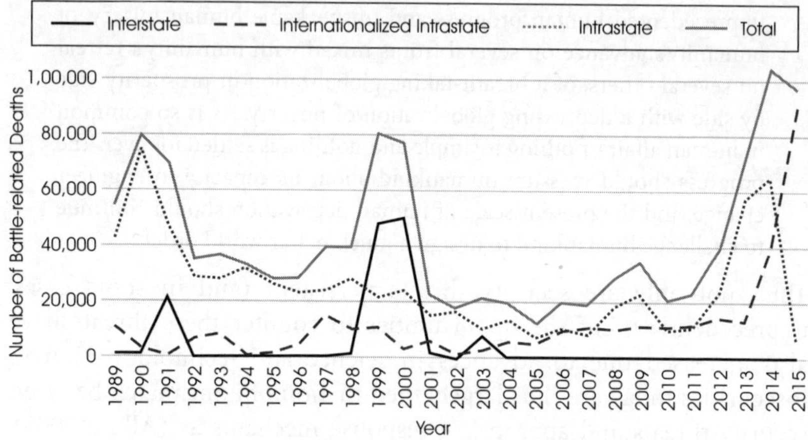

Fig. 20.1: Battle Related Deaths 1989–2015

Source: Uppsala Conflict Database, 2016.

The end of the Cold War also meant that many countries, such as Afghanistan and Vietnam, lost their strategic relevance as battlefields for proxy wars waged between the major powers. As material and political support to militia factions dwindled in these areas, the combatants targeted civilians and humanitarian relief as resources to sustain the war (Anderson 1999). Thus, in these new wars, civilian life, livelihood, and property were not just collateral damage, but became the intended targets of conflict.

> The tendency to avoid battle and to direct most violence against civilians is evidenced by the dramatic increase in the ratio of civilian to military casualties. At the beginning of the 20th century, 85–90 per cent of the casualties in war were military. In World War II, approximately half of all war deaths were civilians. By the late 1990s,

[8]Counted as battle-related deaths is the use of armed force between warring parties in a conflict dyad, be it state-based or non-state, resulting in deaths. For further details, see the Uppsala Conflict Data Program.

> the proportions of a hundred years ago have been almost exactly reversed, so that nowadays approximately 80 per cent of all casualties in wars are civilian. (Kaldor 1999, 106)

Second, population pressure, together with an increase in consumerism, contributed to environmental degradation, a scarcity of basic resources such as water, and induced mass migration. The 1994 Human Development Report noted that by 2050, the world population would have doubled and the global economy would have quadrupled. Food production, energy, and infrastructure would have to grow accordingly to satisfy the needs of this ever-growing population. Eventually, the interrelationship between environmental scarcity and social cohesion became the focus of attention for many scholars such as Homer-Dixon (1994), who studied the impact that the severe depletion of renewable resources and environmental degradation had in exacerbating violent conflicts.

Third, the 1973 Oil Shock showed that non-military factors such as oil[9] could threaten state security and stability. There were a series of energy crises between 1967 and 1979, caused by the instability in the Middle East, primarily the Arab-Israel conflict. The most significant was the 1973 oil shock, when the Arab oil-producing countries (OPEC) decided to impose an embargo on the sale of oil upon the US and its allies who had supported Israel against Egypt and Syria in the Yom Kippur War. The Western industrialised economies were heavily dependent on oil from the Middle East for their energy source. Thus, the embargo did not only cause an energy crisis, but it also led to inflation and economic recession in these economies. The price of crude oil increased from $3 to $12 within a short period (Macalister 2011). The UK experienced an inflation of more than 24 per cent, and there were even talks of using leftover wartime coupons for rationing oil (ibid.). The economic instability led in turn to political instability. Governments were forced to

---

[9]The Arab oil-producing countries in the Middle East decided to boycott the US and the West in retaliation for their support to Israel in the Yom Kippur War against Egypt. The increase in the price of oil, one of the main energy sources, adversely affected every other aspect of the economy, such as transportation, food production, and manufacturing. The inflation and economic recession caused a deterioration in social relations and political instability. Labour unions demanded an increase in wages to keep up with rising prices and the governments had to bail out several industries (Macalister 2011).

reconsider their energy policies and seek ways to end their dependence on the Middle East. Inadvertently, the crisis of 1973 spurred discussions on the negative impact that non-renewable energy resources had on climate change, and the need for cleaner energy sources like wind and solar power.

Fourth, the Human Development Report (1994) noted that threats to human security were no longer confined to the personal, local, or national. Instead, they had become global. Drugs, health issues such as HIV/AIDS, terrorism, pollution, nuclear proliferation, global poverty, and environmental degradation transcend national and political boundaries.

> Their grim consequences travel the world. The same speed that has helped unify the world has also brought many problems to our doorsteps with devastating suddenness. Drug dealers can lauder money rapidly through many countries—in a fraction of the time it takes their victims to detoxify. And terrorists operating from a remote safe haven can destroy life on a distant continent. (UNDP 1994)

Along with threats to human security, the early 1990s also offered opportunities to scholars to seek alternative approaches to security. *First*, the Cold War was over, and with it, the obsessive need to focus on bloc politics. *Second*, most colonised nations had won their independence, and the United Nations membership now stood at 184 countries. Many of these nations sought to embark on a path of nation-building and international politics based on self-determination, national independence, and sovereignty and territorial integrity; opposition to apartheid; non-adherence to multilateral military pacts, struggles against imperialism, colonialism, neo-colonialism, racism, foreign occupation and domination; disarmament; peaceful coexistence, and strengthening of the United Nations; democratisation of international relations; restructuring of the international economic system; and international cooperation on an equal footing (GOI 2012). These countries sought an alternative approach to economic growth and political stability, instead of following the modernisation process of the West. Hence, it is not surprising that the human security approach took root among development economists in the Global South.

Second, the quality of life had improved over the past decades and progress in science and technology made it possible to conceive of a world where everyone enjoys security of life and livelihood. Human development indicators, such as life expectancy, infant mortality, and educational attainment, had improved across countries. By 1992, it was estimated that 60 per cent of people around the world were enjoying satisfactory human development levels (as compared to only 25 per cent in the 1960s) (UNDP 1994).

These quantifiable changes in the political, security, and socioeconomic landscape were accompanied by analytical advances and development in institutional cooperation, which added greater impetus to the growth of the human security approach.

Analytical Advances

This refers to developments in theoretical, qualitative, and quantitative analyses that highlight the causal relationships and interdependencies between various security threats, and form the basis of recommendations and policy action (Alkire 2003). The altered security environment of the 1990s encouraged scholarship on environmental scarcity and violence, humanitarian intervention, and the responsibility to protect, linking relief with development and critical geopolitics. The benefits of a joint analysis of the interrelated variables of human security (such as famine and voice, poverty and conflict) are now clearly recognised (ibid.).

International Cooperation

An elaboration of common goals, collaboration among global development agencies and national governments, public-private partnerships, global summits on human rights, mobilisation of a global civil society in order to protect environmental, social, economic, and political rights, and greater civil-military cooperation in humanitarian interventions were part of a post-Cold War response to an altered security environment. While these responses were often reflexive reactions to impending crises,[10] they established the framework of a collective comprehensive action to tackle post-Cold War human insecurities.

---

[10] For example, comprehensive humanitarian interventions in Rwanda and Bosnia, and the World Bank's Structural Adjustment Programmes (SAPs) in Southeast Asia and Latin America.

Human Security, Human Rights, Development, and Humanitarian Intervention

Figure 20.2 illustrates the linkages between human security, human rights, and development and humanitarian interventions and shows how protection and empowerment work as key strategic pillars in operationalising human security.

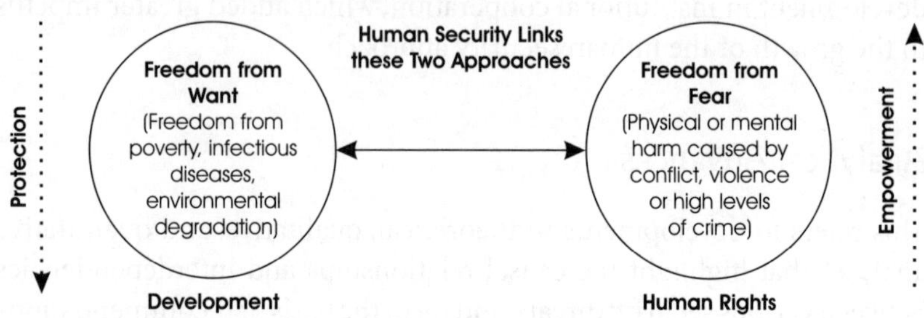

Fig. 20.2: Human Security, Human Rights, Development and Humanitarian Interventions

Source: Author.

The figure also shows that the human security approach provides the link between human rights, development, peace, and humanitarian interventions. Peace-building assures freedom from fear by offering protection from conflict, violence, and crime. Poverty, a vulnerability to infectious diseases, and the threats posed by environmental degradation are mitigated through development, which ensures freedom from want. Human dignity is assured through the protection of basic human rights and, where necessary, humanitarian interventions.

Protection and empowerment may be regarded as the two important cornerstones for achieving the goal of human security (Human Security Unit 2009). The Directorate General of the European Commission for Humanitarian Action and Civil Protection, the ICRC, and the Inter-Agency Standing Committee understand protection as 'all activities aimed at ensuring full respect for the rights of the individual in accordance with the letter and spirit of the relevant bodies of law (i.e. human rights law, international humanitarian law and refugee law)' (DG ECHO 2016). That is, it is the strategies put in place by states, international agencies, NGOs, and the private sector to shield people from harm (CHS 2003). According to the UN Charter and General Assembly Resolution

A/RES/46/182 on 'Strengthening of the Coordination of Humanitarian Emergency Assistance of the United Nations', the primary responsibility of providing protection to citizens lies with the state. It is the main responsibility of each state to take care of victims of natural disasters and other emergencies occurring on its territory. Hence, it has to take a primary role in the initiation, organisation, coordination, and implementation of humanitarian assistance within its territory.

Further, states in need of humanitarian assistance are called upon to facilitate the work of implementing such assistance, in particular the supply of food, medicines, shelter, and healthcare, for which access to victims is essential. Other states in close proximity to the site of the emergency are urged to participate closely in international efforts, with a view to facilitating, to the extent possible, the transit of humanitarian assistance.

Empowerment, on the other hand,

> is the process of enhancing the capacity of individuals or groups to make choices and to transform those choices into desired actions and outcomes. Central to this process are actions which both build individual and collective assets, and improve the efficiency and fairness of the organizational and institutional context which govern the use of these assets. (World Bank 2007)

Empowerment is essentially a bottom-up approach aimed at developing the capacities of individuals and communities to make informed choices and act on their own behalf (Human Security Unit 2009).

Protection and empowerment are mutually reinforcing strategies required to achieve human security and ensure development, peace, and human dignity.

Human Security: Key Characteristics

As discussed above, the term 'human security' has evolved to capture a people-centric approach to security, development, and peace-building. Over the years, however, scholars have defined human security in different ways. Kaldor (2007) mentions two main elements to the concept of human security: freedom from fear and freedom from want. Acharya (2001, 442) traces the meaning and evolution of human security and points to its geo-strategic roots, suggesting a distinction between the

'Eastern' and 'Western' understandings of the term that (can) lead to serious communication gaps, controversy, and suspicion in multilateral settings. We will first list the different dimensions of human security, categorised under 'freedom from fear' and 'freedom from want'.

Dimensions of Human Security: Freedom from Fear

'Freedom from fear' refers to the personal, community, and political securities that safeguard a person from threats to their life, liberty, and freedom of expression.

Personal Security This involves protecting people from physical violence—from states, individuals, sub-state actors, domestic abuse, and predatory adults. The Human Development Report notes that 'perhaps no other aspect of human security is so vital for people as their security from physical violence. In poor nations and rich, human life is increasingly threatened by sudden, unpredictable violence' (UNDP 1994, 30). Personal security may be endangered by threats from the state (physical torture), threats from other states (war), threats from groups of people (ethnic tension), threats from gangs or individuals (crime, street violence), gender-based violence (rape, domestic violence), and threats directed against children.

Community Security This refers to protection from loss of traditional relationships and values. Most people derive sustenance, support, and security from their membership of a social group, such as the family, an organisation, or an ethnic or religious group. These groups define a person's social network, offer practical and emotional support, and even form a part of a person's social identity. For example, in many cultures the extended family system provides social or emotional succour to struggling family members. Religious or ethnic groups constitute social capital that offer sustenance and psychosocial support in the aftermath of a family or social crisis. However, it needs to be noted that at times, communities and traditional groups may perpetuate rituals or practices that are detrimental to an individual's well-being. Oppressive practices such as slave or bonded labour, female genital mutilation, and discriminations related to caste and gender are the best-known examples of harmful traditional practices.

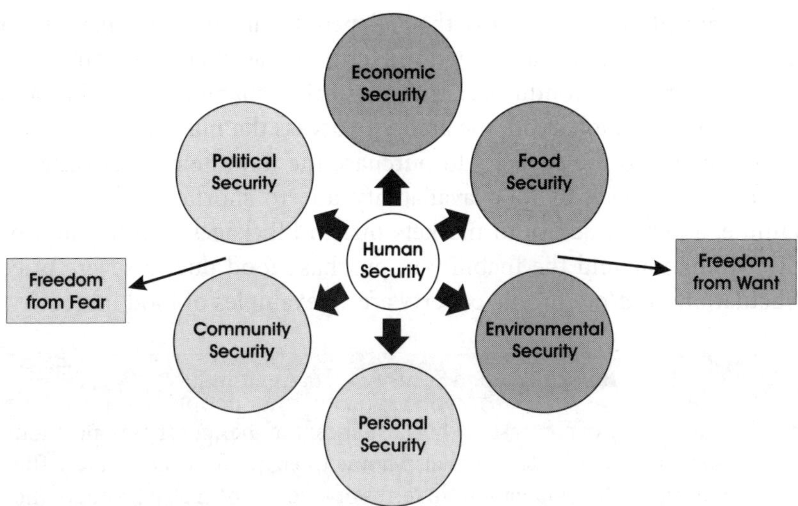

Fig. 20.3: Dimensions of Human Security

Source: UNDP 1994.

Political Security This means ensuring a political environment that protects an individual's basic human rights and restricts state control over freedom of expression, information, and the flow of ideas. State persecution in response to a citizen's political ideology and human rights violations are particular threats to political security.

Dimensions of Human Security: Freedom from Want

This entails protecting an individual's basic needs, such as food, water, and shelter. Freedom from want involves the following dimensions of security.

Economic Security This refers to an assured basic income for individuals, usually from productive, remunerative work. It also includes publicly financed safety nets such as social welfare in case remunerative work is not available. The oil crisis during the 1970s, the Asian financial crisis of 1997, and the recent recession of 2011 are all examples of major economic crises that led to a loss of jobs and livelihoods, and exposed people to economic insecurity.

Food Security This means that all people, at all times, have both physical and economic access to food for basic sustenance. This includes three interrelated conditions: the physical availability of edible and culturally acceptable food; the ability to access the markets where food is available; and the capacity to purchase the food items necessary for sustenance. A lack of food availability due to shortages, drought, or famine, a lack of access to markets due to blockages, conflict, and/or discrimination, and the inability to purchase food due to severe price fluctuations and/or chronic poverty are all examples of food insecurity.

Box 20.1: Food Security Facts about India

India is a country of contrasts. While 22 per cent of the country's population lives below the poverty line, it is also home to eighty-four billionaires. The top 1 per cent of the population (in terms of income) own 50 per cent of the country's wealth. India is the world's second-largest food producer and also the country with the second largest number of undernourished people.

Since its independence, India has made significant progress in eradicating hunger and undernourishment. The Global Hunger Index (2016) captured this positive trend under four key categories: proportion of the population that is undernourished, prevalence of wasting in children below the age of five, prevalence of stunting below the age of five, and under-five mortality rate.

Currently 15.2 per cent of the Indian population is undernourished, that is, they do not receive adequate calories per day. Around 38.7 per cent of children below the age of five are stunted and 15.1 per cent are wasted (low weight for height). Around 4.8 per cent of children die before reaching the age of five.

The Government of India enacted the National Food Security Act (NFSA), 2013 to 'provide for food and nutritional security by ensuring access to adequate quantity and quality of food at affordable prices to people to live a life with dignity'.

Source: Welt Hunger Hilfe, et a. 2016.

Health Security This refers to the ability to maintain one's physical and mental well-being. A robust health service accessible to all is vital for achieving health security. In developing countries, infectious diseases and parasites are a major cause of deaths. In developed countries, diseases related to lifestyles, such as obesity, heart conditions, and diabetes, are more common.

People living in poverty usually have lower heath security. Poverty often implies a lack of proper nutrition, unsatisfactory or unhealthy living conditions, lack of access to proper water and sanitation, greater exposure to the elements (extreme heat or cold), and a lack of access to proper healthcare.

Health security also depends on a country's infrastructure and governance policies concerning the provision of suitable healthcare for all its citizens. For example, Pakistan has launched Sehat Card, a national health programme ensuring that identified underprivileged citizens across the country are given access to healthcare in a swift and dignified manner, with no financial obligations (Rifaq 2017).

Several deadly diseases continue to threaten health security. Cancer, HIV/AIDs, the Zika virus, and Ebola are some that have reached epidemic proportions in recent years.

Box 20.2: The Ebola Virus in West Africa (2014)

The Ebola virus causes an acute, serious illness which is often fatal if left untreated. Ebola virus disease (EVD) first appeared in 1976 in two simultaneous outbreaks, one in what is now Nzara, South Sudan, and the other in Yambuku, Democratic Republic of Congo. The latter occurred in a village near the Ebola River, from which the disease takes its name.

The outbreak that took place in West Africa in March 2014 was the largest and most complex Ebola outbreak since the virus was first discovered in 1976, with the greatest number of fatalities. The outbreak began in Guinea and then spread across land borders to Sierra Leone and Liberia, by air to Nigeria and the USA, and by land to Senegal and Mali.

The most severely affected countries—Guinea, Liberia, and Sierra Leone—had very weak health systems, lacked human and infrastructural resources, and had recently emerged from long periods of conflict and instability. On 8 August 2014, the WHO Director-General declared the West Africa outbreak a Public Health Emergency of International Concern under the International Health Regulations (2005).

Source: World Health Organization.

Environmental Security This has various dimensions:

- Protecting people from the ravages of nature, such as a tsunami or an earthquake.

- Protecting nature from human-induced destruction, such as soil erosion that results from deforestation, contamination caused by oil spills, etc.
- Protecting the environment from long-term deterioration, climate change, and loss of biodiversity that results from anthropogenic activities. The nuclear disaster in Fukushima in 2011, the BP oil spill, and the rising sea levels in the Bay of Bengal due to climate change are all cases in point.

SCOPE OF HUMAN SECURITY AND ITS CHARACTERISTICS

After a review of the contemporary literature, Alkire (2003, 2) stated: 'Human security take [*sic*] its shape from the human being: the vital core that is to be protected. Institutions that undertake to protect human security will not be able to promote every aspect of human well-being. But at very least they must protect this core of people's lives.' This definition helps us to identify the five key elements that define the scope of human security.

The *first* element is *safeguarding*, which means that human security has a deliberately protective nature (ibid., 2). It recognises that people are constantly under threat from events and occurrences beyond their control. However, the impact of these threats or hazards can be minimised through systematic, institutionalised protection. Thus, safeguarding human security involves (*i*) the identification of critical and pervasive threats; (*ii*) wherever possible, taking preventive measures so that the threat does not materialise; (*iii*) mitigation of the threat through a swift response, in order to minimise damages; and (*iv*) responding to the threat to enable the people affected to survive with dignity. A crucial element in safeguarding people from threats is respect for human security (ibid., 3). Thus, human security needs to be mainstreamed in all interventions so that individuals, states, or corporations do not unwittingly undermine it while pursuing other policy objectives.

The *second* important element is the notion of *the vital core*, which is a 'rudimentary but multidimensional set of human rights and human freedoms based in practical reason' (Alkire 2003, 8). Thus, it constitutes freedom from both fear and want. A focus on the vital core conveys that human security is restricted in its purview. It seeks to protect only what may be defined as the fundamental human rights, basic capabilities, and absolute needs of human beings; in other words, survival, livelihood, and basic dignity. Here Alkire (ibid., 3) foresees a tension when organisations, states, or people themselves attempt to rank what constitutes this *vital core*. This tension within, and challenges faced in, defining human security will be dealt with in the next section.

The *third* important attribute is that it pertains to *all human lives*, that is, human security is people-centred, universal, and non-discriminatory. *Fourth*, human security is concerned with *critical and pervasive threats* that pose a risk to the core activities and functions of human lives. These threats can refer to violence during a conflict, soil degradation, or genocide, which affect human lives directly, or indirect threats such as disproportionate spending on the military, which reduces the money available for public services. The threats can also be sudden, such as an economic shock, or protracted, such as chronic poverty or climate change. The final attribute of human security has to do with its relationship with *long-term human fulfilment*. It is acknowledged that human security is limited in scope, and therefore insufficient for all-round human fulfilment. However, the processes of human security should be consistent with ongoing human development. Governance, participation, transparency, capacity building, and institution building should be arranged in a manner that is consistent with human security, while also facilitating long-term human fulfilment.

Simply put, 'human security brings together the human elements of security, rights and development' (Human Security Unit 2009). It will now be easy to identify the distinctive characteristics of human security.

1. *Human security is people-centred*. People are at the centre of analysis; human security is concerned with how people live, the opportunities they have to earn their livelihoods, the extent to which they can freely exercise their choices, and whether they live in peace or under the threat of violence. The approach identifies a diverse range of conditions under which human life and livelihood are threatened.
2. *Human security is multisectoral and interdependent*. In order to understand the full range of insecurities that threaten the lives and livelihoods of human beings, the human security approach looks to different sectors: food, health, environment, personal aspects, community, and political security, and emphasises the

interconnectedness of insecurities in these different sectors in two ways (Human Security Unit 2009). *First*, a domino effect between the different sectors leads to each threat feeding off the others. For example, political insecurity resulting from violent conflict or war can exacerbate economic (poverty), environmental (degradation), and social (loss of community) insecurities. *Second*, there is a spatial interconnectedness between the insecurities. Threats to human security within an area can spread across regions to the nation, and even jeopardise international insecurity.

3. *Human security is comprehensive.* Human security needs to be comprehensive in its policymaking. Since this approach concerns itself with a wide range of threats to people, it cannot tackle them in isolation. Its response to insecurities thus have to be comprehensive and multisectoral in nature.
4. *Human security is universal and context-specific.* The concern of human security is universal, that is, human security concerns itself with all people everywhere, irrespective of location, gender, race, religion, ethnicity, or economic background. At the same time, the approach recognises that insecurities vary across time and space. Thus, it is vital that the solutions offered be context- and actor-specific; in other words, they should be tailored to the needs of people at any given time and location.
5. *Human security is prevention-oriented.* Human security is largely concerned with addressing the root causes of the risks that threaten human survival. It is usually easier and less expensive to tackle potential threats early, rather than intervening after disaster strikes. However, the human security approach does offer protection and ensures human dignity in the context of a crisis.

HUMAN SECURITY: CRITIQUE

Alkire (2003, 22) and Acharya (2014, 451) have summarised the critical voices in the literature on human security.

1. Many scholars have argued that human security is too broad and too vague a concept. Roland Paris (2001, 95) said: 'Human

security is like sustainable development—everyone is for it, but few people have a clear idea of what it means.' Alkire, however, believes that this very vagueness helps to bind together the otherwise disparate understandings of the term.

2. Scholars such as Macfarlane and Khong (2006) argue that the human security approach may do more harm than good, as the international community rarely has the wherewithal or the political will to achieve the lofty goals of human security.
3. Scholars reviewing the human security approach and the literature in general complain that in practice, the specific threats to security under consideration are often selected arbitrarily. This at times makes human security analysis incoherent.
4. Scholars such as Buzan and Little (2001) and realist thinkers within IR criticise the human security approach for neglecting the role of the state. They argue that as the state is the primary provider of security, its survival is key to ensuring the protection of individuals. Human security and traditional state security need not always be in conflict with one another. However, the human security approach does seek to protect individuals in instances where an otherwise secure state does not fulfil its obligation to protect its own citizens.

Conclusion

The human security approach introduced a paradigm shift in security studies within IR. While debates on its meaning and scope continue, there is a general acceptance that the traditional, narrow focus of security is no longer sufficient to analytically capture the transnational, complex threats of the twenty-first century. This approach provides a useful framework to conceptually link the diverse policy aspects of peace-building, development, and human rights by placing human lives at the centre of its analysis. However, it should be noted that the terrorist attacks of 11 September 2001 and the stabilisation agenda have proven detrimental to human security analysis, as the focus has now shifted back to the traditional narrow concept of state-centred security.

21

The United Nations

Anindya Jyoti Majumdar

The United Nations Organization (UNO), popularly known as the United Nations (UN), was established at the end of World War II (1939–45) on 24 October 1945 with its headquarters in New York City. As a global political institution with universal membership and multifarious activities and programmes aimed towards maintaining world peace and the betterment of life, the UN has become a crucial part of contemporary international relations. The UN was set up by the states after the League of Nations, established after World War I (1914–1918), failed to evolve into an effective world organisation. This chapter will discuss the origin of the UN, its structures, and major organs, assess the role it plays in contemporary international politics, and explain the need for reforms in the organisation.

The Origin

Certain favourable trends and developments aimed at the establishment of a global association for peace influenced the pattern of international politics in the nineteenth century. The Congress of Vienna, held after the defeat of Napoleon in 1815, created a system of collective diplomatic consultation through the Concert of Europe. With the major powers of the day—Austria, Prussia, Russia, and the United Kingdom—as its members, the Concert took upon itself the responsibility of preventing or limiting potential armed conflicts. Later, France was admitted to the group as well. Representatives held regular meetings until World War I. The notion of major powers being the self-appointed guardians of global harmony, primarily responsible for international peace and security, stemmed from such developments. In the UN, the Security Council, which comprises five permanent members who have veto power (along with a few non-permanent elected members), reflects this spirit.

Towards the end of the nineteenth century, attempts were made to clarify and codify international law and establish common codes of behaviour on the basis of a broad-based agreement of members in the international community. The Hague Peace Conferences (the first of which was held in 1899 with twenty-six states and the second in 1907 with forty-four states; the third, to be held in 1915, was cancelled because of World War I) created the possibility for an assembly of states (and not just the major powers), which would debate and discuss issues of common concern. The trend culminated in the UN General Assembly; a member of the UN is, *ipso facto*, a member of the General Assembly.

In the latter half of the nineteenth century, a growing spirit of functional cooperation led to the emergence of international institutions geared towards mutual benefit. *Ad hoc* arrangements were sought to be replaced by permanent institutions. For example, the Universal Postal Union was introduced in 1874, and continues to function even today. These institutions provided the basic structure of an international organisation, with their permanent offices and a budget supported by the members. This structure is followed by all global organisations: in the UN, the permanent office is the Secretariat under the Secretary-general, who is the chief administrative officer of the UN.

The first attempt to establish a global organisation, in the form of the League of Nations in 1920, failed for many reasons. The decades after World War I were marked by the rise of extreme exclusivist political ideologies like Nazism and Fascism, along with severe economic crises and constant political instability. The United States' absence from the League made it weak and essentially European in character, and it was often bypassed by the major actors. Operating on the principle of unanimity, which remained elusive, it failed to function effectively and was unable to apply sanctions upon members charged with acts of aggression. The major powers, which had aggressive designs on the world, deserted the League, and World War II made it clear that as a world organisation, the League of Nations had failed. However, many of League's agencies later became specialised agencies of the UN, for instance, the International Labor Organization (ILO) and the Permanent Court of International Justice (PCIJ), which came to be known as the International Court of Justice (ICJ) under the UN.

As World War II persisted, the Allied powers felt the need to unite for peace and security. The process was led by the 'Big Three'—the US, the USSR, and the UK. In January 1942, the Declaration by the United Nations was signed in Washington. The credit for the name 'United Nations' lies with US President Theodore Roosevelt. In subsequent years, while the war raged on, negotiations were carried on and contentious issues such as voting arrangements in the Security Council or membership principles were worked out. In 1944, at the Dumbarton Oaks Conference, the basic structure and principles of the UN were formulated and approved. In February 1945, at the Yalta Conference, permanent members were given the right of veto. Although initially the Soviet Union had claimed separate membership for all its constituent republics, Stalin later scaled down the demand (but he did secure separate membership for Ukraine and Belarus). India, under British rule, had provided soldiers and material resources to the war efforts during both World War I and World War II. In recognition of this action, it was made a member of the League of Nations after World War I. After World War II, it became a founding member of the UN. At the San Francisco Conference, the UN Charter was signed, and the necessary ratification by the Big Five and a majority of the other signatory states was attained on 24 October 1945.

This second attempt to form a global organisation was based on the previous experience and sought to remove the earlier shortcomings. Special care was taken to turn the UN into the hub of all multilateral activities, in the hope that universal membership would reduce any possibility of the UN being ignored or bypassed.

PURPOSES, PRINCIPLES, AND MEMBERSHIP

The purposes of the UN, as enumerated in Article 1 of the UN Charter, include:

- maintenance of international peace and security;

- developing friendly relations among nations based on equal rights;
- achieving international cooperation in solving non-political problems and promoting respect for human rights and fundamental freedoms; and
- becoming a centre for harmonising the actions of nations.

The primary task of maintaining international peace and security makes the UN a political institution, despite the importance given to solving non-political problems. By aspiring to be the centre for the harmonising of all international activities, the UN sought to reduce any possibility of being bypassed.

The principles, as enumerated in Article 2 of the UN Charter, provide clear directions to the members to enable them to behave in a manner conducive to the functioning of the new organisation. The Article proclaims that:

- the organisation is based on the sovereign equality of all nations;
- members should fulfil all obligations in good faith;
- members should settle their disputes by peaceful means;
- members should refrain from the use of force;
- members should provide every assistance to the UN in any action it takes;
- non-members, too, have to act in accordance with these principles; and finally,
- the organisation will not intervene in matters of 'domestic jurisdiction'.

It is clear that the framers of the Charter were very particular about securing the support of both members and non-members for the organisation's aims. However, in case of any violation of such obligations by a member state, even the 'domestic jurisdiction' principle, which respects state sovereignty and ordinarily prevents intervention in the internal affairs of a state by any other party, can be overruled if the Security Council of the UN decides to apply forcible measures like economic sanctions or military action under Chapter VII of the Charter against the offender.

Articles 3–6 provide the rules for membership of the UN. Apart from the original members, who participated in the San Francisco Conference of 1945 or signed the UN Declaration of 1942, membership is open to all peace-loving states that accept the obligations given in the

Charter of the UN. However, a member state against which preventive or enforcement action has been taken may be suspended temporarily, and a member who persistently violates the principles of the UN as contained in its Charter can also be expelled.

The Structure and Organs

The UN, as it emerged in 1945, had six principal organs: (1) the General Assembly; (2) the Security Council; (3) the Economic and Social Council; (4) the Trusteeship Council; (5) the International Court of Justice; and (6) the Secretariat.

Of these, the Trusteeship Council was assigned the task of overseeing the territories placed under its supervision at the end of World War II and of ensuring the progress of these territories towards becoming self-governing entities. In 1994, the last of eleven such territories, Palau, became independent, and having completed its task, the Trusteeship Council became defunct. The Secretary-General of the UN proposed that it be terminated. It may be noted that the administration of each trust territory was governed through a trusteeship agreement with the administering power. The Council played a supervisory role, which included accepting petitions from the people of trust territories, replies to questionnaires and other reports from the administering power, periodic and special missions to the trust territories, and on-the-spot investigations. As a result of these measures, the administering powers moved to make the trust territories politically independent at the earliest.

The General Assembly

The General Assembly is the legislative branch of the UN and comprises all its members. It holds an annual formal session in September every year. It may also call special sessions on particular issues, as and when required. Emergency special sessions can also be called within twenty-four hours on the request of the Security Council or a majority of its members. While each state can send five delegates, it is entitled to only one vote. Delegates serve on the Committees formed by the General Assembly to debate and discuss specific security, economic, financial, cultural, or humanitarian issues. The Assembly also has special committees and working groups to cater to procedural and administrative matters.

The Assembly has the main deliberative function of considering and recommending measures that will ensure cooperation in the maintenance of peace and security; international collaboration on economic, social, cultural, and human rights issues; the development and codification of international law; and the peaceful settlement of disputes. Deliberation, however, usually leads to the formulation of general principles or resolutions. In addition, the Assembly performs certain supervisory, financial, electoral, and constituent functions as it receives reports from other UN organs, approves the UN budget, elects the non-permanent members of the Security Council and the judges of the ICJ (jointly with the Security Council), and has the power to amend the Charter by two-thirds majority, which includes the permanent members of the Security Council. However, the Charter did not envisage a role for the Assembly in enforcing peace and security. In fact, the Assembly cannot discuss a dispute that is under consideration in the Security Council. However, if the Security Council fails to fulfil its obligations, the General Assembly is empowered, by virtue of the 'Uniting For Peace Resolution' (1950), to consider any matter involving threat to peace, breach of peace, or act of aggression, and to make the appropriate recommendations for collective measures, including the use of armed forces when necessary. This Resolution was invoked in a few cases in the 1950s.

The General Assembly serves as a platform where any state can air its views on any issue and where collective bargaining takes pre-eminence. Negotiations also take place in smaller caucus groups or through informal, behind-the-scenes diplomatic channels, to garner support for a resolution to be passed by a large majority or for consensus at the time of voting on the open forum of the Assembly. A blend of negotiations, political manoeuvring, and legislative debate makes it a space for parliamentary diplomacy, which maximises agreement and accommodates a diversity of interests. These resolutions help build world public opinion and provide a direction for the efforts of the international community.

The Security Council

The Security Council is primarily responsible for maintaining international peace and security; hence, it also functions as an arena for international power politics. The Council has five permanent members: the US, Russia, the UK, France, and China (commonly called the P5). The 1945 Charter provided for six non-permanent members, to be elected for a two-year term. The UN membership rose from fifty-one to 113 in 1965, and the number of non-permanent members was increased to ten. As membership of the UN grew dramatically at the end of the Cold War, it can be argued that the Council, with its fifteen members, is too small and unrepresentative, given that UN membership now stands at 193. Moreover, the contemporary arrangement of five permanent members does not reflect current realities, as other powerful states such as Germany, Japan, India, and Brazil have also staked claims for permanent membership.

The voting procedure in the Security Council has been subject to much controversy. The current process ensures the predominance of the P5 and goes against the principle of sovereign equality of all nations in the UN. Decisions on procedural matters are made by the affirmative vote of any nine members. However, for a proposal to be adopted on all other matters (that is, on substantive issues), nine votes are required in favour of it, *including* those of the five permanent members. As a result, any one permanent member can nullify a decision supported by all others. This is referred to as the veto power of the P5. However, the important question is whether a matter is substantive or procedural; a permanent member, by using the veto, can ensure that a matter is discussed under the substantive category, and then use the veto again to invalidate the proposal. This is referred to as the 'double veto' of the P5.

The Security Council has the authority to enforce measures against a state charged with acts of aggression. Chapter VI of the UN Charter prescribes peaceful means of settlement of disputes, which include diplomatic processes and settlement by law. Under Chapter VII, the Council can apply measures such as the partial disruption of economic, transport, and communication links, and the severance of diplomatic relations. If these prove inadequate, the Council can recommend air, sea, and land operations by forces belonging to UN members. Members are bound to carry out the measures decided upon by the Security Council. The Security Council resorted to war in 1950 to protect South

Korea from North Korea, and again in 1991 to protect Kuwait from Iraq. However, often, in challenging situations where peaceful measures were not enough and the use of force was opposed by one or the other big power, the Council authorised peacekeeping operations, which fall somewhere between peaceful methods and coercive action. Over the years, peacekeeping operations have been used to settle disputes within and between states, and the scope of such operations has been expanded to include peacemaking and peace-building as well. However, the provision for a Military Staff Committee under the aegis of the Security Council as envisaged by the Charter never materialised.

The Economic and Social Council

During the San Francisco Conference, the smaller powers saw to the expansion of the economic and social functions of the UN, and the Economic and Social Council (ECOSOC) was upgraded as a principal organ of the UN. The ECOSOC has increasingly become a crucial organ that performs wide-ranging tasks to address economic and social issues. The Council initiates studies and reports concerning international economic, social, cultural, educational, and health issues. Promoting a better life in its myriad aspects in every part of the world and ensuring economic, social, and cultural progress is an arduous, and often elusive, task. But the ECOSOC continues to make recommendations to the General Assembly and to member states, publish reports, and convene conferences seeking a resolution to economic and social challenges.

The Council coordinates the activities of specialised agencies of the UN and seeks to work in tandem with international non-governmental organisations and negotiate with inter-governmental agencies. ECOSOC has regional Economic Commissions for Africa, Europe, Latin America, and the Caribbean, and Economic and Social Commissions for Asia and the Pacific and Western Asia to help develop projects in these regions. ECOSOC has functional commissions to cater to specific issues like human rights, the status of women, population and development, narcotic drugs, crime prevention and criminal justice, science and technology for development, and sustainable development. It has a wide network of standing committees, expert bodies, funds, and programmes that work on a wide range of issues.

However, the ECOSOC functions under the authority of the General Assembly and may be accused of duplicating the activities of Assembly Committees. Critics often point out that despite the verbose debates, these committees offer little by way of practical results. Nevertheless, ECOSOC's programmes have been vital for the welfare and sustenance of many developing nations, and the UN's success and utility are often judged on the basis of its performance.

The International Court of Justice

The International Court of Justice (ICJ) is the main judicial organ of the UN. All members states are also members of the Statute of the ICJ. The Court is constituted of fifteen judges in a manner that represents all principal forms of civilisation and legal systems. All decisions of the Court are made on the basis of majority opinion. The Court works towards the judicial settlement of disputes in accordance with international law. It exercises jurisdiction over all cases submitted to it voluntarily. This is called voluntary jurisdiction. National courts enjoy compulsory jurisdiction insofar as the parties can be summoned to the Court. In the international arena, states are sovereign and cannot be compelled to appear before the ICJ. However, states may also confer compulsory jurisdiction upon the ICJ through a declaration, but can place many conditions and reserve many areas out of the jurisdiction of the Court. Although states generally prefer diplomatic means over legal methods to settle their disputes, they have taken recourse to the ICJ when diplomatic avenues proved inadequate. The Court contributes to the development of international law through its decisions and opinions, and provides for the rule of law in international relations.

The Secretariat

The Secretariat functions as the main office of the UN, and is headed by the Secretary-General. It provides all the services necessary for the effective functioning of the UN system, the organs of the UN, and its subsidiary bodies. Divided into several major departments, each headed by an Under-Secretary-general or an official of similar rank, the Secretariat runs the administration. By producing reports and documents, statistical publications, and information bulletins, and providing technical expert advice, in addition to the usual secretarial and translation services, the Secretariat facilitates deliberations and administers the implementation of the policies adopted by UN bodies. In short, the huge UN bureaucracy located in New York, as well as the branch offices and regional commission secretariats, make plans, allocate resources, appoint personnel, and oversee projects, all within the scope of the rules and responsibilities framed by the General Assembly. The loyalty of the international civil servants of the UN resides with the organisation; they are forbidden to seek or receive instructions from any government.

The Secretary-General is not merely the Chief Administrative Officer of the UN; he also plays important political roles. He is responsible for preparing the UN budget and the initiatives he takes and the proposals he offers can go beyond a mere administrative function and enter the political realm. The Secretary-General and his staff can also take recourse to quiet diplomacy while thrashing out the details of a policy. Since a number of states might be involved in a particular project, continuous negotiations may take place on an extensive scale in order to ensure greater coordination and reduce disagreement. This becomes an important task for the Secretary-General and his staff. Further, the permanent representatives of various member states are in constant touch with the Secretary-General, who plays an important role in consensus-building in the UN.

The importance of the Secretary-General has increased over the years. Article 98 of the UN Charter states that the Secretary-General '... shall perform such other functions as are entrusted to him...' by the other organs of the UN, which have greatly expanded the area and scope of functions of the office of the Secretary-General. More importantly, Article 99 enables him to '... bring to the attention of the Security Council any matter which in his opinion may threaten the maintenance of international peace and security'. This provision not only gives him the right to initiate discussions on a potential or actual crisis, but also allows him to propose specific measures to resolve the crisis. As he investigates an international conflict in order to assess its possible impact and evaluate the possible options before the international community, he often becomes the main channel of communication, if not a bridge, between the disputing parties and the UN. Secretaries-General function as mediators, and much of the diplomatic negotiations are carried out through them. Peacekeeping activities require immense coordination among the dispatching states and the UN, administrative efficiency, and budgetary control. Finally, the personality factor also contributed to the growth of the role of the Secretary-General, as many of them widened the scope of activities beyond the Charter provisions by taking initiatives to resolve international disputes, not merely as chief administrators but also as diplomats and advocates of core human values.

Trygve Lie, Dag Hammarskjold, U Thant, Kurt Waldheim, Javier Perez de Cueller, Boutros Boutros-Ghali, Kofi Annan, Ban Ki-moon—all these Secretaries-General had to manage the forces at work at a specific time in international politics. The nature of the threats and challenges has changed in the post-Cold War period, and these issues demand able stewardship from the chief executive officer. However, the amount of political support he gets from the members, especially from the Big Five states, often determines the outcome of his initiatives. The present incumbent, Antonio Guterres, may also find the going tough, given the immense and intense disputes and conflicts raging currently, the uncertainties related to emerging power equations, and the common international concerns over climate change, depleting resources, international terrorism, economic disparities, and the COVID-19 pandemic that swept the world in 2020–23.

Specialised Agencies of the UN

When the UN was being formed, a number of autonomous international agencies were already in existence. These were attached to the UN and a few others were created as and when the necessity arose. The UN (primarily through the ECOSOC) was made a coordinating body with the power to seek regular reports from these specialised agencies, and also to make suggestions and oversee their functioning. For effective collaborative action to counter a common challenge, a dedicated platform is regarded as more appropriate, and the specialised agencies of the UN function as such dedicated platforms. However, while specialised agencies have states as members, not all states are members of all the specialised agencies. These agencies have independent governing bodies, and are dissimilar in their structures and methods of functioning. In general, they have three main bodies:

1. An assembly or a conference where all members of the agency are represented.
2. An executive council or a governing body responsible for the continuity of programmes.
3. An office or a secretariat.

Some of these agencies have created a place for themselves in international politics: the International Monetary Fund (IMF), the International Bank for Reconstruction and Development (IBRD), International Labour Organization (ILO), World Health Organization (WHO), and the United Nations Educational, Scientific and Cultural Organization (UNESCO) are very familiar names in contemporary international politics. However, global organisations are often dependent on their donors, and thereby vulnerable to politicisation and manipulation. The WHO was accused of having a 'China bias' during the COVID-19 pandemic, and allegations were made about its ineffective role during this period. This even led US President Donald Trump in 2020 to suspend US funding for WHO and eventually withdraw from the organisation (this decision was reversed when Joe Biden took over as US President in 2021). As Trump returned to power for a second term, he issued an executive order again in 2025, stating that the US would withdraw from the organisation.

There is almost no field that has not been touched by the activities of the UN. The UN General Assembly has also established programmes and funds for very specific purposes, with their own administrative boards in charge. Popular programmes include the UN Development Programme (UNDP), the UN Environment Programme (UNEP), World Food Programme (WFP), and the UN Conference on Trade and Development (UNCTAD). Funds include the most popular UN Children's Fund (UNICEF) and the UN Population Fund (formerly, the UN Fund for Population Activities, or UNFPA). All these are intergovernmental organisations (IGOs) that are a part of the UN, and must be distinguished from the NGOs operating in many fields of common human concern.

An Assessment

Almost everybody will readily agree that the UN is not a perfect institution. At the end of World War II, the Charter of the UN was framed 'to save succeeding generations from the scourge of war', and a code of conduct was framed for member states to follow. In case of a dispute, members are required to shun armed conflict and settle their differences peacefully; the UN Charter even suggests various ways to settle disputes. However, there is always the possibility of unprovoked aggression. The UN operates on the principle of collective security, wherein an attack against one state is considered an attack against all, that is, an act of aggression against a member state is regarded as an act of aggression against all the members of the UN. Punitive actions are taken collectively by all the members against the offender. A threat or breach of peace or act of aggression is determined by the Security Council, the perpetrator/s are identified, and collective action is taken by the members.

Such actions, however, are meaningful only when the great powers, that is, the P5, agree on the collective measures. The end of World War II saw the rise of two superpowers hostile to one another, and an ideological contest ensued with military ramifications. A bipolar world led by two hostile hegemons and their allies made it difficult for the UN to foster lasting peace and stability. Under these circumstances, the principle of unanimity among the great powers suffered a serious setback. Depending on political expediency, the P5 may oppose one another and prevent a coordinated policy to end a dispute. For example, in the Iraq War that began in 2003, the US formed a coalition of willing states and invaded Iraq when it became clear that no such mandate was forthcoming from the UN. Yet another drawback has been the tendency towards selective engagement: the major powers take their time deciding whether to get involved in a crisis, or whether to stay away completely.

Under these trying circumstances, the UN has come up with innovative methods. Peacekeeping is one such innovation, where multinational forces under UN command are used to contain and halt international armed conflicts within states or a region. The purpose of the soldiers is not to launch war but to usher in peace, by setting up buffer zones, maintaining order, monitoring armistices, brokering contacts between the conflicting parties, and providing humanitarian aid. In fact, an expansion in functions led to the induction of different categories of personnel, and activities such as monitoring and facilitating elections to bring in normality in a troubled state have increased. Peacekeeping as a measure has not been mentioned in the Charter, however, and it falls between the peaceful measures suggested in Chapter 6 and the forcible measures suggested in Chapter 7. Since Dag Hammarskjold, the second Secretary-General of the UN, peacekeeping has been regarded as belonging to 'Chapter 6½'. The UN Peacekeeping Forces (often referred to as Blue Berets or Blue Helmets) have undertaken missions in various of the world's conflict zones. In 1988, the UN Peacekeeping Forces was awarded the Nobel Prize for Peace.

One can argue that the new challenges that arose in the later decades of the twentieth century could not have been envisaged in 1945, which is why the UN has remained a state-based institution that was ill-equipped to tackle the challenges posed by civil wars, ethnic and religious conflicts, cross-border terrorism, and state versus non-state conflicts. However, as the idea of conflict and security changed, so did the nature of peacekeeping. Human security became pre-eminent in the post-Cold War period, and rampant human rights violations in countries where the state itself is either unable or unwilling to protect its citizens placed an urgent responsibility on the international community. Under these circumstances, unanimous consent becomes impossible to achieve, and the UN may be compelled to intervene, violating the principle of domestic jurisdiction. This has led to a greater role of the UN in peace-building, which includes post-conflict reconstruction and the rebuilding of domestic administration and civil society. From the late 1980s, UN missions in Africa, Latin America and the Caribbean, Asia, the Middle East, and Europe have been very different from the earlier missions, which primarily ensured a ceasefire between the disputing parties. Termed 'second-generation peacekeeping', UN involvement now includes the defence of rights and well-being of individuals within their own countries. As a result, even though the Charter remains an essentially state-based inter-governmental arrangement, the UN has changed into an institution that transcends the domestic jurisdiction of states. However, this creates a huge economic burden on the UN, with many states fearing that peacekeeping activities might impede the UN's development programmes and bring it to the brink of bankruptcy.

The UN provides states with the most important platform to promote collaboration and coexistence. Through discussions, debates, and dialogue, the UN provides states with opportunities to settle their differences through parliamentary diplomacy. It helps build global public opinion and creates an environment that facilitates reconciliation.

The specialised agencies of the UN play a critical and indispensable role in fostering international cooperation and facilitating the collaborative programmes of states in areas of common concern, such as health, education, environment, science and technology, and transport and communication. UN efforts to protect and promote human rights, offer aid and support to refugees and internally displaced persons, provide technological assistance to developing states, and the humanitarian support it extends to vulnerable populations are commendable. The UN has been instrumental in leading the world community towards a better future.

It is true, though, that in view of the ambitious aims and objectives proclaimed in the Preamble to the UN Charter, the achievements of the UN have been modest at best. However, the efficacy and relevance of the UN can be appreciated only when one imagines a world without its presence. The UN continues to offer a compromise between ideal principles and pragmatic choices in the contemporary period as well.

The UN is now pursuing the Sustainable Development Goals (SDGs), which came into effect in 2016. Its targets are to be achieved by 2030. The goals include: eradicating poverty in all its forms; attaining food security and ending hunger and malnutrition; promoting good health, quality education, gender equality, clean water and sanitation, clean energy, decent work, and economic growth. The vital issues of climate change, sustainable cities, and peaceful, just, and inclusive societies are also a part of the SDGs. While these goals are not easy to achieve, substantial collective effort in this direction will make the world a safer and better place.

A belief in the UN system has been an important plank of India's foreign policy as well. India is committed to playing a leading role in the fight against racism, colonialism, hegemonic politics, and an imbalanced economic order. A strengthened UN is in India's best interests. India has regularly contributed to the UN's peacekeeping measures and participated in most of its initiatives. India believes, however, that the Security Council must be broadened, and as the most populous country of the world, the largest democracy, and a growing economic powerhouse, it has a natural claim to permanent membership of the Security Council. This requires mobilising worldwide support, which might take some time. There are regional powers who steadfastly oppose the inclusion of nations like India, Germany, Japan, and Brazil, fearing a greater regional dominance of these states if they become permanent members of the UN.

REFORMS OF THE UN

Apart from the fact that the UN Security Council is too small and unrepresentative of contemporary realities and an expansion of the Security Council is urgently necessary to maintain its legitimacy, it is often argued that the UN has become too cumbersome a system, with too many agencies that are a financial drain on the existing resources. Some of the missions have become irrelevant and useless, and streamlining the system has become a necessity. One may remember in this context that in 1947, India had referred the dispute with Pakistan over Kashmir to the UN, which led to the formation of the United Nations Military Observer Group in India and Pakistan (UNMOGIP) that came to this region in January 1949 to supervise the ceasefire between India and Pakistan. Since then, India and Pakistan have fought wars in 1965, 1971, and 1999, and there have been surgical strikes and retaliations against cross-border terrorist attacks; ceasefire violations therefore have become a rule rather than an exception in this region. The very usefulness of such a mission, after almost seventy-five years with a cost that has exceeded \$100 million, has been repeatedly questioned. However, terminating the mission requires a Security Council resolution, which has not materialised yet. UNMOGIP can be cited as an example of a failed UN mission that is still being maintained at a high cost.

If the UN is to be a viable organisation suited to the requirements of the twenty-first century, then administrative, programmatic, and structural reforms are called for. Former Secretary-General Kofi Annan appointed a High Level Panel in 2003, and on the basis of the recommendations put forward in its report submitted in 2004, various reform proposals were introduced in 2005. After decades of discussion, however, little progress has been made in this respect, despite a plethora of official and unofficial suggestions for reform of the UN system. We shall now consider some of the meaningful suggestions.

Certain reforms were easy to implement, especially administrative and programmatic reforms targeted towards cutting costs and enhancing efficiency. These measures mostly include:

- streamlining and consolidating departments by merging similar agencies;
- reducing the number of UN staff and personnel;
- inserting sunset provisions so that the bodies no longer needed could be disbanded without delay once their objective is achieved;
- bringing all in-country UN agencies in a particular state under one UN House;
- introducing result-based budgeting and reducing the quantity, length, and frequency of the reports produced by various UN bodies.

The Millennium Summit of 2000 focussed on the six fundamental values of freedom, equality, solidarity, tolerance, respect for nature, and shared responsibility, leading to the Millennium Development Goals, according to which specific projects were undertaken in partnership with civil society, covering peacekeeping, development, and democratisation. It was emphasised that the UN should facilitate action by involving local and regional organisations (IGOs and NGOs), rather than taking up the responsibility on its own. The SDGs also emphasise partnerships between governments and civil societies.

While the Trusteeship Council and the non-existent Military Staff Committee can be removed, it was suggested that the General Assembly and the ECOSOC be trimmed by reducing the number of representatives and the number of elected members, respectively. However, Kofi Annan proposed the establishment of a Peace-Building Commission that would cover the proactive peace-making, peacekeeping, and post-conflict peace-building efforts of the UN.

A matter of urgent debate is the expansion of the Security Council. When the UN was formed in 1945 with fifty-one members, the Security Council had eleven members, including the big five states. In 1965, the number of non-permanent members was increased from six to ten when the UN members stood at 117. By 2011, the UN had 193 members after the inclusion of South Sudan, but membership of the Security Council remains static at fifteen. A number of new states have emerged in the twenty-first century. Kofi Annan's proposal called for an expansion of the Security Council by increasing the membership to twenty-four. This can be achieved in two ways:

1. Adding six more permanent seats (none with veto power, though) and three more non-permanent seats for a two-year term;
2. Creating a category of eight renewable four-year term seats and one new two-year term non-permanent seat. This option did not gather much support, as the emerging major powers preferred permanent seats on the Council.

The proposal inspired several middle powers to lobby for the permanent seats. Germany and Japan were regarded as the two major contenders, but emerging aspirants and regional powers like India, Brazil, Nigeria, and Egypt came forward as well, fuelling opposition from their respective regional adversaries. As Japan, India, Germany, and Brazil formed a group to campaign for permanent seats, China, Pakistan, Italy, and Argentina formed a group to oppose them. India's foreign policy was geared towards garnering greater support from the states in her favour. However, it became clear over time that no such reform could take place without the concurrence of the P5, and they are in no hurry to bring new permanent members into the Security Council.

The veto power exercised by permanent members has always been a matter of controversy, and scholars and commentators have put forward a number of suggestions. While some call for abolishing the veto power completely or introducing a collective veto of two or three members together, others are in favour of inducting more permanent members with veto power into the Council. The practice, however, is not going to change soon, as the existing permanent members are unwilling to give up their privilege, or extend it to fresh incumbents.

Any structural reform would require amending the UN Charter. Articles 108 and 109 make any such amendment a rigid process. Amendments have to be adopted by two-thirds of the General Assembly and ratified in accordance with constitutional processes by two-thirds of the UN members, including all the permanent members of the Security Council. So far, the Charter has been amended to increase the membership of the Security Council (in 1965) and of ECOSOC (in 1965 and 1973). However, through the non-implementation of certain provisions (such as Article 47, which calls for the establishment of a Military Staff Committee), adopting resolutions amounting to structural changes (like the Uniting for Peace Resolution 1950 in the General Assembly), and the creation of subsidiary bodies (*ad hoc* and permanent commissions, programmes, and funds, thereby expanding the scope of UN activities), the UN has avoided the rigid process of amendment, while furthering its role in the desired direction.

Bibliography

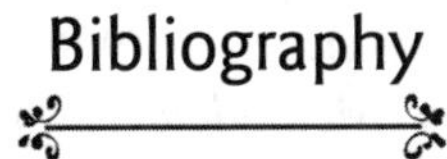

Abraham, J. 2016.. 'Global warming is melting the Greenland Ice Sheet, fast'. *The Guardian*, 25 August. Available at https://www.theguardian.com/environment/climate-consensus-97-per-cent/2016/aug/25/global-warming-is-melting-the-greenland-ice-sheet-fast (accessed July 2025).

Acharya, A. 1999. 'Culture, Security, Multiculturalism: The Asean Way'. In Keith Krause (ed.), *Culture and Security: Multilateralism, Arms Control and Security Building*. London: Frank Cass.

_____. 2001. 'Human Security: East versus West'. *International Journal* 56 (3), 442–60.

_____. 2014. 'Human Security'. In J. Baylis, S. Smith, and P. Owens (eds), *The Globalization of World Politics*, 448–61. Oxford: Oxford University Press.

Acharya, A., and B. Buzan (eds). 2010. *Non-Western International Relations Theory: Perspectives on and beyond Asia*. London and New York: Routledge.

Ackerly, B., M. Stern, and J. True (eds). 2005. *Feminist Methodologies for International Relations*. Cambridge: Cambridge University Press.

Adler, E.. 1997. 'Imagined (Security) Communities: Cognitive Regions in International Relations'. *Millennium: Journal of International Relations* 26 (2), 249–79.

Adler, E., and M. Barnett (eds). 1998. *Security Communities*. Cambridge: Cambridge University Press.

African Union (AU). n.d. 'About the African Union'. Available at https://au.int/en/overview (accessed August 2025).

Ajami, F. 1993. 'The Summoning'. *Foreign Affairs* 72 (4), 2–9.

Akinsanya, A., and A. Davies. 1984. 'Third World Quest for a New International Economic Order: An Overview'. *The International and Comparative Law Quarterly* 33 (1), 208–17.

Alexander, Y., and D. Alexander. 2015. *The Islamic State: Combating the Caliphate without Borders*. Lanham: Lexington Books.

Alker, H. 1996. *Rediscoveries and Reformulations: Humanistic Methodologies for International Studies*. New York: Cambridge University Press.

Alkire, S. 2003. *A Conceptual Framework for Human Security*. Oxford: CRISE, University of Oxford.

Allison, G. T. 1971. *Essence of Decision: Explaining the Cuban Missile Crisis*. Boston: Little, Brown.

Allison, G. T., and P. Zelikow. 1999. *Essence of Decision: Explaining the Cuban Missile Crisis*. Princeton, New Jersey: Pearson PTR.

Amin, S. 1974. *Accumulation on a World Scale*. New York: Monthly Review Press.

Anderson, A. 1998. 'Cosmopolitanism, Universalism, and the Divided Legacies of Modernity'. In Pheng Cheah and Bruce Robbins (eds), *Cosmopolitics: Thinking and Feeling Beyond the Nation*. Minneapolis: University of Minnesota Press.

Anderson, B. 1983. *Imagined Communities: Reflections on the Origins and Spread of Nationalism*. London: Verso.

———. 2012. 'Guest Lecture: Nationalism and Time'. UCD School of Sociology, 19 September. Available at https://www.youtube.com/watch?v=pndcJMsIVR8 (accesed August 2025).

———. 2013. *About Nationalism*. Retrieved from Anthropology Online: https://www.youtube.com/watch?v=cNJuL-Ewp-A&list=PL6e5-2gH5bfpOeY1fdDMGJW5x6dGBZ1ZZ&index=1

Anderson, M. 1999. *Do No Harm: How Aid Can Support Peace—Or War*. London: Lynne Rienner.

Anderson, P. 1992. *A Zone of Engagement*. London: Verso.

Angell, N. 1912. *The Great Illusion: A Study of the Relation of Military Power to National Advantage*. London: W. Heinemann.

Anheier, H., M. Glasius, and M. Kaldor. 2001. 'Introducing Global Civil Society'. In H. Anheier, Marlies Glasius, and Mary Kaldor (eds), *Global Civil Society*. Oxford: Oxford University Press.

Antlov, H., and T.-W. Ngo. 2000. *The Cultural Construction of Politics in Asia*. Richmond: Curzon Press.

Alliance of Small Island States (AOSIS). 2015. 'About'. Available at http://aosis.org/about/ (accessed August 2025).

Appadurai, A. 1990. 'Disjuncture and Difference in the Global Cultural Economy'. *Theory, Culture, and Society* 7 (2–3), 295–310.

Appadurai, A. 1997. *Modernity at Large: Cultural Dimensions of Globalisation*. New Delhi: Oxford University Press.

Apter, D. E. 1987. *Modernization, Dependency and Postmodern Politics*. Beverly Hills, CA: Sage Publications.

Arendt, H. 1967. 'Truth and Politics'. *The New Yorker*, 25 February.

Association of South East Asian Nations (ASEAN). 2017. 'About ASEAN'. Available at https://asean.org/about-asean (accessed August 2025).

Ashley, R. K. 1984. 'The Poverty of Neorealism'. *International Organization* 38 (2), 225–86.

_____. 1987. 'The Geopolitics of Geopolitical Space: Toward a Critical Social Theory of International Politics'. *Alternatives* 12 (4), 403–34.

_____. 1988. 'Un-tying the Sovereign State: A Double Reading of the Anarchy Problematique'. *Millennium: Journal of International Studies* 17 (2), 227–62.

Axelrod, R. 1984. *The Evolution of Cooperation*. New York: Basic Books.

Axworthy, L. 2001. 'Introduction'. In R. McRae and D. Hubert (eds), *Human Security and the New Diplomacy: Protecting People, Promoting Peace*, 3–15. London: McGill-Queen's University Press.

Ayoob, M. 1991. 'The Security Problematic of the Third World'. *World Politics* 43 (January).

Kaveji, H. 1996. *The State, War, and the State of War*. New York: Cambridge University Press.

Backstrand, K., and E. Lovbrand. 2016. 'The Road to Paris: Contending Climate Governance Discourses in the Post-Copenhagen Era'. *Journal of Environmental Policy and Planning* 21 (5), 519–32.

Bacon, A. 2025. 'Trump announces tariffs of 30% on Mexico and the European Union'. *CNN*, 13 July. Available at https://edition.cnn.com/2025/07/12/business/trump-tariff-mexico-european-union (accessed July 2025).

Bajpai, K. 2000. 'Human Security: Concept and Measurement'. Kroc Institute Occasional Paper 19: OP:1, 1–64.

_____. 2012. 'Global Terrorism'. In B. S. Chimni and S. Mallavarapu (eds), *IR: Perspectives for the Global South*. New Delhi: Pearson.

Balachandran, V. 2020. 'How to Read Chinese Incursions'. *The Tribune*, 19 July.

Baldwin, D. A. (ed.). 1993. *Neorealism and Neoliberalism: The Contemporary Debate*. New York: Columbia University Press.

Bandyopadhyaya, J. 1993. *A General Theory of International Relations*. New Delhi: Allied Publishers.

Banerjee, D. (ed.). 1999. *Confidence Building Measures in South Asia*. Colombo: Regional Centre for Strategic Studies.

Baran, P. A. 1957. *The Political Economy of Growth*. New York: Monthly Review Press.

Barash, D. P. 2013. *Approaches to Peace: A Reader in Peace Studies*. New York: Oxford University Press.

Barber, B. R. 2010. *Jihad vs McWorld*. New York: Times Books.

Barkawi, T., and M. Laffey. 2002. 'Retrieving the Imperial: Empire and International Relations'. *Millennium: Journal of International Studies* 31 (1), 109–27.

Barnett, M. N. 1996. 'Identity and Alliances in the Middle East'. In Peter J. Katzenstein (ed.), *The Culture of National Security: Norms and Identity in World Politics*. New York: Columbia University Press.

______. 2002. *Eyewitness to a Genocide: The United Nations and Rwanda*. Ithaca, New York: Cornell University Press.

Barth, F. (ed.). 1969. *Ethnic Groups and Boundaries*. Boston: Little Brown.

Bartley, R. L. 1993. 'The Case for Optimism'. *Foreign Affairs* 72 (4), 15–18.

Basu, R. 1994. *The United Nations: Structure and Functions of an International Organization*. New Delhi: Sterling Publishers.

Bayly, C. A. 2002. 'Archaic and Modern Globalization in the Eurasian and African Arena, c. 1750–1850'. In A. G. Hopkins (ed.), *Globalization in World History*. London: Pimlico.

______. 2004. *The Birth of the Modern World, 1780–1914. Global Connections and Comparisons*. Oxford: Blackwell.

Baylis, J., S. Smith, and P. Owens. 2014. *Theories of World Politics*. Oxford: Oxford University Press.

BBC. 2025. 'A Really Simple Guide to Climate Change', 30 July. Available at http://www.bbc.com/news/science-environment-24021772 (accessed July 2025).

Behera, N. 2010. 'Re-imagining IR in India'. In Amitav Acharya and Barry Buzan (eds), *Non-Western International Relations Theory: Perspectives on and beyond Asia*. New York: Routledge.

Berger, S. 2000. 'Globalization and Politics'. *Annual Review of Political Science* 3 (1), 43–62.

Berman, P. 2003. *Terror and Liberalism*. New York: W. W. Norton & Company.

Bernard Jr., P. 2006. 'Canada and Human Security: From the Axworthy Doctrine to Middle Power Internationalism'. *American Review of Canadian Studies* 36 (2), 233–61.

Bertucci, M. E. 2015. 'Latin America's New Era of Regionalism'. *Americas Quarterly*, 3 February. Available at https://www.americasquarterly.org/fulltextarticle/latin-americas-new-era-of-regionalism/ (accessed June 2025).

Best, E., and T. Christiansen. 2014. 'Regionalism in International Affairs'. In J. Baylis, S. Smith, and P. Owens (eds), *The Globalization of World Politics: An Introduction to International Relation*, 401–16. Oxford: Oxford University Press.

Bhagwati, J. 2004. *In Defense of Globalization*. New Delhi: Oxford University Press.

Bially Mattern, J. 2000. 'Taking Identity Seriously'. *Cooperation and Conflict* 35 (3), 299–308.

Biersteker, T. J. 2002. 'State Sovereignty and Territory'. In Walter Carlsnaes, Thomas Risse, and Beth A. Simmons (eds), *Handbook of International Relations*. New York: Sage.

Biersteker, T. J., and C. Weber. 1996. *State Sovereignty as a Social Construct*. Cambridge: Cambridge University Press.

Black, R. 2015. 'A Brief History of Climate Change'. *BBC News*, 20 September. Available at http://www.bbc.com/news/science-environment-15874560 (accessed July 2025).

Blinkhorn, M. 2006. *Mussolini and Fascist Italy*. New York: Routledge, 3e.

Blum, A. L. 1988. 'Gilligan and Kohlberg: Implications for Moral Theory'. *Ethics* 98 (3), 472–91.

Bodenheimer, S. 1971. 'Dependency and Imperialism: The Roots of Latin American Underdevelopment'. In K. T. Fann and D. C. Hodges, *Readings in U.S. Imperialism*. Boston: Porter Sargent.

Bohman, J. 2005. 'Critical Theory'. Available at http://plato.stanford.edu/entries/critical-theory/ (accessed August 2025).

Bonner, S. E. 2011. *Critical Theory: A Very Short Introduction*. New York: Oxford University Press.

Borzel, T. A. 2016. 'Theorizing Regionalism: Cooperation, Integration and Governance'. In T. A. Borzel and T. Risse (eds), *Oxford Handbook of Comparative Regionalism*. Oxford: Oxford University Press.

Bourdieu, P. 2003. *Counterfire: Against the Tyranny of the Market*. New York: Verso Books.

Brass, P. R. 1991. *Ethnicity and Nationalism: Theory and Comparison*. New Delhi: Sage Publications.

Breuilly, J. 2011. 'Nationalism'. In J. Baylis, S. Smith, and P. Owens, *The Globalization of World Politics*. Oxford: Oxford University Press.

Broecker, W. 1975. 'Climate Change: Are We on the Brink of a Pronounced Global Warming?' *Science* 189 (4201), 460–63.

Bronner, S. E. 2017. *Critical Theory: A Very Short Introduction*. Oxford: Oxford University Press.

Brooks, S. G. 1997. 'Dueling Realisms (Realism in International Relations)'. *International Organization* 51 (3), 445–77.

Brown, C. 1997. *Understanding International Relations*. London: Macmillan.

Brown, S. 1988. 'Feminism, International Theory, and International Relations of Gender Inequality'. *Millennium: Journal of International Studies* 17 (3), 461–75.

Bucher, B., and U. Jasper. 2017. 'Revisiting "Identity" in International Relations: From Identity as Substance to Identifications in Action'. *European Journal of International Relations* 23 (2), 391–415.

Bullock, A. 1991. *Hitler: A Study in Tyranny*. London: Penguin.

Burchill, S., and A. Linklater. 2005. 'Introduction'. In Scott Burchill, Andrew Linklater, Richard Devetak, Jack Donnelly, Matthew Paterson, Christian Reus-Smit and Jacqui True, *Theories of International Relations*, 1–28. Basingstoke: Palgrave Macmillan.

Busby, J. W. 2007. *Climate Change and National Security: An Agenda for Action*. New York: Council on Foreign Relations. Available at https://ciaotest.cc.columbia.edu/wps/cfr/0002812/index.html.

Buzan, B., and R. Little. 2001. 'Why International Relations has Failed as an Intellectual Project and What To Do about It'. *Millenium: Journal of International Studies* 30 (1), 19–39.

Buzan, B., and L. Hansen. 2009. *The Evolution of International Security Studies*. Cambridge: Cambridge University Press.

Buzan, B., C. Jones, and R. Little. 1993. *The Logic of Anarchy: Rethinking Neorealism*. New York: Columbia University Press.

Buzan, B., O. Wæver, and J. de Wilde. 1998. *Security: A New Framework for Analysis*. Boulder, CO: Lynne Rienner.

Calvocoressi, P. 1988. *World Politics since 1945*. London: Longman.

Campbell, D. 1992. *Writing Security: United States Foreign Policy and the Politics of Identity*. Minneapolis: University of Minnesota Press.

———. 1998. *National Deconstruction: Violence, Identity, and Justice in Bosnia*. Minneapolis, MN: University of Minnesota Press.

Caney, S. 2010. 'Climate Change and the Duties of the Advantaged'. *Critical Review of International Social and Political Philosophy* 13 (1), 203–28.

Cardoso, F. H., and E. Faletto. 1967. *Dependência e Desenvolvimentona América Latina*. Rio de Janeiro: Zahar.

Carment, D. 1994. 'The Ethnic Dimension in World Politics: Theory, Policy and Early Warning'. *Third World Quarterly* 15 (4), 551–82.

Carment, D., and P. James. 1997. 'The International Politics of Ethnic Conflict: New Perspectives on Theory and Policy'. *Global Society: Journal of Interdisciplinary International Relations* 11 (2), 205–32.

Carnoy, M. 1997. 'Foreword'. In P. Freire, *Pedagogy of the Heart*. London: Bloomsbury.

Carr, E. H. 1947. *The Twenty Years' Crisis, 1919–1939*. London: Macmillan.

Carter, N. T. 2010. 'Climate Change and the Politics of the Global Environment'. In M. Beeson and N. Bisley (eds), *Issues in 21st Century World Politics*, 52–65. Hampshire: Palgrave Macmillan.

Cassen, B. 2004. 'Repenser les forums sociaux'. *Libération*, 12 January.

Castells, M. 1996. *The Information Age, Vol. I: The Rise of the Network Society*. Oxford: Blackwell.

Cederman, L.-E., and J. Wucherpfenning. 2017. 'Inequalities Between Ethnic Groups, Conflict, and Political Organizations'. *Ethnopolitics* 16 (1), 21–27.

Cerny, P. G. 1996. 'What Next For the State?' In E. Kofman and G. Young, *Globalization: Theory and Practice*. London: Pinter.

Chandler, D. 2004. *Constructing Global Civil Society: Morality and Power in International Relations*. London: Palgrave-Macmillan.

———. 2012. 'Resilience and Human Security: The Post-Interventionist Paradigm'. *Security Dialogue* 43 (3), 213–229.

Chase-Dunn, C. K., and P. Grimes. 1995. 'World-Systems Analysis'. *Annual Review of Sociology* 21, 387–417.

Chase-Dunn, C. K., and T. D. Hall. 1997. *Rise and Demise: Comparing World-Systems*. Boulder: Westview.

Chatterjee, P. 2013. 'A Conversation with Partha Chatterjee, moderated by Karuna Mantena'. Yale University, 20 November. Available at https://www.youtube.com/watch?v=jaZn9IqPJZg (accessed August 2025).

Chatterjee, S. 2005a. 'Ethnic Conflicts in South Asia: A Constructivist Reading'. *South Asian Survey* 12 (1), 75–89.

_____. 2005b. 'Global Images: "Realism" Contra "Culture"?' *Economic and Political Weekly* 40 (52), 5497–5504.

_____. 2008. 'Intra-State/Inter-State Conflicts in South Asia: The Constructivist Alternative to Realism'. In Navnita Chadha Behera (ed.), *International Relations in South Asia: Search for an Alternative Paradigm*, 177–208. New Delhi: Sage.

_____. 2009. 'Domestic Preferences and Foreign Policy: The Left Position on Indo-US Nuclear Deal'. In Nalini Kant Jha (ed.), *Nuclear Synergy: Indo-US Strategic Co-operation and Beyond*. New Delhi: Pentagon Press.

_____. 2011. 'Deconstruction and Double Reading of the South Asian Security Order'. In E. Sridharan (ed.), *International Relations Theory and South Asia: Security, Political Economy, Domestic Politics, Identities, and Images*, Vol. 2. New Delhi: Oxford University Press.

_____. 2014. 'Western Theories and the Non-Western World: A Search for Relevance'. *South Asian Survey* 21 (1–2), 1–19.

_____. 2019. *India's Spatial Imaginations of South Asia: Power, Commerce, and Community*. New Delhi: Oxford University Press.

Chatterjee, S., and S. Maitra. 2020. 'Identity, Conflicts and Security'. In Anindya Jyoti Majumdar and Shibashis Chatterjee (eds), *Peace and Conflict Studies*, 97–119. New Delhi: Routledge.

Chaturvedi, S. 2011. 'Hybridity, Imaginations, and Diasporic Otherness: Challenges for International Relations Theory'. In E. Sridharan (ed.), *International Relations Theory and South Asia: Security, Political Economy, Domestic Politics, Identities, and Images*, Vol. 2. New Delhi: Oxford University Press.

Chay, J. (ed.). 1990. *Culture and International Relations*. New York: Praeger.

Cheah, P., and B. Robbins (eds). 1998. *Cosmopolitics: Thinking and Feeling Beyond the Nation*. Minneapolis: University of Minnesota Press.

Chen, C. C. 2011. 'The Absence of Non-western IR Theory in Asia Reconsidered'. *International Relations of the Asia-Pacific* 11 (1), 1–23.

Chilcote, R. 1981. 'Issues of Theory in Dependency and Marxism'. *Latin American Perspectives* 8 (3/4), 3–16.

Chomsky, N. 2015. 'Nation State is an Artificial Construct', 13 July. Available at https://www.youtube.com/watch?v=GO37VVzYbYc (accessed August 2025).

Child Health Services (CHS). 2003. *Human Security Now*. New York: United Nations.

Christensen, T. J. 1996. *Useful Adversaries: Grand Strategy, Domestic Mobilization, and Sino-American Conflict, 1947–1958*. Princeton: Princeton University Press.

Christensen, T. J., and J. Snyder. 1990. 'Chain gangs and Passed Bucks: Predicting Alliance Patterns in Multipolarity'. *International Organization* 44 (2), 137–68.

Clausewitz, Carl von. 1832. *On War*, edited and translated by Michael Howard and Peter Paret. Available at chrome-extension://efaidnbmnnnibpcajpcglclefindmkaj/https://www.usmcu.edu/Portals/218/EWS%20On%20War%20Reading%20Book%201%20Ch%201%20Ch%202.pdf (accessed May 2025).

Cohen, B. J. 2014. *Advanced Introduction to International Political Economy*. Cheltenham: Edward Elgar Publishing Limited.

Cohen, S. P. 2004. *The Idea of Pakistan*. Washington D.C.: Brookings Institution Press.

Cohn, C. 1987. 'Sex and Death in the Rational World of Defense Intellectuals'. *Signs* 12 (4), 687–718.

_____. 2011. '"Feminist Security Studies": Toward a Reflexive Practice"'. *Politics & Gender* 7 (4), 581–86.

Council on Foreign Relations. 2024. 'Mercosur: South America's Fractious Trade Bloc'. Available at https://www.cfr.org/backgrounder/mercosur-south-americas-fractious-trade-bloc (accessed August 2025).

Cox, M. 2018. *The Post-Cold War World: Turbulence and Change in World Politics since the Fall*. London: Routledge.

Cox, R. W. 1981. 'Social Forces, States and World Orders: Beyond International Relations Theory'. *Millennium: Journal of International Studies* 10 (2), 126–55.

_____. 1983. 'Hegemony and International Relations: An Essay on Method'. *Millennium: Journal of International Studies* 12 (2), 162–75.

_____. 1987. *Social Forces in the Making of History*. New York: Columbia University Press.

Cox, R. W., and T. J. Sinclair. 1996. *Approaches to World Order*. Cambridge: Cambridge University Press.

CRED. 2015. *The Human Cost of Natural Disasters*. Louvain: Centre for Research on Epidemiology of Disasters.

Cueva, A., J. Villamil, and C. Fortin. 1976. 'A Summary of "Problems and Perspectives of Dependency Theory"'. *Latin American Perspectives*, 3 (4), 12–16.

Danilin, I. V. 2018. 'Emerging Technologies and their Impact on International Relations and Global Security'. Hoover Institution, 3 October. Available at https://www.hoover.org/research/emerging-technologies-and-their-impact-international-relations-and-global-security (accessed August 2025).

Das, S. K. 2003. *Ethnicity, Nation and Security: Essays on Northeastern India*. New Delhi: South Asian Publishers.

De Keersmaeker, G. 2017. *Polarity, Balance of Power and International Relations Theory*. London: Palgrave Macmillan.

Demeritt, D. 2001. 'The Construction of Global Warming and the Politics of Science'. *Annals of the Association of American Geographers* 91 (2), 307–37.

Der Derian, J. 1992. *Antidiplomacy: Spies, Terror, Speed, and War*. Oxford: Blackwell.

_____. 1995. 'A Reinterpretation of Realism: Genealogy, Semiology Dromology'. In J. Der Derian (ed.), *International Theory*. London: Palgrave Macmillan.

_____. 2009. *Critical Practices of International Theory: Selected Essays*. Abingdon: Routledge.

Derrida, J. 1978. *Dissemination*, Barbara Johnson (trans.). Chicago: The University of Chicago Press.

_____. 1981. *Writing and Difference*, A. Brass (trans.). Chicago: University of Chicago Press.

Desch, M. C. 1998. 'Culture Clash: Assessing the Importance of Ideas in Security Studies'. *International Security* 23 (1), 141–70.

Despres, L. A. (ed.). 1975. *Ethnicity and Resource Competition in Plural Societies*. The Hague: Montana Publishers.

Deutsch, K. W. 1957. *Political Community and the North Atlantic Area*. Princeton, N.J.: Princeton University Press.

Devetak, R. 1996a. 'Critical Theory'. In S. Burchill, A. Linklater, R. Devetak, J. Donnelly, M. Paterson, C. Reus-Smit, and J. True (eds), *Theories of International Relations*. New York: St. Martin's Press.

Devetak, R. 1996b. 'Postmodernism'. In S. Burchill, A. Linklater, R. Devetak, J. Donnelly, M. Paterson, C. Reus-Smit, and J. True (eds), *Theories of International Relations*, 167–81. New York: St Martin's Press.

DG ECHO. 2016. *Humanitarian Protection: Improving Protection Outcomes to Reduce Risks for People in Humanitarian Crises.* Brussels: European Commission.

Donnelly, J. 2000. *Realism and International Relations*. Cambridge: Cambridge University Press.

Dos Santos, T. 2002. *La Teoría de la Dependencia: Balance y Perspectivas*. Buenos Aires: Plaza and Janes.

Down to Earth. 2012. 'The Brundtland Report: A 25-year-old Milestone', 4 April.

Doyle, M. W. 1986. 'Liberalism and World Politics'. *American Political Science Review* 80 (4), 1151–69.

Duffield, J. S. 1999. 'Political Culture and State Behaviour: Why Germany Confounds Neorealism'. *International Organization* 53 (4).

Duffield, J. S., T. Farrell, R. Price, and M. Desch. 1999. 'Correspondence: Isms and Schisms: Culturalism versus Realism in Security Studies'. *International Security* 24 (1), 156–80.

Dunne, T. 2001. 'Liberalism'. In J. Baylis and S. Smith (eds), *The Globalization of World Politics: An Introduction to International Relations*. Oxford: Oxford University Press, 2e.

Dunne, T., and B. Schmidt. 2001. 'Realism'. In J. Baylis, and S. Smith. *The Globalization of World Politics: An Introduction to International Relations*, 99–112. Oxford: Oxford University Press, 2e.

Dutli, M. T. 1990. 'Captured child combatants'. IRRC, 278 (September–October), 421–34. Available at https://international-review.icrc.org/sites/default/files/S002086040007594Xa.pdfEconomic (accessed August 2025).

Economic Cooperation Organization (ECO). 2017. 'About ECO'. Available at https://eco.int/history/ (accessed August 2025).

Economic Community of West African States (ECOWAS). n.d. 'ECOWAS in Brief'. Available at https://au.int/en/recs/ecowas (accessed August 2025).

The Economist. 2013. 'What was Mercantilism?', 23 August. Available at https://www.economist.com/blogs/freeexchange/2013/08/economic-history (accessed August 2025).

Elliott, G. 2008. *Ends in Sight: Marx/Fukuyama/Hobsbawm/Anderson (Between the Lines)*. London: Pluto Press.

Elman, C., and M. F. Elman. 1997. 'Lakatos and Neorealism: A Reply to Vasquez'. *The American Political Science Review* 91 (4), 923–26.

Elshtain, B. J. 1988. 'The Problem with Peace'. *Millennium: Journal of International Studies* 17 (3), 441–49.

Emmett, D. 1954. 'The Concept of Power: The Presidential Address'. *Proceedings of the Aristotelian Society* (n.s.) 54, 1–26.

Encyclopædia Britannica. 2013. 'Commission on Global Governance'. Available at https://www.britannica.com/topic/Commission-on-Global-Governance (accessed July 2025).

———. 2017a. 'Washington Consensus'. Available at https://www.britannica.com/topic/Washington-consensus (accessed August 2025).

———. 2017b. 'Industrial Revolution'. Available at https://www.britannica.com/event/Industrial-Revolution (accessed August 2025).

———. 2017c. 'State-Sovereign Political Entity'. Available at https://www.britannica.com/topic/state-sovereign-political-entity (accessed August 2025).

———. 2021. 'Political Economy'. Available at https://www.britannica.com/topic/political-economy/Historical-development (accessed August 2025).

Enloe, C. 2000. *Maneuvers: The International Politics of Militarizing Women's Lives*. Berkeley: University of California Press.

Escobar, A. 2001. 'A Brief Response to Ray Kiely's "Reply to Escobar"'. *Development* 43 (4), 1–14.

Etefa, T. 2019. 'Ethnicity as a Tool: The Root Causes of Ethnic Conflict in Africa—A Critical Introduction'. In T. Etefa, *The Origins of Ethnic Conflict in Africa. African Histories and Modernities*, 1–27. London: Palgrave Macmillan.

European Union (EU). n.d. 'Principles, Countries, History: Aims and Values'. Available at https://europa.eu/european-union/about-eu/eu-in-brief_en (accessed August 2025).

Evans, P. B., D. Rueschemeyer, and T. Skocpol. 1985. *Bringing the State Back In*. New York: Cambridge University Press.

Falk, R. 1999. *Predatory Globalization: A Critique*. Cambridge: Polity Press.

———. 2003. 'Regionalism and World Order: The Changing Global Setting'. In F. Söderbaum and T. M. Shaw (eds), *Theories of New Regionalism: A Palgrave Reader*, 63–80. London: Palgrave Macmillan Ltd.

Falkner, R. 2019. 'The Unavoidability of Justice and Order in International Climate Politics: From Kyoto to Paris and Beyond'. *The British Journal of Politics and International Relations* 21 (2), 270–78.

Fawcett, L., and A. Hurrell. 1995. *Regionalism in World Politics*. Oxford: Oxford University Press.

Fearon, J., and A. Wendt. 2002. 'Rationalism vs. Constructivism: A Skeptical View'. In W. Carlsnaes, T. Risse, and B. A. Simmons (eds), *Handbook of International Relations*. London: Sage.

Featherstone, M. 1990. *Global Culture: Nationalism, Globalization and Modernity*. London: Sage.

Featherstone, M., S. Lash, and R. Robertson (eds). 1995. *Global Modernities*. New York: Sage.

Ferraro, V. 2008. 'Dependency Theory: An Introduction'. In Giorgio Secondi (ed.), *The Development Economics Reader*, 58–64. London: Routledge.

Fidler, D. P. 2021. 'Vaccine Nationalism and Global Health Diplomacy: Inequities, Interests, and Geopolitics'. *Ethics & International Affairs* 35 (3), 367–80.

Finlan, A. 2004. *The Collapse of Yugoslavia, 1991–1999*. Oxford: Osprey Publishing.

Follett, M. P. 1934. *Dynamic Administration*. London: Management Publications Trust Ltd.

Foster, J. B. 2002. 'The Rediscovery of Imperialism'. *New York Monthly Review* 54 (6), 1–16.

Foucault, M. 1978 [1976]. *The Will to Knowledge: The History of Sexuality*, Vol. 1, R Hurley (trans.). New York: Pantheon Books (Random House).

Fox, J. 2005. 'Paradigm Lost: Huntington's Unfulfilled Clash of Civilizations Prediction into the 21st Century'. *International Politics* 42 (4), 428–57.

Frank, A. G. 1972. 'The Development of Underdevelopment'. In James D. Cockcroft, Andre Gunder Frank, and Dale Johnson (eds), *Dependence and Underdevelopment*. Garden City, New York: Anchor Books.

Frank, A. G., and B. Gills. 1993. *The World System: Five Hundred Years or Five Thousand?* London: Routledge.

Frankel, J. 1977. *International Relations in a Changing World*. Oxford: Oxford University Press.

Freedman, J. 2010. 'Mainstreaming Gender in Refugee Protection'. *Cambridge Review of International Affairs* 23 (4), 589–607.

Freedman, L. (ed.). 1994. *War*. New York: Oxford University Press.

_____. 2012. 'Defining War'. In Julian Lindlay-French and Yves Boyer (eds), *The Oxford Handbook of War*. Oxford: Oxford University Press.

Friedman, T. L. 2015. 'Paris Climate Accord Is a Big, Big Deal'. *The New York Times*, 16 December. Available at https://www.nytimes.com/2015/12/16/opinion/paris-climate-accord-is-a-big-big-deal.html (accessed August 2025).

Fukuyama, F. 1989. 'The End of History?' *The National Interest* 16, 3–18.

_____. 1992. *The End of History and the Last Man*. New York: Free Press.

_____. 1995. 'Reflections on the End of History, Five Years Later'. *History and Theory* 34 (2), 27–43.

Gaddis, J. L, 2007. *The Cold War*. London: Penguin Books.

Gangal, A. n.d. 'The Gandhian Concept of Human Security and Peace: Quest for Amity Amidst Globalisation and Weapons of Mass Destruction', University of Jammu.

George, J. 1993. 'Of Incarceration and Closure: Neo-Realism and the New/Old World Order'. *Millennium: Journal of International Studies* 22 (2), 197–238.

_____. 1994. *Discourses of Global Politics: A Critical (Re)introduction to International Relations*. Boulder, Colorado: Lynne Reiner.

_____. 1995. 'Realist Ethics, International Relations, and Post-modernism: Thinking Beyond the Egoism-Anarchy Thematic'. *Millennium: Journal of International Studies* 24 (2), 195–224.

George, J., and D. Campbell. 1990. 'Patterns of Dissent and the Celebration of Difference: Critical Social Theory and International Relations'. *International Studies Quarterly* 34 (3), 269–93.

George, N., K. Lee-Koo, and L. Shepherd. 2019. 'Gender and the UN's Women, Peace and Security Agenda'. In Caron E. Gentry, Laura J. Shepherd and Laura Sjoberg (eds), *The Routledge Handbook of Gender Security*, 311–22. New York: Routledge.

George, S. 2002. 'The Global Citizen's Movement'. *New Agenda* 6 (Second Quarter).

GHA. 2016. 'Global Humanitarian Assistance Report 2016'. Bristol: Development Initiatives. Available at https://reliefweb.int/report/world/global-humanitarian-assistance-report-2016 (accessed July 2025).

Ghimire, K. B. 2005. 'The Contemporary Global Social Movements: Emergent Proposals, Connectivity and Development Implications'. Civil Society and Social Movements Programme, Paper No. 19, August, United Nations Research Institute for Social Development. Available at https://www.unrisd.org/80256B3C005BCCF9/(httpAuxPages)/F0F8C2DF84C2FB2DC1257088002BFBD9/$file/ghimire.pdf (accessed August 2025).

Giddens, A. 1985. *Nation-State and Violence*. Berkeley: University of California Press.

_____. 2008. 'The Politics of Climate Change'. Policy Network Paper, September, 1–19.

Gill, S. (ed.). 1993. *Gramsci, Historical Materialism and International Relations*. Cambridge and New York: Cambridge University Press.

Gilligan, C. 1982. *In a Different Voice: Psychological Theory and Women's Development*. Cambridge, MA: Harvard University Press.

Gilpin, R. 1981. *War and Change in World Politics*. Cambridge: Cambridge University Press.

_____. 1984. 'The Richness of the Tradition of Political Realism'. *International Organization* 38 (2), 287–304.

_____. 2001. *Global Political Economy: Understanding the International Economic Order*. Princeton: Princeton University Press.

Glaser, E. 2014, 'Bring Back Ideology: Fukuyama's "End of History" 25 Years On'. *The Guardian*, 21 March. Available at https://www.theguardian.com/books/2014/mar/21/bring-back-ideology-fukuyama-end-history-25-years-on (accessed August 2025).

Golan, G. 1997. 'Militarization and Gender: The Israeli Experience'. *Women's Studies International Forum* 20 (5–6), 581–86.

Goldfrank, W. L. 2000. 'Paradigm Regained? The Rules of Wallerstein's World-System Method'. *Journal of World-Systems Research* XI (2), 150–95.

Gomez, O. A., and D. Gasper. 2013. *Human Security: A Thematic Guidance Note for Regional and National Human Development Report Teams*. Washington, D.C.: UNDP.

Gourevitch, P. 1978. 'The Second Image Reversed: The International Sources of Domestic Politics'. *International Organization* 32 (4), 881–912.

Government of India (GOI). 2012 'History and Evolution of Non-Aligned Movement', 22 August. New Delhi: Ministry of External Affairs, GOI. Available at https://www.mea.gov.in/Speeches-Statements.htm?dtl/20349/History+and+Evolution+of+NonAligned+Movement (accessed July 2025).

———. 2013. 'Andean Community'. New Delhi: Ministry of External Affairs, Government of India. Available at https://www.mea.gov.in/Portal/ForeignRelation/Andean_Community_11_08_2022.pdf (accessed August 2025).

Grantham Research Institute on Climate Change and the Environment. 2022. *What is the UN Framework Convention on Climate Change (UNFCCC)?* London: London School of Economics and Political Science. Available at https://www.lse.ac.uk/granthaminstitute/explainers/what-is-the-un-framework-convention-on-climate-change-unfccc/#:~:text=The%20ultimate%20goal%20of%20the,and%20economies%20to%20develop%20sustainably (accessed July 2025).

Green, D., and L. Luehrmann. 2007. *Comparative Politics of the Third World: Linking Concepts and Cases*. London: Lynne Rienner Publishers.

Greer, S. L., E. J. King, E. Massard da Fonseca, and A. Peralta-Santos. 2021. *Coronavirus Politics: The Comparative Politics and Policy of COVID-19*. Michigan: University of Michigan Press.

Grieco, J., R. Powell, and D. Snidal. 1993. 'The Relative-Gains Problem for International Cooperation'. *The American Political Science Review* 87 (3), 727–43.

Griffin, R. (ed.). 2009. *Fascism*. Oxford: Oxford University Press.

Griffiths, M. 1995. *Realism, Idealism and International Politics: A Reinterpretation*. London: Routledge.

———. 1999. *Fifty Key Thinkers in International Relations*. London: Routledge.

Gurr, T. R. (ed.). 1980. *Hand Book of Political Conflict: Theory and Research*. New York: The Free Press.

Gurr, T. R., and B. Harff. 2000. *Ethnic Conflict in World Politics*. Boulder, Colorado: Westview Press, 2e.

Guzzini, S. 1998. *Realism in International Relations and International Political Economy: The Continuing Story of a Death Foretold*. London: Routledge.

Haacke, J. 1996. 'Theory and Praxis in International Relations: Habermas, Self-Reflection, Rational Argumentation'. *Millennium: Journal of International Studies* 25 (2), 255–89.

Haas, E. B. 1958. *The Uniting of Europe*. Stanford, CA: Stanford University Press.

_____. 1961. 'International Integration: The European and the Universal Process'. *International Organization* 15 (3), 366–92.

_____. 1964. *Beyond the Nation State*. Stanford, CA: Stanford University Press.

Haas, P. M. 1992. 'Introduction: Epistemic Communities and International Policy Coordination'. *International Organization* 46 (1), 1–35.

Hall, S. 1997. 'The Local and the Global: Globalization and Ethnicity'. In Anthony King (ed.), *Culture, Globalization, and the World-System: Contemporary Conditions for the Representation of Identity*, 19–40. Minneapolis: University of Minnesota Press.

Halliday, F. 1988. 'Hidden from International Relations: Women and the International Arena'. *Millennium: Journal of International Studies* 17 (3), 419–28.

_____. 1994. *Rethinking of International Relations*. London: Macmillan.

Hansen, L. 1997. 'A Case for Seduction?: Evaluating the Poststructuralist Conceptualization of Security'. *Cooperation and Conflict* 32 (4), 369–97.

_____. 2000. 'Past as Preface: Civilizational Politics and the Third Balkan War'. *Journal of Peace Research* 37 (3), 345–62.

Haque, M. 2002. 'Globalization, New Political Economy and Governance: A Third World Viewpoint'. *Administrative Theory and Praxis* 24 (1), 103–24.

Harding, S. 1986. *The Science Question in Feminism*. Ithaca, BY: Cornell University Press.

Harithas, B., K. Meng, E. Brown, and C. Mouradian. 2025. 'Liberation Day Tariffs Explained'. Centre for Strategic and International Studies, 3 April. Available at https://www.csis.org/analysis/liberation-day-tariffs-explained (accessed July 2025).

Hartsock, N. C. M. 1983. *Money, Sex and Power: Toward a Feminist Historical Materialism*. Boston, MA: Northeastern University Press.

Harvey, D. 1989. *The Condition of Post-Modernity: An Enquiry into the Origins of Cultural Change*. Oxford: Blackwell.

Hay, C. 2002. *Political Analysis: A Critical Introduction*. London: Palgrave.

Haynes, J. 2019. *From Huntington to Trump: 30 Years of the 'Clash of Civilizations'*. New York: Lexington Books.

He, B. 2020. 'Regionalism as an Instrument for Global Power Contestation: The Case of China'. *Asian Studies Review* 44 (1), 79–96.

Hehir, A. 2010. *Humanitarian Intervention: An Introduction*. Hampshire: Palgrave Macmillan.

Held, D. 1995. *Democracy and the Global Order: From the Modern State to Cosmopolitan Governance*. Stanford: Stanford University Press.

Held, D., and A. G. McGrew. 2000. 'The Great Globalization Debate: An Introduction'. In David Held and A. G. McGrew (eds), *The Great Globalization Debate: An Introduction*, 1–50. Cambridge: Polity Press.

Held, D., A. G. McGrew, R. Higgott, et al. 1993. 'Globalization and the Liberal Democratic State'. *Government and Opposition* 28 (2), 261–88.

Henderson, E. A., and R. Tucker. 2001. 'Clear and Present Strangers: The Clash of Civilizations and International Conflict'. *International Studies Quarterly* 45 (2), 317–38.

Hermon, C. C. 2000. *Terrorism Today*. London: Frank Cass.

Herz, J. 1951. *Political Realism and Political Idealism: A Study in Theories and Realities*. Chicago: University of Chicago Press.

Higate, P. 2019. 'Men, Masculinity, and Global Insecurity'. In Caron E. Gentry, Laura J. Shepherd, and Laura Sjoberg (eds), *The Routledge Handbook of Gender Security*, 70–82. New York: Routledge.

Hirsch, F., and J. H. Goldthorpe. 1978. *The Political Economy of Inflation*. Boston, M.A.: Harvard University Press.

Hirschman, A. O. 1958. *The Strategy of Economic Development*. New Haven and London: Yale University Press.

———. 1967. 'The Principle of the Hiding Hand'. Available at https://www.nationalaffairs.com/storage/app/uploads/public/58e/1a4/a29/58e1a4a298835643416368.pdf (accessed June 2025).

———. 1970. *Exit, Voice, and Loyalty: Responses to Decline in Firms, Organizations, and States*. Boston: Harvard University Press.

Hirst, P. 2000. 'Globalization, Nation State, Political Theory'. In Noel O' Sullivan (ed.), *Political Theory in Transition*. London and New York: Routledge.

Hirst, P., and G. Thompson. 1996. *Globalisation in Question: The International Economy and the Possibilities of Governance*. Cambridge: Blackwell.

Hobden, S. 1998. *International Relations and Historical Sociology: Breaking down Boundaries*. London: Routledge.

Hobsbawm, E. (1992). *Nations and Nationalism Since 1780: Programme, Myth, Reality*. Cambridge: Cambridge University Press.

Hoetink, H. 1975. 'Resource Competition, Monopoly, and Socioracial Diversity'. In Leo A. Despres (ed.), *Ethnicity and Resource Competition in Plural Societies*. The Hague: Montana Publishers.

Hoffman, J. 1998. *Sovereignty*. Minneapolis: University of Minnesota Press.

Hoffman, M. 1987. 'Critical Theory and the Inter-Paradigm Debate'. *Millennium: Journal of International Studies* 16 (2), 231–49.

_____. 1988. 'Conversations on Critical International Relations Theory'. *Millennium* 17 (1), 91–95.

Hollis, M., and S. Smith. 1990. *Explaining and Understanding International Relations*. Oxford: Clarendon Press.

Holsti, K. J. 1995. *International Politics: A Framework for Analysis*. Englewood Cliffs, NJ: Prentice-Hall.

_____. 1996. *The State, War, and the State of War*. Cambridge: Cambridge University Press.

Holzgrefe, J., and R. O. Keohane. 2003. *Humanitarian Intervention: Ethical, Legal and Political Dilemmas*. Cambridge: Cambridge University Press.

Homer-Dixon, T. 1994. 'Environmental Scarcities and Violent Conflict: Evidence from Cases'. Peace and Conflict Studies Programme, University of Toronto, 5–40.

Hooghe, L., and G. Marks. 2019. 'Grand Theories of European Integration in the Twenty-first Century'. *Journal of European Public Policy* 26 (8), 1113–33.

Hoogvelt, A. 1997. *Globalization and the Post-Colonial World*. London: Macmillan.

Hopkins, A. 2002. 'The History of Globalization and the Globalization of History'. In A. G. Hopkins (ed.), *Globalization in World History*. London: Pimlico, 2002.

_____. 2010. 'The Historiography of Globalization and the Globalization of Regionalism'. *Journal of the Economic and Social History of the Orient* 53 (1/2), 19–36.

Hoshiro, H. 2019. 'Does Regionalization Promote Regionalism? Evidence from East Asia'. *Contemporary Journal of East Asian Studies* 8 (2), 199–219.

Hudson, F. N., and L. Huber. 2019. 'Gender in International Security Organizations'. In Caron E. Gentry, Laura J. Shepherd, and Laura Sjoberg (eds), *The Routledge Handbook of Gender Security*, 373–84. New York: Routledge.

Hudson, V. M. (ed.). 1997. *Culture and Foreign Policy*. Boulder, Colorado: Lynne Rienner.

Human Security Unit. 2009. *Human Security in Theory and Practice*. New York: The United Nations Trust Fund for Human Security.

Huntington, S. P. 1993. 'The Clash of Civilizations'. *Foreign Affairs* 72 (3), 22–49. Available at https://www2.kenyon.edu/Depts/Religion/Fac/Adler/Politics/Huntington-Clash.htm (accessed July 2025).

_____. 1996. *The Clash of Civilizations and the Remaking of the World Order*. New York: Simon and Schuster.

Hurrell, A. 1995. 'Explaining the Resurgence of Regionalism in World Politics'. *Review of International Studies* 21 (4), 331–58.

Hurrell, A., and N. Woods. 1999. *Inequality, Globalization and World Politics*. Oxford: Oxford University Press.

Inter-American Defense Board (IADB). n.d. 'About Us; History'. Available at https://jid.org/en/historia/ (accessed August 2025).

ICRtoP. 2017. *Key Developments on the Responsibility to Protect at the United Nations from 2005–2014*. New York: International Coalition for the Responsibility to Protect. Available at http://www.responsibilitytoprotect.org/index.php/about-rtop/the-un-and-rtop.

Ikenberry, J. 2003. 'Global Civil Society?' *Foreign Affairs*, November–December 2003. Available at http://www.foreignaffairs.com/articles/59214/g-john-ikenberry/global-civil-society (accessed August 2025).

International Monetary Fund (IMF). n.d.(a). 'About the IMF'. Available at http://www.imf.org/en/About (accessed August 2025).

_____. n.d.(b). 'World Economic Outlook'. Available at http://www.imf.org/en/Publications/WEO/Issues/2017/04/04/world-economic-outlook-april-2017 (accessed August 2025).

_____. 2025. 'World Economic Outlook: A Critical Juncture Amid Policy Shifts'. April. Available at https://www.imf.org/en/Publications/WEO/Issues/2025/04/22/world-economic-outlook-april-2025 (accessed June 2025).

Inayatullah, N., and D. L. Blaney. 1996. 'Knowing Encounters: Beyond Parochialism in International Relations Theory'. In Yosef Lapid and Freidrich Kratochwil (eds), *The Return of Culture and Identity in IR Theory*. Boulder, Colorado: Lynne Rienner Publishers.

International Crisis Group. 2017. 'Myanmar's Rohingya Crisis Enters a Dangerous New Phase', 7 December. Available at https://www.crisisgroup.org/asia/south-east-asia/myanmar/292-myanmars-rohingya-crisis-enters-dangerous-new-phase (accessed 16 July 2025).

IPCC. 2007a. 'Climate Change 2007: Synthesis Report'. Available at https://www.ipcc.ch/site/assets/uploads/2018/02/ar4_syr_full_report.pdf (accessed July 2025).

_____. 2007b. 'Is Sea Level Rising?' Available at https://www.ipcc.ch/publications_and_data/ar4/wg1/en/faq-5-1.html (accessed July 2025).

Iriye, A. 1997. 'Cultural Internationalism and World Order'. New York: John Hopkins University Press.

Jackson, R., and G. Sørensen. 2003. *Introduction to International Relations: Theories and Aproaches*. New Delhi: Oxford University Press.

Jameson, F., and M. Masao (eds). 1998. *The Culture of Globalization*. Durham: Duke University Press.

Jetschke, A., and P. Murray. 2012. 'Diffusing Regional Integration: The EU and Southeast Asia'. *Western European Politics* 35 (1), 174–91.

Johnston, A. I. 1995. *Cultural Realism: Strategic Culture and Grand Strategy in Chinese History*. Princeton, N.J.: Princeton University Press.

_____. 1998. *Cultural Realism: Strategic Culture and Grand Strategy in Chinese History*. Princeton, N.J.: Princeton University Press.

Jorgensen, D., and O. Corry. 2016. 'Beyond "Denierd" and "Believers": Towards a Map of the Politics of Climate Change'. *Global Environmental Change* 32, 165–74.

Kaldor, M. 1999. *New and Old Wars: Organized Violence in the Global Era*. Stanford: Stanford University Press.

_____. 2003. 'The Idea of Global Civil Society'. *International Affairs* 79 (3), 583–93.

_____. 2007. *Human Security*. Cambridge: Polity Press.

Kaplan, M. 1961. 'Is International Relations a Discipline?' *The Journal of Politics* 23 (3), 462–76.

Kaplan, R. D. 1994. 'The Coming Anarchy'. *Atlantic Monthly* 273 (2), 44–76.

Katzenstein, P. J. 2005. *A World of Regions: Asia and Europe in the American Imperium*. Ithaca, NY: Cornell University Press.

_____ (ed.). 1996. 'Introduction: Alternative Perspectives on National Security'. In Peter Katzenstein (ed.), *The Culture of National Security: Norms and Identity in World Politics*, 1–32. New York: Columbia University Press.

Katzenstein, P., R. J. Jepperson, and A. Wendt. 1996. 'Norms, Identity, and Culture in National Security'. In Peter J. Katzenstein (ed.), *The Culture of National Security*, 33–75. New York: Columbia University Press.

Keane, J. 2001. 'Global Civil Society?' In Helmut Anheier, Marlies Glasius, and Mary Kaldor (eds), *Global Civil Society*, 23–47. Oxford: Oxford University Press.

Kegley, C. W., and E. R. Wittkopf. 2004. *World Politics: Trends and Transformation*. Wadsworth: Belmont.

Keller, F. E. 1985. *Reflections on Gender and Science*. New Haven, CT: Yale University Press.

Kennedy, P. 2017. *The Rise and Fall of Great Powers*. London: William Collins.

Keohane, R. 2015. 'The Global Politics of Climate Change: Challenge for Political Science'. *PS: Political Science & Politics* 48 (1), 19–26.

_____ (ed.). 1983. *Neorealism and Its Critics*. New York: Columbia University Press.

Keohane, R., and J. Nye. 1971. *Transnational Relations in World Politics*. Cambridge, Massachusetts: Harvard University Press.

_____. 1977. *Power and Interdependence: World Politics in Transition*. Boston: Little, Brown.

Keohane, R. O. 1984. *After Hegemony: Cooperation and Discord in the World Political Economy*. Princeton: Princeton University Press.

_____. 1988. 'International Institutions: Two Approaches'. *International Studies Quarterly* 32 (4), 379–96.

Kindleberger, C. P., and R. N. McCauley. 1978. *Manias, Panics, and Crashes: A History of Financial Crises*. New York: John Wiley and Sons. Available at https://delong.typepad.com/manias.pdf (accessed June 2025).

Kirkpatrick, J., A. Weeks, and G. Piel. 1993. 'The Modernizing Imperative: Tradition and Change'. *Foreign Affairs* 72 (4), 22–26.

Kissinger, H. 1994. *Diplomacy*. New York: Simon & Schuster.

Knorr, K., and J. Rosenau. 1969. *Contending Approaches to International Politics*. Princeton, New Jersey: Princeton University Press.

Knorr, K., and S. Verba (eds). 1961. *The International System: Theoretical Essays*. Princeton. N.J.: Princeton University Press.

Kofman, E., and G. Young. 1996. *Globalization: Theory and Practice*. London: Pinter.

Kohl, U. 2019. 'Territoriality and Globalization'. In S. Allen, D. Costello, M. Fitzmaurice, P. Gragl, and E. Guntrip (eds), *The Oxford Handbook of Jurisdiction in International Law*. Oxford: Oxford University Press.

Koon-hong, D. C. 2014. 'The Role of Global Civil Society in Bringing Global Democratic Order'. *E-International Relations*, 29 December. Available at www.e-ir.info/2014/12/29/the-role-of-global-civil-society-in-bringing-global-democratic-order/ (accessed August 2025).

Krasner, S. D. 1996–97. 'Compromising Westphalia'. *International Security* 20 (3), 115–51.

_____. 1999. *Sovereignty: Organized Hypocrisy*. Princeton, N.J.: Princeton University Press.

_____ (ed.). 1983. *International Regimes*. Ithaca, NY: Cornell University Press.

Kratochwil, F., and J. G. Ruggie. 1986. 'International Organization: A State of the Art on an Art of the State'. *International Organization* 40 (4), 753–76.

Kratochwil, F. 1986. 'Of Systems, Boundaries, and Territoriality: An Inquiry into the Formation of the State System'. *World Politics* XXXIX (1), 27–52.

Krause, K. (ed.). 1999. *Culture and Security: Multilateralism, Arms Control and Security Building*. London: Frank Cass.

Krause, K. and M. C. Williams. 1996. 'Broadening the Agenda of Security Studies: Politics and Methods'. *Mershon International Studies Review* 40 (2), 229–54.

Krickovic, A. 2015. 'All Politics is Regional: Emerging Powers and the Regionalization of Global Governance'. *Global Governance* 21 (4), 557–77.

LaHaye, L. 2008. 'Mercantilism'. Library of Economics and Liberty (Econlib). Available at http://www.econlib.org/library/Enc/Mercantilism.html (accessed August 2025).

Lahiry, S. 2020. 'The Changing Narrative of Security Discourse'. *World Affairs* 183 (2), 183–205.

Lampe, M. 2010. 'Explaining Nineteenth-Century Bilateralism: Economic and Political Determinants of the Cobden–Chevalier Network'. World Trade Organization. Available at https://www.wto.org/english/res_e/publications_e/wtr11_forum_e/wtr11_11jan11_e.htm (accessed August 2025).

Langenhove, L. V. 2010. 'The Transformation of Multilateralism Mode 1.0 to Mode 2.0'. *Global Policy* 1 (3), 263–70.

Lapid, Y., and F. Kratochwil (eds). 1996. *The Return of Culture and Identity in IR Theory*. London: Lynne Rienner.

Larsen, J. A. (ed.). 2005. *Arms Control: Cooperative Security in a Changing Environment*. New Delhi: Viva Books.

Larson, D. W. 2022 [2017]. 'Social Identity Theory: Status and Identity in International Relations'. *Oxford Research Encyclopedia of Politics*. Available at https://oxfordre.com/politics/view/10.1093/acrefore/9780190228637.001.0001/acrefore-9780190228637-e-290#acrefore-9780190228637-e-290 (accessed August 2025).

Lavoy, P. K., S. D. Sagan, and J. J. Wirtz (eds). 2000. *Planning the Unthinkable*. Ithaca, NY: Cornell University Press.

Layne, C. 1994. 'Kant or Cant: The Myth of the Democratic Peace'. *International Security* 19 (2), 5–49.

Lebow, R. N. 2010. *Why Nations Fight*. Cambridge: Cambridge University Press.

Lechner, F. J., and J. Boli (eds). 2020. *The Globalization Reader*. Hoboken, N.J.: John Wiley & Sons.

Leiserowitz, A., E. Maibach, and C. Roser-Renouf. 2009a. *Global Warming's Six Americas: An Audience Segmentation*. New Haven, CT: Yale University Press.

______. 2009b. *Climate Change in the American Mind: Americans' Climate Change Beliefs, Attitudes, Policy Preferences, and Actions*. New Haven, CT: Yale University Press.

Lemke, D. 2002. *Regions of War and Peace*. New York: Cambridge University Press.

Levy, J. 1988. 'Domestic Politics and War'. *The Journal of Interdisciplinary History* 18 (4), 653–73.

______. 2002. 'War and Peace'. In W. Carlsnaes, T. Risse, and B. A. Simmons (eds), *Handbook of International Relations*. London: Sage.

Lewis, N. 2013 'The 1870–1914 Gold Standard: The Most Perfect One Ever Created'. *Forbes*, 3 January. Available at https://www.forbes.com/sites/nathanlewis/2013/01/03/the-1870-1914-gold-standard-the-most-perfect-one-ever-created/#25abd6e64a6a (accessed August 2025).

Lijphart, A. 2008. *Thinking about Democracy: Power Sharing and Majority Rule in Theory and Practice*. London and New York: Routledge.

Lindberg, L. N., C. S. Maier, and B. Barry. 1985. *The Politics of Inflation and Economic Stagnation: Theoretical Approaches and International Case Studies*. Washington, D. C.: Brookings Institution.

Lindley-French, J., and Y. Boyer (eds). 2012. *The Oxford Handbook of War*. Oxford: Oxford University Press.

Linklater, A. 1993. *Beyond Realism and Marxism: Critical Theory and International Relations*. New York: St. Martin's Press.

_____. 1996. 'The Achievements of Critical Theory'. In S. Smith, K. Booth, and M. Zalewski (eds), *International Theory: Positivism and Beyond*. Cambridge: Cambridge University Press.

_____. 1998. *The Transformation of Community*. Cambridge: Polity Press.

Luna, K. C., G. Haar, and D. Hilhorst. 2017. 'Changing Gender Role: Women's Livelihoods, Conflict and Post-conflict Security in Nepal'. *Journal of Asian Security and International Affairs* 4 (2), 175–95.

Lyotard, J.-F. 1984. *The Postmodern Condition: A Report on Knowledge*. Minneapolis: University of Minnesota Press.

Macalister, T. 2011. 'Background: What Caused the 1970s Oil Price Shock?' *The Guardian*, 3 March. Available at https://www.theguardian.com/environment/2011/mar/03/1970s-oil-price-shock (accessed July 2025).

MacFarlane, S. N., and Y. F. Khong. 2006. *Human Security and the UN: A Critical History*. Bloomington: Indiana University Press.

Maibach, E., C. Roser-Renouf, and A. Leiserowitz. 2009. *Global Warming's Six Americas 2009: An Audience Segmentation Analysis*. New Haven: George Mason University, Yale University Press.

Majumdar, A. J. 2003. 'Nuclear Terror'. In Omprakash Mishra and Sucheta Ghosh (eds), *Terrorism and Low Intensity Conflict in South Asian Region*. New Delhi: Manak.

_____. 2009. 'The Profile of Terrorism in the 21st Century'. In Debnarayan Modak (ed.), *Terrorism: Concepts and Problems*. Kolkata: Progressive Publishers.

Majumdar, A. J., and S. Chatterjee (eds). 2021. *Peace and Conflict Studies: Perspectives from South Asia*. New York: Routledge.

Mamdani, M. 2004. *Good Muslim, Bad Muslim: Islam, the USA and the Global War against Terror*. New Delhi: Permanent Black.

Mann, M. 1984. 'The Autonomous Power of the State: Its Origins, Mechanisms and Results'. *European Journal of Sociology/Archives Européennes de Sociologie/EuropäischesArchivfürSoziologie* 25 (2), 185–213.

Mann, M. E, R. S. Bradley, and M. K. Hughes. 1999. 'Northern Hemisphere Temperatures during the Past Millennium: Inferences, Uncertainties, and Limitations'. *Geophysical Research Letters* 26 (6), 759–62. Available at https://www.researchgate.net/publication/201169897_Northern_hemisphere_temperatures_during_the_past_millennium_Inferences_uncertainties_and_limitations_Geophysical_Research_Letters (accessed July 2025).

Manno, J. 2004. 'Political Ideology and Conflicting Environmental Paradigms'. *Global Environmental Politics* 4 (3), 155–59.

Mansfield, E. D., and J. Snyder. 2002. 'Democratic Transitions, Institutional Strength, and War'. *International Organization* 56 (2), 297–337.

Martinez-Vela, C. 2001. 'World Systems Theory'. *ESD* 83, 1–5. Available at https://web.mit.edu/esd.83/www/notebook/WorldSystem.pdf (accessed August 2025).

Maruska, H. J. 2010. 'When are States Hypermasculine?' In Laura Sjoberg (ed.), *Gender and International Security: Feminist Perspectives*, 235–55. New York: Routledge.

Mason, J. W. 1996. *The Cold War: 1945–1991*. London: Routledge.

McGrath, M. 2020. 'Climate change: China aims for "carbon neutrality by 2060"'. *BBC News*, 23 September. Available at https://www.bbc.com/news/science-environment-54256826 (accessed July 2025).

McGrew, A. 1997. 'Globalization and Global Politics'. In John Bayliss and Patricia Owens (eds), *Global Politics: Globalization and the Nation-State*. Oxford: Oxford University Press.

———. 2014. 'The Logic of Economic Globalisation'. In J. Ravenhill (ed.), *Global Political Economy*. Oxford: Oxford University Press.

McKie, R. 2016. 'Scientists Warn World Will Miss Key Climate Target'. *The Guardian*, 6 August. Available at https://www.theguardian.com/science/2016/aug/06/global-warming-target-miss-scientists-warn (accessed August 2025).

McLellan, D. 1998. *Marxism after Marx: An Introduction*. London: Macmillan, 3e.

McLuhan, M., and E. McLuhan. n.d. *Laws of Media: The New Science*. Toronto, Buffalo, London: Toronto University Press. Available at https://monoskop.org/images/e/ec/McLuhan_Marshall_McLuhan_Eric_Laws_of_Media_The_New_Science.pdf (accessed August 2025).

McLuhan, M., and B. R. Powers. 1989. *Transformations in World Life and Media in the 21st Century*. New York: Oxford University Press.

McWilliams, W. C., and H. Piotrowski. 2006. *The World since 1945: A History of International Relations*. Boulder, CO: Lynne Rienner.

Mearsheimer, J. J. 1994. 'The False Promise of International Institutions'. *International Security* 19 (3), 5–49.

_____. 2001. *The Tragedy of Great Power Politics*. New York: W. W. Norton and Company.

Merriam-Webster. 2017. 'Stagflation'. Available at https://www.merriam-webster.com/dictionary/stagflation (accessed August 2025).

Merriman, J. 2009. 'Hist 202: European Civilization, 1648–1945'. Open Yale Courses. Available at https://www.youtube.com/watch?v=7a6j17VWhBc (accessed August 2025).

Miller Center. n.d. 'Edward R. Stettinius Jr. (1944–1945)', University of Virginia. Available at https://millercenter.org/president/fdroosevelt/essays/stettinius-edward-1944-secretary-of-state (accessed August 2025).

Miller, D. 2008. 'Nationalism'. In J. S. Dryzek, B. Honig, and A. Phillips (eds), *The Oxford Handbook of Political Theory*, 529–45. Oxford: Oxford University Press.

Ministry of Foreign Affairs of Japan. 2009. *The Trust Fund for Human Security.* Tokyo: Global Issues Cooperation Division.

Mishra, O., and S. Ghosh (eds). 2003. *Terrorism and Low Intensity Conflicts in South Asian Region*. New Delhi: Manak.

Mitra, S. 1997. 'Legitimacy, Governance and Political Institutions in India after Independence'. In Subrata K. Mitra and Dietmar Rothermund (eds), *Legitimacy and Conflict in South Asia*. New Delhi: Manohar.

_____. 2012. 'Sub-National Movements, Cultural Flow, the Modern State and the Malleability of Political Space: From Rational Choice to Transcultural Perspective and Back Again'. *Transcultural Studies* (2), Heidelberg.

Mitrany, D. 1966. *The Working Peace System*. Chicago: Quadrangle Books.

Mockaitis, T. R. 2012. 'Terrorism, Insurgency and Organized Crime'. In Paul Shemella (ed.), *Fighting Back: What the Governments Can Do about Terrorism*. New Delhi: Foundation Books/Cambridge University Press.

Moore, J. A., and J. Pubantz. 2008. *The New United Nations: International Organization in the Twenty-First Century*. New Delhi: Pearson.

Moore, M. 2004. 'Sub-State Nationalism and International Law'. *Michigan Journal of International Law* 25 (4), 1–23.

Moore, S. 2014. 'India's Role in the International Climate Negotiations'. Planet Policy, Brookings Institute, 26 November. Available at https://www.brookings.edu/blog/planetpolicy/2014/11/26/indias-role-in-the-international-climate-negotiations/ (accessed July 2025).

Moravcsik, A. 1997. 'Taking Preferences Seriously: A Liberal Theory of International Politics'. *International Organization* 51 (4), 513–53.

Morgan, P. M. 2003. *Deterrence Now*. Cambridge: Cambridge University Press.

Morgenthau, H. J. 1947. *Scientific Man Versus Power Politics*. Chicago: Chicago University Press.

———. 1948. *Politics among Nations: The Struggle for Power and Peace*. New York: Alfred Knopf.

Mukherjee, S., and I. Mukherjee. 2008. *International Relations*. Kolkata: World Press Private Limited.

Munck, R. 1981. 'Imperialism and Dependency: Recent Debates and Old Dead-Ends'. *Latin American Perspectives* 8 (3/4), 162–79.

Mungiu-Pippidi, A., and D. Mindruta. 2002. 'Was Huntington Right? Testing Cultural Legacies and the Civilization Border'. *International Politics* 39 (2), 193–213.

Murphy, C. N., and D. R. Nelson. 2001. 'International Political Economy: A Tale of Two Heterodoxies'. *The British Journal of Politics and International Relations* 3 (3), 393–412.

Murray, R. 1971. 'Internationalization of Capital and the Nation-state'. *New Left Review* 67 (May–June), 84–108.

Murthy, C. S. R. 2020. *India in the United Nations: Interplay of Interests and Principles*. New Delhi: Sage.

NASA. 2015. 'Study: Mass Gains of Antarctic Ice Sheet Greater than Losses'. NASA Science Editorial Team, 5 November. Available at https://science.nasa.gov/science-research/earth-science/water-energy-cycle/cryosphere/study-mass-gains-of-antarctic-ice-sheet-greater-than-losses/ (accessed July 2025).

———. 2016. 'What are Climate and Climate Change?' Available at http://www.nasa.gov/audience/forstudents/5-8/features/nasa-knows/what-is-climate-change-58.html (accessed July 2025).

National Snow and Ice Data Center (NSIDC). 2016. 'Quick facts, basic science, and information about snow, ice, and why the cryosphere matters'. Boulder: University of Colorado. Available at https://nsidc.org/cryosphere/quickfacts/icesheets.html (accessed July 2025).

Negri, A., and M. Hardt. 2000. *Empire*. Cambridge, MA: Harvard University Press.

Neufeld, M. 1993. 'Reflexivity and International Relations Theory'. *Millennium* 22 (1), 53–76.

Nicholas, H. G. 1979. *The United Nations as a Political Institution*. London: Oxford University Press.

Nicholson, H. 1969. *Diplomacy*. London: Oxford University Press.

Niebuhr, R. 1932. *Moral Man and Immoral Society*. New York: Charles Scribner's Sons.

The Nobel Prize. 2007. 'The Nobel Peace Prize 2007'. Available at http://www.nobelprize.org/nobel_prizes/peace/laureates/2007/ (accessed August 2025).

Nye, J. 1971. *Peace in Parts: Integration and Conflict in Regional Organizations*. Boston: Little Brown and Company.

_____. 1995. 'International Regionalism'. In L. Fawcett and A. Hurrell, *Regionalism in World Politics: Regional Organizations and International Order*. Oxford: Oxford University Press.

_____. 2004. *Soft Power: The Means to Success in World Politics*. New York: Public Affairs.

Nye, J. S., and R. O. Keohane. 1971. 'Transnational Relations and World Politics'. *International Organization* 25 (3), 721–48.

Organization of American States (OAS). n.d. 'Who We Are'. Available at http://www.oas.org/en/about/who_we_are.asp (accessed August 2025).

Obuchi, K. 1998. 'The Asian Crisis: Meeting the Challenges to Human Security'. In A. Sen (ed.), *Why Human Security*. Tokyo: Harvard University.

Overseas Development Institute (ODI). 1980. 'The Brandt Commission: Briefing Paper', 17 March. Available at https://odi.org/en/publications/the-brandt-commission/ (accessed July 2025).

Organisation of Economic Cooperation and Development (OECD). 2020. 'Common Ground between the Paris Agreement and the Sendai Framework: Climate Change Adaptation and Disaster Risk Reduction'. Paris: OECD. Available at http://www.oecd.org/environment/climate-change-adaptation-and-disaster-risk-reduction-3edc8d09-en.htm (accessed July 2025).

O'Hagan, J. 1995. 'Civilisational Conflict? Looking for Cultural Enemies'. *Third World Quarterly* 16 (1), 19–38.

Ohmae, K. 1996. *The End of the Nation State: The Rise of Regional Economics*. New York: The Free Press.

Olson, W., and A. J. R. Groom. 1991. *International Relations Then and Now: Origins and Trends in Interpretation*. London: HarperCollins.

Organski, A. F. K. 1958. *World Politics*. New York: Alfred A. Knopf.

Owen, J. M. 1994. 'How Liberalism Produces the Democratic Peace'. *International Security* 19 (2), 87–125.

Oxford Reference. n.d. 'Imagined Community'. Available at http://www.oxfordreference.com/view/10.1093/oi/authority.20110803095958187 (accessed August 2025).

Palmer, N. D., and H. C. Perkins. 1985. *International Relations: The World Community in Transition*. New Delhi: CBS Publishers.

Parashar, S., J. A. Tickner, and J. True (eds). 2018. *Revisiting Gendered States: Feminist Imaginings of the State in International Relations*. Oxford: Oxford University Press.

Paris, R. 2001. 'Human Security: Paradigm Shift or Hot Air?' *International Security* 26 (2), 87–102.

Passmore, K. 2014. *Fascism: A Very Short Introduction*. Oxford: Oxford University Press, 2e.

PBS. 2014. 'The Crash: Timeline of the Panic'. *Frontline*. Available at http://www.pbs.org/wgbh/pages/frontline/shows/crash/etc/cron.html (accessed August 2025).

Pereira, J. C. 2017. 'The Limitations of IR Theory Regarding the Environment: Lessons from the Anthropocene'. *Revista Brasileira de Politica Internacional* 60 (1), 1–15. Available at https://www.scielo.br/j/rbpi/a/wrLfprF5ZbjwpRgMHb76BkH/ (accessed July 2025).

Peterson, V. S. 1992a. 'Transgressing Boundaries: Theories of Knowledge, Gender and International Relations'. *Millennium: Journal of International Studies* 21 (2), 183–206.

_____ (ed.). 1992b. *Gendered States: Feminist (Re)Visions of International Relations Theory*. Boulder, CO: Lynne Rienner.

_____. 1999. 'Political Identities/Nationalism as Heterosexism'. *International Feminist Journal of Politics* 1 (1), 34–65.

Peterson, V. S., and J. True. 1998. 'New Times and New Conversations'. In M. Zalewski and J. Parpart (eds), *The Man Question in International Relations*, 14–28. Boulder, CO: Westview Press.

Phadnis, U. 1990. *Ethnicity and Nation-building in South Asia*. New Delhi: Sage Publications.

Phillips, N. 2020. 'Global Political Economy'. In J. Baylis, S. Smith, and P. Owens, *The Globalization of World Politics: An Introduction to International Relations*. Oxford: Oxford University Press.

Pierson, P. 1994. *Dismantling the Welfare State: Reagan, Thatcher and the Politics of Retrenchment in Britain and the United States*. New York: Cambridge University Press.

Pitt, W. R. 2003. 'Blood Money'. *truthout*, 27 February. Available at https://truthout.org/articles/william-rivers-pitt-blood-money/ (accessed July 2025).

Posen, B. R. 1984. *The Sources of Military Doctrine: France, Britain, and Germany between the World Wars*. Cornell, Ithaca: Cornell University Press.

_____. 1993. 'Nationalism, the Mass Army and Military Power'. *International Security* 18 (2), 80–124.

Prah, K. K. 2004. 'African Wars and Ethnic Conflicts: Rebuilding Failed States'. Human Development Occasional Papers (1992–2007), HDOCPA-2004-10. Human Development Report Office (HDRO), United Nations Development Programme (UNDP).

Przeworski, A., and M. Wallerstein. 1988. 'Structural Dependence of the State on Capital'. *American Political Science Review* 91 (3), 11–30.

Putnam, R. D. 1988. 'Diplomacy and Domestic Politics: The Logic of Two-level Games'. *International Organization* 42 (3), 427–60.

Rajaratnam, B., J. A. Romano, M. Tsiang, and N. S. Diffenbaugh. 2015. 'Debunking the Climate Hiatus'. *Climatic Change* 133 (2), 129–40.

Ramet, S. P. 2018. *Balkan Babel: The Disintegration of Yugoslavia from the Death of Tito to the Fall of Milosevic*. New York: Routledge.

Ramsbotham, O., T. Woodhouse, and H. Miall. 2016. *Contemporary Conflict Resolution*. Cambridge: Polity Press.

Randall, V., and R. Theobald. 1998. *Political Change and Underdevelopment: A Critical Introduction to Third World Politics*. Durham: Duke University Press, 2e.

Rapoport, D. C. 2004. 'The Four Waves of Modern Terrorism'. In Audrey K. Cronin and James M. Ludes (eds), *Attacking Terrorism: Elements of a Grand Strategy*. Washington: Georgetown University Press.

Ravenhill, J. 2010. 'International Political Economy'. In C. Reus-Smit and D. Snidal, *The Oxford Handbook of International Relations*. Oxford: Oxford University Press.

Ravenhill, J. 2014. *The Study of Global Political Economy*. Oxford: Oxford University Press.

Ray, J. L. 1995. *Democracy and International Conflict: An Evaluation of the Democratic Peace Proposition*. Columbia, SC: University of South Carolina Press.

Reardon, B. 1985. *Sexism and the War System*. New York: Teacher's College Press.

Rengger, N. J. 1988. 'Going Critical? A Response to Hoffman'. *Millennium: Journal of International Studies* 17 (1), 81–89.

Reus-Smit, C. 2019. 'International Relations Theory Doesn't Understand Culture'. *Foreign Policy*, 21 March. Available at https://foreignpolicy.com/2019/03/21/international-relations-theory-doesnt-understand-culture/# (accessed August 2025).

Richardson, J. L. 2001. *Contending Liberalisms in World Politics: Ideology and Power*. Boulder, Colorado: Lynne Reinner.

Richter, J., and C. Wagner (eds). 1998. *Regional Security, Ethnicity and Governance*. New Delhi: Manohar.

Rifaq, F. 2017. 'Prime Minister's National Health Program, Pakistan'. Ministry of National Health Services, Regulations and Coordination, Government of Pakistan. Available at https://p4h.world/app/uploads/2023/02/2017_12_07_Faisal_Rafiq-PMNHP_HSA_Conference2017.x80726.pdf (accessed July 2025).

Risse, T. 2016. 'The Diffusion of Regionalism'. In T. A. Borzel and T. Risse, *The Oxford Handbook of Comparative Regionalism*. Oxford: Oxford University Press.

Robertson, R. 1992. *Globalization: Social Theory and Global Culture*. London: Sage.

Roberts, A. 2010. 'Lives and Statistics: Are 90% of War Victims Civilians?' *Survival* 52 (3), 115–36.

Rodrik, D. 1997. *Has Globalization Gone Too Far?* Washington D.C.: Institute for International Economics.

Rogel, C. 1998. *The Breakup of Yugoslavia and the War in Bosnia*. Westport, CT: Greenwood Press.

Rosato, S. 2003. 'The Flawed Logic of Democratic Peace Theory'. *The American Political Science Review* 97 (4), 585–602.

Rose, G. 1998. 'Neoclassical Realism and Theories of Foreign Policy'. *World Politics* 51 (1), 144–72.

Rosenau, J. N. (ed.). 1969. *Linkage Politics: Essays on the Convergence of National and International Systems*. New York: The Free Press.

_____. 1990. *Turbulence in World Politics: A Theory of Change and Continuity*. Princeton, New Jersey: Princeton University Press.

_____. 1995. 'Governance in the Twenty-first Century'. *Global Governance* 1 (1), 13–43.

_____. 1997. 'The Complexities and Contradictions of Globalization'. *Current History* 96 (613), 360–64.

Rosenau, J. N., and K. Knorr (eds). 1969. *Contending Approaches to International Relations*. Princeton, N.J.: Princeton University Press.

Ross, J. 2001. 'Is Canada's Human Security Policy Really the "Axworthy" Doctrine?' *Canadian Foreign Policy Journal* 8 (2), 75–93.

Rubenstein, R. E. 2017. 'State Security, Human Security and the Problem of Complementarity'. In E. Jacob (ed.), *Rethinking Security in the Twenty-First Century*. New York: Palgrave Macmillan.

Rubenstein, R. E., and J. Crocker. 1994. 'Challenging Huntington'. *Foreign Policy* 96, 113–28.

Ruddick, S. 1989. *Maternal Thinking: Towards a Politics of Peace*. Boston, MA: Beacon Press.

Ruggie, J. 1982. 'International Regimes, Transactions and Change: Embedded Liberalism in the Post-War Economic Order'. *International Organization* 36 (2), 379–415.

_____. 1983. 'Review of Kenneth N. Waltz, *Continuity and Transformation in the World Polity: Towards a New-Realist Synthesis*', *World Politics* 35 (2), 261–85.

_____. 1993. 'Territoriality and Beyond: Problematizing Modernity in International Relations'. *International Organization* 47 (1), 139–74.

_____. 1998. 'What Makes the World Hang Together? Neo-Utilitarianism and the Social Constructivist Challenge'. *International Organization* 52 (4), 855–85.

Rusconi, I. 2023. 'The Rohingya Crisis in Myanmar: Analysing the Use of Citizenship Status as Lawfare'. *The Defence Horizon Journal*, 16 March. Available at https://tdhj.org/blog/post/rohingya-myanmar-lawfare/ (accessed 16 July 2025).

Russett, B. M., J. R. Oneal, and M. Cox. 2000. 'Clash of Civilizations, or Realism and Liberalism Déjà Vu? Some Evidence'. *Journal of Peace Research* 37 (5), 583–608.

Saba, R. 2006. 'A Closer Look: Professor seeks stronger U.N.' *UCLA Daily Bruin*, 17 October. Available at http://dailybruin.com/2006/10/17/a-closer-look-professor-seeks/ (accessed August 2025).

Sahadevan, P. 1998. 'Internationalization of Ethnic Conflicts in South Asia: A Conceptual Enquiry'. *International Studies* 35 (3), 317–42.

Said, E. W. 2001. 'The Clash of Ignorance'. *The Nation*, 22 October. https://www.thenation.com/article/archive/clash-ignorance/ (accessed August 2025).

Samaddar, R. 1998a. *The Marginal Nation: Transborder Migration from Bangladesh to West Bengal*. New Delhi: Sage Publications.

_____. 1998b. 'The Failed Dialectic of Territoriality and Security, and the Imperatives of Dialogue'. *International Studies* 35 (1), 107–22.

_____ (ed.). 2004. *Peace Studies: An Introduction to the Concept, Scope, and Themes*, Vol. 1. New Delhi: Sage.

Sassen, S. 1996. *Losing Control? Sovereignty in an Age of Globalization*. New York: Columbia University Press.

Schechterman, B. 1991. 'Ethno-Nationalism and International Relations Textbook Literature'. *Journal of Political Science* 19 (1), 4–17.

Schimdt, B. C. 2008. 'International Relations Theory: Hegemony or Pluralism?' *Millennium: Journal of International Studies* 36 (2), 295–304.

_____. 2012. 'The First Great Debate'. Available at http://www.e-ir.info/2012/09/28/the-first-great-debate/ (accessed August 2025).

_____. 2013. 'On the History and Historiography of International Relations'. In Walter Carlsnaes, Thomas Risse, and Beth A. Simmons (eds), *Handbook of International Relations*. Los Angeles: Sage, 2e.

_____ (ed.). 2012. *International Relations and the First Great Debate*. London: Routledge.

Schmitter, P. C. 2005. 'Ernst B. Haas and the Legacy of Neofunctionalism'. *Journal of European Public Policy* 12 (2), 255–72.

Scholte, J. A. 1993. *International Relations of Social Change*. Buckingham: Open University Press.

_____. 2000. *Globalization: A Critical Introduction*. London: Macmillan.

Schweller. R. L. 1998. *Deadly Imbalances: Tripolarity and Hitler's Strategy of World Conquest*. New York: Columbia University Press.

Schwiening, S., and M. McKee. 2021. 'Vaccine Nationalism and the Dynamics of European Integration'. *European Journal of Public Health* 31 (3), 517–19.

Sen, A. 2000. *Why Human Security?* Tokyo: Harvard University Press.

______. 2002. 'Does Globalization Equal Westernization?' *The Globalist*, 25 March. Available at https://www.theglobalist.com/does-globalization-equal-westernization/ (accessed August 2025).

Senghaas, D. 1998. 'A Clash of Civilizations: An Idee Fixe'. *Journal of Peace Research* 35 (1), 127–32.

Service, R. 1999. *The Russian Revolution, 1900–1927*. London: Macmillan, 3e.

Seth, S. 2011. 'Postcolonial Theory and the Critique of International Relations'. *Millennium: Journal of International Studies* 40 (1), 167–83.

Shanghai Cooperation Organization (SCO). n.d. 'About SCO: General Information'. Available at https://eng.sectsco.org/20170109/192193.html (accessed August 2025).

Shannon, T. R. 1996. *An Introduction to the World-System Perspective*. Boulder, Colorado: Westview Press.

Sheehan, M. 1988. *Arms Control: Theory and Practice*. Oxford: Basil Blackwell.

Shemella, P. (ed.). 2012. *Fighting Back: What Governments Can Do about Terrorism*. New Delhi: Foundation Books / Cambridge University Press India.

Shirer, W. L. 1991. *The Rise and Fall of the Third Reich*. London: Random House.

Scholte, J. A. 1993. *International Relations of Social Change*. Buckingham: Open University Press.

Shue, H. 2014. *Climate Justice: Vulnerability and Protection*. Oxford: Oxford University Press.

Shurke, A., and G. Noble. 1997. *Ethnic Conflict in International Relations*. New York: Praeger.

Sikimic, S. 2015. 'Profile: What is the GCC?' *Middle East Eye*, 12 February. Available at http://www.middleeasteye.net/news/profile-what-gcc-18030284 (accessed August 2025).

Singer, J. D. 1960. 'Discussions and Reviews: Theorizing about Theory in International Politics'. *Journal of Conflict Resolution* 4 (4), 431–42.

______. 1961. 'The Level-of-Analysis Problem in International Relations'. *World Politics* 14 (1), 77–92.

Singh, S. 2017. 'Rethinking the "Normative" in United Nations Security Council Resolution 1325: Perspectives from Sri Lanka'. *Journal of Asian Security and International Affairs* 4 (2), 219–38.

Sjoberg, L. (ed.). 2009. 'Introduction to Security Studies: Feminist Contributions'. *Security Studies* 18 (2), 183–213.

_____. 2010. *Gender and International Security: Feminist Perspectives.* New York: Routledge.

_____. 2012. 'Feminist IR 101: Teaching through Blogs'. *International Studies Perspectives* 14 (3), 1–11.

_____. 2013. *Gendering Global Conflict: Toward a Feminist Theory of War*. New York: Columbia University Press.

_____. 2019. 'Gender, Feminism and War Theorizing'. In Caron E. Gentry, Laura J. Shepherd and Laura Sjoberg (eds), *The Routledge Handbook of Gender Security*, 59–69. New York: Routledge.

Sklair, L. 1991. *Sociology of the Global System*. London: Prentice-Hall.

Smith, A. D. 2000. 'Towards a Global Culture?' In D. Held and A. McGrew (eds), *The Global Transformation Reader: An Introduction to the Globalization Debate*. London: Polity Press.

Smith, M. 1986. *Realist Thought from Weber to Kissinger*. Baton Rouge: Louisiana State University Press.

Smith, S. 1995. 'The Self-Images of a Discipline: A Genealogy of International Relations Theory'. In Ken Booth and Steve Smith (eds), *International Relations Theory Today*, 1–37. Cambridge: Polity Press.

_____. 2015 [2011]. 'Six Wishes for a More Relevant Discipline of International Relations'. In Robert E. Goodin (ed.), *The Oxford Handbook of Political Science*. Oxford: Oxford University Press.

Smith, S., and M. Hollis. 1991. *Explaining and Understanding International Relations*. Oxford: Oxford University Press.

Smith, S., K. Booth, and M. Zalewski (eds). 1996. *International Theory: Positivism and Beyond*. Cambridge: Cambridge University Press.

Smith, T. 1979. 'The Underdevelopment of Development Literature: The Case of Dependency Theory'. *World Politics* 31 (2), 247–88.

Snyder J. 1991. *Myths of Empire: Domestic Politics and International Ambition*. Studies in Security Affairs. Ithaca: Cornell University Press.

Snyder, G. 2002. 'H. Mearsheimer's World-Offensive Realism and the Struggle for Security'. *International Security* 27 (1), 149–73.

Snyder, J., and E. Mansfield. 1995. 'Democratization and the Danger of War'. *International Security* 20 (1), 5–38.

Söderbaum, F. 2012. 'Theories of Regionalism'. In M. Beeson and R. Stubbs (eds), *The Routledge Handbook of Asian Regionalism*. Gothenburg: Routledge.

Söderbaum, F., and T. M. Shaw. 2003. *Theories of New Regionalism: A Palgrave Reader*. London: Palgrave McMillan.

Sola Pool, I. de. 1990. *Technologies Without Boundaries*. Cambridge, MA: Harvard University Press.

South Asian Association of Regional Cooperation (SAARC). 2009. 'About SAARC'. Available at https://www.saarc-sec.org/index.php/about-saarc/about-saarc (accessed August 2025).

Sørensen, G. 1998. 'IR theory after the Cold War'. *Review of International Studies* 24 (5), 83–100.

_____. 2001. 'War and State-Making: Why Doesn't It Work in the Third World?' *Security Dialogue* 32 (3), 341–54.

Stephen, R. 1995. *Ethnic Conflict and International Relations*. Brookfield V.T.: Dartmouth Pub Co.

Stephey, M. J. 2008. 'A Brief History of the Bretton Woods System'. *TIME*, 21 October. Available at http://content.time.com/time/business/article/0,8599,1852254,00.html (accessed August 2025).

Sterling-Folker, J. 2007. 'Neoliberalism'. In Tim Dunne, Milja Kurki, and Steve Smith (eds), *International Relations Theories: Discipline and Diversity*, 114–31. Oxford: Oxford University Press.

Stern, J. 1999. *The Ultimate Terrorists*. Boston, MA: Harvard University Press.

Stettinius, E. R., Jr. 1945. 'Report to the U.S. Government on the San Francisco Meeting that Established the United Nations: San Francisco'. Cited in M. V. Ramana, 'Nuclear Weapons Create and Exacerbate Human Insecurity'. *Heinrich Boll Stiftung*, 21 November 2024. Available at https://www.boell.de/en/2024/11/21/nuclear-weapons-create-and-exacerbate-human-insecurity#:~:text=In%201945%2C%20when%20the%20United,victory%20spells%20freedom%20from%20fear (accessed August 2025).

Stiglitz, J. E. 2002. *Globalization and its Discontents*. New York: W. W. Norton and Co.

_____. 2006. *Making Globalization Work*. London: Penguin Books.

Strandsbjerg, J. 2010. *Territory, Globalization and International Relations: The Cartographic Reality of Space*. New York: Springer.

Strange, S. 1976. 'The Study of Transnational Relations'. *International Affairs* 52 (3), 333–45.

_____. 1986. *Casino Capitalism*. New York: Basil Blackwell.

_____. 1988. *States and Markets*. London: Pinter.

Strange, S. 1996. *The Retreat of the State: The Diffusion of Power in World Economy*. New York: Cambridge University Press.

Stroeve, J. 2015. 'Arctic sea ice extent settles at fourth lowest in the satellite record'. NSIDC, 6 October. Boulder: University of Colorado. Available at http://nsidc.org/news/newsroom/PR_2015meltseason (accessed July 2025).

Stubbs, R., and G. Underhill (eds). 1994. *Political Economy and the Changing Global Order*. London: Macmillan.

Sussex, M. 2004. 'Cultures in Conflict? Re-evaluating the "Clash of Civilizations" Thesis After 9/11'. In Peter Shearnan and Matthew Sussex (eds), *European Security after 9/11*. Aldershot, UK: Ashgate.

Swank D. 2002. *Global Capital, Political Institutions and Policy Change in Developed Welfare States*. New York: Cambridge University Press.

Sweney, M. and L. O'Carroll. 2025. 'US will impose 35% tariffs on Canadian imports, Trump says in letter'. *The Guardian*, 10 July. Available at https://www.theguardian.com/us-news/2025/jul/10/us-canada-tariffs-trump (accessed July 2025).

Sylvester, C. 1994. *Feminist Theory and International Relations in a Postmodern Era*. Cambridge: Cambridge University Press.

Telhami, S. 2002. 'Kenneth Waltz, Neorealism and Foreign Policy'. *Security Studies* 11 (3), 158–70.

Terhalle, M., and J. Depledge. 2013. 'Great-Power Politics, Order Transition, and Climate Governance: Insights from International Relations Theory'. *Climate Policy* 13 (5), 572–90.

Thakur, R. and T. G. Weiss. 2015. 'Framing Global Governance, Five Gaps'. In M. Steger (ed.), *The Global Studies Reader*. New York: Oxford University Press.

Thompson, K. 1952. 'The Study of International Politics: A Survey of Trends and Developments'. *Review of Politics* 14 (4), 433–67.

Tickner, J. A. 1988. 'Hans Morgenthau's Principles of Political Realism: A Feminist Reformulation'. *Millennium: Journal of International Studies* 17 (3), 429–40.

———. 1992. *Gender in International Relations: Feminist Perspectives on Achieving Global Security*. New York: Columbia University Press.

———. 2001. *Gendering World Politics: Issues and Approaches in the Post-Cold War Era*. New York: Columbia University Press.

Tickner, J. A. 2005. 'Feminism meets International Relations: Some Methodological Issues'. In Brooke A. Ackerly, Maria Stern, and Jacqui True (eds), *Feminist Methodologies for International Relations*, 19–41. Cambridge: Cambridge University Press.

______. 2018. 'Rethinking the State in International Relations: A Personal Reflection'. In Swati Parashar, J. Ann Tickner, and Jacqui True (eds), *Revisiting Gendered States: Feminist Imaginings of the State in International Relations*, 19–32. Oxford: Oxford University Press.

Topik, S. 1998. 'Dependency Revisited: Saving the Baby from the Bathwater'. *Latin American Perspectives* 25 (6), 95–99.

Touraine, A. 1985. 'An Introduction to the Study of Social Movements'. *Social Research* 52 (4), 749–87.

True, J., and M. Tanyag. 2019. 'Violence against Women/Violence in the World: Toward a Feminist Conceptualization of Global Violence'. In Caron E. Gentry, Laura J. Shepherd and Laura Sjoberg (eds), *The Routledge Handbook of Gender Security*, 15–26. New York: Routledge.

True, J. 2005. 'Feminism'. In Scott Burchill, Andrew Linklater, Richard Devetak, Jack Donnelly, Matthew Paterson, Christian Reus-Smit and Jacqui True, *Theories of International Relations*, 213–34. Basingstoke: Palgrave Macmillan.

______. 2012. *The Political Economy of Violence against Women*. New York: Oxford University Press.

Uppsala Conflict Data Program (UCDP). n.d. 'Number of Conflicts: 1975–2024'. Uppsala: Department of Peace and Conflict Research, Uppsala University. Available at https://ucdp.uu.se/ (accessed August 2025).

UCDP Dataset Download Center, Uppsala University. Available at https://ucdp.uu.se/downloads/ (accessed July 2025).

United Nations (UN). n.d.(a). 'About the Responsibility to Protect'. Office on Genocide Prevention and the Responsibility to Protect. Available at https://www.un.org/en/genocide-prevention/responsibility-protect/about (accessed August 2025).

______. n.d.(b). 'The United Nations Charter'. Available at https://www.un.org/en/about-us/un-charter (accessed August 2025).

______. n.d.(c). 'United Nations Conference on Environment and Development, Rio de Janeiro, Brazil, 3–14 June 1992'. Available at https://www.un.org/en/conferences/environment/rio1992 (accessed August 2025).

United Nations (UN). n.d.(d). 'Member States'. Available at https://www.un.org/en/about-us/member-states (accessed August 2025).

———. n.d.(e). 'Growth in United Nations Membership'. Available at https://www.un.org/en/about-us/growth-in-un-membership (accessed August 2025).

———. n.d.(f). 'Migrants: Protect, NOT Marginalize'. Available at https://www.un.org/en/fight-racism/vulnerable-groups/migrants#:~:text=The%20UN%20Migration%20Agency%2C%20International,movement%20is%20voluntary%20or%20involuntary (accessed August 2025).

———. 1974. 'Resolution adopted by the General Assembly: 3201 (S-VI). Declaration on the Establishment of a New International Economic Order'. UN Document A/RES/S-6/3201. New York: The United Nations. Available at http://www.un-documents.net/s6r3201.htm (accessed August 2025).

———. 1979. 'Convention on the Elimination of All Forms of Discrimination against Women New York, 18 December 1979'. Available at https://www.ohchr.org/en/instruments-mechanisms/instruments/convention-elimination-all-forms-discrimination-against-women (accessed 15 July 2025).

———. 1987. 'International Conference on the Relationship between Disarmament and Development'. In *The United Nations Disarmament Yearbook*. New York: The United Nations Office for Disarmament Affairs. Available at https://www.un-ilibrary.org/content/books/9789210579919s005-c003 (accessed August 2025).

———. 1997. *The UN Conference on Environment and Development (1992)*. New York: The United Nations. Available at https://www.un.org/en/conferences/environment/rio1992 (accessed July 2025).

———. 2009. 'United Nations Security Council Resolution 1888 (2009), S/RES/1888(2009)'. United Nations: SHE Stands for Peace. Available at https://www.un.org/shestandsforpeace/content/united-nations-security-council-resolution-1888-2009-sres18882009 (accessed August 2025).

———. 2015. 'United Nations at 70: Moments and Milestones', UN Headquarters, 17 October–1 December. Available at https://www.un.org/en/exhibits/united-nations-70-moments-and-milestones (accessed August 2025).

UNDP. 1994. *Human Development Report*. New York: Oxford University Press. Available at https://hdr.undp.org/content/human-development-report-1994 (accessed August 2025).

_____. 1998. *Human Development Report 1998: Consumption for Human Development*. New York: UNDP. Available at https://hdr.undp.org/content/human-development-report-1998 (accessed August 2025).

_____. 2020. '13 Climate Action'. Sustainable Development Goals, 16 December. Available at https://www.undp.org/sustainable-development-goals/climate-action (accessed July 2025).

UNDRR. 2020. *Sendai Framework for Disaster Risk Reduction 2015–2030*, 16 December. New York: United Nations Office for Disaster Risk Reduction. Available at https://www.undrr.org/publication/sendai-framework-disaster-risk-reduction-2015-2030 (accessed July 2025).

UNFCCC. 2014a. 'Kyoto Protocol: Targets for the first commitment period'. Available at http://unfccc.int/kyoto_protocol/items/3145.php (accessed July 2025).

_____. 2014b. 'Cancun Climate Change Conference, November 2010'. Available at https://unfccc.int/conference/cancun-climate-change-conference-november-2010 (accessed July 2025).

_____. 2020. 'About Carbon Pricing'. Available at https://unfccc.int/about-us/regional-collaboration-centres/the-ciaca/about-carbon-pricing (accessed July 2025).

_____. 2022. 'UN Climate Change Annual Report 2022', 5 June. Bonn: UNFCCC Secretariat.

UNHCR. 'The 1951 Refugee Convention'. Available at https://www.unhcr.org/about-unhcr/overview/1951-refugee-convention (accessed July 2025).

United Nations Office for Disaster Risk Reduction (UNDRR). 2015. 'Ten-year review finds 87% of disasters climate-related', 6 March. Available at https://www.unisdr.org/archive/42862 (accessed August 2025).

UNISDR. 2016. 'Human Security Network'. Available at https://www.preventionweb.net/organization/human-security-network (accessed July 2025).

United States Environmental Protection Agency. 2016. 'Overview of Greenhouse Gases'. Available at https://www.epa.gov/ghgemissions/overview-greenhouse-gases (accessed July 2025).

UN Women. 2015. 'Preventing Conflict, Transforming Justice, Securing the Peace: A Global Study on the Implementation of United Nations Security Council Resolution 1325'. Available at chrome-extension://efaidnbmnnnibpcajpcglclefindmkaj/https://wps.unwomen.org/pdf/en/CH00.pdf (accessed August 2025).

Van Evera, S. 1994. 'Hypotheses on Nationalism and War'. *International Security* 18 (4), 5–39.

_____. 1999. *Causes of War: Power and the Roots of Conflict*. Ithaca, London: Cornell University Press.

Vasquez, J. A. 1983. *The Power of Power Politics: From Classical Realism to Neotraditionalism*. London: Frances Pinter, and New Brunswick, NJ: Rutgers University Press.

_____. 1998. *The Power of Power Politics: From Classical Realism to Neotraditionalism*. Cambridge: Cambridge University Press.

Vaughan, A. 2015. 'Global Carbon Dioxide Levels break 400ppm Milestone'. *The Guardian*, 6 May. Available at https://www.theguardian.com/environment/2015/may/06/global-carbon-dioxide-levels-break-400ppm-milestone (accessed August 2025).

Vernengo, M. 2006. 'Technology, Finance and Dependency: Latin American Radical Political Economy in Retrospect'. *Review of Radical Political Economics* 38 (4), 551–68.

Vernon, R. 1971. *Sovereignty at Bay: The Multinational Spread of U.S. Enterprises*. New York: Longman.

_____. 1981. 'Sovereignty at Bay Ten Years After'. *International Organization* 35 (3), 517–29.

_____. 1991. 'Sovereignty at Bay: Twenty Years After'. *Millennium* 20 (2), 191–95.

Veseth, M. 2001. 'What is International Political Economy?' In D. N. Balaam and M. Veseth, *Introduction to International Political Economy*. New Jersey: Prentice Hall.

Viner, J. 1937. *Studies in the Theory of International Trade*. London: George Allen and Unwin.

Viotti, P. R., and M. V. Kauppi. 1990. *International Relations Theory: Realism, Pluralism, Globalism*. New York: Macmillan.

Viser, M., D. J. Lynch, and E. Francis. 2025. 'Trump says he'll slap 30% tariffs on Mexico, European Union on Aug. 1'. *The Washington Post*, 12 July. Available at https://www.washingtonpost.com/politics/2025/07/12/trump-tariffs-mexico-european-union/ (accessed July 2025).

Vogler, J. 2014. 'Environmental Issues'. In J. Baylis, S. Smith, and P. Owens, *The Globalization of World Politics: An Introduction to International Relations*, 341–56. Oxford: Oxford University Press, 6e.

Waever, O. 1996. 'The Rise and Fall of the Inter-Paradigm Debate'. In Steve Smith, Ken Booth, and Marysia Zalewski (eds), *International Theory: Positivism and Beyond*, 149–85. Cambridge: Cambridge University Press.

_____. 1998. 'The Sociology of a Not So International Discipline'. *International Organization* 52 (4), 687–727.

Waever, O., B. Buzan, M. Kelstrup, and P. Lemaitre. 1993. *Identity, Migration and the New Security Agenda in Europe*. London: Pinter.

Walker, R. B. J. 1988. *One World, Many Worlds: Struggle for a Just World Peace*. Boulder, Colorado: Lynne Reinner.

_____. 1993. *Inside/Outside: International Relations as Political Theory*. Cambridge University Press: Cambridge.

Wallerstein, I. 1974. *The Modern World-System*, Vol. 1. New York: Academic Press.

_____. 1980. *The Modern World-System*, Vol. 2. New York: Academic Press.

_____. 1989. *The Modern World-System*, Vol. 3. San Diego: Academic Press.

Walt, S. M. 1985. 'Alliance Formation and the Balance of World Power'. *International Security* 9 (4), 3–43.

_____. 1988. 'Testing Theories of Alliance Formation: The Case of Southwest Asia'. *International Organization* 2 (2), 275–316.

_____. 1997. 'The Progressive Power of Realism'. *American Political Science Review* 91 (4), 931–35.

Waltz, K. W. 1959. *Man, the State, and War*. New York: Columbia University Press.

_____. 1979. *Theory of International Politics*. Reading Mass.: Addison-Wesley.

_____. 1990. 'Realist Thought and Neorealist Theory'. *Journal of International Affairs* 44 (1), 21–37.

_____. 1993. 'The Emerging Structure of International Politics'. *International Security* 18 (2), 44–79.

_____. 1996. 'International Politics is not Foreign Policy'. *Security Studies* 6 (1), 54–57.

_____. 1997. 'Evaluating Theories'. *The American Political Science Review* 91 (4), 923–26.

Walzenbach, G. 2016. 'Global Political Economy'. *E-International Relations*, 29 December. Available at http://www.e-ir.info/2016/12/29/global-political-economy/ (accessed August 2025).

Weeks, A. 1993. 'Do Civilisations Hold?', *Foreign Affairs* 72 (4). Available at https://www.foreignaffairs.com/articles/united-states/1993-09-01/do-civilizations-hold (accessed July 2025).

Weiner, M. 1992–93. 'Security, Stability and International Migration'. *International Security* 17 (3), 91–126.

———. 1996. 'Bad Neighbor, Bad Neighborhoods: An Enquiry into the Causes of Refugee Flows'. *International Security* 21 (1), 5–42.

Weiss, C. 2005. 'Science, Technology and International Relations'. *Technology in Society* 27 (3), 95–313.

Weiss, T. G., et.al. 2016. *The United Nations and Changing World Politics*. Boulder: Westview Press.

Welt Hunger Hilfe, International Food Policy Research Institute, and Concern Worldwide. 2016. *The Global Hunger Index*. Washington D.C.: Welt Hunger Hilfe, International Food Policy Research Institute, and Concern Worldwide.

Wendt, A. 1987. 'The Agent-Structure Problem in International Relations Theory'. *International Organization* 41 (3), 335–70.

———. 1992. 'Anarchy is What States Make of It: The Social Construction of Power Politics'. *International Organization* 46 (2), 391–425.

———. 1994. 'Collective Identity Formation and the International State'. *The American Political Science Review* 88 (2), 384–96.

———. 1999. *Social Theory of International Politics*. Cambridge: Cambridge University Press.

Wendt, A., and I. Shapiro. 1997. 'The Misunderstood Promise of Realist Social Theory'. In K. Monroe (ed.), *Contemporary Empirical Political Theory*. London: University of California Press.

The White House. 2025. 'Unleashing American Energy'. Presidential Actions, Executive Orders, 20 January. Available at https://www.whitehouse.gov/presidential-actions/2025/01/unleashing-american-energy/ (accessed August 2025).

Whiting, A. 2013. 'Peacekeeping: A Brief Guide'. *Thomson Reuters Foundation News*, 21 September. Available at https://news.trust.org/item/20130919155317-qsnfr/ (accessed August 2025).

Whitworth, S. 2004. *Men, Militarism, and UN Peacekeeping: A Gendered Analysis*. Boulder, CO: Lynne Rienner Publishers.

Wibben, T. R. A. 2004. 'Feminist International Relations: Old Debates and New Directions'. *Brown Journal of World Affairs* X (2), 97–114.

Wilcox, F. O. 1965. 'Regionalism and the United Nations'. *International Organization* 789.

Williams, P. D. 2011. *War and Conflict in Africa*. London: Polity Press.

_____. 2016. 'Global and Regional Peacekeepers'. Discussion Paper Series on Global and Regional Governance. New York: Council on Foreign Relations.

Wohlforth, W. C. 1993. *The Elusive Balance: Power and Perceptions during the Cold War*. Ithaca, NY: Cornell University Press.

Woods, N. 2014. 'International Political Economy in an Age of Globalization'. In J. Baylis, S. Smith, and P. Owens (eds), *The Globalization of World Politics*, 243–57. Oxford: Oxford University Press.

The World Bank. n.d.(a) 'GDP Growth (Annual %)'. The World Bank Group. Available at https://data.worldbank.org/indicator/NY.GDP.MKTP.KD.ZG (accessed August 2025).

_____. n.d.(b). 'Who We Are'. Available at https://www.worldbank.org/ext/en/who-we-are (accessed August 2025).

_____. 2007. *Empowerment in Practice: Analysis and Implementation*. Washington D.C.: The World Bank. Available at https://documents.worldbank.org/en/publication/documents-reports/documentdetail/286191468315851702/empowerment-in-practice-from-analysis-to-implementation (accessed July 2025).

World Health Organization (WHO). n.d. 'About WHO: Governance'. Available at https://www.who.int/about/governance (accessed August 2025).

Wright, Q. 1955. *The Study of International Relations*. New York: Appleton-Century-Crofts.

World Trade Organization (WTO). n.d.(a) 'Regional Trade Agreements'. Available at https://www.wto.org/english/tratop_e/region_e/regfac_e.htm (accessed August 2025).

_____. n.d.(b). 'Principles of the Trading System'. Available at https://www.wto.org/english/thewto_e/whatis_e/tif_e/fact2_e.htm#seebox (accessed August 2025).

_____. 2007. *World Trade Report 2007*. Available at https://www.wto.org/english/res_e/booksp_e/anrep_e/wtr07-2b_e.pdf (accessed August 2025).

Zakaria, F. 1998. *From Wealth to Power: The Unusual Origins of America's World Role*. Princeton, NJ: Princeton University Press.
Zalewski, M. 1996. 'All these Theories, Yet the Bodies Keep Piling Up: Theory, Theorists, Theorizing'. In Steve Smith, Ken Booth, and Marysia Zalewski (eds), *International Relations Theory: Positivism and Beyond*, 340–53. Cambridge: Cambridge University Press.
Zehfuss, M. 2002. *Constructivism in International Relations*. Cambridge: Cambridge University Press.

Index